Roy E. Garton
Mirages in the Desert

Beihefte zur Zeitschrift für die alttestamentliche Wissenschaft

Herausgegeben von
John Barton, Reinhard G. Kratz, Nathan MacDonald,
Carol Newsom and Markus Witte

Band 492

Roy E. Garton

Mirages in the Desert

The Tradition-historical Developments of
the Story of Massah-Meribah

DE GRUYTER

ISBN 978-3-11-063715-1
e-ISBN (PDF) 978-3-11-046335-4
e-ISBN (EPUB) 978-3-11-046266-1
ISSN 0934-2575

Library of Congress Cataloging-in-Publication Data
A CIP catalog record for this book has been applied for at the Library of Congress.

Bibliografische Information der Deutschen Nationalbibliothek
The Deutsche Nationalbibliothek lists this publication in the Deutsche Nationalbibliografie; detailed bibliographic data are available in the Internet at http://dnb.dnb.de.

© 2018 Walter de Gruyter GmbH, Berlin/Boston
This volume is text- and page-identical with the hardback published in 2017.
Printing and binding: CPI books GmbH, Leck

♾ Printed on acid-free paper
Printed in Germany

www.degruyter.com

In memory of my dad,
George Vance Garton, Jr.,
Who taught me never to give up on my dreams

יהוה נתן ויהוה לקח יהי שם יהוה מברך

Contents

List of Abbreviations —— XI

Acknowledgments —— XV

Chapter One: Introduction —— 1
1.1 The Texts of the Massah-Meribah Tradition —— 1
1.2 The Diversity of the Tradition in the Hebrew Bible —— 4
1.3 The Gap in Scholarship —— 9
1.3.1 Within Classic Historical-Critical Studies —— 10
1.3.2 Within Revisionist Studies —— 16
1.3.3 Summary —— 22
1.4 What to Do and Where to Begin? —— 22

Part I Deuteronomy as the Foundation

Chapter Two: Preliminary Considerations —— 29
2.1 Why Begin with Deuteronomy? —— 29
2.2 Currents and Cautions in Pentateuchal Studies —— 29
2.3 The Formation of Deuteronomy —— 37
2.3.1 The Interior Prologue: Early-Deuteronomy and the Numeruswechsel —— 41
2.3.2 The Exterior Miscellaneous Epilogues —— 46
2.4 Summary: The Advantages of Beginning with Deuteronomy —— 49

Chapter Three: The M-Mt's Reminiscences within Deuteronomy's Interior Prologue —— 51
3.1 Introduction to the Interior Reminiscences —— 51
3.2 Deuteronomy 6:16 —— 52
3.2.1 Textual Criticism of Deut 6:16 —— 52
3.2.2 Literary Analysis of Deut 6:4–25 —— 53
3.2.3 Tradition-historical Analysis of Deut 6:16 —— 63
3.3 Deuteronomy 8:15 —— 65
3.3.1 Textual Criticism of Deut 8:15 —— 65
3.3.2 Literary Analysis of Deut 8:1–20 —— 65
3.3.3 Tradition-historical Analysis of Deut 8:15 —— 72

3.4	Deuteronomy 9:22 —— 73
3.4.1	Textual Criticism of Deut 9:22 —— 73
3.4.2	Literary Analysis of Deut 9:1–10:11 —— 73
3.4.3	Tradition-historical Analysis of Deut 9:22 —— 78
3.5	Reconstructing the Framework of the M-Mt's Tradition-historical Development (Part 1) —— 81

Chapter Four: The M-Mt's Reminiscences within Deuteronomy's Exterior Miscellaneous Epilogues —— 84

4.1	Introduction to the Exterior Reminiscences —— 84
4.2	Deuteronomy 32:13 —— 86
4.2.1	Is Deut 32:13 a M-Mt Text? —— 86
4.2.2	Text Criticism of Deut 32:13 —— 88
4.2.3	Literary Analysis of Deut 32:1–43 —— 95
4.2.4	Tradition-historical Analysis of Deut 32:13b —— 103
4.3	Deuteronomy 32:51 —— 104
4.3.1	Text Criticism of Deut 32:51 —— 104
4.3.2	Literary Analysis of Deut 32:48–52 —— 105
4.3.3	Tradition-historical Analysis of Deut 32:51 —— 119
4.4	Deuteronomy 33:8 —— 120
4.4.1	Textual Criticism of Deut 33:8 —— 120
4.4.2	Literary Analysis of Deut 33:8–11 —— 122
4.4.3	Tradition-historical Analysis of Deut 33:8b —— 134
4.5	Reconstructing the Framework of the M-Mt's Tradition-historical Development (Part 2) —— 135

Part II   Beyond Deuteronomy: The M-Mt in the Remainder of the Pentateuch

Chapter Five: Toward Assessing the M-Mt Texts in the Remainder of the Pentateuch —— 141

5.1	Introduction to the Remaining M-Mt Texts within the Pentateuch —— 141
5.2	What is the Relationship between the M-Mt Narratives? —— 142
5.2.1	The Verbal and Conceptual Correspondence of the M-Mt Narratives —— 143
5.2.2	Additional Features Affecting the Relationship of the M-Mt Narratives —— 146
5.3	Determining the Relationship between the M-Mt Narratives —— 149

5.4 Synopsis: Four Dynamics of the Relationship between the M-Mt Narratives —— **156**

Chapter Six: The Non-P M-Mt Narrative in Exodus 17:1–7 and its Related Texts —— 157
6.1 An Approach toward Assessing Exodus 17:1–7 —— **157**
6.2 Textual Criticism of Exodus 17:1–7 —— **158**
6.3 Literary Analysis of Exodus 17:1–7 in Relation to its Broader Literary Contexts —— **160**
6.3.1 The Travel Notice of Exod 17:1abα and the Wilderness Itinerary of Numbers 33 —— **161**
6.3.2 The Double Etiology of Exod 17:2, 7 and the ריב Elements of Num 20:3a, 13 —— **182**
6.3.3 The Dtr Core of Exod 17:2–7* and the Complaints of Numbers 11 —— **188**
6.4 Toward a Synthesis: The Literary History of Exodus 17:1–7 Aligned with Deuteronomy's M-Mt Tradition-historical Framework —— **197**

Chapter Seven: The Priestly M-Mt Narrative in Numbers 20:1–13 and its Related Texts —— 202
7.1 An Approach toward Assessing Numbers 20:1–13 —— **202**
7.2 Textual Criticism of Numbers 20:1–13 —— **203**
7.3 Literary Analysis of Numbers 20:1–13 in Relation to its Broader Literary Contexts —— **205**
7.3.1 The Failure of Moses and Aaron in Num 20:12 and their Deaths outside the Land in Num 20:22–29 and 27:12–23 —— **209**
7.3.2 The Assemblies against Moses and Aaron in Num 20:2–3 and Numbers 16–17 —— **218**
7.3.3 The Travel Notice of Num 20:1, the Scouts Story of Numbers 13–14, and the Wilderness Itinerary of Numbers 33 —— **224**
7.3.4 The מריבה Coordination of Num 20:3–5*+13a and Exod 17:2–7* —— **229**
7.3.5 The Formation of the קדש Episode of Num 20:1–11*+13b in Light of Exod 17:2–7's Formative Stages —— **231**
7.4 Toward a Synthesis: The Literary History of Numbers 20:1–13 and its Relationship to Exodus 17:1–7 and Deuteronomy's M-Mt Tradition-historical Framework —— **232**

Chapter Eight: Conclusion —— 236
8.1   Summary and Implications of the Current Study —— 236
8.2   Trajectories for Further Study —— 241

Appendices

Appendix A —— 245
   Rhythm and Translation of the Ur-ריב of Deuteronomy 32 —— 245

Appendix B —— 247
   Quantitative Analysis of the Verbal and Conceptual Correspondences of Exod 17:1–7 and Num 20:1–13 —— 247

Appendix C —— 253

Appendix D —— 260
   Exodus 17:1-7 by Stages of Literary Development —— 260

Appendix E —— 264
   Numbers 20:1–13 by Stages of Literary Development —— 264

Bibliography —— 269

Index of names —— 293

Index of ancient sources —— 296

List of Abbreviations

General

→	(Indicates direction of diachronic relationship)
‖	(Indicates parallelism)
≈	(Indicates 'almost equal to')
*	(Indicates a textual parameter is composite)
Dt	Deuteronomic
Dtr	Deuteronomistic
Dtr Supp	Deuteronomistic Supplement
DtrH	Deuteronomistic History
Early-P	Early Priestly material
HexRed/*HexRed*	the Hexateuchal Redactor/*Hexateuchal Redaction*
HexSupp/*HexSupp*	the Hexateuchal Supplementer/*Hexateuchal Supplement*
Mm	Masorah magna
M-Mt	Massah-Meribah tradition
Non-P	Non-Priestly material
P	Priestly material
P*	Priestly oriented
P^G	Priestly Grundschrift
PentRed/*PentRed*	the Pentateuchal Redactor/*Pentateuchal Redaction*
Post-P	Post-Priestly material
Post-PentRed/*Post-PentRed*	Post-Pentateuchal Redactor(s)/*Post-Pentateuchal Redaction(s)*
Pre-HexSupp/*Pre-HexSupp*	the Pre-Hexateuchal Supplementer/*Pre-Hexateuchal Supplement*
Ur-Deut	*Ur*-Deuteronomy

Ancient Witnesses

α'	Aquila
θ'	Theodotion
σ'	Symmachus
Ant.	*Jewish Antiquities*
A	Codex Alexandrinus
B	Codex Vaticanus (Brooke & McLean, *The Old Testament in Greek according to the Text of the Codex Vaticanus* [London: Cambridge, 1906–1940])
Det.	*Quod deterius potiori insidari soleat*
G	Old Greek (*Septuaginta: Vetus Testamentum Graecum*; auctoritate Academiae Scientiarum Gottingensis editum)
G^{Mss}	Manuscripts witnessing to the Old Greek
Hel. Syn. Pr.	*Hellenistic Synagogal Prayers*

L.A.B.	*Liber antiquitatum biblicarum* (Pseudo-Philo)
LXX	Septuagint
M^A	Aleppo Codex
M^L	Leningrad Codex
MT	Masoretic Text
MMT	*Miqṣat Ma'aśê ha-Torah*
S	Syriac
Smr	Samaritan Pentateuch (A. F. Von Gall, *Der Hebräische Pentateuch der Samaritaner* [Giessen: Alfred Töpelman, 1918])
T	Targum (all extant Targumim agree)
T^F	Fragment Targum to the Pentateuch (M. L. Klein, *The Fragment-Targums of the Pentateuch* [2 vols.; Rome: Biblical Institute, 1980])
T^Gnz	Fragments from Cairo Geniza
T^J	Targum Pseudo-Jonathan
T^N	Targum Neofiti
T^O	Targum Onkelos
V	Vulgate

Secondary Sources

AB	Anchor Bible
ABRL	Anchor Bible Reference Library
AnBib	Analecta biblica
ATANT	Abhandlungen zur Theologie des Alten und Neuen Testaments
ATD	Das Alte Testament Deutsch
AYBRL	Anchor Yale Bible Reference Library
BAR	*Biblical Archaeological Review*
BBB	Bonner biblische Beiträge
BDS	Bibal Dissertation Series
BETL	Bibliotheca ephemeridum theologicarum lovaniensium
Bib	*Biblica*
BWA(N)T	Beiträge zur Wissenschaft vom Alten (und Neuen) Testament
BZAR	Beiträge zur Zeitschrift für Altorientalische und Biblische Rechtsgeschichte
BZAW	Beihefte zur Zeitschrift für die alttestamentliche Wissenschaft
ConBOT	Coniectanea biblica: Old Testament Series
DJD	Discoveries in the Judaean Desert
DSD	*Dead Sea Discoveries*
EdF	Erträge der Forschung
ECC	Eerdmans Critical Commentary
EHS.T	Europäische Hochschulschriften: Reihe 23, Theologie
EstBib	*Estudios bíblicos*
ETL	Ephemerides theologicae lovanienses
EWE	Erwägen, Wissen, Ethik
FAT	Forschungen zum Alten Testament
FAT2	Forschungen zum Alten Testament 2. Reihe

FRLANT	Forschungen zur Religion und Literatur des Alten und Neuen Testaments
GKC	*Gesenius' Hebrew Grammar.* Edited by E. Kautzsch. Translated by A. E. Cowley. 2d. ed. Oxford, 1910.
HALC	History, Archaeology, and Culture of the Levant
HALOT	Koehler, L., W. Baumgartner, and J. J. Stamm, *The Hebrew and Aramaic Lexicon of the Old Testament.* Translated under the supervision of M. E. J. Richardson. 4 vols. Leiden, 1994–1999.
HAT	Handbuch zum Alten Testament
HbS	Herders biblische Studien
HeBAI	*Hebrew Bible and Ancient Israel*
Hiph	Hiphil
HRCS	Hatch, E. and H. A. Redpath. *Concordance to the Septuagint and Other Greek Versions of the Old Testament.* 2 vols. Oxford, 1897. Suppl., 1906. Reprint, 3 vols. in 2, Grand Rapids, 1983
HS	*Hebrew Studies*
HSM	Harvard Semitic Monographs
HTR	*Harvard Theological Review*
JBL	*Journal of Biblical Literature*
JDT	*Jahrbücher für deutsche Theologie*
JETS	*Journal of the Evangelical Theological Society*
JHS	*Journal of Hebrew Scriptures*
JNSL	*Journal of Northwest Semitic Languages*
Joüon	Joüon, P. and T. Muraoka. *A Grammar of Biblical Hebrew.* 3d repr. to 2d ed., with corrections. Subsidia biblica 27. Rome, 2011.
JPSTC	JPS Torah Commentary
JQR	*Jewish Quarterly Review*
JSOTsup	Journal for the Study of the Old Testament: Supplement Series
KTU	*Die keilalphabetischen Texte aus Ugarit.* Edited by Manfied Dietrich, Oswald Loretz, and Joaquín Sanmartín. Münster: Ugarit-Verlag, 2013.
LD	Lectio divina
LHB/OTS	Library of Hebrew Bible / Old Testament Studies
MdB	Le Monde de la Bible
MtS	Marburger theologische Studien
OBO	Orbis biblicus et orientalis
ÖBS	Österreichische biblische Studien
OTL	Old Testament Library
OTS	Old Testament Studies
OtSt	Oudtestamentische Studiën
PFES	Publications of the Finnish Exegetical Society
PJ	*Palästina-Jahrbuch*
RB	*Revue biblique*
SBL	Society of Biblical Literature
SBLABS	Society of Biblical Literature Archaeology and Biblical Studies
SBLAIL	Society of Biblical Literature Ancient Israel and its Literature
SBLDS	Society of Biblical Literature Dissertation Series
SBLEJL	Society of Biblical Literature Early Judaism and its Literature
SBLSBL	Society of Biblical Literature Studies in Biblical Literature

SBLSCS	Society of Biblical Literature Septuagint and Cognate Studies
SBLTCS	Society of Biblical Literature Text-Critical Studies
SBS	Stuttgarter Bibelstudien
SBTS	Sources for Biblical and Theological Study
SJ	Studia Judaica
SGWB	Studien zur Geschichte der Wissenschaften in Basel
SKG.GK	Schriften der Königsberger Gelehrten Gesellschaft. Geisteswissenschaftliche Klasse
SOTSMS	Society for Old Testament Studies Monograph Series 5
SubBi	Subsidia biblica
TGl	*Theologie und Glaube*
Trad	*Tradition*
Traj	Trajectories
UTb	Uni-Taschenbücher
VT	*Vetus Testamentum*
VTSup	Supplements to Vetus Testamentum
WBC	Word Biblical Commentary
WMANT	Wissenschaftliche Monographien zum Alten und Neuen Testament
ZAW	*Zeitschrift für die alttestamentliche Wissenschaft*

Acknowledgments

The following study represents a slightly revised version of my doctoral dissertatation, submitted under the same title to Baylor University in the spring of 2015. As this project reaches its final stage, I am keenly aware of how indebted I am to so many who have contributed so much. I am reminded of the words John Donne penned in his Meditation XVII, "No man is an Iland, intire of itselfe; every man is a peece of the Continent, a part of the maine; if a Clod bee washed away by the Sea, Europe is the lesse [.]"[1] Although the analogy is hyperbolic, many are the *peeces* without whom this study would be *the lesse.*

To begin, few have sacrificed more than my extended family. To my mother, grandmother, siblings, and in-laws, thank you for your enduring patience, constant faith, and generous support. I could not have asked you to give up more than you did: a decade, with but brief twice-a-year visits from Deb and me, and only the occasional phone call or other electronic communication to intervene. Since the births of Warren and Grant, the time and distance has become particularly palpable.

I also would like to extend my gratitude to my friends and colleagues with whom I have studied and served at Baylor University. Thank you for listening to me rave about Massah-Meribah over the last several years, for encouraging me to press on, yet keep my priorities duly ordered. My thanks especially goes to John E. Anderson, David P. Melvin, W. G. Hulbert, Kyle Welty, and Jangho Jo. Thank you for sharing office space, entertaining "Gartonian hypotheses," asking keen questions, critiquing charts, and engaging in much-needed witty banter. Annual conferences will ever be the highlight of my academic calendar largely on account of you.

Many professors have mentored and encouraged me on this journey and/or have directly contributed to this undertaking. I am grateful for the late Ruth Ann Foster, who first sparked my interest in the Massah-Meribah tradition via the temptation narratives in the gospels. I would also like to thank David E. Garland, W. Dennis Tucker, Jr., Todd D. Still, and Terry York, not only for their words of encouragement, but also for allowing me to serve the Truett community during the years this project took to complete. I especially wish to thank my dissertation director, James D. Nogalski, to whom I owe an immeasurable debt of gratitude. Thank you for your unending tutelage; for affording me opportunities too numerous to list; and for inspiring excellence in everything from writing undergraduate

---

1 John Donne, *Devotions upon Emergent Occasions* (ed. John Sparrow; 1624; repr., London: Cambridge University Press, 1923), 98.

Hebrew exams to writing this dissertation. Thank you for being my *Doktorvater* in every sense of the word. To the remaining members of my committee—Lidija Novakovic, Stephen B. Reid, William H. Bellinger, Jr., and Kelly R. Iverson—your careful reading and critical insights are greatly appreciated. Special thanks also goes to Joel S. Burnett for reading and commenting on the manuscript, and as well to the Glenn O. and Martell B. Hilburn Endowed Graduate Research Scholarship Fund for supporting my research.

Over the last year and a half, I have gained new friends at De Gruyter who also warrant recognition. I am especially grateful for the assitance of Sophie Wagenhofer and Johannes Parche in preparing the manuscript for publication. All remaining errors are, of course, my own.

Finally, words cannot begin to express my love and gratitude for my wife, Deb, and our two sons, Warren and Grant. Thank you, Sweetheart, for always believing in me and loving me, even in those stress-filled moments when I was not making it easy to do either or both. Thank you for shouldering so many responsibilities; I could not have done this without you. You are my rock that has followed me about, my source of all that is sweet in this life; and through this academic sojourn I have lacked nothing, all on account of you. To Warren and Grant, I love you more than life itself. You are the greatest gifts of joy I have ever received, and your calls to "come play" were a singular source of motivation to finish what I had started. Now that Daddy's "infinity work" is finally done, let's go hiking and find some treasure; let's go play hide-and-seek, and I'll be surprised to find you in the same hiding spot each and every time.

Chapter One: Introduction

1.1 The Texts of the Massah-Meribah Tradition*

Few traditions are so prevalent in the Hebrew Bible, and yet have garnered so little direct scholarly attention, as that of the divine provision of water from a rock during ancient Israel's desert sojourn. The narrative forms of this tradition occur in Exod 17:1–7 and Num 20:1–13, with the former set at Massah and Meribah and the latter at the waters of Meribah. Beyond these two narratives, numerous texts within the Hebrew Bible explicitly evoke the Massah-Meribah tradition (M-Mt)[1]: Num 20:24; 27:12–14; Deut 6:16; 9:22; 32:51; 33:8; Ezek 47:19; 48:28; Ps 81:8, 17; 95:8–11; 106:32.[2] As well, allusions to this tradition occur in many other biblical texts: Num 33:14–15; Deut 8:15; 32:13; Isa 48:21; Ps 78:15–16, 20; 105:41; 114:8; Neh 9:15, 20. Finally, there is evidence of intertextual echoes in Isa 7:10–14; 43:20; Jer 14:1–12, 19–22; and Ezek 16:13, 19 (cf. Deut 32:13).[3] To-

---

* This study uses MT versification to cite texts within the Hebrew Bible.
1 One should not confuse this abbreviation with the standard abbreviation for the *Miqṣat Maʻaśê ha-Torah* (MMT). This scroll, also designated as 4QMMT, consists of six fragmentary manuscripts, numbered 4Q394–4Q399 (MMT[a-f]). The Massah-Meribah tradition does not appear in 4QMMT, so the current study will not treat it. For a full treatment of the content of this scroll, see Elisha Qimron and John Strugnell, *Qumran Cave 4.V: Miqṣat Maʻaśê ha-Torah* (DJD X; Oxford: Clarendon, 1994).
2 At times, scholars have emended two further texts so that they would then evoke the M-Mt: namely, Deut 33:2 and 2 Kgs 11:6. In Deut 33:2, the phrase "with myriads of holy ones" (מרבבת קדש) has occasionally prompted reconstructions based on G's rendering of the MT's קדש as Καδης (= קדש) instead of ἡγιασμένοι (cf. LXX Deut 33:3) or some other Greek equivalent. The emendation then pertains to מרבבת (with myriads), shifting it to מרבת (defective) to create Meribath Kadesh (e.g., C. J. Labuschagne, "The Tribes in the Blessing of Moses," in *Language and Meaning: Studies in Hebrew Language and Biblical Exegesis: Papers Read at the Joint British-Dutch Old Testament Conference at London, 1973* [ed. James Barr; OtSt 19; Leiden: Brill, 1974], 99). As McCarthy correctly notes, however, 1) the form is most often "מי מריבה (Num 20:13, 24; Deut 33:8; Pss 81:8; 106:32) or מי מריבות קדש (Ezek 47:19) or מי מריבת קדש (Deut 32:51; Ezek 48:28)," and 2) not even G renders מרבבת in this way, reading instead σὺν μυριάσιν (= מרבבת). (Carmel McCarthy, *Biblia Hebraica Quinta, Fascicle 5: Deuteronomy* [Stuttgart: Deutsche Bibelgesellschaft, 2007], 155*). As for 2 Kgs 11:6, the 1599 Geneva Bible emended the *hapax legomenon* מסח in the phrase בית מסח ("the house of defense" [?]) to מסה to form the phrase "the house of Massah." There is, however, no earlier manuscript that supports this emendation.
3 For a summary of the intertextual indicators in these texts, see p. 6 n. 13 and p. 241 n. 13 below.

gether, these texts show the power of the M-Mt within the collective, imaginative memories of ancient Israel, the force of which is detectable not only in the Pentateuch, but in the Prophets and Writings as well.

The challenges of reconstructing the stages of the M-Mt's tradition-historical development are formidable, three of which merit preliminary consideration. First, unlike the widely attested exodus tradition,[4] it is clear that the M-Mt did not achieve consistent formulation prior to, or even immediately after, its codifications. Instead, the M-Mt continued to be a "living" tradition, the imaginative reflections and appropriations of which extend well beyond the confines of the Hebrew Bible.[5] The fact that the M-Mt continued to be malleable after its codifications leads one to expect a certain level of diversity within the Hebrew Bible itself. Even so, the pluriformity of the M-Mt within the Hebrew Bible is staggering (cf. §1.2).

A second challenge to reconstructing the developments of the M-Mt is a logical outgrowth of the first challenge: namely, the question of where to begin. The last three decades have witnessed the erosion (if not collapse) of the classic historical-critical foundations upon which one could reconstruct the preliterary and literary developments of the Pentateuch and its traditions. Indeed, left in the wake of the revisionist work of the last thirty-five years is a foundational void, one which diachronic scholars must carefully and modestly negotiate if progress is to be made in uncovering the complicated prehistory of the biblical text.[6] No

---

[4] Despite the frequency of their occurrence within the Hebrew Bible, the formulae that evoke the exodus tradition can be classified under one of the two following expressions. The first uses the hifil of עלה (41 times); the second and more prevalent form uses the hifil of יצא (83 times) (John Wijngaards, "הוציא and העלה: A Twofold Approach to the Exodus," VT 15.1 [1965]: 91–102; cf., Roy E. Garton, "Rattling the Bones of the Twelve: Wilderness Reflections in the Formation of the Book of the Twelve," in *Perspectives on the Formation of the Book of the Twelve* [ed. Rainer Albertz, James D. Nogalski, and Jakob Wöhrle; BZAW 433; Berlin : de Gruyter, 2012], 241–243).

[5] That the M-Mt continued to enthrall the imagination of readers beyond the confines of the Hebrew Bible is also clear. Allusions to it are extant in the Apocrypha (Wis 11:4–10; 2 Esd 1:17–20), the New Testament (1 Cor 10:4; Heb. 3:7–11 [cf. Ps 95:8–11]), the Pseudepigrapha (4 Ezra 1:20; L.A.B. 10:7; Hel. Syn. Pr. 12:74), Josephus (*Ant.* 20.8.10 [cf. Ps 95:8–11]), and Philo (*Det. 115–118*). Moreover, similar to Isa 7:10–14 and Jer 14:1–9, 19–22, the M-Mt continued to inspire intertextual appropriations (Jdt 8–11; Matt 4:1–11 ‖ Luke 4:1–13). For a preliminary assessment of these texts, see p. 241 n. 13.

[6] Recently, David M. Carr summed up this situation well: "The mid- to late-twentieth-century consensus that formerly held about the history of the development of the Hebrew Bible – for example, the various tradition-centers and institutional contexts for the formation of early traditions, early J and E source documents for the Pentateuch, an exilic context for the formation of Deuteronomistic History, the assignment of the bulk of early prophetic writings to the prophets

longer can the tradition historian afford to presume the validity of source critical reconstructions, the primacy of etiology, or evolutionary growth models. Granted, a number of studies have engaged the M-Mt to limited extents from other vantage points, such as tradition blocks or form-critical patterns. Yet for various reasons, none have successfully accounted for the diversity of the M-Mt in the biblical texts themselves. Toward this end, it is necessary to survey past research on the M-Mt, with particular attention paid to the methodological frameworks so far employed toward explicating its developments (cf. §1.3).

A third challenge meriting preliminary concern is the issue of defining this study's method (cf. §1.4). Among the approaches of critical biblical inquiry, tradition-history remains notoriously difficult to define procedurally on account of what Douglas Knight calls the "the multiplicity of the phenomenon."[7] As I have summarized elsewhere, by this turn of phrase, he means that "tradents can pass down practically any inheritable datum (*traditum*), whether oral or written, through an array of techniques that constitute the traditioning process (*traditio*)."[8] Such a dynamic process at least partly explains why no consensus has emerged regarding the parameters of tradition history's scope and method.[9] Is the subject of investigation oral or literary in nature, or both? On the one hand, if oral, does it pertain only to the oral prehistory of a specific literary work (*Überlieferungsgeschichte*), or should it concern itself more broadly with the evolution of the ideas, motifs, or themes within a tradition (*Traditionsgeschichte*)?[10] As well, one ought to question whether these two meth-

---

themselves (e.g., Amos, Hosea), etc. – no longer holds" (*The Formation of the Hebrew Bible: A New Reconstruction* [New York: Oxford University Press, 2011], 3).

[7] Douglas Knight, "Introduction: Tradition and Theology," in *Tradition and Theology in the Old Testament* (ed. Douglas Knight; Philadelphia: Fortress Press, 1977), 2. Knight goes on to ask, "What cannot be considered a matter of tradition? The term is applied as readily to oral and written literature (of all genres) as it is to customs, habits, beliefs, moral standards, cultural attitudes and values, [and] social and religious institutions" ("Introduction," 2). Similarly, Odil Hannes Steck states that "Der Begriff "Traditions-geschichte" ist infolge der Mehrdeutigkeit seines ersten Wortbestandteiles in der exegetischen Literatur alles andere als eindeutig festgelegt" (*Exegese des alten Testaments: Leitfaden der Methodik: Ein Arbeitbuch für Proseminare, Seminare, und Vorlesungen* [12., überarbeitete und erweiterte Auflage 1989; Neukirchen-Vluyn: Neukirchener Verlag, 1971], 127).

[8] Garton, "Rattling the Bones," 239; cf. p. 3 n. 7 above.

[9] For a succinct treatment on the variety of scholarly perspectives on the scope and method of tradition history, see Douglas A. Knight, *Rediscovering the Traditions of Israel* (3rd ed.; SBLSBL 16; Atlanta: Society of Biblical Literature, 2006), 17–20.

[10] Here, Knight cites the definitions of *Überlieferungsgeschichte* and *Traditionsgeschichte* according to Sellin-Fohrer and Barth-Steck (Knight, *Rediscovering Traditions*, 18–19; Ernst Sellin and Georg Fohrer, *Einleitung in das alte Testament: begründet von Ernst Sellin; neubearbeitung*

ods of inquiry are as mutually exclusive as formative practitioners have made them out to be.¹¹ On the other hand, if one's study extends into the literary stages, at what stage of literary production and development does one transition from the concerns of tradition history to those of another discipline? This last question then raises the issue of tradition history's relationship to other critical methods. Should it be one characterized by sharp distinctives apart from the other methods, or should one expect a certain level of overlap?

The present study is not concerned with resolving these issues, so there is no attempt to do so. Rather, the challenge at hand merely requires the limning of a tradition historical approach that, despite this lack of methodological uniformity in the field, is nevertheless both transparent and capable of consistent application, and yet is sufficiently flexible to account for the diversity of the M-Mt itself. It is to the matter of this immense diversity that this study now turns.

1.2 The Diversity of the Tradition in the Hebrew Bible

Just within the Hebrew Bible, the iterations of the M-Mt demonstrate a startling diversity. The narratives in Exodus 17 and Numbers 20, though deriving from the same oral tradition, have had separate, yet at times intertwined literary developments, the results of which have come to embody the precedent failures of both ancient Israel and her leaders respectively. In Exod 17:1–7, the people use the absence/provision of water as a divining rod determining Yahweh's absence/presence among them; in Num 20:1–13, however, the tradition has evolved to explain why Moses and Aaron were forbidden to enter the Promised Land (cf. Num 20:24; 27:12–14; Deut 32:51). One can see further diversity in the different geographical locations associated with these narratives. The Exodus narrative not only has the

---

von Georg Fohrer [11th ed.; Heidelberg: Quelle & Meyer, 1969], 28–31; O. H. Steck, (*Exegese des alten Testaments: Leitfaden der Methodik: Ein Arbeitbuch für Proseminare, Seminare, und Vorlesungen* [13th, rev. ed.; Neukirchen-Vluyn: Neukirchener Verlag, 1993], 63–64.

11 Carr's research into the role that memory plays in the formation of written texts reveals this bifurcation as inadequate for describing the "*oral-performative* and *communal* context" in which ancient Israel would have learned its "*written* tradition": "This stress on the role of *memory* in the formation of *written* texts involves overcoming a dichotomy, all too common in studies of the ancient world, between orality/memorization and writing/literacy. Though scholars decades ago deconstructed the idea that there was a 'great divide' between orality and literacy, a remarkable number of high-quality publications still work with a strong distinction between the two [...] Scholars of antiquity are just at the beginning of exploring the interface between writing, performance, memorization, and the aural dimension of literary texts" (Carr, *Formation of the Hebrew Bible*, 5).

dual etiologies of Massah and Meribah, but is also set at Rephidim near the wilderness of סין (Exod 17:1; cf. Num 33:14) and is somehow proximate to Horeb (Exod 17:6). The Numbers narrative, however, has the single etiology of Meribah situated at Kadesh within the wilderness of צן (Num 20:1; cf. 33:36).

The six reminiscences of this tradition within Deuteronomy demonstrate even greater diversity. In Deut 6:16, the people's testing Yahweh at Massah is the archetypal failure of the wilderness generation; while in Deut 8:15–16, it is Yahweh who tested the people, leading them into the wilderness without water, and slaking their thirst with water from the flinty rock (מצור החלמיש). The location of Massah within ancient Israel's wilderness sojourn becomes an issue in Deut 9:22, Deuteronomy's third remembrance of the M-Mt. Here, Massah appears in a historical recitation that spans from the exodus out of Egypt to the failed initial entry into the land (Deut 9:7–23). Along the way, the failure at Massah occurs *after* the Horeb event, and *between* two similar provocations that occurred at Taberah and then at Kibroth-hattaavah. The narratives that correspond to these additional provocations are in Numbers 11, where the story of Massah is noticeably missing. The fourth instance in Deuteronomy lies couched within the Song of Moses (Deut 32:1–43). Here the bard portrays Yahweh as the divine צור (32:4, 15, 18, 30, 31), who not only found and guided his people in the wilderness, but also nourished them with honey from the crag (סלע) and oil from flinty rock (חלמיש צור) (Deut 32:13; cf. Ezek 16:13, 19). Immediately following the Song of Moses is a fifth iteration of the M-Mt (Deut 32:51), one closely related to the narrative in Numbers 20. Once again, the M-Mt functions as the rationale for Moses' disqualification from entering the Promised Land—a rationale that within Deuteronomy also exhibits tradition-historical developments (cf. Deut 1:34–37; 3:21–22, 26; 4:21–22). The sixth and final reminiscence of this tradition within Deuteronomy lies within one of most obscure texts in the Hebrew Bible: the Blessing of Moses in Deuteronomy 33.[12] In the Levite portion of the Blessing (Deut 33:8–11), Massah and Meribah are names of the location where Levi (or the Levites) purportedly chose covenant fidelity over familial fidelity; the precise narrative details of this event, however, are no longer extant.

Outside the Pentateuch, the reminiscences of the M-Mt only increase the diversity by which this tradition finds expression. Within the Latter Prophets, the most overt occurrences are in Deutro-Isaiah and Ezekiel. In Isa 48:21, the prophet recalls that the wilderness ancestors did not thirst (צמא) at all on account of Yah-

---

[12] Recently, Harald Samuel went so far as to declare that "Das Kapitel [i.e., Dtn 33] gehört zweifelsohne zu den enigmatischsten in der Hebräischen Bibel" (*Von Priestern zum Patriarchen: Levi und die Leviten im alten Testament* [BZAW 448; Berlin–Boston: de Gruyter, 2014], 63).

weh's providing water from the rock (*contra* Exod 17:3; Num 20:2, 5). Although the Isaianic tradents do not situate this tradition geographically, the opposite is true for the tradents of Ezekiel: Ezek 47:19 and 48:28 only relay the toponyms, not the narrative components, associated with the tradition. This absence is a function of the *Gattungen* wherein these toponyms reside; as boundary lists, one does not expect traditional associations spelled out. What is curious, however, is the orthography of the toponym in Ezek 47:19 as nowhere else is Meribah-Kadesh spelled as מריבות קדש. (The place name מריבת קדש in Ezek 48:28 also occurs in Num 27:14b and Deut 32:51). Finally, it is within the Latter Prophets that one detects varying degrees of the tradition being utilized intertextually, specifically in Isa 7:10–14; Jer 14:1–12, 19–22; and Ezek 16:13, 19 (cf. Deut 32:13).[13]

Within the Writings, most of the reminiscences of the M-Mt are preserved in the Psalter, specifically Books III–V. In Book III (Pss 73–89), two psalms preserve such reminiscences—namely, psalms 78 and 81—both of which are part of the Asaphite collection (Pss 50 + 73–83). In Psalm 78, the center of the Psalter,[14] the psalmist recalls the wonders Yahweh performed during the desert sojourn and the forgetfulness of the wilderness generation. In v. 15, the psalmist remembers that the deity supplied water from the *rocks* in the wilderness (צרים במדבר), as opposed to a singular *rock* (cf. Exod 17:6). In parallel fashion, v. 16 relays the same wonder had occurred with a crag (מסלע; cf. Num 20:8–11). Then curiously vv. 19–20 refers to אלהים (not Moses!) striking a rock (צור; cf. Exod 17:6) so that water gushed out. Finally, in v. 35—the center verse of the Psalter—Israel's ancestors at last remember כי־אלהים צורם, "that God was their Rock" (cf. Deut 32:15, 18, 30–31).

---

13 The case for intertextuality, however, requires a cumulative argument and a method of inquiry that does not suit the current study. Consequently, only a cursory introduction can be afforded here. In Isa 7:10–14, the dialogue between King Ahaz and the prophet demonstrates an awareness of Deut 6:16, which in turn appears to inspire the symbolic naming of עמנו אל (Isa 7:14) via the pre-literary etiology of Massah and the tradition as reflected in the Song of Moses (cf. Exod 17:7; Deut 32:10–14). Jeremiah 14:1–12, 19–22, on the other hand, appropriates the literary etiology of Massah (cf. Jer 14:9; Exod 17:7) in a public lament designed to secure the divine provision of water during a severe drought. Finally, in Ezekiel 16, the tradition emerges in an intertextual appropriation of the Song of Moses, where the deity recalls providing personified Jerusalem with bread, honey, and oil during the days of her youth (cf. Ezek 16:19; Deut 32:13). See also p. 241 n. 13 below.

14 By Masoretic counting, Ps 78:35/36 is the center of Psalter (see the Masoretic notation חצי הספר). As well, Beat Weber argues that this psalm was intentionally redacted to be the center of the Psalter and so does not occupy this position by mere coincidence ("Psalm 78 als 'Mitte' des Psalters? – ein Versuch," *Bib* 88 [2007]: 305–325).

In Psalm 81, the psalmist associates Yahweh having tested (√בחן) Israel על־מי מריבה in v. 8 (cf., Num 20:13; Deut 33:8; Ps 106:32) with the issuance of honey (דבש) from the rock (צור) in v. 17. The association of these particular tradition components not only affirms reading Deut 32:13 within the M-Mt, but it also slightly diversifies it. Instead of honey from the rock (Ps 81:16), the Song of Moses has honey issuing forth from a crag (סלע) and oil from the flinty rock (חלמיש צור).

Three reminiscences of the tradition occur in Book IV of the Psalter (Pss 90–106). The first instance is Ps 95:8–9, which recalls how ancient Israel's ancestors hardened their hearts at Meribah and Massah respectively and the consequences of doing so. Specifically, for the psalmist, the ancestor's testing (√נסה) Yahweh at Massah and Meribah was the primary rationale for the deity's rejecting the wilderness generation, who as a result would never enter into Yahweh's rest (Ps 95:10–11; cf. Num 14:26–35).[15]

The remaining two instances of this tradition in Book IV arise in the twin psalms that conclude it. In the historical recitation of Psalm 105, the psalmist recalls Yahweh's prodigal and wondrous deeds (נפאלות / עלילות) on behalf of ancient Israel (vv. 1, 2, 5). Beginning with the covenant with Abraham, the psalmist rehearses the exploits of Yahweh, who eventually delivers Israel from Egypt and provisions them during their sojourn according to whatever they ask (vv. 37–42). The final wonder the psalmist evokes, however, is the deity opening a rock (פתח צור) for water to flow like a river in the desert (v. 41; cf. Isa 43:20), "for (כי) he remembered his holy covenant with Abraham his servant" (v. 42). In short, in Psalm 105, the psalmist not only recalls the tradition positively, but also uniquely ties it to the covenant of the ancestral narratives.

Conversely, in the historical recitation of Psalm 106, the psalmist decries the failure of ancient Israel's ancestors to perceive Yahweh's נפאלות or remember his חסד while in Egypt (v. 7). This forgetfulness comes to typify the wilderness generation's relationship with their deity during their desert sojourn (cf. vv. 13, 21, 45). After their deliverance at the Reed Sea (vv. 7b-12), they quickly forgot Yahweh's deeds, refused to wait for his counsel, craved wantonly, and tested God in the wilderness (v. 14; cf. Num 14:22). The psalmist proceeds erring grievances in an order that, with the exception of the Golden Calf (vv. 19–20) and the Meribah (vv. 32–33) stories being misplaced, reflects the narratives in Numbers 11–25 (cf. Ps 106:13–33) and, more generally, the cycle of judges (Ps 106:34–46; cf.

---

15 This failure to enter Yahweh's rest (κατάπαυσις in the LXX) is an important theme in the book of Hebrews, which quotes extensively from the Septuagint version of Psalm 95 (Heb 3:7b–4:15).

Judg 2:16–16:31). As for these two misplaced stories, both relate in varying degrees to the M-Mt: the Meribah reflection is obvious, but many scholars believe the Levites' role in the Golden Calf story (cf., Exod 32:26–29) to be the closest parallel to the M-Mt reflected in Deut 33:8–10.¹⁶ Returning to the explicit reference of the מי מריבה in vv. 32–33, the psalmist blames the wilderness generation for Moses' misfortune, for they had embittered (√מרה) Moses' spirit (cf. Num 20:1–13).

The Psalter's last reminiscence of the M-Mt occurs within Book V (Pss 107–150), namely Ps 114:8. Set in the context of ancient Israel's exodus from Egypt (v. 1), the tradition serves as an intertext inspiring the psalmist to juxtapose the reactions of watery and rocky entities to divine presence throughout the psalm. The reactions of the seas and the Jordan (vv. 3, 5) are collated with reactions of the mountains and hills (vv. 4, 6). In the last two verses, the psalmist commands the ארץ to tremble before the Lord (אדון), the God of Jacob (אלוה יעקב), who turned the rock (צור) into a pool of water and the flint (חלמיש) into a spring of water.

Finally, the last reminiscences one encounters in surveying the Hebrew Bible for the M-Mt are in Nehemiah 9. Here, the scribe Ezra leads a prayer of communal lament, reciting Yahweh's exploits from creation (v. 6) through the "prophets" (vv. 26–31). In Neh 9:15, the divine provision of water from a crag (סלע), along with the bread (לחם) from heaven, is recalled after the Sinai event (v. 14–15) but prior to the initial command to enter land and the people's refusal to do so (vv. 15b-17). This arrangement parallels the reminiscence within Deut 9:22–23, which again bears resemblance to Numbers 11–14. The parallelism, however, breaks down in Neh 9:18–20, which contains a second, more allusive echo of the tradition. Specifically, it is here—that is, after the wilderness generation's refusal to enter the land—that the writer of this prayer recalls the Golden Calf incident (v. 18) and that Yahweh continued to provide them manna for their mouths and water for their thirst (v. 20).

Cumulatively, the texts iterating the M-Mt within the Hebrew Bible display the M-Mt's remarkable elasticity. Points of divergence can be detected along these fundamental lines: *agency, location, substance of issuance, source of issuance, canonical awareness,*¹⁷ and *interpretative significance.* Secondarily, one

---

16 See p. 128 n. 128 below.
17 The term "canonical awareness" does not imply awareness of a closed canon, as though the texts in question had achieved their final form. Rather, this term refers to an awareness of precursory collections which were seminal to the formation of the Pentateuch. The advantage of *canonical*, as opposed to *corpus*, is that the term "canonical" better reflects the import that these precursors held for their tradents. The presupposition here is that the tradents responsible

must also contend with the diversity of vocabulary, etiologies, orthography, and the evidence for intertextual appropriations. These tensions within the literary reflections of the M-Mt strain the bonds of credulity, yet there is little room for doubting their genetic relationship. The question, of course, is how did this immense diversity come about? What were the processes of transmission whereby the M-Mt found its varied expressions? Only in answering these questions can one then begin to imagine the literary-social milieu of the tradents responsible for them and begin to grasp the historical and theological import of this tradition for these tradents and their readers.

1.3 The Gap in Scholarship

Given its frequency, distribution, and diversity of expression, it comes as no surprise that some scholars doubt the feasibility of successfully tracing the developments of the M-Mt. Brevard Childs' reservations regarding this task are particularly salient:

> There is such a variety in the Old Testament's use of the Meribah tradition that one can suspect a complex history of tradition lying behind the present narrative [i.e., Exod 17:1–7]. Unfortunately the evidence for tracing this development is no longer available, and one is left with a variety of hypotheses which have little chance of being established or disproved.[18]

From Childs' perspective, then, tracing this tradition is complicated for two reasons: not only is there the diversity of expression discussed above, but also there is insufficient evidence for doing so.

Childs' measured skepticism is slightly ironic. Granted, the varied forms in which this tradition finds expression pose serious challenges for anyone attempting to trace it, but the problems of doing so do not stem from a lack of evidence. On the contrary, one could almost contend that there is too much evidence! There are too many awkwardly shaped pieces in the proverbial puzzle box; too many to piece back together into a single, two-dimensional picture of

---

for these precursors did not necessarily preserve all available materials in library fashion, only those materials that they held to be authoritative.

18 Brevard S. Childs, *The Book of Exodus: A Critical, Theological Commentary* (OTL; Louisville: Westminster Press, 1974), 306. John Durham expresses a similar sentiment regarding the tradition history of Exod 17:1–7, for the "multiplicity of opinion [. . .] makes clear that the shifts and currents present in this section render any universally acceptable source or tradition analysis an impossibility. The evidence is ambiguous; the points of departure are too elusive" (*Exodus* [WBC 3; Waco: Word Books, 1987], 229).

linear growth. Yet this critique may simply be bypassing the heart of Childs' demurring. In reading between the lines, what Childs appears to be saying is that there is no acceptable diachronic foundation whereby to negotiate *the variety in the Old Testament's use of the [Massa-]Meribah tradition.*

Further, despite the impression Childs would give, there is in fact a dearth of studies *focused* on this tradition.[19] Instead, studies touching upon the M-Mt have largely done so in tangential fashion as part of larger programs of research, particularly the discovery of the Pentateuch's formative stages. Although admittedly heuristic, the division of these studies under the terms "classic historical-critical" and "revisionist" proves useful for underscoring our method below (cf. §1.4).

1.3.1 Within Classic Historical-Critical Studies

Although one can no longer make sharp distinctions along critical disciplinary lines,[20] by far and away the foremost methodological approach scholars have applied toward the study of the M-Mt is that of *source criticism*. For most of the twentieth century, the exponents of Gunkel's tradition-historical and form critical methods (*Überlieferungsgeschichte* and *Gattungsforschung* respectively) presupposed the framework of the Graf-Wellhausen hypothesis.[21] The major works of Hugo Gressmann (1913), Gerhard von Rad (1938, 1957), Martin Noth (1948, 1958), Sigo Lehming (1961), George W. Coats (1968), Childs (1974), and Propp (1987) all assume, albeit progressively to lesser and lesser degrees, the veracity of the findings of source critical inquiry.[22] Gressmann, who was the first to at-

---

[19] Sigo Lehming's brief article on the topic is the lone exception ("Massa und Meriba" ZAW 73 [1961]: 71–77).
[20] Childs makes a similar observation (*Introduction to the Old Testament as Scripture* [Philadelphia: Fortress, 1979], 119).
[21] As did Hermann Gunkel himself, who believed his investigation into the oral composition of Genesis to compliment the Graf-Wellhausen documentary hypothesis (*Schöpfung und Chaos in Urzeit und Endzeit: Eine religionsgeschichtliche Untersuchung über Gen 1 und Ap Joh 12* [Göttingen: Vandenhoeck & Ruprecht, 1895]; *Genesis: Übersetzt und Erklärt* [3rd ed.; Göttingen: Vandenhoeck & Ruprecht, 1910]).
[22] Hugo Gressmann, *Mose und seine Zeit: Ein Kommentar zu den Mose-Sagen* (FRLANT 18; Göttingen: Vandenhoeck & Ruprecht, 1913); Gerhard von Rad, *Das formgeschichtliche Problem des Hexateuchs* (BWA(N)T 4.26; Stuttgart: W. Kohlhammer, 1938); *Theologie des alten Testaments* (2 vols.; 2nd ed.; 1957; repr., München: Chr. Kaiser, 1958); Martin Noth, *Überlieferungsgeschichte des Pentateuch* (Stuttgart: W. Kohlhammer, 1948); *Das zweite Buch Mose: Exodus* (ATD 5; Göttingen: Vandenhoeck & Ruprecht, 1958); Lehming, "Massa und Meriba," 71–77; George W. Coats, *Rebellion in the Wilderness: The Murmuring Motif in the Wilderness Traditions of the Old Testament* (Nashville: Abingdon, 1968); Childs, *Exodus*; William H. Propp, *Water in the Wilderness:*

tempt a tradition-history in the vein of Gunkel, relied heavily on source critical analyses.²³ Twenty-five years later, however, von Rad pronounced a stalemate (*Stillstand*) among source-critical scholars, which he overcame through the isolation of the "*kleine geschichtliche Credo.*"²⁴ Yet as influential as his "discovery" and his subsequent *Theologie* were in their time, they shed little light on the topic at hand because von Rad paid only scant attention to the M-Mt.²⁵ Instead,

---

A Biblical Motif and its Mythological Background (HSM 40; Georgia: Scholars Press, 1987). This method's most recent and stalwart champion is Joel S. Baden, whose concern with this tradition is limited to identifying the sources to which certain M-Mt texts belong. As for the tradition's developments, he simply concludes "that some form of testing occurred" at Massah-Meribah, but "the nature of this testing was a matter on which traditions varied" (*J, E, and the Redaction of the Pentateuch* [FAT 68; Tübingen: Mohr Siebeck, 2009], 175). Baden's more recent contribution, *The Composition of the Pentateuch* (AYBRL; New Haven: Yale University Press, 2012), makes no further remarks on the developments of this tradition.

23 In *Mose und seine Zeit*, Gressmann divides the narrative of Moses into twenty-nine separate legends (*Sagen*) and proceeds to extract the earliest literary layers along classic source critical lines. Only then does he proceed to reconstruct tradition cycles (*Sagenkranze*) into which these legends first coalesced (*Mose und seine Zeit*, 1–344).

24 Von Rad, *Das formgeschichtliche Problem*, 1. Already well-known, von Rad's thesis needs only to be summarized: Deut 26:5b-9 preserves the earliest form of this ancient Israelite creed, which rehearses "der Hauptdaten der Heilsgeschichte": Israel's ancestral beginnings, Egyptian enslavement, divine deliverance from Egypt, and subsequent entrance into the Promised Land. Later forms can be found in Deut 6:20–24 and Josh 24:2b-13, with adaptions in Exod 15:4–5, 8–10a, 12–16; 1 Sam 12:8; Pss 78, 105, and 136. Together, these texts attest to the creed having been recited on cultic occasions, as well as to the existence of a canonical form for Israel's salvation-history. Striking, of course, is the absence of any component reminiscent of the Sinai Tradition until postexilic recitations (cf. Neh 9:13–14; Ps 106) (*Das formgeschichtliche Problem*, 4–5, 8–11). It is at this point that von Rad's findings reinforce those Wellhausen and Gressmann regarding the secondary nature of the Sinai Tradition; although, he is careful not to confuse the priority of the Sinai Tradition with its antiquity: "Über das absolute Alter der beiden Traditionen ergibt sich aus unseren Festsellungen noch nichts […] Was wir aussagen können, ist lediglich dies, daß zwei Traditionen vorliegen, von denen die eine sekundär in die andere eingearbeitet ist" (*Das formgeschichtliche Problem*, 17).

25 Whatever the reason for this neglect, it certainly was not on account of the tradition's lack of antiquity. For von Rad the fact that the "sakralen Überlieferungen von Kadesh"—including the stories of Massah and Meribah—never became an actual tradition-complex (*eigentlichen Überlieferungsbildung*) could itself be a sign of their high antiquity. Specifically, von Rad sees the verbal roots of the etiologies (נסה "prüfen" or "erproben"; ריב "prozessieren") as evidence for legal cases having once been decided within the district of Kadesh; then granting priority to Deut 33:8–10, he attributes the preservation of these traditions to the Levites, who had in some way proved their worth at Massah and Meribah (*Theologie des alten Testaments*, 1.19 n.19, 19–20, 22). Elsewhere, as far as I can tell, the only other place where von Rad gives sustain attention to a text relevant to this tradition in his *Die Priesterschrift im Hexateuch: Literarisch*

it is Martin Noth who first provided a way forward for exploring this tradition. In fact, Noth's central thesis in *Überlieferungsgeschichte des Pentateuch*—namely, that the traditions of the Pentateuch had coalesced around five major themes—remains one of his most enduring legacies.²⁶ Yet like Gunkel, Gressman, and von Rad before him, Noth could not envision such pre-literary processes culminating into the final text without imaging the classic source documents constituting an intermediate stage—documents which revisionist scholars have increasingly either rejected or radically redefined (see §1.3.2).²⁷ Noth's commentary on Exodus is an example of this persistent presupposition, as in it he pays meager attention to the traditioning process and instead again focuses on source critical matters.²⁸

The brief article by Sigo Lehming, "Massa und Meriba," represents a slight increase in the energies scholars had previously devoted toward this tradition. In his study, Lehming proceeds backward from the latest to the earliest narrative forms of this tradition (*from* Num 20:2–13 and Exod 17:1–7 *to* Deut 33:8–9). In his analysis, the development of the M-Mt began as a result of a misunderstand-

---

untersucht und theologisch gewertet (BWA(N)T 4.13; Stuttgart: W. Kohlhammer, 1934), 117–119, which is primarily source critical in nature.

26 Likewise, Noth's thesis also requires only summary attention: he begins by isolating five themes (*Hauptthemen*) around which ancient Israel's traditions coalesced (*aneinandergereiht*). Citing Galling and von Rad, he dismisses the themes of "*Erzvätergeschichte*" and "*Offenbarung am Sinai*" as secondary. Likewise, the theme of "*Führung in der Wüste*" is also secondary, as it depends on the themes of "*Herausführung aus Ägypten*" and "*Hineinführung in das palästinische Kulturland*," with the former of the two having priority on account of its prevalence. Interestingly, if Noth had not dismissed "das Thema der Urgeschichte" as a post-literary addition to the Pentateuch, he would have had six major themes instead of five (*Überlieferungsgeschichte des Pentateuch*, 48–50, 63–64; cf. Kurt Galling, *Die Erwählungstraditionen Israels* [BZAW 48; Giessen: A. Töpelmann, 1928], 63 f.; von Rad, *Das formgeschichtliche Problem*, 11 ff.).

27 Noth was more cautious than von Rad regarding the codification of the Pentateuchal traditions. For von Rad, it was the Yahwist of the so-called "Solomonic Enlightenment" who merged these traditions; Noth, on the other hand, sees this merger first taking place in a "*Grundlage*" (G) during the time of the tribal amphictyony, but he is reticent as to whether G represents an oral or literary production. Once beyond these initial stages, however, both Noth and von Rad's compositional theories do not deviate substantially from that of Wellhausen (cf. *Das formgeschichtliche Problem*, especially 31–33, 37–42, 46–49, 62–64; Noth, *Überlieferungsgeschichte des Pentateuch*, 247–250).

28 In his commentary on Exodus, Noth is not concerned with the developments of the Massah-Meribah tradition; he merely posits the tradition's historical origin to lie in a locale where there was a gushing spring. Specifically, Noth imagines nomadic shepherds gathered at this location to resolve disputes; these nomads in turn were so amazed at the spring's gushing force that they attributed it to the miraculous. In the end, Noth provides no grounds for this reconstruction (*Exodus*, 112).

ing: "Massah" and "Meribah" derive from wordplay (*Wortspiel*) in Deut 33:8 where they are not place-names.[29] The JE redactor then added the "Massah" elements in Exod 17:2, 7; and P practically copied (*abgeschrieben*) Exod 17:1–7, modifying it for his purpose. Lehming's reconstruction has rightly drawn criticism, however, as his thesis treats the synonymous pair unequally: while Massah never existed, Meribah in turn is treated as the grounding etiology of the Exodus narrative.[30] Despite this logical flaw, one can at least commend Lehming on recognizing the importance of this tradition.

George W. Coats is among the first to undertake a thoroughgoing investigation of the developments of the M-Mt, as opposed to merely seeking its earliest detectable form. He does so, however, from the broader complex of Noth's *Führung in der Wüste* (cf. p. 12 n. 26 above) and the secondary motif of the murmuring traditions within it.[31] As for his method, Coats still begins with a source critical analysis; he then reconstructs the M-Mt's developments via the form-critical components of the resulting strata. Then in an unexpected twist Coats concedes the majority of these developments to have taken place prior to any literary stage —a goodly amount of literary analysis only to conclude the writers of the object analyzed had nearly no hand in the shaping of its contents.[32]

---

29 Lehming, "Massa und Meriba," 71, 74–75, 76–77.
30 See John Van Seters, *The Life of Moses: The Yahwist as Historian in Exodus-Numbers* (Louisville: Westminster John Knox, 1994), 196.
31 Coats proposes that the murmuring motif within the wilderness traditions developed along the following lines: initially, the wilderness traditions were positive recollections of Yahweh's aid in wilderness; a pro-Jerusalem J source then recast these traditions as negative accounts of rebellious murmuring in order to form a polemic against the northern kingdom; after the destruction of the northern kingdom, a Deuteronomistic influence couched the stories as tests depicting Israel's lack of faith; and finally the postexilic period saw a further broadening of this Deuteronomistic interpretation as an explanation of the exile (*Rebellion in the Wilderness*, 249–254). S. J. DeVries rightly critiqued Coats' historical reconstruction, however, as the use of the murmuring motif in a possible anti-Ephramite polemic does not necessitate that it was founded for that purpose ("The Origin of the Murmuring Tradition," *JBL* 87 [1968]: 51–58). Similarly, the same critique applies to Fritz, who argues that J introduced the murmuring motif into the wilderness tradition in order to warn the monarchy against rebelling against God, since such actions can result in the same divine punishment that the exodus generation experienced (Volkmar Fritz, *Israel in der Wüste: Traditiongeschichtliche Untersuchung der Wüstenüberlieferungen des Jahwisten* [MtS 7; Marburg: N. G. Elwert, 1970], 117–123).
32 Specifically, Coats argues that the form-critical components operative in J (Exod 17:1b-7) developed in four stages: first the etiology, then the miraculous aid, then the murmuring motif, and then a Deuteronomistic expansion (the Massah elements) and reinterpretation (an illustration of Israel's lack of faith). He then argues for a similar process for P [Num 20:1–13], but with two exceptions: P's version never came under the influence of the Deuteronomists, and P's reinterpretation explained why Moses and Aaron never enter the Promised Land (*Rebellion in the Wil-*

Likewise, Brevard Childs also treats our tradition under the rubric of the wilderness murmurings, but he is his markedly more skeptical of source critical solutions to the problem of the M-Mt's developments. Instead, he relies more heavily on *form-critical analysis*, through which he detects two distinct oral patterns underlying the structure of the murmuring stories.³³ These patterns, says Childs, had mutually influenced each other in the oral stages, and yet both were retained and further adapted by J and P sources.³⁴ In the end, like von Rad and Noth before him, Childs could not envision the journey from oral tradition to the text's final form without the intermediate production of continuous source documents.³⁵ As well, since the studies of Coats and Childs are in pursuit of larg-

---

derness, 53–83). Yet in the end, Coats concludes that the three primary levels in J's "Meribah and Massah traditions"—i.e. the etiology, the miracle, and the murmuring motif—"were in all probability already combined before the tradition reached literary form" (*Rebellion in the Wilderness*, 70).

33 Childs, *Exodus*, 306–307. The first oral pattern Childs describes as arising from a genuine need among the people and culminates in "God's miraculous provision", while the second is introduced without this basis and ends with Moses' intercession to mitigate divine punishment (*Exodus*, 258). This distinction along the lines of positive and negative components is by no means original, as the work of Coats aptly demonstrates (cf. p. 14 n. 31 above). The difference between Coats and Childs is primarily in how each envisions the role of etiology: Coats sees etiology as foundational, with the narrative being inspired from it; Childs, however, argues the opposite. Since the etiology echoes the dispute not the miracle, he concludes that the tradition expounded in Exodus 17 "did not develop from the etiology, but the etiology subsequently attached itself to the tradition" (*Exodus*, 307).

34 Specifically, Childs sees the following tradents utilizing this tradition: J collected and further redacted its material in such a way that the Pattern I stories lead up to the Golden Calf narrative (Exodus 32) and Pattern II follows thereafter; the "Deuteronomic school" expanded the parenetic function of the tradition, using it to motivate obedience from a people rebellious from their inception (Deut 9:24); and finally P not only has its own versions of the J stories (thereby retaining the oral patterns), but it also expands the scope of the tradition by adding new ones (e.g., Numbers 16) (*Exodus*, 259–263).

35 In fairness, one should recall that the sharp critique of Rolf Rendtorff, who nuanced the incompatibility of the presuppositions operative within the tradition-historical and source critical tasks, was not yet available. The latter, says Rendtorff distinguishes "mehrere durchlaufende literarische Quellen innerhalb des Pentateuch," ergo beginning with the Pentateuch in its final form (*Endgestalt*); the former, however, begins at the opposite end of the process, namely with the "einzelnen, ursprünglich selbständigen 'kleinsten Einheiten',", and traces the process of their development (*Überlieferungsbildung*) up to their final form (*Endstadium*) (*Das überlieferungsgeschichtliche Problem des Pentateuch* [BZAW 147; Berlin: de Gruyter, 1976], 1). In other words, what Gunkel, Gressman, von Rad, and Noth had considered a mere methodological extension, in retrospect was mechanically forced. Rendtorff therefore issues the call for "a thorough study of the formation and editing of the discrete larger units [...] whereby each is first con-

er agendas (Childs more so than Coats), they do not attend to the developments of the M-Mt to the extent warranted by the diversity preserved within the Hebrew canon.

William H. Propp (1987) approaches the topic from an even broader perspective than do Coats and Childs: the motif of water in the wilderness. He begins by briefly surveying the ancient Near Eastern texts that reflect a pattern of *Chaoskampf* followed by divine issuance of fertile waters.[36] He then looks at the biblical texts, proceeding from texts reflecting the least specific tradition components to texts with the most specific components.[37] The advantage of this approach is that it allows Propp to draw out functional associations at each level of specificity instead of defaulting to the framework of the Documentary Hypothesis, although it is clear he still presumes its general validity.[38] In this sense, Propp reflects the ongoing decline of the currency of the Graf-Wellhausen hypothesis. Regardless, his study is more of a *Motivgeschichte* than a *Traditionsgeschichte* per se.[39]

---

sidered on its own, without prior decision about its belonging to a larger complex or perhaps to one or more 'sources'" (*Problem des Pentateuch*, 28; translation mine).

36 Propp, *Water in the Wilderness*, 1–2.

37 Specifically, Propp moves from looking at those texts reflecting the motif of divine creation of water in the desert (chapter 1), to those texts where that provision is granted specifically to the Exodus generation or is said to have issued from a mountain (chapter 2), and finally to those texts that associate the provision with a particular place (chapter 3) (Propp, *Water in the Wilderness*, 6).

38 In his treatment of the most specific texts (i.e. etiological), it is clear that Propp still uses the Documentary Hypothesis as a foundation for formulating his tradition historical conclusions. For example, for Propp both Exod 15:23–26 and 17:2–7 are foundationally E, the later of the two in conjunction with Exodus 32 (the golden calf and the "testing of the Levites"; cf. Deut 33:8) represents a "new tale of apostasy appropriate to [the Elohist's] needs" (*Water in the Wilderness*, 69; cf. 52 and 81–82 n. 103). As well, Propp says that the priestly version of Massah-Meribah (Num 20:1–13) contains "little independent tradition" and is rather "a polemical re-writing of various JE materials repugnant to the Zadokite priesthood" (*Water in the Wilderness*, 67).

39 A short essay by Wolfmann Hermann could be included in this survey, as it briefly summarizes the debate regarding literary history of Exod 17:1–7. It does so, however, only to show the etiological question in v. 7bβ (היש יהוה בקרבנו אם אין) to be a late addition to the text and thereby establish the need to limn the tradition history behind the question. It is does not, however, seek to trace the development of the M-Mt and so is of limited value here (see *Ex 17,7bβ und die Frage nach der Gegenwart Jahwes in Israel* in *Alttestamentlicher Glaube und biblische Theologie: Festschrift für Horst Dietrich Pruess zum 65. Geburstag* [ed. Jutta Hausmann and Hans-Jürgen Zobel; Stuttgart: Kohlhammer, 1992], 46–55).

1.3.2 Within Revisionist Studies

That the last three decades have witnessed a paradigm shift within Pentateuchal studies away from the classic documentary hypothesis is so widely acknowledged that it needs little introduction here.[40] Albert de Pury summarizes the situation well:

> No, there had never been a Solomonic "Yahwist" (J) or a [sic] 8th-century Northern "Elohist" (E), and if a non-Priestly Pentateuchal global narrative could be presumed at all, a presupposition in itself disputed by some scholars (Rendtorff and his students), that narrative had to be brought down to the vicinity of Deuteronomistic literature (Perlitt, H. H. Schmid), i.e. at least to the reign of Josiah and more probably to exilic (Van Seters) or postexilic times (Rose). Only the Priestly source – P or, more precisely, P[G] (the Grundschrift, or first "edition" of that source) – survived the collapse as a more or less intact literary entity[.][41]

Although caveats could be made to this synthesis of the currents within Pentateuchal studies—a more careful statement, for example, would have used the term "Priestly *material*" rather than "Priestly source"—de Pury's assessment succinctly relays both the shift in the paradigm and the major exponents responsible for it. Embedded in many of these and other revisionist studies are treatments of the major texts preserving the M-Mt, but none have focused on the M-Mt to the exclusion of other agendas. Only a few merit attention here.

Aaron Schart (1990) provides a *redactional analysis* of the Wilderness Narrative, one that attempts to give methodological priority to the synchronic "Ana-

---

[40] A number of surveys from the last two decades give witness to the near demise of the documentary hypothesis, save for the continued consensus on what constitutes priestly (P) and non-priestly (Non-P) materials (e.g., John Van Seters, *The Pentateuch: A Social-Science Commentary* [Traj 1; Sheffield: Sheffield Academic, 1999], 58–85; Mark S. Smith with contributions by Elizabeth M. Block Smith, *The Pilgrimage Pattern in Exodus* [JSOTSup 239; Sheffield: Sheffield Academic, 1997], 144–179; though he disagrees with these trajectories, Ernest W. Nicholson, *The Pentateuch in the Twentieth Century: The Legacy of Julius Wellhausen* [New York: Clarendon-Oxford, 1998], 97 f.; Thomas B. Dozeman, *Exodus* [ECC; Grand Rapids: Eerdmans, 2009], 35–43).
[41] In Albert de Pury, "P[G] as the Absolute Beginning," in *Les Derniérs Rédactions du Pentateuque, de L'Hexateuque et de L'Ennéateuque* (ed. Thomas Römer and Konrad Schmid; BETL 203; Paris: Leuven University, 2007), 100. De Pury cites Rendtorff, *Problem des Pentateuch*; Erhard Blum, *Die Komposition der Vätergeschichte* (WMANT, 57), Neukirchen-Vluyn, Neukirchener, 1984; Lothar Perlitt, *Bundestheologie im Alten Testament* (WMANT, 36), Neukirchen-Vluyn, Neukirchener, 1969; Hans Heinrich Schmid, *Der sogenante Jahwist: Beobachtungen und Fragen zur Pentateuchforschung*, Zürich, Theologischer Verlag, 1976; John Van Seters, *Abraham in History and Tradition*, New Haven, CT – London, Yale University Press, 1975; and Martin Rose, *Deuteronomist und Jahwist:Untersuchungen zu den Berührungspunkten beider Literaturwerke* (ATANT, 67), Zürich, Theologischer Verlag, 1981.

lyse des Endtextes" and yet still values the insights to be gleaned from diachronic analysis.⁴² His insistence that literary analysis not privilege the earliest strata over the *Endtext*, but should begin with it, is an appreciable step forward toward synchronic-diachronic methodology.⁴³ Yet after Schart treats the narrative "Ringstruktur" around Sinai—a structure in which the Massah-Meribah texts play a pivotal role⁴⁴—he immediately transitions to dividing the text according to the classic source-critical divisions with results that deviate little from those of the historical critics before him.⁴⁵ His findings regarding the developments of the M-Mt are therefore limited.

A sharp contrast to Schart's redactional analysis is the approach of Erhard Blum. Released concurrently in 1990, Blum's published *Habilitationsschrift* uses "relief" analysis (*Reliefbeschreibung*), whereby he gives priority to consecu-

---

42 Specifically, Aaron Schart states that "Am Beginn der Textarbeit muß die Analyse des Endtextes stehn. Ist dies richtig, so folgt daraus die Umgruppierung des traditionellen Methodenkanons, so daß mit den synchronen Arbeitsgängen (Form- und Traditionskritik) begonnen wird" (*Mose und Israel im Konflikt: Eine Redaktionsgeschichtliche Studie zu den Wüstenerzählungen* [OBO 98; Göttingen: Vandenhoeck & Ruprecht, 1990], 26).

43 For Schart's discussion on the "Primat des Endtextes" in relation to diachronic analyses, see *Mose und Israel*, 23–26.

44 Schart sees a six-fold ring structure framing the "Theophanie, Bund und Gesetz" at Sinai: A. Wasserumwandlung (Exod 15:22–25) ∥ A'. Brunnen (Num 21:16–18); B. and B'. Wasser aus de Felsen (Exod 17:1–7 ∥ Num 20:1–13); C. Krieg: Amelek – Israel (Exod 17:8–16) ∥ C'. Krieg: Israel – Amelek (Num 14:39–45); D. and D'. Entlastung des Mose (Exodus 18 ∥ Numbers 11); E. der Midianiter Jitro kehrt zurück (Exod 18:27) ∥ E'. der Midianiter Hobab will nicht mitziehen (Num 10:29–32); and F. Ankunft am Sinai (Exod 19:1–2) ∥ F'. Aufbruch vom Sinai (Num 10:11–23). Schart also recognizes parallel components that do not fit this schema; namely, the issue of Sabbath keeping or breaking (cf. Exod 16:16–31; Num 15:32–36); and the manna and meat narratives (cf. Exod 16:1–15; Numbers 11) (*Mose und Israel im Konflikt*, 52–53). In the end, Schart concludes that this ring structure served as a "Kompositionsprinzip" by which the relationship between Yahweh is fundamentally changed: Israel is now covenantally responsible to Yahweh for its behavior (*Mose und Israel im Konflikt*, 53).

For an interesting synchronic reading of how the first half of Israel's wilderness journey alters its identity, see Arie Leder, "The Desert Itinerary Notices of Exodus: Their Narrative, Semiotic, and Theological Functions," *EstBib* 68 (2010): 291–311.

45 Schart proceeds backwards in time through the material, from most certain to least certain: the late exilic/early postexilic "Priesterschrift" (Ch. 4), the "D-Schicht," which includes a late preexilic/early exilic redaction of JE (so "Dje") and a late postexilic redaction of P (so "Dp") (Ch. 5), and the post-722 BCE, preexilic "jehowistischen Schicht" (Ch. 6). The stages he envisions for the formation of the Wilderness Narrative are then seven-fold: J and E (which no longer can be delineated), JE, Dje, P, Dp, and a final redaction (Ch. 7). As for the texts relevant to the M-Mt, Schart assigns them as follows: JE (Exod 15:22–25a; 17:1b, 3–6), Dje (Exod 17:2, 7), P (Num 20:1–13, a revision of Exod 17:1b, 2–6 [JE]); and Dp (Exod 15:25b-26) (*Mose und Israel*, 243–253).

tive cross-references and connections and then to whatever appears to be a diachronic addition.⁴⁶ As a result, two types of Tetrateuchal material emerge: 1) non-priestly material, which he labels "K^D" (*D-Komposition*) on account of its parallel relationship to "deuteronomischen bzw. deuteronomistischen Traditionsbildung,"⁴⁷ and 2) priestly material, which he dubs "K^P" (*P-Komposition*). His conclusion is that K^D—though it had used previously written collections of materials⁴⁸—was largely a postexilic work that presupposed the Deuteronomistic History and was secondarily integrated into its framework.⁴⁹ Later, the priestly writers incorporated K^D into K^P, preserving the disjunctures between the two according to the dictates of Persian *Reichsautorisation*, and thereby bringing the Pentateuch to its approximate final form.⁵⁰

The breadth and depth of Blum's work readily lends itself to superlative characterization.⁵¹ Yet the texts preserving and/or relating to the M-Mt prove unwieldy; they are the exceptions that unfortunately do not prove the rule of his formation theory.⁵² Blum's reticence to reconstruct the literary stages of Exod 17:1b-7 (K^D) is but one example: while he allows the existence of names and founding etiological structure of episode to be prior to K^D, he insists that the

---

46 Blum, *Studien zur Komposition*, 18.
47 Blum, *Studien zur Komposition*, 36.
48 Blum specifically cites the *Vätergeschichte* and the *Moseerzählung* as narrative complexes which authors of K^D inherited (*vorgegeben*) (*Studien zur Komposition*, 213–218).
49 Blum, *Studien zur Komposition*, 164.
50 Blum, *Studien zur Komposition*, 360. Blum indicates that while the integration of K^D into K^P was a decisively formative step toward the canonical Torah, it by no means represents the end of the Pentateuch's shaping (*Studien zur Komposition*, 361). Nicholson succinctly summarizes Blum's formation theory: "The stages in the formation of the Pentateuch suggested by Blum—early written traditions, Deuteronomy, the Deuteronomistic History, K^D, K^P—and the 'paradigm' his study advances is correspondingly different [than Wellhausen's]: an originally independent Tetrateuch (K^D) composed subsequent to Deuteronomy and the Deuteronomistic History and only secondarily combined with the latter" (*Pentateuch in the Twentieth Century*, 174).
51 Together with his published dissertation—*Die Komposition der Vätergeschichte* (WMANT 57; Neukirchener: Neukirchener Verlag, 1984)—Blum's two volumes mark a singular contribution to critical Pentateuchal studies. Jean-Louis Ska has called Blum "a new Wellhausen" ("Un nouveau Wellhausen?" *Bib* 72 [1991], 253–263); Van Seters calls it a "massive *tour de force*" in Pentateuchal studies (review of Erhard Blum, *Studien zur Komposition des Pentateuchs*), *JBL* 111 (1992): 122.
52 Granted, Blum attributes Exod 17:1b-7 to K^D, but Deut 6:16 and 9:22 he also believes belongs to K^D, with "Massah" in 9:22 possibly being a marginal gloss; the derivation of Deut 8:15 he says is questionable, while Deut 32:48–52 clearly belongs to K^P, along with Num 20:1–13 (a "Midrasch zu Dtn 33:8"!), 27:12–14, and Numbers 33 (*Studien zur Komposition*, 121 n.81 [Numbers 33]; 148f. [Exod 17:1b-7], 149 n. 202 [Deut 6:16; 9:22], 174 [Deut 8:15], 227 [Num 27:12–14; Deut 32:48–52], 276–277 [Num 20:1–13; Deut 33:8]).

text's current form is more likely the result of "einer durchgehenden Neuerzählung" than a "literarkritisch abzuhebenden Redaktion."[53] In the end, Blum concludes that regardless of whether one is willing to attribute this production to K^D, one must concede that Exod 17:1b-7 seamlessly integrates "in das Anliegen der Hauptkomposition."[54] It is for this very reason, that Blum later rationalizes his refusal to speculate on "die Destillation älterer und ältester Überlieferungen"[55] in diachronic fashion—the time for which he deems to have not yet come. In short, Blum makes no attempt to trace the developments of the M-Mt.

Likewise, John Van Seters' use of *comparative historiography* affords no way forward for the task at hand. In his *Life of Moses: The Yahwist as Historian in Exodus – Numbers* (1994), Van Seters carries forward his of argument that the notion of "editors" or "redactors" is an anachronistic retrojection of scholars to understand tensions within biblical texts—tensions more readily explained comparatively in light of antiquarian historiographies in the broader ancient Mediterranean world.[56] For Van Seters, a single exilic author, whom he dubs the "Yahwist,"[57] compiled ancient traditions in the process of authoring an antiquarian history, one supplementing the already extant Deuteronomistic History.[58]

---

[53] Blum, *Studien zur Komposition*, 150–151.
[54] Blum, *Studien zur Komposition*, 151. For Blum, the similarities of theme and structure shared by Exod 15:22–25a (Marah) and 17:1b-7 (Massah-Meribah), coupled with the two etiologically framed complaint stories found in Numbers 11, form a remarkable structural relationship around the Sinai-pericope (*Studien zur Komposition*, 151).
[55] Blum, *Studien zur Komposition*, 214–215. Now this is not to say that Blum denies the producers of K^D having access to such traditions; on the contrary, he concedes this could be the case, but it remains "nicht mehr al seine Möglichkeit" (*Studien zur Komposition*, 217).
[56] John Van Seters, *Prologue to History: The Yahwist as Historian in Genesis* (Louisville: Westminster John Knox, 1992); cf. "The Redactor in Biblical Studies: A Nineteenth Century Anachronism," *JNSL* 29 (2003): 1–19. Van Seters permits only a *passive* role for so-called "redactors," whom he believes merely preserved and edited extant textual materials with minimal creative genius. Regrettably, he does not restate his arguments for this perspective in *The Life of Moses*, but rather assumes them throughout (*The Life of Moses*, ix). This understanding, as Konrad Schmid rightly critiques, "ist zwar überzogen und verkennt die gegenwärtige Forschungsdiskussion um die sachliche Profilierung des Phänomens der 'Redaktion' alttestamentlicher Literatur" (*Literaturgeschichte des Alten Testaments: Eine Einführung* [Darmstadt: Wissenschaftliche Buchgesellschaft, 2008], 47).
[57] Van Seters' Yahwist is not unlike the Yahwist of the so-called "*Solomonische Aufklärung*" envisioned by von Rad. Von Rad began formulating this idea in *Das formgeschichtliche Problem*, 75–76. For a brief survey of where von Rad uses this terminology, see Jean-Louis Ska, *Introduction to Reading the Pentateuch* (trans. Pascale Dominique; Winona Lake: Eisenbrauns, 2006), 120 n. 93.
[58] Van Seters, *Prologue to History*, 98–99, 328–333.

What this reconstruction means for the M-Mt, as Van Seters spells it out, is quite dissatisfactory. For Van Seters, "there is no earlier tradition behind the Ex. 17:1–7 story, apart from the simple statement about God's provision of water in the wilderness."[59] It is, instead, the creation of the Yahwist, along with the murmuring motif as a whole—a creation inspired by Deut 8:15, 9:21 and 33:8 and "developed, by means of the artificially created place-names Massah and Meribah, to include within the murmuring motif the themes of testing God and contending with Moses."[60] Such a conclusion prompts one to ask whether Van Seters' assessment amounts to anything more than a shrugging of the shoulders at the tradition-historical process.[61]

William Johnstone represents another *redactional* treatment of the texts relevant to this tradition, but the processes he describes are radically different than Schart's (see p. 16 above). Building on his earlier thesis (1996[62]), Johnstone argues that Deuteronomy contains reminiscences of the earliest literary version of the Tetrateuch.[63] Thus, methodologically, Johnstone begins his investigation with Deuteronomy. Since Deut 9:22 situates the events at Massah between Taberah and Kibroth-hattaavah (cf. Num 11:3–4), Johnstone contends that the non-P portions of Exod 17:1–7 were once *textually* located between Num 11:3 and 11:4. Later, the P redactor resituated these non-P portions, along with the

---

59 Van Seters, *The Life of Moses*, 197, 316. It is important to remember that Van Seters is only concerned with the writing of the Yahwist, so he does not tend to the P M-Mt narrative in Num 20:1–13 with any level of detail.

60 Van Seters, *The Life of Moses*, 195–197. The irony is that while Van Seters rebuffs Lehming's thesis (*The Life of Moses*, 196), he arrives at a remarkably similar conclusion. His only innovation is that he treats both toponyms in Exod 17:7 as creations of the Yahwist.

61 At best, since he dismisses most of the texts relevant to the tradition as later than J—namely, Deut 6:16; 9:22–24; 32:51, 33:8 [?]; Num 20:1–13 (he does not discuss Num 20:24; 27:12–14; or most of the references outside the Pentateuch, save for Ps 78:16, 20 and Isa 43:20) (*The Life of Moses*, 191–198)—his attributing the creation of the M-Mt to J falls prey to his own critique: it is "speculative, at best, with little control" (*The Life of Moses*, 193).

62 William Johnstone, "From the Sea to the Mountain: Exodus 15,22–19,2: A Case-Study in Editorial Techniques," in *Studies in the Book of Exodus: Redaction – Reception – Interpretation* (ed. Marc Vervenne; BETL 126; Leuven: Leuven University, 1996), 245–263.

63 Essentially, Johnstone contends that 1) monarchial institutions/rites passed down oral tradition, which 2) an exilic Deuteronomistic circle then codified into a pre-P continuous narrative coterminously with the creation of Deuteronomy. This D-version of the Tetrateuch, however, can now only be recovered from the reminiscences within Deuteronomy, since it has undergone 3) a thorough editing by the postexilic P-editors ("The Use of the Reminiscences in Deuteronomy in Recovering the Two Main Literary Phases in the Production of the Pentateuch," in *Abschied vom Jahwisten: Dis Komposition des Hexateuch in der jüngsten Diskussion* [ed. Jan Christian Gertz, Konrad Schmid, and Markus Witte; BZAW 315; Berlin: de Gruyter, 2002], 243–249).

rest of Exod 15:22–19:2, in order to show that Israel had rebelled against Yahweh from the beginning of the wilderness sojourn, not just after the Sinai event.[64] While innovative, Johnstone's thesis suffers on a number of fronts.[65] At the moment, it is sufficient to note that Johnstone's interest in the M-Mt is quite limited and, to be fair, that his intention was not to reconstruct the history of its developments.[66]

One final study deserves recognition: David Frankel's *The Murmuring Stories of the Priestly School: A Retrieval of Ancient Sacerdotal Lore* (2002). As the title indicates, this study operates within the framework of the murmuring motif, but from the unique vantage of the P materials.[67] His revisionist tendencies emerge in his *source-critical analyses* that ground his study, throughout which he recovers successive priestly strata and their tradition-historical implications.[68]

---

[64] Johnstone, "From the Sea to the Mountain," in Vervenne, *Studies in Exodus*, especially 247–259; idem, "Reminiscences in Deuteronomy," in Gertz, Schmid, and Witte, *Abschied vom Jahwisten*, 261. For a discussion of how Johnstone has variously nuanced his thesis, see p. 80 n. 72 below.

[65] First, I agree with Dozeman that Exod 17:1–7 in its final form does not appear to be a rebellion episode in the same sense as the episodes at Teberah and Kibroth-hattaavah in Num 11:1–3, 4–35 (*Exodus*, 356). Additional editorial processes, both for Exod 17:1–7 and Numbers 11, need to be considered. Second, it is not clear how Johnstone intends to account for the formation of Num 20:1–13 and Deut 33:8; he merely states that the D-version of this story is to be "reassembled" minus any "P-additions" (Johnstone, "Reminiscences in Deuteronomy," in Gertz, Schmid, and Witte, *Abschied vom Jahwisten*, 261). Finally, Johnstone utilizes the whole of Deuteronomy synchronically, despite 1) the widely held consensus regarding what this study dubs Deuteronomy's "centrifugal" growth (cf. chapter 2) and 2) the diversity of the reminiscences of the Massah-Meribah tradition within Deuteronomy, which in turn requires some explanation.

[66] Since at least 1987, Johnstone's agenda has been to demonstrate that the reminiscences within "Deuteronomy/DtrH enable the reconstruction of a pre-P version of sections of Exodus" ("From the Sea to the Mountain," in Vervenne, *Studies in Exodus*, 1). For further interactions Johnstone's thesis in relation to the M-Mt, see pp. 79–81 and 188–191 below.

[67] David Frankel, *The Murmuring Stories of the Priestly School: A Retrieval of Ancient Sacerdotal Lore* (VTSup 89; Leiden: Brill, 2002). Specifically, Frankel attends to the priestly murmuring stories in "Ex. 16 (the Manna), Num. 13–14 (the Scouts), Num. 16–17 (the Korah stories), and and Num. 20 (the waters of Merivah)" (*Murmuring Stories*, 11). His purpose is to flush out Childs' earlier observation "that at certain points in the Pentateuch the priestly material seems to be dependent upon the non-priestly material, whereas at other points it seems totally independent" (*Murmuring Stories*, 6; cf. Childs, *Introduction to the Old Testament*, 123).

[68] Frankel divides the P materials into three categories: 1) independent *"early priestly narratives"* that exhibit no influence from Non-P material and may even predate it; 2) a secondary priestly layer, not only responsible for combining the originally independent P and non-P narrative materials, but also for editorially supplementing each in order "to help combine the two traditions"; and 3) "late, *post-editorial*" insertions written in the P style that disrupt the "coher-

Thus, not unlike Van Seters' perspective of the Yahwist, Frankel places a much higher premium on the creative role of the priestly school in the formation of these stories.⁶⁹ The value of Frankel's work resides in his demonstrating the priestly tradents to have been in possession of their own written traditions; he therefore rightly challenges the common presuppositions that all priestly material is late, whether exilic or postexilic, and is derivative of non-P material. In the end, the source-critical insights Frankel affords pertain mainly to the literary developments of Num 20:1–13, and his work does not attempt to trace the M-Mt in total.

1.3.3 Summary

A conclusion that one can draw from this survey is that scholars have yet to treat the Massah-Meribah story as a tradition in its own right. Instead, past research has proceeded along the axes of two broader standpoints: either as part of attempts to reconstruct the formative stages of the Pentateuch as a whole (Noth, Blum, Van Seters) or in part (Gressmann, Schart, Johnstone); or as part of studies intent on discovering the developments of a particular genre (Coats, Childs, Frankel) or specific motif (Propp). Though the above survey is certainly not exhaustive,⁷⁰ it underscores the need for a sustained tradition-historical investigation of the M-Mt and its influence on its own terms.

1.4 What to Do and Where to Begin?

The prevalence and pluriformity of the M-Mt within the Hebrew Bible merits renewed and focused scholarly attention. Past scholarship has primarily attended to the variant expressions of the M-Mt through the findings of source criticism, but now one can no longer assume the veracity of this method's central tenets. Further, previous studies engaging the M-Mt have most often done so as a by-

---

ent combination of priestly and non-priestly materials" (Frankel, *Murmuring Stories*, 6–9; italics original).

69 On account of parameters, Frankel leaves open the issue of the implications that his thesis has for the Pentateuch's formation (*Murmuring Stories*, 6).

70 A more recent example is the synchronic work of Christian Kupfer, *Mit Israel auf dem Weg durch die Wüste: Eine leserorientierte Exegese der Rebellionstexte in Exodus 15:22–17:7 und Numeri 11:1–20:13* (OtSt 61; Leiden: Brill, 2012), who provides a *reader-response* analysis via insights of reception theorists Umberto Eco and Wolfgang Iser.

product of another research agenda. This study sets out to rectify these missteps in light of the currents and cautions afforded by recent Pentateuchal scholarship.

Naturally, at this point of the current study the principal question of methodology looms large. What becomes immediately apparent is the need for a diachronic framework whereby to reconstruct the framework of the M-Mt's formative stages. That was after all what the documentary hypothesis afforded early tradition historians: a means by which to determine the priority of the *traditum* in one text over the *traditum* in another via each text's source critical characteristics. Establishing a viable alternative diachronic framework is the major task of Part One (chs. 2–4).

Chapter two explores several points of consensus which have either survived the breakdown of the documentary hypothesis or have emerged over the course of its downfall. Currents and cautions within Pentateuchal studies in general and in Deuteronomic studies in particular set up the presuppositions that are fundamental to the central thesis of this study: namely, that a framework outlining the major tradition-historical developments of the M-Mt is detectable across the parameters of Deuteronomy's macro-redactional developments. In other words, this study begins with the diversity and distribution of the M-Mt preserved within Deuteronomy, as seen in Deut 6:16; 8:15; 9:22; 32:13; 32:51; and 33:8.

The M-Mt texts inside Deuteronomy find their location within two major blocks fundamental to the book's literary history. *Chapter three* focuses on the M-Mt texts within the first of these blocks, which this study calls the "interior historical prologue" (Deuteronomy chs. [4] 5–11). As the interior prologue itself evinces several layers of micro-redactional activity, establishing the relative chronological relationship of Deut 6:16; 8:15; and 9:22 occupies the central concern of this chapter. Only after this task is accomplished can one proceed to extract and situate diachronically the major developments of the M-Mt that these reminiscences preserve.

Likewise, *chapter four* attends to the M-Mt texts within a second major block of textual material in Deuteronomy's macro-redactional growth—a block this study calls the "exterior miscellaneous epilogues" (Deuteronomy chs. 31–34). The textual material within this block sufficiently differs from that of the interior prologue to warrant separate treatment. Not only is this material supplemental to Deuteronomy, but two of the major pericopes—i.e., the Song and Blessing of Moses (Deut 32:1–44 and ch. 33 respectively)—most likely existed prior to their becoming addendums to the book. A similar verdict holds true for Deut 32:51, which bears an undeniable relationship with the priestly material in Num 27:12–14. Once again, only after the relative chronological relationship of these iterations is established can one proceed to augment the framework discovered in the previous chapter.

Part Two of this study (chs. 5–7) explores the material developments of the M-Mt texts in the remainder of the Pentateuch, with special focus on M-Mt narratives in Exod 17:1–7 and Num 20:1–13. Throughout, the framework of the M-Mt's tradition-historical developments detected in Deuteronomy is brought to bear as a bench mark whereby to gage the literary tensions in each narrative. In this respect, the second part of this study corroborates the findings of the first via the framework's ability to anticipate and negotiate the tensions in these narratives in accordance to the developments of the M-Mt through time.

Chapter five outlines the challenges inherent to tracing the diachrony of the M-Mt narratives individually. Yet ironically, the material and diachronic relationship of the two M-Mt narratives in relation to each other is foundational for an informed separate treatment of Exod 17:1–7 and Num 20:1–13. The verbal and conceptual correspondence between the two narratives is a case in point: not only do shared features confirm their genetic relationship, but the non-aligned features within each text indicate significant independent material development. Additionally, despite their separate developments, the internal tensions within the two M-Mt narratives correspond to one another according to type and proximity. Finally, there is the need to account for how each narrative is anchored into the Pentateuch via immediate and broader literary contexts that display lexical and conceptual connections to each M-Mt narrative.

Accounting for the features outlined in chapter five—i.e., the congruities, incongruities, internal tensions, and contextual moorings—in the literary histories of the M-Mt narratives form the challenge undertaken in chapters six and seven respectively. *Chapter six* investigates the stages of Exod 17:1–7's literary growth in tandem with 1) the texts that anchor this narrative into its current position in the Pentateuch (Exod 15:22–17:7; Num 33:14), and 2) the texts that Deut 9:22 recalls as having at one time anchored an earlier form of this narrative in an earlier collection (Num 10:33–11:35). Similarly, *chapter seven* examines the stages of Num 20:1–13's literary growth in light of 1) the texts mooring it into the Pentateuch (Num 20:22–29; 27:12–14; 33:36–49), and 2) the texts which preserve connections that suggest an earlier form and location of this narrative (Numbers 12–14, 16–17). For both chapters, the framework detected in Deuteronomy of the M-Mt's tradition-historical developments serve as a guide whereby to align the stages involved in Exod 17:1–7's and Num 20:1–13's literary and tradition-historical growth.

By way of a conclusion, *chapter eight* provides a synthesis of the study and its broader implications. Not only is the framework for the formative stages of the M-Mt's tradition-historical development detectable in Deuteronomy, but as well the processes whereby this tradition developed through time has broad ramifications for the formation of the Pentateuch as a whole. The study then concludes with the implications this framework has for diachronically situating the M-Mt reminiscences beyond the Pentateuch in the remainder of the Hebrew Bible, as well as a trajectory for future studies into the echoes and appropriations of the M-Mt that lie beyond the Hebrew Bible.

Part I **Deuteronomy as the Foundation**

Chapter Two:
Preliminary Considerations

2.1 Why Begin with Deuteronomy?

With the great diversity of the M-Mt reflected in Deuteronomy, why privilege this starting-point over others? What stands to be gained as opposed to beginning somewhere else? To answer these questions effectively requires an awareness of certain currents and cautions within Old Testament scholarship, both within Pentateuchal studies (§2.2) in general and within Deuteronomy studies (§2.3) in particular. Deuteronomy's distinctive literary profile within the Pentateuch, coupled with its internal demarcations for its own macro-redactional developments, affords some unique advantages for tradition-historical inquiry, particularly the M-Mt. There are, of course, some challenges to grounding the current study in this way. An upfront disclosure of these advantages and challenges is therefore requisite for the tasks of the next two chapters: namely, the assessment of the M-Mt as it is reflected in Deuteronomy, first within the book's *interior prologue* (chs. 5–11) in chapter three, and then within its *miscellaneous epilogues* (chs. 31–34) in chapter four.

2.2 Currents and Cautions in Pentateuchal Studies

Histories of research are necessary for all fields of biblical inquiry, but perhaps none more so than that of Pentateuchal research.[1] A recent and welcomed entry

---

[1] Although extremely dated, Eissfeldt's "The History of Pentateuchal Criticism" remains an indispensable survey of classic Pentateuchal research (Otto Eissfeldt, *The Old Testament: An Introduction including the Apocrypha and Pseudepigrapha, and also the works of similar type from Qumran* [trans. P. R. Ackroyd; 3d; Tübingen: Mohr, 1934; repr., New York: Harper & Row, 1965], 158–176). Select surveys since then include R. N. Whybray, *The Making of the Pentateuch: A Methodological Study* (JSOTSup 53; Sheffield: JSOT Press, 1987); Joseph Blenkinsopp, *The Pentateuch: An Introduction to the First Five Books of the Bible* (ABRL; New York: Doubleday, 1992), 1–30; Ernest Nicholson, *The Pentateuch in the Twentieth Century: The Legacy of Julius Wellhausen* (New York: Clarendon-Oxford, 1998); John Van Seters, *The Pentateuch: A Social-Science Commentary* (Traj 1; Sheffield: Sheffield Academic, 1999), 30–87; Alexander Rofé, *Introduction to the Composition of the Pentateuch* (trans. H. N. Bock; Sheffield: Sheffield Academic, 1999); Albert de Pury, ed., *Le Pentateuque en question: Les origines et la composition des cinq premiers livres de la Bible à la lumière des recherches récentes* (3d; Geneva: Labor et Fides,

to this ever-growing body of literature is the essay by Reinhard G. Kratz in the seminal volume *The Pentateuch: International Perspectives on Current Research* (2011).² Kratz's survey is extensive; his assessment, judicious; and in it he affords a number of insights regarding common grounds within Pentateuchal studies, both current and emerging, as well as trajectories for future research. Three such insights are pivotal for answering the question "*Why begin with Deuteronomy?*": namely, 1) the consensus regarding the integrity of the textual materials that now constitute the Pentateuch, 2) the currency of tradition history as an analytical method, and 3) the value of relative chronology in critical biblical inquiry.

Throughout his essay, Kratz frames his discussion with the refrain, "To be able to understand a text one should know where/how it begins and where/how it ends"³—an English rendering of a statement made by Erhard Blum, and one Kratz regards as central for Pentateuchal exegetes.⁴ The relevance of this refrain to the current question coincides with the integrity of the textual materials that make up the Pentateuch itself. According to Kratz, the "*magnus consensus*" detects three distinct literary strata within the Pentateuch: the book of Deuteronomy, the Priestly materials, and the Covenant Code (Exodus 20–23).⁵ Further, "as far as the beginning and the ending of these literary entities are concerned," asserts Kratz, "things tend to be most clear in Deuteronomy[.]"⁶ The remaining materials then are the "non-Priestly (non-P) and non-Deuteronomic (non-D) texts in Genesis, Exodus (Exod 1–24), and Numbers," which together

---

2002); Thomas Römer and Konrad Schmid, eds., *Les dernièrs rédactions du Pentateuque, de l'Hexateuque et de l'Ennéateuque* (BETL 203; Paris: Leuven University, 2007).

2 Reinhard G. Kratz, "The Pentateuch in Current Research: Consensus and Debate," in *The Pentateuch: International Perspectives on Current Research* (ed. Thomas B. Dozeman, Konrad Schmid, and Baruch J. Schwartz; FAT 78; Tübingen: Mohr Siebeck, 2011), 31–61.

3 Kratz uses this refrain to varying extents at least eleven times ("Pentateuch in Current Research," in Dozeman, Schmid, and Schwartz, *The Pentateuch*, 31, 33, 34, 37, 40 n. 30, 41, 50, 52, 55, 56).

4 Kratz, "Pentateuch in Current Research," in Dozeman, Schmid, and Schwartz, *The Pentateuch*, 31, citing and translating Erhard Blum, "Pentateuch – Hexateuch – Enneateuch? Oder: Woran erkennt man ein literarisches Werk in der hebräischen Bibel," in *Les Dernièrs Rédactions du Pentateuque, de L'Hexateuque et de L'Ennéateuque* (ed. Thomas Römer and Konrad Schmid; BETL 203; Paris: Leuven University, 2007), 67. For the German, see p. 37 below.

5 Kratz, "Pentateuch in Current Research," in Dozeman, Schmid, and Schwartz, *Pentateuch*, 34–35.

6 Kratz, "Pentateuch in Current Research," in Dozeman, Schmid, and Schwartz, *Pentateuch*, 34.

comprise "the core of the literary-historical problems of the Pentateuch" and within which Kratz believes lie "the oldest parts of the Pentateuch."[7]

In addition to the positive identification of these three major strata (i.e., the Covenant Code, Deuteronomy, and P) and the division of the remaining texts into two profiles (non-P and non-D), Kratz observes another consensus, which no doubt stems from the legacy of Martin Noth (cf. p. 12 above): namely, that before the Pentateuch was shaped into a continuous narrative, its "single parts"—i.e., the "primeval history, patriarchs, Moses and exodus with or without entry into the land"—"originally existed as independent traditions." The processes involved in merging these traditions into an integrated, continuous whole represent secondary developments.[8]

It is easy to overlook the subtle implications that these general consensuses have for the task of reconstructing the history of the M-Mt, yet they are quite significant. Here, a heuristic analogy may prove helpful, one that parallels texts and tradents to land and landlords. Given the distribution of texts that preserve reminiscences of the M-Mt across the Pentateuch,[9] only those within Deuteronomy (especially within the interior prologue) are properties of a common domain of textual proprietors; i.e., the Deuteronomic(-istic) (*Dt/Dtr*) tradents or school of tradents. No other set of M-Mt texts in the Pentateuch—indeed, the entire Hebrew Bible!—can lay claim to such a relationship. The advantage that this common proprietary domain affords to the task of tracing the M-Mt is as follows: if

---

[7] The debate of the value and accuracy of any set of terminologies cannot be resolved here. Such is especially the case with the terms "Deuteronomic" and "Deuteornomistic." Except when citing secondary scholarship that does otherwise, the current study uses "Deuteronomic" (abbreviated "Dt") to refer to textual materials added to Deuteronomy's pre-existing legal core—which this study refers to as *Urdeuteronomium* (abbreviated "Ur-Deut")—in the production of the first edition of Early-Deuteronomy (see Fig. 2.1 below). The term "Deuteronomistic" (abbreviated "Dtr"), however, refers to redactional materials added to this Deuteronomic form of Deuteronomy, materials which often evince connections to the so-called Deuteronomistic History. For scholars who have abandoned this distinction between "Deuteronomic" and "Deuteornomistic," see Raymond F. Person, *The Deuteronomic School: History, Social Setting, and Literature* (SBLSBL 2; Atlanta: Society of Biblical Literature, 2002), 4–7; Thomas Römer, *The so-called Deuteronomistic History: A Sociological, Historical and Literary Introduction* (2005; repr., London–New York: T & T Clark, 2007), 17 n. 3.

[8] Specifically, Kratz states that "[o]nly in a second step were these traditions integrated into the literary and also conceptual context of a continuous narrative, connected with the other parts of the Pentateuch, and in the course of it reworked and supplemented and joined to the canonical entity of the Torah" ("Pentateuch in Current Research," in Dozeman, Schmid, and Schwartz, *Pentateuch*, 35).

[9] Namely, Exod 17:1–7; Num 20:1–13; 20:24; 27:12–14; Deut 6:16; 8:15; 9:22; 32:13, 48–52; 33:8.

these texts exhibit any diversity within the tradition components they preserve, then there is a higher degree of probability that these diversities reflect the development or adaption of a *single* tradition[10] (especially Deut 6:16; 8:15; 9:22[11]). Outside such a domain, the tradition-historian must admit the possibility of there once having been *multiple* traditions that, while similar, were originally wholly separate (cf. Exod 17:1bβ-7; Num 20:1–13; 20:24; 27:12–14).[12]

---

[10] A valid question at this point pertains to my understanding of what constitutes a "tradition" and the nature of its transmission. As to the former, I admit a qualified debt to Douglas Knight: a verbal tradition, about which tradition-history within biblical critical inquiry is primarily concerned, is any inheritable datum and/or set of data (*traditum*) transmitted from one person and/or group (*tradent/s*) to another through a variety of oral and/or written processes (*traditio*) (cf. pp. 3–4 above; Douglas Knight, *Rediscovering the Traditions of Israel* [3rd ed.; SBLSBL 16; Atlanta: Society of Biblical Literature, 2006], 5–23). As to the latter, Siegfried Wiedenhofer eloquently describes this social act, specifically in times of crisis when tradents look to the past to understand their present and envision their future: "Zwar sind Traditionen immer auch vergangenheitsorientiert: als Repetition, Gewohnheit, Routine und Erinnerung. Aber gerade in Krisenzeiten wird sichtbar, dass sie gleichzeitig nie ohne Gegenwartsbezug und Zukunftsbezug existieren. Sie sind immer Antwort auf eine Frage, ein Akt der Rezeption oder Nicht-Rezeption, ein Akt der Selektion, ein Akt der Interpretation und Imagination, ein Akt der Transformation, ein Akt der Proklamation und des rituellen Vollzuges, ja auch ein Akt der Konstruktion, der Fabrikation und der Erfindung, ein Akt der Interaktion und Kommunikation und in all dem ein sozialer Akt" ("Tradition – Geschichte – Gedächtnis. Was bringt eine komplexe Traditionstheorie?" *EWE* 15 [2004]: 238).

[11] The other M-Mt texts within Deuteronomy—namely 32:13, 48–52; 33:8—lie inside the miscellaneous exterior epilogues. A feature all these texts share is the likelihood of having existed prior to their incorporation into Deuteronomy. As such, one cannot assume the Dt/Dtr authorship of these passages (cf. §2.3.2 below).

[12] This admission in no way posits that Exod 17:1bβ-7 on the one hand and Num 20:1–13; 20:24; and 27:12–14 on the other hand are actually separate, non-intersecting traditions. Rather it merely acknowledges the possibility of the arguments levied by those who would see these texts as reflecting separate, distinct historical events (e.g., M. Margaliot, "The Transgression of Moses and Aaron – Num. 20:1–13," *JQR* 74 [1983]: 200; Nathaniel Helfgot, "'And Moses Struck the Rock': Numbers 20 and the Leadership of Moses," *Trad* 27 [1993]: 51–53; Rafael-Anthony Lloréns, "'Water from the Rock': A Comparative Analysis of Exodus 17:1–7 and Numbers 20:1–13" [Thesis, New Orleans Baptist Theological Seminary, 2008], 98); Timothy R. Ashley argues that the similarities between the two narratives are to be expected, since they both revolve around water deprivation; but the differences attest to the author's desire "for his readers to understand, in subtle ways [...] that although Exod. 17:1–17 and Num. 20:1–13 relate similar events, they are discrete incidents" (*The Book of Numbers* [NICOT; Grand Rapids: Eerdmans, 1992], 378–379); cf. Martin Emmrich, who echoes Ashley on this point ("The Case against Moses Reopened," *JETS* 46 [2003]: 53).

A second of Kratz's insights that merits consideration pertains to the methods scholars are currently favoring in the historical-critical investigation of these textual materials:

> As far as the methodology is concerned, it can be regarded as consensus that all stages of the *tradition* should be investigated and as far as possible identified within the (Masoretic) text as we have it now and not in a vague – oral or written – prehistory of this text. Using the terminology of *traditional* Old Testament exegesis, we can state that we observe a shift away from *tradition history* and a focus on literary and redaction history.[13]

Two observations regarding this assessment are immediately warranted. To begin with, the variety of ways in which Kratz uses the lemma "tradition" again underscores the need for precision when using this term: in its first occurrence, it appears to refer to the Pentateuch as a whole; in its second appearance, it serves as a synonym for "classical"; and in its final instance, it forms part of the compound title of the methodology Kratz declares to be in decline.[14]

Additionally, one should recognize that Kratz's sharp distinction between tradition history and literary and redaction history is somewhat forced, as it ignores the overlap in scope that many scholars believe tradition-historical inquiry has with compositional analysis.[15] A simple restriction of tradition history to the

---

13 Kratz, "Pentateuch in Current Research," in Dozeman, Schmid, and Schwartz, *Pentateuch*, 35 (italics mine). The force of Kratz's critique appears directed against such tradition-historical studies as Hermann Gunkel, *Genesis: Übersetzt und Erklärt* (3d ed.; Göttingen: Vandenhoeck & Ruprecht, 1910); Hugo Gressmann, *Mose und seine Zeit: Ein Kommentar zu den Mose-Sagen* (FRLANT 18; Göttingen: Vandenhoeck & Ruprecht, 1913); Gerhard von Rad, *Das formgeschichtliche Problem des Hexateuchs* (BWA(N)T 4.26; Stuttgart: W. Kohlhammer, 1938); and Martin Noth, *Überlieferungsgeschichte des Pentateuch* (Stuttgart: W. Kohlhammer, 1948). More recent examples include William Johnstone, "The Use of the Reminiscences in Deuteronomy in Recovering the Two Main Literary Phases in the Production of the Pentateuch," in *Abschied vom Jahwisten: D's Komposition des Hexateuch in der jüngsten Diskussion* (ed. Jan Gertz, Konrad Schmid, and Markus Witte; BZAW 315; Berlin: de Gruyter, 2002); and Joel S. Baden, *J, E, and the Redaction of the Pentateuch* (FAT 68; Tübingen: Mohr Siebeck, 2009) (cf. Kratz, "Pentateuch in Current Research," in Dozeman, Schmid, and Schwartz, *Pentateuch*, 43 n. 40).
14 The elasticity with which Kratz uses the word "tradition" is unfortunate, but not atypical. See pp. 3–4 above for a brief discussion of the complexities regarding the term.
15 According to Knight (*Traditions of Israel*, 18, 18 n. 8), the perspective that tradition history encompasses "the whole history of a literary piece – from its earliest beginnings as independent units of oral tradition, through its development, growth, and composition at the oral and written levels, and on to its redaction and finalization in its present form"—is quite common. Notable exemplars include Martin Noth, Gerhard von Rad, A. H. Gunneweg, Helmer Ringgren, Rolf Rendtorff, Clause Westermann, Otto Kaiser, Odil Hannes Steck, among others. To be fair to Kratz, however, Knight advocates a more limited scope for tradition history, preferring instead the word "*Literaturgeschichte*" as the "all-inclusive term" (*Traditions of Israel*, 22–23; see also Van Seters,

domain of oral transmission is erroneous, as it presumes that traditions immediately lose their ability to develop and adapt once they have been written down. Methodologically then, the implication is that any stage—whether oral or written—that exhibits tradition-historical development, reinterpretation, and/or reapplication is within the purview of tradition-historical study. Thus, while there are certainly methodological distinctions between tradition-historical analysis and literary and redactional analyses, at times the tradition historian may have need of the procedures and tools employed by those concerned with compositional analysis.

It is in the context of these methodological concerns that another advantage of beginning with Deuteronomy emerges: given the above consensus regarding the book's distinctive literary/stratigraphic profile, the tradition-historical tensions in the texts reflecting the M-Mt within Deuteronomy are real. They are, as Kratz aptly put, within the *Masoretic text as we have it now*; they are not mere reconstructions based on a *vague—oral or written—prehistory of this text*. Consequently, one must either demonstrate how the tradition components in the multiple M-Mt texts within Deuteronomy statically cohere with one another so that there is no diversity within Deuteronomy, or accept the likelihood that the M-Mt continued to evolve and adapt within the *Sitz im Leben* of the tradents in possession of Deuteronomy, despite the fact that certain of the M-Mt's components were already transcribed.[16]

The Pentateuch, 48–49). Even so, the criterion for identifying a tradition's *terminus ad quem*, according to Knight, is not the point of its *initial* written codification. "Rather, the criterion is that the tradition is separated from its life context and has been made a part of a *relatively static* written composition" (*Traditions of Israel*, 22; italics mine).

Here, Knight is at least partly correct: written texts do exert some stabilizing influence on traditions, but only for those tradents who have primary or secondary access to them, whether through literacy or aural presentation respectively. Implicit in this statement is the recognition that the veracity of any sharp distinction between oral and written stages in the life of a tradition is hardly demonstrable; a written exemplar of a tradition no more removes a tradition from the oral sphere than does a printed Bible preclude modern day parents from orally rehearsing and embellishing their child's favorite bedtime Bible story. In this sense then, one cannot say that texts relay the *unchanging* finger prints of a tradition; they are instead snapshots, reflections of the state of a tradition at the time of their being written. In this way, the texts within Deuteronomy (and beyond) that reflect the M-Mt are merely "reminiscences" of the M-Mt, not its embodiment.

16 A third option, albeit no more than hypothetical, is also conceivable. One could imagine a single milieu which is aware of numerous similar, yet distinct iterations of this tradition existing simultaneously, a context from which would emerge all of the Dt/Dtr texts that current study ascribes to the M-Mt. In such a scenario, the orality of the M-Mt has evolved in a non-linear fashion, and any relationship the M-Mt texts in Deuteronomy have to one another would have been

Such is not the case, however, for the remainder of the Pentateuchal M-Mt texts. Granted, there are undeniable tradition-historical tensions within each of the two narratives (Exod 17:1–7; Num 20:1–13) individually, but the stages of development that produced these tensions cannot be extrapolated without the reconstruction of each narrative's compositional history. Again, the significance of this observation is subtle and the earlier analogy to land and landlords may prove useful once more: instead of renovating a single property over and over again as the M-Mt developed, the proprietors of Deuteronomy appear to have constructed / introduced additional textual properties. This process is fundamentally different than what either of the M-Mt narrative exponents underwent: both Exod 17:1–7 and Num 20:1–13 have undergone a number of extensive revisions, making the recovery of the M-Mt's *Traditionsgeschichte* much more problematic should the tradition-historical investigation begin with either of them.

So far, this chapter has engaged Kratz's insight on the compositional and methodological currents within Pentateuchal scholarship. A third insight that both informs this study and grants credence to beginning with Deuteronomy derives not from any consensus that Kratz observes. Rather it is born from a caution that he levies and a recommendation he gives in hopes of moving the conversation forward. Here, although arguably tangential, a brief introduction to the context of this caution and recommendation may be helpful. In his response to Blum's *Reliefbeschreibung*, Kratz grants that something must be made of the "numerous narrative, conceptual, and literary cross-references that are found in a plethora of monumental narrative contexts from Genesis to 2 Kings and that play a central part in the literary- and redaction-historical analysis of the Pentateuch."[17] Such texts, he says, may not be redactional at all, but may instead indicate "separate literary contexts" or "general knowledge of the narration."[18]

Though no consensus appears forthcoming, Kratz insists that what is not helpful is the assumption that the writers all had a "general and widespread knowledge of the tradition"[19]—by which he appears to mean extant written

---

artificially imposed by later editors/readers, who (whether by error or necessity) conflated the iterations. This option is highly problematic as it would necessitate several centers of tradition-historical development existing simultaneously. Further, since provisionally the early explicit evocations and allusions of the M-Mt across the Hebrew canon tend to align with either the non-P M-Mt or the P M-Mt (but not both), while only later iterations evince combinations of both, a scenario in which the M-Mt developed independently in only two milieus (i.e., non-P and P) stands as most likely (cf. p. 241 n. 11 below).

17 Kratz, "Pentateuch in Current Research," in Dozeman, Schmid, and Schwartz, *Pentateuch*, 57.
18 Kratz, "Pentateuch in Current Research," in Dozeman, Schmid, and Schwartz, *Pentateuch*, 58.
19 Kratz, "Pentateuch in Current Research," in Dozeman, Schmid, and Schwartz, *Pentateuch*, 58.

texts. Regardless, he then outlines some guidelines whereby future studies may be better grounded. The first of these prescriptions is to describe the relationship of these cross-references as either *intratextual* (i.e., references occurring "within the context of the same work") or *intertextual* (i.e., references that exist "between two separate contexts")—a point that bears revisiting beyond the confines of the current study.[20]

More fundamental than terminology for Kratz, however, is the need to redirect the task of dating a text chronologically. It is common practice among scholars to assign specific, absolute dates (or date ranges) to biblical texts in light of historical reconstructions—reconstructions that in turn rely on the same biblical texts to make them (note the circularity). Instead of dating texts *absolutely*, Kratz stresses that future studies on the Pentateuch should focus on dating these texts *relatively* by establishing the direction of dependence; i.e., whether a text relies on another text, thereby making it relatively younger than the text upon which it relies. Only when one has mapped the "relative chronology of the literary stages of the formation of the Pentateuch," should an attempt be made to align these individual stages with periods within ancient Israel's history in an absolute chronological fashion.[21]

Again, a case-in-point is Deuteronomy. Since the first of half of the nineteenth century, the absolute dating of Deuteronomy (in whole or in part) has been a keystone in discussing the formation of two distinct bodies of textual material: the Torah and the Former Prophets.[22] The recounting of these conversa-

---

[20] Kratz, "Pentateuch in Current Research," in Dozeman, Schmid, and Schwartz, *Pentateuch*, 58. Although for a preliminary sketch of the evidence for the intertextual engagement of M-Mt texts within the Hebrew Bible, see p. 241 n. 13 below.

[21] Kratz, "Pentateuch in Current Research," in Dozeman, Schmid, and Schwartz, *Pentateuch*, 59.

[22] Since W. M. L. de Wette's *Dissertatio* (1805), scholars have commonly asserted that the earliest version of Deuteronomy (*Urdeuteronomium*) was originally an independent Pentateuchal source dating to the Josianic reform in the late seventh century B.C.E. (De Wette, "Dissertatio critico-exegetica qua Deuteronomium a prioribus pentateuchi libris diversum, alius cuiusdam recentioris auctoris opusesse monstratur" [Ph.D. diss., Jena, 1805], 1–16; repr. in *Biblische Theologie und historisches Denken: Wissenschaftsgeschichtliche Studien aus Anlass der 50. Wiederkehr der Basler Promotion von Rudolf Smend* [ed. M. Keßler and M. Wallraff; SGWB.NF 5; Basel: Schwabe Verlag, 2008], 182–192). That this chronological anchor remains a mainstay among most critical scholars is almost axiomatic and finds only occasional challengers; most recently, Juha Pakkala, who acknowledges this consensus and argues for a post-monarchic date ("The Date of the Oldest Edition of Deuteronomy," *ZAW* 121 [2009]: 390, 400).

Regarding Deuteronomy's role as the cornerstone in the formation of both the Torah and the Former Prophets, one cannot escape the influence of Martin Noth's *Überlieferungsgeschichtliche Studien. I. Die sammelnden und bearbeitenden Geschichtswerke im Alten Testament* (SKG.GK 18; Halle: M. Niemeyer, 1943) and its subsequent fallout. Here, Römer and de Pury's history of

tions is here unnecessary. Rather, what is important is that in contrast to the endless debates regarding the *absolute* dates for the formation of these textual materials, the scholarly discussion about the *relative* stages of development within Deuteronomy itself is considerably stable (see §2.3 below). This stability affords a particular advantage in studying the M-Mt, for the texts reflecting the M-Mt within Deuteronomy are located across the boundaries of at least two of the book's major developmental stages, the delineation of which now requires attention.

2.3 The Formation of Deuteronomy

In his contribution to the volume *Les Dernières Rédactions du Pentateuque, de L'Hexateuque et de L'Ennéateuque*, Erhard Blum states that "Um einen Text verstehen zu können, sollte man wissen, wo/wie er anfängt und wo/wie er aufhört."[23] How one answers this question, he insists, is often tied to which text one generally treats as a literary unit.[24] This same observation—which frames Kratz' survey on the Pentateuch (cf. p. 30 n. 3 above)—applies particularly well to Deuteronomy, with only minor adaptation: *in order to understand a Dt/Dtr text within Deuteronomy, one should know where/how it begins and where/how it ends. Further, how a scholar determines such parameters within Deuteronomy is often tied to which texts s/he deems to display literary unity.*

---

research on Dtr historiography is indispensable, and in it they give the following valuation to Noth's volume: "Rétrospectivement, on peut dire qu'il s'agit là sans doute du livre qui, au cours de ce siècle [i.e., the *twentieth*], aura influencé le plus profondément et le plus durablement les études vétérotestamentaires" (Thomas Römer and Albert de Pury, "L'Historiographie deutéronomist (HD): Historie de la recherche et enjeux de débat," in *Israël construit son histoire: L'historiographie deútéronomiste à la lumière des recherches récentes* [ed. Albert de Pury, Thomas Römer, and Jean-Daniel Macchi; MdB 34; Geneva: Labor et Fides, 1996], 31). Alternatively, see also Römer's helpful essay "The Book of Deuteronomy," in *The History of Israel's Traditions: The Heritage of Martin Noth* (ed. Steven McKenzie and M. Patrick Graham; JSOTSup 182; Sheffield: Sheffield Academic, 1994), 178–212.

23 Blum, "Pentateuch – Hexateuch – Enneateuch," in Römer and Schmid, *Rédactions du Pentateuque*, 67. As noted earlier, Kratz deems this observation as pivotal for current Pentateuchal studies (cf. p. 30 n. 3).

24 Blum, "Pentateuch – Hexateuch – Enneateuch," in Römer and Schmid, *Rédactions du Pentateuque*, 67. Blum has recently reiterated this truism in his contribution to *Pentateuch, Hexateuch, or Enneateuch?* ("Pentateuch – Hexateuch – Enneateuch? Or: How Can One Recognize a Literary Work in the Hebrew Bible," in *Pentateuch, Hexateuch, or Enneateuch? Identifying Literary Works in Genesis through Kings* [ed. Thomas B. Dozeman, Thomas Römer, and Konrad Schmid; SBL 8; Atlanta: Society of Biblical Literature, 2011], 43).

The locus of such debates, not surprisingly, is in the details of Deuteronomy's literary growth[25]—that is, at the *micro-redactional* level.[26] What is striking, however, is the near consensus among scholars regarding the broad strokes of this process at the *macro-redactional* level. Two scholars vet this enduring currency on Deuteronomy rather well: Moshe Weinfeld and Thomas Römer. In the early 1990's, Moshe Weinfeld observed there to be "a general agreement in regards to Deut 4:44–28:68. It is believed that these chapters constitute the original book, which was later supplemented by an additional introduction (1:6–4:40) and by varied material at the end of the book (chaps. 29–30)."[27] Granted, there is no agreement on the precise textual parameters of this development, as redactional additions are detectable across all stages. Yet a survey of literature since Weinfeld's observation indicates an enduring, widespread agreement that Deuteronomy's macro-redactional material growth transpired

---

[25] A useful synopsis of three key interlocutors—namely, Mayes, Preuss, and Nielsen—is in Antony F. Campbell and Mark A. O'Brien's *Unfolding the Deuteronomistic History: Origins, Upgrades, Present Text* (Minneapolis: Fortress, 2000), 39–99. Though certainly no substitute for consulting each work directly, this volume provides an excellent visualization of the conclusions drawn by A. D. H. Mayes, *Deuteronomy* (NCB; Grand Rapids: Eerdmans, 1979), Horst D. Preuss, *Deuteronomium* (EdF 164; Darmstadt: Wissenschaftliche Buchgesellschaft, 1982), and Eduard Nielsen, *Deuteronomium* (HAT I/6; Tübingen: Mohr-Siebeck, 1995).

[26] This use of the term "micro-redaction" is informed by the methodological process Richard D. Nelson envisioned for the formation of proto-Deuteronomy (for Nelson, chs. 5–26, 28). Due to the multiplicity of viewpoints within Deuteronomy, the book is "resistant to analysis into clearly defined and mutually exclusive stages of literary development." Instead of successive redactional layers, Nelson therefore posits "microredaction" [sic] as the literary process that shaped proto-Deuteronomy through "accretion by small steps and changes by minor increments." Only after its public release during the Josianic reform did Deuteronomy undergo successive "monarchic and exilic additions," which Nelson describes as clearly discernible (*Deuteronomy* [OTL; Louisville: Westminster John Knox, 2002], 7–8). As such, in this study, the term "micro-redactional" describes the editorial accretions to texts within Ur-Deuteronomy that exhibit these tensions, but do not form any clear redactional layer. Conversely, "macro-redactional" in this study refers to the process whereby large textual blocks entered Deuteronomy in the formation of the whole, blocks which most scholars agree were subsequent additions to the book's primitive legal corpus embedded in chs. 12–26 (cf. Fig. 2.1 on p. 41 below).

[27] Moshe Weinfeld, *Deuteronomy 1–11: A New Translation with Introduction and Commentary* (AB 5; New York: Doubleday, 1991), 10. Weinfeld continues, describing chs. 31–34 as "usually divided" into "Deuteronomic material" (31:1–13, 24–29; 32:45–47; and ch. 34) and "ancient material appended to the book" (31:14–23; 32:1–43, 48–52; 33:1–29). As well, Weinfeld further nuances his limning of the general consensus that Deut 4:44–28:68 constitutes the "original book," noting "chaps. 5–28 are not homogenous either" (*Deuteronomy 1–11*, 10). For Weinfeld's discussion of the heterogeneity of these chapters, see *Deuteronomy 1–11*, 10–13.

by accretion from the inside out—what this study describes as being *centrifugal* in nature. Here, Thomas Römer summarizes the evidence for this process well:

> In its present form, the book of Deuteronomy is the result of a long redactional process, which is indicated by the following points: the book has at least two prologues (chs 1–3 [4] and 5–11) and several conclusions (chs 26; 27–28; 30–34). Numerous laws in the core of the book (chs 12–26) do not presuppose the historical introductions (esp. chs 1–4; 9–10), which tend to integrate Deuteronomy into a larger historical perspective, with several allusions to parallel episodes in Exodus and Numbers. These chapters underwent several stages of editions, as can be shown by inconsistent statements or changes of style. In this context, one has to mention the so-called *Numeruswechsel*; this term designates the frequent alternation of second personal singular and plural forms of address. This criterion is often used in order to determine the successive stages of growth within Deuteronomy: thus, it is often claimed that the texts in the *plural* belong to exilic redactors, whereas texts recurring with a *singular* form of address should be seen as belonging to the original book of Deuteronomy. But this view is certainly oversimplified.[28]

Already the careful reader will notice the different terminologies and textual parameters Weinfeld and Römer use.[29] Still, the overlap sufficiently attests to an enduring consensus regarding at least two stages in Deuteronomy's macro-redactional development: 1) the Dt authors took an preexisting body of legal material (embedded in chs. 12–26) and framed it with an exterior (now interior) historical, paraenetic prologue (chs. 5–11) and covenantal epilogue (chs. 27–30), thereby forming the first edition of Deuteronomy as a book; 2) the addition of the current exterior frame (chs. 1–3 [4]; 31–34) then occurred through subsequent processes (cf. Fig. 2.1 below).

Here a caveat is especially warranted, if not mandated. Not unlike Römer's warning against the unqualified use of the *Numeruswechsel* to determine Deuter-

---

28 Römer, *The so-called Deuteronomistic History*, 73. Van Seters provided a similar survey in 1999: "This yields the following broad outline of development: (a) Laws in 12–26 are the oldest. (b) First framework of 5–11, 28 equals the second stage. (c) Second framework, 1–4 plus 29–31, 34 equals the third stage. (d) Later additions: the ceremonial curse, 27; the two poems, 32–33; some secondary expansions. This scheme is generally considered to be an oversimplification of the book's literary history. Its development was, in fact, quite complex and calls for further internal scrutiny to determine whether there are additional signs for literary stratification within the larger units" (*The Pentateuch*, 90).
29 What Weinfeld calls an "original book" (4:44–28:68), Römer further limns as a "core" (chs. 12–26) supplemented with the innermost prologue (chs. 5–11) and conclusion (chs. 26; 27–28). Weinfeld's "additional introduction (1:6–4:40)" and "varied material at the end of the book (chaps. 29–30)" roughly correspond to Römer's outermost prologue (chs. 1–3 [4]) and conclusions (chs. 30–34) (Weinfeld, *Deuteronomy 1–11*, 10; Römer, *The so-called Deuteronomistic History*, 73).

onmic literary strata,[30] the above outline of Deuteronomy's macro-redactional literary developments also borders upon oversimplification, and again, the debate hinges on where/how many of these blocks of texts begin and where/how they end.[31] Such is especially the case for the interior prologue (chs. 5–11), over which there is considerable debate regarding its micro-redactional stages. Yet it is in this block of material that one finds the first set of M-Mt texts within Deuteronomy (Deut 6:16; 8:15; 9:22). As such, the task of establishing the relative chronology of these M-Mt texts, both to each other and their surrounding literary context, marks a distinct challenge—one that occupies the following chapter. The second set of M-Mt texts—namely, Deut 32:13; 32:48–52; and 33:8—resides within Deuteronomy's exterior epilogues (chs. 31–34), a block of textual material that faces its own unique challenges in this regard. Yet even in the face of ongoing debates, areas of general agreement which inform this study emerge regarding both these blocks of material.

---

30 Römer rightly observes that there are numerous texts in Deuteronomy in which one cannot extract the second person masculine plural (2mp) portions and thereby recover the earlier second person masculine singular (2ms) sentence. His choice of an illustration of this conundrum, however, is a bit unfortunate. Römer deems it impossible to reconstruct an "original sentence in the singular" of Deut 12:1: אלה החקים והמשפטים אשר תשמרון לעשות בארץ אשר נתן יהוה אלהי אבתיך לך לרשתה כל־הימים אשר־אתם חיים על־האדמה (*The so-called Deuteronomistic History*, 74). However, if one extracts 1) the first relative clause up through לעשות and 2) the remainder of the verse from כל onward (both underlined), what remains is intelligible: אלה החקים והמשפטים בארץ אשר נתן יהוה אלהי אבתיך לך לרשתה, *These are the statutes and ordinances in the land which Yahweh the God of your fathers gave you to inherit*. Römer's warning is still warranted, however, as many scholars agree this phenomenon requires case-by-case evaluation (cf. p. 45 n. 44 below).

31 See p. 39 n. 28 above for Van Seters' similar caution. Still, the acceptance of this outline of Deuteronomy's material is quite prevalent; it even forms the organizing principle for the essays collected in Duane L. Christensen, ed., *A Song of Power and the Power of Song: Essays on the Book of Deuteronomy* (SBTS 3; Winona Lake: Eisenbrauns, 1993). Even Karel van der Toorn's recent four stage development for the book of Deuteronomy generally aligns with this centrifugal development: The "Covenant Edition" framed an original corpus (chs. 12–26*) with 4:45 + 6:4–9 and ch. 28 (this edition is what van der Toorn considers to be *Urdeuteronomium*); the "Torah Edition" added 4:44, inserted ch. 5, and expanded upon ch. 28 up through 29:28; the "History Edition" then added chs. 1–3 and 31–34; finally, the "Wisdom Edition" inserted chs. 4* and 30 (Karel van der Toorn, *Scribal Culture and the Making of the Hebrew Bible* [Massachusetts: Harvard University, 2007], 150–172). Van der Toorn's cursory treatment is of limited value to the current study, however, as it omits Deut 6:10–11:32 from its discussion.

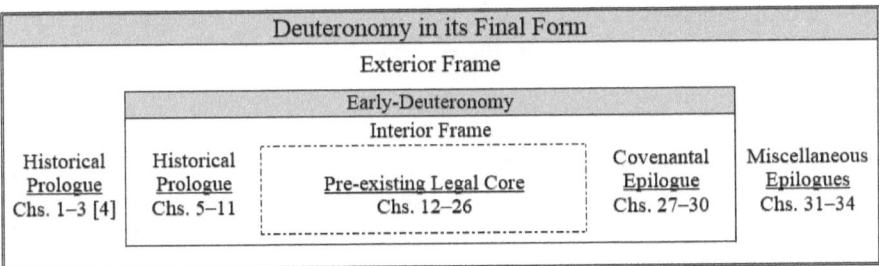

Fig. 2.1: Deuteronomy's Macro-Redactional Formation

2.3.1 The Interior Prologue: Early-Deuteronomy and the Numeruswechsel

As it currently stands, the interior prologue functions as a parenesis that 1) exhorts Israel to keep (שמר) and/or do (עשׂה) the commands of Yahweh when they enter the land they are to possess (ירשׁ), and 2) warns of the consequences for failing to do so.[32] Yet despite its functional uniformity, the textual materials that make up the interior prologue are far from homogeneous. Several tensions, in fact, point to a complex history of development, including multiple introductions to the law (cf. 5:1–5; 6:1–3), sets of law codes (cf. 5:6–21; 6:4–7:26), and wilderness histories (cf. 8:2–20; 9:7–10:11; 11:2–7), as well as the infamous *Numeruswechsel*. Consequently, foremost among the diachronic tasks relevant to the interior prologue is the isolation and chronological assignment of the varied literary strata that now constitute chs. 5–11.[33]

No consensus appears forthcoming regarding the internal prologue's micro-redactional stages, although there are points of general agreement across the spectrum of positions. One such point is the relative antiquity of Deut 6:4–5. There is a long list of scholars who agree that these verses once constituted some of the book's earliest content, if not its first non-introductory, material content: e.g., Lohfink (1963); García López (1977); A. D. H. Mayes (1979), Horst D. Preuss (1982), Thomas Römer (1992, 2005), Eckart Otto (1999), Reinhard G. Kratz (2000), Ansgar Moenikes (2002, 2006), Richard D. Nelson (2002), Timo Vei-

---

[32] For parenesis on keeping/doing the commands of Yahweh, see Deut 5:1; 6:1; 7:11–13; 8:1; 11:8–9, 22–25; for warnings for failing to do, see Deut 8:11, 19–20; 11:16–17.
[33] Kratz identifies this task as the focus in current "exegesis on Deuteronomy" ("Pentateuch in Current Research," in Dozeman, Schmid, and Schwartz, *The Pentateuch*, 39.

jola (2004), and David Carr (2010).³⁴ Now the intent of this inventory is not to dismiss the diversity intrinsic to these scholars' reconstructions,³⁵ nor is this

---

34 Norbert Lohfink, *Das Hauptgebot: Eine Untersuchung literarischer Einleitungsfragen zu Dtn 5–11* (AnBib 20; Rome: Pontifical Biblical Institute, 1963); 289; Gottfried Seitz, *Redaktionsgeschichtliche Stüdien zum Deuteronomium* (BWA(N)T 5. Folfe, 13. Heft; Stuttgart: W. Kohlhammer, 1971), 73; Félix García López, "Analyse littéraire de Deutéronome, V-XI," *RB* 84 (1977): 499; Mayes, *Deuteronomy*, 48; Preuss, *Deuteronomium*, 69; Thomas Römer, "Le Deutéronome à la quête des origines," in *Le Pentateuque: débats et recherches: XIVe Congrìs de l'ACFEB, Angers (1991)* (ed. Pierre Haudebert; LD 151; Paris: Cerf, 1992), 67; *The so-called Deuteronomistic History*, 78–81; Eckart Otto, *Das Deuteronomium: Politische Theologie und Rechtsreform in Juda und Assyrien* (BZAW 284; Berlin: de Gruyter, 1999), 68–69, 359–360; Reinhard G. Kratz, *Komposition der erzählenden Bücher des Alten Testaments: Grundwissen der Bibelkritik* (UTb 2157; Göttingen: Vandenhoeck & Ruprecht, 2000), 128–130; Ansgar Moenikes, *Tora ohne Mose: Zur Vorgeschichte der Mose-Tora* (BBB 149; Berlin: Philo, 2004), 202; "Das Tora-Buch aus dem Temple. Zu Inhalt, geschichtlichen Hintergrund und Theologie des sogenannte Ur-Deuteronomium," *TGl* 96 (2006): 50; Nelson, *Deuteronomy*, 4–5; Timo Veijola, *Das fünfte Buch Mose: Deuteronomium / Übersetzt und erklärt von Timo Veijola* (ATD 8/1; Göttingen: Vandenhoeck & Ruprecht, 2004), 2–3; originally David Carr (*Writing on the Tablet of the Heart: Origins of Scripture and Literature* [New York: Oxford University, 2005], 135), although he now sees v. 5 as a secondary expansion based on the Songs 1:7; 3:1–4 (*The Formation of the Hebrew Bible: A New Reconstruction* [New York: Oxford University Press, 2011], 147 n. 110, 437; cf. *The Erotic Word: Sexuality, Spirituality, and the Bible* [New York: Oxford University, 2003], 190 n 25).

35 A few clarifications are necessary. First, given the parameters of the current study, the following survey does not reflect the full extent of proto-Deuteronomy as each scholar reconstructs it. Secondly, the consensus regarding Deut 6:4–5 devolves unnecessarily over two debates. The first occurs over terminology, as several scholars prefer to limit the terminology of "Ur-Deuteronomy" or "Proto-Deuteronomy" to sections of the legal core, while materials framing chs. 12–26 constitute an edition (e.g., Seitz). Others, however, call the first "book" form of Deuteronomy "Proto-Deuteronomy," while admitting the incorporation of pre-existing materials (e.g., Mayes). The current study prefers the latter, though there is little to be gained for the insistence upon any set of terminology to exclusion of another. The second debate revolves around the matter of what constituted the original introductory superscription to the earliest "book" stage of Deuteronomy, and whether Deut 4:45 made up any part of it. This debate is more tangible, and scholarship can be divided along the following lines:

Scholars who incorporate *Deut 4:45* in their reconstructions include Mayes, who cites "4:45; 6:4–9, 20–24; 7:1–3, 6, 17–24; 8:7–11a, 12–14, 17–18a; 9:1–7a, 13–14, 26–29; 10:10–11" as the texts relevant to the original book (*Deuteronomy*, 48); Preuss, who lists 4:45; 6:1*, 4–9, 20–24 (*Deuteronomium*, 69); Veijola, who lists only 4:45 and 6:4–5 (*Deuteronomium*, 2–3); and van der Toorn (*Scribal Culture*, 152). A few scholars, however, cite other possible introductions: Kratz insists that *Deut 5:1aα¹* ("And Moses called all Israel and spoke to them") originally introduced Deut 6:4–5 ("Hear, Israel" ...) (*Komposition*, 130); and Nelson describes chs. 6–11 as part Deuteronomy's "primary material," after which he strips away "obvious" secondary materials (6:18–19; 8:1; 9:8–10:11; 11:8), thereby tacitly rendering *Deut 6:1* as the starting point of proto-Deuteronomy (*Deuteronomy*, 4–5).

list in any way exhaustive, as there are a number of scholars who argue for alternative starting points.[36] Even so, across the spectrum of scholarly opinion, there is strong agreement that Deut 6:4–5 represents a vestige of the first version of Deuteronomy as a book.

As for the rest of the textual materials within the interior prologue, the field of scholarship remains quite contentious.[37] Certainly there are points of general agreement between select scholars, but the force of such agreements is insufficient to command even a limited consensus. Instead, the need to perform careful literary analysis persists, and here is where a second point of overlapping agree-

---

Scholars who avoid reconstructing a superscription include Römer, who only mentions Deut 6:4f.* (Römer, "Le Deutéronome," in Haudebert, *Le Pentateuque*, 78–81); Eckart Otto, whose terminologies differ, but whose redactional breakdowns nevertheless correspond: a pre-existent Deuteronomy (13:2–10* and 28:15*, 20–44*)—which he understands to be a subversive appropriation of Neo-Assyrian loyalty-oaths for the bolstering of Israel's loyalty to Yahweh—undergoes an expansion under Josianic "dtn Reformsprogramms" (which begins with 6:4f.) (Otto, *Das Deuteronomium*, 68–69, 359–360); and Ansgar Moenikes, who limits the "Vorderer Rahmenteil" to 6:4–5, 17, 20–22, 24–25 (*Tora ohne Mose*, 202; "Tora-Buch aus dem Temple": 50).

36 Foremost here is Eduard Nielsen, who finds remnants of Ur-Deuteronomium as early as the first chapter and as late as the last. Granting priority to the current major structural framework of Deuteronomy, he states that the frames radiating out from the two central legal sections (i.e., the laws relating to the *Kult-zentralisationsgesetz* [Deut 12:1–19:13] and the legislation to regulate Israel's life in promise land [19:14–25:19]) "mag in sehr hohem Maße das "Ur-Deuteronomium" widerspiegeln." Nielsen sees the following frames: The parenesis on life in the wilderness (chs. 6–11) ‖ the blessings and cursings of ch. 28; the historical recitation (1:6–3:29) ‖ Joshua's appointment and Moses' death (31:1–8, 14–15, 23; 34:1–12); and the transcription of the law (31:9–13) ‖ the introduction to the law in 1:1–5. The poems of chs. 32 and 33 constitute a later insertion (*Hineinfügung*) (Nielsen, *Deuteronomium*, 3). The strength of Nielsen's reconstruction is the value it places on Deuteronomy's current literary structure, but that structure is not so tightly knit as to warrant his conclusions.

One could count Alexander Rofé as contributing to the above consensus, except he sees the Decalogue of Deuteronomy 5 as part of the first expansion upon the pre-existing legal corpus. The book discovered during Josiah's reign (D_1) was merely a legal code (12:8–12; 14:22–23, 28–29; 15:19–23; 16:1–17; 26:1–11), followed by "a brief blessing and cursing" (28:3–6, 16–19), and perhaps the "covenant in land of Moab" (28:69–30:20). Much of the material this study locates within the interior prologue Rofé attributes to a secondary expansion during Josiah's lifetime (D_2), specifically 5:1–6:9; 7:1–11; 8:1; 11:22–25; 11:32–12:1. Rofé, however, leaves his rationale for the delineation of specific strata unstated in many places (*Deuteronomy: Issues and Interpretation* [OTS; London: T. & T. Clark, 2002], 6–9).

37 Raymond F. Person, Jr. states the problem succinctly in his discussion of the challenges facing redaction historians who reconstruct the literary stages of the Dtr History: "The problem lies in the inability of redaction criticism to distinguish one Deuteronomic redactor from another Deuteronomic redactor, since all Deuteronomic redactors use similar Deuteronomic language and themes!" (*Deuteronomic School*, 4).

ment emerges: namely, the continued use of the *Numeruswechsel* as a tool for reconstructing literary strata, with the second singular address presumably characteristic of older textual material and the second plural indicative of relatively younger material.

The use of the *Numeruswechsel* as a diachronic indicator is a long standing practice.[38] Yet since the time of G. Minette de Tillesse's influential essay "Sections 'Tu' et Sections 'Vous' dans le Deuteronome" (1962),[39] renewed debate has ensued about whether this criterion is adequate for demarcating literary strata. Since then, several counter proposals have emerged, but none have succeeded in vanquishing its use along the above lines.[40] Foremost among such proposals is Norbert Lohfink's. Lohfink considers the alternation of second person pronouns to be a stylistic device, with the plural form of address heightening the tension for the individual hearers, who are momentarily (and ironically) being singled out from the community.[41]

---

38 Scholars have been utilizing this phenomenon as diachronic criterion since the classic works of C. Steuernagel (*Der Rahmen des Deuteronomiums: Literarcritische Untersuchungen über seine Zusammensetzung und Entstehung* [Halle: J. Krause, 1894]) and W. Staerk (*Das Deuteronomium – Sein Inhalt und seine literarische Form: Eine kritische Studie* [Leipzig: Hinrichs, 1894]). For summaries of each, see H. G. Mitchell, "The Use of the Second Person in Deuteronomy," *JBL* 18 (1899): 62–63; Eissfeldt, *The Old Testament*, 225–226.
39 G. Minette de Tillesse, "Sections "tu" et sections "vous" dans le Deutéronome," *VT* 12 (1962): 29–87.
40 A number of surveys relaying the history of research on the *Numeruswechsel* are available, so it is not necessary to recount to any large extent here. For research prior to Noth, see Christopher T. Begg, "The Significance of the Numeruswechsel in Deuteronomy: The "Pre-History" of the Question," *ETL* 55 (1979): 116–124. For the state of the question up through the 1970's, see the five volume (!) dissertation of Christopher T. Begg, "Contributions to the Elucidation of the Composition of Deuteronomy with special attention to the significance of the Numeruswechsel" (Ph.D. diss., Katholieke Universiteit te Leuven, 1978). More recently, see Timothy A. Lenchak, *"Choose Life!": A Rhetorical-Critical Investigation of Deuteronomy 28,69–30,20* (AnBib 129; Rome: Pontificio Ist Biblico, 1993), 12–16; Römer and Pury, "L'Historiographie deutéronomist," in Pury, Römer, and Macchi, *Israël construit son histoire*, 89–91; David P. Wright, *Inventing God's Law: How the Covenant Code of the Bible Use and Revised the Laws of Hammurabi* (Oxford: Oxford University, 2009), 324 n. 3 (on p. 484). The breadth of studies listed above is indicative of the sustained prevalence of this criterion.
41 Norbert Lohfink, *Das Hauptgebot*, 30–31, 239–258; followed recently by Moenikes, *Tora ohne Mose*, 66 n. 187, and Lenchak, *"Choose Life!"*, 16. Mayes critiques Lohfink's thesis fairly, observing that in some texts (e.g., Deut 4:1–40) the phenomenon is clearly "a stylistic feature of a single author," but noting that in many passages the *Numeruswechsel* corroborates separate evidence for the "assignment of sections to different authors" (e.g., Deut 7:11; 8:1) (*Deuteronomy*, 36). Other explanations appealing to stylistics involve quotations/citations (e.g., Jeffrey Stackert, *Rewriting the Torah: Literary Revision in Deuteronomy and the Holiness Legislation*

More cautionary than any appeal to rhetorical styling, however, is the inescapable fact that this phenomenon is not unique to Deuteronomy. It occurs elsewhere, not only in the Hebrew Bible (e.g. within the Covenant Code and the book of Leviticus[42]), but also in ancient extrabiblical sources (e.g., the Hittite and Sefîre treaties[43]). The implication, especially in light of the latter, is clear: one cannot assume pronominal vacillation only occurs as a result editorial activity.

Nevertheless, several scholars continue to hold that *Numeruswechsel* may serve as a useful indicator of editorial activity when corroborated with additional criteria.[44] The reason for scholars' continued, albeit cautious use of the *Numeruswechsel* as a criterion is quite simple: the evidence demands an explanation, yet no single explanation for the phenomenon as it is extant in Deuteronomy has proven capable of carrying the full weight of its varied presence within the book. In short, consideration of such pronominal shifts is warranted as part of a thorough analysis of the M-Mt texts in Deuteronomy.

[FAT 52; Tübingen: Mohr Siebeck, 2007], 128 n. 42), and even structural markers in metrical analysis (Duane L. Christensen, *Deuteronomy 1:1–21:9* [2d. ed.; WBC 6 A; Nashville: Thomas Nelson, 2001], xcix-ci).

42 Laws within the Covenant Code (Exod 20:23–23:19) prefer the second singular, but see the vacillations in Exod 22:20–33 and 23:9–31. As well, legislation within Leviticus is almost exclusively in the second plural, but see for example Lev 2:5–9, 13–16; 18:7–23. Mitchell lists several examples of this phenomenon outside of Deuteronomy within the Hebrew Bible ("Second Person in Deuteronomy," 63–66).

43 Peter T. Vogt, *Deuteronomic Theology and the Significance of Torah: A Reprisal* (Winona Lake: Eisenbrauns, 2006), 9; Lenchak adds *Oedipus* 23.2–3, Xenophon 25.1, and the *Illiad* 27.1–2 ("*Choose Life!*", 15 n. 67); Mayes notes specifically Sefîre 1B, lines 21–45 (*Deuteronomy*, 35–36); Römer observes the same in Assyrian treaties (*The so-called Deuteronomistic History*, 74); for additional references see Klaus Baltzer, *The Covenant Formulary in Old Testament, Jewish and Early Christian Writings* (Philadelphia: Fortress, 1971), 33 n. 71.

44 Mark O'Brien advises due caution when using the *Numeruswechsel*, suggesting each occurrence be "cross checked against additional criteria where possible" (The *Deuteronomistic History Hypothesis: A Reassessment* [OBO 92; Göttingen: Vandenhoeck & Ruprecht, 1989], 51 n. 13); see also, Nelson (*Deuteronomy*, 5–6). Cautious sentiment can also be seen in Van Seters, who postulates that the *Numeruswechsel* may be useful for identifying strata at the earliest stages of Deuteronomy's development, "But once both [pronominal] forms were present in the text side by side, any subsequent writer may have felt free to use whichever form suited them, or even a mixture of both" (*The Pentateuch*, 92); similarly, Römer *The so-called Deuteronomistic History*, 74; see also Stackert, *Rewriting the Torah*, 128 n. 42. Kratz lists the phenomenon as the first of three criteria by which to identify Ur-Deuteronomy; his other criteria include Deuteronomy's dependency on the Covenant Code and its tendency to demand the centralization of the cult (*Komposition*, 121–122).

2.3.2 The Exterior Miscellaneous Epilogues

The exterior epilogues are a miscellany comprised of two well-defined blocks of poetic material—namely, the Song of Moses (Deut 32:1–43) and the Blessing of Moses (Deut 33:2–29)—framed by narrative and superscriptive materials (Deut 31:1–30; 32:44–33:1; 34:1–12) that are loosely connected to one another and to the book's exterior prologue via the related themes of Moses' impending death and Joshua's subsequent succession.[45] This state of composition precipitates its own challenges and scholarly trends, a few of which require brief attention here.

First, scholars generally agree that most of the materials within this exterior frame *entered* Deuteronomy rather late, either as Dtr or post-Dtr additions to the original book.[46] Yet the situation is decidedly more complex from the standpoint

---

[45] These themes not only link the exterior epilogues to the non-poetic materials that come before, but also serves as a foil to the book's exterior prologue (chs. 1–4). Not unlike the M-Mt texts within Deuteronomy, these texts also evince tradition-historical diversity. In the exterior prologue, for instance, Moses blames the people for his not being allowed to enter the land of promise. Yahweh was angry with Moses on account of the people's rebellion (Deut 1:19–40 names the rebellion in Kadesh-barnea; cf. Deut 3:23–29 and 4:21–22). Throughout Deuteronomy's first four chapters, there is no expression of Moses' culpability, and with exception of 4:21–22, each instance serves to explain Joshua's rise to leadership. In the exterior epilogues (chs. 31–34), however, the rational for Moses' exclusion from the land is not uniform. In ch. 31:1–22, there is no awareness of either Moses' sin or the people's wilderness rebellion (31:23–30 clearly disrupts the context; cf. 31:22 and 32:1). Instead, Moses does not enter the Promised Land on account of his age and failing health (cf. 31:2, 14, 16a), and again Moses' death is used to explain Joshua's rise to leadership (Deut 31:14–16). In ch. 34, the reason for Moses' preclusion from the land remains unstated, only that while he was aged, he was *not* decrepit (v.7). It is only in Deut 32:51 that Moses' punishment is a direct result of he and Aaron breaking faith (מעלתם) at Meribath-Kadesh (cf. Num 20:1–13). (Incidentally, while Aaron shares in this sin and punishment in Deut 32:51, his death is recorded without rationale in Deut 10:6.)

[46] Mayes goes so far as to assert that "in no case can pre-deuteronomistic material be seen here [i.e., 31:1–34:12]" (*Deuteronomy*, 371); Christensen identifies this trend as his third major impulse in the modern study of Deuteronomy (Duane L. Christensen, "Deuteronomy in Modern Research: Approaches and Issues," in *A Song of Power and the Power of Song: Essays on the Book of Deuteronomy* [ed. Duane L. Christensen; SBTS 3; Winona Lake: Eisenbrauns, 1993], 5); Van Seters characterizes the field as consigning chs. 31 and 34 to the Dtr History (along with chs. 1–4, 29), while chs. 32–33 are cast as later additions (*The Pentateuch*, 90, 94); see also Stephen B. Chapman (*The Law and the Prophets: A Study in Old Testament Canon Formation* [FAT 27; Tübingen: Mohr Siebeck, 2000], 155); Nelson, *Deuteronomy*, 8–9; Kratz, *Komposition*, 135; Römer, who treats 31:1–8; 34:1–6* and chs. 32, 33 as exilic and postexilic additions respectively (*The so-called Deuteronomistic History*, 132–133, 181).

of the M-Mt texts located within these epilogues. Deuteronomy 32:13 and 33:8 reside within the Song and Blessing of Moses respectively, and the Song and Blessing most likely existed in some written form prior to, and independent of, their current literary contexts.[47] In others words, one cannot gage the relative ages of Deut 32:13 and 33:8, and the stages of the M-Mt that they reflect, based *solely* upon their location within the book of Deuteronomy. A more careful examination of each text is therefore required (cf. §4.2 and §4.4).

Likewise, the case for Deut 32:51 is also challenging; yet it is here that a second consensus emerges. Up until recently, scholars have largely followed Noth in taking Deut 32:48–52 to be a post-Dtr/priestly expansion that recapitulates Num 27:12–14 (cf. §4.3).[48] Its purpose, as Mayes succinctly notes, is "to recover the connection between the announcement of Moses' death (Num 27:12–14) and the actual account of his death (the priestly portions of Dt. 34) [...] The section thus belongs to the time of the formation of the Pentateuch."[49] This consensus, as will be discussed later (§4.2.2), has come under recent attack from several continental scholars, so that one can neither safely presume that Deut 32:51 is in some way priestly, nor that it reflects the latest stage of the tradition.

The notion that the priestly literature was the last major stratum to enter the Pentateuch has, of course, been dominant since the time of Wellhausen.[50] More-

---

[47] On this point, scholars largely agree; the date for each text's original composition, however, is another matter (cf. §4.2 and §4.4). For the Song of Moses, dates within critical scholarship range from the pre-monarchic to the exilic or postexilic periods; see the extensive history of research in Paul Sanders, *The Provenance of Deuteronomy 32* (OtSt 37; Leiden: Brill, 1996), 1–57. Similarly, proposed dates for the tribal sayings in the Blessing of Moses range from the pre-monarchic to the monarchic periods; see most recently, Stefan Beyerle, who posits an early eleventh century origin (*Der Mosesegen im Deuteronomium: Eine text-, kompositions- und formkritische Studie zu Deuteronomium 33* [BZAW 250; Berlin: de Gruyter, 1997], 279–280); and David A. Robertson, who sees evidence from the eighth century (*Linguistic Evidence in Dating Early Hebrew Poetry* [SBLDS 3; Missoula: Society of Biblical Literature, 1972], 49–54).
[48] Noth, *Überlieferungsgeschichtliche Studien*, 190f. See for example, Mayes, *Deuteronomy*, 394; Preuss, *Deuteronomium*, 61; Weinfeld, *Deuteronomy 1–11*, 10; Nielsen, *Deuteronomium*, 284–285; Kratz, *Komposition*, 111; Nelson, *Deuteronomy*, 378.
[49] Mayes, *Deuteronomy*, 394.
[50] After *Julius Wellhausen* had convincingly shown in his *Geschichte Israels* 1) that the Yahwist was more primitive than the Elohist, and 2) that the Priestly Code was later than Deuteronomy (*Geschichte Israels: in zwei Bänden* [Berlin: Druck und Verlag von G. Reimer, 1878], 1.35–40, 371), the essentials of the "Newer Documentary Hypothesis" as the source critical theory for Pentateuchal formation became a scholarly mainstay for nearly a century. This hypothesis—sometimes prepended with "Graf-Wellhausen" on account of Karl Heinrich Graf's influence on Wellhausen—is only "newer" in comparison to the former documentary hypothesis. The earlier model was largely the product of Jean Astruc, J. Gottfried Eichhorn, and Carl David Ilgen in the

over, this is perhaps the singular tenet of Wellhausen's theory that has survived the revisionist movement relatively unscathed (cf. §1.3.2 above). Yet as also noted earlier, David Frankel rightly raises the question whether the tradents of P might have been in possession of their own literary traditions from the beginning, especially their own murmuring traditions,[51] including the M-Mt. In other words, one must consider whether Deut 32:51 reflects an earlier stage of the P's M-Mt than its association within the priestly stratum would typically lead one to presume (§4.3).

---

last half of the eighteenth century (Jean Astruc, *Conjectures sur les mémoires originaux dont il paroit que Moyse s'est servi pour composer le livre de la Genèse* [Brussels, 1753]; J. Gottfried Eichhorn, *Einleitung ins Alte Testament* [3 vols.; Leipzig: Bey Weidmanns erben und Reich, 1780–1783]; Carl David Ilgen, *Die Urkunden des jerusalemischen Templearchivs in ihrer Urgestalt. 1, Die Urkunden des ersten Buchs von Moses in ihrer Urgestalt* [Halle: Hemmerde & Schwetschke, 1798]). With Ilgen as the exception, this first documentary hypothesis posited only two continuous sources behind the Pentateuch—the Elohist source (E) and the Yahwist source (J)—distinguishable by the use of the divine name (either אלהים or יהוה), by narrative stylistic differences (including distinct vocabulary beyond the divine name), and by doublet narratives. (Ilgen had two "E" sources, which did not catch on until Hupfeld.) Afterwards, four major shifts lead from the older hypothesis to the newer hypothesis: 1) Wilhelm Martin Leberecht DeWette's isolation of Deuteronomy (D) as a third Pentateuchal source (with the order of EJD); 2) Hermann Hupfeld's dividing the Elohist source into earlier (E^1) and later (E^2, now "P") strands, so resulting in four sources (with the order PEJD); 3) Graf's arguing that Deuteronomy shows awareness of the combined J and E but not E^2/P, ergo P is later than D (with the order of EJDP); and finally 4) Wellhausen's opinion of J being more primitive than E renders the "newer" model complete with the famous order of JEDP (cf., de Wette, "Dissertatio critico-exegetica qua Deuteronomium, 1–16; Hermann Hupfeld, *Die Quellen der Genesis und die Art ihrer Zusammensetzung* [Berlin: Wiegandt und Grieben, 1853]; Karl H. Graf, *Die Geschichtlichen Bücher des Alten Testaments: Zwei historisch-kritische Untersuchungen* [Leipzig: T. O. Weigel, 1866], 8–9 f.; Wellhausen, *Geschichte Israels*, 35–40, 371). Wellhausen provided the source critical work informing his synthesis in a series of articles first published in *Jahrbücher für deutsche Theologie*: "Die Composition des Hexateuchs" *JDT* 21 (1876), 392–450, 531–602, and *JDT* 22 (1877) 407–479. Eventually, these articles were collectively released under the title *Skizzen und Vorarbeiten* (Berlin: G. Reimer, 1885) and then revised and expanded in *Die Composition des Hexateuchs und der historischen Bücher des Alten Testaments* (Berlin, 1889).

51 See pp. 21–22 above; David Frankel, *The Murmuring Stories of the Priestly School: A Retrieval of Ancient Sacerdotal Lore* (VTSup 89; Leiden: Brill, 2002), 2.

2.4 Summary: The Advantages of Beginning with Deuteronomy

The crucial role that Deuteronomy's literary developments continue to play in discussions regarding the formation of Pentateuch and Former Prophets is beyond question. As Thomas Römer aptly put two decades ago, "Le Deutéronome reste la *pierre de touche* de toutes les théories sur la formation de la Torah et sur le movement dtr."[52] It is from within these conversations that several currents and cautions within critical scholarship emerge, the basis of which inform this study in the following ways and answer the question *Why begin with Deuteronomy?*:

1. Deuteronomy is the clearest discernible literary entity among the textual materials that were foundational to the formation of the Pentateuch. There is no debate as to its specific literary parameters, or even whether it originally had an independent existence outside the developing Pentateuch.

2. Most of Deuteronomy's textual material is the property of a single school of tradents. As such, it affords a more solid foundation for discerning diachronic tradition-historical developments than the M-Mt texts outside of Deuteronomy which do not inherently share the same literary milieu.

3. The M-Mt texts within Deuteronomy reside within two of the book's macro-redactional blocks: the interior historical prologue (chs. 5–11) and exterior miscellaneous epilogues (chs. 31–34). The relative chronological relationship between these two blocks of material serve as a preliminary guide for assigning relative chronological priority to the M-Mt texts within the interior prologue (Deut 6:16; 8:15; 9:22), as they entered at an earlier stage of Deuteronomy's literary history than did the M-Mt texts located within the exterior epilogues (Deut 32:13, 51; 33:8). Each block of material, however, is in possession of its own micro-redactional history, which requires separate and careful consideration. The interior prologue has undergone several editings, which in turn require additional criteria for their discernment.

4. The *Numeruswechsel*—the frequent vacillation between the second person singular and plural forms of address—is a literary phenomenon that may be indicative of diachronic literary development in Deuteronomy, especially within the interior prologue. The use as this criterion, however, needs corroboration with other diachronic indicators.

5. Although the exterior epilogues have entered Deuteronomy at a relatively later date than did the interior prologue, the Song and Blessing of Moses (32:1–

---

52 Römer, "Le Deutéronome" in Haudebert, *Le Pentateuque*, 66.

43; ch. 33) have prehistories that must be taken into consideration when assessing the M-Mt texts within them (32:13; 33:8). The tradition-historical reminiscences within them could be later, coterminous to, or earlier than, their counterparts within the interior prologue. Similar concerns pertain to the Deut 32:51, since Deut 32:48–42 closely resembles Num 27:12–14 and the priestly writers may have been stewards of their own set of wilderness traditions. As such, one must consider the possibility that the tradents of Deuteronomy may not have been aware of the divergent M-Mt components embedded in Deut 32:13, 51; 33:8 until the incorporation of the exterior epilogues into Deuteronomy.

In conclusion, the currents and cautions within Pentateuchal and Dt/Dtr studies afford a unique opportunity to study the diversity and development of the M-Mt within the Dt/Dtr school of tradents. For certain, each M-Mt text within Deuteronomy presents its own challenges and so requires careful literary analysis using every available critical tool, but in the end a framework for establishing the *Traditionsgeschichte* of the M-Mt is detectable. It is to the tasks of textual, literary, and tradition-historical analyses for each of the M-Mt texts within Deuteronomy that this study now turns. Chapter three treats the M-Mt texts inside the book's interior prologue (Deut 6:16; 8:15; 9:22), while chapter four attends to the M-Mt texts inside the book's exterior epilogues (Deut 32:13, 51; 33:8).

Chapter Three:
The M-Mt's Reminiscences within Deuteronomy's Interior Prologue

3.1 Introduction to the Interior Reminiscences

The texts preserving reminiscences of the M-Mt within Deuteronomy's interior historical prologue (chs. 5–11) are Deut 6:16; 8:15; and 9:22. Engaging these M-Mt texts leads to an immediate observation that is both obvious and yet worth mentioning: for the tradents of Deuteronomy, the M-Mt was a well-known tradition, one they could safely assume their readers and hearers would know. Thus, these proprietors did not find it necessary to rehearse every aspect of the M-Mt.[1] Reminiscences of the M-Mt were sufficient to accomplish their theological agenda—reminiscences comprised of various combinations of M-Mt components, including *agency, location, substance of issuance, source of issuance, interpretative significance,* and *canonical awareness.*

Although Deut 6:16; 8:15; and 9:22 do not possess each of these M-Mt components, what they do preserve reflects diversity within the M-Mt. Consequently, it is not enough when comparing these texts merely to observe the differences in the tradition components that they reflect. One must assess the relative chronological relationship of these texts in order to sequence the changes the M-Mt has undergone through time. Once diachronically mapped, these changes allow one to deduce the stages of the M-Mt's development from the perspective of the Deuteronomic / Deuteronomistic (Dt/Dtr) proprietors responsible for the shaping of Deuteronomy's interior prologue. The same task is mandated for the reminiscences within Deuteronomy's exterior epilogues, although the epilogues' distinct literary history presents challenges that warrant separate consideration (chapter 5). Together, the findings of the current chapter and the next facilitate the reconstruction of a tradition-historical framework descriptive of M-Mt's *Traditionsgeschichte* (cf. §3.2 and §4.2).

Complicating the task of uncovering the relative chronological relationship of the M-Mt reminiscences within the interior prologue is the fact that this block of textual material is itself the product of several editorial stages. The di-

---

[1] The force of this observation holds true for most of the M-Mt texts within the Hebrew Bible: their tradents presumed an awareness of the M-Mt to such a degree that they only needed to iterate select M-Mt components to evoke the M-Mt and interact with it. The exceptions, of course, are the narrative exponents themselves in Exod 17:1–7 and Num 20:1–13.

versity of the M-Mt reminiscences within the interior prologue is evidence of the complex literary history that lies behind chs. 5–11. The following sections attend to this challenge for each of the interior prologue's M-Mt reminiscences—Deut 6:16 (§3.2); 8:15 (§3.3); and 9:22 (§3.4), respectively—and their broader literary contexts. Methodologically, attention to this task unfolds in three phases: *text criticism* of the individual text; a detailed *literary analysis* of the material growth of each text's broader literary context; and finally a *tradition-historical analysis* of the M-Mt reminiscences that each text preserves. While a detailed reconstruction of the material growth of Deuteronomy 5–11 is beyond the scope of the current study, the results of the following investigation reveal the relative chronology of these reminiscences to proceed as follows: Deut 8:15 is earlier than Deut 6:16, while Deut 6:16 is earlier than Deut 9:22 (or Deut 8:15→6:16→9:22).[2]

3.2 Deuteronomy 6:16

3.2.1 Textual Criticism of Deut 6:16

$^{Deut\ 6:16}$לא תנסו את־יהוה אלהיכם כאשר נסיתם במסה:

The text critical task as it applies to Deut 6:16 suffers from the paucity of ancient textual witnesses that preserve the text. Despite Deuteronomy's apparent importance within the Qumran community, Deut 6:16 is not (or is no longer) represented within its scrolls.[3] The major witnesses that do preserve Deut 6:16, however,

---

2 For an overview of the reconstruction this study advocates for the stratigraphic growth of the broader literary contexts in which these M-Mt texts reside, see Table 3.3 Proposed Stratification of Deut 6:4–25; 8:1–20; 9:1–10:11 on p. 78 below.

3 Hanne von Weissenberg contends that the importance of Deuteronomy at Qumran "is indicated by the number of copies found in the Qumran library, where it is one of the four most popular scriptural books alongside the books of Psalms, Isaiah, and Genesis" ("Deuteronomy at Qumran and in MMT," in *Houses Full of All Good Things: Essays in Memory of Timo Veijola* [ed. Juha Pakkala and Martti Nissinen; PFES 95; Göttingen: Vandenhoeck & Ruprecht, 2008], 520). Yet no extant scroll from Qumran preserves Deut 6:16, even though many scrolls preserve portions of Deuteronomy that are within the proximity of Deut 6:16; e.g., both Murphyl (Mur4) and 4Qphyl^c (4Q130) have 6:4–9; 4Qphyl^o (4Q142) has 6:7–9; and 4QDeut^p (4Q43) has 6:4–11. For a complete list of scrolls preserving portions of Deuteronomy, see David L. Washburn, *A Catalog of Biblical Passages in the Dead Sea Scrolls* (SBLTCS 2; Atlanta: Society of Biblical Literature, 2002), 56–75; alternatively, see Emanuel Tov et al., *The Texts from the Judaean Desert: Indices and an Introduction to the Discoveries in the Judaean Desert Series* (DJD 39; Oxford: Oxford University Press, 2002), 189–191.

vary on whether the address is second singular (2ms) or second plural (2mp).[4] The inclination to shift Deut 6:16's address to 2ms is understandable, however, since the singular address dominates much of the broader literary context. In fact, for all of Deut 6:4–25[5] one only encounters the 2mp in vv. 14, 16–17, and 20: the address in vv. 14 and 16 is wholly 2mp, while all but the last word of v. 17 (צוּךָ) uses 2mp, and in v. 20 only the last word (אתכם) is 2mp. In the end, standard text-critical principles[6] incline preference toward the 2mp in each of these verses as preserved in the Masoretic Text (MT), leaving critical scholars to question the literary integrity of the pericope as a whole.

3.2.2 Literary Analysis of Deut 6:4–25

Fundamentally, the endeavor to explain each individual instance of 2mp address in Deut 6:4–25 must begin with a single question: Do the literary characteristics of this instance stand out so starkly against its current literary context so as to insist upon its heterogeneity, or is there an aspect of the broader pericope (e.g. form, rhetoric, etc.) which holds open the possibility of the instance in question being homogenous to the text surrounding it? Naturally, the absence of any such unifying aspect increases the likelihood of multiple hands having been involved in a text's formation. The opposite scenario, on the other hand, affords evidence for the possibility of a single hand having written a text that merely appears composite to modern sensibilities.

G. Minette de Tillesse's study represents a particular watershed among those attempting to explain the sudden shifts to 2mp within Deuteronomy—the so-called *Numeruswechsel* phenomenon. De Tillesse argues that most of the 2mp verses within Deut 4:44–30:20 are secondary Dtr insertions to an otherwise continuous singular

---

[4] Most prefer the plural (so Smr S T), but some contextually harmonize to the singular (so G V) (Carmel McCarthy, *Biblia Hebraica Quinta, Fascicle 5: Deuteronomy* [Stuttgart: Deutsche Bibelgesellschaft, 2007], 23).
[5] That Deut 6:4 marks the beginning of a new section is longstanding in scholarship. Félix García López observes "De l'avis unanime des exégètes, *Deut.*, vi, 4 ouvre une nouvelle unité ou section. Même N. Lohfink, qui defend l'unité des chaps. v-vi, est obligé de reconnaître qu'avec vi, 4 commence quelque chose de nouveau" ("Deut., VI et la tradition-rédaction du Deutéronome," *RB* 85 [1978]: 162).
[6] Namely, the rules of *manuscript ponderantur, non numerantur* ("manuscripts are to be considered for their worth and not reckoned according to their number") and *lectio defficilior praeferenda* ("the more difficult reading is to be preferred"). On the logic, application, and challenges for both of these "rules," see Emanuel Tov, *Textual Criticism of the Hebrew Bible* (3rd, rev. and exp.; Minneapolis: Fortress, 2012), 39 n. 34, 273–282.

text. But these interpolations "ne sont pas non plus des additions accidentelles d'un quelconque rédacteur; mais qu'elles sont l'oeuvre d'un auteur [namely, the Dtr], qui a consciemment suivi son idée et l'a exprimée chaque fois que l'occasion s'en présentait."[7] The force and simplicity with which de Tillesse argues commands respect, and his thesis soon found a number of tentative followers.[8] Nevertheless, Römer and de Pury rightly critique this thesis as "trop schématique," [9] as a comparison of de Tillessee's study with the 2mp sections within Deut 6:4–25 shows. De Tillessee argues that Deut 6:14 and 16–17a disrupt the paraenetic unity of vv.13+15+18, but his argument ignores v. 17b (2ms) and it does not attend to the sudden shift to 2mp with the last word of v. 20.

Gottfried Seitz, despite his redactional proclivities, represents in this instance a decisive shift toward seeing the 2mp of Deut 6:14, 16–17 as compositionally intrinsic to its current literary context, specifically vv. 10–18. Seitz begins by rejecting Lohfink's assessment that vv. 4–9 are extraneous to the pericope—a result of Lohfink detecting a new *Gattung* in vv. 10–16, 20–25.[10] The problem with

---

[7] G. Minette de Tillesse, "Sections "tu" et sections "vous" dans le Deutéronome," *VT* 12 (1962): 72. De Tillesse unfolds his argument in three sections. In the first, he shows 1) that the 2mp sections can be removed without damage to the "contextualité" of the 2ms sections, and 2) that together these 2mp sections share "une préoccupation théologique particulière absente des sections-*Tu*." In his second section, he concludes that there is a "un sérieux indice les occurences [i.e., of "parallelisms litteraires"] où les sections-*Vous* et Dtr sont littéralement d'accord *contre* les sections-*Tu*." Then in his final section, he demonstrates 1) that the differences between the 2mp and 2ms sections are not just literary, but also theological in nature, and 2) that this theology again reveals "l'intime appartenance des sections-*Vous* à l'histoire dtr" (De Tillesse, "Sections "tu et sections "vous"," 34–35, 47, 83).
[8] Cf. E. W. Nicholson, *Deuteronomy and Tradition* (Philadelphia: Fortress, 1967), 25–34.
[9] In the same breath, Thomas Römer and Albert de Pury go on to critique the future use of the *Numeruswechsel* as a criterion for limning stratification, citing F. García López and Yoshihide Suzuki as examples: "et la critique littéraire, opérant avec le critère du *Numeruswechsel*, produisit une multiplicité de couches dt et dtr échappant à tout contrôle" ("L'Historiographie deutéronomist (HD): Historie de la recherche et enjeux de débat," in *Israël construit son histoire: L'historiographie deutéronomiste à la lumière des recherches récentes* [ed. Albert de Pury, Thomas Römer, and Jean-Daniel Macchi; MdB 34; Geneva: Labor et Fides, 1996], 89; cf., F. García López, 'Analyse littéraire de Deutéronome V-XI,' *RB* 84 [1977], 481–522 and 85 [1978], 5–49; Y. Suzuki, *The 'Numeruswechsel' Sections in Deuteronomy* [Ph.D. diss., Claremont Graduate School, 1982]).
[10] The *Gattung* in question is Lohfink's so-called "Gebotsumrahmung." This form—of which Deut 6:10–25 is the clearest example—is said to have emerged from the preliterary context of ancient Israel's cultic preaching-tradition (*Predigttradition*). Its primary form takes the shape of two כי clauses: the first introduces a condition (6:10–11), which is then followed by an instruction (6:12–16); the second introduces an observer's question (6:20), which is then followed by a prescribed response (6:21–25). The remaining portions of Deut 6:4–25 are not part of the form, but rather reflect optional elements that can attach to it: vv. 4–9 are likely

Lohfink's proposal, as Seitz sees it, is that the *Kinderfrage* in Deut 6:20 presumes some form of cultic action, which in turn can only be found in Deut 6:4–9.¹¹ Instead, Seitz argues that Deut 6:4–9 and 6:20–25 are closely bound together, as sign (*Zeichen*) and question (*Frage*). The question then is what to do with the intervening textual material (vv. 10–19), and it is here that Seitz makes a fairly novel observation. The content and style of vv. 10–18 exhibit a chiastic arrangement, while v. 19 appears to be from a later hand:

v.	10a	Ancestral Promise (*Väterschwur*);
	10b + 11	Description of the Land (*Landbeschreibung*);
	12 f.	Warning and Positive Counterpart (*Gegenstück*) introduced by השמר לך פן;
	14	Prohibition (Plural);
	15	Rationale (*Begründung*) (Singular);
	16	Prohibition (Plural);
	17 f.	Legal Exhortation (*Gebotsparänese*) introduced by שמור תשמרון;
	18b.	Purpose Statement (*Zweckangabe*) regarding the Good Land; Ancestral Promise.¹²

"einleitende Sätze," while vv. 17–19 are "verbindende Sätze (Paränetische Formeln) zwischen den beiden Bedingungsgefügen" (Norbert Lohfink, *Das Hauptgebot: Eine Untersuchung literarischer Einleitungsfragen zu Dtn 5–11* [AnBib 20; Rome: Pontifical Biblical Institute, 1963], 113–118).

The fact that Deut 6:14, 16–17 is 2mp is irrelevant to Lohfink. He clearly separates 6:16 from 6:17—with v. 16 being part of the form and v. 17 an extraneous after-thought—even though the 2mp address continues into v. 17. In other words, Lohfink is simply not concerned with accounting for the *Numeruswechsel* in this passage. For this reason, it is Seitz, not Lohfink, who is decisive for reading the 2mp as intrinsic to its current literary context.

11 Gottfried Seitz (*Redaktionsgeschichtliche Studien zum Deuteronomium* [BWA(N)T 5. Folfe, 13. Heft; Stuttgart: W. Kohlhammer, 1971], 71–72) derives his critique from Soggin's brief observation that *Kinderfragen* in the Hebrew Bible are not expressions of random curiosities, but in fact are "Katechismusähnliche Frage" that always follows an ancient cultic ritual that requires further explanation or instruction by a father or teacher; cf. Exod 12:26; 13:14; Deut 6:20; Josh 4:6; 4:21; 22:24 (cf. J. Alberto Soggin, "Kultätiologische Sage und Katechese im Hexateuch," *VT* 10 [1960]: 341–347).

In fairness, Lohfink is aware of Soggin's thesis and recognizes the problems it creates for his own. Lohfink defends his position by pointing to other texts (Deut 4:9 ff; 6:7 ff; 11:19 ff) where instruction to transmit cultic knowledge to the coming generation without a *Kinderfrage* within a conditional clause introducing it. "So ist denkbar, daß die Einführung der Kinderfrage in unseren Texten [i.e., Deut 6:20] nur ein rhetorisches Mittel ist" (Lohfink, *Das Hauptgebot*, 115–116). The force of Lohfink's defense, however, is weakened substantially by the fact the question is a rhetorical device in both Soggin's and Lofink's argued forms, but only Soggin's is clearly demonstrable outside of Deuteronomy 6, while Lohfink already admits Deut 6:10–25 to be the "deutlichsten und umfassendsten" example of his (*Das Hauptgebot*, 113).

12 Seitz, *Redaktionsgeschichtliche Studien*, 73.

A number of scholars have since gravitated toward seeing all or part of vv. 10–19 as either having a concentric structure itself or constituting a component of a chiasm on a much larger scale. Mayes, for example, follows Seitz closely in this regard, with the exception that he sees Deut 6:10–18 entering Deuteronomy with Deut 4:1–40, as part of his proposed second Deuteronomistic editing.[13] (Seitz believes 6:10–18 entered the book at the same as the Decalogue in chapter 5.[14]) Likewise, Nelson, who does not cite Seitz, arrives at a very similar envelope structure.[15] Nielsen, on the other hand, believes vv. 10–13 (with vv. 4–9, but not vv. 14–19) was once the beginning of a much larger chiasm, which in turn constituted the original "dt Paränese" (Deut 6:4–13 + 7:1–6* + 8:7–13,* 17–18* + 10:12–21*).[16]

One could certainly increase the list of advocates for either side of the debate over whether the 2mp texts in Deuteronomy 6 are homogenous or heterogeneous to the dominant 2ms context.[17] The most forceful arguments for Deut 6:14,

---

13 A. D. H. Mayes, *Deuteronomy* [NCB; Grand Rapids: Eerdmans, 1979], 45–46, 175; in more detail, "Deuteronomy 4 and the Literary Criticism of the Deuteronomy," *JBL* 100 [1981]: 35–36).

14 Seitz, *Redaktionsgeschichtliche Studien*, 73–74.

15 Richard D. Nelson describes the "envelope structure" as follows: "'Swore to your fathers' (vv. 10a and 18bβ), the good land (vv. 10b-11 and 18bα), careful obedience (vv. 12–13 and 17–18a)) and "do not" (vv. 14 and 16) enclose v. 15 in a chiastic pattern" (*Deuteronomy* [OTL; Louisville: Westminster John Knox, 2002], 92 n. 12).

16 The center of this "schönen chiastischen Aufbau" is the prohibition against foreign intermarriage (7:1a, 3, 6), around which are the warnings not to forget Yahweh upon entering the land (6:10–13 ‖ 8:7–11a, 12, 13, 17–18a), which are in turn framed by the commands to love and fear Yahweh (6:4–9 ‖ 10:12, 20, 21a) (Eduard Nielsen, *Deuteronomium* [HAT I/6; Tübingen: Mohr-Siebeck, 1995], 89). Although Nielsen's isolation of these materials as deuteronomic appears at first glance sporadic, Campbell and O'Brien detect several overlaps with the strata isolated by both Mayes and Preuss, specifically that 1) Deut 7:1a, 6*; 8:7–11a, 17–18a are Dt; and that 2) Deut 6:14–19; 7:4–5, 7–8, 12a, 25–26; 8:1, 11b, 19–20; 9:7b-8, 20, 22–24; 10:13–19, 21b-22; 11:1–28, 31–32 are Dtr or later (Anthony F. Campbell and Mark A. O'Brien, *Unfolding the Deuteronomistic History: Origins, Upgrades, Present Text* [Minneapolis: Fortress, 2000], 57–63).

17 For other scholars who see the Deut 6:14, 16–17 as later than its surrounding 2ms context, see Eduard Nielsen, who considers Deut 6:14–19 to be post-Dtr but calls v. 16 "besonders ungeschickt, weil dort [i.e., Exod 17:1–7] der Durst des Volkes in der Wüste der Hintergrund für die Zweifel des Volkes ist: Ist Jahwe bei uns (mit seiner Hilfe)?, während hier das gesättigte Volk am Ernst der göttlichen Drohung zweifeln möchte" (*Deuteronomium*, 91); Timo Veijola, who attributes Deut 6:14, 15b, 17a to the early postexilic DtrB and Deut 6:15a, 16 to an even later hand (Timo Veijola, *Das fünfte Buch Mose: Deuteronomium / Übersetzt und erklärt von Timo Veijola* [ATD 8/1; Göttingen: Vandenhoeck & Ruprecht, 2004], 188, 189–191). One may also include García López, who not only isolates vv. 14–19 from its surrounding context, but also de-

16–17 being homogeneous to its immediate surroundings, however, continue to be the arguments proffered by Seitz and Mayes. Yet upon closer inspection, neither solution outweighs the evidence for the heterogeneity of Deut 6:10–18.

Beginning with Seitz,[18] the chiastic features of Deut 6:10–18 are not as tight as his outline would lead one to assume (see p. 55 above), especially within the two innermost frames (v. 14 ‖ v. 16 and vv. 12–13 ‖ vv. 17–18a). The content of the prohibitions in vv. 14 and 16 are parallel only in their 2mp address and the negative particle לא. Moreover, the 2mp ends not with v. 16 but with v. 17, yet Seitz designates vv.17–18a as parallel to the 2ms content of vv. 12–13. Granted, vv. 17–18a and vv. 12–13 do have the lemmas שמר and יהוה אלהים in common, but the parallelism of their remaining content is implicit at best and so requires further evaluation.

In contrast to the inexact chiastic features of the two innermost frames, the two outermost frames (vv. 10b-11 ‖ v. 18bα and v. 10a ‖ v. 18bβ) cohere quite well. The extended *Landbeschreibung* of vv. 10b-11 parallels the description of the land in v.18bα (למען ייטב לך ובאת וירשת את־הארץ הטבה) and shares the lemma טוב as well (cf. vv. 10b, 18bα). Further, the reference to Yahweh having sworn to give the land to ancient Israel's fathers in the outermost frame (v. 10a ‖ v. 18bβ) is strikingly similar:

6:10a   יביאך יהוה אלהיך אל־הארץ אשר נשבע לאבתיך לאברהם ליצחק וליעקב
6:18bβ (את־הארץ חתבה) אשר־נשבע יהוה לאבתיך

In short, the chiastic features of the interior frames (cf. v. 14 ‖ v. 16 and vv. 12–13 ‖ vv. 17–18a) are demonstrably weaker than those of the exterior frames (cf. vv. 10b-11 ‖ v. 18bα and v.10a ‖ v. 18bβ).

At this point, evidence begins to converge that discredits the claim that the 2mp is intrinsic to Deut 6:10–19, for the junctures where this chiasm is weakest correspond precisely to vv. 14, 16–17. In fact, contrary to what one might other-

---

tects two layers within vv. 14–19 (Deut 6:14, 15b, 17a, 18–19 is primary; 6:15a, 16, 17b is secondary) ("Deut., VI," 168–173). Although García López has rightly received strong criticism—e.g. Alexander Rofé, who critiques him for a "too prompt and too bold use of the critic's scissors" (*Deuteronomy: Issues and Interpretation* [OTS; London-New York: T. & T. Clark, 2002], 30 n. 14)—one can still appreciate the careful eye he gives to possible stylistic, lexical, thematic, and traditional tension within the text.

For scholars who read Deut 6:14, 16–17 as some way homogenous to its literary surroundings, see presumably Carsten Vang, who sees the "greater part" of Deuteronomy 1–28 as comprising proto Deuteronomy ("The So-called 'Ur-Deuteronomy' – Some Reflections on its Content, Size, and Age," *Hiph* 6 [2009]:18); Christensen's prosodic analysis also fits into this category (*Deuteronomy 1:1–21:9* [2nd ed.; WBC 6a; Nashville: Thomas Nelson, 2001]).

18 For Maye's argument, see p. 61 below.

wise expect, the removal of vv. 14 and 16 and the modification of v. 17 actually strengthens the chiasm's interior integrity in two areas: the central rationale and the immediate interior frame.

In Deut 6:15, the central rationale is that Yahweh is a jealous god (קנא אל), which in the current text immediately follows the reformulation of the *first* commandment in v. 14 (לא תלכון אחרי אלהים אחרים; cf. Exod 20:3; Deut 5:7). This arrangement is unusual, however, in that the rationale of Yahweh being a jealous god typically follows the *second* commandment (Exod 20:4; Deut 5:8) (cf. Table 3.1 below).

Table 3.1: The Rationale of the 2nd Commandment

Exod 20:5a	Deut 5:9a	Deut 6:13+15a
לא־תשתחוה להם ולא <u>תעבדם</u> <u>כי אנכי יהוה אלהיך אל קנא</u>	לא־תשתחוה להם ולא <u>תעבדם</u> <u>כי אנכי יהוה אלהיך אל קנא</u>	¹³את־יהוה אלהיך תירא ואתו <u>תעבד</u> ובשמו תשבע: ¹⁵<u>כי אל קנא יהוה אלהיך</u> בקרבך

When one removes Deut 6:14, thereby adjoining v. 13 to v. 15, a constellation of vocabulary emerges that would otherwise go unnoticed, yet is readily found elsewhere. The notice that Yahweh is a "jealous god" (אל קנא) regularly follows prohibitions against "worship" (√שחה) and/or "service" (√עבד) to graven images, especially after the second commandment (Exod 20:5a; Deut 5:9a; cf. Exod 34:14; Josh 24:19).[19] In the case of Deut 6:13, 15, this formula finds a positive expression advocating service to Yahweh since he is a "jealous god." Finally, the subsequent threat of Yahweh's wrath / punishment in v. 15b offers further corroboration that this formula was original to the chiasm, for it is the component that typically concludes this form (cf. Exod 20:5b; Deut 5:9b; Josh 24:19b-20).

Reconstructing any biblical text, as attempted above, always requires caution and humility on the part of the exegete. This maxim is particularly salient for the task of reconstructing the immediate interior frame that once surrounded this chiasm's central rationale (now vv. 13+15; contra Seitz[20]). One cannot simply

---

[19] Exceptions to this formulation may include Ezek 39:25 and Nah 1:2; in the former, Yahweh says he will become jealous for his holy name (וקנאתי לשם קדשי); in the latter, the prophet merely declares Yahweh to be a jealous and avenging god (אל קנוא ונקם יהוה). The clearest and most significant exception is in Deut 4:24, where "כי יהוה אלהיך אש אכלה הוא אל קנא" is not in the context of divine service / worship, but yet is still set in the context of the second commandment (cf. Deut 4:23b).

[20] If one grants the above argument for associating vv. 13 and 15, it is likely that together they formed the original center of this chiasm. Seitz, however, includes v. 13 in the parameter of his

excise Deut 6:16–17 because of their 2mp address[21]; each verse requires separate consideration.

The matter is simplest with v. 16. As stated earlier, its connection to the current literary context is quite loose, with its 2mp address (cf. vv. 14 and 17) and the negative particle לא (cf. v. 14) offering the only obvious connections to the surrounding text, and these are merely stylistic features. Content wise, v. 16 offers little to moor it to its current context, raising the question *"Why it is here in the first place?"* One possible answer is that the redactor responsible for v. 16 may have been inspired by the otherwise unnecessary בקרבך at the end of v. 15a. The etiology of Exod 17:7 says that Moses named the place "Massah" because they had tested (√נסה) Yahweh saying "Is Yahweh among us (בקרבנו) or not?"[22] It is possible then that v. 15a triggered the recollection of the M-Mt, perhaps coterminous to the time when the prophetic tradition began envisioning Israel's cultic failures as beginning in the wilderness.[23] Regardless of its motivation, Deut 6:16 hardly bears the stamp of originality.

---

frame "12f. Warnung und positives Gegenstück, eingeleite פן לך השמר" (*Redaktionsgeschichtliche Studien*, 73; cf. also p. 55 above).

[21] Contrary to De Tillesse, Deut 6:17a does not "continue la même monition" from v. 16; it merely carries the same address. As well, v. 17b is more than a "simple reprise stéréotypée de vi, 2, 20," as a comparison with Deut 8:11 clearly shows (Tillesse, "Sections "tu" et sections "vous"," 36, 36 n.1).

[22] Other scholars have observed this connection as well: García López, "Deut., VI," 170–171; Veijola, *Deuteronomium*, 190. Both García López and Veijola make too much of this connection, arguing that the redactor is responsible for both the formulation of v. 15a and v. 16. The need to illustrate "göttlichen Zornesgericht" of v. 15bα with a concrete example does not explain how the said redactor arrived at choosing M-Mt narrative in Exod 17:1–7 for this currently ill-fit illustration—ill-fit because Yahweh in no way exacts his wrath in this instance. On this point, Nielsen agrees (cf. the quote on p. 56 n. 17 above). Most likely, the trigger בקרבך (v. 15a) has literary priority over against v. 16, which in turn suggests that some from of the etiological question in Exod 17:7bβ-γ is intrinsic to the early stages of the non-P M-Mt narrative's literary development (*contra* Wolfram Herrmann, "Ex 17,7bβ und die Frage nach der Gegenwart Jahwes in Israel," in *Alttestamentlicher Glaube und biblische Theologie: Festschrift für Horst Dietrich Pruess zum 65. Geburstag* [ed. Jutta Hausmann and Hans-Jürgen Zobel; Stuttgart: Kohlhammer, 1992], 51).

[23] A few prophetic texts recall a time when tradition held that ancient Israel was faithful to Yahweh during most or all of the wilderness sojourn, but unfaithful to Yahweh on entry into the land (e.g., Jer 2:2–8; Ezekiel 16, especially vv. 4–8, 43 [?]; Hos 2:16–17 [14–15]; 9:10; 11:1–5; 13:4–6; *contra* Jer 22:21 and Ezek 23:8 where Israel is said to have been disloyal from her youth). Hosea particularly reflects the prophetic debate as to when Israel began to be unfaithful (cf., Roy E. Garton, "Rattling the Bones of the Twelve: Wilderness Reflections in the Formation of the Book of the Twelve," in *Perspectives on the Formation of the Book of the Twelve*

But such is not the case with v. 17, for at least two reasons. First, as noted earlier, v. 17 does exhibit some lexical similarity to v. 12, especially with the lemma שמר: v. 12 begins with השמר לך, while v. 17 starts off with שמור תשמרון את־מצות יהוה אלהיכם. Thus, removing v. 17 entirely would weaken the chiasm at this particular point, especially since what would remain (v. 18a) is in no way parallel to vv. 12.

Secondly, there is trace evidence that v. 17 may have *originally* been 2ms. To begin with, one should not forget that v. 17b suddenly and otherwise inexplicably reverts to 2ms with its final word: צוך. Additional evidence emerges when one considers the striking similarity between vv. 12 and 17 to Deut 8:11–14. In Fig. 3.1 below, one can immediately see the verbatim correspondence of Deut 6:12a and 8:11a (letter "A"), while the verbal parallels between 6:17 and 8:11b are certainly present (letter "B"), but not as overt as the correspondence between 6:12a and 8:11a. Conversely, verbal parallels to 6:12a frame 8:12–14a (letter "α"), while most of 6:12b finds exact representation in 8:14b (letter "C").[24] Putting aside for the moment the issues of Deuteronomy 8's formation process and the direction of dependence (see p. 69 n. 50 below), the point here is that there is a clear relationship between Deut 6:12, 17 and 8:11–14; yet Deut 8:11–14 is cast wholly in 2ms. Moreover, Deut 6:12, 17 would be too, were it not for v. 17, which is predominantly in 2mp, but then unexpectedly shifts back to the 2ms on the last word, as though the whole of v. 17 was originally 2ms from the start.[25]

A. D. H. Mayes affords an alternative explanation to the *Numeruswechsel* in Deut 6:17, as well as an argument for the unity of Deut 6:10–18 (19)[26] as a whole. Through a stylistic and lexical comparison, Mayes concludes that the author of

---

[ed. Rainer Albertz, James D. Nogalski, and Jakob Wöhrle; BZAW 433; Berlin: de Gruyter, 2012], 246).

[24] The remainder of Deut 8:12 (i.e., after פן) contains language similar to Deut 6:11: תאכל ושבעת (8:12a) ‖ ואכלת ושבעת (6:11c); ובתים טובים תבנה (8:12b) ‖ ובתים מלאים כל־טוב (6:11a). The content of Deut 8:13–14aα, however, bears only a conceptual correspondence (*prosperity*) to Deut 6:11b.

[25] A mechanism explaining this shift should be sought. Although speculative, I suggest that the redactor responsible for inserting Deut 6:14, 16 *may*, in the process of so doing, have continued transcribing in the 2mp beyond v. 16, effectively rewriting most of v. 17 into the 2mp. If this redactor was the same hand responsible for Deut 4:1–40, whose use of the second person is fairly erratic, such an oversight may not have warranted the trouble of correcting it, but merely a shift back to the 2ms of his received text.

[26] Mayes is ambivalent regarding whether v. 19 is homogeneous to vv. 10–18. In his 1979 commentary, he says v. 19 was probably subsequent to the chiasm of vv. 10–18 (*Deuteronomy*, 175). In his 1981 article, however, he does not make this distinction, merely stating there to be "sufficient contact between 6:10–19 and 4:1–40 to indicate unity of authorship" ("Deuteronomy 4," 35).

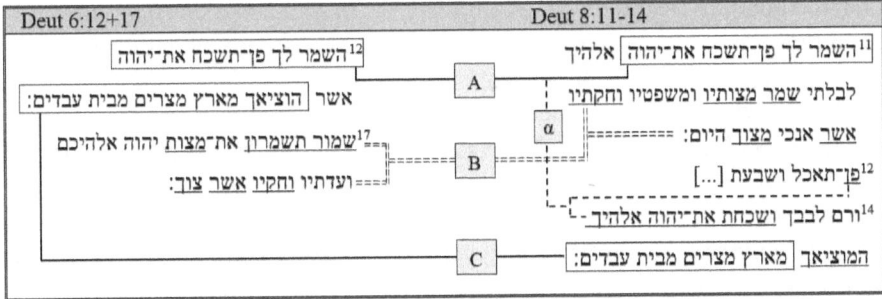

Fig. 3.1: Deut 6:12+17 and 8:11–14

Deut 4:1–40 is also responsible for a literary stratum that extends across the book of Deuteronomy, including the whole of Deut 6:10–19.²⁷ Mayes demonstrates that Deut 4:1–40 and 6:10–19 share a surprising number of traits:

> There is common allusion to the Decalogue and concern with the worship of other gods (the remainder of 6:4–25 does not presuppose the Decalogue); there is the same change from singular to plural form of address at decisive points in order to introduce emphasis (the prohibition of the worship of other gods in v. 14, and the prohibition of testing Yahweh with the general demand to keep the commandments in vv. 16–17); there is the same concern that settlement in the land and familiarity with its benefits will bring failure to keep fresh the memory of it as the gift of Yahweh who demands obedience (4:25; 6:10–12); there is common reference to the oath to the patriarchs (4:31; 6:10; 18); and there is the shared thought that nations have been dispossessed in order that Israel might have the land (4:38; 6:19). Finally, the two passages share a considerable stock of terminology: fear (4:10; 6:13); (the gods of) the peoples (4:19; 6:14); a jealous God (4:24; 6:15); destroy (4:26; 6:15); diligently keep (4:9; 6:17); that it may go well with you (4:40; 6:18); good land (4:22; 6:18).²⁸

As noted earlier, Mayes appropriates Seitz' thesis that Deut 6:10–18 (19) forms a chiasm; the above critiques levied against Seitz are therefore applicable to Mayes as well and need not be reiterated here. Instead, Mayes' contribution toward the

---

27 Mayes limns this strata as follows: "4:1–40; 6:10–19; 7:4–5, 7–15, 25–26; 8:1–6, 11b, 14b-16, 18b-20; 10:12–11:32 (omitting 10:19, 11:29–30); 26:16–19; 27:9–10; 28:1–6, 15–19; 29:1–30:20; 32:45–47" ("Deuteronomy 4," 48). According to Mayes, three aspects of this strata reveal the purpose for its composition: the "desire to inculcate obedience to the law"; the attempt to regulate "relationship between Yahweh and Israel" through "covenant or treaty thought forms and terminology"; and the similarity of thought to the "prophets of the exile" to advocate fidelity to Yahweh and the hope of restoration in the context of the sixth century exile ("Deuteronomy 4," 48–51).
28 Mayes, "Deuteronomy 4," 35–36.

understanding of Deut 6:10–19 as a unified composition stands encapsulated in the quote above. Yet despite this impressive list of overlapping features, two aspects of Mayes' argument fail to convince. The first aspect Mayes readily admits, but handily downplays: the fact that the overlap in vocabulary is not "exclusive to the particular editorial layer to which 4:1–40 and other passages belong."[29] The same critique especially applies to the themes of *worship to other gods* and the *oath to the fathers*, which pervades Deuteronomy outside the stratum Mayes identifies.[30] Again, this challenge is the bane of all who use language and themes to differentiate Dt/Dtr strata.[31]

A greater challenge to Mayes' thesis, however, lies in his statement that Deut 6:10–19 exhibits the same rhetorical usage of the *Numeruswechsel* as does Deut 4:1–40—that is, for effect and emphasis.[32] Yet a closer inspection shows the *polarity* of the shifting does not consistently correspond to the content being relayed. For example, Deut 4:23a (השמרו לכם פן־תשכחו) clearly parallels 6:12a (השמר לך פן־תשכח), yet the former is 2mp while the latter is 2ms, and the shift in address for both texts occurs in the context of entering the land of promise (cf. 4:22b; 6:10–12). Likewise, the polarity is reversed for the threat of utter destruction should Israel fail to remember Yahweh's covenant / Yahweh himself in 4:26 (השמד תשמדון) and 6:15 (והשמידך). If these shifts punctuate an effect or affect some emphasis, and if they are the product of a single hand, should the polarities then not correspond when shifts are made to affect similar content? The presence of the *Numeruswechsel* in these texts is clear; that it intentionally introduces emphasis at decisive points in both texts is not.[33]

---

29 Mayes reasons that the author is firmly rooted in Deuteronomistic thought and is an inheritor of its corresponding thought and vocabulary. As such, the similar vocabulary is at best corroborative with other points of evidence for his thesis (Mayes, "Deuteronomy 4," 36 n. 49).

30 The following are instances that fall outside the boundaries of Mayes' proposed stratum (cf. p. 61 n. 27 above): *worship to other gods* (Deut 5:7; 13:2, 6; 17:3; 18:20; 28:14, 36; 31:18, 20) and *oath to the fathers* (Deut 1:8, 35; 9:5; 10;11; 26:3; 28:11; 31:20–23; 34:4).

31 See p. 43 n. 37 above for Person's apt appraisal of the challenge facing redaction critics who use language and themes as the determinative criteria for detecting strata in the Deuteronomistic History.

32 Mayes only illustrates what he means by "effect and emphasis" from the shifts in Deut 4:1–40. Eventually, his description of this phenomenon becomes strained due to the frequency and irregularity of the *Numeruswechsel* in ch. 4. In the end, one is left with the impression that Mayes has appealed to the least common denominator, one without controls outside of Mayes himself ("Deuteronomy 4," 29–30).

33 An additional challenge addressed below (see p. 77) is that Mayes' proposed stratum does not account for the difference in the agencies of M-Mt in Deut 6:16 and 8:15.

In summary, the heterogeneity of Deut 6:10–19 remains demonstrable at precisely v. 14 and, more importantly for the current study, v. 16. These verses appear to be the latest substantive material additions to Deut 6:4–25*[34], the relative chronological development of which likely transpired according to the following stages: 1) to vv. 4–5 (*Ur-Deut*), were added 2) the texts of the *Kinderfrage*, namely vv. 6–9 + 20–25 (*Dt*); afterwards an editor inserted 3) the paraenetic chiasm (vv. 10–13 + 15 + 17–19; *early Dtr*), into which a final editor added 4) the 2mp prohibitions (vv. 14 + 16; *late Dtr*).[35] The structure of the original chiasm, into which vv. 14 and 16 were inserted, is the ancestral promise (v.10a ‖ 18bβ), the description of the land (vv. 10b-11 ‖ 18bα), the parenesis (v. 12 ‖ 17), and the central mandate (vv. 13+15).

3.2.3 Tradition-historical Analysis of Deut 6:16

The tradents of Deuteronomy, presuming an awareness of the M-Mt among their readers, selectively incorporated tradition components to accomplish their theological ends rather than rehearsing the whole tradition. Deuteronomy 6:16 only preserves two such components: namely, *agency* (i.e., who tested whom) and *lo-*

---

34 The matter of Deut 6:20–25 heterogeneity is widely recognized (cf. Table 3.2 on p. 76 below). The central question is where precisely the original *Kinderfrage* terminated textually. While the current argument does not hinge on this debate, two observations made elsewhere in this chapter may help clarify this debate. First, the infinitive clause of v. 24aβ—ליראה את־יהוה אלהינו—thematically coheres with the center of the paraenetic chiasm in 6:13+15, which in turn presumes the second commandment (cf. pp. 57–58 above). Secondly, it is possible that v. 24aα+b may have originally continued into Deut 8:2 f. (cf. p. 67 n. 48 below). Evidence for this connection is that the idea of Yahweh commanding something for Israel's good in 6:24b—לטוב לנו כל־הימים לחיתנו הזה—resonates well with Deut 8:2–18, especially v. 16. As well, without Deuteronomy 7, the historical recitation given in answer to the *Kinderfrage* continues uninterrupted from Deut 6:21–24 + 8:2–18: after the exodus and rationale (6:21–23) follows the reception of law (6:24) and then the wilderness sojourn in preparation for inhabiting the land (8:2–18). Deuteronomy 7 digresses from this historical recitation by giving instructions for the conquest of the land. Thus, it is likely that the paraenesis of Deut 8:2–18 once immediately followed the *Kinderfrage* of Deut 6:4–9 + 20–25*.
35 Any assignment of absolute chronology is, of course, tentative in nature, but the *Sitz im Leben* wherein the *Kinderfrage* (vv. 7–9 + 20–25*) would likely be most meaningful is preexilic, perhaps Josianic (*Dt*). The paraenetic chiasm (vv. 10–13 + 15 + 17–19) possibly reflects an early exilic context (*early Dtr*), during which time an explanation for the execution of Yahweh's jealous wrath warrants explanation. Finally, the concern about worshipping gods of the surrounding people (העמים אשר סביבותיכם) and testing Yahweh (with experiential knowledge of Yahweh's wrath) bears the imprint of a late exilic–early postexilic (*late Dtr*) setting (see Table 3.2 below for a comparison to other relevant strata).

cation (i.e., where the recalled event took place). In Deut 6:16, it is the people who inappropriately tested (√נסה) Yahweh, and that failure took place at the site etiologically known as *"the testing"* (בַּמַּסָּה has the assimilated definite article), most often translated simply as "Massah."[36] This curious feature ought not to be overlooked, as nowhere else in the Hebrew Bible is מסה definite.

Finally, although an argument from silence, one should not overlook the fact that Deut 6:16 and its immediate context demonstrates no *canonical awareness* of the priestly version of the M-Mt narrative in Num 20:1–13. Instead, if inspired by בקרבך in v. 15, Deut 6:16 affords the possibility that whoever inserted it was aware of a precursor of Exod 17:1–7, one perhaps devoid of Meribah elements.[37] Further, it is likely that Deut 6:16 reflects a time when the M-Mt had achieved the notoriety of reflecting an ancestral failure of epic proportions—one that serves as a paradigmatic warning with grave consequences should its lesson go unlearned (*interpretative significance*).[38]

---

36 All major modern versions render בַּמַּסָּה with a *preposition* + "Massah," presuming בְּמַסָּה. The only modern version I am aware of that translates the assimilated definite article is the Douay-Rheims American Edition (1899), which reads from the Latin Vulgate (*in loco temptationis*). Although the Hebrew pointing is a late tradition in its own right, one must contend with the current definiteness of במסה. Does בַּמַּסָּה represent the more ancient reading, which the Masoretes received and accurately transcribed, or is it more likely that בְּמַסָּה was at some point in time (un)intentionally downgraded (toponymically speaking) to the present בַּמַּסָּה? Any answer must remain speculative, but the toponym "Massah" and its tradition occur with such frequency in the canon that had בְּמַסָּה been the vocalic tradition, it is difficult to imagine a mechanism (text-critically or theologically) that would prompt its permanent revision to בַּמַּסָּה. Had בְּמַסָּה been original, any revision to the more generic בַּמַּסָּה would likely have undergone correction back to בְּמַסָּה. The fact the generic בַּמַּסָּה remains in the MT despite the prevalence of Massah as a specific toponym suggests that בַּמַּסָּה is the more ancient and traditional vocalization of במסה in Deut 6:16.

37 Contra the prevailing insistence that the "Meribah" elements are primary in Exod 17:1–7; e.g., Martin Noth, *Das zweite Buch Mose: Exodus* (ATD 5; Göttingen: Vandenhoeck & Ruprecht, 1958), 111; George W. Coats, *Rebellion in the Wilderness: The Murmuring Motif in the Wilderness Traditions of the Old Testament* (Nashville: Abingdon, 1968), 55; and Erik Aurelius, who observes that "Im Thema ריב und dem Namen Meriba wird normalerweise der traditionsgeschichtliche Kern von Ex 17:1–7 erblickt" (*Der Fürbitter Israels: Eine Studie zum Mosebild im Alten Testament* [ConBOT 27; Stockholm: Almqvist & Wiksell, 1988], 172).

38 Duane L. Christensen arrives at a similar conclusion, calling the incident at Massah "a paradigmatic warning for all time" (*Deuteronomy 1:1–21:9*, 151). Christensen, however, does not observe the difference in *interpretative significance* that Deut 9:22 brings to the development of the M-Mt (see p. 83 below).

3.3 Deuteronomy 8:15

3.3.1 Textual Criticism of Deut 8:15

Deut 8:15 המוליכך במדבר הגדל והנורא נחש שרף ועקרב וצמאון אשר אין־מים מצור החלמיש:

Unlike with Deut 6:16, portions of Deut 8:15–16 are extant from the remains of Qumran. Though quite fragmentary—4QDeut^e [4Q32] more so than 5QDeut [5Q1]—the evidence at Qumran supports the 2ms address within these verses, as well as the dominance of the 2ms in the larger context. The other major ancient witnesses predominantly follow the MT; minor variants include 1) the insertion in the Old Greek of the demonstrative pronoun ἐκείνης after the rendering of והנורא (an apparent assimilation to Deut 1:19's כל־המדבר הגדול והנורא ההוא), and 2) the Samaritan Pentateuch's omission of the vav-conjunction of ועקרב.[39] Yet this agreement among the witnesses does not bar the likelihood that behind Deuteronomy 8 stands a complex history of literary development.

3.3.2 Literary Analysis of Deut 8:1–20

Since the time of Lohfink's *Das Hauptgebot* (1963), scholars have widely recognized the structural artistry of Deut 8:1–20. Lohfink observes two principles of organization within this chapter: 1) a concentric or chiastic organization of the basic train of thought (*Gedankengang*) into thematic blocks; and 2) a concentric organization in the repetition of particular catchwords (*Stichwortrepetitionen*) (see Fig. 3.2 below).[40] At the center of each organizational scheme is the parenesis of v. 11, which according to Lohfink, and along with vv. 7–18, serves as a commentary on Deut 6:10–19.[41]

Lohfink's two schemes, however, are not without problems, as the parallels between the two do not consistently overlap. There are no catchwords connecting the parallel sections on the arable land (C ‖ C'); instead, the catchwords of C' (v.12) find their parallel in v. 10, which Lohfink conveniently excludes from his

---

39 Carmel McCarthy, McCarthy, *BHQ Deuteronomy*, 28–29.
40 Lohfink, *Das Hauptgebot*, 194–195. Note that *Figure 3.2.: Lohfink's Concentric Models for Deuteronomy 8* is an adaptation of Lohfink's charts in *Das Hauptgebot*, 195.
41 Lohfink, *Das Hauptgebot*, 196. For an illustration of the relationship between Deut 6:10–19 and 8:7–18, specifically as it concerns 6:12, 17 and 8:11–14, see p. 61 above. The current study, however, understands the dependency to proceed in opposite direction: Deut 6:10–13, 15, 17–19 (*early Dtr*) is a commentary on Deut 8:2–18 (*Dt*).

thematische Blöcke		Stichwortrepetitionen
A. Paränese (v.1)	v.1	כל־המצוה אשר אנכי מצוך היום
	1	אשר־נשבע לאבתיכם
B. Wüste (vv. 2-4)	2	וזכרת את־
	2	הליכך ... במדבר
	3	ויאכלך את־המן אשר לא־ ... ידעון אבתיך
C. Kulturland (vv. 7b-9)		[None present]
	10	ואכלת ושבעת ... הטבה
D. Paränese (v. 11)	11	פן־תשכח את־יהוה אלהיך ... שמר מצותו ...
		אשר אנכי מצוך היום
C'. Kulturland (vv. 12f)	12	פן־תאכל ושבעת ... טובים
B'. Wüste (vv. 14b-16)	15	המוליכך במדבר ...
	16	המאכלך מן במדבר אשר לא ידעון אבתיך
	18	וזכרת את־
	18	אשר־נשבע לאבתיך
A'. Fluch (vv. 19f)	19	אם־שכח תשכח את־יהוה אלהיך ... היום

Fig. 3.2: Lohfink's Concentric Models for Deuteronomy 8

schema on thematic blocks.[42] A similar misalignment occurs with the mention of the oath to the ancestral fathers, which first appears in the parenesis of v. 1b (A) but not in the parallel warning in vv. 19–20 (A'). Instead, the parallel occurs at the end of v. 18, which Lohfink again does not incorporate into his schema of thematic blocks.[43]

Additional parallels are extant in Deut 8:1–20, some of which support Lohfink's thesis, while others do not. One can easily cite למען ענתך לנסתך (v. 2b) as parallel to למען ענתך ולמען נסתך (v. 16b), and do so without eroding the concentricity of the catchwords Lohfink identifies. Likewise, on a conceptual level, one can detect parallels in the descriptions of the arable land as follows: husbandry (v.8–9a) and ore (v. 9b) ‖ husbandry (v. 13a) and ore (v. 13b). On the other hand, several verbal pairings do not cohere well with Lohfink's thesis. For example, the verbal repetitions between v. 2 and vv. 4–6 in themselves suggest a concentric arrangement for the first wilderness section (vv. 2–6): הדרך אשר לדעת את־אשר (v. 4b)[44] ‖ הליכך (v. 2aα); ארבעים שנא (v. 2aβ) ‖ ללכת בדרכיו (v. 6bα);

---

[42] Deut 8:10 is a positive pareneis, thematically and syntactically linked to the praise of the land (*Lob des Landes*) but made formally distinct by וברכת את־יהוה אלהיך. Both Mayes and Nelson read vv. 7–10 as an extend protasis to v. 11, but it is difficult to read וברכת את־יהוה אלהיך as a part of this protasis. The ancient Israelites blessing Yahweh for his gift of the land cannot serve as a conditional element warranting the warning not to forget Yahweh (v.11) (Mayes, *Deuteronomy*, 192; Nelson, *Deuteronomy*, 105–107).

[43] Altogether, Lohfink excludes vv. 5–7a, 10, and 17–18 from schema relaying the thematic blocks in Deuteronomy 8.

[44] Lohfink says "*ze 'arbā'îm šānā* in 8, 2 und 4 bildet eine Stitchwortinklusion" (*Das Hauptgebot*, 190), but he does not incorporate this element in either of his concentric models.

ושמרת (v. 2by) ‖ התשמר מצותו אם־לא (v. 5a); and וידעת עם־לבבך (v. 2bβ) ‖ בלבבך את־מצות יהוה אלהיך (v.6a).⁴⁵ Similarly, one may detect a conceptual frame around the second wilderness block (vv. 14–17): ואמרת בלבבך כחי ועצם (v. 14a) ‖ ורם לבבך ידי עשה לי את־החיל הזה (v. 17). In short, Deut 8:1–20 evinces a richer, more complex literary structure than even Lohfink describes, one that cautions against the insistence upon exact parallelism.⁴⁶

Despite the artistry it displays, Deuteronomy 8 is not without its share of literary tensions. The presence of the *Numeruswechsel* in vv. 1, 18–19, coupled with the extrinsic nature of vv. 1, 18–19's material content,⁴⁷ leads to the conclusion that these verses reframe vv. 2–18.⁴⁸ Additionally, several scholars agree that vv. 2–18 are the product of merging the warnings against two distinct types of forgetfulness: the primary parenesis warns against the hubris of forgetting Yahweh's role in securing the bountiful land of promise (vv. 7–11a, 12–18), while the

---

45 Félix García López, Veijola, and Nelson also see similar framing devices for vv. 2–6 (Félix García López, "Yahvé, fuente última de vida análisis de Dt 8," *Bib* 62 (1981): 50–52; Timo Veijola, "'Der Mensch lebt nicht vom Brot allein:' Zur literarischen Schichtung und theologischen Aussage von Deuteronomium 8," in *Bundesdokument und Gesetze: Studien zum Deuteronomium* [ed. G. Braulik; HbS 4; Freiburg: Herder, 1995], 154–155; Nelson, *Deuteronomy*, 1).

46 Robert H. O'Connell's complex structural analysis is a case and point. He identifies twelve tiers (lettered A–L‖L'–A') which enclose vv. 7b-9 as the center of the Deuteronomy 8's concentric structure. While thought-provoking, his thesis fails to persuade, primarily on account that the land description of vv. 7b-9 is conceptually parallel to vv. 12b-13b, the latter of which O'Connell is not able to incorporate into his proposed asymmetric concentric structure ("Deuteronomy VIII 1–20: Asymmetrical Concentricity and the Rhetoric of Providence," *VT* 40 [1990]: 439–445).

47 Deuteronomy 8:1 is but a précise to vv. 2–18, while the threat of vv. 18–19 is nearly *non sequitur* to vv. 2–18. Nelson also observes this disconnect, noting that "the theme of going after other gods and perishing falls outside the topic of chapter 8 and returns to the outlook of chapter 7 (cf. 4:25–26; 6:14–15)" (*Deuteronomy*, 114). The threat of Deut 8:19–20 ties chapter 8 to Yahweh's promise to dispossess the people groups already occupying the land (Deut 7:1–2a, 16–24) and the commands against making alliances with them (7:2b-4) or despoiling their idols (7:25–26).

48 Seitz, *Redaktionsgeschichtliche Studien*, 79; Aurelius, *Der Fürbitter Israels*, 21–22. One critique of this observation is that Deut 8:2 presumes a context similar to Deut 8:1; without 8:1, vv. 2–18 have no clear introduction. A solution to this problem emerges when one recognizes that 8:2 may have once been a continuation of Deut 6:24aα+b. If such is the case, Deut 8:1 not only joins Deuteronomy 7 to 8:2f., it also constitutes what David M. Carr would call a "resumptive repetition" of 6:23b-24aα. If an ancient editor deemed his supplement to the text to be significant enough, said editor may transition back to the inherited text through a resumptive repetition of the material (in this case Deut 6:23b-24aα+b) from which he digressed (*Reading the Fractures of Genesis: Historical and Literary Approaches* [Louisville: Westminster John Knox, 1996], 28).

caution not to forget Yahweh's commandments (vv. 2–6, 11b) appears to be a secondary line of reasoning.[49]

The rationale for Deut 8:1, 19–20 framing an already extant 8:2–18 is reasonably secure. The same does not hold true, however, for the apparent tension between the two types of forgetfulness. Latent in this reading of Deuteronomy 8 is the assumption that a single writer would probably not have interlaced 1) the concern for keeping (שמר√) the commands (מצות) of Yahweh (vv. 1, 6, 11b), particularly the first and second commandments (vv. 19–20), with 2) a parenesis on remembering (זכר√) (or conversely, not forgetting [שכח√]) Yahweh and his deeds (vv. 2–5, 7–11a, 12–18). Yet in a bit of irony, this assumption *forgets* that Deu-

---

[49] See Seitz, *Redaktionsgeschichtliche Studien*, 79–81; Mayes, *Deuteronomy*, 189–190; Nelson, *Deuteronomy*, 110; cf. Nielsen, *Deuteronomium*, 104–108. Although he does not cite him, Nelson follows Neilsen (*Deuteronomium*, 107) by further dividing vv. 7–11a, 12–18 into strata: "Verses 12–16 separate v. 11a from its logical continuation in vv. 17–18 ('lest you forget ... and you say'). At the same time, vv. 14bβ-16 break into a similar connection between v. 14bα and v. 17 ('you forget Yahweh your God ... and you say'). This analysis demonstrates that vv. 7–11, 17–18 constitute the earliest text and were supplemented in turn by vv. 12–14bα (a catalog of progress in the land that continues and replicates the theme of vv. 7–10) and vv. 14bβ-16 (a hymnic story of the wilderness that contrasts with vv. 12–13)" (*Deuteronomy*, 110 n. 4). Nelson's second stage (vv. 11a + 12–14bα + 17–18) fails to convince on two grounds. First, this second stage would not read as smoothly as he indicates, as פן־תשכח את־יהוה אלהיך (v.11a) becomes redundant with פן־ [...] ושכחת את־יהוה אלהיך (vv. 12a + 14bα). Secondly, this stage breaks up the well-attested formula "יהוה + העלה + הוציא / ממצרים" in v. 14b (cf. John Wijngaards, "הוציא and העלה: A Twofold Approach to the Exodus," *VT* 15 [1965]: 91–102), which in conjunction with "מבית עבדים" is already attested in Deut 6:12 (cf. Fig. 3.1 above). In other words, it seems unnecessary to divide vv. 12–16 into secondary and tertiary supplements (vv. 12–14bα and vv. 14bβ-16 respectively), as vv. 14bα-17 reads more smoothly with v. 14bβ than without it.

One may also cautiously add Veijola to the above roster. Veijola limits vv. 7a, 10a, 11a, 14bβ, 17–18a as the framework instead of the whole of vv. 7–11a, 12–18, but the theme by which he demarks this unit is still "das Leben in der materiellen Fülle des verheißenen Landes als Bedrohung für die Identität Israels." The content of v. 16, for Veijola, entered at the hand of a *Bearbeiter*, who felt compelled to describe the land's material wealth and its psychological effects on the residents in comparison to the wilderness experiences (Veijola, *Deuteronomium*, 213). This editor was responsible for vv. 7b-9, 10b, 12–14abα, 15–16, and took the forgetting in his older text to mean "die Vernachlässigung des offenbarten Willens seines Gottes in Gestalt der 'Gebote, Recte und Satzungen'" (Veijola, "'Der Mensch lebt nicht von Brot allein'," in Braulik, *Bundesdokument und Gesetz*, 151–152). Subsequent redactions followed with the DtrB's addition of vv. 1, 11b, 18b, 19–20 (commandment texts), and then finally vv. 2–6 (a parenthetical theological tractate) (*Deuteronomium*, 211, 215–221; "'Der Mensch lebt nicht von Brot allein'," in Braulik, *Bundesdokument und Gesetz*, 150–158). Veijola's textual splicing appears too exacting given the structural artistry of ch. 8, as well it continues the assumption that the dual foci of forgetting Yahweh's deeds and Yahweh's commandments could not have stemmed from the same hand.

teronomy from its earliest stage is a law code cast as commandments of Yahweh. This fact mitigates much of the tension that so many scholars have seen in 8:1–20 and undermines any attempt to reconstruct Deuteronomy 8's composition history along these axes.

Further evidence for the interlacing of these concerns can be marshaled from the foundational stages of Deuteronomy 6. Common within the scholarly literature on Deuteronomy 8 is the recognition that Deut 8:7–18 is in some way related to Deut 6:10–19; it is the direction of dependence which remains the center of debate.[50] Yet what has so far gone unnoticed is that the whole of Deut 8:2–18

---

50 For scholars who see Deut 8:7–18 as dependent on Deut 6:10–19, see Lohfink, who states that "Dtn 8, 7–18 ist ein Kommentar zu Dtn 6, 10–19" (*Das Hauptgebot*, 192); Reinhard Achenbach, *Israel zwischen Verheißun und Gebot: Literarkritische Untersuchungen zu Deuteronomium 5–11* (EHs.T 422; Frankfurt am Main: Peter Lang, 1991), 321; Veijola, *Deuteronomium*, 212, 212 n. 525.

Félix García López, on the other hand, argues that the similar style, terminology, and formulations of the 6:10–13 and 8:7–18 (as well as 7:17–19) are traits "qui plaident en faveur d'un même auteur pour ces textes ("Analyse littéraire de Deutéronome, V-XI," 492); cf. presumably Vang, "The So-Called 'Ur-Deuteronomy'," 18.

For scholars who see this relationship but avoid ascribing dependency, see Moshe Weinfeld and Nelson, (*Deuteronomy 1–11: A New Translation with Introduction and Commentary* [AB 5; New York: Doubleday, 1991], 396; Nelson, *Deuteronomy*, 8, 107). Weinfeld asserts that the dependence of Deut 8:7–18 on 6:10–15 "can hardly be proved." Instead, he prefers to describe the relationship of these two texts as *overlapping*, not just verbally but also structurally. The two progress according to the following structure: an introduction (כי יביאך יהוה אלהיך אל־הארץ [6:10] ‖ כי יהוה אלהיך מביאך אל־ארץ טובה [8:7]); then the description of the land (6:10b-11 ‖ 8:7b-9 [Weinfeld omits vv. 12b-13]), which ends with the phrase ואכלת ושבעת (6:11 ‖ 8:10 [Weinfeld omits v. 12a]); afterwards there is a warning not to forget Yahweh (6:12 ‖ 8:11 [Weinfeld omits v. 14b, 19]), and both texts conclude with the threat of annihilation as punishment for idolatry (6:14–15 ‖ 8:19–20) (*Deuteronomy 1–11*, 396–397). Weinfeld, as noted above, ignores several undermining elements in making his case. Nelson, on the other hand, observes the relationship but makes no comment on the direction of dependency (*Deuteronomy*, 107).

For scholars who argue that Deut 6:10–19 is dependent on Deut 8:7–18*, see Mayes and Aurelius. Mayes sees Deut 6:10–19 as dependent on Deut 8:7–11a, 12–14a, 17–18a. For Mayes, the whole of Deut 6:10–18 (19) stems from the same hand as Deut 4:1–40, which is a part of the last major redaction of the Book. The founding portions of Deut 8:7–18 (8:7–11a, 12–14a, 17–18a) were therefore already extant for the writer of Deut 6:10–18 (19) to draw upon (*Deuteronomy*, 192; "Deuteronomy 4," 37–39). For a critique of Mayes thesis, see pp. 61–63 above. Aurelius argues for this direction of dependence on other grounds. He notes that 8:12b portrays ancient Israel as actively having to build their own houses in the land—houses which in 6:10–11 Israel passively inherits; 8:7–18 is therefore the older of the two texts, as otherwise it would be difficult to explain why 6:10–11's passive portrayal was not carried on into 8:12b (*Der Fürbitter Israels*, 30). Although this rationale relies heavily on the verb תבנה (8:12b), Aurelius' reasoning is sound.

also expounds upon the underpinnings of Deut 6:4–9, 20–25. Though the *Kinderfrage* does not use the lemmas זכר or שכח (cf. 6:6–7+20–25), one cannot deny that its purpose is to transmit key cultic knowledge to the next generation so that it is *remembered* or conversely not *forgotten*. And what is so important for future generations to remember? The answer in both texts is the same: the deeds of Yahweh that fulfilled the ancestral promise (cf. 6:23; 8:1, 18), from the liberation from Egypt (cf. 6:23–24a; 8:14b) to the possession of the land (cf. 6:23b; 8:7–10, 12–13).[51] Further, the vehicle that is instrumental to the success or failure of this task is also the same in both texts: namely, the commands of Yahweh. In Deut 6:6–9, 20, 24–25, it is the commands of Yahweh that prompt the *Kinderfrage*, which in turn transmits the knowledge of Yahweh and his deeds to the next generation. While in Deut 8:2–6, 11–18, the failure to keep (שמר) Yahweh's commands nullifies this process, resulting in ancient Israel forgetting Yahweh and his exploits on their behalf.

One could draw further parallels between Deut 6:4–9, 20–25 and Deut 8:2–18,[52] but such is not necessary for the immediate argument. The differing types of forgetfulness do not clearly evince strata within Deut 8:2–18. Instead, they are thematic relics which were already extant in the earliest stages of the Deuteronomy's formation as a book; i.e., Deut 6:4–5 (*Ur-Deut*) → 6:4–9, 20–25 (*Kinderfrage*). Consequently, it is quite possible that a single editor was predominantly responsible for the artistry and content of Deut 8:2–18,[53] while a later hand in-

---

51 The deeds of Yahweh which are noticeably absent from Deut 6:4–9, 20–25, and yet which Deut 8:2–18 expounds, pertain to ancient Israel's wilderness sojourn (Deut 8:2–4, 15–16). Yet here too the concerns of the earliest stages of ch. 6 are evident. According to Deut 8:2, Yahweh's purpose for the wilderness sojourn is the humbling and testing of Israel's heart (לבב) to see whether they would keep (שמר) his commandments (מצבות); in fact, the concern for the condition of ancient Israel's heart pervades Deut 8:2–18 (vv. 2, 5, 14, 17). Deuteronomy 6:5–6 also evinces this concern (cf. Deut 6:24–25; 8:6–7a), which in turn mandates the teaching of Yahweh's commands to Israel's sons (6:7–9).
52 E.g. the emphases of fearing Yahweh (cf., 6:24; 8:6b) and Israel's enduring welfare (6:24; 8:16), and more loosely the image of childrearing (cf. 6:7–9, 20–21; 8:5).
53 One element does stand out as most likely secondary, however. Throughout Deut 8:2–18, the author makes no distinction between generations in the wilderness; instead a single generation is presumed. The exception is 8:16aβ, אשר לא־ידעון אבתיך, which seems strangely out of place. What benefit is there in stating that the fathers did not know what the manna was, unless it was the fathers who ate it? Yet in 8:16aα it is the current generation who ate the manna, not the fathers. Only two explanations present themselves: either the אבתיך refers to the ancestral fathers who are prior to the wilderness generation (which is, of course, highly unlikely), or the relative clause is a later interpolation stemming from a time when the Wilderness Tradition had transitioned to having two wilderness generations and when the manna tradition (cf. Exod

corporated the exterior frame of vv. 1, 19–20. Stylistically and thematically, this later hand evinces the same characteristics of the editor responsible for inserting Deut 6:14, 16.⁵⁴ Likewise, the content, structure, and style of Deut 8:2–18 bears some of the trappings of the hand that produced the chiasm of Deut 6:10–13, 15, 17–19.

It is tempting, for the sake of simplicity, to attribute Deut 8:2–18 and Deut 6:10–19* to the same hand. This conclusion, however, proves to be premature as the two texts have fundamentally different perspectives on the role Israel is to play in the building of the land's infrastructure. In the description of land in Deut 8:7–18, Israel has to build its "good houses" (ובתים טובים תבנה; cf. v. 12b); yet in the land description in Deut 6:10–13, this component of the land's infrastructure is pre-existent: the Promised Land already has "great and good cities" which Israel did not build (ערים גדלת וטבת אשר לא־בנית; cf. 10b)! The land description in 6:10 continues to exclude Israel's involvement in the land's full houses (ובתים מלאים כל־טוב אשר לא־מלאת), hewn cisterns, and planted fields (6:11). Thus, as Aurelius correctly observes, Deut 6:10–13 portrays the land's infrastructure as an "unverdienter Gabe," and if these verses were to serve as the *Vorlage* to Deut 8:7–18, it becomes difficult to explain why this notion of the land's unmerited qualities did not carry over to 8:7–18.⁵⁵ Instead, the direction of dependence is easier to explain from 8:7–18 to 6:10–13: while 8:12 indicates that Israel built its own houses, 6:10–13 stands as a theological supplement preconditioning the reader to understand this activity to have taken place on a limited scale in light of Yahweh's fulfillment of the ancestral promise. In short, it is more likely that 8:2–18 inspired 6:10–13, 15, 17–19 which accounts for their similar content, structure, and style and yet explains this difference regarding Israel's roles in the development of the land.

In summary, the relative chronological relationship of Deut 6:4–25 and 8:1–20 unfolds as follows: Deut 8:2–18 depends on 6:4–5 (*Ur-Dt*) and is cotemporaneous with the *Kinderfrage* in 6:6–9, 20–25* (*Dt*); the chiasm of Deut 6:10–13, 15, 17–19 is from an *early Dtr* hand; and Deut 8:1, 19–20 is a frame that stems from the same *late Dtr* hand as the 2mp prohibitions in Deut 6:14, 16. Thus, the relative chronological relationship of the M-Mt texts within Deut 6:4–25 and 8:1–20 is that 8:15 is earlier than 6:16.

16:1–36; Num 11:7–8) was firmly affixed to the first generation which Yahweh rejected in the wilderness of Paran (Num 14:20–36).
54 Namely, 1) a preference for the 2mp form of address, 2) the ability to extend chiastic structures, and 3) a profound concern for the dictates of the first and second commandments (cf. 6:14; 8:1, 19–20).
55 Aurelius, *Der Fürbitter Israels*, 30. For further details see p. 69 n. 50 above.

3.3.3 Tradition-historical Analysis of Deut 8:15

The above literary analysis chronologically situates the reminiscence of the M-Mt in Deut 8:15 as relatively earlier than that preserved in Deut 6:16. This literary priority aids in understanding the tradition-historical differences between the two texts. In Deut 8:15–16, it is Yahweh who furnishes the *agency* for the test, which the tradent understands to be both appropriate and intended for the enduring good of the people (v. 16b, למען ענתך ולמען נסתך להיטבך באחריתך). In Deut 6:16, the polarity of agency reverses with the people testing Yahweh. This shift represents a radical development in the M-Mt, the rationale for which one can only speculate. Regardless, the wilderness reflections in Deut 8:2–18 in no way indict the wilderness generation of cultic failure; instead, the implication throughout is that the textual proprietors at this point understood Israel's first failure have taken place after their entrance into the Promised Land. Yahweh's leading and provisioning of Israel through the desert is a test of Israel's faithfulness (8:2, 15–16), yet Moses' rhetoric is not charged with accusation, but rather warning: Do not forget Yahweh's deeds and commands once you enter the land and prosper. There is no remembrance of failure in the wilderness, only prolepsis of the failures to come.

As for *canonical awareness*, Deut 8:15 provides no indication that its author was to any extent aware of either of the two M-Mt narrative exponents, whether Exod 17:1–7 or Num 20:1–13. Not only is the direction of the agency reversed, but the description of the *source of issuance* is strikingly different. The non-P account prefers צור (Exod 17:6, 2x), while the P narrative uses סלע (Num 20:8–11, 5x). Yet Deut 8:15 describes Yahweh issuing water (*substance of issuance*) "from the flinty rock" (מצור החלמיש)—a description that finds approximate parallels only in Deut 32:13 (מחלמיש צור) and Ps 114:8 (... חלמיש הצור). Further, it may not be insignificant that Deut 8:15 does not anchor its reflection to any definite geographic *location* (cf. הצור בחרב in Exod 17:6) or particular region (cf. Exod 17:1; Num 20:1). Together, these three tradition components (agency, source of issuance, and *in absentia* location), in conjunction with the above literary analysis and Deut 8:15's other distinctive elements,[56] increase the likelihood that this verse preserves a particularly

---

[56] Two further features stand out in Deut 8:15: 1) the mention of desert "scorpions" (עקרב), the memory of which occurs in no other wilderness text; and 2) the sequence of the wilderness events it recalls. When both manna and the M-Mt are present, the typical sequence in the Hebrew Bible situates the M-Mt after the Manna tradition. The arrangement of the reflections in Deut 9:22 and Ps 78:13–31, however, raise the possibility that the reversal of this sequence in Deut 8:15 is more than a byproduct of its chiastic structuring (8:3–4 ∥ 8:15–16). It may,

early, if not the earliest, reflection of the M-Mt within Deuteronomy's interior prologue.

3.4 Deuteronomy 9:22

3.4.1 Textual Criticism of Deut 9:22

ובתבערה ובמסה ובקברת התאוה מקצפים הייתם את־יהוה: ^{Deut 9:22}

Like Deut 6:16, the text-critical task for Deut 9:22 garners no assistance from the material remains of Qumran. A major lacuna occurs in 4QDeut^c (4Q30) from 9:20–28, and from the one fragment that does preserve any part of Deut 9:22 (4Q364 frag. 26a col. ii) only a few letters remain.[57] The one debate among the textual witnesses pertains to whether the divine name is to be followed by the appositive equivalent to אלהיכם.[58] In short, the ancient witnesses offer no aid relevant to the tradition-historical task at hand.

3.4.2 Literary Analysis of Deut 9:1–10:11

A survey of the literary analyses diachronic scholars have proffered for Deut 9:22 and its broader literary context reveals at least three fronts on which scholarship has largely achieved consensus. The first, quite naturally, pertains to the parameters of Deut 9:22's broader literary context. Here, scholars widely agree to Deut 9:1–10:11, with many holding more narrowly to the strictures of Deut 9:7b–10:11.[59] There are a number of reasons for the narrowing of this parameter: 1)

---

in fact, offer further support of Johnstone's thesis that the non-P M-Mt narrative was originally located between Num 11:3 and 11:4. For more details, see p. 80 n. 72 and §6.3.3 below.

[57] Only the first two letters of ובתבערה is clear, after which there is a lacuna until the last two words of the verse (i.e., את יהוה) (DJD XIII, 237; plate XIX).

[58] Most witnesses prefer the shorter reading (Smr G V S T), though a few G^{Mss} attest to the longer; Naḥal Ḥever is damaged so as to make the reading uncertain (BHQ Deuteronomy, 32; see also p. 78* in BHQ Deuteronomy on why G should also read the appositive).

[59] Tillesse, "Sections "tu et sections "vous"," 37; Lohfink, Das Hauptgebot, 210–211; Félix García López, "Analyse littéraire de Deutéronome, V-XI," RB 85 (1978): 18–30; Aurelius, Der Fürbitter Israels, 17–18; Suzanne Boorer, The Promise of the Land as Oath: A Key to the Formation of the Pentateuch (BZAW 205; Berlin: de Gruyter, 1992), 272–297; Nielsen, Deuteronomium, 112–119; Veijola, Deuteronomium, 238; Nelson, Deuteronomy, 119.

Deut 9:1–7a is parenesis, while 9:7b–10:11 is historical narrative; 2) in 9:1–7bα Israel is addressed in the 2ms, while Israel is address in the 2mp from 9:7bβ up through the last word of 10:10 (השחיתך); and 3) in 9:1–6 Moses is relaying instructions for the conquest of the land—a theme that the wilderness failures of 9:7–10:10 disrupts and Deut 10:11 resumes. A second front, and one that warrants only brief mention, is the general opinion that Deut 9:20, 10:6–7, and 10:8–9 are particularly late, perhaps glossic.[60] Finally, and most significantly for the current study, there is a strong agreement that Deut 9:7b-8 + 22–24 also constitute a late insertion, especially vv. 22–24.[61] Scholars cite a number of evidences for this insertion as well: 1) the overlapping vocabulary of Deut 9:7b-8 + 22–24[62]; 2) the frame these verses create around Israel's failure with

---

A notable exception is Seitz, who sees too many connecting lines (*Verbindungslinien*) to isolate 9:1–6 from the material that follows, as though 9:7–10:11 merely disrupts the flow of 9:1–6 +10:12–13. Instead Seitz argues for the following strata: an original hortatory speech of Moses in the 2ms (9:1–7a, 13–14, 26–29; 10:10, 12–13); a secondary parallel strand representing the Horeb event in the 2mp (9:9, 11, 12, 15–17, 21 [18–19]; 10:1–5, 11); after these strands were woven together (*verflochten*), later hands added 9:7b, 22–24; 9:20; and 10:6–9 (*Redaktionsgeschichtliche Studien*, 56–57). Here, Mayes follows Seitz closely, with the exception that he casts the second strand (Dtr) as an *elaboration* upon the first (Dt), as opposed to each strand initially being independent (so Seitz) (*Deuteronomy*, 195).

60 Lohfink treats 9:20 (?) and 10:8–9 as "*levitischen Glossen*," while 10:6–7 come from an even later hand (*Das Hauptgebot*, 209, 291); see also, Seitz, *Redaktionsgeschichtliche Studien*, 57; García López, "Analyse littéraire" (1978), 22, 25–30; Mayes, *Deuteronomy*, 196, 201, 205–206; Horst D. Preuss, *Deuteronomium* (EdF 164; Darmstadt: Wissenschaftliche Buchgesellschaft, 1982), 49–50; Aurelius, *Der Fürbitter Israels*, 18, 44; Neilsen, who does not distinguish 9:20 as later than its surrounding textual material, but does consider 10:6–9 to be late (*Deuteronomium*, 112–113); Veijola, *Deuteronomium*, 225, 239–241; Nelson, *Deuteronomy*, 120 n. 1. Even Robert H. O'Connell agrees 10:6–7 and 10:8–9 are later insertions (!), though he incorporates vv. 6–7 as a possibly original "parenthetical inset" since its "structural position and allusive function are analogous to ix 26aβ-29" ("Deuteronomy IX 7–X 7, 10–11: Panelled Structure, Double Rehearsal and the Rhetoric of Covenant Rebuke," *VT* 42 [1992]: 492 n. 2; 506 n. 10).

61 Lohfink, *Das Hauptgebot*, 210; Seitz, *Redaktionsgeschichtliche Stüdien*, 57; Mayes, *Deuteronomy*, 196, 197–198; Preuss, *Deuteronomium*, 49; Aurelius, *Der Fürbitter Israels*, 14–15; Boorer, *Promise of the Land*, 279, especially 279 n. 175; Achenbach, *Verheißun und Gebot*, 363–365; Nielsen, *Deuteronomium*, 115, 116; Veijola, *Deuteronomium*, 238; Nelson, *Deuteronomy*, 119, 120 n. 1.

62 Lohfink observes parallels to vv. 22–24 in both v. 7a and v. 7b, parallels which Boorer summarizes succinctly: "These consist of : v. 7a הקצפת את־יהוה אלהיך / v. 22 מקצפים הייתם את־יהוה; vv. 7b, 24 ממרים הייתם עם־יהוה; and v. 7b ... מן־היום/ v. 24b ... מיום" (cf. Lohfink, *Das Hauptgebot*, 210; Boorer, *Promise of the Land*, 276 n. 164). García López sees an additional parallel in the use of the formula וב + toponym: ובהרב in v. 8a ‖ ובקברת התאוה ובמסה ובתבערה in v. 22 ("Analyse littéraire" [1978], 23).

molten calf (9:9–19+21) and the disruption vv. 22–24 creates in the continuing narrative (9:25–10:5);[63] and 3) the shift in perspective these verses bring to the significance of Israel's failure with the molten calf—that is, from it being ancient Israel's paradigmatic failure, to it being but one example (albeit a pivotal one) in a pattern of ongoing behavior since the day they left Egypt (vv. 7b, 24).[64]

The composite nature of Deut 9:1–10:11 is all but certain, and Deut 9:7–8, 20, 22–24, and 10:6–9 stand out as particularly indicative of this heterogeneity.[65] Yet here is where the consensus dissolves, as determining the relative chronological relationship of these materials marks a distinct challenge. This task becomes more formidable when faced with the necessity of aligning these texts to their respective strata that extend across the interior historical prologue (chs. 5–11) (see Table 3.2 below).

For Lohfink, who describes the strata according to stages (*Phasen*) as opposed to terms of Deuteronomism,[66] the foundational text (*Grundtext*) of Deuteronomy included the earliest layer of Deut 9:1–10:11 (9:9–18, 21, 25–29; 10:1–5, 10–11). This layer comes from the hand of the book's author (*Verfasser*), who was also responsible for expanding 6:4b-5 to Deut 6:1–25. A later reviser (*Überarbeiter*) added Deut

---

63 For example, Lohfink casts vv. 22–24 as a "keine Digression" in the context of an already existing narrative, one structured into five strophes by the refrain "40 Tage und 40 Nächte" (9:9, 11, 18, 25; 10:10) (*Das Hauptgebot*, 214–215, 217).

64 See especially Boorer, *Promise of the Land*, 291–293. Boorer states that "the addition of Deut 9:7–8, 22–24 has the effect of transforming the incident at Horeb, unfolded at the earlier level, into one example of the rebelliousness of Israel which was characteristic of Israel throughout the whole wilderness period. Deut 9:7–8, 22–24 form a generalizing framework around the portrayal of the specific event at Horeb outlined in Deut 9:9–21" (*Promise of the Land*, 291).

65 There are, of course, scholars who would argue otherwise. O'Connell is perhaps the foremost example. He argues for an overarching structure of A-B-A'-B', with A∥A' (9:7–8a∥9:22–24) framing B (9:8b-21) with "a compound inverse frame comprising two triadic frames (a-b-a'// a"-b'-b")." The internal structure of section B—which "presents a concentric compound inverse frame (i.e., c-d-d'//d"-c'-c")"— "is extended by the addendum of the B' section (ix 25-x 7, 10–11) whose structure is only a permutation of the preceding B-section." O'Connell critiques Lohfink throughout as failing to discern this pattern—a pattern the majority of scholars since O'Connell have continued not to see ("Paneled Structure," 494, 495, 497; for critiques of Lohfink, see O'Connell's notes 3, 4, 9).

66 For Lohfink, the earliest stage (Ph. A) lays outside and prior to Israel's existence in the *Modelle* that informed the *Gattungen* and *Formen* of Deuteronomy 5–11. The next phase is the formation of basic institutions (*grundlegenden Institutionen*) and *Gattungen* within Israel itself (Ph. B), while phase C is the formation of covenant documents (*Bundesurkunden*) and similar texts. The drafting of the foundational text (*Grundtextes*) by an author (*Verfasser*) then follows (Ph. D), and afterwards an editing *Überarbeiter* (Ph. E). An additional editing where Deut 5:1–11:25 was joined (*verbindungen*) to chs. 12–28 (Ph. F). The final two phases pertain to glosses (Ph. G) and later additions (Ph. H) (Lohfink, *Das Hauptgebot*, 289–291).

Table 3.2: Recent Proposals for the Stratification of Deut 6:4–25; 8:1–20; 9:1–10:11

Ch.	Lohfink (1963)[i]	Seitz (1971)[ii]	G. López (1977/8)[iii]	Mayes (1979)[iv]	Preuss (1982)[v]	Neilsen (1995)[vi]	Veijola (2004)[vii]
6	Ph. C - 6:4ᵇ-5 Ph. D - 6:1-4ᵃ, 6-25	DtnÜ - 6:4-9, 20-24* DtrÜ - 6:1-3, 10-18	pr - 6:4-9 ré - 6:10-13 Dt - 6:20-24 b-m - 6:14-19	Dt - 6:4-9, 20-24 Dtr2 - 6:10-19	G - 6:1*, 4-9, 20-24 Erg - (6:10-13?) DtrÜ - 6:14, (15?), (6:16?), 17-18 sZ - (6:15?), (16?), 25	Dt - 6:4-9, 10-13 (n)Dtr - 6:14-19, 20-25	UrDt - 6:4-9* DtrH(?) - 6:21-25* DtrN - 6:10-13* DtrB - 6:5, 14, 15ᵇ, 17ᵃ, 18, 20 sP - 6:15ᵃ, 16
8	Ph. E - 8:1-20	DtnÜ - 8:2-6, 11ᵇ sS - 8:7-11ᵃ 12-18 DtrÜ - 8:1, 19-20	pr - 8:7-8, 10ᵇᵃ, 14ᵇᵇ, 16ᵃˣ ré - 8:9-10abβ, 11ᵃ, 12-14ᵇᵃ, 17-18ᵃ Dt - 8:2-6 b-m - 8:1, 19-20	Dt - 8:7-11a, 12-14, 17-18a Dtr2 - 8:1-6, 11b, 15-16, 18b-20	Erg - (8:2-6?), 7-18* DtrÜ - 8:1, (2-6?), 19ᵃᵇ-20 sZ - 8:11ᵇ	Dt - 8:7-11ᵃ, 17-18ᵃ (n)Dtr - 8:1-6, 11ᵇ-16, 18ᵇ-20	kK(?) - 8:7, 10ᵃ, 11ᵃ, 14ᵇ, 17-18ᵃ Erg - 8:7ᵇ-9, 10ᵇ, 12-14ᵃᵇᵃ, 15-16 DtrB - 8:1, 11ᵇ, 18ᵇ, 19-20 sR - 8:2-6
9 & 10	Ph. D - 9:9-18, 21, 25-29, 10:1-5, 10-11 Ph. E - 9:1-8, 22-24 Ph. G - 9:20(?), 10:8-9 Ph. H - 10:6-7	DtnÜ - 9:1-7ᵃ, 13-14, 26-29; 10:10 DtrÜ - 9:9, 11, 12, 15-17, 21, (18-19); 10:1-5, 11 sZ - 9:7ᵇ, 20, 22-24; 10:6-7, 8-9	pr - 9:1-3 ré - 9:4-7ᵃ Dtr - 9:9-19, 21, 25-29; 10:1-5, 10-11 tar - 9:7ᵇ-8, 20, 22-24; 10:6-9	Dt - 9:1-7a, 13-14, 26-29; 10:10-11 Dtr1 - 9:2(?), 9-12, 15-19, 21, 25; 26-29; 10:1-5 (sZ) - 9:7b-8, 20, 22-24; 10:6-7, 8-9	Erg - 9:1-3, (4-6?), (7ᵃ?) DtrÜ - 9:8, 9ᵃ, 10, 13-14, 15ᵃᶜ, 16-17, 21, 25, 26-29; (10:1-5?), 10ᵃᵇ, 11 sZ - (9:7ᵃ?), 7ᵇ, 9ᵇ, 11, 15ᵇ, 18-19, 20, 22-24, 25ᵇ; 10:6, 7, 8-9ᵃ, 9ᵇ, 10c	(n)Dtr - 9:1-6, 7-29; 10:5, 8-11 P - 10:6-9	DtrN - 9:9-12ᵃᵃᵇ, 15, 16ᵃˣ, 17, 21ᵃᵃᵇ; 10:1-5 DtrB - 9:7ᵃ*, 8*, 12ᵇᵃ, 13-14, 16ᵃᵃᵃᵇ, 18-19, 21ᵃᵃᵃ; 10:10-11 sR - 9:1, 3-6* gZ - 9:2, 4ᵇ, 20, 7ᵃ*, 7ᵇ, 8; 22-24; 10:6-7, 8-9

ABBREVIATION KEY: i. Lohfink: Phase (Ph.). Cf. *Das Hauptgebot*, 153–166, 189–218, 289–291. See p. 75 n. 66 below for a description of these phases. ii Seitz: dtn Überarbeitung (DtnÜ), dtr Überarbeitung (DtrÜ); später Stück (sS); später Zusatz (sZ). Cf. *Redaktionsgeschichtliche Studien*, 51–74, 79–81, 91, 91 n. 116, 303–311. iii García López: unités primitives (pr); réélaboration (ré); redaction deutéronomique (Dt); benediction et malediction (b-m); redaction deuteronomiste (Dtr); tardif (tar). Cf. "Analyse littéraire," (1977) 491–522 and (1978) 18–49. vi Mayes: Deuteronomic (Dt); first Deuteronomistic editor (Dtr1); second Deuteronomistic editor (Dtr2); late editions (sZ). Cf. *Deuteronomy*, 41–49, 175–181, 189–207. v Preuss: singular Grundschicht (G); Ergänzungsschicht (auch sing.) und Zusätze zu ihr (Erg); plural dtr Überarbeitung (DtrÜ); später Zusätze (sZ). Cf. *Deuteronomium*, 49–50. vi Neilsen: Vor- und Früh-Deuteronomisches (none present); Deuteronomisches (Dt); Deuteronomistisches und Nach-Deuteronomistisches ((n)Dtr); Priesterschriftliches (P). Cf. *Deuteronomium*, 18, 84–94, 104–119. vii Veijola: Ur-Deuteronomium (UrDt); Deuteronomistischer Historiker (DtrH); Nomistischer Deuteronomist (DtrN); Prophetischer Deuteronomist (none present); Bundestheologischer Deuteronomist (DtrB); kleinen Kriegsansprache (kK); Veijola links to Deut 7:1b*, 17–19, 21); Ergänzung (Erg); späten Redaktionsschrift (sR); glossenhaften Einzelzusätzen (gZ); späteren Phase (sP). Cf. *Deuteronomium*, 2–6, 174–193, 199, 208–241.

9:1–8, 22–24, presumably along with the whole of 8:1–20. Thus, for Lohfink, Deut 6:16 is earlier than 8:15 and 9:22, while 8:15 and 9:22 are in turn cotemporaneous. From a tradition-historical standpoint, however, this reconstruction fails to convince: how could the agency of testing shift from an earlier stage in which Israel alone is the agent (6:16) to a later stage in which either Yahweh (8:15) or Israel (9:22) could correctly be said to be the agent? The interpretative significance of the M-Mt which these texts reflect further undermines Lohfink's chronology: in 8:15–16 Yahweh tests Israel out of his beneficence, while in 6:16 and 9:22 Israel's actions toward Yahweh are clearly provocative.

The problem of agency also complicates Mayes' reconstruction, and to an even greater extent Nielsen's. Mayes attributes both Deut 6:16 and 8:15 to his second Dtr (Dtr2), while 9:22 enters as a late addition "of unidentifiable authorship."[67] The inescapable problem, however, is the difference in the agencies of the M-Mt reflected in 6:16 and 8:15. Though Mayes' vision of Dtr2 attempts to explain the *Numerusweschel* on rhetorical grounds, it cannot explain the vacillation of the agency within these two tradition-historical reflections. In Deut 6:16, Israel's testing of Yahweh "בְּמַסָּה" is a paradigmatically negative event, yet in 8:15 Yahweh's testing Israel at the same traditional event is for Israel's ultimate good. These two texts represent radically different interpretations of the M-Mt.[68]

More convincing, rather, is that Deut 6:16; 8:15: and 9:22 each reflect different stages of the development and interpretation of the M-Mt. Both Seitz and García López agree that the relative chronology proceeds from 8:15, to 6:16, to 9:22; though their arguments are strikingly different. One might also cautiously add Preuss and Veijola to their number.[69] Regardless, there is a consensus among these scholars that Deut 9:22 is markedly later than 8:15 and most likely later than 6:16 as well (cf. Table 3.2 above).

A brief summation of the relative chronological findings for Deut 9:22 and its broader literary context in construct with the previous M-Mt texts and their broader literary contexts is here in order. Taken together, Deut 6:4–25; 8:1–20; and 9:1–10:11 are the products of at least six successive stages of literary growth

---

67 Mayes, *Deuteronomy*, 196.
68 Compounding this error is Nielsen, who cast all three of the M-Mt texts—Deut 6:16; 8:15; and 9:22—within a single range, which he labels Dtr to post-Dtr (Nielsen, *Deuteronomium*, 18, 88, 106, 112).
69 Both Preuss and Veijola regard Deut 8:15 as a supplement (*Erg*) that dates earlier than either 6:16 or 9:22, but their treatments of 6:16 and 9:22 leave their relative chronological relationship to each other unclear. Preuss sets off 6:16 as a possible late addition (*sZ*), but he is certain 9:22 is a late addition. Veijola considers 6:16 to have entered at a later stage (*sP*), while 9:22 was glossic addition (*gZ*) (cf. Table 3.2 above).

(see Table 3.3 below): 1) Deut 6:4–5 is the earliest (*Ur- Deut*); 2) Deut 6:4–9, 20–25*; 8:2–18*; 9:1–6*; 10:12f.* contain the *Kinderfrage* and the materials with an active stance toward Israel's construction within the land (*Dt*); 3) Deut 6:10–13, 15, 17–19 are slightly later, shifting Israel's role in the land from active to passive and demonstrating an awareness of the rationale for the second commandment (Deut 5:9), but there is no explicit awareness of Israel's failure in the wilderness (*early Dtr*); 4) Deut 6:14, 16; 8:1, 19–20; 9:7a, 8–19, 20, 25–29; 10:1–5, 10–11 bear the stylistic shiftings of Deut 4:1–40, and likewise focus specifically on Israel's failure to keep the first and second commandments in the wilderness at Horeb (*late Dtr*); 5) Deut 9:7b, 22–24 are later still, insisting Israel's failures in the wilderness were not limited to Horeb (or even Baal-Peor; cf. Deut 4:3–4) but were pervasive throughout the wilderness sojourn (*Dtr Supp*); and finally 6) Deut 9:20; 10:6–7, 8–9 appear to be late glosses (perhaps *post-Dtr* or *priestly*).

Table 3.3: Proposed Stratification of Deut 6:4–25; 8:1–20; 9:1–10:11

Strata	Deut 6:4-5	Deut 8:1-20	Deut 9:1–10:11
Ur-Deut	6:4-5		
Dt	6:4-9 + 20-25*	8:2-18*	9:1-6*; 10:12f.*
Early Dtr	6:10-13 + 15 + 17-19		
Late Dtr	6:14, 16, 17 (2mp revision)	8:1, 19-20	9:7a, 8-19, 20, 25-29; 10:1-5, 10-11
Dtr Supp			9:22-24
Glossic			Deut 9:20; 10:6-7, 8-9

3.4.3 Tradition-historical Analysis of Deut 9:22

The only explicit tradition-historical component that Deut 9:22 preserves is the *location* via the toponym מסה in וּבְמַסָּה. The vocalization here is significant as it most likely represents an advancement of the tradition from the generic בַּמַּסָּה in 6:16 (cf. §3.2.3). It may be tempting to explain the different vocalization in 6:16 as a memory variant, since the agency and second person address (2mp) are the same in each. Further, an additional similarity is that both reminiscences rhetorically serve as illustrations of past cultic infidelity: 6:16 is tethered to the prohibition of idolatry in 6:14 specifically, and more broadly to 6:12–15; likewise, 9:7b+22–24 expands upon the wilderness generation's idolatry with the molten calf at Horeb (9:8–10:11). Nevertheless, despite these similarities, the *interpretative significance* that Massah plays in Deut 9:22 suggest that this reminiscence stems from a later stage of tradition-history than that in Deut 6:16.⁷⁰ In Deut 6:16, the generic "at the testing" (בְּמַסָּה) stands as the lone wilderness tradition in its immediate context; the editor responsible for it most likely judged the nascent M-Mt to be a failure of special significance. Yet within the context of Deut 9:7–10:11, that infamy has passed to the failure at Horeb, and the editor responsible for 9:7b, 22–24 adduces the episode "at Massah" (וּבְמַסָּה) as but one failure among many.

The order of the wilderness events as they occur in Deut 9:7–24 also warrants consideration, as it may reflect an awareness of the developing canon. Sequentially, the wilderness traditions this text relays are as follows: the exodus from Egypt (v. 7b), which is then followed by the failures at Horeb (vv. 8f.); Taberah, Massah, and Kibroth-hattaavah (v. 22); and Kadesh-barnea (v. 23). The Tetrateuchal narratives that correspond to these failures are in Exod 17:1–7* (Massah); Exodus 32–34 (Horeb/Sinai); Num 11:1–3 (Taberah); Num 11:4–34 (Kibroth-hattaavah); and Numbers 13–14 (Kadesh-barnea; cf. Num 32:7–15). Two observations are immediately warranted: 1) this range of texts includes both non-P (Exod 17:1–7*; Exodus 32–34; Num 11:1–34) and P (Numbers 13–14*; 32:7–15) narrative materials⁷¹; and 2) Massah is the only component of this list in Deut 9:7–24 that does not align with the current sequence of corresponding narratives outside Deuteronomy. This evidence is what leads William

---

70 David M. Carr shows that the oral-written transmission of "culturally-centered literary theological texts" in the ancient world transpired over time through "compositional expansion, occasional conflation / combination, harmonization and coordination within themselves and with other texts," and through smaller-scale changes he calls "memory variants" (e.g., the exchange of synonymous words, variation of word order, rearrangement of lines, or minor shifts in grammatical elements such as prepositions and conjunctions) (*The Formation of the Hebrew Bible: A New Reconstruction* [New York: Oxford University Press, 2011], 145). This evidence leads him to caution against focusing on redactional layers and expansions within biblical texts, and instead to encourage minimal relative dating between separate scrolls or clearly identifiable larger strata. "It is a fantasy," Carr states, "to think that we could approach precision in reconstructing every stage in the development of the biblical text, however much we might wish to do so" (*Formation of the Hebrew Bible*, 148). Yet as Carr later acknowledges, "Deuteronomy is a multi-layered, selective, and highly theological recasting of previous stories [... the back-references to which] still suggest the *existence* of early Israelite wilderness traditions, perhaps even a composition featuring wilderness stories, and these back-references can be used to identify potential wilderness texts that might show other signs of early origins" (*Formation of the Hebrew Bible*, 481). Thus, while memory variants may account for differences within texts reflecting the M-Mt outside of Deuteronomy, one cannot so easily dismiss variances of the M-Mt within Deuteronomy.
71 A helpful list of P-narrative material occurs in William H. C. Propp, "The Priestly Source Recovered Intact," *VT* 46 (1996): 477.

Johnstone to conclude that, prior to P's editing of the Pentateuch and Exod 17:1–7, the Massah narrative was once located between Num 11:3 and 11:4.⁷²

Given this awareness of the developing canon, the implications that this reminiscence may have for the development of M-Mt are enormous. For each overt provocation in the Deut 9:7–24, the narrative corresponding to it concludes with a lethal expression of divine wrath (c.f., Exod 32:26–28, 35; Num 11:1b, 33–34; 14:20–35). The lone exception is the narrative of Massah as it currently stands in Exod 17:1–7. Once again, like Deut 6:16, the M-Mt appears strangely out of place in 9:22.⁷³ For both texts, the reader is left to wonder how the M-Mt can meet the editor's rhetorical purpose, especially since in the M-Mt's narrative expressions (Exod 17:1–7; Num 20:1–13) the people do not suffer any direct negative consequence for having murmured against Yahweh or Moses.

---

72 A noticeable evolution has taken place in Johnstone's theory. In his 1996 essay, Johnstone argues that the pre-P portion of Exod 17:1–7 was physically located between Num 11:3 and 11:4 ("From the Sea to the Mountain: Exodus 15,22–19,2: A Case-Study in Editorial Techniques," in *Studies in the Book of Exodus: Redaction – Reception – Interpretation* [ed. Marc Vervenne; BETL 126; Leuven: Leuven University, 1996], 247–259). In his 1998 volume, however, he only speaks of transposition of Exod 17:7 (*Chronicles and Exodus: An Analogy and its Application* [JSOTSup 275; Sheffield: Sheffield Academic, 1998], 246, 248). Again, in an even more recent essay (2002), he argues that the narrative that corresponds to Deut 9:22 and 33:8 must be 1) "reassembled" from the stories of Marah (Exod 15:22–26), Massah (Exod 17:1–7; Num 20:1–11), and the molten calf at Horeb (Exod 32:25–29), and 2) repositioned to its original location between Num 11:3 and 11:4 ("The Use of the Reminiscences in Deuteronomy in Recovering the Two Main Literary Phases in the Production of the Pentateuch," in *Abschied vom Jahwisten: Die Komposition des Hexateuch in der jüngsten Diskussion* [ed. Jan Gertz, Konrad Schmid, and Markus Witte; BZAW 315; Berlin: de Gruyter, 2002], 261).

Aside from the short itinerary of Deut 9:22 and its correspondence to Numbers 11, one of the key evidences that Johnstone evokes for his argument is that Deuteronomy recalls no complaint/rebellion narrative prior to Horeb; rather "it is the construction of P," who wanted to "elevate Sinai as the location not of the covenant with the redeemed and initially responsive people as in D, but of the revelation of the Law (Johnstone, "Reminiscences in Deuteronomy," in Gertz, Schmid, and Witte, *Abschied vom Jahwisten*, 261; cf., *Chronicles and Exodus*, 243). This line of reasoning is faulty from the start: Deut 9:7 recalls Israel as having provoked YHWH in the wilderness from the day they left the land of Egypt; yet even Johnstone concedes that, in the "D-version" of the wilderness trek, Israel arrives at Horeb on day three after the exodus (cf. Exod 15:22a-bα + 19:2b; "Reminiscences in Deuteronomy," in Gertz, Schmid, and Witte, *Abschied vom Jahwisten*, 262). In other words, the memory of Israel provoking YHWH to prior Horeb is already embedded in the reminiscences of Deut 9:7–10:11*; *it is not a construction of P*. Instead, the people's complaint in Exod 14:11–12 (non-P) may be in mind here, as here Israel uses rhetoric similar to her later provocations (cf. Exod 16:3 ‖ Num 11: 4–6, 18, 20 [Kibroth-hattavah]; Exod 17:3 ‖ Num 20:4–5 [Massah-Meribah]; Exod 32:1, 23 (?) [Horeb]; Num 14:2–4 [Kadesh-barnea]; Num 21:5 [fiery serpents]).

73 See Neilsen's comments cited on p. 56 n. 17 above.

Logically, only two possible explanations emerge for consideration, though both are admittedly speculative. Either the M-Mt in Exod 17:1–7 once ended with divine wrath against the people, a component lost or relocated over the course of its tradition history, or the M-Mt in Exod 17:1–7 never had such a component but was understood to have been an instance of inappropriate provocation nevertheless. Johnstone prefers the first option, using Deut 33:8 as the clue that leads to identifying Exod 32:25–29 as this lost piece of the tradition-historical puzzle. Deuteronomy 33:8 uniquely ties the Levites to the M-Mt, which is here cast in terms that some find evocative of the Levite's bloody role in executing Yahweh's wrath against their fellow Israelites at Horeb (Exod 32:25–29). Consequently, Johnstone concludes "that the narrative matching the reminiscence of enraging the LORD at Massah in Deut 9,22, cf. 33,8, is to be reassembled, shorn of its P-additions, from Ex 17,1–7; 32,25–29; 15,22–26; Num 20,1–11, and relocated in its original position after Num 11,3."[74] This hypothesis, however, places an immense interpretative weight on an extraordinarily ambiguous text (see §4.4 below), and as well ascribes to the P redactor an unprecedented role in the compiling and insertion of the literary materials that now constitute Exod 15:22bβ–19:2a.[75] In the end, a more balanced approach would be to reconstruct the M-Mt's developments by diachronically aligning the reminiscences across the macro-structural development of Deuteronomy as a whole, rather than to found the M-Mt's prehistory on its most elusive exponent.

3.5 Reconstructing the Framework of the M-Mt's Tradition-historical Development (Part 1)

The relative chronological relationship of the texts that preserve reminiscences of the M-Mt within Deuteronomy's interior prologue proceed, earliest to latest, from Deut 8:15, to 6:16, and finally to 9:22. This relative chronology is crucial, as it provides the controls whereby one may negotiate the varying tradition components and thereby reconstruct the framework of the earliest literary stages of the M-Mt's *Traditions-geschichte* from the Dtr perspective.[76] The six tradition components the tradents used to evoke the M-Mt within Deuteronomy's interior

---

74 Johnstone, "Reminiscences in Deuteronomy," in Gertz, Schmid, and Witte, *Abschied vom Jahwisten*, 261.
75 Johnstone goes so far as to call Exod 15:22bβ–19:2a an "insertion" at the hand of P ("Reminiscences in Deuteronomy," in Gertz, Schmid, and Witte, *Abschied vom Jahwisten*, 262).
76 This statement does not deny the possibility of the M-Mt having earlier oral stages—only their demonstrability.

prologue are *agency, substance of issuance, source of issuance, location, interpretative significance*, and *canonical awareness*.

Stage 1: As the earliest exponent of the M-Mt within the interior prologue, Deut 8:15 (*Dt*) reflects a time when the M-Mt was a part of a developing cycle of traditions. In this cycle, Yahweh "tests" (נסה√) Israel (*agency*) with instances of privation, only in turn to prove his faithfulness by miraculously meeting those needs. In the wilderness, Israel's subsistence naturally required water, a need which the deity meets miraculously through an eruption of "water from the flinty rock" (מים מצור החלמיש) (*substance and source of issuance*). The description of the *location* situating the M-Mt at this stage bears mythic undertones—happening "in the great and terrible wilderness" (במדבר הגדל והנורא) as opposed to at any specific geographic location. The *interpretative significance* of the M-Mt pales slightly in comparison to the manna tradition (8:3, 16), which respectively opens and closes the parallel wilderness descriptions (8:3–4 ‖ 15–16). Explicit textual, *canonical awareness* is not demonstrable at this point, save in the general terms of a metanarrative framework: i.e., exodus from Egypt, then wilderness sojourn, then entry into the good land. Yet this metanarrative is distinct from its final form in the Pentateuch as it presumes Israel's innocence in the wilderness: Yahweh tests Israel in the wilderness for their good, so that they might not forget Yahweh when they enter the land.

Stage 2: Striking changes in the M-Mt have taken place at this stage, no doubt requiring a significant amount of reflection for their development. In this regard, it may not be insignificant that Deut 6:16 (*late Dtr*) enters into its current literary surroundings as a tertiary expansion to what was originally just Deut 6:4–5 (see Table 3.3 above). Foremost among these changes is the reversal of the M-Mt's *agency*, from Yahweh testing Israel, to Israel testing Yahweh. The details as to how Israel tests Yahweh are left unstated, including any particulars regarding the *substance* and *source of issuance*. Nevertheless, it is not presumptuous to conjecture a scenario revolving around water deprivation. After all, the foundational aspects of Yahweh providing water from a rock in the wilderness are already in existence, and there can be no doubt that they eventuate into an episode about Israel murmuring over the lack of water in the wilderness. The *location* at this stage remains vague, with the vocalization of בְּמַסָּה ("at the testing"), which may preserve the memory of when "Massah" was not yet a proper toponym. The association of this location with בקרבך in Deut 6:15 may evince *canonical awareness* of an early narrative version of Exod 17:1–7, or at least the developing etiology in Exod 17:7. It remains difficult, however, to determine whether at this stage the M-Mt had achieved special notoriety as the paradigmatic failure of the first wilderness generation, or if the insertion of 6:16 was merely a product of intertextuality. Regardless, the *interpretative sig-*

3.5 Reconstructing the Framework of the M-Mt's Tradition-historical Development

nificance—despite the fact that the repercussions of Israel's failure remain unstated—clearly serves as a warning to future generations. Since Ps 95:8–11 remembers the M-Mt as the moment that doomed the first wilderness generation, it is possible that Deut 6:16 tacitly warns of similar consequences.

Stage 3: Changes to the M-Mt at this stage reflect the beginnings of stabilization within the Dt-Dtr school of tradents. In Deut 9:22 (*Dtr supp*), the direction of the *agency* is the same as it is in Deut 6:16, and likewise the details of the M-Mt such as *source* and *substance of issuance* remain in the realm of presupposition. Further concretizing of the M-Mt, however, is evident with the *location*, with the emergence of the toponym in the phrase "and at Massah" (וּבְמַסָּה) over and above the more general "at the testing" (בַּמַּסָּה). The tradents at this stage appear to have been *canonically aware* of a written precursor of the Pentateuch, one in which the M-Mt is situated after the failure at Horeb and between the failures of Taberah and Kibroth-hattaavah (cf. Num 11:1–35). In this context, the *interpretative significance* of the M-Mt has flagged: it is no longer the decisive failure in the wilderness; the tradition about the molten calf at Horeb is. Instead, the M-Mt retains significance as part of a larger pattern of behavior—namely, the first wilderness generation's rebellion against Yahweh.

Detection of these three stages of the M-Mt's tradition-historical development is possible only because the conservative nature of the traditioning-processes which the Dt-Dtr tradents used in the tending of their traditions. Rather than revising again and again their earliest iteration of the M-Mt (Deut 8:15) as the M-Mt developed, these tradents incorporated additional iterations—ones reflecting the current state of the M-Mt—as they reverently supplemented their received text. Consequently, the above stages represent the framework of the M-Mt's *Traditionsgeschichte* as it transpired within the purview of the Dt-Dtr tradents. Additional stages are possible, even likely, but they are not demonstrable from the texts within Deuteronomy's interior prologue. Instead, evidence for such stages must be sought in the book's exterior miscellaneous epilogues, the investigation of which is the concern of the following chapter.

Chapter Four:
The M-Mt's Reminiscences within Deuteronomy's Exterior Miscellaneous Epilogues

4.1 Introduction to the Exterior Reminiscences

The texts preserving reminiscences of the M-Mt within Deuteronomy's exterior miscellaneous epilogues (chs. 31–34) are Deut 32:13; 32:51; and 33:8. Along with their broader literary contexts, these texts are the products of two literary processes that are strikingly different from those that shaped the M-Mt texts within Deuteronomy's interior historical prologue (chs. 5–11): namely, literary appropriation and canon formation.[1] While the relevant pericopes inside chs. 5–11 are the product of a series of editorial expansions in a continual process of *Fortschreibung*, such is not the case with the germane pericopes inside chs. 31–34. Most likely, earlier forms of the Song and Blessing of Moses (Deut 32:1–43 and 33:2–29) were in circulation prior to being incorporated into Deuteronomy, while Deut 32:48–52 appears to reiterate and expand upon Num 27:12–14. Thus, one cannot assume these texts to be the sole literary genius of Deuteronomy's textual proprietors. Also, since Deut 32:48–52 now functions as a resumptive repetition of Num 27:12–14, one must consider a second literary process that distinguishes the formation of chs. 31–34 from that of chs. 5–11: namely, the incorporation of Deuteronomy into a multi-scroll collection (or multi-scroll collections) in the process of canon formation.[2]

---

[1] This observation in no way denies the availability or the appropriation of pre-existing material within Deuteronomy's interior prologue. The Decalogue in Deut 5:6–21, appropriated from Exod 20:2–17, is a clear example of this phenomenon. Instead, the observation here pertains to the formation of the paraenetic sections within the interior prologue that preserve reminiscences of the M-Mt (i.e., Deut 6:4–25; 8:1–20; 9:1–10:11).

[2] I do not mean here to advocate or assume the validity of what Konrad Schmid calls the Noth-von Rad "separation model," which argues that two distinct collections of scrolls—namely, the so-called "Tetrateuch" and the "Deuteronomistic History"—fed into the formation of the primary history, Genesis–Kings (Konrad Schmid, "The Emergence and Disappearance of the Separation between the Pentateuch and the Deuteronomistic History in Biblical Studies," in *Pentateuch, Hexateuch, or Enneateuch? Identifying Literary Works in Genesis through Kings* [eds. Thomas B. Dozeman, Thomas Römer, and Konrad Schmid; SBL 8; Atlanta: Society of Biblical Literature, 2011], 11–24). Over the last forty years, challenges to this model have steadily risen alongside those that eroded the favor of the Graf-Wellhausen Documentary Hypothesis. (For recent examples, see Thomas Römer, ed., *The Future of the Deuteronomistic History* [BETL 147; Leuven-Louvain: Leuven University Press, 2000]; Dozeman, Römer, and Schmid, *Pentateuch, Hexateuch, or*

suance is nearly always potable water, "and then the reference is always to events in the wilderness."[7] This consistency is remarkable, given the prevalence and distribution of the M-Mt throughout the Hebrew Bible (cf. §1.1 above), and warrants the careful consideration of whether Deut 32:13 could be a M-Mt text.

Lest the difference in the *substance of issuance* be an insurmountable obstacle—i.e., that it is "honey" issuing from the rock, not "water" as it is elsewhere in the M-Mt—one ought to consider a second bit of evidence. In the Ugaritic Baal Cycle, Baruch Margalit has found evidence which allows one to read דבש ("honey") and שמן ("oil") in Deut 32:13b as mythological metaphors for "sweet water" rather than physical honey:

> In describing the empirical signs of Baal's revival and return from the land of the Dead (*arṣ. dbr*), the text in [*KTU*] 1.6:III:6f.//12f. states: *šmm. šmn. tmṭrn // nḥlm. tlk. nbtm* = "The heavens rained ›oil‹ // The brooks flowed with ›honey‹" […] This usage has its precise, and striking, parallel in Deut 32,13b.[8]

---

7 Sanders, *Deuteronomy 32*, 170–171. The only exceptions beyond Deut 32:13b are Ps 81:17 (the only other biblical text in which honey issues from a rock) and Job 26:9 (the only biblical text in which oil issues from a rock). Job 26:9 has no detectible connection to the M-Mt, so Sanders rightly does not entertain it. As for Ps 81:17, Sanders declares that it "relates to blessings in Canaan rather than blessings in the wilderness," but he cites no evidence to substantiate this conclusion (*Deuteronomy 32*, 389). A structural analysis of Psalm 81, however, shows that Ps 81:17 is rhetorically parallel to Ps 81:8b's explicit mention of מי מריבה and represents the deity's promise to provide sustenance in exchange for fidelity as he had done before in the wilderness.
8 Margalit, "Ugaritic Contributions," 401–402. Margalit continues to argue that the semantic use of the constellation of terms (*šmn* ‖ שמן and *nbt* ‖ דבש) in both texts is metaphorical and rhetorically identical: namely, that both sets of terms connote "sweet water." The reason why scholars have overlooked this comparison is the proclivity to interpret Deut 32:13b too literally, thereby failing to recognize the "co-opting" of this Canaanite idiom for life-giving fresh water. Margalit then proffers a bold thesis: "The parallelism סלע-צור which we find in Deut 32:13 corresponds to, and takes up, the synonyms for ›rock‹ used consistently and respectively in Ex 17 and Num 20. This is hardly a matter of chance. The conclusion can only be that in Deut 32,13 ›oil‹ and ›honey‹ are poetic metaphors for ›fresh-‹/›sweet-water‹ suitable for drinking" ("Ugaritic Contributions," 402–403). He then cites the semantic parallels in Deut 8:15 and Ps 81:17b as further corroboration for his thesis. Finally, to counter the objection that the Promised Land is formulaically described as "a land of milk and honey" (ארץ זבת חלב ודבש), Margalit argues for repointing of חלב from the traditional חָלָב ("milk") to an unconventional חֵלֶב ("fat"). His rationale is that milk is not a product of agriculture but of animals—"No land flows with ›milk‹"—and that outside this presumed formula "Nowhere in the Bible is ›milk‹ a symbol of fertility" ("Ugaritic Contributions," 404).

Beyond the possibility of "honey" and "oil" being metaphors for Yahweh's provision of water, Margalit's conclusions are overstated and largely unsubstantiated. The value of Margalit's work here is its contribution toward recovering the mythic background that was original to Deut 32:13b.

In short, the Baal Cycle shows that in the early Canaanite milieu the terms for "honey" and "oil" could operate as metaphors for divinely provided potable water. When read against this background, the feasibility of reading Deut 32:13 as a M-Mt text continues to improve.

To his credit, Sanders does engage this evidence in limited fashion; he even concedes that it lends "some support" for Deut 32:13 reflecting the same phenomenon as do other passages within the M-Mt.[9] Eventually, Sanders decides in favor of the traditional reading of Deut 32:13–14 as a description of Canaan, thereby excluding it from the Wilderness Tradition in general and the M-Mt in particular.[10] There are, however, several points of additional evidence which one ought to take into consideration, including 1) the mythological overtones elsewhere original to the Song, 2) the profiles of the ancient witnesses that read Deut 32:13 as a description of Canaan, and 3) the indefinite construction על במותי ארץ in contrast to the Dt and Dtr pattern of evoking the Promised Land (cf. §4.2.2.); as well as 4) the Song's fundamental genre, 5) the internal and external evidence of its textual growth, and finally 6) the chiastic structure of Deut 32:4–18 (cf. §4.2.3.). Taken together, this evidence holds open the possibility that Deut 32:13b preserves a reminiscence of the M-Mt.

4.2.2 Text Criticism of Deut 32:13

ירכבהו על־במותי ארץ ויאכל[הו] תנבת שדי [Deut 32:13]
וינקהו דבש מסלע ושמן מחלמיש צור:

The pluriformity of the Song extant among the ancient witnesses is remarkable and commands much text-critical attention, especially toward the anti-polytheistic emendations that were made to MT Deut 32:8 and 32:43.[11] The significance

---

[9] Specifically, Sanders concedes that KTU 1.6:iii.6–7, 12–13 "gives some support to the view that Deut 32:13b refers to the same kind of events as the passages of the Hebrew Bible about the flowing of water from a rock" (Sanders, *Deuteronomy 32*, 171 n. 372).

[10] Sanders concludes that the "traditional interpretation is preferable" on account that Deut 32:13b is framed by material (i.e., vv. 13a+14) that "relates to blessings in Canaan rather than blessings in the wilderness" (*Deuteronomy 32*, 389). However, the meaning of phrase על במותי ארץ (v. 13aα) is not clear, which Sanders at first readily admits and yet then declares with certainty that for ארץ the rendering of "'land' is preferable to the translation 'earth'" (*Deuteronomy 32*, 168–169). Sanders provides no evidence for this assertion. See pp. 92–94 below for the difficulties of reading this phrase as a direct evocation of the Promised Land.

[11] The source of contention for Deut 32:8 is MT's and Smr's reading of בני ישראל as compared to בני אלוהים (in 4QDeut^j), possibly [...] בני אל (in 4QDeut^q), υἱῶν θεοῦ (in G$^{848\ 106c}$), and ἀγγέλων θεοῦ

of these specific emendations for MT Deut 32:13 lies in the heightened awareness of the Song's original mythological overtones, which in turn should shape the debate over whether v. 13b preserves a reminiscence of M-Mt. As for text-critical issues in Deut 32:13 itself, three types of variants are extant within the readings of the ancient witnesses: 1) the shifts in the implied subject noun represented by MT's ויאכל and וינקהו, 2) interpretations and/or exegetical expansions to the text, and 3) changes in the definiteness of the construct phrase במותי ארץ.

To begin, the variance in the subject nominatives within the readings most likely occur for syntactical or theological reasons.[12] The MT shifts its implied subject noun from the deity in the first hemistich (v. 13aα) to Israel with יאכל in the second hemistich (v. 13aβ), and finally back to the deity in in the third and fourth hemistiches via ינקהו (v. 13b). The Smr, however, adds a 3ms pronominal suffix to יאכל (יאכלהו) and shifts ינקהו to hifil by adding the *yod* preforma-

---

(G^Mss). See also (cf. ג.[בולות עמים ...מעי] שו[אל ...מבני, "more than the sons of God who he[ar ...the bo]undaries of the people" in 1QH^a XXIV 33–34 (Eileen M. Schuller and Carol A. Newsom, *The Hodayot (Thanksgiving Psalms): A Study Edition of 1QH^a* [SBLEJL 36; Atlanta: Society of Biblical Literature, 2012], 74–75; cf. Emanuel Tov, *Textual Criticism of the Hebrew Bible* [3d, rev. and exp.; Minneapolis: Fortress, 2012], 249 n. 78). The evidence leads to the conclusion that the original reading was probably either בני אלהים or בני אלים, with the MT and Smr resulting from what Emanuel Tov calls an "anti-polytheistic alternation" (*Textual Criticism*, 248–249; for the history of the debate, see Sanders, *Deuteronomy 32*, 156–158). A similar correction likely occurred in MT Deut 32:43, where two cola appear to have been deleted in comparison to 4QDeut^q and G: following the MT's הרנינו שמים עמו would have been the polytheistic parallel colon והשתחוו לו כל אלהים, "and bow down to him, all (you) gods" (4QDeut^q; cf. G's καὶ προσκυνησάτωσαν αὐτῷ πάντες υἱοὶ θεοῦ); a second deletion occurred between MT's third and fourth cola (i.e., ולמשנאי ישלם, "and those who hate him he will requite" in 4QDeut^q; cf. G's καὶ τοῖς μισοῦσιν ἀνταποδώσει) (Tov, *Textual Criticism*, 249–250; Sanders, *Deuteronomy 32*, 248–256; Carmel McCarthy, *Biblia Hebraica Quinta, Fascicle 5: Deuteronomy* [Stuttgart: Deutsche Bibelgesellschaft, 2007], 152*–153*).

12 McCarthy poses two options for these verbal shifts: either MT is to be preferred as the *lectio difficilior*, or the shift in MT reflects a "scribal initiative for theological motives" (*BHQ Deuteronomy*, 143*)—motives which McCarthy understandably leaves to speculation. It is difficult to imagine, however, what would prompt a scribe to strip away Yahweh's role in feeding the Israelites by rewriting ויאכ(י)להו to ויאכל and yet not prompt a similar revision of וינקהו to either וינק or וינקו (cf. G's ἐθήλασαν). This shift therefore does not appear to have been theologically motivated. Alternatively, Sanders suggests the possibility that the pronominal suffix of ירכבהו in the first colon (v.13aα) could serve as a "double-duty suffix" that modifies the verb in the second colon (v.13aβ). If such is the case, the consonantal text for יאכל would remain the same, but be read as a hifil (יַאֲכֵל?) that elliptically carries forward the force of the earlier pronominal suffix הו- to rendered "he fed [him]") (Sanders, *Deuteronomy 32*, 169). As this literary device does not occur elsewhere in the immediate context where one would expect it (e.g. vv. 10b, 11b, 13bα), it is more likely that the MT has suffered the loss of the pronominal suffix הו- through haplography on account of the similarity of first two letters of the word that follows (תנובת).

tive (ויּנקהו), resulting in the respective readings of "he fed him" and "he caused him to suckle." Together, these changes sustain the focus on the Yahweh's actions throughout and avoid the attribution of female physiology to the deity.[13] The same rationales explain G's ἐψώμισεν αὐτοὺς for יאכל (presuming יאכילם) and ἐθήλασαν for ינקהו (presuming ינקו)[14]: the focus remains on Yahweh's actions through v.13aβ, while G's rendering of v.13b reorients the feminine imagery toward the land (cf. the feminine γῆς in v. 13aα), thereby removing the deity from the image of suckling entirely.[15] Similarly, the Targum Onkelos (T⁰)—which tends to follow the MT more closely than all the other targumim[16]—reads אוכילינון and יהב להון for the MT's יאכל and ינקהו respectively.[17] These changes in T⁰ again reflect the desire to sustain the focus on the Yahweh's ac-

---

13 Sanders attributes the LXX's ἐθήλασαν to the same motives (*Deuteronomy 32*, 170).
14 Cf. John W. Wevers, ed., *Deuteronomium* (vol. III, 2 of *Septuaginta: Vetus Testamentum Graecum; auctoritate Academiae Scientiarum Gottingensis editum*; Göttingen: Vandenhoeck & Ruprecht, 1977), 348. See also Sanders comments on the LXX's ἐθήλασαν (*Deuteronomy 32*, 170).
15 Wevers believes the translators took Deut 32:13b as "interruptive" within their *Vorlage*. The reason he makes this assertion is that the list of produce in Deut 32:14a does not have a controlling verb, and the verb in the last line (LXX ἔπιον for MT's תשתה) only modifies the last line. "The translator was aware of the problem," argues Wevers, "and tied the first four lines [of v. 14] to v. 13 as modifiers of a verb; the nearer one is ἐθήλασαν, but sensibly these should be taken as additions to the products of the fields; accusative modifiers are βούτυρον and γάλα 'butter (of cattle) and milk (of sheep). In other words, the translator took lines three and four of v. 13 as interruptive; thus butter and milk also constitute modifiers of ἐψώμισεν" (*Notes on the Greek Text of Deuteronomy* [SBLSCS 39; Atlanta: Scholars Press, 1995], 517). Wevers reconstruction is complicated by the fact that γάλα is not only a liquid, but the one most naturally associated with the action of suckling.
16 Israel Drazin, *Targum Onkelos to Deuteronomy: An English Translation of the Text with Analysis and Commentary* (New York: Ktav Publishing House, 1982), 1; Alexander Sperber, *The Bible in Aramaic: The Pentateuch according to the Targum Onqelos, vol. 1* (Leiden: Brill, 1992), 348.

Although the T⁰ tends to follow the MT more closely than the other targumim, its version of the Song deviates substantially from the MT's. McCarthy observes that for Deut 32:13 the other targumim (T^NJF) are closer to the MT than T⁰ (McCarthy, *BHQ Deuteronomy*, 143*). Of these, the Fragment-Targum (T^F) follows the Masoretic tradition the closest: ארכב יתהון על במתא דארעא, ואייכיל יתהון עללת תפנוקי מלכין ואייניק יתהון מין [דבש מין] כיפה <ו>משח יתהון מין כיף שמיר טינרא: "He made them ride on the high places of the earth; and He fed them the yeild of royal delicacies; and he made them suck [honey from] the rock; and He anointed them [with oil] from the rock of flint stone" (Michael L. Klein, *The Fragment-Targums of the Pentateuch according to their Exant Sources* [2 vols.; AnBib 76; Rome: Biblical Institute Press, 1980], I:226, II:183).
17 See also Targum Neofiti (T^N), which has אייכל יתהון and אייכל יתהון, and Targum Pseudo-Jonathan (T^J), which likewise has אייכל יתהון but then אוניק יתהון.

tions and to disassociate the deity from the feminine image of suckling.[18] Regrettably, none of the many fragments from the Judean Desert that preserve portions of the Song shed any light on this matter.[19]

Another variant quickly detectable within the ancient readings is the proclivity toward interpretation and/or exegetical expansion. Here, the somewhat odd construction על־במותי ארץ is a case in point.[20] While the Smr adds only the definite article to the *nomen rectum*, the other versions employ a greater level of literary interpretation. In the LXX Deut 32:13,[21] one would expect ἐπὶ τὰ ὕψη τῆς γῆς ("upon the high places of the earth"); after all, this is the rendering the LXX gives for על־במותי ארץ in Mic 1:3 and for על־במתי ארץ in Amos 4:13.[22] The LXX Deut 32:13, however, interprets its *Vorlage*. Instead of employing the more

---

18 Rather than reassigning the implied subject noun (cf. G), the T⁰ disassociates the deity from this feminine image by replacing the verb "to suckle" (√ינק) with a more neutral verb "to give" (√יהב).

19 The fragments of the Song found in the Judean Desert include the following portions from the Song: 1QDeut^b (1Q5) has Deut 32:17–29 (cf. DJD I:60); 4QDeut^b (4Q29) has Deut 32:1–3 (cf. DJD XIV:9, 13–14); 4QDeut^c (4Q30) has Deut 32:3 (cf. DJD XIV: 15, 33); 4QDeut^j (4Q37) has Deut 32:7–8 (cf. DJD XIV:76, 90); 4QDeut^K1 (4Q38) has Deut 32:17–18, 22–23, 25–27 (cf. DJD XIV:92, 97–98); 4QDeut^q (4Q44) has Deut 32:9–10(?), 37–43 (cf. DJD XIV:137–142; Patrick Skehan W., "A Fragment of the "Song of Moses" (Deut. 32) from Qumran," *BASOR* 136 [1954]: 12–15); 4QpaleoDeut^r (4Q45) has Deut 32:6–8, 10–11, 13–14, 22(?), 33–35 (cf. DJD IX:132, 146–147, 150); and 4Qphyl^n (4Q141) has Deut 32:14–20, 32–33 (cf. DJD VI:73–74). Of these eight witnesses, only 4QpaleoDeut^r (4Q45) contains any part of Deut 32:13, but it is too fragmentary to be of value at this particular point. See p. 93 below for further discussion of this lone witness.

20 What makes this construction odd, as the Masoretes pointed out, is that plural inflection of בָּמָה in MT Deut 32:13's על־במותי ארץ contains both masculine and feminine terminations (cf. GKC §87 s and 95o; Daniel S. Mynatt, *The Sub Loco Notes in the Torah of Biblia Hebraica Stuttgartensia* [BDS 2; Louisville: Bibal Press, 1994], 215–216).

21 Timothy H. Lim provides a summary profile of Alexandrian LXX Deuteronomy. Conservative and in places slavish, but not as "barbaric and unintelligible" as Aquila, the LXX Deuteronomy intervenes interpretively to varying degrees within its major sections: "it is infrequent in the first eleven chapters. In the legal section (chs 12–26), the divergences are of a technical nature [. . .] In the final section (chs 27–34), the interpretative elements are most numerous and they reflect the intention of the translator to express Yahweh's love for his dispersed people" ("Deuteronomy in the Judaism of the Second Temple Period," in *Deuteronomy in the New Testament: The New Testament and Scriptures of Israel* [ed. Maarten J. J. Menken and Steve Moyise; LNTS 358; London: T & T Clark, 2007], 19–20).

22 It is worth noting that in the context of both Mic 1:3 and Amos 4:13, the construction על־במ(ו)תי ארץ denotes the cosmological place of Yahweh's theophanic appearance, not the Promised Land as a specific geographical location.

literal ὕψη for במותי,²³ the LXX uses ἰσχὺν ("strength") thereby interpreting the produce listed in Deut 32:13aβ-14 as the natural resources or "strengths" of the Promised Land. Likewise, the T° also interprets על־במותי ארץ in terms of strength: אשרינון על תוקפי ארעא ("I made them dwell on the strong places of the earth").²⁴ Yet instead of natural resources, the T° understands the fertility language of Deut 32:13aβ-14 as the spoils (ביזת) of ancient Israel's conquest against the indigenous rulers of the land.²⁵

Despite these early interpretations, it is not clear that the Dtr editors would have understood the phrase על־במותי ארץ as indicative of the Promised Land. Throughout Deuteronomy, as well as in the DtrH, it is always a definite form of ארץ that *directly* evokes the Promised Land (e.g., הארץ אשר נשבע לאבתיך in Deut 6:10).²⁶ Indefinite forms of ארץ that refer to the Promised Land only do so *indirectly* as appositives when they syntactically follow one or more of the following elements: *a*) the definite הארץ or האדמה that does directly evoke the Promised Land, *b*) a reference to Yahweh's oath or act of giving / bringing Israel to the land, or *c*) explicit toponyms or specific geographical boundaries that span the Promised Land.²⁷ Yet על־במותי ארץ in Deut 32:13 is not preceded by any such element.²⁸

---

23 Although Aquila (α') does have ἐπὶ τὸ ὕψωμα τῆς γῆς (cf. Wevers, ed., *Septuaginta Deuteronomium*, 348). Elsewhere, G's phrase τὴν ἰσχὺν τῆς γῆς occurs only in Odes 2:13 (= Deut 32:13) and in Dan 11:19 in Theodotion (θ') where the king of the north turns his face back to the strength of his own land (εἰς τὴν ἰσχὺν τῆς γῆς αὐτοῦ). The context of Dan 11:19 (θ') does not illuminate why the Septuagint translators would choose ἰσχὺν to translate במותי in Deut 32:13; Deut 32:13 is the only instance the translators did so (cf. Hatch and Redpath, "ἰσχὺς," *HRCS* 1:694–695).

Interestingly, the LXX Isa 58:14 renders this phrase loosely as ἐπὶ τὰ ἀγαθὰ τῆς γῆς ("upon the good places of the land"). Yet here the connection to the Promised Land is more overt: since MT Isa 58:14b is syntactically parallel to MT Isa 58:14a, the phrase נחלת יעקב אביך (v. 14b) may be understood to clarify על־במותי ארץ (v. 14a) in appositive fashion.

24 Drazin, *Targum Onkelos to Deuteronomy*, 274.

25 Drazin, *Targum Onkelos to Deuteronomy*, 274–276.

26 To paraphrase Waltke and O'Connor, a noun is definite if it is (1) a proper noun, (2) bears the affix article [ה] or a pronominal suffix, or (3) is in construct with a noun made definite by either (1) or (2) (Bruce K. Waltke and M. O'Connor, *An Introduction to Biblical Hebrew Syntax* [Winona Lake: Eisenbrauns, 1990], §13.4, p. 239).

27 For the instances that follow *a*) a definite form of ארץ or אדמה, see Deut 11:9–12; 26:9, 15; 27:3; Josh 5:6; 2 Kgs 18:32. For indefinite forms that follow *b*) a reference to Yahweh's oath or act of giving (√נתן), see Deut 6:3; 8:7–9; 11:9–12; 26:9, 15; 27:3; Josh 5:6; 24:13. Finally, for indefinite instances following *c*) explicit toponyms or specific geographical boundaries, see Deut 33:28; 2 Sam 3:12 (in context of 2 Sam 3:10).

28 Another evidence that undercuts reading על־במותי ארץ as indicative of the Promised Land is the syntactical position of ארץ within the construct chain במותי ארץ. In the *nomen regens* posi-

It is for this reason one must consider a third variant within the readings of Deut 32:13, one which generally goes overlooked: the rendering of MT's indefinite construct phrase על־במותי ארץ as definite within the major versions.²⁹ Granted, it is difficult to render this phrase indefinitely, which may have contributed to the ubiquity of this particular variance: the Smr, the LXX and its recensions, and targumim all render the phrase as definite.³⁰ Yet the Masoretic preference for the indefinite is attested in both the Leningrad Codex (M^L) and Aleppo Codex (M^A). Regrettably, no confirmation for the MT is possible from 4QpaleoDeut^r, the only scroll from Qumran to preserve fragments of Deut 32:13. Though a fragment clearly preserves the *resh* and *tsade* of ארץ, only a trace of the *aleph* remains.³¹ Still, none of the standard mechanisms that typically prompt parablepsis could produce the loss of the definite *heh* (ה) from ארץ in the MT from a presumed proto-MT *Vorlage*.³² Further, since instances of this indefinite phrase are also extant in the Isa 58:14, Amos 4:13, and Mic 1:3, it is more likely that MT's indefinite construction is preferable and reflects cosmological space rather than any specific geographical location.³³

---

tion, ארץ commonly receives definiteness on account of its *nomen rectum* being a specific toponym (e.g., ארץ כנען, ארץ אפרים, or ארץ יהודה) or gentilic (e.g., ארץ הכנעני, ארץ האמרי, or פלשתים). In the *nomen rectum* position, ארץ most often results in the loss of any particularity, exporting instead a universal (e.g., מלכי־ארץ or שפטי ארץ) or cosmological (e.g., אפסי־ארץ or כל־גבולות ארץ) parameter to its *nomen regens*. Deuteronomy 32:13a has ארץ as a *nomen rectum*—על־במותי ארץ—and as such does not lend itself to the particularization of its *nomen regens*, במותי. Instead, the construct phrase על־במותי ארץ serves as a cosmological reference to the "high places" or "heights," just as the phrase does in the Prophets (cf. Isa 58:14; Amos 4:13; Mic 1:3).
29 The Masoretic vocalization אָרֶץ is not definite; it is the pausal form of אֶרֶץ, as indicated in MT Deut 32:13 with the disjunctive accent זָקֵף קָטוֹן over the *aleph*. Segolate nouns often experience a vowel shift when in pause, specifically from *segol* under the first radical to *qamets* (cf. Joüon, §32c). For commentary on the massorah's notes on where this shift with ארץ occurs elsewhere, see McCarthy, *BHQ Deuteronomy*, 47*.
30 For example, the Smr has על במתי הארץ; B and G has τὴν ἰσχὺν τῆς γῆς; α' has τὸ ὕψωμα τῆς γῆς; T^F has במתא דארעא; T^O has תוקפי ארעא; T^J has כרכי ארע דישראל.
31 Patrick W. Skehan rates the *aleph* as probable, with trace ink of the letter's fulcrum still visible (DJD IX: 131, 147; cf. Plate XXXVI, fragment no. 38). For a list of the fragments from the Judean Desert that preserve portions of the Song, see p. 91 n. 19 above.
32 Within the immediate textual context of Deut 32:13aα's על במותי ארץ, there is no adjacent letter ה or earlier occurrence of ארץ to prompt haplography. Homoiarcton, as well, is highly unlikely.
33 Additional support for this reading again emerges from the Baal Cycle. Sanders notes (without explanation) that a similar expression again appears in KTU 1.4:vii.34 as *bmt 'r[ṣ]* (Sanders, *Deuteronomy 32*, 389 n. 472). Upon closer inspection, line 34b's *bmt 'r[ṣ]* is parallel to line 33 – 34a's *ġrm] qdmym*, which Mark S. Smith and Wayne T. Pitard reconstruct as "ancient mountains" (*The Ugaritic Baal Cycle: Volume II: Introduction with Text, Translation and Commentary*

In sum, several text-critical issues are salient for determining whether Deut 32:13 possibly preserves a reminiscence of the M-Mt. Not only is the MT's indefinite construct phrase על־במותי ארץ in v. 13aα to be preferred, but it also does not univocally signal ancient Israel's transition into the Promised Land in historical-recitative fashion. The distinctive pattern for evoking the Promised Land within Deuteronomy and the DtrH further corroborates this conclusion. Instead, it is more likely that the phrase represents the mythological heights onto which Yahweh descends, as is attested by the usage of the phrase in Mic 1:3 and Amos 4:13. This phrase then combines with Deut 32:13a (ויאכל[הו] תנובת שדי)[34] to form the cosmological scope of Yahweh's gracious provisions: from the mythic high places of the earth to the fields below.

Further, the demonstrable textual changes to the Song within the ancient witnesses, including those within the Masoretic tradition, offer additional support for this reading of Deut 32:13a. Together, these changes suggest the earliest form of the Song was deeply embedded with a polytheistic cosmology.[35] It is within this mythological purview that Deut 32:13's semantic parallels with the Ugaritic Baal Cycle find greater value, despite the chronological distance between KTU 1.1–1.6 and the Song.[36] Given this context, the feminine image of Yahweh suckling Israel remains preferable, with דבש מסלע ושמן מחלמש צור serving as a metaphor for the deity's provision of potable water.[37]

---

of KTU/CAT 1.3–1.4 [VTSup 114; Leiden: Brill, 2009], 675). This notion of the "high places of the earth" or "ancient mountains" (הררי־קדם) occurs as well in the Blessing of Moses (Deut 33:15–16).

[34] The verb either carries forward the pronominal suffix of ירכבהו in elliptic fashion, or more likely has suffered the loss of הו- through haplography (cf. p. 89 n. 12 above).

[35] Namely, the textual changes made to proto-MT Deut 32:8, 43 (cf. p. 88 n. 11 above), the elimination of the feminine imagery from the deity suckling in Deut 32:13b (cf. pp. 89–91 above), and the interpretive renderings of Deut 32:13's במותי ארץ (cf. pp. 91–93 above).

[36] For discussion on the relevance of the Ugaritic Baal Cycle to Deut 32:13, see pp. 87–88 and p. 93 n. 33 above. Conservative dates for the six tablets that make up the Ugaritic Baal Cycle are between 1400 to 1350 BCE (Mark S. Smith, *The Ugaritic Baal Cycle: Volume 1: Introduction with Text, Translation and Commentary of KTU 1.1–1.2* [VTSup LV; Leiden: Brill, 1994], 1). For a discussion of the preexilic dating of the Song, see §4.2.3 below.

[37] The nature of this metaphor is both fundamental, yet delightfully complex. Over the course of the Song, the archetypal image of a nursing mother takes on a number of surprising changes: 1) the mother in this metaphor is Yahweh, a *male* deity (cf. Deut 32:18); 2) yet Yahweh himself is metaphorized six times by the *non-reproductive* vehicle (or metaphorizing idea) "Rock" (צור; cf. Deut 32:4, 15, 18, 30, 31, 37); 3) this male Rock then suckles Israel, not with milk (חלב), but *honey* and *oil* (דבש and שמן)—the very same vehicles used to represent Baal's sweet water in the Baal Cycle (cf. pp. 87–88 above); and finally to complete the metaphor 4) the apparatus through which the Rock "lactates" is not a breast (שד), but a *crag* (סלע) and *flinty rock* (חלמש

4.2.3 Literary Analysis of Deut 32:1–43

Already text-critical and comparative evidence warrants one keeping an open mind as to whether Deut 32:13 reflects the M-Mt. Analysis of the Song's foundational genre, the broad strokes of its literary development, as well as the structural organization of its earliest detectable form also lend support for this reading.

In his survey of studies on the Song's genre, Sanders has shown that the enterprise to classify most or all of the Song under a single genre—especially covenant lawsuit, or rîb[38]—while at times fruitful for clarifying the relationship of certain of the Song's components, has proven largely unsuccessful.[39] Instead, the Song as it currently stands is a mixed-genre that incorporates elements of several genres, but especially the prophetic rîb.[40] The desire to classify the Song's genre, however, persists and has given rise to the functional taxonomy of calling the Song a *didactic hymn* or *poem*.[41]

צור)—now synecdoches of the deity himself, and materials through which liquid sustenance does not typically flow.

38 Foremost is the attempt to classify the Song under the rîb or covenant lawsuit genre and therefore comparable to Isa 1:2–20, Jer 2:4–13, Mic 6:1–8 or even Ps 50. Sanders cites H. B. Huffmon, G. E. Wright, J. Harvey, and W. Beyerlin as examples (*Deuteronomy 32*, 86 n. 86), to which one may also add Mayes (*Deuteronomy* [NCB; Grand Rapids: Eerdmans, 1979], 380–382.

The rîb pattern, however, cannot account for the forms in the Song's latter half, which is why Wright and Harvey argue the rîb stops after v. 29 and v. 25 respectively. Mayes, who calls the Song an "extended rîb," outlines the rîb proper as follows: introduction and summoning of witnesses (vv. 1–3); a preview of the legal case (vv. 4–6); the prosecution recalls the good actions of Yahweh (vv. 7–14); the indictment levied against Israel (vv. 15–18); guilty verdict and sentence to total destruction (vv. 19–25) (Mayes, *Deuteronomy*, 380).

39 Sanders, *Deuteronomy 32*, 84–96. S. A. Nigosian's assessment "most of the past efforts to determine the *Gattung* of the Song have been fruitless" is an overstatement.

40 Mark Biddle succinctly describes this complexity: "the Song presents a bewildering mixture of archaic speech forms and late prophetic and wisdom vocabulary, of first person divine speech and third person speech about God, of legal, wisdom, and liturgical genres, and [...] of theological perspectives from Israel's earliest period alongside ideas typical of the late monarchial period" (*Deuteronomy* [SHBC; Macon: Smyth & Helwys, 2003], 469).

41 As examples, Sanders cites J. R. Boston, S. Carillo Alday, and C. J. Labuschagne (*Deuteronomy 32*, 91–93). Recent exemplars included Nigosian, who deems the Song to be a "unique genre: a 'covenantal lawsuit' inverted to forge a salvation oracle and the whole presented in the didactic mode" (i.e. a *didactic poem*) ("Song of Moses," 8); see also Nelson, *Deuteronomy*, 369–370; Biddle, *Deuteronomy*, 469; Matthew Thiessen, "The Form and Function of the Song of Moses (Deuteronomy 32:1–43)," *JBL* 123 (2004): 401–424; Brian Britt, *Rewriting*

One possible solution would to be treat the Song diachronically, with the more ancient *rîb* (Deut 32:1–26*[42]) being foundational to the Song's compositional formation. Granted, the Song's highly polished nature[43] renders speculative the yield of any such endeavor; yet there are trace tensions which invite such an investigation. Foremost of these tensions is the sudden shift away from the *rîb*'s dire forecast at v. 27 toward that of a more hopeful future.[44] It is this tran-

---

Moses, 148–158; and more recently Matthew E. Gordley, *Teaching through Song in Antiquity* (WUNT2 302; Tübingen: Mohr-Siebeck, 2011), 168–172.

A word of caution here is in order when classifying texts in the Hebrew Bible as "didactic hymn." First, Gordley observes that didactic hymnody remains ill-defined due to the "lack of scholarly discussion of this particular category, with definitions of the scope, contents, and function of texts within this category" (*Teaching through Song*, 4). This dearth leads Gordley to limn his own definition: "Didactic hymns, prayers, and poetry are compositions which employ the stylistic and/or formal conventions of praise and prayer, but whose primary purpose was to convey a lesson, idea, or theological truth to a human audience" (*Teaching through Song*, 5). Secondly, the earliest exemplars of this genre derive from the Homeric and Hesiodic literature of the 6th-7th and 7th-8th centuries BCE respectively (*Teaching through Song*, 28 n. 1)—pivotal centuries to the formation of Deuteronomy 32. A genetic relationship between the two milieus ought to be established prior to critiquing the Song through this lens; that the same literary conventions could evolve independently would again require further study. In the absence of formal criteria, the classification of a text as *didactic hymn* or *poem* hinges on one's general impression of that text's didactic quality.

42 The current study demarks the *rîb* proper as concluding with v. 26 for the following reasons. First, 1QDeutᵇ's א]שבית and Smr's אשבית cast doubt on MT Deut 32:26b's אשביתה having been originally cohortative. Contra Duane L. Christensen, this emendation does carry significance as scholars frequently use the parallelism of this known verb to clarify the *hapax* of v. 26a's אפאיהם (*Deuteronomy 21:10–34:12* [WBC 6B; Nashville: Thomas Nelson, 2002], 802 n. 26.b.; for a discussion of v.26a's אפאיהם, see McCarthy, *BHQ Deuteronomy*, 147*). Second, without the cohortative, v. 26 becomes declarative: אמרתי אפאהם אשבית מאנוש זכרם ("I said, 'I will cut them to pieces; I will remove the memory of them from among men"). As such, v. 26 then sustains Yahweh's determination to annihilate his people, a resolve that does not clearly shift until v. 27 pivots the Song's focus to the fate of the unnamed enemy. Finally, presuming אפאיהם carries the sense of "piercing through" (cf. *HALOT*, 907, which links the root פאה to the Arabic *fw/y* "to split [by a blow of the sword]"), the image of the sword that bereaves in v. 25 finds culmination in v. 26a. Thus, v. 26 carries forward the tenure or imagery of vv. 21–25 (cf. p. 96 n. 44 below.)

43 For examples of synchronic analyses that demonstrate the prosodic artistry of the Song as a whole, see Sanders, *Deuteronomy 32*, 258–294; J. P. Fokkelman, *Major Poems of the Hebrew Bible: At the Interface of Hermeneutics and Structural Analysis: Volume 1: Ex. 15, Deut. 32, and Job 3* (SSN 37; Assen: Van Gorcum, 1998), 54–149; Christensen, *Deuteronomy 21:10–34:12*, 788–821.

44 Scholars widely recognize this shift, but typically locate it as taking place in v. 26; e.g. Norbert Lohfink, "Der Bundesschluß im Land Moab: Redaktionsgeschictliches zu Dt 28, 69–32, 47," *BZ* 6 (1962): 53; Mayes, *Deuteronomy*, 389; Eduard Nielsen, *Deuteronomium* (HAT I/6; Tü-

sition which prompts descriptions of the Song's *rîb* as being "broken," "extended," or "inverted."⁴⁵ Thus, for the moment, one can set aside vv. 27–43 as a secondary expansion to Deut 32:1–26*, one likely deriving from a late exilic to early postexilic era when Israel's fortunes would again reflect divine favor. One can do the same for v. 2, which implicitly forecasts this optimistic turn of events.⁴⁶

A second tension emerges in v. 20, where the *rîb* transitions to its final stage: the sentencing of the accused (vv. 20–26). It is here, in a first person divine speech in v. 20a, that Yahweh initially announces that he will take a passive stance toward Israel's punishment: "I will hide my face from them; I will see what their end *will be* (אסתיר פני מהם אראה מה אחריתם) ⁴⁷). As Nelson correctly observes, this posture suggests a "passive waiting for developments." ⁴⁸ Yet what immediately follows in vv. 21–26 is anything but *laissez-faire.* The tenor of Yahweh's speech suddenly and inexplicably darkens; in talionic fashion, Yahweh outlines an active agenda of exacting punishment, one which will culminate in Israel's obliteration. In short, this subtle shift advocates for a preexilic *termi-*

---

bingen: Mohr-Siebeck, 1995), 286; Nelson, *Deuteronomy*, 375. Nigosian, however, reads v. 26 as the end of the *rîb* ("The Song of Moses," 11). David M. Allen notes that the "precise terminus is disputed, but some form of shift in the argument occurs in 32:26–27" (*Deuteronomy and Exhortation in Hebrews: A Study of Narrative Re-presentation* [WUNT2 238; Tübingen: Mohr Siebeck, 2008], 32–33). That this study locates this transition in v. 27 as opposed to v. 26 (cf. p. 96 n. 42 above) in no way undermines the consensus that a diachronic shift has in fact taken place.

45 Initially, G. E. Wright describes the *rîb* as "broken," but later he also describes it as "expanded" ("Lawsuit of God," in Anderson and Harrelson, *Israel's Prophetic Heritage*, 40, 66). Mayes, on the other hand, takes a more neutral stance describing it only as having been expanded (*Deuteronomy*, 381). More recently, Nigosian described the *rîb* as "inverted" in that it was appropriated "to forge a salvation oracle" ("Song of Moses," 8).

46 Sanders' principle assessment is correct: "If one regards 32:25–43 as a secondary addition and assumes that the song's message is pessimistic, one has to drop at least verse 2" (*Deuteronomy 32*, 347). The similes of the poet's "teaching" (לקחי), a term that elsewhere only occurs in wisdom literature; cf., James R. Boston, "The Wisdom Influence upon the Song of Moses," *JBL* 87 [1968]: 201) being "like rain" (כמטר), "like dew" (כטל), "like droplets" (כשעירם), and "like showers" (כרביבים) presage the optimistic conclusion of the Song's final form. Sanders' rationale for v. 2's being fundamental to the Song, however, does not follow; that v. 2 contributes to the "beautiful structure" of the Song is as much evidence for a skillful redactor as it is for homogeneity (*Deuteronomy 32*, 347).

47 Like in v. 26 (cf. p. 96 n. 42 above), the MT has the cohortative in v. 20 (so אסתירה). Support for the shorter form comes from Smr, which according to McCarthy, "tends to use the lengthened impf. with ו as a clear expression of past time (at least thirty-eight times in Deuteronomy)" (*BHQ Deuteronomy*, 145*). Regrettably, 1QDeutᵇ is too fragmentary at this point (cf. frgs. 16–17) to determine if it attests the shorter form as it does for v. 26. It is clear, however, that the redactors who framed the Song (cf. Deut 31:17–18) did not read Deut 32:20 as cohortative.

48 Nelson, *Deuteronomy*, 373.

nus ad quem for v. 20, while vv. 21–26 appear to be *vaticinia ex eventu* of the catastrophes of the early exile.

Finally, a third tension (or rather *set* of tensions) that emerges is the abrupt shifts to second person address within the Song, specifically to the 2mp in vv. 6aα, 7aβ, 17bβ[49] and to the 2ms from 3ms in vv. 14b and 15aβ. Regarding the shifts to the 2mp, not only do these instances of the *Numeruswechsel* phenomenon all occur within the *rîb* portion of the Song, but they are all located in sections that 1) exhibit some degree of logical inconsistency regarding the identity of Israel's father(s) and that 2) introduce a protracted chronological perspective to the *rîb*.[50] Granted, these incongruities by themselves are insufficient to merit excising vv. 6aα, 7aβ, 17bβ from the *rîb*, but taken in construct with the

---

49 The second person plural also occurs in the imperatives of vv. 1aα (האזינו), 3b (הבו), 39aα (ראו), and 43aα (הרנינו), as well as in the pronominal suffixes of v. 38b (ויעזרכם ... עליכם). These instances, however, do not represent a shift from the second person singular. For vv. 1aα, 3b, and 43aα, one expects a plural imperative to address a plural addressee: in v. 1aα האזינו addresses השמים (cf. Isa 1:2); v. 3b presumes the same cosmic entities in v. 1; and הרנינו in v. 43aα addresses the plural גוים. The second person plurals in vv. 38b-39aα appear in first person divine speech directed at Israel—the last time Israel is spoken to directly in the Song—but Israel has not been the subject of second person speech (singular or plural!) since v. 18 and so does not constitute a sudden shift from the second singular.

50 For Deut 32:6–7, the second person address oscillates from plural to singular in both verses: in v. 6, the address shifts from plural in v. 6a (via תגמלו) to singular in v. 6b (via ך- suffixes); a similar pattern occurs in v. 7, which shifts from plural in v. 7aβ (via בינו) to singular in v. 7b (via שאל and ך- suffixes), but the singular imperative זכר in v. 7aα slightly complicates this pattern. Smr and G, however, have plural forms for all of v. 7a, which suggests that MT may have suffered the loss of a ו- from זכר on account of how many times ו occurs in v. 7a (7x!) (*contra* McCarthy, who judges Smr and G reflect harmonization of syntax; cf. *BHQ Deuteronomy*, 93, 140*). For Deut 32:17–18, the address shifts from the plural in v. 17bβ (via the כם- suffix on אבתיכם) to the singular in the verbs and suffixes in v. 18.

The logical consistency in both sections becomes strained around the lemme אב. The "father(s)" only appears in the Song in vv. 6–7 and 18, yet the precise referent is different in each instance. In v. 6, the poet asks הלוא־הוא אביך with Yahweh as the referent; yet the same form (אביך) appears in the imperative phrase שאל אביך ויגדך (v. 7bα), where the *current generation's fathers* is the referent, as their availability to "ask" about the about the "days of old" (ימות עולם) and the "years of generation *to* generation" (שנות דור־ודור) makes clear. In v. 17bβ, however, אבתיכם appears to refer to the *ancestral fathers* whose cultic infidelities lie in the distant past, but yet are somehow committed with newer gods who had only recently arrived (חדשים מקרב באו, v. 17bα)—gods with whom the ancestors were either "not acquainted" (לא שערום; reading √שער III, possibly related to the Arabic *šaʿara*, "know, be cognizant"; cf. *HALOT*, 353 and J. H. Tigay, *Deuteronomy* דברים [JPSTC; Philadelphia: Jewish Publication Society, 1996], 306) or "did not dread" (reading √שער I, *HALOT*, 353).

distribution of the second person across the Song,⁵¹ one may suspect the hand responsible for vv. 27–43 was also likely at work at these junctures where second plural unexpectedly occurs. Such may also be the case for the unexpected shifts to 2ms address in vv. 14b and 15aβ, both of which bear the trappings of interpolation.⁵²

Taken together, these tensions suggest the Song to be the product of three major stages: 1) the foundational *rîb* (vv. 1, 3–20*) was a preexilic composition that warned of Yahweh's impending judgment in open-ended fashion⁵³; the devastation of the exile, however, led to the Song undergoing 2) an early exilic expansion (vv. 1, 3–26*), the despair of which remains palpable both in vv. 21–26 and the frames that seat the Song (i.e., Deut 31:16–22 and 31:27–29⁵⁴); and only

---

51 The dominant second person profile of the *rîb*, where it occurs in reference to Israel, is singular (cf. vv. 6b, 7aα [although perhaps originally plural; see p. 98 n. 50 above], 14bβ, 15aβ, 18); while second person references to Israel in the Song's latter half are exclusively plural (cf. vv. 38b-39aα).

52 The following emendations to the MT appear likely and are reflected in Fig. 4.1 below: *Minuses* (–): v. 2, for reasons observed on p. 97 n. 46 above; v. 6a is not only in the second plural, but was likely an interpolation added to presage vv. 21bβ, 28–29; v. 7a, for reasons cited on p. 98 n. 50; v. 14b disrupts its immediate third person context with content that only serves to presage vv. 32–33; likewise, v. 15aβ is extremely disruptive to its immediate context, and though it has no lexical echo in the Song its conceptual reversal appears in v. 24a. *Additions* (+): וישבט...יאכל+ (v. 15aα by reconstruction) appears in Smr, G, 4QPhylⁿ, and T^NF. McCarthy suggests it was omitted through haplography, though the mechanism prompting such an ellipsis is not clearly represented (McCarthy, *BHQ Deuteronomy*, 94, 144). *Adjustments* (*): אלוהים for MT's ישראל (v. 8bβ) is attested at Qumran and in G^mss and is generally accepted by scholars (cf. p. 88 n. 11); MT's אבתיכם (v. 17b) is difficult to explain given the 2ms address surrounding its immediate context and hardly seems original; and lastly for a discussion on emending to אסתיר (v. 20a) for MT's cohortative אסתירה, see p. 97 n. 47 above. For a representation and translation this reconstruction, see Appendix A: Rhythm and Translation of the Ur-ריב of Deuteronomy 32.

53 While open-ended, this pre-exilic ending of the song—i.e., Deut 32:20—is by no means dependent on what follows. Other oracles, both positive and negative, conclude in similar fashion (e.g. Num 23:10; Jer 5:31). Moreover, the threat פני מהם אסתיר(ה) is anything but oblique. In several texts this phrase operates as a portent sign of divine wrath or as the explanation of personal anguish or national catastrophe: e.g. Gen 4:14; Isa 8:17–22; 54:8; Ezek 39:23–24, 29; Ps 13:2–3; 27:9; 30:8–10; 44:25–26; 88:15–19; 89:47; 104:29). Here, the initial frame seating the Song in Deut 31:16–22 is particularly salient: the people's idolatry (31:16; cf. 32:16–18) prompts Yahweh to turn his face away (31:17–18; cf. 32:20), sealing the people's unspecified fate (31:17ay, 21aα; cf. 32:20a), which in turn prompts the people to recognize that God is no longer in their midst (31:17b – הלא על כי־אין אלהי בקרבי מצאוני הרעות האלה; cf. the non-P M-Mt narrative etiology in Exod 17:7by). In short, while no doubt ominous, Deut 32:20 constitutes a fitting end to the Ur-ריב.

54 Space precludes a thorough development of the external evidences that also support this model for the Song's literary development. Suffice it say, the literary frames that seat the

at the portents of a) the fall of Babylon (making the nation in effect "לא־עם"; cf. Deut 32:21) and b) Israel's imminent return from exile did the Song undergo 3) its final major revision with the addition of vv. 2, 27–43, which transformed the Song from a *rîb* into a *didactic hymn* on Israel's salvation-history.

Additional evidence in support of this model emerges via a structural analysis of the *rîb*'s earliest form. Embedded in Deut 32:1, 3–20* is a concentric organization of lexemes, concepts, and modes of address that unfolds alongside and within the genre components that typify the *rîb* pattern (see Fig. 4.1 below). Textual emendations aside,[55] the clearest parallels to emerge are levels D ∥ D', E ∥ E', and F ∥ F' (vv. 6b-18). *Level D ∥ D'* (vv. 6b-7b ∥ 17b-18) is characterized by the second person address and directly confronts ancient Israel with the tes-

---

Song in its current position within Deuteronomy (especially Deut 31:16–22; 31:27–29 stands out as tertiary to my eye) only demonstrate knowledge of the Song's foundational *rîb*; e.g., the people going after foreign gods in 31:16 (אלהי נכר; cf. 32:12); Yahweh's decision to hide his face in 31:17, 18 (והסתרתי פני מבם ... ואנכי הסתר אסתער פני; cf. 32:20); the accusation of Israel having eaten, been sated, and grown fat in 31:20 (ואכל ושבע ודשן; cf. +32:15aα and MT 32:15aα); Israel's spurning (√נאץ) Yahweh in 31:20bβ finds parallel in Yahweh's spurning them (32:19)—the only two times in Deuteronomy where this verbal root occurs; the ominous threat of many troubles in 31:17, 21, 29 (cf. 32:20); the call to the heaven and earth as witness in 31:28 (ואעידה את־השמים ואת־הארץ [...]; cf. 32:20). See the studies of Norbert Lohfink, "Der Bundesschluß im Land Moab," 32–56, especially 52–53; Jon D. Levenson, "Who Inserted the Book of the Torah," *HTR* 68 (1975): 204–221; Sanders, *Deuteronomy 32*, 336–348; Nelson, *Deuteronomy*, 360.

Sanders, however, rejects the idea that the redactors responsible for the Song's introductions (31:16–22, 27–29) were in possession of an earlier form of the Song on account of the positive implications of 32:2. "It is hardly thinkable," argues Sanders, "that the redactors of the song's introductions in chapter 31 knew a version of the song which comprised at least 32:1 and 32:10–25 and probably also 32:5 but in which 32:2 would be lacking" (*Deuteronomy 32*, 347). It is for this reason that he is later forced to concluded that these redactors must also have known of the "more optimistic parts" of the Song, but chose "not to allude to 32:2 and 32:26–43" because of their work "took place under conditions of extreme hopelessness" (*Deuteronomy 32*, 348). This logic does not follow and merits reconsidering. Instead, it is more likely that these redactors inserted the Ur-ריב (Deut 32:1, 3–20*) because its unmitigated warning resonated with their dire circumstance. Also, since the Song's introductory frames presage Deut 32:21–26 in general terms, rather than in explicit lexical terms, it is possible that these same redactors are also responsible for the Song's early exilic expansion (i.e. Deut 32:21–26*) which shifts Yahweh's punitive role from being passive (32:20) to active with the many troubles made explicit in 32:21–26.

55 Recognition of the concentric structure is not dependent on the success of the proposed textual emendations, as most of the parallel components emerge despite them. Nevertheless, at times these changes do strengthen the correspondence of certain levels; e.g. if MT's vv. 14b and 15aβ are interpolations (cf. p. 99 n. 52 above), the distribution of second person address becomes delimited to level D ∥ D' (vv. 6–7 ∥ 17–18).

timony and failures of her fathers (אבתיך). Level E ‖ E' (vv. 8–9 ‖ 15–17a) exhibits a nexus of divine beings and their corresponding nations, with Level E exploring the mythic grounds for proper relationships between these deities and their nations, and conversely Level E' revealing Jacob/Jeshurun's failure on this front. Finally Level F ‖ F' (vv. 10–11 ‖ 13–14) showcases Yahweh's great care for his inheritance, with vv. 10–11 moving spatially from the desert wilds up to the heights of soaring eagles, while vv. 13–14 reverses the direction of that spatial movement from the earth's mythic heights down to the lush valleys below. The use of animals as tropes—i.e. the simile of Yahweh as an eagle (כנשר; v. 11), and the implicit metaphor of a "heifer" for Israel (vv. 13–15a)[56]—also characterizes this level. Together, these levels frame the central tenet underlying the entire rîb (Level G): it was Yahweh alone, and no other god, who guided Jacob in the wilderness (v. 12).

The presence of these overt parallels prompts investigation into whether this organization in any way extends outward from vv. 6b-18, and indeed it does in levels A ‖ A', B ‖ B', and C ‖ C' (vv. 1+3 ‖ 19–20), though admittedly the closing elements of these levels do not exhibit the same level of concentric rigidity as vv. 6–18. The rejection motif of Level C ‖ C' does resume in v. 19 immediately after component D' (vv. 17b-18), but the shift to the first person divine address in v. 20a is reminiscent of poet's first person address Level A (v. 1).[57] Afterwards, the parallelism returns to the rejection motif in v. 20b via the portrayal of Israel as a perverse generation (דור) (C') in whom there is no faithfulness (לא אמן), which is in contradistinction to the characterization of Yahweh as "a God of faithfulness" (אל אמונה) in v. 4bα (Level B ‖ B'). In short, only component A' is out of sequence with this concentric organization—a shift that rhetorically reveals Yahweh as not only the plaintiff within the rîb's proceedings, but also judge and jury in the climatic verdict and sentencing of Israel, the accused.

In sum, while the rîb no doubt possesses a level of chronological narrative progression, the structure of its major components evinces a concentric pattern

---

[56] Admittedly, the certainty of this metaphor does not arise until v. 15a's וישמן ישרון ויבעט, but once recognized, it possible to read the metaphor as beginning in v. 13a where it serves to clarify the phrase ירכבהו על במותי ארץ. Typically, the verb √רכב connotes the action of mounting or riding upon an animal or chariot. In what way that Yahweh would "ride" or "mount" Israel remains obscure until v. 15a portrays Jeshurun growing fat and kicking (√בעט) like an unspecified animal. A similar metaphor occurs in Hos 10:11, where Yahweh harnesses (√רכב) the heifer Ephraim to plow.

[57] A further parallel may be the prophet's invocation for earth to hear the words of his mouth (אמרי פי). Since the prophet serves as Yahweh's herald, his words are the words of Yahweh. Thus, the otherwise formulaic ויאמר introducing Yahweh's speech in v. 20a (level A') is parallel to אמרי פי in v. 1aβ (level A).

ריב-Components	Embedded Concentric Organization of Reconstructed Ur - ריב				Emendations MT –/+/*	Parallel Components
I. Invocation (vv. 1+3)	A.	1	האזינו השמים ואדברה	ותשמע הארץ אמרי פי	{– v. 2	A. – *1st person address* – אמרי (v.1aβ)
		3	כי שם יהוה אקרא	הבו גדל לאלהינו		
II. Intro to Plaintiff (v.4)	B.	4	הצור תמים פעלו	כי כל דרכיו משפט		B. – [Character of deity] – אל אמונה (v.4bα)
			אל אמונה ואין עול	צדיק וישר הוא		
III. Arraignment (vv. 5-6)	C.	5	שחת לו לא בניו מומם	דור עקש ופתלתל		C. – [Rejection motif] – לא בניו (v. 5aβ) – [Perverse] דור (v. 5b)
	D.	6b	הלוא הוא אביך קנך	הוא עשך ויכננך	{–v. 6a	D. – *2nd person address* – אביך (vv. 6bα, 7bα)
		7b	שאל אביך ויגדך	זקניך ויאמרו לך	{– v. 7a	
IV. Grounds of Accusation (vv. 7-14)	E.	8	בהנהל עליון גוים	בהפרידו בני אדם		E. – [Proper divine-nation relationships] – יעקב (v. 9b)
			יצב גבלת עמים	למספר בני אלוהים	{*אלוהים: MT has ישראל	
		9	כי חלק יהוה עמו	יעקב חבל נחלתו		
	F.	10	ימצאהו בארץ מדבר	ובתהו ילל ישמן		F. – [Deity's providential care] – [Spatial motion: ארץ (v. 10aα) ↑ sky] – [Animal simile: כנשר]
			יסבבנהו יבוננהו	יצרנהו כאישון עינו		
		11	כנשר יעיר קנו על גוזליו ירחק	יפרש כנפיו יקחהו ישאהו על אברתו		
	G.	12	יהוה בדד ינחנו	ואין עמו אל נכר		G. – [Central thesis: יהוה בדד]
	F.'	13	ירכבהו על במותי ארץ	ויאכלהו תנובת שדי	{*ויאכלהו: MT has ויאכל	F.' – [Deity's providential care] – [Spatial motion: שדי (v. 13a) ↓ במותי ארץ] – [Animal metaphor: heifer (cf. Hos 10:11)]
			וינקהו דבש מסלע	ושמן מחלמיש צור		
		14	חמאת בקר וחלב צאן	עם חלב כרים ואילים		
			בני בשן ועתודים	עם חלב כליות חטה	{– v.14b	
V. Indictment (vv. 15-18)	E.'	15	יאכל יעקב וישבע	וישמן ישרון ויבעט	{+יאכל...וישבע	E.' – [Improper divine-nation relationship] – יעקב (+v. 15aα) & ישרון (v. 15aβ)
			ויטש אלוה עשהו	ונבל צור ישעתו	{– v. 15aβ	
		16	יקנאהו בזרים	בתועבת יכעיסהו		
		17a	זבחו לשדים לא אלה	אלהים לא ידעום		
	D.'	17b	חדשים מקרב באו	לא שערום אבתיך	{*אבתיך: MT has אבתיכם	D.' – *2nd person address* – *אביך (v. 17bβ)
		18	צור ילדך תשי	ותשכח אל מחללך		
VI. Verdict & Sentencing (vv. 19-20)	C.'	19	וירא יהוה וינאץ	מכעס בניו ובנתיו		C.' – [Rejection motif]
	A.'	20a	ויאמר אסתיר פני מהם	אראה מה אחריתם	{*אסתיר: MT has אסתירה	A.' – *1st person address* – ויאמר (v. 20aα)
	C.' + B.'	20b	כי דור תהפכת המה	בנים לא אמן בם		C.' – [Perverse] דור (v. 20bα) B.' – לא אמן בם (v. 20bβ)

Fig. 4.1: The Concentric Organization of Deut 32:1, 3–20

that is especially evident in vv. 6–18. This organization further cautions against artificially restricting the reminiscences within Deut 32:13 to being only about the Promised Land. The spatial movement of Level F ‖ F' (vv. 10–11 ‖ 13–14) portrays Yahweh's faithful and providential care for Israel across cosmological boundaries: from the desert wilds to the heights where eagles soar, from the mythic high places of the earth to the verdant valleys below. In short, the focus is on Yahweh's actions, not the specific geographical locations where certain historical events took place.[58] It is within these nearly boundless parameters that one can say Deut 32:13b preserves a reminiscence of the M-Mt.

4.2.4 Tradition-historical Analysis of Deut 32:13b

The above literary analysis posits the reminiscence of the M-Mt in Deut 32:13b is a relic of a preexilic prophetic *rîb* that was redacted into the growing book of Deuteronomy during the early exilic period. As such, the relative chronology of Deut 32:13b is at least cotemporaneous with the M-Mt reminiscence preserved in Deut 8:15 (*Dt*). This chronology comports well when one compares the few tradition-historical components preserved in Deut 32:13b with those preserved in Deut 8:15 (cf. §3.3.3. above). Like Deut 8:15, the M-Mt reminiscence in Deut 32:13b also records the *source of issuance* as "from the flinty rock," though the expression differs slightly (cf צור מחלמיש in 32:13bβ with מצור החלמיש in 8:15).[59] Additional similarities include the reticence to anchor the M-Mt to a specific geographic *location*, as well as there being no *canonical awareness* of either of the two M-Mt narrative accounts.

The immediate difference between Deut 32:13b and Deut 8:15 (as well as other M-Mt reminiscences) is the *substance of issuance:* namely honey (דבש) and oil (שמן). The Baal Cycle, however, shows that the issuance of honey and oil from a deity could serve as a metaphor for the divine provision of potable

---

[58] Von Rad recognized as much when he concluded that in this section "ergeht sich das Lied in eindrucksvollen Vergleichen [i.e., of Yahweh's providential care for Israel], doch ohne damit auf irgendeine konkretere geschichtliche Situation Bezug zu nehmen" (*Das fünfte Buch Mose: Deuteronomium* [ATD 8; Göttingen: Vandenhoeck & Ruprecht, 1964], 141).

[59] The only other biblical text that employs the lemma חלמיש in conjunction with the M-Mt is Ps 114:8. Here, however, חלמיש is an independent nominative in a parallel relationship to צור, not a *nomen regens* or *nomen rectum* in construct with צור as is the case in Deut 32:13b and 8:15 respectively. Like Ps 114:8, Deut 32:13b provides a nominative parallel to צור חלמיש, but the parallel is the word סלע, not צור. Deuteronomy 8:15 does not have a nominative parallel for צור החלמיש.

water (cf. pp. 87–88 above). The variance in the substance of issuance may therefore be superficial.

The only actual difference between these two reminiscences is that Deut 32:13b does not interpret Yahweh as testing Israel through his divine provisions, while Deut 8:15 does. Still, at least one aspect of *agency* is comparable between the two texts: neither one recalls this tradition as a moment of national failure. For Deut 8:15 and its broader literary context, Israel's failure results from forgetting Yahweh's deeds and commands once they enter the land; there is no failure in the wilderness. Likewise, in Deut 32:13b-18, it is the culmination of Yahweh's divine provisions that surfeits Jacob/Jeshurun and leads *non sequitur* to their kicking (√בעט) in rebellion against Yahweh. There is no clear indication of Israel having failed prior to or during their suckling at the rock.

4.3 Deuteronomy 32:51

4.3.1 Text Criticism of Deut 32:51

^{Deut 32:51}על אשר מעלתם בי בתוך בני ישראל במי־מריבת קדש מדבר־צן על אשר
לא־קדשתם אותי בתוך בני ישראל:

Unlike the Song itself, the narrative materials that form the closing frame around the Song (Deut 32:44–47, 48–52) evince relative stability among the ancient witnesses that are extant. Such is especially the case with Deut 32:51, where the explanation for Moses and Aaron's exclusion from the Promised Land recurs as part of what is now a resumptive repetition of Num 27:12–14 (cf. §4.3.2. below). The only significant variant pertains to MT's בי, "with/against me" in MT Deut 32:51aα. While the Smr, V, and S all follow MT, the G and the targumim attempt to mitigate the accusation levied against Moses. Instead of accusing Moses and Aaron of being unfaithful to Yahweh (so MT), the LXX softens the tone with ἠπειθήσατε τῷ ῥήματί ("you disobeyed/disbelieved my word").[60] Similarly, T^{ONJF} all utilize the *Memra* (מימר)—the "Word" of Yahweh, whether hypo-

---

[60] McCarthy attributes the change to exegesis (*BHQ Deuteronomy*, 98, 154*). Although it is possible that this change represents a harmonization with MT Num 27:14's מריתם פי, which G renders similarly with παρέβητε τὸ ῥῆμά; α' Deut 32:51 employs παρέβητε instead of ἠπειθήσατε perhaps for the same reason (cf. Wevers, ed., *Septuaginta Deuteronomium*, 361). Regardless, since in MT Num 27:14 Moses rebels (√מרה instead of √מעל) against Yahweh's word (פ; metonymy) rather than Yahweh himself, attributing the changes in G's Deut 32:51 to exegesis may be overstating the translator's role at this point.

statized or not⁶¹—to mitigate Moses' offence as an act of disobedience against Yahweh's *word* rather than overt rebellion against the deity himself.⁶² Thus, the variance pertains to the nature of Moses' failure, not the tradition complex to which it is tied.

4.3.2 Literary Analysis of Deut 32:48–52

Two diachronic questions dominate discussions regarding the pericope in which Deut 32:51 lies: 1) What is the direction of influence between Deut 32:48–52 and Num 27:12–14? and 2) To what layer of narrative framing material does Deut 32:48–52 belong? Each question in turn requires close consideration, as they are crucial for nuancing the tradition-historical framework by which the M-Mt developed. To preview, this study concludes that Deut 32:48–52 is most likely composite. Initially, a post-P Hexateuchal redactor (HexRed) constructed Deut 32:48–50, 52 with some degree of an awareness of the P* materials that now reside in Num 20:1–13*; 22–29*; and 27:12–23*, as well as the Dtr's exterior prologue in Deuteronomy and original conclusion in chs. 1–3, and 34 respectively. Secondarily, a post-Pentateuch redactor (post-PentRed) inserted Deut 32:51, redirecting the rationale for why Moses was not permitted to enter the land.

4.3.2.1 What is Deut 32:48–52's Relative Diachronic Relationship to Num 27:12–14? There is no doubt that Deut 32:48–52 is somehow related to Num 27:12–14

---

61 The status of the *Memra* as an intermediate hypostasis within the targumic literature has long been debated; for a recent discussion, see Daniel Boyarin, "The Gospel of the Memra: Jewish Binitarianism and the Prologue of John," *HTR* 94 [2001]: 252–261, who concludes the *Memra* to be a divine mediator akin to Wisdom and the Logos. Raymond E. Brown, whom Boyarin cites as representing the scholarly consensus on the nature of the *Memra*, insists that in T⁰ the *Memra* "is not a personification, but the use of *Memra* serves as a buffer for divine transcendence" (*Gospel According to John (i-xii): Introduction, Translation, and Notes* [AB 29; New York: Doubleday, 1966], 524). Boyarin, however, correctly critiques the incongruity inherent in this stance: "if the *Memra* is just a name that simply enables avoiding asserting that God himself has created, appeared, supported, saved, and thus preserves his absolute transcendence, then who, after all *did* the actual creating, appearing, supporting, saving? Either God himself, in which case, one has hardly 'protected' him from contact with the material world, or there is some other divine entity, in which case, the *Memra* is not just a name" ("The Gospel of the Memra," 255).
62 T⁰ has במימרי דסריבתון / דשקרון ("because you acted falsely / rebelled against my *Memra*); Tᴺ has סרבתון בשם ממרי ("you rebelled against the name of my *Memra*"); Tʲ has דשקרתון במימרי ("because you acted falsely against my *Memra*"); Tᶠ has סרבתון בשם מימרי ("you rebelled against the name of my *Memra*").

(see Fig. 4.2 below), but as Preuss observes "Ihr Verhältnis zu Num 27, 12–14 ist nicht leicht zu bestimmen."[63] In the past, however, classic historical-critical scholarship typically assigned the whole of Deut 32:48–52 to P with confidence on account of this text's strong resemblance to Num 27:12–14, which was also attributed to P.[64] Recent studies have significantly complicated this conclusion, however. Not only is Deut 32:48–52 related to Num 27:12–14, but it is also fundamentally connected to Deut 34:1–9*, a text which appears to be related in some way to Num 27:15–23 and yet demonstrates either multiple layers or at least multiple hands in collaborative effort.

Here, a summary and critique by David M. Carr regarding this recent scholarship is both illustrative and cautionary.[65] "An increasing number of scholars," he demurs, argue that Deut 34:1*, 7–9 cannot be "the original end of P" on account that vv. 7 and 9 depend on texts that are already later than P^G: to begin, v. 7's calculation of Moses' lifespan depends on Gen 6:3 and combines "Moses age at the exodus (Exod 7:7; P) and the D figure of 40 years in the wilderness" (so Nihan, Schmid); and v. 9's report of Joshua's appointment depends on Num 27:15–23; yet Num 27:15–23 is also later than P^G because 1) it builds on Num 27:12–14 which appears to depend on Deut 32:48–52 (so Achenbach, see pp. 111–112 above), 2) it contains phrases elsewhere seen only in texts that are also deemed to be late[66] (so Frevel, Nihan); and 3) both it and Num 20:22–29

---

[63] Horst D. Preuss, *Deuteronomium* (EdF 164; Darmstadt: Wissenschaftliche Buchgesellschaft, 1982), 169.

[64] John E. Harvey summarizes this logic well: "The reigning assumption is 'P is later than D; it therefore follows that where P language exists in D there exists a redaction by P'[... and] represents P's attempt to round off the Pentateuch" [John E. Harvey, *Retelling the Torah: The Deuteronomistic Historian's Use of Tetrateuchal Narratives* (JSOTSup 403; London-New York: T & T Clark, 2004], 23). Lothar Perlitt cites this consensus as far back as Bernard Stade in the nineteenth century ("Priesterschrift im Deuteronomium," *ZAW* 100 [1988]: 65), but early to mid-twentieth century examples include Otto Eissfeldt, von Rad (who thinks Deut 32:48–52 is a variant P text), and Martin Noth (cf. Eissfeldt, *The Old Testament: An Introduction including the Apocrypha and Pseudepigrapha, and also the works of similar type from Qumran* [trans. P. R. Ackroyd; 3d; Tübingen: Mohr, 1934; repr., New York: Harper & Row, 1965], 189; Rad, *Deuter-onomium*, 144; Noth, *Überlieferungsgeschichtliche Studien. I. Die sammelnden und bearbeitenden Geschichtswerke im Alten Testament* [Schriften der Königsberger Gelehrten Gesellschaft. Geisteswissenschaftliche Klasse 18; Halle: M. Niemeyer, 1943], 190–206).

[65] David M. Carr, *The Formation of the Hebrew Bible: A New Reconstruction* (New York: Oxford University Press, 2011), 138.

[66] Carr goes on, "even if one held with the alternative position that Deut 32:48–52 is a late resumptive repetition of Num 27:12–14 linking Deuteronomy with a narrative strand in Numbers, several authors have still argued for the late character of Num 27:15–23 because it features phrases otherwise seen only in a series of other texts that are held (by those authors) to

(the report of Aaron's death) depend on Num 20:1–13 (Moses and Aaron's failure at Kadesh); yet Num 20:1–13 is also considered later than P^G because of v. 13's use of ויקדש בם "presupposes a post P H in Lev 22:32" and 20:12's use of "the H-stem of אמן, which is a leitmotif of Exodus 4" (so Römer and Brettler, Nihan), which in turn depends on P^G's "depiction on the first two plague signs" (so Gertz).[67]

Carr remains suspicious of such scholarship, which he describes as using "cumulative claims of textual dependence,"[68] for three reasons. First, it presumes that P's original conclusion must have been retained, when in fact such preservation is "not typical of documented cases of such large-scale appropriation and/or conflation of documents."[69] Second, it relies too heavily on isolated lexical or conceptual similarities that could be the products of processes other than direct literary dependence.[70] Finally, Carr observes that as "the chain of posited textual dependencies grows, the overall argument grows progressively weaker."[71] In the end, Carr himself does not attempt to resolve this diachronic

---

be late, a series that includes Num 16:22 (אלהי הרוחות לכול הבשר, 'gods of the spirits and of all flesh'); Num 31:16 and Josh 22:16–17 (עדה יהוה), and 1 Kgs 22:27 (כצאן אשר אין־להם רעה; Num 27:17)" (*Formation of the Hebrew Bible*, 138–139).

67 Carr cites Christophe Nihan, *Priestly Torah to Pentateuch: A Study in the Composition of the Book of Leviticus* (FAT2 25; Tübingen: Mohr Siebeck, 2007), 22–25; Konrad Schmid, "The Late Persian Formation of the Torah: Observations on Deuteronomy 34," in *Judah and the Judeans in the Fourth Century B.C.E.* (ed. Oded. Lipschits, Gary Knoppers, and Rainer Albertz; Winona Lake: Eisenbrauns, 2007), 248–249; Reinhard Achenbach, *Die Vollendung der Tora: Studien zur Redaktionsgeschichte des Numeribuches im Kontext von Hexateuch und Pentateuch* (BZAR 3; Wiesbaden: Harrassowitz Verlag, 2003), 557–567; Christian Frevel, *Mit Blick auf das Land die Schöpfungerinnern: zum Ende der Priestergrundschrift* (HbS 23; Freiburg: Herder, 2000), 281; Thomas Römer and Marc Z. Brettler, "Deuteronomy 34 and the Case for a Persian Hexateuch," *JBL* 119 (2000), 407; and Jan Christian Gertz, *Tradition und Redaktion in der Exoduserzählung: Untersuchungen zur Endredaktion des Pentateuch* (FRLANT 186; Göttingen: Vandenhoeck & Ruprecht, 2000), 314.
68 Carr, *Formation of the Hebrew Bible*, 138. One should note that Carr is not denying the value of diachronic studies; instead, he is merely advocating that we ground future studies on "documented cases of transmission history" (*Formation of the Hebrew Bible*, 3–9).
69 Carr, *Formation of the Hebrew Bible*, 139.
70 Carr, *Formation of the Hebrew Bible*, 139.
71 Carr, *Formation of the Hebrew Bible*, 139. By way of example, Carr argues that even if there was a 70% chance for each of the dependencies related to Deut 34:1, 7–9 being accurate individually, there is only a 24% chance that the cumulative string of literary dependencies is accurate: assuming a 70%^{A} chance that Deut 34:9 depends on Num 27:15–23; then a 70%^{B} chance that Num 27:15–23 depends on Num 20:22–29; then a 70%^{C} chance that Num 20:22–29 depends on Num 20:1–13; and finally, a 70%^{D} chance that Num 20:1–13 depends on Exod 4:1–9, 27–31 (70%^{A} × 70%^{B} = 49%; 49% × 70%^{C} = 34.3%; 34.3% × 70%^{D} = 24%).

quandary[72]; nevertheless, his summary of the complexities involved affords a voice of cautious modesty to anyone attempting to do so. In this vein, the following attends to the relative chronology for the M-Mt texts involved—i.e., Num 20:1–13*; 27:12–14; and Deut 32:38–52.* A treatment of Deut 32:48–52's relationship to Deut 34:1–9 will then follow (§4.3.2.2).

Assuming some degree of dependency, only three configurations emerge as likely: either 1) all the relevant texts in Numbers depend on Deut 32:48–52*; or 2) Num 27:12–14 depends on Deut 32:48–52*, which is in turn dependent on Num 20:1–13*; or finally 3) Deut 32:48–52* depends on the Numbers texts. Christophe Nihan, against whom Carr appears to direct tacitly much of his critique, is a key proponent of the first configuration. Nihan argues for multiple post-P redactions to the Torah: Deut 32:48–52 is post-P, but it is *earlier* than the Holiness Code (H, which is also post-P) because it does not display H's distinctive style; Numbers 20 and 27, however, belong to a post-P layer which is *later* than H, one that combines Priestly and Deuteronomistic traditions (so Deut 32:48–52 → Numbers' texts).[73] This configuration, however, does not take account of the profile of the non-aligned portions of Deut 32:48–52 (see Fig. 4.2 below). Not only are there several more non-aligned portions in Deut 32:48–52 than in Num 27:12–

While illustrative of his point, Carr's statistical argument is dubious from the start: all the passages from Numbers (20:1–13, 22–29; 27:15–23) are priestly oriented (P*) and evince their own internal tensions which likely attest to a process of *Fortschreibung* similar to that evident within Deuteronomy. One cannot simply treat each text as a separate sequential layer; Num 20:22–29 and 27:12–14 presume the expansion of Num 20:12 (see §7.3.1 below), and to a more limited extent so does Num 27:15–23 (Joshua's ordination). In short, there may not be as many major redactional layers intrinsic to this argument as Carr represents.

72 To be fair, Carr only cites this debate for the purpose of legitimizing his critique of studies that advocate for more than two or three major redactional stages of any given text (*Formation of the Hebrew Bible*, 144–145); it is not within the scope of his study to limn the relative chronological relationship of the texts under consideration.

73 Christophe Nihan, *Priestly Torah to* Pentateuch, 570–572. Nihan ascribes to multiple post-P redactions to the Torah, but occasionally fails to specify to which one he is referring. The sigla is mine, not Nihan's, and represents the relative chronology that at times Nihan leaves for deduction. In this instance, Nihan clearly locates the "theocratic revision" (post-P^3; ca. 350 BCE) as younger than H (post-P^2), but he only implies the diachrony between Deuteronomy and the H. Specifically, he asserts that "there are many post-P additions in Deuteronomy, but none of them exemplifies the distinctive style of HS. Either HS scribes were not authorized to intervene editorially on this scroll or, more simply, they were just not interested in it" (*Priestly Torah to Pentateuch*, 570). In short, Nihan presumes H to be younger than the post-P additions to Deuteronomy (post-P^1). This reconstruction, however, fails to account for the evidence of Deut 32:48–52's literary dependence on Numbers 20. For a detailed engagement with Nihan's argument that Num 20:1–13 is a homogenous composition, see pp. 207–209 below.

14,⁷⁴ but these non-alignments—especially those in vv. 48–51—reflect a lexical profile that is neither wholly Dtr, nor wholly P, but a combination of both. To begin, several components in Deut 32:48–52 stand in sharp relief against the lexicality evinced in the rest of Deuteronomy: בעצם היום הזה (v. 48), כנען (v. 49bα), אחזה (v. 49b), and הר ההר (v. 50b) elsewhere do not occur in Deuteronomy and operate primarily within a priestly semantic domain.⁷⁵ On the other hand, the non-aligned phrase בארץ מואב in Deut 32:49 is well within the Dtr semantic domain (cf. Deut 1:5; 28:69; 32:49; 34:5, 6).⁷⁶ In other words, the post-P redactor re-

---

74 The only clear plus to Num 27:12–14 is the phrase גם־אתה in v. 13aγ. The only other possible plus is the phrase הם מי־מריבת קדש מדבר־צן in. v. 14b, which since the time of Noth has often been considered glossic (cf. Martin Noth, *Das vierte Buch Mose: Numeri* [ATD 7; Göttingen: Vandenhoeck & Ruprecht, 1966], 185; for recent examples, see Schmidt, *Studien zur Priesterschrift*, 215; Peter Weimar, *Studien zur Priesterschrift* [FAT 56; Tübingen: Mohr Siebeck, 2008], 338). Since both Num 20:14b and Deut 32:51 standout of their immediate context, and they evince precise verbal correspondence (aside from the ב preposition), it is likely that both texts represent post-P supplements by late post-Pentateuchal Redactors (post-PentRed). This study attributes the whole of Num 27:14 to these hands (cf. §7.3.1 below).
75 The phrase עצם היום הזה occurs 18 times across the Hebrew Bible: 14 times with the ב preposition (Gen 7:13; 17:23, 26; Exod 12:17, 41, 51; Lev 23:21, 28, 29, 30; Deut 32:48; Jos 5:11; Ezek 24:2; 40:1); three times with עד instead of ב (Lev 23:14; Jos 10:27; Ezek 24:2); and once with את (Ezek 42:2). Perlitt too quickly dismisses the implications of this distribution, when he asserts "so ist klar, daß die Phrase von exilischer Zeit ab in verschiedenen Bereichen gebraucht wurde, also gewissermaßen zeitgenössisch war, jedenfalls kein P-Privileg" ("Priesterschrift," 73). William H. C. Propp assigns all of these Pentateuchal texts (save Deut 32:48) to P ("The Priestly Source Recovered Intact," *VT* 46 [1996]: 477), while Ezekiel's ties to the priestly sphere and use of its language are well-known (cf. Menahem Haran, "Ezekiel, P, and the Priestly School," *VT* 58 [2008]: 211–218; although without accepting Menahem's assertion that P is "an authentic expression" of the priestly school, while Ezekiel is but an "epigonic outgrowth" or "loose extension" of it). In short, the only texts that undermine this phrase being from a priestly semantic domain is Jos 5:11 and 10:27. Perlitt is correct, however, regarding the value of כנען, which is evenly distributed across P* and non-P materials within the Pentateuch. The lemme אחזה, on the other hand, only rarely appears in non-P (only Gen 36:43; 47:11; 50:13, but 36 times in P-oriented materials [P*]). Finally, aside from Deut 32:50b, הר ההר is the exclusive property of P* (Num 20:22, 23, 25, 27; 21:4; 33:37, 38, 39, 41; 34:7, 8; Deut 32:50), and its appearance in Deut 32:50b displays a preference for the P-tradition regarding the place of Aaron's death over against Deut 10:6's מוסרה, which in the itinerary of Numbers 33 is located seven stations before הר ההר (cf. Num 33:31, 37; Eryl W. Davies, *Numbers* [NCB; Grand Rapids: Eerdmans, 1995], 211).
76 Contrary to Mayes, while the phrase בארץ מואב in Deut 34:4 may be "superfluous" syntactically to שמה, it is not likely that it was inserted "by someone expressly noting that Moses did not die in Canaan" (*Deuteronomy*, 413). Instead, this phrase is the preferred expression of the Dtr that only occurs in the exterior macro-redactional frames of the book of Deuteronomy (Deut 1:5; 28:69 [29:1]; 32:49; 34:5, 6). By contrast, the construct phrase ערבת מואב predominantly

sponsible for Deut 32:48–52* utilized both Dtr and P language. This characteristic also explains the toponym הר־נבו (v. 49aβ) and the phrase על־פני ירחו (v. 49aγ), which elsewhere appear in Deuteronomy only in Deut 34:1—a text which, along with Deut 34:7–9*, also evinces editorial activity informed by both Dtr and priestly oriented (P*)[77] traditions (cf. §4.3.2.2 below). Together, these non-aligned portions of Deut 32:48–52 are characteristic of a redactor who is interested in merging Dtr and P* materials.

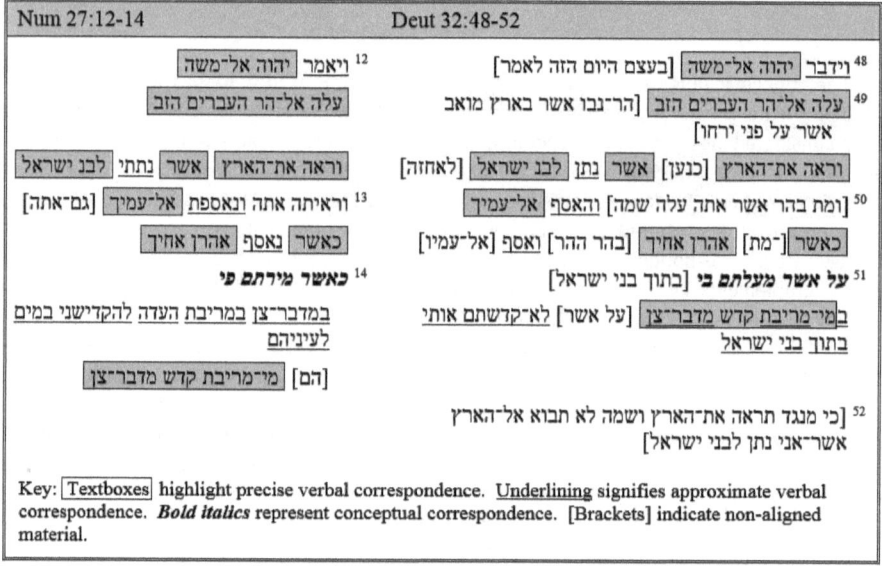

Fig. 4.2: Alignment and Non-alignment of Num 27:12–14 and Deut 32:48–52

This profile is the same one that Nihan sees in Numbers 20 and 27, which at best suggests these texts are cotemporaneous. Such, however, is most likely not the case for either of these M-Mt texts. Had Deut 32:48–52 as a whole inspired

---

occurs (that is, outside of Deut 34:1, 8) only in P* materials (Num 22:1; 26:3, 63; 31:12; 33:48, 49, 50; 35:1; 36:13; but also Josh 13:22).

77 The designation "P*" does not refer to P^G (the priestly *Grundschrift*), the exact closing parameters of which are increasingly being contested; e.g., Otto argues for P^G ending as early as Exodus 29; Pola, M. Bauks, Kratz posit Exodus 40; Zenger suggests Leviticus 9; Köckert and Nihan see Leviticus 16 as the conclusion of P^G; and L. Schmidt, Frevel, and H.-C. Schmitt argue for P^G ending in Deuteronomy 34 (cf. Nihan, *Priestly Torah to Pentateuch*, 23 n. 14, 31). Instead, P* denotes a lexical profile that is "priestly oriented," or typical of materials commonly understood to be distinctive of P* strata, which includes the Holiness Code, P^G, and other P supplements.

Num 20:1–13, one would expect the etiology of מי־מריבת קדש in v. 51 to appear in Num 20:13 in place of מי מריבה; however, it does not. Instead, it is more likely that the phrase מי־מריבת קדש reflects an awareness of the station קדש in Num 20:1 and the etiology מי מריבה in Num 20:13. Thus, it is more likely that Num 20:1–13 is foundational to Deut 32:51 (and Num 27:14) than the other way around. Further, it is difficult to explain the reductions in Num 27:12–14 at the hands of a post-P redactor (regardless of which one), especially since the non-aligned portions of Deut 32:48–51 predominantly reflect P* language and traditions.

A second theoretical sequence scholars have posited is that the direction of dependency flows from Num 20:1–13* to Deut 32:48–52, and from Deut 32:48–52 to Num 20:22–29 and 27:12–24, 15–23. Reinhard Achenbach advocates for this configuration in his study on the formation of the book of Numbers and the role that its redactors played in the finalization of the Pentateuch.[78] Though he initially attributes both Num 20:1–13* (minus v. 12b) and Deut 32:48–52 to the Pentateuch redactor (PentRed), Achenbach later clarifies that Deut 32:48–52 was triggered (*ausgelöst*) and justified (*begründet*) "durch die Legende von Num 20, 1–13."[79] As for Num 27:12–14, which Achenbach assigns to his *theocratic revision* (ThB), he believes it is an abridged variant of Deut 32:48–52 (so Num 20:1–13* → Deut 32:48–52 → Num 27:12–14).[80]

Achenbach dismisses the commonly held position that Deut 32:48–52 is dependent on Num 27:12–14 for a couple of reasons. He first balks at the thesis as

---

[78] Only a brief summary of Achenbach's redactional findings is possible here. Achenbach argues that the Pentateuch is a product of two comprehensive redactions and a substantial revision of the book of Numbers: 1) a Hexateuch redactor (HexRed) joined the exilic DtrL (Noth's *deuteronomistische Landnahmeerzählung*, which had earlier joined Deuteronomy and Joshua) with a nascent Tetrateuch in the early postexilic period, and held out hope for a future prophet who would be like Moses (Deut 18:15); 2) a Pentateuch redactor (PentRed) during the time of Nehemiah then separated Deuteronomy from Joshua, inserted legal codes, and elevated Moses and the Torah to canonical status; and finally 3) a theocratic reviser (*theokratische Bearbeiter*) during the first half of the 4th century added Numbers chs. 1–10, 26–36 and revised chs. 11–25 in order to form a foundational legend legitimizing a "hierokratisch geführten israelitischen Theokratie" (Reinhard Achenbach, *Die Vollendung der Tora*, 629–633). For a more thorough survey, see Christophe Nihan, review of Reinhard Achenbach, *Die Vollendung der Tora: Studien zur Redaktionsgeschichte des Numeribuches im Kontext von Hexateuch und Pentateuch* [http://www.bookreviews.org] (2006).
[79] Achenbach, *Die Vollendung der Tora*, 322, 328; cf. Achenbach's tables of textual strata on pp. 635–637. Eckart Otto also sees Num 27:12–14 as dependent on Deut 32:48–52, *Das Deuteronomium im Pentateuch und Hexateuch: Studien zur Literargeschichte von Pentateuch und Hexateuch im Lichte des Deuteronomiumrahmens* (FAT 30; Tübingen: Mohr Siebeck, 2000), 222–225.
[80] Achenbach, *Die Vollendung der Tora*, 558–561.

being only necessary to support the notion that P knew the DtrH, was literarily dependent on Deut 3:23–28 and Deut 34:1–9*, and yet was responsible for both Deut 34:1a and Num 27:12.[81] The primary critique Achenbach levies against this configuration, however, is that it supposedly cannot explain the discrepancy of the place-names for where Moses died in Deut 32:49 and 34:1.[82] Yet Achenbach leaves unclear how reading Num 27:12–14 as later than Deut 32:48–52 in any way resolves this tension. On the contrary, he asserts the non-aligned texts of Deut 32:48–52 are the result of balancing the context of Deuteronomy 31–34, which Numbers 27 either reduces or avoids altogether.[83]

In the end, Achenbach's argument for the primacy of Deut 32:48–52 over Num 27:12–14 fails to convince, and the complications he cites against the reverse configuration are overstated. To begin, there is no need to subordinate the thesis that Deut 32:48–52 relies on Num 27:12–14 to the thesis that P ends in Deuteronomy 34. Secondly, the quandary of the toponyms in Deut 32:48–52 and 34:1–9 appears once again to be a convergence of Dtr and P* traditions. The traditions in question here, of course, are the location and rationale of Moses' death, the tracing of which across Deuteronomy's exterior prologue and epilogues will aid in isolating the layer(s) to which Deut 32:48–52* belongs (see §4.3.2.2 below).

The third and final configuration is that Deut 32:48–52 is dependent on some form of Num 27:12–14, as well as Num 20:1–13, 22–29. This thesis has long swayed the majority of scholars—a consensus that increases if one disregards the complications of differing sigla.[84] The current study nuances this

---

[81] Achenbach, *Die Vollendung der Tora*, 558; contra Ludwig Schmidt, *Studien zur Priesterschrift* (BZAW 214; Berlin – New York: de Gruyter, 1993), 211–221.
[82] Achenbach, *Die Vollendung der Tora*, 558. Specifically, Achenbach states that "Dabei ergibt sich aber die Unstimmigkeit, daß die Lokalisierung im Abarim-Gebirge in Dtn 32,48–52; 34,1ff. die beiden Bergenamen Nebo und Pisga zu integrieren vermag, in Num 27, 12 diese Funktion voraussetzend aber nur vom Abarim-Gebirge die Rede ist" (*Die Vollendung der Tora*, 558).
[83] Achenbach states the Numbers texts "reduziert die Begründung für die Beschauung des Landes durch Mose und spart den den Kern der Aussage, nämlich den Befehl zu sterben (v.50aα) und die Ansage Dtn 32,52, Mose solle nicht ins Land hinüberkommen, aus. Die übrigen Textüberschüsse der Version des Deuteronomiums sind weitgehend auf den Ausgleich zum Umfeld von Dtn 31–34 zurückzuführen (v.48b. 49aβγ), der in Num 27 unterbleibt" (*Die Vollendung der Tora*, 560).
[84] Since the time of Noth's *Überlieferungsgeschichtliche Studien*, most scholars have held Deut 32:48–52 to be a secondary repetition of Num 27:12–14 by a priestly redactor (*Überlieferungsgeschichtliche Studien*, I:190–206.) Initially, even Perlitt agrees with Noth insofar "daß Dtn 32,48–52 "eine sekundäre Wiederholung" ist – allerdings ohne mit ihm den gebenden Text "als ursprüngliches Element des P-Erzählung" zu betrachen" ("Priesterschrift," 75). Building on Perlitt, Philipp Stoellger argued that Deut 32:48–52 belongs to a Dtr redactor, who was pos-

model in two ways: first, it does not assume that Deut 32:48–52 is itself homogenous; and secondly, it does not argue that the purpose of Deut 32:48–52 was to reconnect the Numbers' narrative to the displaced P^G report of Moses' death.[85] Instead, an analysis of Deut 32:48–52 in relation to Deut 34:1–9 suggests that the *rationale* for Moses' and Aaron's deaths outside the land is secondary to Deut 32:48–52*; and what was original to this pericope (vv. 48–50, 52) conflates the Dtr and P* traditions regarding the location of Moses' death. In other words, it is not enough to analyze Deut 32:48–52's relationship with Num 27:12–14. Deuteronomy 32:48–52* inextricably connects to Deut 34:1–9 at the narrative level—a progression that the blessing of Moses (Deut 33:1–29) clearly disrupts. It is thus necessary to determine the stratum within ch. 34 with which Deut 32:48–52* directly corresponds.

4.3.2.2 Deuteronomy 32:48–52's Stratigraphic Relationship with Deut 34:1–9. Scholars frequently understand Deuteronomy 34 to be the product of at least three scribal hands that generally correspond to vv. 1–6, 7–9, and 10–12. This breakdown, however, is overly simplistic, as Félix García López's survey and his own position clearly shows.[86] The current study advocates the following three stages: a *Dtr* layer (vv. 1aα+δ, 1bα, 4a*-b, 5–6) that ties back to the Dtr exterior prologue (Deuteronomy chs. 1–3 [4]), which in turn anticipates Joshua as part of the DtrH; a *HexRed* layer (vv. 1aβ-γ+ε, 1bβ-3, 4a*, 7a, 8–9) that merges Dtr and P* traditions as part of the formation of the Hexateuch, and ties back to Deut 32:48–50, 52; and finally a supplement by PentRed (vv. 7b, 10–12), whose editing is corrective and delimiting in formation of the Pentateuch and seeks to elevate the character of Moses to an incomparable status.

The foundational layer of Deuteronomy 34 lies within Deut 34:1–6* (vv. 1aα+δ, 1bα, 4a*-b, 5*-6) and is tied to the Dtr tradition within Deuteronomy's

---

sibly influenced by a priestly redactor ("Deuteronomium 34 ohne Priesterschrift," *ZAW* 105 [1993]: 29). Likewise, see Harvey's thesis that a Dtr scribe based Deuteronomy 1–3 on his memory of narratives in Numbers that included priestly texts (*Retelling the Torah*, 29–32, 99).

85 Recent proponents who continue to argue that Deut 34:1–9* preserves the so-called missing end of P^G include Christian Frevel, *Mit Blick auf das Land*, especially 380–382; H.-C Schmitt, "Dtn 34 als Verbindungsstück zwischen Tetrateuch und Deuteronomistischem Geschichtswerk," in *Das Deuteronomium zwischen Pentateuch und Deuteronomistischen Geschichtswerk* (ed. Eckart Otto and Reinhard Achenbach; FRLANT 206; Göttingen: Vandenhoeck & Ruprecht, 2004), 181–192; Philippe Guillaume, *Land and Calendar: The Priestly Document from Genesis to Joshua 18* (LHB/OTS 391; London – New York: T & T Clark, 2009), 154–156.

86 See the history of research and divisions advocated by Félix García López, "Deut 34, Dtr History and the Pentateuch," in *Studies in Deuteronomy in Honour of C.J. Labuschagne on the Occasion of his 65th Birthday* (ed. F. García Martínez et al.; VTSup 53; Leiden: Brill, 1994), 47–61.

exterior prologue (chs. 1–3 [4]), where Moses is forbidden to enter the land because of Yahweh's misdirected anger over the people's refusal to take the land (cf. Deut 1:34–37; 3:26–29; 4:21). The connection is particularly clear with Deut 3:27–28, since Deut 34:1aα+δ fulfills Yahweh's instructions in Deut 3:27aα for Moses to go up (√עלה) to the top of Pisgah (ראש הפסגה). Likewise, in Deut 3:27aβ Yahweh commands Moses to view (√ראה) the land from west, to north, to south, and then to the east—instructions that Yahweh facilitates in Deut 34:1bα when he shows (√ראה) Moses all the land (כל־הארץ).[87] It is difficult, however, to determine at which point vv. 1aε, 1bβ-3 entered Deuteronomy 34, as the directions that Yahweh instructs Moses to look in Deut 3:27aβ roughly correspond to the path that Moses' line of sight would have traveled in Deut 34:1aε, 1bβ-3 (see Fig. 4.3 below).[88] Yet it is striking that the parameters of this visual journey are framed by ירחו, which in Deuteronomy only appears in 32:49 and 34:1, 3, and which in construct with the ערבת מואב is typical of P* materials.[89] Consequently, Deut 34:1aε and 1bβ-3 stand out as likely HexRed rather than Dtr.

As for the remaining material in Deut 34:1–6*, Römer and Brettler are correct in their assessment that some form of v. 4 was likely original to the Dtr layer; however, it has been so thoroughly reworked as to prevent reconstruction. The formulation for the Promised Land and the apparent citation of Gen 12:7 argue against v. 4 being entirely Dtr.[90] Yet the repetition of Deut 3:27b in 34:4b

---

[87] Stoellger, as well as Römer and Brettler, also sees this connection (cf. Philipp Stoellger, "Deuteronomium 34 ohne Priesterschrift," *ZAW* 105 (1993): 34; cf., Thomas Römer and Marc Z. Brettler, "Deuteronomy 34 and the Case for a Persian Hexateuch," *JBL* 119 (2000): 404).
[88] Nelson also notes this correspondence: "Moses' geographical survey [in Deut 34:1–3] expands on the command of 3:27 (DH) [...] He looks from right to left, first north, then west, then south" (*Deuteronomy*, 395). More specifically, I would argue that the description of Pisgah as על־פני ירחו (v. 1aε) orients Moses' initial line of sight westward; the phrase את־הגלעד עד־דן (v. 1bβ) shifts Moses' line of sight to the northernmost extremities of the land; the line of sight then turns southward through כל־נפתלי, then ארץ אפרים ומנשה, and כל־ארץ יהודה (v. 2a-bα); the direction then shifts again to the west with the mention of the ים האחרון (v. 2bβ); v. 3 then continues the southward descent to the נגב (v. 3aα), only to turn comparatively eastward to the Dead Sea region between בקעת ירחו and צער (v. 3aβ-γ).
[89] The tripartite geographical phrase ערבת מואב על ירדן ירחו is typical of the materials in Numbers (22:1; 26:3, 63; 31:12; 33:48, 50; 35:1; 36:13). The Dtr exterior prologue prepares one for the mention of ירדן (especially Deut 3:20, 25, 27), as does the *late Dtr* closing from of the Song (Deut 32:47), yet ירדן is noticeably absent from Deuteronomy 34. With the absence of ירחו from the Dtr exterior prologue of Deuteronomy, the concentration of occurrences in Deut 32:49 and 34:1,3 raises the possibility that its inclusion again illustrates the intent of merging Dtr and P* traditions.
[90] Römer and Brettler make a convincing case against Deut 34:4 being Dtr on two grounds: "Nowhere else in Deuteronomy is the promise of the land presented as a quotation (לזרעך

cautions against precluding any form of v. 4 from having originally been a part of the Dtr layer.[91] As for vv. 5*-6, the phrases בארץ מרוב, עבד־יהוה,[92] and בית פעור (cf. Deut 3:29) are Dtr, and the status of Moses' grave being unknown[93] constitute a fitting conclusion to the Dtr frame for Deuteronomy as a whole. Although על־פי יהוה in v.5bβ is elsewhere always associated with P* material, and as such probably reflects a later hand (probably HexRed).[94]

אתננה), introduced by לאמר. Dtr texts elsewhere use infinitive constructs of ירש or נתן [...] Additionally, the text of Deut 34:4 is grammatically problematic, since the MT notes the names of the three patriarchs but continues in the singular לזרעך אתננה, rather than לזרעכם אתננה. This is best explained by suggesting that this is a citation of the promise in Gen 12:7, where the singular is used since Abraham alone is the promise recipient. If this is the case, the inversion of הארץ הזאת of Genesis to זאת הארץ might reflect an application of Seidel's law, which suggests that earlier sources are often quoted chiastically" ("Deuteronomy 34," 405–406). Römer and Brettler's suggestion that the naming of the three patriarchs in place of Dtr's more typical use of the generic אבות, however, remains unconvincing; Deut 1:8; 6:10; 9:5; 29:12 [13]; and 30:20 all use the ancestral father's names in apposition to אבות. Instead, it is the absence of אבות, not the presence of the ancestral father's names, that is distinctive. This critique undermines Römer and Brettler's claim that v. 4 (as well as Deut 1:8; 6:10; 9:5, 27; 29:12; 30:20) was written by the Pentateuch redactor who wanted "to separate Deuteronomy from the following books, since beyond the book of Deuteronomy the אבות are never explicitly identified with the three patriarchs" ("Deuteronomy 34," 406).

91 The syntactical and lexical features of Deut 3:27b and Deut 34:4b are quite close; cf. v. 27b (וראה בעיניך כי־לא תעבר את־הירדן הזה) and v. 4b (הראיתיך בעיך ושמה לא תעבר). These phrases also appear in Deut 32:52a-bα: כי מנגד תראה את־הארץ ושמה לא תבואץ. Harvey also sees this correspondence as indicative of Deut 34:4b being Dtr, but the features of v. 4a undermine his attempt to attribute the entire verse to the Dtr (*Retelling the Torah*, 24 n. 40).

92 The phrase עבד־יהוה does not occur elsewhere in the Pentateuch, but is typical of the book of Joshua. For "Moses" as the עבד־יהוה, see Jos 1:1, 13, 15; 8:31, 33; 11:12; 12:6; 13:8; 14:7; 18:7; 22:2, 4, 5; cf. 2 Kgs 18:12, but also 2 Chr 1:3; 24:6. For Joshua as the עבד־יהוה, see Jos 24:29 and Judg 2:8. For בארץ מואב, see p. 109 n. 76 above.

93 Römer and Brettler note that "the insistence that no one knows the place of Moses' grave 'until today' may well be explained by the Deuteronomistic hostility toward the popular cult of the dead (cf. Deut 18:11 and 26:14, which are typically considered Dtr)" ("Deuteronomy 34," 406). Similarly, Adriane Leveen suggests that the "anonymity [of the grave] prevents the people from developing any special attachment to an area connected to Moses. He must not be worshiped instead of God" (*Memory and Tradition in the Book of Numbers* [New York: Cambridge University Press, 2008], 153).

94 Within the Hexateuch, על־פי יהוה only occurs in Exod 17:1; Lev 24:12; Num 3:16, 39, 51; 4:37, 41, 45, 49; 9:18, 20, 23; 10:13; 13:3; 33:2, 38; 36:5; Deut 34:5; Josh 19:50; and 22:9 (although cf. על־כל־מוצא פי־יהוה in Deut 8:3; את־פי יהוה in Num 14:41; 22:18; 24:13; Deut 1:26, 43; 9:23; Jos 9:14; 15:13; and 17:4; and אל־פי יהוה in Jos 17:4 and 21:3). See F. García López' discussion of על־פי יהוה in the Hexateuch in "La Place du Lévitique et des Nombres dans la Formation du Pentateuque," in *The Books of Leviticus and Numbers* (ed. Thomas Römer; BETL 215; Leuven: Peeters, 2008), 82–98.

The second layer of Deuteronomy 34 frames the foundational Dtr layer and extends it to Deut 34:1–9* (vv. 1aβ-γ+ε, 1bβ-3, 4a*, 7a, 8–9). HexRed begins by supplementing Dtr's version of 34:1a (Dtr = ויעל משה ראש הפסגה ויראהו יהוה את־כל־הארץ[95]) with geographical expressions elsewhere typical of P* materials: מערבת מואב (v. 1aβ); הר נבו (v. 1aγ); and על־פני ירחו (v. 1aε).[96] As discussed above, the survey of the land (vv. 1bβ-3) is also most likely part of this layer, along with the thorough revision of v. 4a. Contrary to most reconstructions, however, the entirety of v. 7 does not align well with this layer.[97] While v. 7a echoes the Dtr tradition in Deut 31:2 of the age at which Moses died, v. 7b corrects the Dtr perspective of Moses being frail and ailing.[98] Verse 7b therefore aligns with the theology of vv. 10–12,[99] which together with v. 7b constitutes the final revision to

---

95 Stoellger, Nielsen, Römer and Brettler, and Philip Y. Yoo agree, although Yoo attributes it to the Yahwist (Stoellger, "Deuteronomium 34 ohne Priesterschrfit," 34; Nielsen, *Deuteronomium*, 308; Römer and Brettler, "Deuteronomy 34," 404; Philip Y. Yoo, "The Four Moses Death Accounts," *JBL* 131 [2012]: 427, 429).

96 For the expression "the plains of Moab" (מערבת מואב), see p. 109 n. 76 above and pp. 174–179 below. Within the Pentateuch "Nebo" (נבו) appears only in Num 32:2, 38; 33:47; Deut 32:49; and 34:1; whereas "Mount Nebo" (הר נבו) only occurs in Deut 32:49 and 34:1. Like הר נבו, the phrase "opposite of Jericho" (על־פני ירחו) only occurs in Deut 32:49 and 34:1, yet ירחו is a typical component of P* expressions for the plains of Moab (cf. p. 114 n. 89 above).

97 See the introductory survey in Perlitt, "Priesterschrift," 65–67; more recently, Propp, "Priestly Source," 477; Römer and Brettler, "Deuteronomy 34," 407–408.

98 The tradition reflected in Deut 31:2 is unique and difficult to place. In the Dtr exterior prologue, Moses' exclusion from entry into the land is a repercussion of Yahweh's anger over Israel's refusal to take the land (cf. Deut 1:34–37; 3:26–29; 4:21); yet in Deut 31:2, Moses declares himself terminally aged and physically incapable of entering the land. Scholars have made too much of the number "120" as dependent on Exod 7:7 (Moses being eighty years old at the exodus) and the Dt tradition of forty years in the wilderness (e. g., Deut 8:1–4); e. g., Nihan, *Priestly Torah to Pentateuch*, 22. Numbers can be easily edited without substantial revision, even omitted by corruption (e. g. 1 Sam 13:1). The tradition on Moses' physical health in Deut 31:2, however, is clearly older than that in Deut 34:7b, so it is at least Dtr; the number of years in Deut 31:2, on the other hand, could easily be a product of later harmonization.

99 Römer and Brettler argue that Deut 34:10 corrects the "Dtr statement in Deut 18:15, which suggests that Yhwh will raise up (יקים) a prophet like Moses. Deuteronomy 34:10, however, insists that Moses is incomparable, and 'no prophet has risen (לא קם) in Israel like Moses […] The incomparability of Moses is the theme of the following verses [i. e., vv. 11–12]. In these verses, Dtr expressions that are elsewhere used to celebrate God's rescue in the exodus are transferred to Moses" ("Deuteronomy 34," 406). Given their observation about this layer correcting earlier content in Deuteronomy and enhancing Moses' status, it is surprising that Römer and Brettler retain all of v. 7 as part of their Hexateuch redaction. Compare Otto, *Das Deuteronomium im Pentateuch und Hexateuch*, 212, 226, who also aligns v. 7 with vv. 10–12; as well, Konrad Schmid, who sees v. 7 as part of the Pentateuchal redaction that reflects the same theological profile as

the chapter by the hand of PentRed. In vv. 8–9, the P* expression ערבת מואב again signals a return to this layer, which is further confirmed by the formulation of the notice regarding the mourning period for Moses (v. 8a) resembling that of Aaron's in Num 20:29.[100] Additionally, the description of Joshua in v. 9a (מלא רוח חכמה) echoes and expands upon that in Num 27:18 (just אשר־רוח בו), while v. 9b employs a Dtr expression (√שמע + אל-preposition) that does not occur in P* materials.[101] Overall, the *modus operandi* of HexRed—that is, to merge Dtr and P* material and traditions—is evident throughout this stratum and lends support to Römer and Brettler's thesis of a priestly-deuteronomistic Hexateuch redaction in the early Persian period.[102]

A comparison of Deut 34:1–9* with Deut 32:48–52* further corroborates this reconstruction (see Fig. 4.3 below). The post-P redactor responsible for merging Dtr and P* traditions in Deut 34:1–9* (HexRed) also appears to have skillfully constructed Deut 32:48–52* using the same redactional processes, the clearest examples of which lie in Deut 32:49–50, 52 and 34:1–5. It may not be a coincidence, however, that HexRed begins Deut 32:48 with a P* expression similar to the Dtr expression that concludes the Dtr material in Deut 34:6, material HexRed would have inherited (see letter A in Fig. 4.3 above). Next, HexRed introduces the Dtr mountain (ראש פסגה) in 34:1 with the P* expression for Moab (ערבת מואב) and then inverts the process in 32:49, clarifying the P* mountain range (הר העברים הזה) with the Dtr expression for Moab (ארץ מואב). Then in catchword fashion, HexRed binds these mergers with the phrases הר־נבו and ירחו אשר על־פני (see letter B).[103] Next, HexRed systematically expands on Dtr's declaration that Yahweh

---

Gen 6:3, which together form "the only literary inclusio that draws a line from the ending of the Torah [...] to the primeval narrative" ("Late Persian Formation of the Torah," 248, 249).

100 The formulation of the notice regarding the mourning period for Aaron (Num 20:29b) resembles the notice for Moses (Deut 34:8a): cf. v. 29b (ויבכו את־אהרן שלשים יום כל בית ישראל) and v. 8a (ויבכו בני ישראל את־משה בערבת מואב שלשים יום).

101 Nihan, *Priestly Torah to Pentateuch*, 22 n. 9.

102 Römer and Brettler assert that both the Hextateuch and Pentateuch redactions "must be viewed within the debate about the publication of an 'official' Holy Scripture for Judaism in the Persian period." The decision for a Pentateuch over a Hexateuch, they argue, was a "compromise due to long and difficult negotiations among different religious parties in Jerusalem and Samaria." They then tentatively suggest that early negotiations were "complicated by the existence of a Dtr-Priestly minority, which coalesced to promote the publication of a Hexateuch" ("Deuteronomy 34," 408–409).

103 In Deut 32:49, הר־נבו clarifies the specific mountain within the Abarim mountain range which Moses ascends, but in Deut 34:1 HexRed positions הר־נבו before ראש פסגה, turning ראש פסגה into an appositive of הר־נבו and thereby equating the two peaks (cf. Num 33:47). The two instances of the phrase אשר על־פני ירחו are unique and derivative of P*'s tripartite ערבת מואב על־ירדן ירחו (cf. p. 114 n. 89 above).

showed Moses all the land (cf. ויראהו יהוה את־כל־הארץ in v. 1bα), by 1) using the series of directions specified in Deut 3:27a (W>N>S>E) as a guide for selecting the locations of Moses' visual journey (Deut 34:1bβ-3), and by 2) adumbrating this journey via his addition of כנען in his appropriation of Num 27:12b (see letter C). One can detect the same technique of inversion in 32:50 + 52 (see letter D): HexRed shapes 32:50aα-β as an expanded form of the syntagm ומת שם from 34:5 (cf. שמה ומת בהר אשר אתה עלה in 32:50aα-β); then in 32:52—itself an inversion of 34:4—HexRed first adumbrates 34:4b and then echoes the motif of the gift of the land in 34:4a.

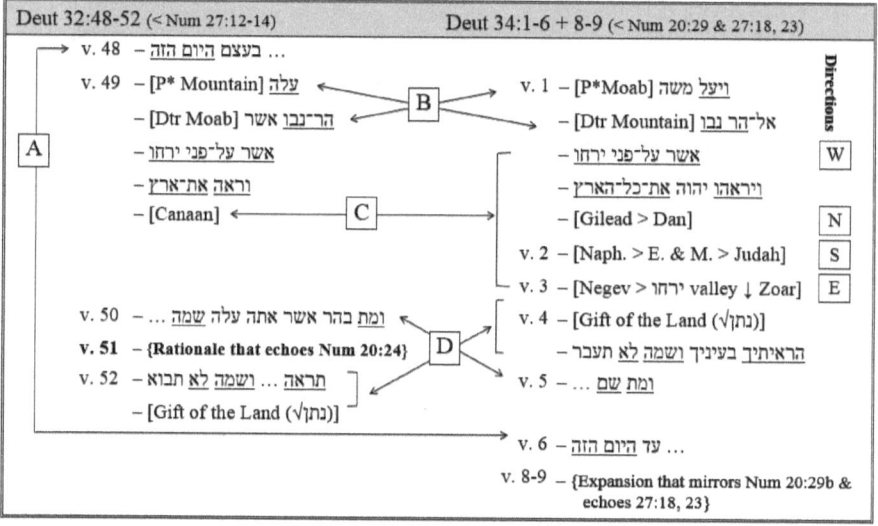

Fig. 4.3: Redactional Processes in Deut 32:48–52 and 34:1–9

Curiously, the only portion of Deut 32:48–52 that does not participate in the above techniques is v. 51, the P* M-Mt rationale for Moses and Aaron's exclusion from entry into the Promised Land. This omission within HexRed's editorial process, however, is not entirely surprising. Several indicators coalesce to suggest that 32:51 is not from same hand as the surrounding material provided by HexRed. Additional indicators include 1) the deterioration in the level of correspondence with Num 27:12–14 at this juncture in Deut 32:48–52 (cf. Fig. 4.2 on p. 110 above); 2) the only precise verbal correspondence is with Num 27:14b, which many note as being glossic (cf. p. 109 n. 74 above), but which this study attributes to a post-Pentateuchal redactor (cf. §7.3.1 below); 3) that otherwise HexRed demonstrates no knowledge of the P* rationale for Moses' exclusion from the Promised Land (cf. §6.3.1 below); and lastly 4) that there is evidence to suggest that the rationale for Moses' exclusion is itself a redactional stratum attributable to post-PentRed (cf. pp. 213–218 below). In short, while internal evidence within Deuteronomy indicates 32:51 stems from a post-P redactor (along with the rest of Deut 32:48–52), it is evidence within the M-Mt texts in Numbers that confirms the trace indications that the post-P redactor responsible for Deut 32:51 is post-PentRed rather than HexRed or PentRed.[104]

Finally, for the sake of a complete treatment, one must briefly turn attention to HexRed's work within Deuteronomy 34. After having merged the Dtr and P* traditions regarding the command and location of Moses' death in Deut 32:48–50, 52 + 34:1–6*, HexRed continues to merge Dtr and P* traditions to formulate Moses' epitaph in Deut 34:7a (cf. Deut 31:2 [Dtr]), the subsequent period of mourning in Deut 34:8 (cf. Num 20:29 [P*]), and the successful transition to Joshua's leadership in Deut 34:9 (cf. Num 27:18 [P*]).

In the end, there is no avoiding the complexities involved in negotiating the relative chronology of Deut 32:48–52 and the P* materials with which it resonates (Num 20:1–13, 22–29; Num 27:12–14, 15–23), as well as the texts within Deuteronomy with which Deut 32:48–52 is intricately connected (Deut 3:27–29 and 34:1–9). Yet the above analysis demonstrates that while 32:48–50, 52 is most likely the product of a post-P Hexateuchal redactor (HexRed), with the M-Mt reminiscence in 32:51 entering Deut 32:48–52 at a later stage. Yet the reminiscence preserved in Deut 32:51 is not only a late entry into Deuteronomy, its correlatives in Num 20:12 and 27:14b also represent late entries into their respective P* M-Mt contexts; i.e., Num 20:1–13 and 27:12–14, respectively. This relative diachronic relationship suggests that the P* M-Mt has its own history of development (cf. §5.3 below) independent of, and most likely simultaneous to, the Dtr developments of M-Mt reflected in Deut 6:16 (*late Dtr*) and 9:22 (*Dtr supp*) (cf. §3.2; §3.4; §3.5 above).

4.3.3 Tradition-historical Analysis of Deut 32:51

Given the development of the M-Mt tradition so far encountered across Deuteronomy—that is, in Deut 6:16; 8:15; 9:22; and 32:13b—it is striking that Deut 32:51 preserves the first clear *canonical awareness* of the P* M-Mt. There is no tradition-historical development within Deuteronomy, however, that leads up to, or tran-

---

[104] For why the current study attributes Deut 32:51 to post-PentRed instead of PentRed, see the argument that Deut 33:8 is PentRed (§4.4.2), yet evinces no awareness of Aaron's failure alongside Moses at מי מריבה (cf. pp. 137–138 and 213–218 below).

sitions to, the P* M-Mt that Deut 32:51 reflects. Thus, although the Dtr and P* versions of the M-Mt no doubt have a common origin, it is clear that for a time the two scribal traditions developed independently of each other.

As for the other tradition-historical components in Deut 32:51, the *substance of issuance* is embedded in the M-Mt *location*, מי־מריבת קדש. The *source of issuance*, however, is noticeably missing, though perhaps it was not necessary as P*'s source and substance of issuance conceptually overlap with the Dtr tradition. There are a few distinctive tradition-historical components of the P* M-Mt of note here: it was Moses and Aaron who had failed, not the people (*agency*; cf. Deut 6:16; 9:22); and they did so at מי־מריבת קדש מדבר־צן, not at a place known as מסה (*location*; cf. Deut 6:16; 9:22); this failure is the reason why Moses and Aaron were not allowed to enter the land—a repercussion that no doubt served as a dire warning to the leaders of later generations (*interpretative significance*). As it stands, this perspective toward the characters of Moses and Aaron is incongruent with that of PentRed in Deut 34:7b, 10 – 12, which aggrandizes Moses' relationship—and as will be seen, also Aaron's relationship (§4.4)—with the deity. In the end, the failure of Moses and Aaron in Deut 32:51 represents the latest M-Mt reminiscence in the book of Deuteronomy.

4.4 Deuteronomy 33:8

4.4.1 Textual Criticism of Deut 33:8

וללוי אמר ^{Deut 33:8}
[הבו ללוי] תמיך ואוריך לאיש חסידך
אשר נסיתו במסה תריבהו על־מי מריבה:

Like the Song, the obliquity of the Blessing of Moses (hereafter "the Blessing") has given rise to numerous variant readings, and such is especially the case for the sayings directed to Levi.[105] The text of MT Deut 33:8a—וללוי אמר תמיך ואוריך לאיש חסידך ("And to Levi he said, 'Your thummim and your urim to your loyal one'")—is particularly unclear, and the addition of a verbal phrase akin to הבו ללוי (attested in 4QDeut[h] and 4QTestimonia; cf. G's singular form, δότε

---

[105] A full treatment of the text-critical issues relevant to the Blessing is not intrinsic to the current study. For fuller treatments see Julie A. Duncan, "New Readings for the "Blessing of Moses" from Qumran," *JBL* 114 (1995): 273–290. Stefan Beyerle, "Evidence of a Polymorphic Text: Towards the Text-History of Deuteronomy 33," *DSD* 5 (1998): 215–232.

Λευι) seems warranted.[106] It is likely that the proximity of the two instances of "ללוי" prompted parablepsis, and the resulting haplography ensued.[107] Still, while the restoration of this phrase identifies the חסיד as a devout Levite, the an-

---

106 The emendation "allows for a smoother flow of the first two cola as follows: [And to Levi he said,] 'Give to Levi your Thummim, and your Urim to your loyal one'" (McCarthy, *BHQ Deuteronomy*, 158*). This emendation has found wide acceptance among scholars: e. g., Mayes, *Deuteronomy*, 402; Russell Fuller, "The Blessing of Levi in Dtn 33, Mal 2, and Qumran," in *Konsequente Traditions-geschichte: Festschrift für Klaus Baltzer zum 65. Geburtstag* (ed. Rüdiger Bartelmus, Thomas Krüger, and Helmut Utzschneider; OBO 126; Göttingen: Vandenhoeck & Ruprecht, 1993), 32; Nielsen, *Deuteronomium*, 294, 297; Nelson, *Deuteronomy*, 381, 384; McCarthy, *BHQ Deuteronomy*, 158*-159*.

Labuschagne's suggestion that the text be amended to וללוי אמרת תמיך ("To Levi thou hast assigned thy Thummim ...") is to be rejected on two grounds: there is no textual evidence supporting it, and the reading of √אמר as "assign" based on 1 Kgs 11:18 and 2 Chr 29:24 is too obscure considering that √אמר bears its typical connotation in the formulaic openings to the tribal blessings of Judah, Benjamin, Joseph, Zebulun, Gad, Naphtali, and Asher (Deut 33:7, 12, 13, 18, 22, 23, 24).

107 So Duncan, "New Readings," 280; Fuller, "Blessing of Levi," in Bartelmus, Krüger, and Utzschneider, *Konsequente Traditionsgeschichte*, 34 n. 18; Nelson, *Deuteronomy*, 384. Alternative positions include Mayes, who wonders whether the omission was deliberate since the Levites were not tested at Massah-Meribah (*Deuteronomy*, 402–403); Nielsen, who postulates that "הבו ללוי mag alte Dittographie sein," but leaves the precise mechanics for how this would come about unclear (*Deuteronomium*, 297); and Beyerle, who questions the legitimacy of using 4QDeut^h (4Q35) and 4QTestimonia (4Q175) to establish a so-called "Urtext" (Beyerle, "Polymorphic Text," 225–226). Beyerle's critique merits a response. Beyerle argues that the addition of הבו ללוי is "hardly intelligible in the canonical shape of the blessing" since the vestments already belong to Levi; it is for this reason that the Greek manuscripts either shifts the second person suffixes to third singular suffixes or omits the suffixes altogether. The tension in G remains, however: Levi (singular) is still told to give to Levi what is already his, and yet the Greek plural δότε Λευι persists; in other words, what the LXX shifts is the pronouns, not the base of its *Vorlage* (νδίδωμι + Λευι = √יהב + ללוי). Additionally, Beyerle avers that the dating issues inherent to 4Q175, the textual differences when comparing 4Q175 and 4Q35, as well as their distinct text-types (4Q35 is a "biblical text," while 4Q175 is "a special kind of pesher") "make it impossible to establish which is the '*Urtext*'" or the direction of dependency, if there is any ("Polymorphic Text," 225–226). However, the argument for the originality of הבו ללוי (as Duncan, Fuller, et al have argued it) is not to establish which of these Qumran manuscripts is the '*Urtext*,' but rather whether they are inheritors of a textual tradition in which הבו ללוי is a part of Deut 33:8. Beyerle's objections are moot within the parameters of this respective conversation.

Perhaps the firmest grounds for rejecting הבו ללוי is 1) that MT is understandable without it, if one takes the ל-preposition on לאיש חסידך as a lamed of possession (so "your Thummim and Urim belongs to your loyal one"); and 2) that Smr follows the MT with the exceptions of some minor orthography and the insertion of a ו. Such rebuttals do not account for the poetic balance that הבו ללוי restores to Deut 33:8 (cf. Duncan, "New Readings," 280 n. 19) or for the parableptic mechanism it provides explaining its loss.

tecedents of the second person components in Deut 33:8 remain ambiguous. The shifts in G and expansions in T[ONJF] are attributable to the translators attempting to clarify these identities and are therefore interpretative.[108] The only other significant variant reading is the occasional tendency to render the MT's תריבהו ("you contended with him") with the verb "to test" (so σ', S, T[OJ]), which McCarthy understands as a move away from anthropomorphic language.[109]

4.4.2 Literary Analysis of Deut 33:8–11

The tight literary correspondences between Deut 32:48–52* and 34:1–9* (§4.3.2.) show the Blessing to be a later insertion into Deuteronomy. Further analysis is required, however, as most of the blessing to Levi (Deut 33:8–11)—in which the M-Mt reminiscence lies—does not appear to be original to the anthology of tribal sayings that surrounds it. Specifically, the syntax, structure, and orthography of vv. 8–10 do not match that of its surrounding literary context. Cross and Freedman summarize this evidence well:

> In [vv.] 8–10 there is a complete break in style, meter and content with the rest of the poem. The relative pronoun (ʾăšer), the sign of the definite accusative (ʾet-), and the article, all suspicious in ancient poetry, occur in these lines. The poetic structure is dubious, and [v.] 9 at least seems to be largely prose. Significant from the point of view of the writers is

---

108 G is the least interpretative: the implied antecedent to the imperative δότε is 2ms instead of 2mp (cf. הבו) and remains anonymous, but it cannot be taken as identical to the 3ms pronouns G uses for the rest of the line (v. 8a). McCarthy understands κύριε as the implied subject of δότε, while Λευι is the antecedent for the 3ms pronouns, rendering the δῆλος (= תמים) and ἀλήθεια (= אורים), as "belonging to Levi rather than to God" (*BHQ Deuteronomy*, 158*); G does not provide a possessive pronoun for the restrictive phrase for "holy man" (τῷ ἀνδρὶ τῷ ὁσίῳ; cf. MT's חסידך), thereby avoiding the implication that the holy man also belongs to Levi; in v. 8b, G shifts to the 3mp verbs thereby attributing the action of ὑπειράζω (= √נסה) and ὑλοιδορέω (= √ריב) either to the Levites or to the people in general.

As expected, the targumim are expansive and interpretative: in T[F] Moses the prophet of Yahweh (משה נבייא דיי) states that Aaron is the pious man (גברא חסידא) on whom Yahweh (implied) vested the Thummim and Urim because Aaron had withstood Yahweh's test and examination at the waters of quarreling at Reqem (במי מצותא די רקם; Reqem is the targummic designation for Kadesh) (Klein, *Fragment-Targums of the Pentateuch*, 1:232, 2:188–189); T[JN] and T[Gzn] provide the same identifications; T[O] is more reserve, leaving the specific identities unstated, but the "man who was found holy before you" (גבר דאשתכח חסיד קדמך) is likewise tested (√נסי ‖ √בחן) and found upright (שלם) and faithful (מהימן) (Drazin, *Targum Onkelos to Deuteronomy*, 298–299). The importance for these identifications is the early interpretation that the devout one is not only a Levite, but the founder of the Aaronides.

109 McCarthy, *BHQ Deuteronomy*, 159*.

the absence of tenth-century spellings and archaic forms in this passage, while the surrounding verses abound in both. How much, if any, of [vv.] 8–11 belongs to the original blessing, must remain in question. The passage is rejected *in toto* as a late addition by some scholars.[110]

Cross and Freedman, however, do not reject vv. 8–11 "*in toto*"; instead, they retain a reconstructed form of v. 11 because it "swarms with archaisms."[111]

The conclusion that Deut 33:8–10 is relatively later than the rest of the Blessing has found wide acceptance,[112] but no consensus appears forthcoming on the date when the Blessing was first composed. Cross and Freedman date it as early as the 11th century B.C.E. on account of the Blessing's archaisms and "affinities with Canaanite literature,"[113] but this position is overly optimistic, especially given that epigraphic evidence for ancient Israel's scribal culture does not become extant until the 9th century B.C.E.[114] More recently, scholarship has increasingly favored later dates, but the proposals vary greatly and range from the early monarchic to exilic periods.[115]

---

[110] F. M. Cross Jr. and David Noel Freedman, "The Blessing of Moses," *JBL* 67 (1948): 203 n. 28.
[111] F. M. Cross Jr. and David Noel Freedman, "The Blessing of Moses," *JBL* 67 (1948): 204 n. 29.
[112] E.g., C. J. Labuschagne, "The Tribes in the Blessing of Moses," in *Language and Meaning: Studies in Hebrew Language and Biblical Exegesis: Papers Read at the Joint British-Dutch Old Testament Conference at London, 1973* (James Barr et al., eds.; OtSt 19; Leiden: Brill, 1974), 111; Mayes, *Deuteronomy*, 402; Preuss, who while cautioning against the optimism of older reconstructions still asserts that "V. 8b-10 sich im jetzigen Kontext jedenfalls nicht alt" (*Deuteronomium*, 170); Kent Sparks, "Genesis 49 and the Tribal List Tradition in Ancient Israel," *ZAW* 115 (2003): 329.
[113] Cross and Freedman, "Blessing of Moses," 192.
[114] See Christopher A. Rollston, *Writing and Literacy in the World of Ancient Israel: Epigraphic Evidence from the Iron Age* (SBLABS 11; Atlanta: Society of Biblical Literature, 2010). Rollston asserts that "there is no evidence for a distinct Old Hebrew national script during the tenth century. Rather [...] such a script is first attested only in the ninth century (*Writing and Literacy*, 44).
[115] In 1982, when Preuss and André Caquot wrote, the proposals for the Blessing's date of composition ranged from the Mosaic to the exilic periods (Preuss, *Deuteronomium*, 170–171; André Caquot, "Les bénédictions de Moïse (Deutéronome 33, 6–25). I – Ruben, Juda, Lévi, Benjamin," *Sem* 32 [1982]: 69–70). Since then scholars have increasingly advocated for the Blessing becoming a written composition in a preexilic context. For example, Nielsen concludes that historical background for the Blessing is to be sought "in der Zeit jedenfalls vor dem assyrischen Angriff, d. h. vor 745 v. Chr." (*Deuteronomium*, 300); Stefan Beyerle argues for a *terminus ad quem* no later than the "Grundschicht des Dtn (ca. letztes Drittel des 7. Jh.s v. Chr.)" and for a *terminus a quo* for the oldest traditions of the Blessings as early as "die erste Hälfte des 11. Jh.s v. Chr." (*Der Mosesegen im Deuteronomium: Eine text-, kompositions- und formkritische Studie zu Deuteronomium 33* [BZAW 250; Berlin-New York: DeGruyter, 1997], 279); Nelson suggests the

The quest for any one absolute date for the Blessing—as understandable as this focus is—is from the start somewhat misguided, as the content and form of the Blessing actually suggests multiple composition dates. Setting aside for the moment the redactional nature of the blessing of Levi, the Blessing as a whole is a collection of eleven tribal sayings which earlier could have once existed individually or in smaller clusters.[116] As well, several scholars agree that the hymnic materials which now frame the tribal sayings (vv. 2–5+26–29) originally formed as an independent psalm.[117] In other words, both the tribal sayings (vv. 6–25*) and the psalmic framework appears to have existed independently, and not only of Deuteronomy, but from each other as well.

The lone exception to this process of scribal appropriation is Deut 33:8–10, the expansion that created the elusive blessing of Levi (vv. 8–11). Not only do vv. 8–10 stand out via their style, meter, and content (so Cross and Freedman), but they also stand disjointed from v. 11 and the rest of the tribal sayings on account of their scope and function. The scope of vv. 8–10 is cultic, as evidenced by 1) the instruction (or petition[118]) to give the Thummim and Urim to "your devout one" (חסידך) in v. 8a, and 2) by the description of the Levites' role as teachers of Yahweh's משפטים and תורה in v. 10. Yet the scope of the tribal sayings in

---

time of the Assyrian conquests during the Divided Monarchy, specifically 732 and 722 B.C.E. (Deuteronomy, 387).

116 Labuschagne argues, for instance, that the northern tribal sayings once constituted "a separate and distinct group that may be called a collection of eulogistic tribal sayings," while the southern tribal sayings "belong to a different category and perhaps also date from a different time" ("Tribes in the Blessing," in Barr, *Language and Meaning*, 102).

117 Scholars have argued that vv. 2–5, 26–29 originally constituted a single psalm since at least Steuernagel (*Übersetzung und Erklärung der Bücher Deuteronomium und Josua und allgemeine Einleitung in den Hexateuch* [HKAT I.3; Göttingen: Vandenhoeck & Ruprecht, 1900], 123), but see also I. L. Seeligmann, "A Psalm from Pre-Regal Times," *VT* 14 (1964): 75–92; Z. Weisman, "A Connecting Link in an Old Hymn: Deuteronomy XXXIII 19a, 21b," *VT* 28 (1978): 365–368; D. L. Christensen, "Two Stanzas of a Hymn in Deuteronomy 33," *Bib* 65 (1984): 382–389; D. N. Freedman, "The Poetic Structure of the Framework of Deuteronomy 33," in *Divine Commitment and Human Obligation, vol. 2: Poetry and Orthography* (ed. J. Huddlestun; Grand Rapids: Eerdmans, 1997), 85–107, originally printed in *The Bible World: Essays in Honor of C. H. Gordon* (G. Rendsburg et al, eds; New York: Ktav, 1980), 25–46.

118 The nature of Deut 33:8's unclear antecedents yields two possible readings. The traditional reading is that Moses is petitioning Yahweh to vest his Thummim and Urim onto a devout Levite. This reading, however, becomes theologically problematic in v. 8b, where Yahweh is then implicated in the testing at "Massah" and the contention at the "waters of Meribah," thereby prompting the pronominal shifts in the ancient witnesses (cf. p. 122 n. 108). Alternatively, one could read Moses as relaying death-bed instructions for Israel to impart the Thummim and Urim to Aaron, who is a Levite and whom Israel had presumably confronted at both these locations (see pp. 130–132 below).

general, and of v. 11 specifically, is predominantly militaristic.[119] Additionally, the rhetorical function of the blessing of Levi undoubtedly serves to safeguard the succession of particular priestly roles. Yet such a program is without parallel in the other tribal sayings: Joseph's dominance is presumed (v. 16), not advocated; and the other tribes do not have social roles ascribed to them.

With the mounting evidence that Deut 33:8–10 is secondary to the Blessing, two questions immediately present themselves. First, at what point in time were vv. 8–10 most likely added? Then, secondly, what is one to do with v. 11? To begin with the second question, Cross and Freedman suggest (for reasons left unexplained) that v. 11 may have been the original blessing of Levi.[120] The problem with this suggestion, however, is that v. 11 contains no identifier linking it to Levi. Instead, a number of scholars argue that v. 11 originally formed the conclusion to the blessing of Judah.[121] Labuschagne, for example, has aptly shown that v. 11 closely follows the form and style of v. 7, and with the emendation of a single stroke (ך for ו) in v. 7b (from ידיו רב לו to ידיך רב לו) the two verses would read seamlessly together.[122] Regardless of v. 11's provenance, Deut 33:8–10 is most likely secondary to v. 11 and the Blessing as a whole.

That Deut 33:8–10 is later than the rest of the Blessing provides a key vantage point for further assessing vv. 8–10 diachronically, as the literary context that surrounds vv. 8–10 most likely dates to a fairly narrow historical context, namely the years of the Divided Kingdom (c. 930's–722 BCE).[123] This timeframe,

---

119 Cf. Labuschagne, "Tribes in the Blessing," in Barr, *Language and Meaning*, 111; Mayes, *Deuteronomy*, 402; Nelson, *Deuteronomy*, 387. Similarly, Labuschagne observes that whereas "Levi" in Gen 49:5–7 denotes a "secular tribe," Deut 33:8 "uses the name Levi to denote the Levites and not the tribe of Levi" ("Tribes in the Blessing," in Barr, *Language and Meaning*, 111).
120 Cross and Freedman, "Blessing of Moses," 194, 204 n. 29; cf. Nelson, *Deuteronomy*, 389–390.
121 As early as Umberto Cassuto, "Il capitolo 33 del Deuteronomio e la festa del Capo d'anno nell'antico Israele," *RSO* 11 (1926–1928): 243; cf., Labuschagne, "Tribes in the Blessing," in Barr, *Language and Meaning*, 108–109; Mayes, *Deuteronomy*, 402; Fuller, "Blessing of Levi," in Bartelmus, Krüger, and Utzschneider, *Konsequente Traditionsgeschichte*, 37.
122 Labuschagne, "Tribes in the Blessing," in Barr, *Language and Meaning*, 108–109. Although there is no manuscript evidence to support this construction, it is clear that the ancient witnesses struggled to understand MT's oblique phrase "ידיו רב לו" (cf. McCarthy, *BHQ Deuteronomy*, 158*).
123 No other timeframe can adequately account for the Blessing's northern perspective, which regards Judah as being separated from his people (v. 7) and yet considers Joseph (Ephraim and Manasseh) to be crown prince over the other tribes (נזיר אחיו ולקדקד יוסף לראש) in v. 16b; cf. Gen 49:26) and militarily capable at an international level (v. 17). These descriptors resonate with an 9th to 8th century BCE context, suggesting the non-Levitical tribal sayings were composed prior to the reduction of the Northern Kingdom into an Assyrian province in 722 BCE. For an alternative

since Deut 33:8–10 is later than its surrounding literary context, therefore constitutes a *terminus a quo* for the creation and insertion of the blessing of Levi into the Blessing as a whole. Here is where the rhetorical function of vv. 8–10 becomes significant, as it allows one to ask, "At which point in ancient Israel's history, from the period of the Divided Kingdom onward, would an editor have most acutely felt the need to advocate and clarify the Levites' role in proper priestly succession and temple service?" Only two periods present themselves as particularly salient: either the period from shortly before the fall of the Northern Kingdom to the failure of Josiah's religious reforms,[124] or sometime after the reconstitution of the cult during the postexilic era.

The earlier period, however, does not stand up to scrutiny. The concern for the Levite within a Judean context is already well-attested within the early portions of Deuteronomy's legal core (chs. 12–26). Yet within this legal core the sociological location of the Levites is quite variegated; there are *peripheral* Levites (12:12–19; 14:27–29; 16:11, 14; 18:6–7; 26:11–13), *localized* levitical priests (21:5; 24:8), and *centralized* levitical priests (17:9, 18:1–2), as well as priests who may not have been Levites at all (26:3–4; cf. 26:11–13).[125] Yet in Deut 33:8–10—a trib-

---

reading, see Etienne Nodet, who suggests the Blessing of Moses fits the postexilic context, with Judah's separation indicative of the returning "peculiar Jews who do not want a relationship with local Israelites" ("Israelites, Samaritans, Temples, Jews," in *Samaria, Samarians, Samaritans: Studies on Bible, History and Linguistics* [ed. Jósef Zsengellér; SJ 66; Berlin–Boston: De Gruyter, 2011], 165).

124 So, Nelson, *Deuteronomy*, 387; Sparks, "Tribal List Tradition," 344; cf. Mayes, *Deuteronomy*, 402, who argues that the blessing of Levi's insertion into the Judah-saying (Deut 33:7+11) "reflects [the] close association of the Levites with Judah which would have come into existence particularly after the fall of the northern kingdom in 721 BC. So the insertion of the blessing on Levi at this point is probably not earlier than this"; also Labuschagne, who argues that the blessing of Levi stems from a glossator who was "probably a refugee Levite who found a home in Judah […] after the fall of the northern kingdom, when many Levites fled to Judah" ("Tribes in the Blessing," in Barr, *Language and Meaning*, 112).

125 This assessment does not presume that Deuteronomy's legal core is a literary unity, as numerous studies have shown the legal core to be composite. A seminal study—that is, with reference to the Levite's variegated social location within Deuteronomy 12–26 and indeed within Deuteronomy as a whole—is Ulrich Dahmen's *Leviten und Priester im Deuteronomium: Literarkritische und redaktionsgeschictliche Studien* (BBB 110; Bodenheim: Philo, 1996). The details of Dahmen's study of study cannot be recounted here. It is sufficient to note that he sees the blessing of Levi as part of a "spätnachexilische," "pro-levitische Redaktion"; cf. *Leviten und Priester*, 398, 404, especially 404 n. 94 in which he states "Unabhängig vom Alter und der Genese Sondertradition des Mose-Segens dürfte dieser Beleg für Levi erst mit Kap. 33 durch diese spätnachexilische Redaktion in das Dtn hineingekommen sein." This dating in no way hinders the current argument, though I would include the insertion of 33:8f with Dahmen's "Aaronidische Zensur" (Dahmen, *Leviten und Priester*, 401, 404) (cf. pp. 130–134 below).

al blessing presumably for all Levites—there is no such sociological dynamic: the priests are either localized or centralized, among whom is a select individual vested with תמים and אורים (v. 8); together, these priests collectively serve to relay Yahweh's משפתים and תורה to Israel, as well as burn incense (קטורה) and offerings (כליל) on Yahweh's altar (v. 10). In the end, either the blessing of Levi is an ancient prescription for northern Levites, localized around rural cultic centers, and so predates the Josianic *Sitz im Leben* of Deuteronomy's legal core; or its prescription is significantly later than the late preexilic era, in which case its presumption of a functioning cult dictates a postexilic, centralized context. Given the literary tensions discussed above, a postexilic setting is all but a foregone conclusion.[126]

Additional corroboration for this setting can be found in the *traditions* that the blessing of Levi reflects. Contrary to prevailing scholarship, the blessing of Levi does not reflect an otherwise lost, ancient *tradition* (singular) regarding the ordination of the Levites to cultic service at Massah-Meribah[127]—a "Levitical M-Mt," to coin a phrase. According to such scholars, Deut 33:8–11 preserves an

---

Additionally, for a more recent survey on the current debate over how to account for this dynamic within Deuteronomy's legal core, see Peter Altmann, "What do the "Levites in your Gates" Have to do with the "Levitical Priests"? An Attempt at European-North American Dialogue on the Levites in the Deuteronomic Law Corpus," in *Levites and Priests in Biblical History and Tradition* (ed. Mark A. Leuchter and Jeremy M. Hutton; SBLAIL 9; Leiden: Brill, 2012), 135–154. For a study that surveys the theme of the Levites across biblical, apocryphal, and qumranic materials, see Harald Samuel, *Von Priestern zum Patriarchen: Levi und die Leviten im alten Testament* (BZAW 448; Berlin–Boston: de Gruyter, 2014).

126 Fuller also suggests this period, but reaches this conclusion through a different avenue. Fuller argues that the language of v. 11a—i.e., ברך יהוה חילו ופעל ידיו תרצה—has parallels in Malachi's discussion of acceptable priestly offerings. "To the tradent of the second temple period the language of 33:11a […] would be considered quite appropriate for discussion of priestly or levitical functions. The second temple period might provide a reasonable period in which to set the shifting of v. 11 from the blessing of Judah to the blessing of Levi" ("Blessing of Levi," in Bartelmus, Krüger, and Utzschneider, *Konsequente Traditionsgeschichte*, 37).

127 There is a large following of scholars who to varying degrees ascribe to this interpretation of Deut 33:8–11; e. g., Joel S. Baden, "The Violent Origins of the Levites: Text and Tradition," in *Levites and Priests in Biblical History and Tradition* (ed. Mark A. Leuchter and Jeremy M. Hutton; SBLAIL 9; Leiden – Boston: Brill, 2012), 109–111; Thomas B. Dozeman, *Exodus* (ECC; Grand Rapids: Eerdmans, 2009), 711–712; David Frankel, *The Murmuring Stories of the Priestly School: A Retrieval of Ancient Sacerdotal Lore* (VTSup 89; Leiden – Boston – Köln: Brill, 2002), 305–306; Nelson, *Deuteronomy*, 389; William Johnstone, *Chronicles and Exodus: An Analogy and its Application* (JSOTSup 275; Sheffield: Sheffield Academic, 1998), 244, 257; John Van Seters, *The Life of Moses: The Yahwist as Historian in Exodus-Numbers* (Louisville: Westminster John Knox, 1994), 316–318; William H. C. Propp, *Water in the Wilderness: A Biblical Motif and its Mythological Background* (HSM 40; Atlanta: Scholars Press, 1987), 53–63.

ancient tradition about the Levites' violent rise to priesthood, which once the narratives of Exod 17:1–7* + 32:25–29* originally explicated.[128] In this reconstructed tradition, the Levites exact Yahweh's punishment for Israel's complaint about the lack of water in the wilderness (Exod 17:1–7*); in response to Moses'

---

[128] There are several permutations for Exod 17:1–7* + 32:25–29's literary dependence on Deut 33:8–11. Baden argues J inserted the Blessing into his document, but did not author it; he then suggests based on form (cf. Numbers 11) that one should relocated J's Exod 32:26–29 (the punishment) to its original location after J's Exod 17:1bβ-7 (the complaint). Somewhat incoherently, Baden later states that "if the story of the Levites [i.e. Exod 32:26–29] does not belong with Exod 17, then we are left to wonder what the author of Deut 33 imagined had happened at Massah and Meribah that involved the Levites" (Baden, "Violent Origins of the Levites," in Leuchter and Hutton, *Levites and Priests*, 105–106, 109–110). Theoretically, either J inserted the Blessing into his document, or the author of the Levi-saying relied on J; one cannot have it both ways. Dozeman, however, is not clear on the diachronic relationship of these texts: while he accepts Cross and Freedman's early date for Deut 33:8–10, he treats Deut 33:8–11 as part of the Non-P History, which includes Exod 17:1–7 and 32:25–29 (*Exodus*, 390, 711–712). Similarly, Johnstone's assessment of Deut 33:8–11 is also unclear, but he asserts it preserves the memory of when the pre-P narrative of Exod 17:1–7* (originally situated after Horeb between Num 11:1–3 and 11:4–34) was followed by Exod 32:25–29; P relocated both Exod 17:1–7* and 32:25–29 to their current locations (*Chronicles and Exodus*, 255–257; cf. pp. 20–21, 80 n. 72 above and pp. 188–190 below). Van Seters confidently asserts that the Jahwist "construed" the single event in Deut 33:8–9 into two events in Exod 17:1–7* and 32:25–29*: Exod 17:1–17* is "an elaboration of the remarks about 'testing' and 'striving' in Deut 33:8," while Exod 32:25–29 is an accretion to the Golden Calf narrative "intended to explain their dissemination as *gērîm* (resident aliens without land) among the tribes, and their installation in the priesthood" (*The Life of Moses*, 316–317).

A most unusual reconstruction is posited by Frankel, who appears to accept Exod 32:26–29 as original to the Golden Calf narrative (contra the majority of scholarship). According to Frankel, Deut 33:8–9 preserves the earliest memory of the M-Mt, which was originally about an act of idolatry, not water deprivation. The non-P materials (for reasons left unexplained) first associated מריבה with the motif of water provision, which in turn inspired P's revision of Num 20:1–13*. Originally in the Dt tradition, Moses and Aaron were refused entrance into the land because of Israel's idolatry; this tradition was echoed in Ps 106:31–32 and identified as taking place at מי מריבה, where God makes an oath (√בטא) against Moses because of Israel's idolatry (cf. Deut 4:21–22; see also 6:14–16, where injunctions about idolatry are followed by the parenesis of Massah). The P supplementer to Num 20:1–13* opposed the idea of Moses being punished for Israel's sin, so he fabricated "a sin committed by Moses and Aaron (for Aaron was already a character in the tradition and he too would die outside the land) for which they were punished" (*Murmuring Stories*, 310, 305–310). While provocative, Frankel's reconstruction lacks any discernible controls beyond his own reading.

In the end, all the above reconstructions not only presume the antiquity of Deut 33:8–10 over Exod 17:1–7* and 32:25–29, but also place enormous burden on these verses as reflecting a single tradition-historical event, which is something even the targumim do not attempt to do (cf. T^ONJF on Deut 33:8–9).

beckon, the Levites then rise up and slaughter 3,000 Israelites, without any regard for ties of kinship (Exod 32:25–29). Thus, while Israel had failed by inappropriately complaining against Yahweh, the Levites had passed Yahweh's test in their violent zeal on behalf of Yahweh.

There are several difficulties that render this reading problematic. First, as already discussed above, all internal evidence within the Blessing points to Deut 33:8–10 being particularly late, most likely postexilic. Yet scholars who utilize Deut 33:8–10 to reconstruct the earliest form of the M-Mt by necessity must assume the blessing of Levi is extremely early. Second, the above reading requires Yahweh to perform the action of the 2ms verbs נסיתו and תריבהו, yet the antecedents for the pronominal subjects in Deut 33:8 are notoriously unclear. Considering that no other M-Mt text recalls the deity engaging an individual or particular tribe in this way, [129] it is procedurally preferable to clarify the antecedents in Deut 33:8 by the weight of the other M-Mt texts, even more so if Deut 33:8–10 is postexilic as this study argues. Thirdly, the overlap between Deut 33:8–11 and Exod 32:25–29 is miniscule: a) in Deut 33:9, there is nothing explicitly violent in the devout Levite declaring לא ראיתיו to his father and mother, nor in his having no regard (לא הכיר) for his brothers or not knowing (לא ידע) his son (sons, *qere*)[130]; b) the purported actions of the Levites in Deut 33:9 (לא + √ראה, √נכר, √ידע) do not align with those they took against the other tribes in Exod 32:27–29—that is, for each man to take (√שים) a sword, go back and forth (√שוב + √עבר), and kill (√הרג) his brother (אחיו), his friend (ראהו), his neighbor (קרבו), and even his son (בנו); and c) the familial relations mentioned in the two texts do not fully correspond, for while Exod 32:26–29 mentions brother and son, no mention is made of the first two relations listed in Deut 33:9, namely father (אב) and mother (אם). In the end, the closest lexical parallels are that both brother and son are objects of the Levites' actions (cf. Exod 32:27, 29; Deut 33:9b) and the aspect of the Levites being "blessed" (ברכה ‖ √ברך; cf. Exod 32:29 and Deut 33:11 respectively). Fourth and finally, the amount of textual rearrangement this reading presupposes—i.e. that at some point Exod 32:26–29 was severed from Exod 17:1–7* and then inserted 32:26–29 into the Gold Calf narrative—

---

129 In Deut 8:15–16, Yahweh tests all the people of Israel, not an individual or specific tribe.
130 Even if this language is formulaic for legal disinheritance, the interpretation that the enactment of it was intrinsically violent is deductive from the Levite's violent roles in the stories of Dinah (Gen 34:25–31) and Israel's failure at Horeb (Exod 32:25–29) (Nelson, *Deuteronomy*, 390).

stands as too heavy of a burden for an oblique tribal saying like Deut 33:8 – 11 to bear.[131]

Rather than reconstructing just one tradition, it is much easier to read Deut 33:8 – 10 as interacting with multiple texts across the Pentateuch in intertextual fashion. The clearest of these texts, of course, are references to the events at מסה (Exod 17:1 – 7) and at מי מריבה (Num 20:1 – 13*). Yet in neither text, as they currently stand, does Yahweh test (√נסה) or contend (√ריב) with a devout Levite, whether Moses or Aaron.[132] Instead, it is the congregation in Num 20:2 – 3 that gathers (√קהל) against Moses and Aaron, and quarrels (√ריב) explicitly against Moses and implicitly against Aaron (cf. the 2mp forms in accusations in Num 20:4 – 5). Likewise, in Exod 17:2 – 3, Israel only grumbles against Moses, but here the redactor (PentRed; cf. p. 138 below) responsible for Deut 33:8 may also have inferred Aaron's presence via the people's plural imperative תנו־לנו in MT Exod 17:2.[133] Thus, one can read Deut 33:8 as either 1) Moses instructing

---

[131] Nevertheless, several possible connections are extant between the non-P M-Mt narrative in Exod 17:1 – 7 and the Golden Calf narrative, as Nathan MacDonald has recently shown. These connections, as Nathan lists them, include the mention of Horeb (Exod 17:6; 33:6); the matter of Yahweh's presence amidst Israel (17:7; 33:3, 5; 34:9); the attribution of the exodus from Egypt "solely to Moses" instead of Yahweh (17:3; 32:1, 7, 23; 33:1); the role of the elders of Israel (17:5; 24:9 – 11); drinking from a flow of water associated with Horeb (17:6; 32:20); and finally, the reversal of two posturings: 1) from Yahweh standing on a rock before Moses (17:6) to Moses standing before Yahweh (33:21; 34:2), and 2) from Moses passing before the people (17:5) to Yahweh passing before Moses (33:19, 22) (cf. "Anticipations of Horeb: Exodus 17 as Inner-Biblical Commentary," in *Studies on the Text and Versions of the Hebrew Bible in Honour of Robert Gordon* [ed. Geoffrey Khan and Diana Lipton; VTSup 149; Leiden–Boston: Brill, 2012], 12 – 14). Such connections hint at the artistry of the non-P wilderness corpus of which the Deuteronomistic proprietors were aware; they do not suggest, and MacDonald does not argue for, an early Levitic M-Mt tradition.

[132] That Moses and Aaron are Levites is well-known (cf. Exod 2:1; 4:14), but only Aaron is ever called "the Levite" (Exod 4:14).

[133] Here, Samuel's assertion that originally Deut 33:8 could only refer to Moses, "nicht Aaron und auch nicht Angehörigen des Stammes Levi generell," is overstated (*Von Priestern zum Patriarchen*, 69). Though Aaron is not overtly mentioned in Exod 17:1 – 7, the people's demand for Moses to "give[2mp] us water" in MT Exod 17:2 (תנו־לנו מים) may be read to imply Aaron's presence. Admittedly, complicating this reading is the fact that several manuscripts have a singular imperative instead of a plural; cf. 4QpaleoExod^M, Smr, G, S, T^j, V. Nevertheless, the MT is the *lectio difficilior*, and since Aaron is active in the pericopes that surround Exod 17:1 – 7 (cf., Exod 16:2; 17:10 – 12), the MT is to be preferred, and Aaron's presence alongside Moses can be inferred. (Although, the literary history of Exod 17:1 – 7 indicates that the 2mp תנו may have originally addressed Moses and the deity [cf. p. 184 below; Num 21:5].) Although Samuel's reading of Deut 33:8 – 11 is markedly similar to my own (see pp. 130 – 134 below), his conclusion is compromised by the failure to note that the phrase "מי מריבה" (Deut 33:8bβ) does not appear

the Israelites to give their תמים and אורים to an Aaronide, whose founder is Aaron the Levite (הבו ללוי, so 4QDeut^h, 4QTestimonia, and G), *or* 2) Moses declaring that these vestments belong to such an individual (taking ל on MT's לאיש as a *lamed* of possession).[134] This Aaronide is their devout one (חסידך)—a term found nowhere else in the Pentateuch[135]—whose founder the Israelites had tested at מסה and quarreled with at מי מריבה.[136]

Admittedly, the intertextual echoes in Deut 33:9 are not as overt as those in v. 8. Early midrash, however, does not lend support for reading Deut 33:9 as a continuation of the M-Mt referenced in Deut 33:8.[137] One text that scholars have

---

in Exod 17:1–7, but in Num 20:13. Granted, Exod 17:7 mentions both מסה and מריבה, while Num 20:13 does not; but מסה and מי מריבה in Deut 33:8 does not precisely correspond to either Exod 17:7 or Num 20:13. Instead, Deut 33:8 draws on both Exod 17:7 and Num 20:13.

134 The phrase תמיך ואוריך in Deut 33:8 is unusual for two additional reasons: first, the sequence is reverse from the usual order of Urim and Thummim (cf. Exod 28:30; Lev 8:8; Ezra 2:63 = Neh 7:65); and second, these vestments are elsewhere never modified by possessive pronouns. Further, nowhere in the Hebrew Bible do the terms Urim or Thummim appear in a construct phrase which would in any way clarify the identity of the 2ms pronominal suffixes on these terms in Deut 33:8. In fact, there is no indication within the Hebrew Bible that the Urim and Thummim were considered Yahweh's possession instead of Israel's, which the typical reading of Deut 33:8 as a petition to Yahweh to bestow his Thummim and Urim on Levi requires. In short, reading v. 8 as Moses' instruction for Israel to give their Thummim and Urim to an Aaronide Levite, or conversely that they belong to such an individual, is wholly within the bounds of possibility. That elsewhere the Urim and Thummim are a part of the high priest's accoutrements (cf., Exod 28:30; Lev 8:8; Num 27:21, probably also Ezra 2:63 = Neh 7:65) lends further support for reading Deut 33:8 as a benefaction to Aaronide priests as opposed to the Levites in general.
135 The lemme חסיד occurs in thirty-two verses in the Hebrew Bible, twenty-five of which are in the Psalter: Deut 33:8; 1 Sam 2:9 (2x); 2 Sam 22:26; Jer 3:12; Mic 7:2; Pss. 4:4; 12:2; 16:10; 18:26; 30:5; 31:24; 32:6; 37:28; 43:1; 50:5; 52:11; 79:2; 85:9; 86:2; 89:20; 97:10; 116:15; 132:9, 16; 145:10, 17; 148:14; and 149:1, 5, 9; 2 Chr 6:4.
136 Again, T^JNF and T^Gzn also understand the חסיד as Aaron; cf. p. 122 n. 108 above.
137 The targummim interpret Deut 33:9 variously: T^O interprets the actions of the Levites toward father, mother, brothers, and sons in the context of jurisprudence—family on whom they had no compassion (לא רחים) when they are guilty of the law (כד חבו מן דינא); curiously, T^F states the Levites' did not show favor toward their father and mother in the case of Tamar (לא נסיב אפין בדינא דתמר), yet the Levites play no role in Genesis 38; this has prompted suggestions of a scribal error of "תמר" for "חמור" (cf. Gen 34:2) so that the text refers to the story of Dinah instead; T^F then references the Levite's impartiality toward their brothers in the incident of the calf (בעובא דעיגלא; cf. Exod 32:26–29) and toward theirs sons in the incident of Zimri (בעובא דזימרי; cf. Num 25:7–15) (Klein, *Fragment-Targums of the Pentateuch*, I:232, II:189, 189 n. 123); like T^O, T^N states that the Levites did not favor their father and mother in legal cases, but then T^N follows T^F in referencing the incidents of the calf and Zimri in relation to their impartiality toward their brothers and sons respectively. The primary significance here is that early

failed to consider and yet bears striking resemblance to the familial language in Deut 33:9 is Lev 21:1–4, 10–12. In Lev 21:1–4, the Aaronide priests (הכהנים בני אהרן) are only permitted to defile themselves (טמא√) for immediate family: לאמו ולאביו ולבנו ולבתו ולאחיו ולאחתו הבתולה הקרובה אליו (vv. 2b-3aα). Yet in Lev 21:10–12, the Aaronide high priest (הכהן הגדול מאחיו)—who has been consecrated to wear the priestly garments (הבגדים), which includes the Urim and Thummim (cf. Exod 28:3, 30)—is forbidden to defile himself for his father and mother (לאביו ולאמו לא יטמא; v. 11b). Although the whole list of relatives is not recapitulated at this point, the contrast of Lev 21:1–4 stands in the foreground, and the reversal of the introductory pair (from לאמו ולאביו to לאביו ולאמו) most likely serves as a synecdoche for the entire list. The implications these verses have for reading Deut 33:8–9 are far more compelling than any attempt to recreate a "Levitical M-Mt": Moses commands Israel to vest as their high priest a devout Aaronide, who is a Levite by lineage (v. 8a; cf. Exod 4:14), whose founder Israel had tested at Massah and quarreled with at Meribah (v. 8b), and whose familial ties are to be severed in high priestly service to Yahweh (v. 9a). In the end, this reading not only comports well with Deut 33:8–9a's consistent use of the singular to refer to this devout individual, but it also establishes these verses as programmatic of the Aaronide priesthood's ascendency during the late Persian period.[138]

The remainder of the insertion that constitutes the blessing of Levi (Deut 33:9b-10) is of little consequence for the study of the M-Mt in Deut 33:8. Nevertheless, in the interest of providing a full reading, one should note that Deut 33:9b marks a sudden change on two fronts: 1) the Levites are referred to in the plural instead of the singular,[139] and 2) Yahweh emerges as the clear antecedent to the 2ms pronouns. These shifts prompt some scholars to suggest that vv. 9b-10 stem from a different literary hand than the one responsible for vv. 8–9a.[140] Once one recognizes vv. 8–9a to be programmatic of the Aaronide high priest, however, the suggestion of a tertiary layer becomes unnecessary. The priestly roles prescribed in v. 10 are supportive and combine functions that can

---

interpreters did not read Deut 33:9 as continuing to describe the M-Mt tradition referenced in v. 8.

138 For a recent discussion of the rise of the Aaronides and their influence in shaping the Torah, see James W. Watts, "Scripturalization and the Aaronide Dynasties," *JHS* 13.6 n.p. [cited 15 July 2013] On Online: http://dx.doi.org/10.5508/jhs.2013.v13.a6.

139 In v. 11, reference to the Levites again occurs in the singular, but this shift is most likely a byproduct of PentRed appropriating v. 11 from the blessing of Judah.

140 E.g., Mayes, *Deuteronomy*, 402; Nielsen, *Deuteronomium*, 294; Nelson, *Deuteronomy*, 389–390; Dahmen, *Leviten under Priester*, 197–201; Samuel, *Von Priestern zum Patriarchen*, 71.

typify either Aaronide or Levitical priests in general.[141] In other words, one can detect the same Aaronide program in vv. 9b-10 as is in vv. 8–9a, but at a subordinate priestly level.[142] As such, it appears that the purpose of the blessing of Levi is to facilitate the Aaronide absorption of the Levites in the creation of a reconciled priesthood, while at the same time maintaining Aaronide ascendancy (cf. Num 8:6–26).[143]

In summary, there are several indicators which suggest that the M-Mt embedded in Deut 33:8 is part of an insertion that is particularly later than the literary context that surrounds it. The style, content, meter, scope, and function of Deut 33:8–10 are quite distinctive from the rest of the tribal sayings that make up the

---

141 Although the Aaronides are commanded to teach Yahweh's חקים (Lev 10:10–11), the task of teaching and tending to Yahweh's תורה is more characteristic of the Levites (e.g., Deut 17:18; 31:9, 24–26; Neh 8:7–9; 2 Chr 31:4). Conversely, while the Levites can offer sacrifices (Jer 33:18; 2 Chr 31:2), the offering up of smoke (√קטר; cf. קטורה in Deut 33:10) and burnt offerings (כליל) is the monopoly of the Aaronides (e.g., Exodus 29–30, Leviticus 1–9). That the word כליל is in parallel construct with קטורה in Deut 33:10 is particularly reminiscent of the grain offering Aaron and his sons are to offer up in smoke every morning and evening (Lev 6:13–16 [20–23]).
142 Cf. Dahmen, who sees vv. 9b-10 as part of a post-exilic pro-Levitic redaction (along with Deut 10:8f. and 24:14) that reclaims for the Levites their roles in teaching and participating in sacrificial cult (*Leviten und Priester*, 201). I agree that the priestly Levites benefit in vv. 9b-10 via a unique conflation of terminological activities (cf. p. 133 n. 141 above), but I do not see the rhetorical agenda of these verses as wholly distinct from vv. 8–9a. Rather, vv. 8–9a portray the eponymous ancestor Levi with strictly Aaronide terms and traditions, thereby circumscribing the highest priestly office to the Aaronides; while vv. 9b-10 relegate the Levites to subordinate priestly duties. In short, the rhetorical agenda is the same for both the singular and plural sections of the blessing of Levi: the absorption of the Levites in the creation of a reconciled priesthood, while at the same time maintaining Aaronide ascendancy.

Samuel arrives at a similar conclusion but through a different argument: even though Deut 33:8 reclaims for the Levites (via the figure of Moses) the high priestly functions (cf. *Von Priestern zum Patriarchen*, 73), "Die Erwähnung der Urim und Tummim läßt andererseits ganz natürlich an den Hohenpriester und damit Aaron denken—jedenfalls in einem Pentateuch, der die Priesterschrift voraussetzt" (*Von Priestern zum Patriarchen*, 77); the Aaronide vestments, along with the final priestly supplement of Deut 10:6–9, suggests the possibility that for these supplementers "aaronidische Interessen" would have stood in the background of Deut 33:8–11, and that they would have viewed Aaron as איש חסידך in v. 8 (cf. *Von Priestern zum Patriarchen*, 77).
143 The appropriation of the patriarch Levi as the priestly archetype develops over the course of the second temple period and is beyond the scope of the current study; see James Kugel, who traces these developments from Malachi 2 through the *Testament of Levi* ("Levi's Elevation to the Priesthood in Second Temple Writings," HTR 86 [1993]: 1–64). Alternatively, Leveen asserts that the root of these priestly tensions—especially as represented in Numbers—could stem from as early as "the period of Hezekiah with the influx of priests from the north," but likely continued for centuries into the "rebuilding of the Second Temple with the reinstitution and realignment of a priestly leadership" (*Memory and Tradition*, 63 and pp. 58–64).

Blessing. Further, not only do vv. 8–9a interact with literary texts across the Pentateuch (i.e., Exod 16:2–17:13; Lev 21:1–12; and Num 20:1–13*), but they appear along with vv. 9b-10 to be Aaronide programmatic texts. The blessing of Levi is therefore most likely a postexilic composition. Add to these indicators the observation that Deut 33:8 aggrandizes Aaron in much the same way that PentRed did the figure of Moses (cf. Deut 34:7b, 10–12), and it may not be too much to credit PentRed with composing Deut 33:8–10 coterminously to his having inserted the Blessing into its current textual location.

4.4.3 Tradition-historical Analysis of Deut 33:8b

The above literary analysis drastically undermines the likelihood of a "Levitical M-Mt" having ever existed. Instead, for the first time in Deuteronomy, there is explicit *canonical awareness* of the existence and relative textual location of non-P and P* M-Mt narratives: in v. 8bα, the testing (נסה√) at מסה evokes the non-P M-Mt narrative in Exod 17:1–7*; while in v. 8bβ, the quarrelling (ריב√) at מי מריבה evokes the P* M-Mt narrative in Num 20:1–13*.[144] Thus, in Deut 33:8b, מסה and מי מריבה are the *locations* of non-P's M-Mt and P*'s M-Mt respectively, not mere wordplays as Lehming proposed.[145]

Further tradition components that mirror the M-Mt narratives include the *substance of issuance* and *agency*. The substance of issuance is retained in the toponym from P*'s M-Mt narrative, מי מריבה (cf. Num 20:13); while the *source of issuance* is again left to the reader's recollection. The *agency* of the testing, although distinctive compared to the other M-Mt texts in Deuteronomy, is derivative of the people having quarreled against Moses and (presumably) Aaron in Exod 17:2 and Num 20:3. The precise *interpretative significance* for citing these exemplars of the M-Mt tradition, however, remains unclear. Perhaps PentRed cited the M-Mt narratives since they artistically approximate the span of Aaron's faith-

---

[144] Although Exod 17:7 also includes the etiological toponym מריבה, it does not employ the construct phrase מי מריבה, which appears variously in priestly texts, but not in dt/Dtr texts (Num 20:13; 27:14; Ezek 47:19; 48:28; cf. Pss 81:8; 106).

[145] Sigo Lehming, "Massa und Meriba," *ZAW* 73 (1961): 76–77. Curiously, Lehming feels compelled to reconstruct עלי־מיin the phrase על־מי מריבה (Deut 33:8bβ) to a hypothetically more original "לים". Had he recognized that מי + מריבה* is typical of M-Mt in P* texts, perhaps he would have reconsidered his idea that מריבה in Deut 33:8b is merely a concept (*Begriff*) as opposed to a name. See pp. 12–13 above for further critique of Lehming's thesis.

ful service during the wilderness sojourn?¹⁴⁶ The appellation "חסיד" would then serve to exonerate Aaron from any perceived wrong during this span of service—an interpretation the targummim explicate for Deut 33:8.¹⁴⁷

4.5 Reconstructing the Framework of the M-Mt's Tradition-historical Development (Part 2)

In Part One of Reconstructing the Framework (§3.5.), this study found that the three M-Mt reminiscences within Deuteronomy's interior prologue stem from three different periods, each in turn reflecting a different stage in the tradition-historical development of the M-Mt: Deut 8:15 (*Dt*), 6:16 (*late Dtr*), and 9:22 (*Dtr Supp*). The reminiscences preserved in Deuteronomy's exterior epilogues both supplement and add to these stages: Deut 32:13 is coterminous with 8:15 (*Dt*) or perhaps slightly earlier; while Deut 32:48–50, 52 is the work of *HexRed*, Deut 32:51 stems from an even later hand than Deut 33:8 which is *PentRed*; 32:51 is therefore a late *post-PentRed* addition and constitutes the latest reminiscence in Deuteronomy as a whole. Thus, Deuteronomy is witness to five literary stages in the development of M-Mt's *Traditionsgeschichte*.

Stage 1: It is not necessary to recapitulate every aspect of this stage. Summarily, at this early stage Yahweh tests Israel (*agency*) in the wilderness via water deprivation, only to provide water (*substance of issuance*) miraculously from a flinty rock or crag (*source of issuance*); there is no culpability or failure, however, on the part of Israel until their entry into the land. Both Deut 8:15 and 32:13 align to varying degrees with this tradition-historical profile, but they also evince a number of other similarities: both texts relay ancient Israel's early history in

---

146 Aaron's first appears in the Wilderness Tradition in conjunction with the manna episode in Exodus 16; the conflict at the waters of Meribah in Numbers 20 is Aaron's final episode before his death (Num 20:22–29). The M-Mt narratives comprise an artistic, albeit somewhat imprecise frame for this time.

147 Drazin notes this possibility for T⁰, which adds the phrase "and he was upright" (והוה שלים) immediately after the reference to Israel's holy one (presumably Aaron) being tested at "the trials"; and which further adds "and he was found faithful" (ואשתכח מהימן) after the reference to the "water of contention" (Drazin, *Targum Onkelos to Deuteronomy*, 299 n. 35); cf. Tʲ, which has the same additions. Likewise, Tᶠ adds the phrases "and who stood up to the test" (וקם בניסיונא) as well as "and you found him to be faithful" (ואישתכחת מהימן) (Klein, *Fragment-Targums of the Pentateuch*, 1:232; 2:188–189). Note that Tʲ has the same supplements as T⁰, while Tᴺ reads the same as Tᶠ.

broad metanarrative strokes with little historical specificity[148]; both texts employ mythic language regarding the setting of the M-Mt rather than relaying a specific toponym (*location*); and as well, there is no *canonical awareness* of either of the two M-Mt narratives (i.e., Exod 17:1–7; Num 20:1–13), or for that matter of a developing Pentateuchal or Hexateuchal collection. This stage therefore most likely reflects the oral foundation in the earliest literary stage of the M-Mt (see §3.3.3; Stage 1 in §3.5; §4.2.2 above).

Stage 2: No further evidence regarding this stage is extant in Deuteronomy beyond Deut 6:16 and its immediate literary context. Nevertheless, for the sake of completion, a summary restatement is warranted. At this intermediate stage, the *agency* of Dtr's M-Mt has shifted drastically from Yahweh to Israel, from divine orchestration to an incident of national failure (cf. Deut 8:15; 6:16). The *location* of the M-Mt is only now embryonic, no more than a cognate accusative (נסה√; cf. בְּמַסָּה); but it is sufficient to suggest the *canonical awareness* among the Dtr textual proprietors of an early form of the non-P M-Mt narrative in Exod 17:1–7* (cf. §3.2.3; Stage 2 in §3.5; above). The *interpretative significance*, as well, has reached a zenith as the M-Mt here represents the paradigmatic failure of the first wilderness generation.

Stage 3: As reflected in Deut 9:22, it is at this stage that the Dtr/non-P M-Mt is beginning to stabilize and to be situated canonically. The *agency* remains the same as at Stage 2, as presumably does the *source* and *substance of issuance*. Additionally, there is the concretization of the Dtr/non-P M-Mt *location* (מַסָּה), as well as the collocation of the M-Mt among other murmuring traditions (*canonical awareness*), though at this stage it appears to have held a post-Horeb position. This textual arrangement, however, fundamentally reshaped the M-Mt's *interpretative significance* from that of pinnacle failure to an instance of patternistic behavior (cf., §3.4.3; Stage 3 in §3.5).

Stage 4: This stage of the M-Mt development is reflected in the Blessing of Levi in Deut 33:8, which evinces the earliest *canonical awareness* of the P* M-Mt within Deuteronomy.[149] Regardless of its authorship,[150] it is clear that this var-

---

[148] In Deut 8:2–18, the historical metanarrative moves from the exodus out of Egypt, to care in the wilderness, to satiety and infidelity in the Promised Land. A similar metanarrative is reflected in Deut 32:1–20*, which moves from primordial allotment of the nations, to discovery and care in the wilderness, to satiety and infidelity (presumably in the Promised Land).

[149] Since Deuteronomy does not contain any texts that preserve reminiscences of the P* M-Mt's developmental stages, inquiry into the formative stages of the P* M-Mt must turn to P* M-Mt narrative in Num 20:1–13 and all its related texts beyond Deuteronomy (i.e., Exod 17:1–7; Num 20:24; 27:12–14; 33:14, 36, 38–39, 46). This undertaking is the focus of chapter seven of this study.

iant expression of the M-Mt entered Deuteronomy at a time when the P* M-Mt had not yet reached its full development. There is no *awareness* of Aaron's (and Moses') failure at מי מריבה; instead, the people have tested Aaron at both Massah and Meribah, yet Aaron still remains devout (חסיד). In other words, not only does Deut 33:8 carry the implication that the M-Mt had earlier split into two separate literary traditions,[151] but it also recalls a time when the P* M-Mt did not conclude with the failure of Moses and Aaron (cf. §7.3.1), but instead focused on the people's challenging Aaron and Moses (§7.3.2). Thus, the *interpretative significance* of the M-Mt for the author of Deut 33:8 is its support for the Aaronide program which it advocates. To this extent, Deut 33:8 aggrandizes Aaron in much the same way that Deut 34:7b, 10 – 12 aggrandizes Moses.

Stage 5: In contrast to Deut 33:8, the stage of the P* M-Mt which Deut 32:51 reflects is not intermediate, but rather the final stage of the P* M-Mt's tradition-historical development. Here, the *agency* of P* M-Mt has shifted compared to the earlier M-Mt reminiscences, from an instance of national failure (cf. Deut 6:16; 9:22; and 33:8 [?]) into a costly momentary indiscretion on the part of Israel's founding leaders, which in turn provides an explanation for why Moses and Aaron died outside the Promised Land (*interpretative significance*). For Moses this rationale is also a corrective: Moses was neither too aged to enter the land (Deut 31:2; cf. Deut 34:7 [PentRed]), nor punished for the sins of others (Deut 1:34 – 37; 3:26 – 29; 4:21), for his fate was not contingent upon others; only his own failure could merit such an outcome (cf. Num 20:12; 27:14; Deut 32:51). Thus, this alteration of the P* M-Mt not only presumes PentRed's elevating

---

150 In §7.3.1 below, evidence is marshalled to suggest that Deut 32:51 is part of a larger redaction, whereby post-PentRed transformed the P* M-Mt into the rationale for why Moses and Aaron were not allowed to enter the Promised Land. This redactor accomplished this feat by first shifting the *agency* of the P* M-Mt narrative, from a failure of the congregation to that of Moses and Aaron; afterwards, post-PentRed only need to amend the death notices of Aaron (Num 20:24b) and Moses (Num 27:14; Deut 32:51) respectively. Given this redaction, it is likely that Deut 32:48 – 50+52 (HexRed) originally had no connections to the M-Mt.

151 Although not attested in Deuteronomy, analysis of the M-Mt texts beyond Deuteronomy in the remainder of the Pentateuch corroborates the bifurcation of the M-Mt's *Traditionsgeschichte* at its earliest written stage. Thus, while the non-P and P* M-Mt no doubt stem from the same oral tradition, they appear to have emerged in separate literary forms and then undergone further literary developments independently from one another until such a time when they were coordinated (cf. §6.3.2 and §7.3.4). This process of separate literary emergence, independent development, and subsequent coordination accounts for the verbal and conceptual correspondences the two M-Mt narratives have when compared to one another (cf. 5.2.1).

Moses to canonical status, but it also contends with the tension that this creates on account of Moses' exclusion from the land.[152]

In summary, the M-Mt texts in Deuteronomy give witness to at least five stages in M-Mt's *Traditionsgeschichte*. Stage 1 is the earliest literary expression of the oral M-Mt tradition: a positive tradition of divine testing and subsequent provision (Deut 32:13b; 8:15 [*Dt*]). Stage 2 initiates the literary developments of the M-Mt, most likely in two independent contexts, by Dtr/non-P and P* respectively. At this stage, the Dtr/non-P M-Mt reflects the agency shifting from divine to human, as well as early etiological development (Deut 6:16 [*late Dtr*]). By stage 3, however, the Dtr/non-P M-Mt etiology Massah has concretized and its corresponding narrative has found its early location within the non-P corpus of wilderness narratives (Deut 9:22 [*Dtr Supp*]). Stage 4 displays awareness of two distinct versions of the M-Mt: the Dtr/non-P M-Mt at מסה as reflected in Exod 17:1–7 and the P* M-Mt at מי־מריבה as reflected in Num 20:1–13* (Deut 33:8 [*PentRed*]). Significantly, at this fourth stage, the P* M-Mt tradition has not yet achieved its final form; there is no awareness of Moses and Aaron's failure (cf. Num 20:12), and the interpretive significance that Deut 33:8 reflects indicates its author understood the P* M-Mt narrative as evidence of Aaron's faithfulness. It is only at the fifth and final stage of the M-Mt that Deuteronomy reflects Moses and Aaron's sin and its consequence has entered the P* M-Mt (Deut 32:51 [*post-PentRed*]).

In the second part of this study, the M-Mt texts outside Deuteronomy in the remainder of the Pentateuch demonstrate two intermediate stages in the M-Mt's development, stages between the third and fourth stages reflected in Deuteronomy. In the first of these stages the Dtr/non-P and P* M-Mt undergo coordination (pre-Hex Supp); in the second, the Dtr/non-P narrative experiences transposition in the emergence of the Hexateuch (HexRed) (§6.3). Though Deuteronomy itself does not bear direct witness to these stages, the framework detected in Deuteronomy for the M-Mt tradition-historical development logically anticipates these intermediate stages. Thus, the reminiscences in Deuteronomy establish a framework whereby to negotiate the diachrony of M-Mt text lying outside the perspective of Deuteronomy's macro- and micro-redactional growth. It is with this framework in mind that the second part of this study attends to the remaining M-Mt texts in the Pentateuch.

---

[152] This tension is especially poignant for Moses, whom Achenbach aptly describes as "größer als Aaron," citing Numbers 12 (*Die Vollendung der Tora*, 334). In Exod 7:1, Aaron is Moses' prophet, but Num 12:6–8 describes Moses' relation to Yahweh as closer than the prophets; finally, Deut 34:10 asserts Moses' superiority to the prophets after him, who have not known Yahweh face to face.

Part II **Beyond Deuteronomy:
The M-Mt in the Remainder of the
Pentateuch**

Chapter Five:
Toward Assessing the M-Mt Texts in the Remainder of the Pentateuch

5.1 Introduction to the Remaining M-Mt Texts within the Pentateuch

Part One of this study attended to the reminiscences of the M-Mt embedded within the book of Deuteronomy: Deut 6:16, 8:15; 9:22; 32:13b, 51; 33:8. Evidence from several methods of inquiry—including redaction criticism (at both the macro- and micro-redactional levels), text criticism, and literary analysis (with attention to both literary tensions and unifying factors)—established the relative chronological relationship of these texts in regards to each of their surrounding literary contexts and their relationship to one another. This chronology provided a means whereby to negotiate the diversity of the M-Mt reminiscences preserved within Deuteronomy, thereby establishing the framework of the M-Mt's tradition-historical developments, at least from the perspective of Deuteronomy's scribal proprietors.

The second part of this study now turns to evaluating the M-Mt texts in the rest of the Pentateuch beyond Deuteronomy—namely, Exod 17:1–7; Num 20:1–13, 24; 27:12–14; 33:14, 36.[1] Yet to limit this part of the study to these M-Mt texts only, as though to set the parameters of our investigation, proves too restrictive. Not only do the M-Mt narratives relate to one another—as do also Num 20:24 and 27:12–14 to Num 20:1–13, and Num 33:14, 36 to Exod 17:7 and to Num 20:1–13 respectively—but all these texts are also thematically and lexically anchored to their broader literary contexts in some surprising ways. It is therefore insufficient to treat the M-Mt narratives as isolated pericopes. Instead, not only must one investigate each narrative's history of development individually as discreet literary units, but one must also treat these developments in relation to the other M-Mt related texts and to their moorings within their broader literary contexts throughout the Pentateuch.

The subsequent chapters are but a foray in the undertaking of the above mandate, with *chapter six* attending to Exod 17:1–7 and its related texts, and

---

[1] The scope of this study precludes a detailed investigation into the remainder of the M-Mt texts within the Hebrew Bible: Isa 48:21; Ezek 47:19; 48:28; Ps 78:15–16, 20, 35; 81:8, 17; 95:8–11; 105:41; 106:32; 114:8; and Neh 9:15, 20. See §8.3 below for a preliminary assessment of these texts and a trajectory for their further study.

chapter seven attending to Num 20:1–13 and its related texts. In both chapters the findings of the first part of this study—i.e., the framework for the stages of the M-Mt's *Traditionsgeschichte* as reflected in Deuteronomy—are brought to bear in order to approach a new synthesis.

Yet underlying both of these inquiries is the central question of how these M-Mt narratives relate to each other in first place—a relationship that doubtlessly factors into the history of the development of at least Num 20:1–13, if not Exod 17:1–7 as well. It is to this dynamic relationship that the study now turns.

5.2 What is the Relationship between the M-Mt Narratives?

Few scholars doubt that the non-P M-Mt narrative in Exod 17:1–7* and the P* M-Mt narrative in Num 20:1–13* share the same tradition-historical origin.² George W. Coats asserts

> There can be no doubt that the unit here [i.e. Num 20:1–13] is parallel to the tradition in Exod. 17:1–7, for exactly the same outline is to be found in both cases: (1) The setting involves the lack of water. (2) The people "strive" with Moses. (3) They also murmur against their leaders. (The P form uses קהל instead of לון and directs the murmuring against both Moses and Aaron.) (4) Moses appeals to Yahweh. (5) Yahweh give instructions for finding water. (6) Moses carries out the instructions before witnesses by striking a rock. (7) The narrative is concluded with an aetiological explanation of the place name.³

Yet as Coats succinctly states, there are "few points of verbatim agreement" from which to establish literary dependency.⁴ For Coats, the solution lies along source critical and literary analytical lines: Exod 17:1bβ-7 and Num 20:2–13 are fundamentally parallel versions of the same "Meribah tradition," with each text in possession of no clear internal doublets, and in turn the product of J and P editing their received traditions.⁵

---

2 For detractors, see p. 32 n. 12 above.
3 Cf. George W. Coats, *Rebellion in the Wilderness: The Murmuring Motif in the Wilderness Traditions of the Old Testament* (Nashville: Abingdon, 1968), 71. Coats' statement that "exactly the same outline is to be found in both [narratives]" is slightly overstated: his sixth parallel is "Moses carries out the instructions [of Yahweh] before witnesses by striking the rock," but in Num 20:8 Yahweh commands Moses and Aaron to speak to the rock, not to strike it.
4 Coats, *Rebellion in the Wilderness*, 71.
5 Coats, *Rebellion in the Wilderness*, 53–56, 71–73. Like Noth, Coats also considers the Massah elements in Exod 17:2bβ, 7 to be a secondary Deuteronomistic addition, giving priority instead to the Meribah (*Rebellion in the Wilderness*, 55; cf. Martin Noth, *Das zweite Buch Mose: Exodus* [ATD 5; Göttingen: Vandenhoeck & Ruprecht, 1958], 111). Yet this conclusion is predi-

Upon closer examination, however, the task of assessing the relationship between these narratives is significantly more complex than Coats' observations imply. Coats only observes four places of precise verbal parallelism between the narratives,[6] yet a closer comparison of the two M-Mt narratives demonstrates a level of correspondence that demands further nuancing (§5.2.1). Additionally, one must also observe two other shared features: 1) the strikingly similar internal literary tensions—similar both in type and proximity—that the two narratives exhibit, and 2) the fact that both narratives are lexically and thematically moored to literary contexts that are broader than one might initially presume (§5.2.2). These features merit careful consideration prior to characterizing the nature of the relationship between Exod 17:1–7 and Num 20:1–13 (§5.3), not alone to tracing their formative literary stages in subsequent chapters.

5.2.1 The Verbal and Conceptual Correspondence of the M-Mt Narratives

The M-Mt narrative exponents of Exod 17:1–7 and Num 20:1–13 evince a dynamic verbal and conceptual correspondence which undermines bald characterization (cf. Fig. 5.1 below). To begin, while there are a few instances of *verbatim correspondence*, none are beyond the measure of a few words. Moreover, many of these word-for-word parallels are to some extent formulaic; such instances may be incidental to the writing of these texts rather than instances of intentional quotation. *Approximate verbal correspondence*, which employs the same lexemes but with distinctive inflections, is more prevalent than verbatim corre-

---

cated on no more than that "Massah" elsewhere appears primarily in Deuteronomy; the exception, of course, is Ps. 95:8. This distribution, however, does not establish the "Massah" elements in 17:2bβ, 7 as secondary additions to the text. One could, in fact, argue quite the opposite via the same line of argumentation: that the Meribah elements are secondary on account that the texts mentioning "Meribah" are either priestly or have priestly ties (e.g., Num 20:13, 24; 27:14; Ezek 47:19; 48:28); the exceptions, of course, being the demonstrably late texts in Deuteronomy (32:51; 33:8) and psalmic literature (81:8; 95:8; 106:32), whose generic quality precludes clear association with either non-P or P oriented materials. Thus, since the Exod 17:2b-7 is clearly non-P material, one could just as easily conclude that it is the "Meribah" elements in 17:2bβ, 7 that are secondary, not the "Massah" elements (for further discussion, see §6.3 below).

6 Specifically, Coats notes the following parallels: Num 20:3a parallels Exod 17:2a; Num 20:5aα parallels Exod 17:3b; though "slightly rearranged" Num 20:5a parallels Exod 17:1bβ; and the narrative introduction to Yahweh's response in Num 20:7 parallels the same in Exod 17:5aα. "Beyond these points," states Coats, "there is no evidence of contact in the literary structure of the two narratives" (*Rebellion in the Wilderness*, 72).

spondence. Many of these approximate correspondences also contain formulaic expressions, which likewise may not reflect a deliberate echo of the correlative text. Where lexical correspondence is not demonstrable, often there is *conceptual correspondence* between comparable actions or ideas. Here too, formulaic language plays a role and must be taken into consideration when assessing intentional correspondence. Finally, there is significant material within both narratives that does not correspond verbally or conceptually. The prevalence and distribution of such *non-aligned material* also warrants consideration when calculating the similarity and dissimilarity of these texts.

The diagram below divides Exod 17:1–7 and Num 20:1–13 into eleven narrative sections (§1–§11), eight of which are present in both M-Mt narratives, while three are not (cf. §2, §5, and §10). Each section is then analyzed for the types of correspondence the correlative portions within each narrative display: *verbatim correspondence, approximate verbal correspondence, conceptual correspondence,* and *non-aligned material.* This approach allows one to quantify and compare each type of correspondence, thereby facilitating a more nuanced characterization of the M-Mt's material relationship.

Here, a summary of the findings using this approach is sufficient for the task at hand.[7] To begin, only 18 words exhibit verbatim correspondence and shared structural proximity.[8] Yet most of these words are arguably formulaic in nature, which in turn may not be the product of one text's literary dependence upon the other.[9] Only one verbatim phrase stands out as non-formulaic—וירב העם עם־משה

---

[7] For a thorough section-by-section analysis, see Appendix B: Quantitative Analysis of the Verbal and Conceptual Correspondences of Exod 17:1–17 and Num 20:1–13 on pp. 247–252 below.

[8] These words are as follows: בני־ישראל (17:1a ‖ 20:1a; 17:7bα ‖ 20:13aβ); מים (17:1bβ ‖ 20:2a); ממצרים (17:2aα ‖ 20:3a); וירב העם עם־משה ויאמרו (17:3bα ‖ 20:5aα); משה (17:4aα ‖ 20:6aα; 17:6bα ‖ 20:9a); יהוה אל־משה (17:5aα ‖ 20:7a); and את־יהוה (17:7bβ ‖ 20:13aβ).

[9] Of the eighteen words exhibiting verbatim correspondence, the following words appear in formulas across Exodus and Numbers: בני־ישראל (17:1aα ‖ 20:1aα; cf. 17:7bα ‖ 20:13aβ) appears in construct with כל־עדת (e.g., Exod 16:1, 2, 9, 10; Num 13:26; 14:7; 15:25; 17:6; 25:6; 26:2; 27:20; twice more in apposition in Num 20:1, 22); ויאמרו (17:2aα ‖ 20:3bα) as a speech formulary needs no substantiation; ממצרים + למה (17:3bα ‖ 20:5aα) in relation to √עלה is also in Num 21:5, but the murmuring question also occurs with the √יצא (Exod 14:11; Num 11:20); יהוה אל משה (17:5a ‖ 20:7) frequently occurs in speech formularies (57x with וידבר; 62x with ויאמר); את־יהוה [17:7bβ ‖ 20:13aβ]) is expected syntactically (cf. Exod 17:2, 7; Num 11:20; 20:13); and single word instances of verbatim correspondence—i.e. מים (17:1bβ ‖ 20:2) and משה (17:4aα ‖ 20:6aα; 17:6bα ‖ 20:9a)—are more likely to be incidental than intentional. In other words, the appearance of these expressions within both M-Mt narratives—although they exhibit both verbal and structural correspondence—is insufficient to establish direct literary dependence.

5.2 What is the Relationship between the M-Mt Narratives?

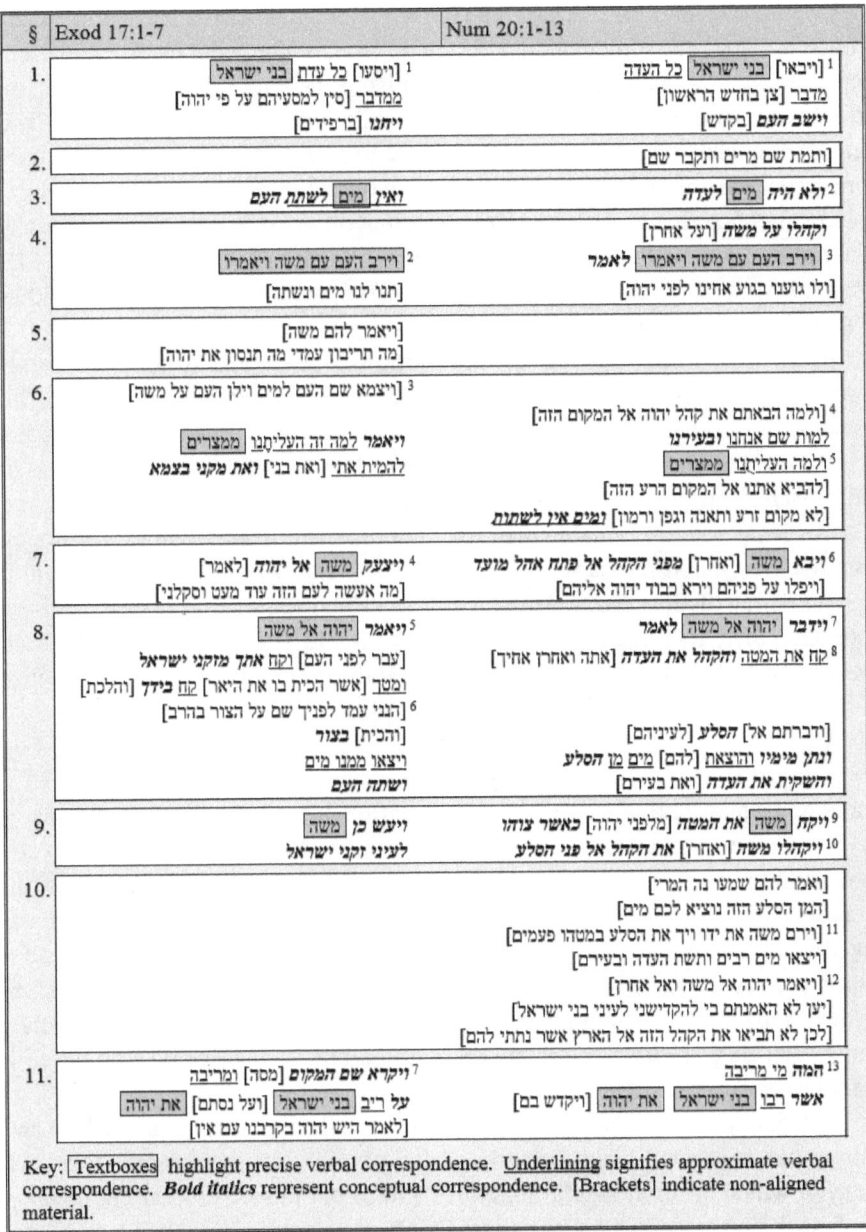

Fig. 5.1: The Verbal and Conceptual Correspondences of Exod 17:1–7 and Num 20:1–13

(17:2aα‖20:3a)—as it only occurs here in the M-Mt narratives. Thus, this single phrase provides the only evidence for direct literary dependence via quotation, though quotation is not the only interpretative possibility (cf. §6.3.2 below). Approximate verbal correspondence is also fairly limited, with just 16 words in Exod 17:1–7 being lexically, yet imprecisely related to 17 words in Num 20:1–13. Loose conceptual correspondence, however, is demonstrably more prevalent in Numbers 20 than Exodus 17, with 46 words in Num 20:1–13 overlapping conceptually (but not lexically) with 21 words in Exod 17:1–7. Finally, 65 words of Exod 17:1–7's total 133 words are unique, non-aligned material, while 111 words of Num 20:1–13's total 192 words are non-aligned.

In the end, when assessed quantitatively (see Appendix B), one can safely assert—without any presupposition regarding sources, redactional strata or insertions, or other forms of editing—that the verbal and conceptual overlaps between Exod 17:1–7 and Num 20:1–13 only comprise approximately 50% or less of their discreet literary units. Conversely, approximately 50% of Exod 17:1–7 and 60% of Num 20:1–13 remains distinctly non-aligned. In other words, although they tell very much the same story, Exod 17:1–7 and Num 20:1–13 articulate it in remarkably distinct ways. Any attempt to sketch the literary history of these texts and their relationship to one another should strive to account for both these incongruities and congruities, including the precise verbal correspondence of וירב העם עם־משה (17:2aα‖20:3a).

5.2.2 Additional Features Affecting the Relationship of the M-Mt Narratives

Two additional shared features—that is, beyond the verbal and conceptual (in)congruties outlined above (cf. §5.2.1)—contribute to the challenge of characterizing the nature of the relationship between the M-Mt narratives, features for which literary analysis should make an account. These additional features are 1) that both narratives exhibit similar internal tensions at similar junctures, and 2) that they are both thoroughly integrated into their respective broader literary contexts.

Not only do Exod 17:1–7 and Num 20:1–3 evince considerable verbal and conceptual correspondence, but they also exhibit several internal tensions, many of which occur at similar junctures within both texts. Proceeding linearly, the first shared internal tension pertains to the travel notices for both texts (17:1a-bα; 20:1a), which although relating to the itinerary of Numbers 33, nevertheless evince geographical and/or chronological displacement when compared to other texts.¹⁰ Secondly, both texts have internal redundant material located at approximately the same point in their respective narratives: namely, the people's complaint (Exod 17:2–3; Num 20:2b-5).¹¹ Lastly, both texts have etiologies with components that stand disjointed from the narratives they now conclude (Exod 17:7bγ; Num 20:13b).¹² That both texts have similar literary tensions at similar

---

10 For Exod 17:1a, the displacement is primarily geographical: the travel notice situates the narrative at Rephidim, but the narrative itself is set near Horeb (Exod 17:6), as though the Israelites had already arrived at the Mount of God. Yet narratively the Israelites do not arrive as Sinai/Horeb until Exod 19:1–2. Several scholars over the years have posited that P modified the original travel notice introducing Exod 17:1b-7 (e.g., Van Seters, *The Life of Moses: The Yahwist as Historian in Exodus-Numbers* [Louisville: Westminster John Knox, 1994], 155–156, who was building on G. I. Davies, "The Wilderness Itineraries and the Composition of the Pentateuch," *VT* 33 [1983]: 1–13, who in turn was building on Otto Eissfeldt, *Hexateuch-synopse* [Leipzig, 1922], 139–146). More recent exemplars include Thomas B. Dozeman and William Johnstone. Dozeman argues that in the non-P history the station of Rephidim originally followed upon Elim (Exod 15:27), which is now without an "accompanying narrative" due to P recontextualing the Manna narrative to the wilderness of Sin (Exod 16:1; 17:1a) (*Exodus* [ECC; Grand Rapids: Eerdmans, 2009], 359–360). For Johnstone's thesis regarding Exod 17:1–7 originally being a post-Horeb event, see §6.3.3 below.

The complexities regarding Israel's arrival at Kadesh in the wilderness of Zin (Num 20:1) are at least two-fold. First, Israel has already arrived at Kadesh in Num 13:26, but here the station is located within the wilderness of Paran (cf. Gen. 14:6–7)—a station not relayed in the itinerary of Numbers 33 (cf. Num 12:16; 13:26; 33:17–18). "The main problem," as Angela R. Roskop aptly describes, "is that we have find *two* double arrivals. The Israelites arrive in the wilderness of Paran twice, once in Num 10:12 and again in Num 12:16. They also arrive at Kadesh twice, once implied by Num 13:26 [...] and again in Num 20:1" (*The Wilderness Itineraries: Genre, Geography, and the Growth of Torah* [HACL 3; Winona Lake: Eisenbrauns, 2011], 278–279). Second, the chronological component in Num 20:1's travel notice appears truncated, as it records the month during which Israel arrived at Kadesh, but not the year (cf. Exod 40:17; Num 1:1; 9:1; 10:11; 33:38; Deut 1:3).
11 Noth notes the presence of clear doublets in Exodus 17 (vv. 1bβ-2 with v. 3) and Numbers 20 ("vgl. besonders V. 4 mit V. 5, auch V. 3a mit V. 2b und 3b") (Noth, *Exodus*, 110; *Das vierte Buch Mose: Numeri* [ATD 7; Göttingen: Vandenhoeck & Ruprecht, 1966], 127). Yet neither Noth, nor any other scholar to my awareness, has noticed the confluence of these redundancies occurring at the same narrative juncture within both texts—the very juncture within each text that grounds their corresponding etiologies (cf. Exod 17:2, 7; Num 20:3, 13).
12 To begin, the etiology in Exod 17:7 does not "relate to the water from the rock, but to the dispute" (Brevard S. Childs, *The Book of Exodus: A Critical, Theological Commentary* [OTL; Louisville: Westminster, 1974], 307). Moreover, nothing in the narrative proper prepares one for the question היש יהוה בקרבנו אם־אין (v. 7bγ). Likewise, the etiology in Num 20:13 does not derive from the primary crisis of water deprivation, but instead from the people's dispute. Even so, in Num 20:3 the people's dispute is with Moses (and Aaron), but in v. 13 Yahweh is the target of the people's dispute. Moreover, v. 13b declares Yahweh was sanctified among them, but this assertion contradicts v. 12 in which Yahweh accuses Moses and Aaron of failing to sanctify him among the people.

junctures may not be a coincidence, and methodologically one should at least consider whether they stem from overlapping editorial processes. In other words, in tracing the literary history of both texts, one should seek to explain not only the verbal and conceptual (in)congruities between them, but their shared literary tensions as well.

Another feature for which one must strive to account—aside from verbal and conceptual (in)congruities and shared internal literary tensions—is the way in which both narratives are lexically and conceptually integrated into their respective broader literary contexts, contexts which are both immediate and extended. Regarding its immediate literary context, Exod 17:1–7 concludes a series of episodes about deprivation in the wilderness (Exod 15:22–17:7), with each episode lexically tied to the other via the verbs נסה (Exod 15:25; 16:4; 17:2, 7) and לון (Exod 15:24; 16:2, 7, 8; 17:3).[13] At a broader level, Exod 17:5's clarification of the staff being the one Moses had used to strike the Nile at least evinces awareness of the tradition behind Exod 7:14–24, if not dependence on the text itself, a text which many scholars now judge to be particularly late.[14] Finally, Exod 17:1's travel notice links the episode to the itinerary in Numbers 33 (cf. Num 33:14).

Likewise, immediate and broader literary connections also moor Num 20:1–13 in its position in the Pentateuch. Numbers 20:1 begins a series of loosely connected episodes which are interspersed with the death notices of Israel's founding leaders: Miriam's death notice is embedded in the narrative's travel notice in 20:1b; Aaron's death is reported in Num 20:22–29, and Moses' death is commanded in Num 27:12–14.[15] At a broader level, the travel notice in Num 20:1

---

13 Some loose lexical connections in material subsequent to these episodes may be seen in Exod 17:8 via רפידם (cf. רפידים in Exod 17:1); in Exod 20:20 via the deity's intent to test [√נסה] Israel; and Num 14:22 via the tradition of Israel having tested [√נסה] Yahweh ten times.
14 Christophe Nihan observes a long-held consensus among scholars that "the motif of Moses' staff in Num 20:8aα, 9 and 11a is redactional" (e.g., Wilhelm Rudolph, Noth, Zenger, Ludwig Schmidt, Artus, Frevel); he then cites Gertz as demonstrating convincingly "that this motif is redactional in the whole Pentateuch" (*From Priestly Torah to Pentateuch: A Study in the Composition of the Book of Leviticus* [FAT2 25; Tübingen: Mohr Siebeck, 2007], 26; cf. Jan Christian Gertz, *Tradition und Redaktion in der Exoduserzählung: Untersuchungen zur Endredaktion des Pentateuch* [FRLANT 186; Göttingen: Vandenhoeck & Ruprecht, 2000], 305–321, especially 313–314).
15 The death report of Aaron (Num 20:22–29) and the initial command for Moses' death (Num 27:12–14) have little lexical overlap with the episode of Num 20:1–13. Granted, both texts draw on מי־מריבה from the narrative's etiology in 20:13. Yet, while Yahweh condemns Moses and Aaron for their failure to believe (לא־האמנתם) him in Num 20:12, in 20:22–29 and 27:12–14 Yahweh accuses Moses and Aaron of having rebelled (מריתם) against his command (פי). Regardless whether the failure was unbelief or rebellion, as Davies correctly observes, "the narrative as it now stands does not properly bear out either charge" (Eryl W. Davies, *Num-*

(like Exod 17:1abα) bears some connection to the itinerary report of Numbers 33; yet curiously, Num 33:36–49 displays no awareness of the rationale for why Moses and Aaron were prohibited from entering the land. Less obvious, however, are the connections that link Num 20:1–13 to narratives before it in Numbers 12–14 and 16–17, including the station קדש (20:1; cf. Num 13:26), the fate of Miriam (20:1b; cf. Num 12:1–15), the produce mentioned in Num 20:5 (cf. Num 13:23; Deut 8:8), the assembly against Moses and Aaron (20:2b; cf. Num 16:3), and the rod set before Yahweh's presence (20:9; cf. Num 17:1–10).

In the end, as difficult as it is to assess diachronically Exod 17:1–7 and Num 20:1–13 as discreet units, one cannot posit a literary history that does not also account for the connections these texts have to their broader literary contexts. Add this challenge to those already mentioned—i.e., accounting for the narratives' verbal and conceptual (in)congruities, along with their shared internal literary tensions—and the task of determining the nature of the diachronic relationship of the M-Mt narratives becomes formidable indeed.

5.3 Determining the Relationship between the M-Mt Narratives

Given the state of Pentateuch scholarship today, it is perhaps no surprise that attempts at unravelling this mystery have yet to approach a consensus. Yet even in the heyday of the Documentary Hypothesis, there was little consensus among scholars regarding the *precise* literary history of Exod 17:1–7 and Num 20:1–13. At best, scholars widely agreed to the following general assertions: 1) that the itinerary notices (17:1abα; 20:1) are secondary, and that the notice in Num 20:1 itself is likely composite; 2) that the narratives proper (17:1bβ-7; 20:2–13) are also composites, formed by merging two or more variant, but similar literary traditions; 3) that these otherwise lost narrative precursors can be recovered by a) dissecting each narrative into snippets that evince redundancy and/or literary tension, and then by b) reassembling these snippets according to the predetermined source-critical profiles of J, E (or JE), and P; and finally 4) that Exod 17:1bβ-7 is a result of combining materials from J and E, while Num

---

bers [NCB; Grand Rapids: Eerdmans, 1995], 205). Instead, Num 20:12; 20:24; and 27:14 represent secondary interpretations of Moses' (and Aaron's) actions in light of Yahweh's commands (cf. Num 20:8). For a survey of scholarly opinion on the nature of Moses and Aaron's transgression, see p. 209 n. 18 below.

20:1b-13 exhibits traces of E (v. 1b) and J, but is predominantly P, and bears some relationship with material in Exod 17:1bβ-7.[16]

Since the last quarter of the twentieth century, however, at least two significant shifts have occurred among critical scholars.[17] The first shift was away from

---

[16] Several seminal scholars merit consideration. For Wellhausen, Exod 17:1 belongs to Q [P], while vv. 2 – 7 are JE; in Num 20:1 – 13, vv. 1a, 2, 3b, 6, and probably v. 12 belong to Q, and one may also detect Q's influence in the portions of vv. 8 – 9, 11 that pertain to the staff; "Alles Übrige," he says, "stimmt aus JE" (*Die Composition des Hexateuchs und der historischen Bücher des Alten Testaments* [3d; Berlin: Georg Reimer, 1899], 79 – 80, 106 – 107). Cornill makes further divisions: while Exod 17:1a comes from P, vv. 3 – 6 are "ein wesentlich unversehrtes Stück aus E," and the remainder (vv. 1b, 2, 7) are fragments of J, imported by a redactor from Numbers 20, where they originally stood with the J fragments that remain in Num 20:1aβ, 3a, 5; the remaining material in Num 20:1 – 13 belongs to P (except for Miriam's death notice in v. 1b which belongs to E) ("Beiträge zur Pentateuchkritik," *ZAW* 11 [1891]: 20, 33 – 34). Gray, and to a slightly lesser extent Bacon, follow Cornill (George B. Gray, *A Critical and Exegetical Commentary on Numbers* [ICC; New York: Schribner's, 1903], 258 – 259; Benjamin W. Bacon, "JE in the Middle of the Pentateuch. III. From Egypt to Sinai: Analysis of Exodus XII.37 – XVII.16," *JBL* 11 [1892]: 197 – 200). Wilhelm Rudolph eliminates E, but with results that remain otherwise strikingly similar; in Exodus 17, v. 1a is P, vv. 1b-7* belong to J, while v. 5b is glossic; in Numbers 20, vv. 1 – 13* are mostly P, with the exceptions of v. $1^a\beta^b$ (Miriam's death notice) and some interpolations from Exodus 17 (vv. 3a, 5a, 8aα, 8bα, 9, 11, 13*) (*Der 'Elohist' von Exodus bis Joshua* [BZAW 68; Berlin: Töpelmann, 1938], 36, 87, 275, 277). Noth divides these texts as follows: for Exodus 17, v. 1abα is P; vv. 1bβ-2, 4 – 7 is mostly J, and only v. 3 is E (*Exodus*, 111); and for Numbers 20, v.1aα is in priestly style, but likely editorial (post-P?); vv. 2, 3b, 4, 6, 7, 8aβ, 8bβ, 10, 11b, 12 belong to P; the rest is a "späteren Bearbeitung" of Exod 17:1 – 7 (*Numeri*, 127).

For additional surveys regarding Exod 17:1 – 7 and Num 20:1 – 13, see H. F. Fuhs, Cornelius Houtman, and Olivier Artus (H. F. Fuhs, "Qadesh – Materielen zu den Wüstentraditionen Israels," *BN* 9 [1979]: 61, 65; Houtman, *Exodus* [trans. Sierd Woudstra; 4 vols.; HCOT; Kampen: KOK Publishing, 1996], 2:357 – 359; Artus, *Etudes sur le livre des Nombres: Récit, Histoire et Loi en Nb 13,1 – 20,13* [OBO 157; Göttingen: Vandenhoeck & Ruprecht, 1997], 209 – 214). Fuhs' assessment of Num 20:1 – 13 is particularly telling and reflects the transition to the current trend: he states that attempts at source-critical division "muß als gescheitert betrachen werden" and that one must begin "von der Einheitlichkeit des Stückes, das P angehört […] wobei man darüber streiten kann, ob P nach Ex 17,1 – 7 (J) sekundär überarbeit wurde (Rudolph) oder P selbst 'die jahwistische Version um das Moment der des Mose erweitert' hat (Fritz, vgl. Noth)" (Fuhs, "Qadesh," 65). Nevertheless, variants of the traditional source-critical divisions of Num 20:1 – 13 still persist, as is evident by Ludwig Schmidt, who sees Num 20:1aα*, 2, 3b*, 4, 6, 7, 8a*, 10, 11b, 12 as belonging to the Priesterschrift ("Die Priesterschrift – kein Ende am Sinai," *ZAW* 120 [2008]: 487) and Suzanne Boorer, who sees Num 20:2, 3b, 4, 6, 7, 8aα*β, 10, 11b, 12 as Pg ("The Place of Numbers 13 – 14* and Numbers 20:2 – 13* in the Priestly Narrative (Pg)," *JBL* 131 [2012]: 50).

[17] This observation is not to say that classical source critical conclusions have been universally abandoned; e.g., Horst Seebass, who concludes that older research was correct to assume that "die Endfassung beruhe auf der Fusion von P mit einer Variante zu Ex 17,1 – 7"—a variant that

the assumption of earlier scholars that multiple pre-existing textual versions were spliced together to form Exod 17:1bβb-7 and Num 20:1b-13. Beginning in the 1970 s, critical scholars started understanding these narratives as largely homogenous productions stemming from J/non-P and P traditions respectively, with both texts having but a few redactional supplements.¹⁸ More recently, a second shift has gained momentum: now several scholars doubt the original priestly narrative (P^G) had a version of the M-Mt at all! Instead, scholars like Kratz,

---

was incompletely preserved in order to be able to work with it (*Numeri 10,11 – 22, 1* [vol. 2. Teilband of *Numeri*; BKAT IV/2; Neukirchen-Vluyn: Neukirchener Verlag, 2003], 279).

18 For Exod 17:1 – 7, see Volkmar Fritz, who grants the base text has received additions (especially the vv. 1abα, 3), but asserts that v.1bβ, 2, 4 – 7 "weist keinerlei Anzeichen für zwei parallele Faden auf" (*Israel in der Wüste: Traditiongeschichtliche Untersuchung der Wüstenüberlieferungen des Jahwisten*" [MtS 7; Marburg: N. G. Elwert, 1970], 11); likewise Aurelius (*Der Fürbitter Israels: Eine Studie zum Mosebild im Alten Testament* [ConBOT 27; Stockholm: Almqvist & Wiksell, 1988], 167 – 169); Blum (*Studien zur Komposition des Pentateuch* [BZAW 189; Berlin: de Gruyter, 1990], 148 – 152); Van Seters denies any "earlier tradition behind Ex. 17:1 – 7 story, apart from the simple statement about God's provision of water in the wilderness" (*The Life of Moses*, 197); cf. Dozeman, *Exodus*, 388.

For the essential unity of Num 20:1 – 13, see Fritz, who assigns vv. 1aα, 2 – 13 to P (*Israel in der Wüste*, 29); Blum (*Studien zur Komposition*, 272; cf. p. 153 n. 20 below); Katharine D. Sakenfeld, who suggests only v. 11b to be secondary ("Theological and Redactional Problems in Numbers 20:2 – 13," in *Understanding the Word: Essays in Honour of Bernhard W. Anderson* [ed. J. T. Butler, E. W. Conrad, and B. C. Ollenburger; JSOTSup 37; Sheffield: JSOT Press, 1985], 143); Artus, who sees "la version la plus ancienne" in vv. 2, 4 – 7, 8aβ-γ, 10, 12 in connection to v. 11b, while the author attempting to harmonize Numbers with Deuteronomy inserted vv. 3a, 8aα, 8b, 9, and 11a, which in turn echoes Exod 17:1 – 7 (*Etudes sur le livre des Nombres*, 240 – 243); Christian Frevel, who after a detailed analysis of Num 20:1 – 13, concludes that while there is evidence in the text to suggest that vv. 1a, 2, 3b (without ויאמרו), 4, 6, 7, 8aα*β*b, 10, 11b do not belong to P^G, "doch reichen nicht aus, den alten Konsens aufzugeben" (*Mit Blick auf das Land die Schöpfung erinnern: Zum Ende der Priestergrundschrift* [HbS 23; Freiburg: Herder, 2000], 330); one may include Frankel, though the supplements he posits are more extensive (non-P = vv. 1aβb, 3a, 5*; editor = כל-העדה in v.1, 3b, 5bβ, 13; post-P = vv. 8aβ, 10b, 12) (*The Murmuring Stories of the Priestly School: A Retrieval of Ancient Sacerdotal Lore* [VTSup 89; Leiden – Boston – Köln: Brill, 2002], 278 – 306).

Additionally, it should be noted that scholars representing the second shift also maintain the unity of Num 20:2 – 13; the distinction lies in assigning the entire text to post-P, with no kernel of the M-Mt extant within P^G (see p. 152 n. 19 below). Similarly, several scholars representative of the first shift also argue for Num 20:1 – 13 being a reformulation of Exod 17:1 – 7, but it was P who rewrote the JE traditions (including Exod 17:1 – 7 in Num 20:1 – 13) not a post-P redactor; e.g. Aaron Schart, *Mose und Israel im Konflikt: Eine Redaktionsgeschichtliche Studie zu den Wüstenerzählungen* (OBO 98; Göttingen: Vandenhoeck & Ruprecht, 1990), 117; according to Frankel, this position has been the "tacit assumption" since Noth's "conviction that P is too late to have derived his narrative material from living tradition—an assumption Frankel seeks to rectify in his published dissertation (*Murmuring Stories*, 297).

Achenbach, and Nihan insist that Num 20:1b-13 is entirely redactional—a post-priestly *reformulation* or revision of Exod 17:1–7 designed to clarify why Moses and Aaron were not allowed to enter the Promised Land.[19]

The sustained critique against the piecemeal reconstructions of classic source critical scholarship is rightly levied: one simply cannot extract multiple complete textual traditions behind Exod 17:1–7 and Num 20:1–13. Yet several pieces of evidence also undermine the growing trend to regard Num 20:1–13 as a late reformulation or revision (post-P or otherwise) of Exod 17:1–7, with no living priestly tradition standing behind it. Instead, an intermediate position appears to be more likely, even if demonstrably unwieldy. The first evidence warranting an intermediate position is the metanarrative of the Pentateuch itself. As David Frankel articulates well, the narrative logic in Num 20:1–13 does not fit that of the larger Pentateuchal metanarrative:

---

[19] Although, this position is extant as early as Siegfried Mittmann, who describes Num 20:1–13 as "eine späte Zweckkonstruktion, gestaltet nach dem Vorbild von Exod 17 1–7 und unter Verwendung von sekundärem P-Material, um zu begründen, warum auch Mose und Aaron [...] das ersehnte Ziel der Landverheißung nicht erreichten" (*Deuteronomium 1:1 – 6:3: Literarkritisch und Traditionsgeschichtlich Untersucht* [BZAW 139; Berlin: de Gruyter, 1975], 109). For more recent exemplars, see Eryl W. Davies, who is reticent to distinguish between P^G and P^S in Num 20:1–13, but clearly supports this position to the extent that the text is clearly P* and is an amplification of Exod 17:1–7 (*Numbers*, xlix, 202); Thomas Pola, who concludes that none of the priestly portions in the so-called wilderness murmuring stories (including Num 20:1–13) belong to P^G (*Die ursprüngliche Priesterschrift: Beobachtungen zur Literarkritik und Traditionsgeschichte von P^g* [WMANT 70; Neukirchen-Vluyn: Neukirchener Verlag, 1995], 97, 145); Kratz, who sees Num 20:1–13 as a (priestly) redactor's supplement to the Pentateuch / Enneateuch (*Komposition der erzählenden Bücher des Alten Testaments: Grundwissen der Bibelkritik* (UTb 2157; Göttingen: Vandenhoeck & Ruprecht, 2000), 115); Reinhard Achenbach, who concludes that if v. 12 is redactional (as is widely agreed), upon which the sense of the entire episode depends, "dann ist die Erzählung selbst gleichfalls eine redaktionelle Komposition" (*Die Vollendung der Tora: Studien zur Redaktionsgeschichte des Numeribuches im Kontext von Hexateuch und Pentateuch* [BZAR 3; Wiesbaden: Harrassowitz Verlag, 2003], 309); Christophe Nihan who concludes "there is no trace of an earlier, originally independent narrative in Num 20:1–13 and that in spite of its complexity this text must be regarded as a coherent composition by a late, post-P author [...] The whole account is a sophisticated reformulation of the earlier non-P story of Ex 17:1–7, which seeks to offer an alternative explanation for the death of Moses and Aaron outside the promised land" (*Priestly Torah to Pentateuch*, 29; cf. Christophe Nihan, "La Mort de Moïse (Nb 20,1–13; 20,22–29; 27,12–13) et l'Édition Finale du Livre des Nombres," in *Les dernièrs rédactions du Pentateuque, de l'Hexateuque et de l'Ennéateuque* [ed. Thomas Römer and Konrad Schmid; BETL 203; Paris: Leuven University, 2007], 164–165); and Thomas C. Römer, "Israel's Sojourn in the Wilderness and the Construction of the Book of Numbers," in *Reflection and Refraction: Studies in Biblical Historiography in Honour of A. Graeme Auld* (ed. Robert Rezetko, Timothy H. Lim, and W. Brian Aucker; VTSup 113; Leiden: Brill, 2007), 435–436, 441–443.

Such an assumption, on the contrary, makes the narrative quite incomprehensible. Why are the Israelites so distraught, convinced that they are on the verge of dying of thirst? Did they not recall the way in which Moses provided them with water from a rock in Ex. 17? Should they not simply have asked him to do the trick again? Again, why doesn't Moses immediately reprimand the Israelites for faithlessly forgetting the previous miracle of water provision? Why does he entreat God at the tent of meeting as if clueless as to what may be done? Finally, the rhetorical question of verse 10b, המן הסלע הזה נוציא לכם מים, becomes incomprehensible no matter how it is precisely understood. The Israelites could have responded: Of course you can bring forth water from the rock! That's what you did the last time, so why are you making such an issue over it?![20]

In the end, if Num 20:1–13 is a post-P recasting of Exod 17:1–7, with no priestly narrative for its foundation, one must conclude its authors were either not aware of a collection that approaches the Pentateuch as it is today, or they intentionally created several narrative inconsistencies in spite of their awareness; neither conclusion bears the semblance of probability.

A second evidence undermining the thesis that Num 20:1–13 is a homogeneous, post-P "revision" of Exod 17:1–7 is that Num 20:1–13 does not clearly reflect the editorial tendencies evident elsewhere in documented cases of *revised textual transmission*. Here, Carr's comparative study of documented textual transmission in the ancient world and its implications for the formation of the Hebrew Bible is particularly salient. Carr has shown that when ancient tradents engaged in revised textual transmission, they did so at a macro-editorial level for the purpose of creating new editions or compilations from pre-existing source material.[21] At this level of scribal activity, two editorial and somewhat contradictory tendencies emerge: 1) in instances of verbatim reproduction, the "overall trend was toward preservation and expansion of the tradition,"[22] with deliberate omissions to be

---

20 Frankel, *The Murmuring Stories*, 269. Frankel's critique is specifically levied against Blum's argument that Num 20:1–13 is not a priestly alternative to Exod 17:1–7, but rather an allusion to and continuation of this specific story. More precisely, Blum argues that "beide Episoden in einem kontinuier-lichen Diskurs gelesen werden wollen, wobei das zweite Wunder einerseits als Steigerung/Überbietung [...] des ersten angelegt ist, andererseits erst in diesem Nacheinander seine Aussage entfallen kann." (Erhard Blum, *Studien zur Komposition*, 278). Thus, for Blum, Num 20:1–13 does not merely build on Exod 17:1–7, it intensifies and surpasses it.
21 Examples that Carr cites include Chronicles revised reproduction of Samuel–Kings, the Temple Scroll's restructuring of Deuteronomy's legal core (chs. 12–26 and 28), and Matthew and Luke's use of the Gospel of Mark. David M. Carr, "The Moses Story: Literary Historical Reflections," *HeBAI* 1 (2012): 10 n. 8; cf. David M. Carr, *The Formation of the Hebrew Bible: A New Reconstruction* (New York: Oxford University Press, 2011), 88–90.
22 Carr, *Formation of the Hebrew Bible*, 88. By "tradition," Carr appears to mean "source text."

expected at the beginning and ending materials of the sources they used[23]; but in instances of partial preservation, tradents could incompletely abbreviate, rephrase by memory, reorganize, or even elide selections of their source materials.[24] These trends suggest a more balanced approach to understanding the scribal techniques that were used, for example, to revise Samuel–Kings in the production of Chronicles: the Chronicler was not merely reproducing his earlier sources, but neither was he as "consistently creative as many once thought."[25] Instead, the production of a revised edition of Samuel–Kings (i.e., Chronicles) involved both trends.

If Num 20:1–13 is a post-P revision of Exod 17:1–7, then the scribes who produced this revised edition did not participate in these editorial trends. To begin, although Num 20:1–13 is certainly expansive (cf. v. 10f), it does not reflect the intent to preserve Exod 17:1–7 through verbatim reproduction; as noted earlier, the only instance of non-formulaic, *verbatim correspondence* is a phrase that is only four words long (וירב העם עם־משה in Exod 17:2aα‖Num 20:3a) (cf. pp. 144–146 above). On the other hand, and again as noted earlier, Num 20:1–13 does evince substantial *approximate verbal correspondence* and *conceptual correspondence* with Exod 17:1–7. At first glance, these non-verbatim correspondences could be interpreted as a byproduct of rephrasing Exod 17:1–7 from memory, but this conclusion is not the only possibility. Alternatively, the correspond-

---

23 Carr's study on the Chronicler's use of Samuel–Kings is especially enlightening at this juncture: "As seen in the case of Chronicles in particular, it appears that tradents could alternate between close reproduction/expansion of a given tradition on the one hand and elision of large chunks of it on the other. Insofar as the beginnings and ends of compositions are the best loci to shape audiences' perceptions of a text, they appear to have been loci for particularly intense scribal intervention. A scribe wishing to add significant material to the outset or end of a composition often (though not always!) would be inclined to eliminate distinctive markers of the beginnings (e.g., the label in Mark 1:1) or decisive end of a composition. [...] A nuanced view of documented cases of transmission history must keep both tendencies in view: an overall orientation toward preservation/expansion combined with some omissions, particularly of the original beginnings and ends of compositions, in the process of producing new wholes" (Carr, *Formation of the Hebrew Bible*, 89–90).
24 Carr, *Formation of the Hebrew Bible*, 88–90.
25 Carr, *Formation of the Hebrew Bible*, 75. Carr continues: "In many loci where exegetes might think that a divergence between Chronicles and Samuel–Kings is an exegetical revision by the Chronicler, it is now as or more likely that the given divergence resulted from a memory variant and/or use by the Chronicler of an edition of Samuel–Kings that was different from the editions available to us now. Generally speaking, the Chronicler seems to have stayed *remarkably close to his sources in places where he chose to appropriate them*, even as he appears to have chosen not to reproduce substantial portions of Samuel–Kings that did not fit with his interests" (*Formation of the Hebrew Bible*, 75; italics mine).

ence between these texts could stem from two separate, independent tradents (i.e., non-P and P) expressing the same foundational, yet oral tradition in their own distinctive vernacular.

Finally, the preservation of Exod 17:1–7 itself within the Pentateuch is a third piece of evidence that suggests Num 20:1–13 is not a post-P revision of Exod 17:1–7. A revision would likely displace the older edition, not be inserted into the same metanarrative in which the older edition continues to reside.[26] Again, the editorial techniques of the Chronicler come to bear: The Chronicler did not create a revised edition of Samuel–Kings and then compile it with Samuel–Kings; the revised edition stood as an independent literary product. Granted, the example of Chronicles operates at a considerably larger scale than the individual pericopes under consideration. Even so, the principle holds true at this reduced scale, given a post-P awareness of the Pentateuchal narrative as a whole, which seems likely. In short, the preservation of Exod 17:1–7 within the Pentateuch itself strongly suggests that Num 20:1–13 was never intended to be a revised edition of it per se; instead, the P* scribes responsible Num 20:1–13 must have been in possession of a M-Mt distinct from that preserved in Exod 17:1–7.

---

[26] Recently, Müller, Pakkala, and ter Haar Romeny observed this technique in the transmission of the geographical boundaries listed in Deut 34:1–3. The Smr appears to have replaced the MT's boundary list with its own idealized version—one that not only expands the parameters of the idealized Promised Land, but also brings the boundary list into harmony with Gen 15:18. This instance of "substantial rewriting" is evidence that "editors could replace parts of transmitted texts with new passages," not just make additions to them (Reinhard Müller, Juha Pakkala, and Bas ter Haar Romeny, *Evidence of Editing: Growth and Change of Texts in the Hebrew Bible* [SBLRBS 75; Atlanta: Society of Biblical Literature, 2014], 6). The application to Num 20:1–13 is clear: if this text was the product of a substantial rewriting of Exod 17:1–7, one would expect it to displace Exod 17:1–7, not be relocated within the same multi-scroll narrative.

Alternatively, one may rebut that Num 20:1–13 is a "revised edition" of Exod 17:1–7 in the sense that it was *inspired* by Exod 17:1–17, and that it was artfully created for its place within the Pentateuch as an explanation of Moses and Aaron's exclusion from the land (cf. p. 152 n. 19 above). Yet Num 20:1–13 demonstrates no awareness of Exod 17:1–7 at the metanarrative level. If a post-priestly scribe had been so inspired, recasting Exod 17:1–7 as a kind of chiastic parallel to its literary precursor, then this scribe reforged Exod 17:1–7 so thoroughly as to lead one would to expect a smoother recollection and carrying forward of Exod 17:1–7 (as Blum suggests; cf. p. 153 n. 20 above), but the kernel of Num 20:1–13 does not reflect this level of metanarrative interaction.

5.4 Synopsis: Four Dynamics of the Relationship between the M-Mt Narratives

In summary, for scholars advancing the argument that Exod 17:1–7 and Num 20:1–13 are in some way genetically related, four dynamics of this relationship demand attention: verbal and conceptual correspondences (*congruity*), distinctive non-alignments (*incongruity*), internal tensions that are similar both in type and proximity (*shared internal tensions*), and contextual moorings to broader literary contexts (*connectivity*). Together these four dynamics combine to form a most formidable challenge: In reconstructing each text's *Literargeschichte*, how does one account for their verbal and conceptual correspondence in such a way that in turn culminates in their final distinct literary forms—forms that are also lexically and conceptually tied to their surrounding literary contexts? This question constitutes a literary "Gordian knot," not only for the task of explaining the relationship of Exod 17:1–7 and Num 20:1–13 (and usually in context of the formation of the Pentateuch), but also for that of tracing the M-Mt's tradition-historical development. It is to this difficult task—armed with the framework reflected in Deuteronomy of the M-Mt's tradition historical development (cf. §4.5 above)—that this study now turns.

Chapter Six:
The Non-P M-Mt Narrative in Exodus 17:1–7 and its Related Texts

6.1 An Approach toward Assessing Exodus 17:1–7

The previous chapter outlines four dynamics that challenge any attempt at determining 1) the nature of the relationship of the M-Mt narratives in general and 2) the history of each text's formation in particular. First, on the one hand, Exod 17:1–17 and Num 20:1–13 have remarkably similar outlines, as well as a significant overlap at the verbal and conceptual levels (i.e., *congruity*). Yet secondly, on the other hand, as much as 50% of the material within both narratives remains distinct non-aligned (i.e., *incongruity*). Additionally, one must also consider a third dynamic: that both texts exhibit internals tensions that curiously correspond according to type and proximity (i.e., *shared internal tensions*). Finally, add to these quandaries the fact that both texts connect lexically and thematically to several others within the Pentateuch (i.e., *connectivity*), and the result is a multi-faceted challenge meriting a full study in its own right.

This chapter lays the groundwork for accounting for the above dynamics in Exod 17:1–7 by reconstructing Exod 17:1–7's compositional history. A similar approach to that taken with the M-Mt texts in Deuteronomy is therefore in order: methodologically, the study begins with text-critical (§6.2) and literary (§6.3) analyses, the findings of which then facilitate a tradition-historical analysis of the non-P M-Mt in Exod 17:1–7 as this text developed through time (§6.4). Yet the approach taken in this chapter (and the next) differs from that in Part One of this study in three ways: 1) the literary analysis works backward through time, beginning *from* the latest, clearest stage *to* progressively earlier, more conjectural stages; 2) the investigation into each of these stages unfolds alongside consideration of texts outside of Exod 17:1–7, texts which constitute Exod 17:1–7's broader literary context; and finally 3) the implications of the framework detected in Deuteronomy for the M-Mt's tradition-historical development are brought to bear as corroboration of the ensuing reconstruction of Exod 17:1–7's incremental literary growth. In the end, the results of these inquiries not only suggest that Exod 17:1–7 was the M-Mt narrative with which Deuteronomy's proprietors were intimately familiar, but also that Exod 17:1–7 developed centrifugally via five compositional stages—stages which progress in accordance with the M-Mt tradition-historical framework detected in Deuteronomy.

6.2 Textual Criticism of Exodus 17:1–7

Only a few minor variants are extant,[1] and most of these discrepancies smooth out the strained person numbers within MT Exod 17:2–3. In v. 2aβ, several readings have the people's imperative in the singular (presuming תנה), directed exclusively toward Moses.[2] The MT, however, has the plural (תנו)—as does also the earliest pointed Masoretic text, the "British Museum Codex" (*Or.* 4445)[3]—indicating that the people are addressing Moses and another unnamed entity, presumably either Aaron or God. Given that the context and the readings support תנה over תנו, it is tempting to discredit the reliability of MT's transmission at this point, but there is no clear text-critical mechanism whereby this variant would have entered the MT.[4] The only manuscript from Qumran which may shed light on this specific issue is 4QpaleoExod^m (4Q22), which has תנה. Nevertheless, this manuscript is clearly within the Samaritan tradition, agreeing with most of the expansions in the Smr (save its new tenth commandment in Smr Exod 20:17b).[5] Since the Smr harmonizes the MT with תנה,[6] the reading תנה in

---

[1] For the Hebrew text of Exod 17:1–7, see either Fig. 5.1 on p. 145 above or Appendix D: Exodus 17:1–7 by Stages of Literary Development.
[2] These readings include 4QpaleoExod^m (4Q22), which though fragmentary clearly has תנה ל[נו] (see DJD 9:92 and plate XIV, column XVII); Smr, G, S, T^J, and V also presume a singular imperative.
[3] Not only does the Leningrad Codex B19^A (L) have תנו, but the "British Museum Codex (*Oriental* 4445) also has תנו. This manuscript dates to 820–895 CE and represents the earliest pointed Masoretic manuscript extant. It contains 187 folios covering most of the Pentateuch; of these folios, 122 are original, the span of which covers most of Gen 39:20–Deut 1:33. (The leaves are missing for Num 7:46–73 and 9:12–10:18.) Though occasionally cited in text critical manuals and manuscript catalogues, this codex has not yet received the attention its primacy merits, as there continues to be no critical edition of this important manuscript. This state persists despite Aron Dotan's decades old announcement that a critical edition of Or. 4445 "is almost ready for computerized reproduction" ("Reflections towards a Critical Edition of Pentateuch Codex Or. 4445," in *Estudios masoréticos (X Congreso de la IOMS): En memoria de Harry M. Orlinsky* [ed. E. F. Tejero and M. T. O. Monasterio; TECC 55; Madrid: Instituto de Filogía del CSIC, 1993], 42).
[4] The penultimate and ultimate letters of לנו in MT's תנו־לנו could suggest something akin to *homoioteleuton*, but this error typically results in a minus from the text, not an interchange. As well, it is not likely that the cursive script for *heh* would be confused graphically for a *shureq*.
[5] See the discussion regarding the relationship of 4QpaleoExod^m to Smr in DJD IX:65–70. "The scroll shares all major, typological features with 𝓂 [Smr], including all the major expansions of that tradition where it is extant (twelve), with the single exception of the new tenth commandment inserted in Exodus 20 from Deuteronomy 11 and 27 regarding the altar on Mount Gerizim" (DJD IX:66). Note that the other manuscripts from Qumran which have fragments of Exod

6.2 Textual Criticism of Exodus 17:1–7 — 159

4Q22 is not unexpected, and the weight it carries for establishing the preferable reading is reduced. The plural תנו is the *lectio difficilior* and therefore preferable. Moreover, as will be discussed below, there is evidence to support that תנו originally addressed God and Moses (cf. p. 184 below).

Additional tensions over person numbers appear in the readings for Exod 17:3. Both MT and *Or.* 4445 have direct objects with first singular pronominal suffixes (אתי ואת־בני ואת־מקני) while several readings (G, S, T^J, and V) have first person plural pronouns. The evidence from Qumran is varied: both 4Q22 and 4QExod^c (4Q14) suffer from lacunae at this juncture; 4QpaleoGen-Exod^l (4Q11) has the singular, while the relevant fragment from Reworked Pentateuch^c (4Q365) appears to have the plural.[7] Though rare,[8] other instances of a collective (not specifically עם) representing itself in the singular are extant (e.g., Num 21:2; Josh 17:14). As such, by principle of *lectio difficilior*, the singular reading in MT and *Or.* 4445 retains preference.

17:1–7 include 4QpaleoGen-Exod^l (4Q11), 4QExod^c (4Q14), and 4Q365—all of which suffer from a lacuna at this juncture in their respective texts.

6 August Freiherrn von Gall hrsg, *Der Hebräische Pentateuch der Samaritaner* (Giessen: Alfred Töpelmann, 1918), 151; cf. G, S, T^J, and V which also have a singular form here.

7 In 4Q11, the ink apparently contained iron, resulting in the disintegration of many letters on account of the acidic compounds. The resulting negative space outlines the letters on fragments 17–18, which contain the infinitive phrase להמית אתי; here, the editor specifically notes the *yod* in אתי to be "probable, not but not clear enough for an assured reading" (DJD IX:38; cf. Plate III, frag. 17–18).

For 4Q365, however, the transcription is rated as only "possible," on account that only traces of the bottoms of select letters are visible after the infinitive להמית. The plate, however, is exceptionally clear, and the traces for the word immediately following most likely reflect אותנו instead of אותי. Were the suffix first singular with י, at most there would be a bottom trace of a single vertical beyond the legs of the ת (cf. the completely formed *yods* that are still visible earlier on the same line: ... להמית]ים). Instead, the following traces are preserved: the lower cross portion of the א is clear; then there is the bottom traces of three verticals, with the last vertical hooked to the left (from the letters ות); then raised slightly above this hook is the bottom trace of a short horizontal (from נ); finally, there is the bottom trace of a final vertical (from ו) descending slightly below the preceding horizontal. Since the first direct object marker in the infinitive phrase has a first plural suffix, the remaining pronominal suffixes in this phrase were likely plural too.

8 When the people (עם) represent themselves in speech, they do so foremost in the first person plural; e.g., Exod 15:24; 17:2, 3bα; 19:8, 19; 24:7; 32:1, 22; Num 20:3–5; 21:5, 7; Josh 24:16, 21–22, 24; Judg 20:8–10; 1 Sam 8:19–20; 11:12; 12:19; 2 Sam 18:3; 19:9–10; 1 Kgs 12:16 (cf. 2 Chr 10:16); Jer 16:10; Ezek 24:19; 2 Chr 10:10 (cf. 1 Kgs 12:4). To my knowledge, Exod 17:3bβ is the only instance in the MT in which the collective עם represents itself in speech using first singular forms.

6.3 Literary Analysis of Exodus 17:1–7 in Relation to its Broader Literary Contexts

Similar to Deuteronomy, the major literary tensions extant in Exod 17:1–7 suggest that the stages of this text's literary development were centrifugal in nature[9]; in other words, its material growth transpired by accretion, from the inside out, along the lines of three zones of editorial activity (cf. Fig. 6.1 below). The latest, most assured zone is the travel notice in v. 1aba (§6.3.1). Prior to the penning of the travel notice, however, an etiological framework in vv. 1bβ-2* + 7 (§6.3.2) had already been added to the foundational narrative core in vv. 3–6* (§6.3.3). Yet tensions within the etiological frame and the narrative core suggest that Exod 17:1–7's compositional history cannot be reduced to three simple stages of literary growth. Instead, this narrative exhibits signs of at least five stages of literary growth: 1) a foundational narrative core in vv. 3aα + 4aα + 5a-5b^i + 5^{vii}-6 (*Dt*); 2) the מסה etiology in vv. 1bβ + 2aβ-bα + 2bγ + 7a^{i-iv} + 7bβ-γ (*late-Dtr–Dtr supp*); 3) the מריבה etiology and the murmuring motif in vv. 2aα + 2bβ + 3aβ-b + 4aβ-b + 7a^v-bα (*pre-Hex Supp*); 4) the travel notice in v. 1aba (*HexRed*); and 5) a glossic relative clause that disambiguates the staff in v. 5ba^{ii-vi} (*post-PentRed*) (cf. Appendix D).

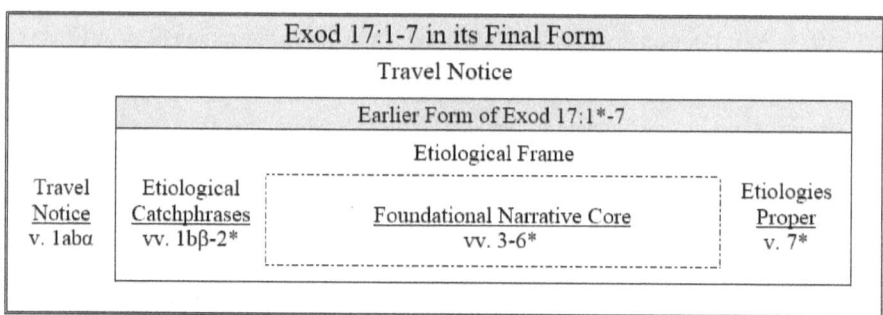

Fig. 6.1: The Three Major Areas of Editorial Activity in Exod 17:1–7

---

9 For Deuteronomy's macro-redactional formation, see §2.3 above. For a preview of the literary tensions within Exod 17:1–7, see §5.2.2 above.

6.3.1 The Travel Notice of Exod 17:1abα and the Wilderness Itinerary of Numbers 33[10]

The complexities that arise from comparing a) the travel notices across Exodus and Numbers with b) the so-called priestly wilderness itinerary in Num 33:1–49 are well-known.[11] Even a synchronic reading of the wilderness sojourn alone evinces several logical inconsistencies that, as Angela R. Roskop aptly describes, "violate the linear character of the itinerary genre, run counter to our knowledge of how bodies move through space [...] and are not present in Num 33:1–49."[12] For the travel notices that introduce the M-Mt narratives, for example, implicit double arrivals emerge. At Rephidim in Exod 17:1, the Israelites are already within the proximity of Horeb, the Mountain of God (Exod 17:6; cf. Exod 3:1), and in Exod 18:5 Moses (and presumably the Israelites) is encamped at הר האלהים. Yet synchronically, they do not enter the wilderness of Sinai and camp at Sinai until Exod 19:1–2. Similarly, in the scouts story (Numbers 13–14), the Israelites are stationed in the wilderness of Paran near Kadesh (מדבר פארן קדשה in Num 13:26). Yet the congregation does not arrive at Kadesh until Num 20:1, which by contrast is set in the wilderness of Zin.

Returning to Exod 17:1abα, the logical disruption at this juncture in the wilderness sojourn only arises on account of the embedded reference to Horeb in 17:6. Had בחרב been omitted in the transmission history, then there would be

---

[10] Scholars frequently apply the term "itinerary" to Exod 17:1abα and the list in Num 33:1–49. This study disambiguates this term by restricting "itinerary" for a series of encampment locations (e.g. Num 33:5–49 but also Num 21:10–20). The term "travel notice" refers to the record of a single stage of the Israelites' trek through the wilderness, from one station to another—a record that typically prepends and anchors individual narratives within the Wilderness Narrative.

[11] For seminal studies regarding this issue see Martin Noth, "Der Wallfahrtsweg zum Sinai," *PJ* 36 (1940): 5–28; George W. Coats, "The Wilderness Itinerary," *CBQ* 34 (1972): 135–152; Frank M. Cross, Jr., *Canaanite Myth and Hebrew Epic: Essays in the History of the Religion of Israel* (Cambridge: Harvard University Press, 1973), 308–325; G. I. Davies, "The Wilderness Itineraries: A Comparative Study," *TynBul* 25 (1974): 46–81; "The Wilderness Itineraries and the Composition of the Pentateuch," *VT* 33 (1983): 1–13; J. T. Walsh, "From Egypt to Moab: A Source Critical Analysis of the Wilderness Itinerary," *CBQ* 39 (1977): 20–33; John Van Seters, *The Life of Moses: The Yahwist as Historian in Exodus – Numbers* (Louisville: Westminster John Knox, 1994), 153–164; and more recently Thomas B. Dozeman, ("The Priestly Wilderness Itineraries and the Composition of the Pentateuch," in *The Pentateuch: International Perspectives on Current Research* [ed. Thomas B. Dozeman, Konrad Schmid, and Baruch J. Schwartz; FAT 78; Tübingen: Mohr Siebeck, 2011], 257–288) and Angela R. Roskop (*The Wilderness Itineraries: Genre, Geography and the Growth of Torah* [HACL 3; Winona Lake: Eisenbrauns, 2011]).

[12] Roskop, *Wilderness Itineraries*, 139.

no disruption. Nevertheless, a literary analysis of Exod 17:1bβ-7's literary growth indicates that the phrase על־הצור בחרב in 17:6aβ belongs to the narrative's earliest literary stage (cf. §6.3.3 below). Instead, it is the travel notice in Exod 17:1abα that is clearly secondary to the narrative, along with the narrative's current position *before* Israel's arrival at Sinai. Recall that Deut 9:22 situates this narrative immediately *after* the people's failure at Horeb (Deut 9:7–21), and this sequence follows well upon the giving of the law on Mount Horeb.[13] Yet it is the sequence of events in Exodus 17–19 that one finds preserved in Num 33:14b-15: ויחנו ברפידם ולא־היה שם מים לעם לשתות ויסעו מרפידם ויחנו במדבר סיני. The need to discuss Exod 17:1abα's diachronic relationship to Num 33:1–49 is therefore paramount.

6.3.1.1 The Wilderness Narrative's Travel Notices and Num 33:1–49 in Recent Research. Scholars have long considered some form of diachronic relationship between the Wilderness Narrative's travel notices and the itinerary in Num 33:1–49 to be a foregone conclusion.[14] Agreement beyond this common assent, however, is difficult. Since Martin Noth, two major camps, each home to a variety of subordinate permutations, have flourished: those who argue that the itinerary is dependent upon the travel notices in the Wilderness Narrative proper (e.g., Noth, Van Seters, E. W. Davies Achenbach, Roskop)[15]; and those who maintain the op-

---

13 The narrative logic would proceed as follows: Yahweh delivers the stone tablets to Moses on Mount Horeb (Deut 9:8–9); shortly after departing Horeb (cf. Num 10:33–11:3), Israel thirsts for water, and Yahweh instructs Moses to take some of the elders and the staff to the rock at Horeb, where he will be standing (cf. Exod 17:6aα-β, הנני עמד לפניך שם על־הצור בחרב).

14 In reference to what he dubs the "non-P" travel notices, G. I. Davies observes that most "have more or less word-for-word parallels in Num. xxxiii 1–49 [...] The parallels are so close as to make a literary relationship between Num. xxxiii and the itinerary-notes which correspond to it *undeniable*, and it is only *the character of that relationship* that needs more careful discussion" ("Wilderness Itineraries and Composition," 6) (italics mine). Although Davies' source-critical labelling here is debated, the level of correspondence between the travel notices and Num 33:1–49 is not.

For surveys of the scholarly discussion, see Philip J. Budd, *Numbers* (WBC 5; Waco: Word Books, 1984), 350–352; Thomas B. Dozeman, *Exodus* (ECC; Grand Rapids: Eerdmans, 2009), 179–182; Roskop, *Wilderness Itineraries*, 3–13.

15 Though Noth is understandably hesitant to assign a date to Num 33:3–49, he does conclude it must be late, "da es bereits die Zusammenarbeitung der verschiedenen Überlieferungselemente der Wanderungserzählung als gegeben voraussetzt" ("Wallfahrtsweg zum Sinai," 27). Van Seters arrives at a similar conclusion, asserting the itinerary to be "entirely dependent upon the Pentateuchal wilderness tradition in its latest and most complex development [...] it is a very late document that made use of the combined presentation of J and P but modified it at places to present its own notions about the itinerary" (*The Life of Moses: The Yahwist as Historian in Exodus – Numbers* [Louisville: Westminster John Knox, 1994], 161). E. W. Davies

posite, namely that the relevant travel notices are dependent upon, or were influence by, the itinerary in Num 33:1–49 (e.g., Cross, G. I. Davies, Budd, Johnstone).¹⁶

---

echoes Noth at this point, but departs from Noth's suggestion that the otherwise unknown stations in Num 33:18b-30a, 41b-47a may reflect a pilgrimage route to and from Sinai (cf. "Wallfahrtsweg zum Sinai," 27–28); here, he follows Budd's suggested provenance (cf. Budd, *Numbers*, 356) of official court records—a record outlining the route for travel in the wilderness in general or perhaps trade in particular (Eryl W. Davies, *Numbers* [NCB; Grand Rapids: Eerdmans, 1995], 342). More recently, Achenbach has argued that Num 33:1–49 developed "zunächst neben und außerhalb der Tora," but its author (*Verfasser*) "gehört in die Phase der spätesten, summarischen Ergänzungen des Pentateuchs, ThB III" (*Die Vollendung der Tora: Studien zur Redaktionsgeschichte des Numeribuches im Kontext von Hexateuch und Pentateuch* [BZAR 3; Wiesbaden: Harrassowitz Verlag, 2003], 625–628). The most recent and expansive study is that of Roskop; she attributes the travel notices, the date formulas, and the itinerary to the Priestly author(s), who adopted the genre of kingly annals to portray "Israel as an army, and Yahweh in the role of the king." Fractures in the travel notices "are not the result of adaptation"—i.e., via a redactor appropriating pre-existing travel notices—"but were created by a number of revisions to this Priestly version." Her conclusion is that "Num 33:1–49 could not have been the source for the itinerary notices in the Wilderness Narrative [...] It is, rather, a summary of the entire Wilderness Narrative, more or less complete." It is the creation of a post-Priestly author, who seeks to set out the definitive, authoritative version of wilderness sojourn, one "that corrects it [i.e., the Wilderness Narrative] back to the shape of the Priestly wilderness narrative as much as possible" (*Wilderness Itineraries*, 223–224, 225). Finally, one may here *functionally* list Matthias Ederer's synchronic study. Although Ederer methodologically eschews "redaktionskritisch arbeit und somit das Instrumentarium der 'hsitorisch-kritischen Exegese," his canonical approach privileges the narratives and travel notices in Exodus and Numbers as "Hypotexten" that the itinerary in Num 33:1–49 as a "Hypertext" rehearses and comments upon (*Aufbrüche zur Exodustheologie: Das Itinerar Num 33.1–49 als theologische Deutung der Wüstenzeit Israels* [SBS 231; Stuttgart: Katholisches Bibelwerk, 2014], 14–17).

16 Cross argues that the priestly redactor responsible for forming the Tetrateuch derived the wilderness travel notices directly from Num 33:1–49; to compensate for the itinerary having more stations than stories which the redactor had inherited, Cross suggests the redactor used "a general locality to embrace a number of stations in the list" (*Canaanite Myth and Hebrew Epic*, 308). G. I. Davies illustrates this technique of abridgement in Exod 17:1. That Israel journeyed from the wilderness of Sin "by stages" (למסעיהם) and then camped at Rephidim (Exod 17:1aβ-bα) is an abridgement of Num 33:12–13, which records Dophkah and Alush as stations between the wilderness of Sin and Rephidim. Thus "by stages" abridges Dophkah and Alush—stations that are in Numbers 33, but missing in the travel notice of Exod 17:1aba. The assessment G. I. Davies gives afterwards encapsulates the body of his work on the notices: "It is therefore necessary to depart from the view which has dominated scholarship for the past century and hold that those itinerary-notes in Exodus and Numbers which are parallel to verses in Num. xxxiii were derived from it" ("Wilderness Itineraries and Composition," 7; cf. *The Way of the Wilderness: A Geographical Study of the Wilderness Itineraries in the Old Testament* [SOTSMS 5; New York: Cambridge University Press, 1979], 59–61; "Wilderness Itineraries: Comparative

Angela R. Roskop, who offers the most recent sustained diachronic examination of the wilderness itineraries, argues strongly against the travel notices in any way stemming from Num 33:1–49. To begin, if a redactor had used the itinerary "to create a coherent version of the wilderness narrative," he would have copied the convention that Num 33:1–49 consistently uses to record Israel's movement from one station to the next: "The verbs נסע and חנה are used in their narrative preterite forms, each followed by a place-name."[17] Yet the travel notices across the Wilderness Narrative occasionally attest other forms (cf. Num 21:12–13a, 18b-20).[18]

Additionally, Roskop argues that if the redactor's intent was to create a coherent Wilderness Narrative modeled after Num 33:1–49, then the redactor undermined his own enterprise by introducing several logical inconsistencies, such as double arrivals, double departures, and narrative transposition without emendation of the itinerary.[19] Not only do the Israelites arrive twice at the moun-

---

Study," 50–51, 78–81; "The Wilderness Itineraries and Recent Archaeological Research," in *Studies in the Pentateuch* [ed. J. A. Emerton; VTSup 41; Leiden: Brill, 1990], 171–174). The primary way Davies' differs from Cross, as Dozeman succinctly notes, "is that for Cross Numbers 33 is the basis for Priestly tradition in Exodus and Numbers, while for Davies Numbers 33 is the basis for a pre-Priestly (i.e., Deuteronomistic) version of itineraries in Exodus and Numbers, with the Priestly influence in Numbers 33 the result of a later redaction" (*Exodus*, 148 n. 9). Budd echoes Davies argument, but contends that it was the priestly *author* who appropriated the Deuteronomistic "list," annotated it, and then used it "as the skeleton on which to fit their own priestly stories of the wilderness period" (*Numbers*, 352–353). Likewise, Johnstone believes that prior to their combining, D and P were in possession of "an overarching view of Israel's itinerary and of the chronology associated with it"; their geographical and chronological frameworks, however, differed radically, so Johnstone argues that it was P, as the later of the two, who was "responsible for the dominating itinerary and chronology in the extant Pentateuch." As for Num 33:1–49, Johnstone finds it satisfactory to attribute "the list in its entirety to P, without any D elements" (*Chronicles and Exodus: An Analogy and its Application* [JSOTSup 275; Sheffield: Sheffield Academic, 1998], 37, 38).

17 Roskop, *Wilderness Itineraries*, 137. Roskop slightly overstates the consistency of the formula (as she describes it) within the itinerary; breakdowns in the pattern occur early in the itinerary's third and fifth travel notices (vv. 7, 9), which in place of √חנה use √שוב and √בוא respectively. Following both travel notices are additional qualifiers; it is within these qualifiers that the verb √נסע again appears.

18 Instead of "√נסע + station of departure," the travel notices in Num 21:12–13a have "משם ונסעו"—a form Roskop finds parallels to in both Middle Assyrian and Egyptian literature. The form of the travel notices in Num 21:18b-20 are verbless, with the מן preposition affixed to the station of departure and with the station of arrival immediately following without an intervening preposition. Roskop finds a parallel for this form in the Old Babylonian tablets from Shemshara (Roskop, *Wilderness Itineraries*, 138).

19 Roskop, *Wilderness Itineraries*, 136–140.

tain of God and twice at Kadesh (see p. 161 above), but they also arrive twice at Moab (Num 21:20; 22:1).²⁰ Likewise, Roskop asserts that there appear to be two departures from Egypt (Exod 13:20; 15:22),²¹ as well as two departures from Sinai / the mountain of Yahweh (Num 10:12, 33). Finally, there is the troublesome transposition of the crossing of the Yam Suf:

> If a redactor used Num 33:1–49 to structure the wilderness narrative, he has moved Yam Suf to a different location on the route. In the wilderness narrative, the Israelites camp at the sea (Exod 14:2) and, once they have crossed, Moses leads them away from it in Exod 15:22, where it is specifically called Yam Suf […] The sea crossing in the Numbers 33 itinerary is indicated in v. 8, but the Yam Suf does not appear until vv. 10–11, *three stops later*. Why would a redactor create this and other geographical problems that are not present in the source document?²²

---

20 Roskop also understands Israel as arriving "in the wilderness of Paran twice, once in Num 10:12 and again in Num 12:16" (*Wilderness Itineraries*, 139; note that G. I. Davies also treats these travel notices as duplicate ["Wilderness Itineraries and Composition," 4]). Yet Num 10:12 says that the Israelites set out "by stages" (למסעיהם) until the cloud (of Yahweh) settled in the wilderness of Paran; the implication of למסעיהם (cf. Exod 17:1) is that there were multiple points where Israel bivouacked before arriving at wilderness of Paran, which is precisely what is reflected by the travel notices that follow Num 10:12 until Num 12:16. Thus, as it currently stands, Num 10:12 is a summary that opens a block of pericopes, which Num 12:16 in turn concludes.

21 Roskop's reading again requires nuancing (cf. p. 164 n. 17 and p. 165 n. 20 above). She understands Israel as departing twice from Egypt, once "into the wilderness of Etham in Exod 13:20," another time "into the wilderness of Shur in Exod 15:22" (*Wilderness Itineraries*, 139). Yet Exod 13:20 portrays Israel bivouacking *at Etham on the edge of the wilderness* (באתם בקצה המדבר); they do not enter the "wilderness of Etham" at this juncture (cf. Num 33:6). In fact, the phrase "מדבר אתם" only occurs in Num 33:8, in place of Exod 15:22's מדבר־שור.

Dozeman's summary is more accurate: In the non-P trek, Etham is at the edge of the wilderness (בקצה המדבר) and the crossing of the sea is the first event in the wilderness sojourn; thus, the arrival at Etham itself represents a departure from Egypt (cf. Exod 13:20; 14:11). The P trek, however, locates the miracle at the sea at Pi-hahiroth (Exod 14:1–2), which is most likely *inside* Egypt; thus, the crossing of the sea is the climatic exit from Egypt, and the entry into wilderness of Shur (Exod 15:22) is the first stage of the wilderness sojourn (cf. "Priestly Wilderness Itineraries," in Dozeman, Schmid, and Schwartz, *The Pentateuch*, 262–266).

22 Roskop, *Wilderness Itineraries*, 139–140. One should note, however, that the Israelites encounter the ים־סוף (at least as a trajectory) elsewhere along their sojourn. In Num 14:25 (cf. Deut 1:40), after the scouts deliver a negative report to Israel, Yahweh commands Israel to turn (√שוב) and set out (√נסע) again for the wilderness "*by* way of the Yam Suph" (דרך ים־סוף). Likewise, after the death of Aaron, the Israelites depart (√נסע) from Mt. Hor "*by* way of the Yam Suph" (דרך ים־סוף) in order to go around Edom (Num 21:4). These other instances of ים־סוף in the travel notices indicate that the ים־סוף served, at least literarily, as a key geographical marker in the mental map of the Israelites. Consequently, the itinerary's record of the Israelites having camped על ים־סוף in Num 33:10–11 (station 6) would at most represent an omission within the narrative,

In the end, these tensions between the travel notices and the itinerary lead Roskop to conclude that "Num 33:1–49 could not have been the source for the itinerary notices in the wilderness narrative [...] It is, rather, a summary of the entire wilderness narrative, more or less complete."[23]

A full response to Roskop's central thesis[24] and her supporting arguments lies beyond the scope of the current study. Yet her conclusion that Num 33:1–49 is a late Priestly summary of the Wilderness Narrative in its nearly completed form is not convincing. Several features of Num 33:1–49 combine to suggest that this text itself is composite,[25] and that at its earliest stage it did not have the Pentateuch as its literary horizon. It is to these features that the current study now turns.

6.3.1.2 Indicators of Num 33:1–49's Composite Nature. The *first feature* that indicates the itinerary is composite, and the one that is most overt, is a cluster of eighteen toponyms (stations 14–31) in Num 33:18b-36a that do not appear in the Wilderness Narrative (see Appendix C fractures 4a-c). Most of these toponyms are unique to the itinerary, with only five toponyms appearing elsewhere in the Hebrew Bible: stations 26–29 in vv. 30b-34a are also in Deut 10:6–7, albeit with slight differences in form and arrangement[26]; and station 31 is also in Deut 2:8, as well as in 1 Kgs 9:26; 22:48 (cf. 2 Chr 8:17; 20:36 respectively). Granted, a few other stations also do not *directly* appear in the Wilderness Narrative—specifically, by the ים סוף (station 6), דפקה and אלוש (stations 8–9), צלמנה and פונן (stations 34–35), and דיבן גד and עלמן דבלתים (stations 38–39). Yet within the Wil-

---

not that a redactor had "moved Yam Suf to a different location on the route" (*contra* Roskop, *Wilderness* Itineraries, 139).

23 Roskop, *Wilderness* Itineraries, 223–224.
24 For Roskop's thesis, see p. 162 n. 15 above.
25 Ulrich Fistill agrees, citing particularly the itinerary's introduction (Num 33:1–4) and conclusion (vv. 48–49), as well as the digression regarding Aaron's age and death and the King of Arad's hearing of the Israelites approach (vv. 38–40) as later additions to the itinerary (*Israel und das Ostjordanland: Untersuchungen zur Komposition von Num 21,21–36,13 im Hinblick auf die Entstehung des Buches Numeri* [ÖBS 30; Frankfurt: Peter Lang, 2007], 132–133). Although the following section (i.e., §6.3.1.2) does not build upon Fistill's work, of which I became only recently aware, instances of similar conclusions or disagreement have been noted. A more thorough engagement with the details of Fistill's thesis regarding the formation of Num 21:21–36:13 cannot be undertaken here.
26 Specifically, the itinerary's מסרות and בני יעקן appear in reverse order in Deut 10:6, as בארת בני־יעקן and מוסרה respectively. The toponyms הר הגדגד and יטבתה occur in the same order in Deut 10:7, but appear as הַגֻּדְגֹּדָה and יטבתה respectively (cf., Appendix C fracture 4b). For a survey of scholarly opinion regarding the direction of dependence, see Roskop, *Wilderness Itineraries*, 225 n. 82.

derness Narrative, there are elements that correspond to these missing stations, and these elements occur at relative junctures in the Wilderness Narrative where one would expect to find these missing stations.[27] The only stations that are in

---

[27] For each of these four junctures—i.e., station 6 and the three clusters (stations 8–9, 34–35, and 38–39)—there is trace evidence within the Wilderness Narrative of which the itinerary may be aware. To begin, station 6 beside (על) the ים סוף (Num 33:10b) may be an inference to the final two words of Exod 15:27's description of station 5, אלים. A comparison of Num 33:9 with Exod 15:27 is here necessary:

ויבאו אילמה **ושם** שתים עשרה עינה מים ושבעים תמרים ויחנו־שם [על־המים] Exod 15:27

[ויסעו ממרה] ויבאו אילמה **ובאילם** שתים עשרה עינה מים ושבעים תמרים ויחנו־שם Num 33:9

As indicated by the underlining, most of the material exhibits verbatim correspondence, while the bolded italics indicate that the particle שם (15:27) is conceptually parallel to the toponym אלים with ב-preposition (33:9). The only non-aligned portions are ויסעו ממרה in 33:9 (the departure portion of the itinerary formula) and significantly על־המים in Exod 15:27b. Thus a confluence emerges: the precise juncture in the Wilderness Narrative where one would expect the ים־סוף (cf. Num 33:10b) to follow, is instead punctuated by Exod 15:27b's notice of Israel bivouacking על־המים—a phrase noticeably missing in Num 33:9's otherwise nearly verbatim echo of Exod 15:27. It is possible then that whoever was annotating 33:9b (cf. pp. 170–179 below) may have understood על־המים in 15:27 to be the ים־סוף. Noth also sees this possible inference (*Numeri*, 211).

Regarding דפקה and אלוש (stations 8–9 in Num 33:12b-13b), one would expect travel notices for this cluster of stations between the departure from the מדבר־סין and the arrival at רפדים in Exod 17:1. Yet the travel notice in 17:1 indicates additional intermediate stages with the phrase למסעיהם על־פי יהוה (v. 1aγ), so Cross, Davies, and even Roskop (Cross, *Canaanite Myth and Hebrew Epic*, 308–309; Davies, "Wilderness Itineraries and Composition," 7; Roskop, *Wilderness Itineraries*, 140–141).

The next omitted cluster is צלמנה and פונן (stations 34–35 in Num 33:41b-42b). Although not as concretely indicated as דפקה and אלוש, scholars frequently identify פונן (Smr, G, and S presume פני) as Khirbet Feinan (also spelled Faynan), a site well-known in the ancient world for its copper mines. Although metal production ceased from the 9th to 4th centuries B.C.E., one must ask if it is coincidence that a narrative about Moses constructing a serpentine *image* from copper alloy (נחשת) should be loosely tied into a context where one would expect to find a travel notice to a well-known copper mine (פונן)? (For a history of the Faynan mines, see Mohammad Najjar and Thomas E. Levy, "Condemned to the Mines: Copper Production and Christian Persecution," *BAR* 37 [Nov / Dec 2011]: 30–39; for the connection between פונן and Num 21:4–9, see Bartlett, J. R., "The Wadi Arabah in the Hebrew Scriptures," in *Crossing the Rift: Resources, Routes, Settlement Patterns and Interaction in the Wadi Arabah* [ed. Piotr Bienkowski and Katharina Galor; LSup 3; Oxford: Oxbow, 2006], 152–154.) As for צלמנה, no clear literary device in the bronze serpent alludes to this station. The action, however, of Moses making an image (צלם) is conceptually (not lexically) present in Num 21:9 and invites speculation in relation to its phonetic contiguity to צלמנה.

The final cluster omitted from the Wilderness Narrative is דיבן גד and עלמן דבלתימם (stations 38–39 in Num 33:45b-46b). The toponym דיבן with no ties to גד appears in Num 21:30; yet in this context דיבן is not a station, but a toponym mentioned in the victory song over Moab (Num 21:27–

no way indicated in the Wilderness Narrative is the large block of stations from Num 33:18b-36a. Thus, stations 14–31 appear secondary to the stations that frame them in the itinerary and that are reflected in the Wilderness Narrative.[28]

For what purpose then were these stations inserted into the itinerary? Their inclusion certainly did not contribute toward the creation of a "definitive version of the wilderness sojourn that corrects it back to the shape of the Priestly wilderness narrative as much as possible,"[29] as Roskop contends. One simply cannot assert that a scribe pulled the stations in Num 33:1–49 (or more precisely in 33:5–49) from the composite Wilderness Narrative in order to create a definitive version, and yet have a block of eighteen total stations—thirteen unique to the Hebrew Bible, and five synchronically appearing later in Deuteronomy—absent from the Wilderness Narrative proper. Indeed, another purpose for these stations must be sought.

A *second feature* of the itinerary not only suggests the itinerary is composite, but also provides a clue to the rationale for inserting the block of eighteen stations: namely, the number and scope of arrival stations reflected in Num 33:5–

---

30). The only appearance of דיבן in the Wilderness Narrative as an area encountered occurs in Num 32:3, 34, in which the בני גד rebuild דיבן along with other sites. One of these sites is Baal-meon (בעל מעון) in Num 32:38, which is listed with the scribal note "name to be changed" (מוסבת שם). This notation, along with the graphic similarity of בעל מעון in Num 32:38 to בעלמן (the ב is the preposition) in Num 33:46b, suggests that a scribe at one time intended to correct בעל מעון to בעלמן. This reconstruction finds support in S and multiple manuscripts of the Smr (Gall lists ABEG³HIMNPQY³ABDEJλ del ρ; cf. Gall, *Pentateuch der Samaritaner*, 350), where בעל מעון appears instead as בעלמון, the *plene* form of the MT Num 33:46's בעלמן. Thus, Num 32:34–38 may demonstrate an awareness of דיבן גד and דבלתימם as stations 38–39 in Num 33:45b-46b. At first glance this position in the Wilderness Narrative appears problematic, since this juncture situates דיבן גד and עלמן דבלתימם *after* Mt. Abarim in the narrative (cf. Num 27:12) while the itinerary has them situated *before* the Mts. of Abarim (station 40 in Num 33:47b). Albertz notes, however, a consensus among scholars "that Num 25–36 or 26–36 are among the latest texts of the Pentateuch," with possible minor exceptions for Num 25:1–5 and select verses from Num 32:1–38 (among which are vv. 34–36a, 37–38), which appear to be non-P material (Rainer Albertz, "A Pentateuchal Redaction in the Book of Numbers? The Late Priestly Layers of Num 25–36," *ZAW* 125 [2013]: 221). Although Albertz notes the continued debate regarding Num 27:12–14 as possibly stemming from the original Priestly source (Albertz, "Late Priestly Layers in Num 25–36," 221 n. 4), the current study concludes that PentRed is to be credited for Num 27:12–14*'s initial *entry* into the Pentateuch (cf. p. 216 n. 33 below).

28 For Fistill, that the itinerary mentions stations "die sich sonst nirgends finden" is evidence that it cannot simply be "eine Summlung von Notizen aus Ex-Num" (*Israel und das Ostjordanland*, 132). He does not consider this cluster of eighteen stations to be redactional.

29 Roskop, *Wilderness Itineraries*, 225.

6.3 Literary Analysis of Exodus 17:1–7 — 169

49. Scholars frequently count forty-two stations in the itinerary,[30] but this number includes רעמסס (Num 33:5a), which is merely the *station of departure* (A) for the first stage of the Israelite's journey. Yet the formula that frames these stages throughout the itinerary focuses on the *stations of arrival* (B), as each of which subsequently serves as the station of departure for next stage of the journey. Davies describes the formula well:

> The itinerary is constructed according to a regular pattern: 'And they set out from A, and encamped in B.' There are forty-one such sentences (with a slight variation in verse 9 – cf. the parallel in Exodus 15:27), and each is linked to the next by the fact that its B-name recurs in the A-position. 'They set out from the Red Sea, and encamped in the wilderness of Sin. They set out from the wilderness of Sin, and encamped at Dophqah. They set out from Dophqah, and encamped at Alush' (verses 11–13), and so on.[31]

Thus, while there are forty-two total stations in these sentences, there are only forty-one sentences, with forty-one arrival stations—one for each stage of the Israelites' sojourn.

The significance of the number of arrival stations, or the terminus of each stage, becomes apparent when one recognizes that the fortieth arrival station is נבו הרי העברים לפני (Num 33:47b)—the station that sets the climactic scene of the Pentateuch itself: the death of Moses (cf. Deut 32:49; 34:1–12). Yet curiously, not only is there no notice of Moses' death at this juncture in the itinerary, as there is for Aaron's death in Num 33:38–39, but the scope of the itinerary clearly shows Moses travelling with the Israelites beyond it! On the forty-first stage of the sojourn, they journey from הרי העברים and encamp at עברת מואב על ירדן ירחו (Num 33:48b).[32] Here, Yahweh commands Moses to give Israel instructions

---

[30] For example Cross, *Canaanite Myth and Hebrew Epic*, 309; Timothy R. Ashley, *The Book of Numbers* (NICOT; Grand Rapids: Eerdmans, 1993), 623–624; Dozeman, "Priestly Wilderness Itineraries," in Dozeman, Schmid, and Schwartz, *The Pentateuch*, 286–287 n. 104. This count is traditional, however, appearing as early as Rashi, who said "do not say that they were moving and wandering from station to station all forty years, and they had no rest, because there are here only forty-two stations" לא תאמר שהיו נעים ומטולטלים ממסע למסע כל ארבעים שנה ולא היתה להם מנוחה, שהרי אין כאן אלא ארבעים ושתים מסעות (cf. Ḥ. D. Chavel, פרושי רש"י על התורה [Jerusalem: Rav Kook, 1983], תקו [506]).

[31] Davies, "Wilderness Itineraries: Comparative Study," 50.

[32] Numbers 33:49's caveat clarifying the geographical range this forty-first stage entails appears parenthetical. The final arrival station in Num 33:48b is עברת מואב על ירדן ירחו, which is repeated precisely in Num 33:50's speech formula that introduces the next pericope. The caveat indicates a range from בית הישמת as far as אבל השטים (Num 33:49), toponyms which evoke the conflict with Sihon and the failure with Baal of Peor respectively. Joshua 12:3 lists בית הישמת as once under the control of the Amorite king, Sihon, the narrative for which is in Num 21:21–34; while אבל השטים (*hapax*) appears to be a longer name for שטים, the location for the failure with

for crossing the Jordan into Canaan (Num 33:50–56), a command which is recalled in Deut 1:3 and then fulfilled by the framing of Deuteronomy as Moses' final instructions to Israel.³³ In other words, the itinerary demonstrates no awareness that Moses would die at הרי העברים לפני נבו, or even that he would die at all. Instead, the arrival at the הרי העברים appears artificially elevated by the insertion of stations 14–31 to the artfully symbolic fortieth stage of the wilderness sojourn, in presaged deference to the final fate of Israel's greatest prophet (cf. Deut 32:48–52; 34:7, 10–12). Such an agenda aligns with the profile of PentRed's aggrandizing ancient Israel's founding leaders³⁴; thus to this hand may be credited the insertion of the block of eighteen toponyms (stations 14–31) in Num 33:18b-36a.

Finally, the digressions from the itinerary constitute a *third feature* that suggests the itinerary is composite. These digressions annotate certain arrival stations in the itinerary—annotations which in turn provide details that echo, or elaborate upon, the portions of the Wilderness Narrative to which the annotated itinerary station corresponds (vv. 3–4, 6bβ, 7aγ-b, 8aβ-bβ, 9bα-β, 14bβ, 36bβ, 37bβ, 38–39, 40, 44bβ, 47bβ, 48bβ, and 49).³⁵ Collectively, at least two *properties*

Baal of Peor in Num 25:1–18. The absence of any allusion to these episodes in the itinerary is striking—especially the conflict with Sihon, given the prevalence of this tradition elsewhere (Num 21:21–34; 32:33; Deut 1:4; 2:24–3:10; 4:46–49; 29:7–8; 31:4; Jos 2:10; 9:10; 12:1–6; 13:8–12, 24–28; Judg 11:19–23; 1 Kgs 4:19; Jer 48:45; Pss 135:11–12; 136:17–22; Neh 9:22). By its narrative representation in Num 21:21–34, one would expect an allusion to this story to occur in the itinerary in Num 33:45 between station 37 (עיי העברים; cf. Num 21:11) and 38 (דיבן גד; cf. p. 167 n. 27 for this station's relation to Num 32:34). This omission, if not dislocation, further calls into question the argument that the itinerary was written to reflect the Pentateuch's final form.

33 Even though cast with expressions typical of the priestly style, the central concerns of the instructions Yahweh commands Moses to relay in Num 33:50–56 are strongly reminiscent of the paraenesis found in the book of Deuteronomy. E. W. Davies agrees: "The general concern of the passage, namely, the need to rid the land of the Canaanites and their religion, is typical of the Deuteronomist as, indeed is the reason given for such drastic action viz., that their presence would pose a perennial threat to Israel's life and well-being (cf. Dt. 7:1 ff.; 12:2 f., 29 ff.; Noth, p. 248)" (Davies, *Numbers*, 348–349).

34 See pp. 116–117 and 134 above. Contra Ederer, who sees the unknown stations as filling "die Ortsnamen mit 'zusätzlichem Leben,'" which in the end only helps portray the wilderness "als 'Lern- und Praxisraum' der Identität und Gottesbeziehung Israels, in dem das Volk das wird, was es sein und bleiben soll" (*Aufbrüche zur Exodustheologie*, 138, 139).

35 Noth also treats some of these annotations as a digression from the formula and thus secondary to it. "Es ist sehr wahrscheinlich," contends Noth, "daß diese Hinweise [i.e., vv. 3–4, 8, 9, 38–39, 40] erst nachträglich hinzugefügt worden sind. Das wird deutlich vor allem an V. 3. 4, da der Unfang von V. 3 den Unfang von V. 5 vorwegnimmt." Noth rightly concludes that "der ursprüngliche Unfang des Stationenverzeichnisses" lies "in V. 5a" (*Das 4.Buch Mose Numeri* [ATD 7; Göttingen: Vandenhoeck & Ruprecht, 1966], 210). To be precise, the di-

of these annotations warrant consideration: namely, a) their distribution within the itinerary, and b) their confluence with significant fractures within the Wilderness Narrative.[36]

The *first property* of this feature to merit consideration is the distribution of these annotations across the itinerary. Strikingly, none of the annotations appears within Num 33:18b-36a, wherein lies the block of eighteen toponyms (stations 14–31) discussed above. Instead, they characterize the surrounding textual material (cf. vv. 6–9, 14, 36b-40, 44, 47, 49). This distribution further corroborates Num 33:18–35 as a later insertion into an earlier form of the itinerary (33:1–18a + 36b-49). Yet since they represent digressions from the formula, it is likely that the annotations are also secondary to what may be dubbed the "*Ur*-Itinerary," which would have likely been no more than the formulary foundational to vv. 5–18a, 36b-37, 41–48 (although see p. 180 n. 54 below).

A *second property* inherent to these annotations lends additional support for their being secondary to some form of *Ur*-Itinerary: each annotation within the parameters of the *Ur*-Itinerary occurs at a juncture that corresponds to significant

---

gressions from the formulary occur in Num 33:3–4, 6bβ, 7aγ-b, 8aβ-bβ, 9bα-β, 14bβ, 36bβ, 37bβ, 38–39, 40, 44bβ, 47bβ, 49; it is for this reason that the current study focuses on Num 33:5–49 as the locus of the itinerary proper. For the composite nature of the itinerary's introduction in vv. 1–4, see p. 180 n. 54 below.

36 One may suggest a third property, but only insofar as it is detectable in select annotations (vv. 14bβ, 36bβ, 38–39, 47bβ). These annotations all interact with geographical *locations* of tradition-historical reminiscences in Deuteronomy: v. 14bβ relocates the non-P M-Mt narrative from a post-Horeb position to a pre-Sinai tradition (cf. Deut 9:22); v. 36bβ equates מדבר צן with קדש, the intrinsic location for the P* M-Mt in Num 20:1, 13 (cf. Deut 32:51; although Deut 32:51 [*post-PentRed*] appears to be dependent on Num 20:1, 13; cf. pp. 118–119 above and §7.3.1 below); vv. 38–39 relocate the death mount of Aaron from מוסרה (cf. Deut 10:6; מסרות, station 26 in Num 33:30b) to הר ההר (cf. Num 20:22–29; Deut 32:50); and lastly v. 47bβ narrows the focus of הרי העברים to the more specific mount נבו (cf. Deut 32:49; 34:1), the death mount of Moses. Aside then from v. 36bβ, these annotations are indicative of a general awareness of Deuteronomy; specifically, they suggest that the scribe responsible for them (*HexRed*) may be recording 1) how his compilation of non-P and P narratives deviated from Deuteronomy (cf. v. 14bβ; vv. 38–39 vs. Deut 10:6 [cf. Deut 32:50 {*HexRed*}]) and 2) how he supplemented the end of Deuteronomy (cf. v. 47bβ vs Deut 32:49; 34:1) in his merging of the non-P and P materials.

In addition to this interaction with the reminiscences within Deuteronomy, it is striking that the itinerary displays no awareness of the failure of Aaron and Moses. Elsewhere, texts recalling Aaron's death on הר ההר are always accompanied with a tradition-historical explanation for his death outside the land that links back to Num 20:1–13 (e.g., Num 20:24; 27:13–14; Deut 32:51). In Num 33:38–39, however, Aaron's death is simply reported (v. 38a); this report is then followed by a date formula and age of death (v. 38b-39) that evinces the style of PentRed in Num 33:3–4.

fractures within the Wilderness Narrative (cf. Appendix C).³⁷ This property requires significant discussion, as most of these annotations pertain to texts that in some way anchor the M-Mt tradition into the Pentateuch. The *non-related* annotations occur early in the itinerary, in vv. 6bβ, 7ay-b, 8aβ-bβ, and 9bα-β. The first three of these non-related annotations all relate to the key texts that reorient the crossing of the sea from אתם to פי החירת,³⁸ while the fourth provides a clue as to why station 6 in Num 33:10b is missing from the Wilderness Narrative.³⁹ The remainder of the annotations, however—namely, vv. 14bβ, 36bβ, 37bβ, 38–39, 40, 44bβ, 47bβ, and 49—carry varying degrees of relevance for the M-Mt and its related texts. These *related* annotations easily divide into three subcategories: first, vv. 14bβ and 36bβ relate to the travel notices anchoring the M-Mt episodes into the Wilderness Narrative; secondly, vv. 37bβ, 38–39, and 40 relate to הר ההר, the priestly location of Aaron's death, which secondarily depends on the P* M-Mt (cf. Num 20:12); and thirdly, vv. 44bβ, 47bβ, 48bβ, and 49 relate to the Israelites' travels in מואב, wherein is the location of Moses' death, which also depends of the P* M-Mt (cf. Num 20:12).

Especially relevant to the M-Mt are the notations for the stations associated with M-Mt narratives in vv. 14bβ and 36bβ. The annotation in Num 33:14bβ generically clarifies רפידם as the location where the Israelites experienced water dep-

---

37 Dozeman observes six such fractures, or "geographical dislocations": "(1) the location of Pi-hahiroth from the confrontation at the sea (Exod 14:1–2); (2) Sin as the setting of the story of manna (Exod 16:1; 17:1); (3) Sinai as the mountain of revelation (Exod 19:1); (4) Paran (Num 10:11–12; 12:16) as the setting for the spy story and the priestly rebellion of Korah; (5) Kadesh as the setting for the death of Miriam and the sin of Moses (Num 20:1); and (6) the plains of Moab as the setting for Priestly legislation on land, inheritance, calendar, war, and judicial processes (Num 22:1)" ("Priestly Wilderness Itineraries," in Dozeman, Schmid, and Schwartz, *The Pentateuch*, 261). Significantly, though not within the scope of Dozeman's study, many of the annotative digressions in Num 33:6–9, 36–49 correspond with these exact fractures; cf. pp. 171 above–181 below.
38 Cf. Exod 13:17, 20; 14:1; 15:22; Num 33:6–9; and fractures 1a-c noted in Appendix C. In the non-P trek, God fears the Israelites will return (√שוב) to Egypt if faced with the prospect of war with the Philistines, and so God leads them toward the ים סוף, from סכת to אתם בקצה המדבר (Exod 13:17, 20); Dozeman notes P reorients this trajectory by having Yahweh command Moses to turn around (√שוב) and bivouacking at פי החירת, at which point the composite narrative of the Israelites crossing the sea ensues (Exod 14:1; Num 33:8) ("Priestly Wilderness Itineraries," in Dozeman, Schmid, and Schwartz, *The Pentateuch*, 262–266). After crossing the ים סוף, the Israelites journey three days into a wilderness: the מדבר-שור, according to Exod 15:22; the מדבר אתם, according to Num 33:8. A detailed reconstruction of the literary history behind these fractures is not possible here; more important for the current argument is the recognition that the annotations in vv. 6bβ, 7ay-b, and 8aβ-bβ correspond to these fractures.
39 See p. 167 n. 27 above; cf. fracture 1c in Appendix C.

6.3 Literary Analysis of Exodus 17:1–7 — 173

rivation, but there is nothing within Num 33:14b that intrinsically tethers רפידם to the M-Mt specifically.⁴⁰ Additionally, רפידם is one station before סיני (cf. Exod 19:1–2; Num 33:15b), but the narrative itself in Exod 17:2–6 is intrinsically set at חרב (cf. Exod 17:6).⁴¹ A similar tension occurs inside the travel notice and itinerary station for the P* M-Mt: both v. 36bβ and Num 20:1 bind קדש to מדבר־צן, yet קדש has already been located near מדבר פארן (cf. Num 13:26).⁴² In short, the travel notices and itinerary stations for both M-Mt narratives appear to be artificial constructions designed to situate the narratives into their current literary contexts.

The annotations in vv. 37bβ, 38–39, and 40 relate to events that unfold in proximity to הר ההר, a location which in turn relates to the M-Mt through the death of Aaron (cf. Num 20:12).⁴³ It is at הר ההר where Aaron presumably dies

---

40 The annotation in Num 33:14bβ (ולא־היה שם מים לעם לשתות) refers only to the primary narrative crisis (cf. Exod 17:1bβ [ואין מים לשתת העם], the original opening of the non-P M-Mt prior to HexRed affixing the travel notice in v. 1abα), not the מסה or מריבה etiologies. Other episodes of water deprivation outside the M-Mt occur at Marah (cf. Exod 15:22bβ; ולא־מצאו מים), on Israel's circuit around Edom (cf. Num 21:5bα; ואין מים לחם כי אין), and at Beer (cf. Num 21:16by; ואתנה להם מים). Noth is therefore likely correct in his observation that the station originally had nothing to do with the narrative that follows (*Das 2. Buch Mose Exodus* [ATD 5; Göttingen: Vandenhoeck & Ruprecht, 1958], 110), though not necessarily on the source-critical grounds from which he argues.

41 Cf. fracture 2b in Appendix C.

42 In its final form, v. 36bβ has the station as מדבר־צן, which the annotation equates with Kadesh (הוא קדש), but the departure station in v. 37a is קדש, not מדבר־צן. Only two possibilities present themselves: either HexRed inherited מדבר־צן in the itinerary, provided the annotation הוא קדש, and then rewrote v. 37a carrying forward his equation in v. 36bβ; or he inherited קדש in the itinerary and substantially rewrote v. 36b so that מדבר־צן appears as the station and קדש as the annotation. Both options present difficulties, but the first option (i.e., rewriting v. 37a) is less difficult. Thus, מדבר־צן is more intrinsic to the itinerary than קדש. The opposite is true for the travel notice in Num 20:1. While מדבר־צן has no connection to the P* M-Mt narrative beyond the travel notice, there are verbal correspondences between the P* M-Mt narrative and קדש: 1) there is an etiological relationship between the toponym קדש in Num 20:1 and ויקדש בם in 20:13; and 2) figs (תאנה) and pomegranates (רמון) in Num 20:5 occur elsewhere in the Wilderness Narrative only in the scouts story (cf. Num 13:23), wherein Israel is bivouacked at מדבר פארן קדשה (Num 13:26) (see §7.3.3 below for the implications of this relationship). Finally, as Noth rightly observes, the fact that Num 20:16 calls קדש—a region known for its springs (modern ʻAin Qadeis)—a "city" (עיר) on the border of אדום gives the impression of "nur vagen Vorstellung von den geographischen Verhältnissen beruhenden" in this statement (*Numeri*, 132–133 and 94). Thus, since the location of קדש was traditionally vague, HexRed situated it in מדבר־צן, adding Num 20:1aαβ to the P* M-Mt travel notice, then annotating the itinerary with Num 33:36bβ, and finally rewriting the departure station of Num 33:37a.

43 In Numbers, the death of Aaron outside the land is an extension of the P* M-Mt tradition in Num 20:1–13. The deity holds Aaron culpable along with Moses for their failure at קדש, the exact nature of which remains a subject of perennial debate (cf. p. 209 n. 18 below).

(vv. 38–39; although cf. Deut 10:6), and from here that the Israelites appear to depart twice in the Wilderness Narrative: once by the דרך האתרים (Num 21:1), prompting the war with king of Arad (Num 21:1–3; cf. Num 33:40), and a second time by the דרך ים־סוף (Num 21:4), which culminates in the bronze serpent episode (Num 21:4–9).[44]

Lastly, the annotations in vv. 44bβ, 47bβ, 48bβ, and 49 clarify certain stations spanning Israel's southern to northern trek *through* מואב.[45] In the same way that vv. 37bβ, 38–39, and 40 relate to the M-Mt via Aaron's death at הר ההר, these מואב annotations are relevant to M-Mt on account of Moses' eventual death atop a mountain in northern מואב (cf. Num 27:12; Deut 3:27; 32:49–50; 34:1–6). This tradition alone—i. e. that Moses died בארץ מואב (Deut 32:49; 34:5–6)—stands in opposition to the tradition that Israel did not enter מואב, but went around it (cf. Num 21:11–13; Judg 11:15–18). Yet the annotations in vv. 44bβ, 47bβ, 48bβ, and 49 not only clarify Israel's trek through Moab, but they also correspond to major fractures within Wilderness Narrative itself.

The first mention of מואב in the Wilderness Narrative occurs in Num 21:11, which sets עיי העברים *outside* of Moab in the wilderness to the east (במדבר אשר על־פני מואב השמש). In the itinerary, v. 44bβ reorients עיי העברים to being *inside* the territory of Moab (בגבול מואב). Aside from this dissonance, Num 21:11 borders a major fracture within the Wilderness Narrative itself: the mélange of materials

---

44 Like רפידם and קדש, the station הר ההר in the itinerary borders on stations that are not in the Wilderness Narrative: namely צלמנה and פונן (stations 34–35; Num 33:41b-43a), which may have inspired the textual location of the Bronze Serpent story (cf. p. 167 n. 27 above and fractures 6a-b in Appendix C).

45 The trajectory of stations 37–41 in the itinerary progresses linearly from southern to northern Moab: *from* עיי עברים (south of the ארמון [or Wādī el-Mūjib]; cf. annotation in Num 33:44bβ), *to* דיבן גד (5 km north of the ארנון at modern Dhiban), then *to* עלמן דבלתים (4 km north of Khirbet Libb), then *to* הרי העברים (the "northeastern corner of the Dead Sea," according to J. Maxwell Miller; cf. annotation in Num 33:47bβ), and then finally *to* עברת מואב, along the ירדן in proximity to ירחו, a range extending from בית הישמת to אבל השחם (modern day Tell ʿAẓeimeh and Tell el-Ḥammām respectively; cf. annotation in Num 33:49) (Burton MacDonald, *"East of the Jordan": Territories and Sites of the Hebrew Scriptures* [ASORB 6; Boston: American Schools of Oriental Research, 2000], 72–90; Miller, "The Israelite Journey through (around) Moab and Moabite Toponymy," *JBL* 108 [1989]: 581, 582 n. 8).

This portrait of Israel's journey contradicts the tradition preserved in Num 21:11–13 and Judg 11:15–18, which insists that the Israelites went *around* Moab, not through it. For studies regarding these conflicting traditions, see Miller, "Moab and Moabite Toponymy," 577–595; Dozeman, "Geography and Ideology in the Wilderness Journey from Kadesh through the Transjordan," in *Abschied vom Jahwisten: Dis Komposition des Hexateuch in der jüngsten Diskussion* (ed. Jan Christian Gertz, Konrad Schmid, and Markus Witte; BZAW 315; Berlin: de Gruyter, 2002), 173–189; Roskop, *Wilderness Itineraries*, 204–215.

that comprise Num 21:12–20.⁴⁶ Particularly troublesome is this text's conflicting perspectives on the extent of Moabite northern territory. While Num 21:13 cites

---

46 In short, Num 21:10–13 portrays a trek around southern Moab, but not without complications: v. 11 situates עיי העברים outside of Moab to the *east*, but the נחל זרד (most likely Wādī el-Ḥesā) marks Moab's *southern* border, while the ארנון in v. 13 constitutes Moab's *northernmost* border (cf. Miller, "Moab and Moabite Toponymy," 588, 590–591; MacDonald, *East of the Jordan*, 73–74). But how can Israel have arrived on the east side of Moab *before* crossing נחל זרד in the south? Regardless of its difficulties, the poetry cited from the Book of the Wars of Yahweh in vv. 14–15 rhetorically functions in support of this circumnavigation. The sojourn then continues in vv. 16–18a, with the digging of Beer and the record of Israel's song to it. Finally, vv. 18b-20 portray a trek northward beyond the ארנון, but here a valley near פסגה is again described as also being "in Moab" (cf. ומבמות הגיא אשר בשדה מואב ראש הפסגה in v. 20a). In other words, not only do Num 21:11 and 33:44 have discrepant portraits regarding עיי העברים and whether it was inside or outside Moabite territory, but this discrepancy is implicit in Num 21:11–20; it is difficult to imagine a circumstance in which עיי העברים is outside of Moab, yet a valley near פסגה is inside Moab.

These difficulties prompt Miller to critique scholars who have wrestled with Num 21:10–20 "for years on the mistaken assumption that it is supposed to make geographical sense. But it simply does not." Instead, following Mittmann, Van Seters, and Davies, Miller argues Num 21:10–20 as a conflation of traditions from Num 33:5–49, Deuteronomy 2–3, and Judges 11. "The result of all this," Miller contends, "is a geographical hodgepodge totally incomprehensible in terms of the geographical realities of southern Transjordan" ("Moab and Moabite Toponymy," 585–587; cf. J. Van Seters, "The Conquest of Sihon's Kingdom: A Literary Examination," *JBL* 91 (1972): 182–197; J. Van Seters, "Once again – the Conquest of Sihon's Kingdom," *JBL* 99 (1980): 117–119; "Siegfried Mittmann, "Num 21,14–21 – eine redaktionelle Kompilation," in *Wort und Geschichte: Festschrift für Karl Elliger zum 70. Geburtstag* (ed. H. Gese and H. R. Rüger; AOAT 18; Neukirchen-Vluyn: Neukirchener Verlag, 1973), 143–149; Davies, "Wilderness Itineraries and Composition," 1–13).

Instead of a conflation of traditions, Roskop insightfully argues that these tensions are a byproduct of three redactions designed to connect Numbers to Deuteronomy, anchor the Balaam episode in Numbers 22–24, and insert the Sihon & Og narrative in Num 21:21–35. To build her case, Roskop observes a confluence between a) the distinctive forms of travel notice in vv. 12–13a and 18b-20 *and* b) the editorial linkages the toponyms in vv. 12–13a and 18b-20 create with material beyond Num 21:11–20. To begin, the formula in vv. 12–13a abbreviates the P* convention by reducing the station of departure to "משם" ("from there"). The stations vv. 12–13a then relay (נחל זרד and ארנון) serve to link Numbers to Deuteronomy (cf. Deut 2:13–14, the only other text to mention נחל זרד; cf. Deut 2:24, 35; 3:8, 12, 16; 4:48 for נחל ארמון). Secondly, the convention in vv. 18b-20 is terser: it eliminates the verbs entirely, and instead prefixes the מן-preposition to the departure station and then sets the arrival station in direct apposition. Three of the toponyms in vv. 18b-20 then provide a link to the Balaam story: במות (Num 22:41), פסגה (Num 23:14), and הישימן (Num 23:28). Her conclusion therefore is that post-P redactors inserted vv. 12–13a and 18b-20 to order to "connect Deuteronomy to Numbers" and "incorporate the Balaam episode into the Wilderness Narrative" respectively. Finally, Roskop argues that Num 21:11b and 13b are glosses added, not to conflate the traditions of Deuteronomy 2 and Judges 11, but to facilitate the inser-

the ארנון as Moab's northernmost border, with the territory north of the ארנון under Amorite control (cf. Judg 11:18), the itinerary in vv. 18–20 terminates in a valley that is *in* Moab and near Pisgah (בשדה מואב ראש הפסגה; Num 21:20) [47] —a peak located north of the ארנון and associated with the tradition of Moses' death (Deut 34:1).

The second annotation related to Moab is Num 33:47bβ, which synchronically echoes Num 27:12,[48] the P* version of Yahweh's command for Moses to ascend a mountain, view the land, and then die (cf. Deut 32:48–52). Yet v. 47bβ reorients the location, from an unspecified peak within the Abarim mountain range (הר העברים הזה; Num 27:12) to a specific peak, Nebo (הרי העברים לפני נבו)—a peak that is equated with Pisgah in Deut 34:1 (cf. Deut 32:49). Here again, the juncture

---

tion of the Sihon and Og narrative (vv. 21–35), which elsewhere is a conflict within Amorite territory as opposed to Moabite territory (Roskop, *Wilderness Itineraries*, 205–208).

Roskop's reconstruction is thought-provoking, but not entirely convincing. A major problem with this reconstruction is the current location of the Sihon and Og story *after* vv. 18b-20 in Num 21:21–35. Outside of Numbers 21, this story always occurs immediately after the crossing of the נחל ארנון (cf. Deut 2:24; Judg 11:18–19). If the redactor responsible for vv. 11b and 13b also inserted the Sihon and Og story, as Roskop contends, surely he would have done so immediately after vv. 13b-15 which confirms the ארמון as the border of Moab; he would not have situated it *after* vv. 18b-20, which portrays the Moabite territory extending beyond the ארנון as far north as פסגה. Instead, it is more likely that the redactor who added vv. 12–13a (HexRed)—which provides toponyms linking Numbers to Deuteronomy—would have followed the pattern of Deuteronomy by portraying the Israelite's peaceful trek *through* Moab before the military encounters with the Amorite kings, Sihon and Og (cf. Deu 2:8–9, 13–18, 24f.). In other words, the intervening materials, especially in vv. 16–20, are most likely later insertions, with the terse itinerary in vv. 18b-20 specifically stemming from the same hand that inserted the Balaam cycle (HexSupp).

A thorough study, of course, is required but beyond the scope of the current study. Provisionally, Num 21:12–13a + 21–24 + 33–35 stem from HexRed. A later hand then added vv. 18b-20 (which terminates in northern מואב near פסגה) along with the Balaam cycle (HexSupp; cf. p. 177 n. 50 below). The opening of the Balaam cycle itself reflects this strange trajectory of Israel having conquered Amorite territory, then travelling north to bivouac in Moabite territory (Num 22:1–3). Later editors are therefore responsible for remaining materials, including vv. 11b and 13b-15, but also vv. 16–18a and the disruption within the Sihon and Og narrative in vv. 25–32 (cf. vv. 24 and 32 regarding settling in Amorite territory and the proximity of Jezer; note the NASB follows G, which has Ιαζηρ for the MT's עז ["strong"], presuming יעזר ["Jezer"]).

47 Numbers 21:20 also adds על־פני הישימן. For the significance of this toponym to the itinerary's literary history, see p. 177 n. 50 below.

48 Formally, Num 33:47b's description of this location—to be precise, הרי העברים לפני נבו—does not closely resemble the description in either Num 27:12 (הר העברים הזה) or Deut 32:49 (הר העברים הזה הר־נבו). The three texts share העברים, so it cannot factor into the decision as to whether Num 33:47b has either of these texts in view. Since the annotation in Num 33:47bβ mentions נבו, it is more likely that reference is being made to Deut 32:49 than it is to Num 27:12.

in the Wilderness Narrative corresponding to v. 47bβ represents a major fracture within the Wilderness Narrative as a whole. After Yahweh's commands to Moses in Num 27:12–13, one expects Moses' prompt ascent up the unspecified Abarim mountain in order to view the land and then die—or, at least to die soon after he installs Joshua *publicly* as his immediate successor (Num 27:15–23)—but Moses does not die in the immediate textual context. Indeed, he continues to act as though he had never received any such a command; likewise, Joshua remains noticeably absent beyond Num 27:15–23, as though he had never received his commission.[49]

The final annotations are vv. 48bβ and 49. Although one could treat vv. 48bβ-49 as a single digression, the repetition of v. 48b's בעברת מואב על ירדן ירחו in v. 50 suggests that v. 49 is an even later addition than the annotation על ירדן ירחו in v. 48bβ.[50] This annotation combines in apposition ירדן and ירחו, which rarely occurs

---

[49] This pronounced delay in Moses' death and Joshua's transition to leadership—along with the repetition of Yahweh's command to Moses (Deut 32:48–52) and Joshua's public installation (Deut 31:7–8, 14–23; 32:44)—suggests two possible explanations for their *entry* into the emerging Pentateuch. Either Num 27:12–14 and 27:15–23 entered the Pentateuch before Deut 32:48–52 and Deut 31:15–23 respectively, or they are later insertions. The current study argues for the latter, though this diachrony pertains to their insertion into the Pentateuch, not necessarily their initial composition (see p. 217 n. 33 below). Ulrich Fistill reaches a similar conclusion: following de Vaulx (*Les Nombres* [SB; Paris: J. Gabalda, 1972], 399–400), Fistill considers Num 27:12–23 to be a part of the "priesterschriftliche Erzählung," which had taken up and processed older traditions; yet Fistill asserts that "Der heutige Standort von Num 27,12–23"—which sets up the death of Moses and the installation of Joshua—"ist hingegen redaktionell bedingt." Why? Because "einige der folgenden Texte entweder den Tod des Mose (vgl. Num 31,1) oder die Beauftragung Josuas (vg. Num 32,28–30; vgl. auch 34,16)" (*Israel und das Ostjordanland*, 109).

[50] The later addition of v. 49 probably derives from a Hexateuch Supplementer (HexSupp), who was responsible for inserting the Balaam and the Baal-Peor stories (Numbers 22–25). Corroboration for this assignment emerges on two fronts: 1) the distribution of the Balaam and Baal-Peor traditions within the Hexateuch, and 2) when one compares the range indicted in v. 49 (מבית הישמת עד אבל השטים) to הישימן in Num 21:20 and שטים in Num 25:1. Regarding distribution of these traditions, the Balaam narrative and its reminiscences appear in Numbers 22–24; 31:8, 16; Deut 23:4–5; Josh 13:22; 24:9–10, and can be divided into strata according to a positive (Num 22:3–20* + 22:35b–24:25*), transitional (Deut 23:4–5; Josh 24:9–10) and negative (Num 22:22–35a; 31:8, 16; Josh 13:22) portrayals of Balaam, which indicate the original pre-existing materials, their insertion as a supplement into the Hexateuch with transitional modifications, and the secondary modifications at the hands of PentRed respectively (cf. Jonathan M. Robker, "The Balaam Narrative in the Pentateuch / Hexateuch / Enneateuch," in *Torah and the Book of Numbers* [ed. Christian Frevel, Thomas Pola, and Aaron Schart; FAT2 62; Tübingen: Mohr Siebeck, 2013], 334–366; for a brief history of research through 1995, see Meindert Dijkstra, "The Geography of the Story of Balaam: Synchronic Reading as a Help to Date a Biblical Text," in *Synchronic or Diachronic? A Debate on Method in Old Testament Studies* [ed. Johannes

outside of post-priestly material, and attaches to the toponym עברת מואב via the preposition על or the prepositional phrase "מעבר + ל".[51] Together, these basic

---

C. De Moor; OtSt 34; Leiden: Brill, 1995], 72–74). Regardless of the precise stratification, it is clear that the redactor who inserted the Balaam narrative had the Hexateuch as his literary horizon. Likewise, the story regarding Israel's failure with the Baal of (Beth-)Peor also has a Hexateuchal literary horizon (cf. Num 23:28, which links the Balaam narrative to events at Peor; Numbers 25; 31:16 [PentRed]; Deut 3:29; 4:3, 46; 34:6; Josh 13:20; 22:7). Note that while בית פעור is never explicitly tied to the failure in Numbers 25, the association between בית פעור, the בעל פעור, and פעור in general is traditional (cf. Jack R. Lundbom, *Deuteronomy: A Commentary* [Grand Rapids: Eerdmans, 2013], 228, who cites Rashi, ibn Ezra, and Rashbam).

Secondly, a comparison of the range indicated in the annotation of Num 33:49 to the toponyms in Num 21:20 and 25:1 further suggests that this annotation stems from HexSupp. The relation of הישימן to בית הישמת is textually evident by their proximity to Pisgah (cf. Num 21:20; Jos 12:3; 13:20), and as early as T[j] the two were conflated. Martin McNamara notes that T[j] gives the longer spelling Beth-Jeshimon for הישימן in Num 21:20, but then renders Beth-Jeshimoth for הישימן in Num 23:28 (*Targum and Testament Revisited: Aramaic Paraphrases of the Hebrew Bible* [Grand Rapids: Eerdmans, 2010], 290). Miller and Dijkstra makes this comparison as well ("Moab and Moabite Toponymy," 582 n. 8; Dijkstra, "Geography of the Story of Balaam," 89 n. 69). Further, MacDonald notes that "Abel-shittim and Shittim are one and the same" and that Beth-Jeshimoth and Abel-shittim mark the southern and northern extremities of the Plains of Moab (*East of the Jordan*, 88–89). It is this at point that a confluence of toponyms in Num 33:49 and Num 21:18b-20 and Num 25:1 becomes apparent: 1) the itinerary in Num 21:18b-20 (which anchors the Balaam story [cf. p. 175 n. 46 above]) ends with a reference to הישימן, to which בית הישמת in Num 33:49 likely refers; and 2) Num 25:1 sets the Baal-Peor story at שטים, to which אבל השטים in Num 33:49 likely refers. Moreover, given that the role of Midian frames the Balaam and Baal-Peor stories (Num 22:4, 7; 25:15–18), it is now possible to read Num 33:49 (which disrupts vv. 48 + 50) as a marker denoting not only the parameters of Israel travels within the plains of Moab, but also the parameters of *HexSupp*'s work in Numbers 21–25. (For Fistill's perspective on the post-priestly redactional role that the Midianite texts play in the formation of the book of Numbers, see *Israel und das Ostjordanland*, 145–154.)

This reading is *contra* Albertz, "Late Priestly Layers in Num 2–36," 229, who argues that the Baal-Peor episode belongs to the Numbers 25–36 redaction. Albertz's argument fails to convince at this point for three reasons: firstly, it is Midian who is initially blamed for the Baal-Peor episode (Num 25:16–18; Balaam is not blamed for this failure until Num 31:16); secondly, Numbers 25 is not framed by the refrain בעברת מואב על ירדן ירחו as is Numbers 26–36 (cf. Num 26:3, 63; 31:12; 33:48, 50; 35:1; 36:13); and thirdly, the Balaam cycle anticipates Numbers 25 via the peak of Peor (ראש הפעור), the third peak Balak takes Balaam in order to curse Israel (cf. Num 22:41; 23:14, 28), a peak described as overlooking הישימן, which in turn affords another connection to Num 33:49.

51 This annotation combines in apposition ירדן and ירחו into ירדן ירחו, an apposition which is all but restricted to post-priestly materials: Numbers 22–36 (cf. 22:1; 26:3, 63; 31:12; 33:48, 50; 34:15; 35:1; and 36:1) and Joshua 13–22 (cf. 13:32; 16:1; 20:8). The only other instance appears in 1 Chr 6:78. Additionally, this annotation clarifies the toponym עברת מואב, to which it is attached using one of two prepositional conventions. In Num 22:1 (HexSupp; cf. p. 175 n. 46 and p. 177 n. 50 above), the phrase is עברות מואב מעבר לירדן ירחו (cf. Jos 13:32), while the three toponyms (i.e., מואב, ירדן, and ירחו) are the regional boundary markers that triangulate the peaks (i.e., הר הערבים, נבו, and פסגה) in the announcement of Moses' death at the end of Deuteronomy (cf. Deut 32:47–49; Deut 34:1), boundary markers which are noticeably absent in the P* version of Moses' death announcement (Num 27:12–14). Once again, the annotation in v. 48bβ corresponds to significant fractures within the Wilderness Narrative,[52] as this specific toponymic triad occurs six times across the late miscellany that is Numbers 26–36* (Num 26:3, 63; 33:48, 50; 35:1; 36:13), and an earlier form of it introduces the Balaam and Baal-Peor narratives in Numbers 22–25 (Num 22:1).[53]

The scope of the current study, though broad, precludes a thorough analysis of each of the fractures to which these annotations correspond. Nevertheless, the fact that all the annotations in Num 33:5–38 do correspond to such fractures suggests that they are no mere random commentary; they are instead a record of a scribe who is actively involved in the compiling processes that produced these fractures in the Wilderness Narrative. Regardless, the three features discussed above—along with the two properties of the third feature—collectively undermine the thesis that Num 33:1–49 is a whole-cloth construction based on the

---

more prevalent עברת מואב על ירדן ירחו occurs in Num 26:3, 63; 33:48, 50; 35:1; 36:13. The only deviance from this form in Numbers 26–36 is Num 31:12, which adds the relative pronoun (עברת מואב אשר על ירדן ירחו), but otherwise follows the more prevalent convention.

52 Additionally, this annotation corresponds to a major fracture between the itinerary and the Wilderness Narrative: in the itinerary, the Israelites do not arrive בעברת מואב על ירדן ירחו (station 41; Num 33:48b) until *after* they have departed from הרי העברים (station 40 in Num 33:47b; cf. fracture 8c in Appendix C); yet the Wilderness Narrative does not portray Israel arriving at הר העברים. Rather, in Num 27:12, הר העברים הזה is the unnamed peak that Yahweh instructs Moses to ascend (Num 27:12) after conducting the second Israelite census, a census which took place בעברת מואב על ירדן ירחו (Num 26:3, 63). (As it stands, the petition of the daughters of Zelophehad in Num 27:1–11 [cf. Num 36:6–13] is a narrative extension of the census that helps frame the insertion of Numbers 26–36* into the emerging Pentateuch.) The implication is that within the final form of the Wilderness Narrative הר העברים הזה is not station at all; it is instead a peak within the proximity of עברת מואב על ירדן ירחו.

53 Albertz correctly observes the two forms of this toponymic triad as indicative of two separate post-priestly redactions. The tripartite phrase עברות מואב מעבר לירדן ירחו in Num 22:1 (cf. Jos 13:32) seated the Balaam narrative into the Hexateuch, while the refrains בעברת מואב על ירדן ירחו in Num 36:3, 63; 33:48, 50; 35:1; 36:13 frames the pre-existing materials (*Vorlagen*) PentRed used in the creation of the Pentateuch ("Das Buch Numeri jenseits der Quellentheorie Eine Redaktionsgeschichte von Num 20–24 [Teil 1]," *ZAW* 123 [2011]: 179–181; "Das Buch Numeri jenseits der Quellentheorie Eine Redaktionsgeschichte von Num 20–24 [Teil II]," *ZAW* 123 [2011]: 340–344; "Late Priestly Layers in Num 2–36," 227–232). This study primarily disagrees with Albertz regarding the assignment of the Baal-Peor episode to PentRed and the specific strata within the Hextateuchal redactions to which Albertz assigns the Balaam story (cf. p. 175 n. 46 and p. 177 n. 50 above and the *Literargeschichte* of Numbers 33 in §6.3.1.3 below).

Pentateuch in its approximate final form. Indeed, it is more likely that the itinerary is the product of multiple editorial stages.

6.3.1.3 Toward a Synthesis: Exod 17:1abα and the Literary History of Num 33:1–49.
The features and properties that indicate Num 33:5–49[54] to be composite (cf. §6.3.1.2 above) also point toward four strata: the "*Ur*-itinerary" (P), HexRed's annotations, HexSupp's annotation in v. 49, and PentRed's expansion in vv. 18b-36a. The foundational stratum (P), or "*Ur*-Itinerary," was probably no more than a titular sentence (v. 1) followed by no more than twenty-three formulaic sentences with a total of twenty-four distinct toponyms (vv. 3aα, 5b-18a*, 36b-48*), with the arrival at מדבר סיני marking the mid-point of the wilderness journey.[55] It was this priestly itinerary that HexRed saw as authoritative, and he expressed as much in his supplement to itinerary's introduction (v. 2). HexRed therefore used the *Ur*-Itinerary as a blueprint for combining the non-P and P wilderness narratives. At junctures in the merger where HexRed had to compromise one of his *Vorlagen*, especially that of the non-P / Dtr tradition,

---

54 Although not the focus of §6.3.1.3, the introduction to the itinerary proper in Num 33:1–4 appears to have gained accretions at each stage of the itinerary's development. Noth comments that v. 2 follows v. 1 awkwardly (ungeschickt), but vv. 3–4 also lead into v. 5 awkwardly (Noth, *Numeri*, 210). Verse 2 uses the same terminology as the annotator responsible for Num 33:14bβ and Exod 17:1abα, specifically למסעיהם על־פי־יהוה—a form which elsewhere appears only in Num 10:12–13, though disrupted by the insertion regarding the cloud of Yahweh settling in Paran (Num 10:11+12b). At first glance, verse 3aα appears to initiate the sojourn with its departure from רעמסס, but then vv. 3aβ-4 interrupt the itinerary formula with a date formula; this disruption is so pronounced that v. 5a resumptively repeats the departure from רעמסס. The type of date formula appears later in the itinerary, after the annotation in v. 38a regarding Aaron's death (which also uses the HexRed phrase על־פי־יהוה; cf. p. 115 n. 94 above and p. 213 n. 24 below).

Provisionally, the following three stages for vv. 1–4's development emerge: v. 1 is the original introduction to the *Ur*-Itinerary (P); v. 2 is a supplement in the style of *HexRed* and validates HexRed's use of P's itinerary as a blueprint for arranging and combining the non-P and P wilderness narratives; v. 3aβ-4's date formula and its annotation on the departure from רעמסס is later still, and probably attributable to PentRed. Note that v. 3aα follows the itinerary formula, while v. 5a adds בני־ישראל; v. 3aα may therefore be original. When PentRed inserted date formula and annotation in vv. 3aβ-4, he found it necessary to pen v. 5a as a resumptive repetition of v. 3aα. Verses 3aβ-5a therefore stem from PentRed; to this same hand may be credited the date and age formulas (vv. 38b-39) that supplement the annotation for Aaron's death.

55 For why v. 3aα receives preference over v. 5a as the original beginning formula, see p. 180 n. 54 above. Regarding the number of formulaic sentences and toponyms, the twenty-three sentences—each with a departing station and an arrival station in an "a → b, b → c" pattern have a combined total of twenty-four distinct toponyms. With this in mind, it may not be coincidental that the arrival at מדבר סיני (station 11) is the twelfth toponym (counting רעמסס, the first point of departure), which would then represent the mid-point of the P wilderness journey.

he left corresponding annotations in the itinerary (vv. 6bβ, 7ay-b, 8aβ-bβ, 9bα-β, 14bβ, 36bβ, 37bβ, 38a, 40, 44bβ, 47bβ, 48bβ). A continuation of this procedure is detectable in HexSupp, who seated the Balaam cycle and Baal-Peor episode into the Wilderness Narrative and inserted a corresponding annotation in the itinerary in v. 49. Along the way, the Hexateuchal redactors exhibit great concern for preserving the contents of their *Vorlagen*, though preference is shown for the priestly arrangement. Later, PentRed radically altered the itinerary by adding eighteen toponyms (vv. 18b-36a) for the sake of elevating Moses and added other annotations characterized by calendric formulas (vv. 3aβ-5a, 38b-39).[56]

The above reconstruction of the stages of Num 33:1–49's composition sets broad parameters for HexRed's editorial activity, but it does not espouse unidirectional dependency for the travel notices in the Wilderness Narrative and the itinerary in Numbers 33 (cf. §6.3.1.1). The evidence is more complex than a single direction of dependency—whether it be the itinerary deriving from the travel notices or vice versa—can account for on its own. Instead, it is more likely that HexRed inherited two separate collections of wilderness traditions (non-P / Dtr and P) and that he used the *Ur*-Itinerary (P) as a blueprint to merge them into a single Wilderness Narrative. Given this scenario, the direction of influence would naturally extend in both ways: the content, arrangement, and even unique stations of the non-P narratives would influence HexRed's supplements to *Ur*-Itinerary; likewise, the *Ur*-Itinerary would influence HexRed's placement of the non-P narratives in relation to the P narratives.

As for the placement of the non-P M-Mt narrative, Deut 9:22 (*Dtr Supp*) preserves the reminiscence of when the מסה episode (not yet מסה ומריבה; cf. Exod 17:7a) occupied a place *after* the events at חרב (cf. Deut 9:8) and *between* the provocations at תבערה and קברת התאוה, the narratives for which occupy Numbers 11. The evidence therefore suggests that the מסה narrative at one time served to connect the non-P narratives of תבערה and קברת התאוה. HexRed then relocated what is now Exod 17:1bβ-7 to its current position—that is, *before* סיני (cf. Exod 19:1f.) and as the final instance of three loosely connected deprivation episodes (Exod 15:22–17:7)[57]—and in the process so anchored it with the travel notice that

---

56 In short, the four strata in Num 33:1–49 are as follows: vv. 1, 3aα, 5b-18a*, 36b-48* (*P*); vv. 2, 6bβ, 7ay-b, 8aβ-bβ, 9bα-β, 14bβ, 36bβ, 37bβ, 38a, 40, 44bβ, 47bβ, 48bβ (*HexRed*); v. 49 (*HexSupp*); vv. 3aβ-5a, 18b-36a, 38b-39 (*PentRed*).
57 Granted, the narratives about the bitter water of מרה (Exod 15:22–26 [non-P]), the provision of manna and quail in מדבר סין (Exod 16:2–36 [a hybrid of non-P & P*]), and the absence of water at מסה and מריבה (Exod 17:1bβ-7 [non-P]) share the themes of wilderness deprivation and non-punished murmuring, and they all employ the verbal roots לון and נסה (cf. Exod 15:24–25; 16:2, 4, 7, 8; 17:2–3, 7), thereby linking the episodes together in catchword fashion

now introduces it (Exod 17:1abα). This transposition, a thesis championed by William Johnstone (cf. §6.3.3 below), represents the final *major* stage of Exod 17:1–7's literary development (cf. Appendix D below).⁵⁸

6.3.2 The Double Etiology of Exod 17:2, 7 and the ריב Elements of Num 20:3a, 13

The first zone of clear editorial activity in Exod 17:1–7 is the travel notice in v. 1abα (§6.3.1); the next area of significant editorial activity one encounters is the double place-name etiology (vv. 2, 7) that frames the narrative core (vv. 3–6). No other text in the Hebrew Bible has two operative place-name etiologies for the same narrative event⁵⁹; thus, this compound etiology is, as Noth describes it, "schwerlich ursprünglich."⁶⁰ On this front, many scholars agree, both on the matter that one etiology must be earlier than the other and which etiology

---

(e.g., Kupfer's discussion of this literary artistry in *Mit Israel auf dem Weg durch die Wüste: Eine leserorientierte Exegese der Rebellionstexte in Exodus 15:22–17:7 und Numeri 11:1–20:13* [OtSt 61; Leiden – Boston: Brill, 2012], 221–222). Nevertheless, there can be little doubt that these artful connections are the product of compiling and editing diverse pre-existing materials. For a survey of critical scholarship, see Dozeman, *Exodus*, 351–357; for Dozeman's own reconstruction, see *Exodus*, 357–364.

58 Although, see p. 196 below for the glossic nature of אשר הכית בו את־היאר in Exod 17:5.
59 See the place- and tribal-name etiologies cited by Golka: Gen 19:37–38; 26:20–22; 29:31–30:24; Exod 15:23–25a; Num 20:13; Deut 3:14; Josh 7:26; Judg 1:26; 2:5; 10:3–5; 15:19; 18:12; and 2 Sam 6:8 (Friedemann W. Golka, "The Aetiologies in the Old Testament: Part 2," *VT* 27 [1977]: 36). It is striking that Golka does not include Exod 17:7 in treatment of etiologies in the Hebrew Bible. This omission may stem from his adherence to Westermann's definition of what constitutes a narrative etiology: an etiological narrative can only be etiological if "the question provoked and the answer given by the aetiology are identical with the arc of tension" of the narrative itself, "which consists of an event which stretches from a tension to its solution" (Friedemann W. Golka, "The Aetiologies in the Old Testament: Part 1," *VT* 26 [1973]: 411; cf. Claus Westermann, "Arten der Erzählungen in der Genesis," pages 9–91 in Claus Westermann, *Forschung am Alten Testament: Gesammelte Studien* [TBAT 24; München: Kaiser, 1964], especially pp. 39–47). The formulaic shape that the etiologies take in Exod 17:2, 7 (i.e., √קרא + שם + place name) follow the basic formula in the texts that Golka lists as proper etiological narratives; thus, even though Exod 17:2, 7 do not follow the arc of tension within the core narrative (Exod 17:3–6), etiological interpretation has taken place. Golka makes room for this possibility in his category "Aetiological Motifs" ("Aetiologies: Part 1," 418–419), but here Golka is much more selective, and again he does not attend to Exod 17:1–7.
60 Noth, *Exodus*, 111.

of the two is the earliest: namely, Meribah.⁶¹ The arguments scholars marshal for this conclusion naturally vary, but the tradition-historical argument of Noth, Coats, and Childs proceeds along the following lines: Aside from Exod 17:7 and Ps 95:8, all instances of the toponym מסה occur in Deuteronomy (Deut 6:16; 9:22; 33:8); therefore, the מסה etiology and its components in Exod 17:2, 7 must be a Dtr supplement.⁶²

There is, however, a fundamental flaw in this argument that Noth and his followers have largely overlooked: the logic behind it is *non sequitur*. Specifically, the profile (P* or non-P / Dtr) and distribution of the toponyms across the Hebrew Bible in no way substantiates the *priority* of one etiology's entry into Exod 17:1–7 over the other. In fact, the same syllogism can be employed to argue that the Meribah etiology is secondary: Aside from Exod 17:7 and Pss 81:8; 95:8; and 106:32, all instances of toponyms derivative of מריבה occur in P* or post-P material (Num 20:13, 24; 27:14; Deut 32:51 [*post-PentRed*] and 33:8 [*PentRed*]⁶³; Ezek 47:19; 48:28); therefore, the מריבה etiology and its components in Exod 17:2, 7 must be a P* or post-P supplement. In other words, this line of argumentation is insufficient on its own for determining which of the two etiologies is primary and which is secondary. Indeed, one must seek other indicators in order to solve this which-came-first conundrum.

One indicator that merits consideration is the editorial process involved in supplementing a preexisting etiology with an entirely new one. Which set of etiologies and etiological components is more integral to Exod 17:2, 7? Or from the opposite perspective, which set would entail the least amount of editorial activity in its incorporation into the text?

---

61 For example, Hugo Gressmann, *Mose und seine Zeit: Ein Kommentar zu den Mose-Sagen* (FRLANT 18; Göttingen: Vandenhoeck & Ruprecht, 1913), 145–150; Sigo Lehming, "Massa und Meriba," *ZAW* 73 (1961): 1–7; Volkmar Fritz, *Israel in der Wüste: Traditionsgeschichtliche Untersuchung der Wüstenüberlieferungen des Jahwisten* (MtS 7; Marburg: N. G. Elwert, 1970), 48; George W. Coats, *Exodus 1–18* (FOTL IIA; Grand Rapids: Eerdmans, 1999), 137–139; Brevard S. Childs, *The Book of Exodus: A Critical, Theological Commentary* (OTL; Louisville: Westminster, 1974), 306–307; and implicitly in Nathan MacDonald, who sees Exod 17:2aβ-3a as secondary to vv. 2aα+bα ("Anticipations of Horeb: Exodus 17 as Inner-Biblical Commentary," in *Studies on the Text and Versions of the Hebrew Bible in Honour of Robert Gordon* (ed. Geoffrey Khan and Diana Lipton; VTSup 149; Leiden–Boston: Brill, 2012), 10 n. 7.
62 This line of argument is at least as early as Noth (*Exodus*, 111); cf. Coats and Childs (George W. Coats, *Rebellion in the Wilderness: The Murmuring Motif in the Wilderness Traditions of the Old Testament* [Nashville: Abingdon, 1968], 55; cf. *Exodus*, 139; Childs, *Exodus*, 306).
63 For the assignment of Deut 32:51 to *post-PentRed* and Deut 33:8 to *PentRed*, see §4.4.2 above.

Admittedly, such an assessment does not produce immediate, unambiguous results (cf. Fig. 6.2 below). At first glance, one may be inclined to restrict the מסה components in v. 2 to the catchphrase in v. 2bγ (מה־תנסון את־יהוה), leading to the initial conclusion that it alone constitutes the מסה component in v. 2 and is therefore most likely a supplement. A closer examination, however, reveals a more complex situation on account that v. 2aβ (ויאמרו תנו־לנו מים ונשתה) does not directly build upon v. 2aα (וירב העם עם־משה). One simply cannot transition *from* a report that the people had a dispute with Moses alone[64] *to* the people levying a demand to Moses and another entity (so תנו).[65] Instead, v. 2aβ is most likely what prompts Moses' retort מה־תנסון את־יהוה in v. 2bγ, thereby clarifying the people's demand as directed to Moses and Yahweh.[66] Thus, vv. 2aβ and 2bγ are co-dependent and most likely entered the text at the same time. As a byproduct, one cannot treat the מסה etiological catchphrase as a simple supplement to the end of v. 2, thereby privileging the מריבה catchphrases (vv. 2aα + 2bβ) as the more integral of two etiologies. Rather, both the מסה and מריבה etiological components in v. 2 are equally integrated, requiring the same amount of editorial activity for their insertion regardless of which one is secondary.[67] Such is not the case, however, for the etiologies proper in Exod 17:7. The מסה etiology (vv. 7a$^{\text{iv-v}*}$ + 7bβ) would be slightly more difficult to insert if the מריבה etiology were primary than if the priority were reversed. As it stands, the מריבה etiology could have been created via a single insertion (v. 7a^{v}-bα). Thus, in v. 7 at least, the מריבה etiology appears supplemental, thereby indicating the primacy of the מסה etiology.

This argument—i.e., that the editorial activity entailed in adding a second etiology to Exod 17:2, 7 point to מסה as foundational and מריבה as supplemental—finds corroboration in three sets of external texts: specifically, Deut 6:16 and 9:22; Num 20:2–5; and Gen 26:20–22. First and foremost, the M-Mt reminiscences in Deut 6:16 and 9:22 anticipate this conclusion. These early iterances of the M-Mt show the מסה etiology to have had a history of development on its own: *from* an etiological event known as "the testing" (cf. בַּמַּסָּה in Deut 6:16) in which the people asked היש יהוה בקרבנו אם־אין (Exod 17:7bγ; cf. בקרבך in Deut 6:15a), *to*

---

[64] Note that the people contend עם־משה alone, not על משה ועל אהרן (cf. Exod 16:2; Num 14:2; 16:3; 17:6–7; 20:2; 26:9) or even באלהים ובמשה (cf. Num 21:5).
[65] Cf. §6.2 above for the conclusion that MT's תנו is preferable to the singular readings in 4QpaleoExod^m (4Q22), Smr, G, S, T^J, and V.
[66] As opposed to Moses and Aaron; cf. Deut 33:8, in which PentRed later interprets תנו as being directed to Moses and Aaron. For a discussion of this reading of the Blessing of Levi, see §4.4.2 above.
[67] Note that v. 2bα (ויאמר להם משה) is formulaic. It is therefore neutral in this reconstruction, as it could have been a product of the construction of either etiology.

6.3 Literary Analysis of Exodus 17:1–7 — 185

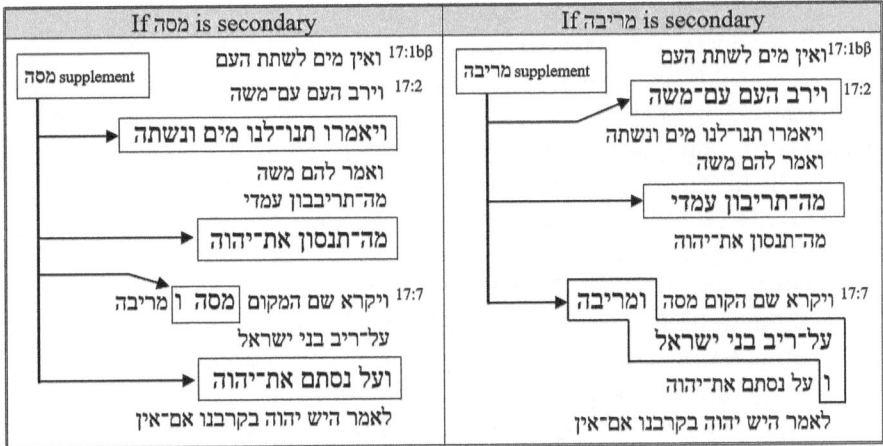

Fig. 6.2: The Editorial Activity Involved in Inserting a Second Etiology into Exod 17:1–7

an etiological place-name proper (cf. וּבְמַסָּה in Deut 9:22), and without any awareness of מריבה.⁶⁸ In other words, the framework in Deuteronomy for M-Mt's tradition-historical development suggests the non-P M-Mt's place-name etiology was מסה before it was מסה and מריבה.

A second external text that corroborates מסה's priority over מריבה is Num 20:2–5. To begin, it is critical to note that Num 20:3a's וירב העם עם־משה is the only extended verbatim correspondence between the P* and non-P M-Mt narratives (Exod 17:2aα ∥ Num 20:3a). Unlike Exod 17:2aα, however, Num 20:3a clearly stands out as secondary to its surrounding narrative context, as it is the first of three duplicates that span Num 20:2–5, each of which resembles a component in the non-P narrative. Together, these three correspondences affect the highest concentration of verbal correspondence between the two M-Mt narratives *within* Num 20:1–13.⁶⁹ A fuller treatment of these duplicates follows in §7.3.4 below, but

---

68 For the conclusions regarding the development of מסה (independently of מריבה) as the *location* for the Dtr M-Mt, see §3.2.3, §3.4.3, and §3.5 above. For how בקרבך at the end of Deut 6:15a may have triggered the reminiscence in Deut 6:16, see p. 59 above.

69 See Appendix B: Quantitative Analysis of the Verbal and Conceptual Correspondences of Exod 17:1–7 and Num 20:1–13 for the following analysis of §3–6 in Num 20:1–13 (§3–6 = vv. 2–5). There are a total of fifty-one words in §3–6: seven of which evince verbatim correspondence (V), five of which evince approximate correspondence (A), eleven of which conceptually correspond (C), and 20 of which remain non-aligned (N) (V/A/C/N = [7/5/11/28]). The resulting percentages for these correspondences is as follows: 13.73% verbatim (7/51 = 13.73%); 9.8% approximate (5/51); 21.57% conceptual (11/51); and 54.9% non-aligned (28/51). The remaining textual material in Num 20:1–13 (§1–2, 7–11) totals to 141 words, which break-

the first and third duplicates are especially germane to the topic at hand. Whereas Num 20:3a evinces verbatim correspondence with Exod 17:2a, the third duplicate component in this section is Num 20:5bβ (ומים אין לשתות) and displays strong verbal correspondence to Exod 17:1bβ (ואין מים לשתת העם). That both phrases are contiguous in the non-P M-Mt narrative (i.e., Exod 17:1bβ-2aα), yet frame in reverse order[70] a highly edited section in the P* M-Mt narrative (Num 20:2–5)—a section edited to reflect the highest degree of correspondence between the two M-Mt narratives—is highly suggestive. Add to this observation the fact that מריבה is less integral than מסה in Exod 17:7 and therefore most likely secondary in Exod 17:2, and the result is a confluence of editorial activity involving מריבה in both M-Mt narratives. In other words, not only are both instances of וירב העם עם משה secondary, but they may well have stemmed from the same scribal hand, a hand intent on coordinating, if not harmonizing, the two M-Mt narratives.

Finally, a third text that corroborates the מריבה etiology is secondary to the מסה etiology in the non-P M-Mt narrative is Gen 26:20–22. This text relays a series of three place-name etiologies for wells Isaac's herdsmen excavated in the valley of Gerar—wells named עשק ("Quarrel"), שטנה ("Hostility"), and רחבות ("Open Spaces").[71] As they currently stand, each of these etiologies—which relate to the M-Mt via the *motif* of water deprivation / provision[72]—is introduced by a reminiscence regarding whether the herdsmen of Gerar disputed (√ריב) the water-rights of the corresponding re-opened well. Yet the presence of the √ריב (ויריבו in vv. 20–21, but רבו in v. 22) in no way affects any of these etiologies. Instead, pre-existing etiologies have been collected and framed by √ריב which secondarily binds the etiologies to the ongoing narrative.[73] In short, the use of √ריב for conflicts involving water sources is tropic,[74] whereas √נסה is not.

---

down to the following correspondences: (11/12/35/83). The resulting percentages of this material is as follows: 7.8% verbatim (11/141); 8.51% approximate (12/141); 24.82% conceptual (35/141); and 58.86% non-aligned (83/141). The correlative additions to Num 20:2–5 result in a 23.53% (= 13.73% + 9.8%) verbal correspondence to §3–6 in Exod 17:1–7 (i.e., vv. 1bβ-3). Comparatively, the remaining textual material in §1–2, 7–11 in Num 20:1–13 only amounts to a 16.31% verbal correspondence (= 7.8% + 8.51%).

70 This editorial technique of inverting textual material that is the subject of citation is sometimes called "Seidel's law"; cf. p. 194 n. 102 below.
71 Gordon J. Wenham, *Genesis 16–50* (WBC 2; Dallas: Word Books, 1994), 192.
72 See William H. Propp, *Water in the Wilderness: A Biblical Motif and Its Mythological Background* (HSS 40; Atlanta: Scholars Press, 1987), 73 n. 30.
73 One could further add Gen 13:7–10, which records the dispute (ריב; cf. Gen 13:7) between Abram's herdsmen and Lot's herdsmen and the subsequent division of the land as the resolution. Note that in v. 10 Lot's criterion for selecting the Jordan Valley is the abundance of water; this suggests that water-rights may have been central to the herdsmen's dispute.

Thus, contrary to long-held critical scholarship (cf. p. 183 n. 61 above), מסה most likely constitutes the primary etiology for the non-P M-Mt narrative, with מריבה serving as a coordinating supplement in both M-Mt narratives.⁷⁵ Yet aligning this coordinating supplement to a particular strata remains particularly difficult. On the one hand, Deut 9:22 (*Dtr Supp*) serves as a *terminus ad quem* for the development of the מסה etiology prior to the entry of the מריבה etiology as a supplement. One therefore might be inclined to assign this supplement to HexRed, who seeks to merge the non-P and P wilderness traditions. The same hand responsible for the post-P travel notice in Exod 17:1abα would therefore also be responsible for the מריבה etiological components in Exod 17:2, 7. On the other hand, however, HexRed's relocation and preservation of this narrative runs counter to the equative force the מריבה etiologies exert on M-Mt narratives. In other words, whoever coordinated these narratives understood them to be literary variants of the same tradition, but this perspective is not reflected by HexRed (and later editors), whose preservation of both M-Mt narratives in general, and relocation of the non-P M-Mt narrative specifically, transforms the M-Mt narratives into distinct wilderness events. An intermediate hand—subsequent to *Dtr Supp*, yet prior to HexRed—may thus be postulated as a pre-Hexateuchal supplement (*pre-Hex Supp*),⁷⁶ one responsible for not only for the creation for מריבה etiology, but for the murmuring motif as well (cf. §6.3.3).

---

74 This trope may be what is reflected in Prov 17:14, פוטר מים ראשית מדון ולפני התגלע הריב נחוש, "Issuing water is the beginning of strife; abandon [it] before the ריב breaks out."
75 See §7.3.5 below for a discussion of מריבה as secondary development of a foundational קדש etiology in Num 20:1–13*.
76 It is beyond the scope of the current study to test such a hypothesis against other materials. Nevertheless, a transitional editorial phase is necessary to explain how the M-Mt narratives were equated via the מריבה etiologies, only to be disambiguated in formation of the Hexateuch. Implicit in the task of joining the non-P/D* and P* literary traditions is an initial comparison and contrast of the two collections. Already it has been observed that HexRed reorients the crossing of the ים־סוף from the first wilderness episode to the climatic scene of Israel's exodus from Egypt (cf. p. 165 n. 21 above). Yet the correspondences between Exod 17:1bβ-2aα and Num 20:2–5 suggest that prior to reorientation of the M-Mt narratives (cf. §6.3.3 and §7.3.3) there was an earlier attempt to coordinate them, perhaps in order to maintain the two canons as separate, yet harmonious literary traditions.
    One can now only speculate as to why a coordination of etiologies transpired for the M-Mt narratives, but not for the manna-quail episodes (Exod 16:2–36 and Num 11:4–35*). Perhaps it is because the P* manna-quail episode in Exodus 16 was never in possession of a developing place-name etiology, thereby negating the need for etiological coordination? Or perhaps the coordination took place at the narrative level, with 1) the integration of the evening provision of quail (vv. 3*, 6, 8*, 12–13*, 20*, 23–24*) into P's story that is otherwise focused on manna, and with 2) the merging of the manna description (Num 11:7–9) into non-P's quail story

6.3.3 The Dtr Core of Exod 17:2–7* and the Complaints of Numbers 11

So far Exod 17:1–7 has exhibited two stages of literary growth: 1) the post-P itinerary (v. 1abα) stems from HexRed, who relocated what is now Exod 17:1bβ-7 into its current position and situated it among the pre-Sinai deprivation narratives (Exod 15:22–17:7); and 2) the מריבה etiology (vv. 2aα + 2bβ + 7a^v-bα) is an earlier pre-Hexateuchal supplement, designed to coordinate the two narrative versions of the M-Mt. The remaining textual material is therefore Exod 17:2aβ-bα + 2by-7a^{iv} + 7bβ-γ, the מסה narrative proper—the majority of which, given the reminiscence in Deut 9:22, was once located between the episodes of תבערה (Num 11:1–3) and קברות התאוה (Num 11:4–35).

The outline of this reconstruction, though not its details, is indebted to the work of William Johnstone. In 1987, Johnstone began arguing that the reminiscences in Deuteronomy "enable the reconstruction of a pre-P version of sections of Exodus."[77] Nearly ten years later in 1996, and as part of this larger agenda, he articulated what he then described as a "radical" hypothesis, one that he would revisit with slight revisions in 1998 and 2002.[78] Specifically, Johnstone contends that Deut 9:22 preserves the memory of when the "original D-form of Exod 17,1–7"[79]—which early on he identified as Exod 17:2, 4–7[80]—was located between

---

(Num 11:4–10*, 13, 18–23, 31–35), which itself is already conflated with a story about the distribution of prophetic leadership (Num 11:11–12, 14–17, 24–30). (For a redaction critical study of Numbers 11, see Benjamin D. Sommer, "Reflecting on Moses: The Redaction of Numbers 11," *JBL* 114 [1999]: 601–624.) Regardless of the explanation, it is significant that M-Mt narratives appear to have had foundational etiologies—מסה in Exod 17:4, but קדש in Num 20:13 (cf. §7.3.4 and §7.3.5 below)—prior to the addition of מריבה etiology, and these pre-existing etiologies may have necessitated that the coordination take place at the etiological level.

77 William Johnstone, "From the Sea to the Mountain: Exodus 15,22–19,2: A Case-Study in Editorial Techniques," in *Studies in the Book of Exodus: Redaction – Reception – Interpretation* (ed. Marc Vervenne; BETL 126; Leuven: Leuven University, 1996), 245. Johnstone cites his article "Reactivating the Chronicles Analogy in Pentateuchal Studies, with Special Reference to the Sinai Pericope in Exodus," *ZAW* 99 (1987): 13–37 as the beginning of his pursuit to demonstrate this thesis.

78 Johnstone initially admits the radical nature of his thesis in "From the Sea to the Mountain," in Vervenne, *Studies in the Book of Exodus*, 261; he leaves this assessment unchanged in his slightly revised republication of this article in *Chronicles and Exodus*, 260; but he is more confident about his thesis in "The Use of the Reminiscences in Deuteronomy in Recovering the Two Main Literary Phases in the Production of the Pentateuch," in *Abschied vom Jahwisten: Dis Komposition des Hexateuch in der jüngsten Diskussion* (ed. Jan Christian Gertz, Konrad Schmid, and Markus Witte; BZAW 315; Berlin-New York: de Gruyter, 2002), 247–273.

79 Johnstone, "Reminiscences in Deuteronomy," in Gertz, Schmid, and Witte, *Abschied vom Jahwisten*, 260.

6.3 Literary Analysis of Exodus 17:1–7

the "Dtr aetiological narrative[s]" of Taberah (Num 11:1–3) and Kibroth-hattaavah (11:4–34).[81] The "P-editor" transposed this narrative, along with reusing other Dtr narratives, in order to create a pre-Sinai wilderness sojourn, to the effect 1) that Israel is now portrayed as complaining *before* Sinai and not just after it as in Deuteronomy, and 2) that Sinai and the giving of Torah becomes the "focal point of the Pentateuch."[82]

While the findings of the current study corroborate a component of Johnstone's thesis—i.e., that what is now Exod 17:1bβ-7 was once located between Num 11:3 and 11:4—two significant differences merit brief attention. First, Johnstone posits that "P" or the "P-editor" is responsible for this transposition, but the current study credits this activity to the post-P HexRed, who while favoring

---

[80] At this point in the development of his thesis, Johnstone excises all of v. 3 solely on account of the לון√ being characteristic of P ("From the Sea to the Mountain," in Vervenne, *Studies in the Book of Exodus*, 257–258; again in *Chronicles and Exodus*, 255). He does not overtly make this argument, however, in "Reminiscences in Deuteronomy." Instead Johnstone merely cites parenthetically the "D-features" in Exod 17:1–7 as being "Horeb in v. 6" and "vv. 2, 4, 5, and 7." In other words, Johnstone still excises v. 3, but he does so implicitly on different grounds ("Reminiscences in Deuteronomy," in Gertz, Schmid, and Witte, *Abschied vom Jahwisten*, 260). Neither of these grounds, however, are sufficient on their own to excise all of v. 3. Granted, v. 3aβb uses לון√, which most frequently occurs in P* texts (cf. Exod 15:24 [non-P] and 17:3 [?] to P* Num 14:2, 27, 29, 36; 16:11; 17:6, 20; Judg 9:18). Yet, the phrase ויצמא שם העם למים in v. 3aα reflects the foundational crisis (water deprivation), which is not dependent on the murmuring motif in v. 3aβb. Instead, v. 3aβb emerges as dependent on v. 3aα only with the people's last word: בצמא ("with thirst"). In short, it is not necessary to excise the whole of v. 3 on account of לון√ or the perceived lack of "D-features." Instead, v. 3aα is intrinsic to the narrative core, and the scribe responsible for inserting the people's murmuring in v. 3aβb has skillfully constructed it so that its final word (בצמא) echoes the first word of v. 3aα (ויצמא).

[81] Johnstone consistently treats Numbers 11 as being related to Deuteronomy, but there is a lack of precision in his sigla and descriptions: He uses "D-composition" and "Dtr" in "From the Sea to the Mountain," in Vervenne, *Studies in the Book of Exodus*, 254–255 and in *Chronicles and Exodus*, 252–253; he describes these episodes as belonging to a "D-version" of the wilderness sojourn in "Reminiscences in Deuteronomy," in Gertz, Schmid, and Witte, *Abschied vom Jahwisten*, 260.

[82] Initially, Johnstone notes that P composed Exod 15:22–19:2 to portray Israel murmuring in the wilderness even before they arrive at Sinai (Horeb), contra Deuteronomy which he says indicates Israel started murmuring at Horeb ("From the Sea to the Mountain," in Vervenne, *Studies in the Book of Exodus*, 254; *Chronicles and Exodus*, 251–252). Later, Johnstone supplements this rationale by noting P's purpose was to "elevate Sinai as the location not of the covenant with the redeemed and initially responsive people as in D, but of the revelation of the Law: Torah is now the focal point of the Pentateuch" ("Reminiscences in Deuteronomy," in Gertz, Schmid, and Witte, *Abschied vom Jahwisten*, 261).

the P tradition is nevertheless merging the non-P and P collections.⁸³ Second, like many scholars, Johnstone uses Deut 33:8 to claim the Levite's punitive role in the Golden Calf narrative (Exod 32:25–29) was originally the punishment "meted out on the people at Massah and Meribah for 'testing' and 'striving' with the LORD."⁸⁴ Yet the current study has shown that the Blessing of Levi is a late entry into the Blessing of Moses as a whole and has within its purview the Pentateuch in its near final form.⁸⁵ As such, Deut 33:8 is not the earliest M-Mt reminiscence, and thus cannot serve to recreate a "Levitical M-Mt"—one in which the Levites are ordained as priests because of their punitive role in a Massah story that originally concluded with what is now Exod 32:25–29.

These differences aside, Johnstone was warrant to explore the literary connections between Exod 17:1–7 and Num 11:1–34, but his approach was regrettably too broad to appreciate the subtle literary features that once likely anchored the non-P M-Mt in Numbers 11.⁸⁶ Granted, Johnstone did observe that the etiologies for תבערה, מסה, and קברות התאוה (cf. Exod 17:7; Num 11:3, 34) use same formula: "X" [ההוא] ויקרא שם המקום.⁸⁷ Yet several additional verbal features in Exod

---

83 Again, Johnstone's sigla requires nuancing: for Johnstone, the "P-editor" is "P"; and as a supplement to the D-version, there never was a continuous, independent P version (P^G) that was devoid of D-material. Yet Johnstone treats the D / pre-P version and P / P-edition as separate literary works: "The D-version and P-edition are two literary works; the latter presupposes the former and supplies a vastly expanded edition of it, rather than [...] Chronicles uses the Deuteronomistic History" ("Reminiscences in Deuteronomy," in Gertz, Schmid, and Witte, *Abschied vom Jahwisten*, 248). The result is a conflation and synonymous usage of the sigla "P" and "P-editor."
84 Johnstone, "Reminiscences in Deuteronomy," in Gertz, Schmid, and Witte, *Abschied vom Jahwisten*, 261. Thus, Johnstone posits two transpositions regarding the D-version of the Massah narrative: when the P-editor relocated the core narrative *from* between Num 11:3 and 11:4 *to* its current position in Exod 17:2–7*, this same editor severed the narrative's punishment and relocated it to Exod 32:25–29. "It is probable," he contends, "that in the process of transposition P has relocated the verses on the punitive slaughter of the rebellious people by the Levites from the same incident [i.e., Massah], as Deut 33.8–9 indicates, to its present position in Exod. 32:25–29" (*Chronicles and Exodus*, 257).
85 See §4.4.2 above, especially pp. 125–134.
86 To be fair, Johnstone's approach was appropriate given the broad parameters of his controlling argument (cf. pp. 188–189 above), but concerning this facet of his argument it is not enough to classify both Exod 17:2–7 and Num 11:1–34 as D-compositions (cf. Johnstone, "From the Sea to the Mountain," in Vervenne, *Studies in the Book of Exodus*, 254–259; *Chronicles and Exodus*, 251–257.
87 Johnstone, "From the Sea to the Mountain," in Vervenne, *Studies in the Book of Exodus*, 258; *Chronicles and Exodus*, 256. This formula occurs elsewhere in the Hebrew Bible only in Gen 28:19 (Bethel); 32:3 (Mahanaim); Num 21:3 (Hormah); and Jos 5:9 (Gilgal).

17:1bβ-7 also resonate with Num 11:1–34.[88] Lexically, the people's question היש יהוה בקרבנו אם־אין (Exod 17:7) finds direct answer in Num 11:20's [89]כי־מאסתם את־יהוה אשר בקרבכם; and the form of the people's demand for water in Exod 17:2 (תנו־לנו מים ונשתה) is used to express their demand for meat in Num 11:13 (תנה־לנו בשר ונאכלה).[90] In short, Exod 17:2–7 is formally, lexically, and even thematically well-suited for a position between Num 11:3 and 11:4, and especially before the קברות התאוה episode (Num 11:4–34).[91]

It is unlikely, however, that the מסה episode proper (Exod 17:2aβ-bα + 2by-7a^iv* + 7bβ-γ) was written whole-cloth between Num 11:3 and 11:4. Instead, literary tensions within the מסה episode and the tradition-historical framework in Deuteronomy suggest that this episode underwent literary development alongside the קברות התאוה tradition (see p. 198 below). Here, it is necessary to recall

---

[88] The thematic resonances are well-known, but still bear mentioning, and include the theme wilderness deprivation and its subordinate motifs of complaint and longing for Egypt; e.g., Coats, *Rebellion in the Wilderness*, 53–71, 96–115. The one feature one would expect to be present in the Exod 17:1–7, but is not, is divine punishment. It is this absence, coupled with the ambiguity of Deut 33:8, that prompts scholars like Johnstone to hypothesize that Exod 32:25–29 was once the punitive conclusion of the Massah episode (cf. p. 190 n. 84 and p. 128 n. 128 above). This speculation is unnecessary, as the absence of this theme may well have been what prompted HexRed to relocate non-P M-Mt narrative to a pre-Sinai / Horeb position in his merging of the non-P and P corpora.

[89] The preposition ב + קרב + pronominal suffix also occurs in the introduction to the קברות התאוה episode in Num 11:4a, where it indicates the presence of a rabble with cravings among the people: והאספסף אשר בקרבו התאוו תאוה. Likewise, in Moses' exasperated reply to Yahweh's instruction to announce to the people that they will eat meat to the point of nausea: ויאמר משה שש־מאות אלף רגלי העם אשר אנכי בקרבו (Num 11:21a). If the non-P M-Mt narrative had once preceded Num 11:4, the preposition ב + קרב + pronominal suffix could serve as a catchword stitching the two episodes together, as the thematic question of who is among Israel unfolds across the two episodes.

[90] Other verbal connections include זקני ישראל (Exod 17:5–6; Num 11:16, 24–25, 30) and the action of striking (√נכה; Exod 17:6; Num 11:33).

[91] As noted earlier (cf. p. 72 n. 56 above), additional support for this position may be detectable in Deut 8:15–16. Although part of the concentric structure of Deut 8:1–20, the reversal of the typical order for the Massah and Manna stories in these verses may preserve the memory of when the Massah episode immediately preceded the Kibroth-hattaavah episode (Num 11:4–34). Additionally, since Deut 8:15 recalls an encounter with fiery (√שרף) serpents and scorpions prior to the Massah and Manna traditions, one may speculate whether there is any tradition-historical connection between this otherwise non-attested tradition (although cf. Num 21:4–9) and the mysterious burning fire of Yahweh (ותבער־בם אש יהוה) at Taberah in Num 11:1–3. This speculation is warranted on account that Num 11:1–3 as a narrative appears remarkably underdeveloped compared to the Massah and Kibroth-hattaavah episodes. If so, then both Deut 8:15–16 and 9:22 recall the arrangement of these episodes as Taberah, then Massah, and then Kibroth-hattaavah.

that the early reminiscences preserved in Deut 6:16, 8:15 and 9:22 reflect significant developments in the agency and location of the M-Mt. In Deut 8:15 (*Dt*), Yahweh is the *agent* testing Israel at an unspecified *location*; the tradition at this stage therefore represents Israel positively. These tradition components shift in Deut 6:16 (*late Dtr*) to Israel being the *agent* who inappropriately tests Yahweh at a *location* simply known as "the testing" (בְּמַסָּה). This improper nominative, however, eventually concretizes into a proper toponym, Massah (וּבְמַסָּה) in Deut 9:22 (*Dtr Supp*) (cf. §3.5 above). Thus, the early stages of the framework detected in Deuteronomy for the M-Mt's tradition-historical development leads one to expect a literary history prior to the codification of the מסה etiology (*late Dtr–Dtr supp*).

Residual traces of these developments are still extant in the literary tensions within the מסה episode proper, but the process of *Fortschreibung* was so thorough as to render speculative any attempt at a precise reconstruction of the episode's earlier literary stages. Nevertheless, one can identify with reasonable confidence three areas wherein secondary accretions to the foundational narrative core are at least probable: 1) the מסה etiology in vv. 2* + 7*; 2) the people's murmuring speech and Moses' response in vv. 3aβ-4*; and 3) the relative clause identifying the staff of Moses in v. 5bα[ii-vi]. Each addition requires brief attention, but for now vv. 3aα + 5a-bα[i] + 5bβ-6 constitutes the approximate remains of the foundational narrative core, a spring tradition that represents Israel positively and corresponds to Deut 8:15 (*Dt*).

As for Exod 17:1bβ-2, scholars since at least the time of Noth have noted its secondary nature to 17:3. Noth argued that vv. 1bβ-2 is a *doublet* of the people's murmuring in v. 3, which "ist ein offensichtlicher Neuanfang" that once must have followed upon a now unspecified location—a location at which the Israelites had previously arrived and to which שם in v. 3 once referred.[92] Coats' study, however, has convincingly shown that "vv. 1bβ-2 and 3–4 are not doublets" resulting from the merger of two separate sources; rather, they are the product of "successive stages in the growth of the tradition."[93] Coats argues correctly that, while v. 3aα does repeat the foundational narrative crisis (i.e., water deprivation), the people's speech to Moses (v. 3aβ-b) and Moses' speech to Yahweh (v. 4aβ-b) do not directly address this crisis; instead, both dialogues reflect the murmuring motif, which in turn is bound (somewhat artificially) to the Meribah etiology.[94] Moreover, the divine response to Moses in vv. 5–6a does not redress

---

[92] Noth, *Exodus*, 110.
[93] Coats, *Exodus*, 137.
[94] Building on J. Begrich's form-critical analysis of the *Gerichtsreden* ("trial speeches") in Deutero-Isaiah, Coats observes that "ריב can be used in a broad sense to include the preofficial quar-

the ensuing rebellion that threatens Moses' life (cf. עוד מעט וסקלני in v. 4b); instead, in vv. 5 – 6a Yahweh relays instructions for how to resolve the foundational crisis, and v. 6b portrays Moses' obedience abating the crisis.[95] In other words, not only is the מסה etiology (vv. 2* + 7*) secondary to the foundational narrative, but so also is the people's murmuring speech against Moses (v. 3aβ-b) and Moses' cry of distress to Yahweh (v. 4aβ-b).[96]

The current study, however, departs from Coats' reconstruction for how these secondary additions entered the text. Coats understands the Meribah etiology as foundational to the narrative, over and above even the provision of water from a rock. In a three stage process, Coats envisions a founding Meribah etiology (little more than "an opening statement that legal cases were resolved at a particular place"[97]), which was first merged with a non-localized spring tradition, then secondarily supplemented with the murmuring motif, and then finally expanded the Dtr מסה components.[98] Yet as noted above (cf. p. 186 above), disputing over water sources is not only a common motif, but it is elsewhere demonstrably secondary to the legends they frame. There is no evidence to suggest the case would be otherwise with Exod 17:1bβ-7. As well, one of the earliest iterances of the M-Mt in Deuteronomy (i.e., Deut 8:15 – 16) leads one to expect the opposite: that a positive spring narrative—one which Coats rightly describes as presuppos-

---

rel that forms the basis of the murmuring," a quarrel that usually takes the form of a question that challenges the past deeds of person against whom the ריב is levied (*Rebellion in the Wilderness*, 57, and also pp. 33 – 36; cf. Joachim Begrich, *Studien zu Deuterojesaja* [BWA(N)T 4 Folge, Heft 25 (77); Stuttgart: W. Kohlhammer, 1938], reprinted in TB 20; München: C. Kaiser, 1963). Coats goes on to note that the demand for water in Exod 17:2 does not conform to this pattern, which suggests that the people have initiated a formal ריב against Moses, as opposed to an informal quarrel. Yet Coats admits that this form of a lawsuit—that is, a ריב followed immediately by a demand—is exceptional, as "the root [ריב] is never again used with a sentence controlled by an imperative" (*Rebellion in the Wilderness*, 57 n. 24). Coats' solution to this breakdown in form is to prioritize the ריב components in Exod 17:2, 7 as the founding layer of Exod 17:1bβ-7, with the spring tradition, the murmuring tradition, and the מסה etiology as subsequent additions to the basic מריבה etiology. For the alternative solution proffered by this study, see p. 195 n. 103 below.

95 Coats, *Exodus*, 138 – 139.
96 Thus, while Herrmann (and others) is correct that the etiological question in 7bβ-γ is not original to the foundational literary layer of the non-P M-Mt narrative, the question itself was most likely part of an expansion undertaken at an early stage of narrative's literary development (cf. Wolfram Herrmann, "Ex 17,7bβ und die Frage nach der Gegenwart Jahwes in Israel," in *Alttestamentlicher Glaube und biblische Theologie: Festschrift für Horst Dietrich Pruess zum 65. Geburstag* [ed. Jutta Hausmann and Hans-Jürgen Zobel; Stuttgart: Kohlhammer, 1992], 51).
97 Coats, *Exodus*, 139.
98 Coats, *Exodus*, 139.

ing "a positive relationship between God and his people"[99]—is foundational, not the מריבה etiology.[100]

Although not contiguously bound, there is evidence to corroborate a connection between the murmuring motif and lawsuit initiated by ריב components in v. 2, which in turn prompt the מריבה etiology in v. 7. Earlier it was noted that the two phrases in Exod 17:1bβ-2aα appear in reverse order and frame Num 20:2–5. Here, in the P* M-Mt narrative, these phrases constitute the *first* and *third* of three duplicate components in Num 20:2–5, which together with their counterparts in Exodus 17 suggest pre-Hexateuchal coordination (*pre-Hex Supp*) of the non-P and P* M-Mt narratives.[101] It is perhaps no coincidence then, given the connection between the people's ריב (v. 2aα) and their murmuring (v. 3aβ-b), that the people's murmuring speech in Exod 17:3b appears in reverse order in Num 20:4b-5aα, the *second* of the three duplicate components in Num 20:2–5.[102] Thus, it appears that same hand responsible for coordinating the M-Mt narratives via the מריבה etiology (*pre-Hex Supp*) may also be credited with inserting the

---

99 Coats, *Exodus*, 139.
100 Childs also expresses doubts regarding this aspect of Coats' reconstruction, at least as Coats first iterated it in *Rebellion in the Wilderness*, 53–71. Specifically, Childs doubts that מריבה etiology "functions in this way within the tradition [...] The tradition did not develop from the etiology but the etiology subsequently attached itself to the tradition of Yahweh's aid in the wilderness" (Childs, *Exodus*, 307).
101 For the earlier discussion of these phrases, see pp. 185–186 above. For a treatment of these phrases as secondary, duplicate components in Num 20:2–5, see §7.3.4 below.
102 The first half of the people's murmuring speech in Exod 17:3bα (למה זה העליתנו ממצרים) is nearly verbatim to Num 20:5aα (ולמה העליתנו ממצרים); the second half of the people's murmuring speech in Exod 17:3bβ (להמית אתי ואת־בני ואת־מקני בצמא) exhibits approximate verbal and conceptual correspondence to Num 20:4b (למות שם אנחנו ובעירנו). For further discussion, see §7.3.4 below.
Christophe Nihan recognizes two of these correspondences: Num 20:3a he says is a quotation of Exod 17:2a, while Num 20:4–5a takes up in reverse order Exod 17:3, in accordance with "the so-called 'law of Seidal'" (*From Priestly Torah to Pentateuch: A Study in the Composition of the Book of Leviticus* [FAT2 25; Tübingen: Mohr Siebeck, 2007], 28; for Seidel's law, see M. Seidel, "Parallels between Isaiah and Psalms," *Sinai* 38 [1955–56], 159–172, 229–240, 272–280, 335–355; reprinted in *Hiqrei Miqra* [Jerusalem: Rav Kook, 1978], 1–90). Nihan does not discuss, however, the strong verbal correspondence between Exod 17:1bβ and Num 20:5bβ, nor that the correlatives in Exod 17:1bβ-3 for all three of these correspondences are secondary to the foundational narrative in Num 20:1–13. Instead, Nihan argues that these correspondences in Num 20:2–5 are a product of rewriting Exod 17:1–7 in the homogenous post-P production of Num 20:1–13 (*Priestly Torah to Pentateuch*, 26–30). For a critical response to Nihan, see pp. 207–209 below.

people's murmuring speech (Exod 17:3aβ-b ‖ Num 20:4b-5aα) and Moses' cry of distress (Exod 17:4aβ-b).[103]

Finally, not only are the מסה etiology (*late Dtr–Dtr supp*) and the murmuring motif (*pre-Hex Supp*) secondary to the foundational narrative (*Dt*), but the relative clause in v. 5 stands out as glossic in nature. Already, Christophe Nihan cites the long-held consensus among historical-critical scholars that the staff in Num 20:8aα, 9, and 11 is secondary to Num 20:8–11 and notes Jan Gertz's recent argument that the staff motif is redactional throughout the whole Pentateuch[104]—a

---

103 An additional feature further supports the notion that the murmuring motif entered the text at the same time as the מריבה etiology: namely their role in the construction of what Coats calls a "preofficial" or "informal" *rib*. Initially, Coats looks for the other components of the ריב form, but concludes "the term *rib* is not obviously appropriate for this kind of legal claim, for the root is never again used with a sentence controlled by an imperative" (*Rebellion in the Wilderness*, 57 n. 24). What Coats fails to notice, however, is that the murmuring question in 17:3 and Moses' cry of distress to Yahweh in 17:4 could serve as the two missing elements of what he describes as a "preofficial stage of the Gerichtsrede": namely, 1) a question directed to the accused challenging a past deed, and 2) some form of response from the accused that acknowledges the complaint, but is often deferred to Yahweh "against whom [the] murmuring is really directed" (*Rebellion in the Wilderness*, 33–40, especially 39–40).

The significance of this observation is two-fold: first, it further corroborates assigning the ריב components and the murmuring motif to the same editorial stage; second, it may proffer an explanation for why this episode does not end with the people's punishment. At the preofficial (or "informal") stage, as Coats summarizes it, "there is no judge present, no witness. The entire process occurs only between the two parties involved. Moreover, if the one succeeds in persuading the other of the validity of his argument, the quarrel is over. It is only in the event that neither can convince the other of the justice of his argument that a transition must be made to official procedure" –i.e., a formal, technical ריב (*Rebellion in the Wilderness*, 34). This stage is precisely what is reflected in the מריבה components in vv. 1bβ-2aα +2bβ, the people's murmuring question in v. 3aβ-b, and Moses' cry of distress to Yahweh in v. 4aβ-b. Here, the people have launched an informal ריב directly against Moses, and Moses' cry of distress to Yahweh in no way denies the validity of the people's murmuring: the situation is dire; Moses acknowledges the validity of the informal ריב; the quarrel may be over, but the impetus for it remains unresolved, and Moses' life is indeed in danger. In short, the components of the ריב in v. 2 and of murmuring motif in vv. 3–4 belong together; they not only constitute a successfully executed informal complaint, but its success explains why the narrative is missing a "punishment" (*contra* scholars who see Exod 32:25–29 as non-P M-Mt's displaced punishment; cf. p. 191 n. 88 and p. 128 n. 128 above).

104 For the redactional nature of the staff in Num 20:8–11, Nihan cites Wilhelm Rudolph, Martin Noth, Erich Zenger, Ursula Struppe, Ludwig Schmidt, Olivier Artus, and Christian Frevel (Nihan, *Priestly Torah to Pentateuch*, 26 n. 24). For Jan Christian Gertz's argument that the staff motif in Pentateuch is entirely a Pentateuchal redaction, see *Tradition und Redaktion in der Exoduserzählung: Untersuchungen zur Endredaktion des Pentateuch* (FRLANT 186; Göttingen: Vandenhoeck & Ruprecht, 2000), 313–314; although Nihan notes that other scholars had al-

consensus with which Nihan slightly disagrees, as he views the whole of Num 20:1–3 to be a late "sophisticated *réécriture* of Ex 17."[105] Although a thoroughgoing analysis of this motif in the Pentateuch cannot be attended to here, the conclusion that the staff is entirely redactional to Exod 17:5–6 is unwarranted. The staff is intrinsic to the foundational narrative, as its instrumentality for striking the rock is essential to the miraculous provision of water. Nevertheless, the relative clause in v. 5bα[ii-vi] (אשר הכית בו את־היאד —(is extraneous to its surrounding text, and indeed v. 5b reads quite smoothly without it: ומטך קח בידך והלכת (v. 5b[i +vii-ix]). Canonically, the only purpose this relative clause serves in Exod 17:5 is to disambiguate the staff Moses uses in the immediate episode as opposed to the one Moses uses in Num 20:8–11. Consequently, the earliest possible hand to which one could credit this gloss is HexRed; given Num 20:9's dependence on Num 17:2–10, however, the editor responsible for this gloss is most likely PentRed (cf. §7.3.2). [106]

---

ready established the redactional nature of the staff motif for individual texts (Nihan, *Priestly Torah to Pentateuch*, 26 n. 25).

105 Nihan, *Priestly Torah to Pentateuch*, 27; although cf. §5.3 above and §7.3 below for arguments rejecting the homogeneity of Num 20:1–13.

106 A thorough study of the staff motif in the Pentateuch is beyond the scope of the current study. Nevertheless, a cursory survey of texts relevant to the miraculous staff (מטה) clearly demonstrates that two sets of traditions have been merged. The staff in Moses' hand transforms into a serpent (Exod 4:2–4, 17), strikes the Nile (Exod 7:14–18, 20), and is stretched (√נטה) toward the sky (Exod 9:23), over land (Exod 10:13; 17:9–12), and over the sea (Exod 14:16) to work miracles. It is this staff to which Exod 17:5 refers, both initially and subsequently more clearly with the insertion of the relative clause in v. 5bα[ii-vi]. Yet several of these traditions regarding Moses' staff overlap with traditions about Aaron's staff: Aaron also transforms his staff into a serpent (Exod 7:9), and he stretches it over (not strikes!) the Nile (Exod 7:19), various water sources (Exod 8:5–6), and land (Exod 8:16–17) in order to work miraculous signs. The merging of these duplicate traditions is typical of HexRed's *modus operandi*, but there is evidence of PentRed merging non-P and P traditions; e.g., the merging of the Dathan-Abiram tradition (non-P) and Korah tradition (P) in Numbers 16–17 (so Rolf P. Knierim and George W. Coats, *Numbers* [FOTL 4; Grand Rapids: Eerdmans, 2005], 204–215). At the very least, the merging of these traditions suggests a history of development (*contra* Gertz, *Tradition und Redaktion*, 313–314), one that cannot be explored here. Nevertheless, it is paramount to note how Aaron uses his staff in these traditions: he typically extends it in an outstretched fashion; only once does he strike an object (i.e., the dust of the land in Exod 8:16), and he never uses it to strike any water source. Consequently, the relative clause in Exod 17:5bα[ii-vi] can only have Moses' staff in view. (One may object here that Exod 7:15 clearly states that the staff Moses is to take in his hand is the one which turned into a serpent, which in the immediate context is Aaron's staff [cf. Exod 7:8–13]; this association may well be the product of merging the two sets of traditions together, since Moses' staff also transforms into a serpent in Exod 4:2–4).

6.4 Toward a Synthesis: The Literary History of Exodus 17:1–7 Aligned with Deuteronomy's M-Mt Tradition-historical Framework

The above literary analyses (§6.3) suggest that the non-P M-Mt narrative in Exod 17:1–7 developed over the course at least five successive stages of literary growth (cf. Appendix D: The Non-P Narrative by Stages of Literary Development). These stages transpired both centrifugally, with the accretions incrementally framing and occasionally supplementing internally the inherited materials, and simultaneously alongside the development of the non-P M-Mt narrative's broader literary contexts. Thus, in the end, these stages of development not only account for the internal tensions within Exod 17:1–7, but they also account for the four dynamics which characterize Exod 17:1–7's relationship with Num 20:1–13—i.e., *congruity*, *incongruity*, *shared internal tension*, and *connectivity* (cf. p. 156 above and pp. 202–203 below).

Stage 1: The first written stage of the non-P M-Mt narrative no doubt emerge from an oral tradition and is now most likely preserved in the foundational narrative core (vv. 3aα + 4aα + 5a-5b^i + 5b^{vii}-6 [*Dt*]). This independent M-Mt narrative reflected a positive tradition in which the people thirst for water, Moses intercedes, and Yahweh provides. In no way are the Israelites culpable of cultic failure or even the focus of narrative; instead, the focus is on Yahweh's provision in the wilderness. This primitive narrative aligns well with the reminiscence in Deut 8:15–16 (*Dt*), which interprets the threats ancient Israel faced in the wilderness as divine tests—tests which included facing "fiery" (שרף) serpents and scorpions, water deprivation, and food deprivation, in that order. This order might recall an original sequence of early non-P narratives in Numbers 11 (cf. p. 191 n. 91), when the Taberah, Massah, and Kibroth-hattaavah episodes were cast as divine tests rather than instances of corporate failure.

Stage 2: The addition of some form of v. 1bβ and the מסה etiological components (vv. 2aβ-bα + 2bγ + 7a^{i-iv} + 7bβ-γ [*late Dtr* to *Dtr supp*]) together reoriented

---

Later, Aaron's staff miraculous buds as a sign of his divine appointment to the priesthood; as a result, Aaron's rod is subsequently retired to the tent of meeting before the testimony as a sign against the Levitic rebels who challenged the Aaronide priesthood (Numbers 16–17, especially 17:2–10). According to Num 20:9, the staff that Moses took to strike the rock was מלפני יהוה, which in context of Num 17:10–11 indicates the staff to be Aaron's. Yet Num 20:11 clearly specifies the staff was originally Moses' staff, not Aaron's. Thus, in the same way that Exod 17:5bα^{ii-vi} disambiguates the staff Moses uses as his own, Num 20:9 also disambiguates the staff Moses uses as specifically Aaron's. It is therefore plausible that the two insertions—i.e., Exod 17:5 bα^{ii-vi} and Num 20:9—stem from the same hand. If so, then both insertions most likely stem from PentRed, as Num 20:9 depends on Numbers 16–17 (*PentRed*) (cf. §7.3.2).

the positive tradition into a negative episode in which the people tested the fidelity and presence of Yahweh. Evidence of the same editorial reorientation is extant for the Kibroth-hattaavah episode, as the etiological anchors frame the episode (Num 11:4, 34), and so are extrinsic to it, while traces of a once positive outcome are still extant in the narrative in Num 11:21–22, 30–31.[107] Further, this reorientation aligns with the tradition-historical development reflected in Deut 6:16 (*late Dtr*) and 9:22 (*Dtr supp*). The triggers in Deut 6:15—i.e., יהוה אלהיך בקרבך (cf. Exod 17:7bγ) in conjunction with the burning (√חרה) of Yahweh's anger (cf. Num 11:1, 10, 33)—inspired the allusion of the nascent מסה episode in Deut 6:16 (*late Dtr*). At this stage of Deuteronomy's M-Mt framework, there is a reversal of the agency in the מסה (not מריבה!) tradition, from Yahweh testing the Israelites to the Israelites inappropriately testing Yahweh. Deuteronomy 9:22 (*Dtr Supp*) reflects the same agency, but then reflects that the budding etiology in Deut 6:16 (בְּמַסָּה) had achieved its full toponymic recognition (וּבְמַסָּה) and that מסה narrative was still located between what is now Num 11:3 and 11:4. In other words, the second stage of Exod 17:1–7's literary development corresponds precisely with the second and third stages (*late Dtr–Dtr supp*) of the M-Mt's tradition-historical framework detected in Deuteronomy.

Stage 3: This stage of Exod 17:1–7's literary growth transformed the non-P מסה episode into the Massah-Meribah episode via the insertion of the מריבה etiology and murmuring motif (vv. 2aα + 2bβ + 3aβ-b + 4aβ-b + 7a^v-bα [*pre-Hex Supp*]). Three of these insertions (i.e., vv. 2aα, 3b, 7a^v-bα) mirror insertions in Num 20:1–13 (cf. §7.3.4 below), and therefore represent an attempt to coordinate two literary versions of this tradition which were at the time located in separate non-P and P corpora. The result of these insertions not only coordinated the non-P and P M-Mt narratives, but they also recast each narrative version as a successfully levied preofficial, informal ריב.[108] Moreover, as it pertains to the non M-Mt narrative, this editorial activity appears to have taken place in the context of

---

[107] For the secondary nature of the negative elements of Kibroth-hattaavah episode, see Knierim and Coats, *Numbers*, 174–177. Evidence for this narrative's earlier positive outcome is readily visible in Moses' response to Yahweh's instruction regarding the provision of meat (Num 11:21–22) and the people's initial reaction to the miraculous provision (Num 11:30–31). Moses' response in vv. 21–22 reflects no awareness of the ironic punishment in v. 20. Moses is only aware that Yahweh has promised the Israelites would eat meat for a month, not the nauseous consequences of doing so (v. 20) and certainly not the plague that followed (v. 33). Moreover, while v. 24 indicates Moses relayed Yahweh's words to the people, the people's response to the miracle in v. 32 in no way demonstrates awareness of these disastrous outcomes.

[108] For a discussion of the form Coats dubs a preofficial, informal ריב, see p. 192 n. 94 and p. 195 n. 103 above. For a discussion of how the ריב and murmuring components in Num 20:2–5 reorient the P M-Mt narrative to this form, see §7.3.4 below.

what is now Numbers 11, prior to the transposition of what is now Exod 17:1bβ-7* into its current textual location. Finally, although there is no reminiscence preserved in Deuteronomy which explicitly reflects this specific stage, the way Deut 33:8 parallels the allusions to מסה and the מי מירבה episodes (Exod 17:1–7 and Num 20:1–13 respectively; cf. §4.4.3 above) may well presume the coordinated relationship this stage supplies.

Stage 4: Similar to the third stage of its literary development, this stage of Exod 17:1–7's literary history is only indirectly represented in Deuteronomy. It is at this stage that HexRed relocated what is now Exod 17:1bβ-7* into its current position, anchoring it with the travel notice of Exod 17:1aba. This transposition is an outgrowth of HexRed's merging the non-P and P wilderness traditions, the effects of which are discernible in Deut 32:48–50, 52 (cf. §4.3.2.1 above). Throughout this undertaking, the foundational priestly itinerary in Num 33:5–49* served as guide for the (re)arrangement of the inherited materials, and the digressions from this formulaic itinerary in vv. 6bβ, 7aγ-b, 8aβ-bβ, 9bα-β, 14bβ, 36bβ, 37bβ, 38–39, 40, 44bβ, 47bβ, 48bβ, 49 are a product of HexRed annotating the foundational itinerary to reflect the changes wrought in the merging of these two collections of wilderness stories (cf. pp. 170–180). In the end, HexRed carefully selected narratives to (re)orient as pre-Sinai / Horeb episodes of deprivation, in turn situating Exod 17:1–7 as the climax of Exod 15:22–17:7.

Stage 5: Evidence of an additional stage in the formation of the Hexateuch is detectable (*HexSupp*; cf. p. 175 n. 46 above), but this subsequent stage in the formation of the Hexateuch did not directly affect the non-P M-Mt narrative in Exod 17:1–7. Instead, it is only with the formation of the Pentateuch that a *fifth and final stage* of Exod 17:1–7's literary development appears: the glossic insertion of relative clause in v. 5bα[ii-vi] (*PentRed*). This insertion disambiguates the staff Moses uses to strike the צור בחרב in non-P M-Mt narrative from the staff in the P* M-Mt narrative: the relative clause in Exod 17:5 identifies the staff as the one Moses had used to strike the Nile, whereas Num 20:9 designates the staff as Aaron's rather than Moses' (cf. p. 196 n. 106).

As will be seen, these clarifications became necessary when PentRed inserted Numbers 16–17 (i.e., the revolt of Korah, Dathan, and Abiram) and recast the P* M-Mt as another instance of the people rebelling against the leadership of Moses and Aaron (cf. §7.3.2). At this stage, however, the failure of Moses and Aaron is still a future development (*post-PentRed*; cf. §7.3.1) and the leadership of Moses and the priesthood of Aaron are again vindicated. This agenda, especially with regard to Aaron's priesthood over the Levites' (cf. Num 16:1, 7, 8, 10), comports well with the subversive Aaronide agenda latent in the Blessing of Levi in general (Deut 33:8–11 [*PentRed*]; cf. §4.4.2) and the positive representation of Aaron in Deut 33:8 in particular.

In summary, Exod 17:1–7's literary history unfolds in relation to its broader literary contexts within the Pentateuch. In five literary stages, Exod 17:1–7 emerged from an oral tradition (*oral foundation*) as a positive story of Yahweh testing Israel (stage 1 [*Dt*]). This independent narrative then developed into a negative story of Israel testing Yahweh at מסה (stage 2 [*Dtr–Dtr Supp*]). A later editor coordinated this "Massah Episode" with an alternative P version of this story via the מריבה etiology and the murmuring motif (stage 3 [*pre-Hex Supp*]). Eventually, an even later redactor merged the non-P and P wilderness collections in the formation of a unified narrative, resulting in the transposition of the non-P M-Mt from what is now Numbers 11 to its current position as the climax of Exod 15:22–17:7 (stage 4 [*HexRed*]). Lastly, a final redactor disambiguated the staff with which Moses struck the rock in Exod 17:5 from the one used in Num 20:8–11 (stage 5 [*PentRed*]).

This reconstruction is no doubt ambitious; yet as ambitious as it is, corroboration for these stages of Exod 17:1–7's literary growth emerges on two fronts. First, these stages not only explain the internal tensions within the narrative itself, but they also diachronically align with the framework detected in Deuteronomy for the M-Mt's tradition-history. Secondly, these stages provide a means to account for the four dynamics—*congruity, incongruity, shared internal tensions*, and *connectivity*—which characterize Exod 17:1–7's and Num 20:1–13's relationship, both to each other and to their respective broader literary contexts within the emerging Pentateuch.

The conceptual *congruity* between the two narratives most likely stems from a shared oral foundation, in which the tradition was a positive expression of Yahweh's testing and provision in the wilderness; as noted above, Exod 17:1–7's earliest literary stage reflects this agency of the M-Mt (Stage 1; cf. Deut 8:15 [*Dt*]). This first literary stage of the non-P M-Mt narrative appears to have been written independently from the first literary stage of the P* M-Mt narrative, which also was most likely a positive tradition (cf. §7.3.5).

The *incongruity* between Exod 17:1–7 and Num 20:1–13 stems from a subsequent period of independent tradition-historical and literary development. For Exod 17:1–7, this took the form of the non-aligned מסה elements in construction of the "Massah Episode" (Stage 2; cf. Deut 6:16 and 9:22 [*Dtr–Dtr Supp*]); for Num 20:1–13, however, it took the form of the non-aligned קדש elements (§7.3.5). Only at a tertiary stage (*pre-Hex Supp*) were these variant expressions of the M-Mt tradition coordinated in separate collections via the מריבה etiology and the murmuring motif, resulting in more precise verbal *contiguity* (Stage 3; presumed by Deut 33:8 [*PentRed*]; cf. §7.3.4).

The *connectivity* of Exod 17:1–7 to its broader literary contexts stems from the final two stages of its literary development—i.e. *HexRed* and *PentRed*—stages which also affected the P* M-Mt narrative (cf. §7.3.2 and §7.3.3). On the one hand, HexRed used the *Ur*-itinerary of Numbers 33 as a guide to merge the non-P and P corpora of wilderness traditions, and in that process transposed Exod 17:1–7 *from* its original location in what is now Numbers 11 *into* it current textual location, as the climax of a series of pre-Sinai wilderness deprivation episodes (Stage 4; presumed by Deut 33:8 [*PentRed*]; cf. §7.3.3). On the other hand, PentRed disambiguated the staff Moses used in both narratives: with a gloss in Exod 17:5 that connects to Exod 7:14–18, 20 and with Num 20:9 (and other components) that connect to Numbers 16–17 (Stage 5; presumed by Deut 32:51 [*post-PentRed*]; cf. §7.3.2).

Lastly, the *shared internal tensions* the M-Mt narratives exhibit stem from their having undergone similar and at times joint editorial processes. The unfolding of these processes in Exod 17:1–7's literary history occupies the current chapter; it is to the unfolding of these processes in the literary history of Num 20:1–13 that this study finally turns.

Chapter Seven:
The Priestly M-Mt Narrative in Numbers 20:1–13 and its Related Texts

7.1 An Approach toward Assessing Numbers 20:1–13

The previous chapter traces the literary history of Exod 17:1–7 in relation to its broader literary contexts within the Pentateuch. This narrative is by no means homogeneous, but is instead the product of at least five stages of literary growth: 1) the *transcription* of a positive oral tradition into the foundational literary narrative; 2) the *independent development* within a non-P collection into a negative episode set at Massah; 3) the *coordination* of this non-P episode with an alternative version of it in a separate P collection via the Meribah etiology and the murmuring motif; 4) the *transposition* of this non-P M-Mt narrative into its pre-Sinai location when the non-P and P collections were merged in the formation of the Hexateuch; and 5) the *disambiguation* of the staff in formation of the Pentateuch (cf. §6.4 above).

The editorial processes involved in these five stages—i.e., transcription, independent development, coordination, transposition, and disambiguation—not only explain the internal tensions within the narrative itself, but diachronically they align with the framework detected in Deuteronomy for the M-Mt's tradition-history. As well, these stages provide an account for the four dynamics—*congruity*, *incongruity*, *shared internal tension*, and *connectivity*—which characterize the relationship of Exod 17:1–7 and Num 20:1–13, both to each other and to their respective broader literary contexts within the emerging Pentateuch (cf. pp. 156 and 197 above).

Yet these findings derive primarily from literary analyses focused on non-P and post-P textual materials. The need therefore follows to limn the literary history of the P* M-Mt narrative in Num 20:1–13 and its related broader literary contexts on their own terms. Only then can one a) corroborate the above reconstruction for how the literary history of Exod 17:1–7 intersects with the literary development of Num 20:1–13, and b) determine to what extent Deuteronomy's framework of the M-Mt's tradition-historical development is descriptive of the P* M-Mt. A continuation of the previous chapter's approach is therefore essential: text-critical (§7.2) and literary (§7.3) analyses facilitate a tradition-historical analysis (§7.4). Likewise, the literary analysis of Num 20:1–13 proceeds stage-by-stage backwards in time, with the limning of each stage unfolding alongside the concurrent development of texts within Num 20:1–13's broader literary context. Along the way, this study's previous findings serve to corroborate the reconstruction of Num 20:1–13's incremental literary growth. In the end, the following analyses confirm 1) that Num 20:1–13 stems from the same oral tradition as does Exod 17:1–7; 2) that like Exod 17:1–7, Num 20:1–13 also experienced an early period of independent development, only to undergo a coordination with Exod 17:1–7* prior to the formation of the Hexateuch; and 3), that the stages of Num 20:1–13's literary growth broadly align with the M-Mt tradition-historical framework detected in Deuteronomy.

7.2 Textual Criticism of Numbers 20:1–13

The text-critical task again suffers from the paucity of manuscript evidence among the Dead Sea Scrolls at this juncture in Numbers.[1] Only two relevant fragments survive: 5/6 ḤevNum (5/6 Ḥev1a) and the relevant portion of the fragmentary 4QNum^b (4Q27). The fragment known as 5/6 ḤevNum dates to the second century C.E. and was once a part of a larger parchment scroll. What now survives, however, is little more than five words of Num 20:7–8 (וידבר יהוה א[ל משה לאמר קח את המטה]והקהל), all of which are identical to the MT.[2]

The second extant witness is part of 4QNum^b, which even in its deteriorated state still represents the "best preserved scroll of the Book of Numbers at Qumran."[3] This mid-to-late first century B.C.E. scroll shares several major interpolations with the Smr,[4] one of which is the interpolation of Deut 3:24–28 immediately following the etiology of Num 20:13, thereby providing Moses' initial response to Yahweh's judgment and Yahweh's concession to let Moses view the

---

[1] For the Hebrew text of Num 20:1–13, see either Fig. 5.1 on p. 145 above or Appendix E: Numbers 20:1–13 by Stages of Literary Development.
[2] See Yigael Yadin, "The Expedition to the Judaean Desert, 1961. Expedition D – The Cave of the Letters"," *IEJ* 12 (1962): 229 and Plate 48D. According to Yadin, this portion of the "Cave of the Letters" had been "ransacked" by Bedouin, who while exiting the east entrance apparently dropped this fragment along with some fragments of Nabatean papyri. The fragment 5/6 ḤevNum dates to the time of Bar Kokhba and follows the MT.
[3] Eugene Ulrich, F. M. Cross, et al, *Qumran Cave 4, VII: Genesis to Numbers* (DJD XII; Oxford: Clarendon Press, 1994), 203. The scroll has suffered the loss of Numbers 1–10 in its entirety, but portions of each chapter from Numbers 11–36 survive. In its current condition, "only nine percent of all the words in Numbers" survives in 4QNum^b (DJD XII, 203).
[4] For a full list, see DJD XII, p. 215.

land.⁵ This interpolation merely harmonizes the narrative with Moses' report of it in Deuteronomy 2–3; the MT is therefore preferable.

Beyond 4QNum^b and Smr, the Septuagint has four minor variants in vv. 4b, 8a, 10b, and 11a, which together sharpen the people's accusations and escalate Moses and Aaron's response to the people.⁶ In MT Num 20:4b, the people ask why Moses and Aaron brought them into the wilderness "to die here, we and our cattle" (למות שם אנחנו ובעירנו); thus in the MT, the people assert their leaders are indirectly responsible for their imminent deaths in the face of wilderness hardships. In LXX Num 20:4b, however, the people's murmuring is more pointed, accusing the leaders of having brought them into the desert "to kill us and our livestock" (ἀποκτεῖναι ἡμᾶς καὶ τὰ κτήτη ἡμῶν, which presumes להמית את (ו)נו ובעירנו). The shift from the Hebrew nominative אנחנו (= ἡμεῖς) to the Greek accusative ἡμᾶς (=א[ו]תנו) may at first appear subtle, but the rhetorical effect sharpens the accusation significantly.⁷ Likewise rhetorical sharpening is detectable in Moses' speech to the people in v. 10. Here, the MT has Moses rallying the people's attention with the imperative שמעו־נא, but the LXX has Moses directing the people's attention to himself with ἀκούσατέ μου, which typically presumes either שמעוני or שמעו אלי.⁸ Finally, the variants in vv. 8b and 11a smooth inconsistencies in the MT, but they also escalate Aaron's role in the narrative. In v. 8a, the LXX has the plural ἐξοίσετε for the MT's 2ms הוצאת, thereby securing Aaron's role in

---

5 See the transcription and reconstruction of column XI, fragments 13i–14 in DJD XII, 225 (cf. Plate XL). Extant fragments cease after Deut 3:27a, but since 4QNum^b follows the Smr in regards to other major interpolations, it is possible, if not likely, that this interpolation originally continued through Deut 3:28 and then was followed by another interpolation from Deut 2:2–6 (DJD XII, 225–226; cf. Smr Num 20:13b; Deut 2:2–6; and Deut 3:24–28 in August Freiherrn von Gall hrsg., *Der Hebräische Pentateuch der Samaritaner* (Giessen: Alfred Töpelmann, 1918), 315–316, 364–365, 369.

6 Other variants include the addition of ועם־אהרן in Num 20:3 in S, but this appears to be an attempt to carry forward Aaron (along with Moses) as the target of people's ריב (cf. v. 2b). There is a lack of confirmation among other witnesses for this addition.

7 Determining priority of one reading over the other is difficult here, since both Exod 17:3 and Num 21:5 portray the people accusing Moses (and God) of actively trying to kill them as well. Nevertheless, a rationale for the MT purposely deescalating the people's rhetoric is not readily apparent; the need for G to escalate it, however, is slightly more pronounced, as it would align it with other instances of the people murmuring, which in turn better precipitates Moses' wrathful response.

8 For examples of the LXX rendering שמעוני with ἀκούσατέ μου, see Gen 23:8; 1 Chr 28:2; 2 Chr 15:2; 20:20; 28:11. For instances where the LXX renders some form of שמעו אלי with ἀκούσατέ μου see Judg 9:7; Isa 46:3, 12; 49:1; 51:1. Other phrases that the LXX renders ἀκούσατέ μου include שמעו לי (Ps 33:12; 34:10; cf. Job 32:10; 34:2), שמעו קולי (Gen 4:23), שמעו שמוע מלתי (Job 21:2), שמעו שמוע אלי (Isa 55:2), and הקשיבו אלי / אלי האזינו (Isa 51:4).

the production of water. In v. 11a, the LXX reflects no possessive pronoun for ῥάβδῳ, while the MT has במטהו ("his staff"), with the pronominal suffix referring to Moses; thus, it is Aaron's staff alone that is operative in the narrative, while the MT oscillates from Aaron's staff in v. 9 to Moses' staff in v. 11. Together these adjustments to their MT *Vorlage* suggest that the Septuagint translators felt the need not only to represent Aaron's involvement more consistently throughout the narrative, but also to escalate the exchanges between the people and Moses so that these exchanges would build up to the narrative outcome: the failure of Moses and Aaron and their subsequent divine punishment.

7.3 Literary Analysis of Numbers 20:1–13 in Relation to its Broader Literary Contexts

Compared to its non-P counterpart, the P* M-Mt narrative in Num 20:1–13 is more thoroughly integrated with its surrounding literary context. Exodus 17:1–7 is only bound to its surrounding context artificially through its superscription (i.e. רפידים in Exod 17:1, 8; 19:2), a couple motifs, and a few catchwords (cf. p. 181 n. 57 above), a byproduct of its material transposition from a post-Horeb/Sinai to pre-Horeb/Sinai location (cf. §6.3.3). Numbers 20:1–13, however, does not appear to have undergone so radical a displacement; instead its material growth occurred organically as supplemental texts entered into its post-Sinai literary horizon (cf. §7.3). Consequently, Num 20:1–13 evinces several material connections to texts that are proximate to it within the scroll of Numbers itself: the phrase ויקהלו על־משה ועל־אהרן in v. 2b and the description of Aaron's staff in v. 9 bind the narrative to the rebellions in Numbers 16–17 (cf. §7.3.2); the list of produce in v. 5b ties the narrative to the scouts story in Numbers 13 (cf. Num 13:23; §7.3.3); and Yahweh's sanctioning Moses and Aaron in v. 12 connects the narrative to the deaths of both Aaron and Moses outside the Promised Land (cf. Num 20:24; 27:14; Deut 32:51) (cf. §7.3.1). Thus, the recent trend among scholars—that is, to view Num 20:1–13 as a homogenous, late post-P revision of Exod 17:1–7 written specifically for its current location—is understandable (cf. p. 152 n. 19 above).

The current study, however, has already indicated that the P* M-Mt narrative is composite. Not only is the literary integrity of Num 20:1–13 compromised by internal tensions, but many of the tensions within it correspond by type and relative proximity to tensions within Exod 17:1–7, thus the dynamic of *shared internal tension* (cf. pp. 146–148 above). Nevertheless, since recent critical scholars like Nihan, Artus, and Frevel see Num 20:1–13 as homogeneous,[9] a fuller survey of the tensions in Num 20:1–13 is warranted, and David Frankel summarizes these tensions well:

> The story's most conspicuous difficulty concerns the definition of the sin of Moses and Aaron. At the same time, other difficulties have been noted. Verse 1 is mysteriously silent about the year of the arrival at the Zin desert. Verse 3a, וירב העם עם משה, repeats what is already related in verse 2b, ויקהלו על משה ועל אהרן, without mentioning Aaron. Verse 4 then abruptly refers once again to both Moses and Aaron (note the plural form of הבאתם). Verse 5 repeats, to a great extent, the contents of verse 4. Both verses express a complaint over the exodus from Egypt and the lack of water in the desert. The command in verse 8 to take the staff is perplexing in light of the command to merely speak to the rock. The reference, in verse 9, to the fact that the staff was kept "before the Lord" associates it with Aaron's rod (Num. 17:25–26). Yet, verse 11 refers to the staff as Moses'. Verse 13's assertion that the Lord was sanctified through the waters of Meribah contradicts the assertion in verse 12 that he was not (יען לא האמנתם בי להקדישני לעיני בני ישראל). Finally, the overall relationship of the story in Num. 20 to the parallel story in Ex. 17 requires clarification.[10]

To these tensions, one should also add the tensions which Num 20:1–13 has with its broader literary context—tensions which would not be present if Num 20:1–13 were a late post-P Pentateuchal production, as scholars like Nihan have argued (cf. pp. 207–209 below). For example, Num 20:1 notes the Israelites arrival at קדש in the wilderness of Zin, yet Num 13:26 portrays קדש as being near the wilderness of Paran.[11] As well, Moses' rhetorical question in Num 20:10b demonstrates no awareness of the non-P M-Mt narrative; if Num 20:1–13 is merely a late, post-P Pentateuchal literary creation, it is inconceivable that Moses would not recall that he had brought forth water from a rock once before.[12] In short, the evidence for Num 20:1–13 being composite is considerable.

---

9 For Nihan, see pp. 207–209 below; for Artus, Frevel and others, see p. 151 n. 18 above.
10 David Frankel, *The Murmuring Stories of the Priestly School: A Retrieval of Ancient Sacerdotal Lore* (VTSup 89; Leiden – Boston – Köln: Brill, 2002), 263. A caveat here is in order: the phrase לפני יהוה does not occur in Num 17:25–26 (Eng. 17:10–11), but in Num 17:22–24 (Eng. 17:7–9). In vv. 22–24, Moses sets the twelve staffs of Israel's tribal heads *before Yahweh in the Tent of Testimony* (לפני יהוה באהל העדת) to reconfirm the deity's choice of Aaron to the priesthood. After Aaron's staff buds and Moses reveals the results in vv. 23–24, Yahweh then commands Moses in v. 25 to return Aaron's staff to its previous position before the testimony to serve as a sign against the sons of the rebels (השב את־מטה אהרן לפני העדות למשמרת לאות לבני־מרי). Thus, when Moses did so in v. 26, he was returning Aaron's staff not just לפני העדות, but also implicitly returning it לפני יהוה. Frankel's summary presumes this logical progress in Num 17:22–26.
11 See p. 147 n. 10 above and §7.3.3 below.
12 Again, Frankel notes this tension as well: "The rhetorical question of verse 10b, המן הסלע הזה נוציא לכם מים, becomes incomprehensible no matter how it is precisely understood. The Israelites

Recently, however, Christophe Nihan has mounted a formidable case for Num 20:1–13 being a homogenous post-Priestly "réécriture" of Exod 17:1–7, with "no trace of an earlier, originally independent narrative."[13] Nihan levies three critiques against previous arguments that Num 20:1–13 is composite. First, he correctly argues that one cannot treat the staff motif as secondary to vv. 8–11, as is so often suggested.[14] Yet here Nihan assumes that the only plausible stratification is one that privileges Moses speaking to the rock as opposed to striking it (cf. §7.3.1).[15] Secondly, Nihan argues that vv. 2–5 form a coherent sequence that is integral to the narrative, but his reading rests upon several more assumptions which do not withstand scrutiny.[16] Thirdly, Nihan observes

---

could have responded: Of course you can bring forth water from the rock! That's what you did the last time, so why are you making such an issue over it?!" (Frankel, *Murmuring Stories*, 269). For more of Frankel's quote, see p. 153 above.

13 Christophe Nihan, *From Priestly Torah to Pentateuch: A Study in the Composition of the Book of Leviticus* (FAT2 25; Tübingen: Mohr Siebeck, 2007), 26–30.

14 See Nihan, *Priestly Torah to Pentateuch*, 26–27.

15 To begin, Nihan notes that scholars who believe Num 20:1–13 is composite typically identify "v. 8aα² (i.e., without קח את־המטה), aβ, (8b), 10, 11b, 12" as the original text in vv. 8–11 (*Priestly Torah to Pentateuch*, 26). Nihan, however, notes that if one excises Yahweh's command to Moses (not Aaron) in v. 8a to take the staff, then the singular address to Moses in v. 8b becomes unintelligible. Here, Nihan cites the LXX's plural address in v. 8b as a "facilitating lesson" that is "unanimously recognized" (*Priestly Torah to Pentateuch*, 26 n. 27; cf. pp. 204–205 above for a text-critical discussion of the Septuagint's adjustments to Num 20:1–13). Further, since v. 11b (which is foundational) depends on v. 8b, then according to Nihan the whole of v. 8 must also be foundational (*Priestly Torah to Pentateuch*, 27).

16 Nihan argues on four grounds that vv. 2–5 is "usually assumed to have been considerably edited but actually form a coherent sequence" (*Priestly Torah to Pentateuch*, 28). First, he says that v. 3a is not a true doublet of v. 2b as is often claimed, but v. 2b portrays the congregation assembling against Moses and Aaron, while v. 3a specifies that the people accused Moses in particular. This focus on Moses is a byproduct of "the general reformulation" of Exod 17:1–7 in Num 20:1–13, since "v. 3a is actually a literal quotation of *Ex 17:2a*." Besides, v. 3a must be original to the narrative, says Nihan, because the etiology in v. 13 depends on it, and the etiology "should belong to the earliest layer of the story." Secondly, scholars often think v. 4 is a late addition to v. 3b, but here Nihan notes that vv. 3b-4 form a murmuring pattern that is already present in Exod 16:3. Thirdly, Nihan says that "there is no tension whatsoever between v. 4 and 5; on the contrary," says Nihan, "v. 5 pursues the motif introduced by v. 4 by opposing Egypts' [sic] fertility to the wilderness' sterility." Moreover, vv. 4–5 reverse the pattern found in Exod 17:3, "following the so-called 'law of Seidel' (i.e., Ex 17:3bβ = Num 20:4; Ex 17:3bα = Num 20:5a)." Thus, for Nihan, vv. 4–5 (along with v. 3a) also demonstrate Num 20:1–13 to be a reformulation of Exod 17:1–7. Fourth and finally, Nihan cites v. 5b as forming an inclusion with v. 2a, "thus rounding off the entire sequence formed by vv. 2–5 and stressing its literary coherence" (all quotes from *Priestly Torah to Pentateuch*, 28; italics original).

that one cannot limit "late, post-P motifs" to vv. 12–13, as though the failure of Moses and Aaron were the only post-P addition; instead, there are post-P motifs and lexemes throughout the whole narrative.¹⁷ Here Nihan's assessment is cer-

---

Throughout these arguments, Nihan makes several assumptions which undermine his argument that vv. 2–5 are homogenous. To begin, he appears to assume that only precise "doublets" is sufficient to create literary tension, but such is not the case in vv. 2–5. For example, as concerning whether v. 3a is a doublet of v. 2b, Nihan is correct that they do not exhibit precise doublet components, but that does not warrant the conclusion that they form a coherent sequence. Why assemble (√קהל) against Aaron, if the accusation (√ריב) the community is going to levy ignores Aaron in order to focus on Moses? Moreover, this reading simply does not unfold in the verses that follow: v. 3b does not contain an accusation against Moses; the accusations one encounters appear in vv. 4–5, which use plural verbs (הבאתם in v. 4a; העליתנו in v. 5a) instead of singular verbs. In other words, vv. 4–5 directs the people's accusation against both Moses and Aaron; thus, v. 3a does not focus the community's accusation toward Moses whatsoever. In the end, vv. 2b and 3a show the community engaging in two sequential combative stances, which is materially redundant, and one must accept (from a synchronic standpoint) either that the focused accusation against Moses is also directed against Aaron, or that the accusations in vv. 4–5 build upon v. 2b, but not v. 3a, in which case one would have to conclude that the accusation that is focused toward Moses alone has been lost. Either way, one cannot read vv. 2b and 3a as a fully "coherent sequence."

A second assumption Nihan makes is that etiological components (vv. 3, 13) belong to the "earliest layer of the story." Coats made the same assumption regarding the מריבה etiology in Exod 17:2, 7 (cf. pp. 192–193 above); yet Deut 6:16, 9:22 and Exod 17:7 demonstrate the מסה etiology developed over time (cf. §3.5 and §6.3.2). Consequently, there is no reason to assume that the etiological components in Num 20:3, 13 were fully formed from the outset of Num 20:1–13's literary history.

Finally, a third and fourth assumption merit brief attention. Since Num 20:3b-4 mirrors the pattern of murmuring in Exod 16:3, Nihan argues that v. 4 cannot be secondary to v. 3b. This reason, however, assumes that Exod 16:3 itself is homogenous, but that is not the case (cf. p. 187 n. 76 above). Likewise, Nihan argues that Num 20:3–4 resemble Exod 17:2–3 because Num 20:1–13 is a reformation of Exod 17:2–3, but this conclusion assumes that the corresponding components in Exod 17:2–3 are foundational to Exod 17:1–7, or at least already present in Exod 17:1–7 when Num 20:1–13 was composed, which this study has already shown not to be the case (cf. §6.3.2–§6.3.3 above).

17 Nihan lists several post-P indicators. There are phrases which link Num 20:1–13 to Numbers 16–17 (*PentRed*; cf. §7.3.2): e. g., v. 3b's use of the √גוע (cf. Num 17:27–28); v. 4's referring to the Israelites as קהל יהוה, which is "never found in P but only in Deut 23 (v. 2, 3, 4, 9) and Num 16:3"; and v. 9's description of the staff as לפני יהוה (cf. Num 17:16–26). Nihan also cites v. 10's *hapax* המרים ("rebels"), the root for which (√מרה) occurs elsewhere in P* materials only in Num 20:24 and 27:14, which he says is dependent on Num 20:1–13. Here, one could also add the phrase לבני־מרי ("to the sons of rebellion") in Num 17:25, which presages Moses' calling the Israelites המרים in Num 20:10. The phrase ויאמרו לאמר in v. 3aβ, however, even though it appears elsewhere in the Pentateuch only in Exod 15:1, is not as convincing. The phrase is formulaic and thus cannot command much weight. (Nihan, *Priestly Torah to Pentateuch*, 28)

tainly accurate, but widespread post-P indicators cannot serve as a litmus test for the narrative's compositional integrity. At most, such indicators suggest that one or more post-P scribe(s) had a hand in shaping Num 20:1–13, whether wholecloth or in part cannot be determined on the presence or prevalence of post-P elements alone. Instead, one must assess the integrity of the narrative as a whole in order to determine whether these post-P indicators are intrinsic to it or in fact create dissonance within it.

The following literary analysis argues that these post-P components in Num 20:1–13 represent incremental accretions to the P^G version of M-Mt narrative, which itself was likely the product of literary developments similar to the first two stages of the non-P M-Mt narrative (cf. pp. 197–198 above). These accretions, however, were not haphazard supplements; rather, at each stage of Num 20:1–13's post-P development, elements were added to enhance the connectivity of the P* M-Mt narrative to texts entering into its broader literary context—beginning with the coordination of non-P and P corpora (*pre-Hex Supp*) through to the final formative stages of the Pentateuch (*post-PentRed*).

To preview, the P* M-Mt narrative evinces the following six stages of literary growth: 1) the foundational narrative core in vv. 2a + 6–8* + 10a + 11* (*early P*; cf. §7.3.5); 2) the קדש elements in vv. 1aγ + 4a* + 5aβ + 13b (P^G; cf. §7.3.5); 3) the מריבה coordination in vv. 3a + 4b + 5bβ* + 13a (*pre-Hex Supp*; cf. §7.3.4); 4) the מדבר־צן travel notice and connective materials added in the emergence of the Hexateuch in vv. 1aαβ + 1b + 5bα (*HexRed*; cf. §7.3.3); 5) the assembly against Moses and Aaron in vv. 2b + 3bβ + 9 + 10b and possibly פעמים in v. 11aβ (*PentRed*; cf. §7.3.2); and 6) the failure of Moses and Aaron via modifying v. 8aγ + adding v. 12 (*post-PentRed*; cf. §7.3.1).

7.3.1 The Failure of Moses and Aaron in Num 20:12 and their Deaths outside the Land in Num 20:22–29 and 27:12–23

The "most conspicuous difficulty" of Num 20:1–13, according to Frankel, is defining the nature of Moses and Aaron's sin,[18] but this task is interpretative and

---

[18] Several factors complicate nuancing the precise nature of Moses and Aaron's sin as it is now preserved in Num 20:12, 24; 27:14; and Deut 32:51. To begin, Num 20:12 is notoriously unclear regarding 1) how Moses and Aaron's actions could be construed as expressing a lack of trust in Yahweh (לא־האמנתם) and 2) in what way Moses and Aaron failed to treat Yahweh as holy before the people (לא + להקדישני בני ישראל) when v. 13 clearly states Yahweh was treated as holy among them (ויקדש בם). Secondly, one must contend with the fact that the nature of this sin is not uniformly represented across the Pentateuch (cf. Num 20:12, 24; 27:14; Deut

32:51). Thus, the failure of Moses and Aaron is most likely the product of multiple hands (cf. p. 212 n. 22 and p. 215 n. 32 below); as such, the endeavor to identify a singular sin that satisfactorily accounts for the vagaries in Num 20:8–13 is somewhat misled from the start. Nevertheless, a survey of the major positions is instructive in that it uncovers the competing components involved in Moses and Aaron's sin for which literary analysis should strive to account.

The survey Frankel provides is especially helpful in this regard in that he critiques several theories which one can group into four categories. The first is the so-called *"cover up" theory*, which posits that a later hand deliberately obscured Moses and Aaron's sin in order to protect their reputations (proposed by Cornill, followed by Bacon, Gray, Kahana, Cross, and Ehrlich). Cornill emended the text so that Moses' speech in v. 10b was originally directed to God not the people, thereby giving expression to the leaders' doubt and sacrilege. Frankel sees this emendation as excessive and agrees with Milgrom and Margaliot that open critique of Israel's leaders is not unusual in the Hebrew Bible. The second category is the inappropriate use of *magic*, which understands Moses and Aaron's failure in terms of either magically striking the rock with the staff (so Loewenstamm, Rofé) or of magically speaking when originally the miracle was supposed to be performed in silence (so Milgrom). Here, Frankel rightly notes that the staff is elsewhere used to perform wonders, so its use in Num 20:1–13 can hardly be deemed magical when the other instances of its use are not. Moreover, contra Milgrom, Moses' speech in v. 10b merely parrots Yahweh's instructions in v. 8; thus, נוציא in v. 10b cannot be read as Moses claiming magical powers for himself and Aaron, since Yahweh himself commands Moses to bring out (והוצאת להם מים) water in v. 8. A third category is *disobedience*, in which Moses fails to follow Yahweh's instruction to speak to the rock, whether because of doubt (so Propp, Lohfink) or righteous rage (so Blum, and to a limited extent Margaliot) expressed in Num 20:10b. In each of these proposals, the purpose for taking the staff was for it to stand on display as a witness against the rebellion (cf. Num 17:25–26). Yet as Frankel rightly observes the text does not state the staff's purpose was such; that Moses and Aaron failed to catch the "extreme subtlety" of Yahweh's instruction hardly warrants the divine punishment meted out against them. Finally, a fourth category is Margaliot's proposal that Moses and Aaron had *desecrated Yahweh's name*. Margaliot argues that the subjects presumed in נוצא in Moses' (and Aaron's!) speech in v. 10b include God. Thus, in direct opposition to the divine plan, v. 10b not only indicates that God is unwilling to provide water, but it also could be misconstrued as God being unable to do so. Moses then strikes the rock twice to prove that God will not provide water, but then God provided water anyway thereby sanctifying himself before the people. Frankel levels several critiques against this reading, but the most convincing is that antecedents of נוצא in v. 10b is most naturally Moses and Aaron, not Moses and God (*Murmuring Stories*, 265–270).

In the end, Frankel understands Moses and Aaron's "primary sin" to be an act of disobedience: instead of relying "on speech alone as commanded," Moses struck the rock with Aaron's staff, and "this was an expression of [their] lack of trust in God. Verse 10b and the reference to sanctification in verse 12 are both late additions" (*Murmuring Stories*, 277–278; cf. pp. 211–214 below, which argues v. 12 is secondary, but v. 10b is intrinsic). Yet the import of Frankel's survey and critical decisions at this juncture is not so much his position; it is the succinct way in which he frames the competing components involved in Moses and Aaron's sin. Other explanations have been proffered since Frankel's survey, such as Boorer's recent explanation—i.e., disobedience as described above, combined with usurping Yahweh by judging the people as "rebels" and by not clearly indicating "that YHWH is behind this miracle" ("The Place of Numbers 13–14* and Numbers 20:2–13* in the Priestly Narrative (Pg)," *JBL* 131 [2012]: 61)—but the competing compo-

begins appropriately from the final form of the text. Yet Num 20:1–13 is composite, so there is no reason to expect the nature of Moses and Aaron's sin to be one dimensional. In fact, it is easier to explain the multiple components involved in this sin as stemming from multiple hands than it is to arrive at a unified reading (cf. p. 209 n. 18 above).

To begin, one must isolate the textual material intrinsic to the sin itself. Surprisingly, from an editorial perspective, the changes and additions necessary to reorient this narrative—that is, from an episode of Israelite rebellion (cf. §7.3.2) to one of Moses' and Aaron's rebellion (cf. Num 20:24; 27:14)—are less substantial, and ergo less intrinsic, than some recent scholars have asserted.[19] The scribes involved would only need to replace the verb in v. 8aγ (from some form of √נכה to ודברתם[20]), transform a direct object marker (את) into the proposition

---

nents remain the same. (Ultimately, the current study agrees with Boorer's primary argument that Num 20:2–13* was a part of Pg, although on different grounds, and her approach of comparing and contrasting the content of Moses' response and the narrative arrangement of Num 20:2–13 with the Pg material in Exodus 16 is insightful. Her description of the nature of Moses and Aaron's sin, however fails to convince: Moses' use of the rod [regardless whether his own or Aaron's] is a visible extension of Yahweh's power with which the people would have been familiar. In short, even in the Pg material there is visible and sufficient indication of Yahweh being "behind" the miracle.)

With the above in mind, a viable literary history of Num 20:1–13 should seek to account for the following components in the development of Moses and Aaron's sin: 1) it should account for role of the staff in the miracle, since Yahweh commands Moses to take it, and yet provides no instruction for what to do with it; 2) it should explain how Moses' (and Aaron's) actions and words represent both a lack of trust in Yahweh and a failure to sanctify him before the people; and 3) it should clarify how v. 13 can assert Yahweh was sanctified when v. 12 accuses Moses and Aaron of failing to do so.

[19] See the discussion in Nihan, *Priestly Torah to Pentateuch*, 26–30, and cf. p. 152 n. 19 above.
[20] Contra Frankel, who advocates excising ודברתם אל־הסלע לעיניהם ונתן מימיו on account that it is redundant with v. 8b. While there are certainly overlapping components, the removal of this phrase from v. 8a would not result in a "smooth sentence," as Frankel argues. Verse 8aα instructs Moses to take the staff, but v. 8b provides no opportunity to use it; some form of v. 8aγ is necessary to make sense of Moses needing to take the staff.

An easier explanation is that an editor has replaced the verb. In light of Exod 17:6, the form one would expect would be either והכית (for Moses only) or והכיתם (for both Moses and Aaron). Other possible actions include "to lift" (√רום) or "to stretch" (√נטה) over (cf. Exod 7:19; 8:5, 12–13; 9:23; 10:13; 14:16; 17:9–11), or perhaps "to cast" (hiphil of √שלך) toward (cf. Exod 4:2–3). What is striking (pun intended) is that Num 20:8 is the only text in the Hebrew Bible in which a physical מטה facilitates speech. In all other instances, the verbs designating the action of מטה requires the one holding the staff to use his hands. The closest parallel to the commands in Num 20:8a to take the staff, gather the assembly, and then speak is the oblique מטות אמר ("rods of speech")

אל,²¹ and then insert v. 12 between what is now vv. 11 and 13.²² The remaining material in Num 20:1–11* + 13 was most likely already extant, as it contains material connections to texts shaped by the *pre-Hex Supp* (cf. §7.3.4), *HexRed* (cf. §7.3.3), and *PentRed* (cf. §7.3.2), while the textual material intrinsic to the sin of Moses and Aaron does not. For this reason, it is apparent that the creation of the literary tradition of Moses and Aaron's sin stems from the hands of post-Pentateuchal redactors (*post-PentRed*).

Evidence corroborating this assignment emerges on several fronts. First, the P* wilderness itinerary in Numbers 33, although evincing the post-priestly hands of HexRed and PentRed, does not show any awareness of Moses and Aaron's sin. One would expect the annotations in Num 33:38–39—which records where Aaron died (v. 38a [HexRed]) and the date and Aaron's age at the time of his death (vv. 38b-39 [PentRed])—to reiterate this rationale for Aaron's death outside the promised land, but they do not.²³

A second piece of evidence indicating the sin tradition to be a creation of a post-PentRed is that the failure of Moses and Aaron does not fit the rhetoric of PentRed, which the current study has shown aggrandizes both leaders (cf.

---

in Hab 3:9aβ, which in light of קשתך ("your bow") in Hab 3:9aα is no doubt metaphoric of divine arrows.

21 This reconstruction presumes v. 8aγ originally read והבית את־הסלע לעיניהם, in which case only the underlined portions would need to be edited to form the current text: ודברתם אל־הסלע לעיניהם. Both Frankel and Artus argue that all of v. 8aγ-δ was added on account of the redundancy that ונתן מימי (v. 8aδ) forms when followed by והוצאת להם מים מן־הסלע in v. 8bα (Olivier Artus, *Etudes sur le livre des Nombres: Récit, Histoire et Loi en Nb 13,1–20,13* [OBO 157; Göttingen: Vandenhoeck & Ruprecht, 1997], 231; Frankel, *Murmuring Stories*, 282). The force of the argument here is not to dispute redundant nature between v. 8aδ and v. 8bα, but to demonstrate the ease with which a scribe could have edited v. 8aγ.

22 Verse 12 disrupts the fluid reading of vv. 11+13. Verse 11 concludes with ויצאו מים רבים ותשת העדה ובעירם, and v. 13 begins with the demonstrative phrase המה מי מריבה which presumes the waters in v. 11. Verse 12 therefore stands out as redactional. Now, this statement in no way suggests that v. 12 stems from a single hand. On the contrary, it merely notes the textual parameters involved in creating the sin of Moses and Aaron, which in v. 12 likely occurred in two phases: the √אמן / √מרה stratum stems from a post-PentRed, while the √קדש addition stems from a later glossator. See p. 215 n. 32 below further discussion.

23 These annotations—which stem from both HexRed (v. 38a) and PentRed (vv. 38b-39) (see the discussions on pp. 171 n. 36, 180 n. 54, 181, 181 n. 56 above)—constitute the only post-P reflection on the Aaron's death that does not reference this rationale. Both of the post-P reminiscences on Moses' death are conditioned by recollections of his failure in the P* M-Mt narrative: Num 27:14 provides this rationale for Num 27:12–13, as does Deut 32:51 for Deut 32:48–52* and 34:1–12.

pp. 116–117, 134, 136–137 above).²⁴ How can the same hand that 1) portrays Moses as a paragon of health at the time of his death (Deut 34:7b; cf. Deut 31:1), and that 2) esteems Moses as the unequaled prophet of God (Deut 34:10–12; cf. Deut 18:18), claim that Moses sinned so egregiously as to merit the same punishment as the first wilderness generation?²⁵ The same argument applies to Aaron as well, as PentRed in Deut 33:8 understands Aaron to be Israel's devout one (חסידך) in relation to this very episode.

The third piece of evidence that corroborates the assignment of the sin of Moses and Aaron to post-PentRed requires more detailed attention. In each of its occurrences within the Pentateuch, the recollection of this sin stands out as secondary to its immediate textual context. Already, this study has demonstrated Deut 32:51 to be later than both Deut 32:48–50, 52 (*HexRed*) and Deut 33:8 and 34:7b, 10–12 (*PentRed*) (cf. §4.3.2.2); thus, Deut 32:51 stands out as a product of editors who continued to shape the Pentateuch after its emergence (so *post-PentRed*). One can also arrive at the same conclusion for the remaining texts that recall this sin: namely, Num 20:12, 24 and 27:14.

---

24 Although it is beyond the scope of the current study to verify, one can provisionally assert that the failure of Moses and Aaron does not fit well with the rhetoric of HexRed either. Latent in the texts this study identifies as HexRed is the theme of Moses and Aaron's unquestioning obedience to Yahweh's command (על־פי יהוה): e.g., Exod 17:1 (cf. §6.3.1.3); Num 10:13 and 33:2 (cf. p. 180 n. 54 above); Num 33:38a (see p. 212 n. 23 above); and Deut 34:5 (cf. pp. 115 and 118 above). For a full list of occurrences of על־פי יהוה within the Hexateuch, see p. 115 n. 94 above. Outside the Hexateuch, this phrase only occurs in 2 Kgs 24:3. For further discussion of this aspect of HexRed's profile, see pp. 215 below.

25 In this regard, Nihan is quite correct: "Contrary to a widespread opinion [...] Moses' and Aaron's crime is certainly not a minor sin" (Nihan, *Priestly Torah to Pentateuch*, 29 n. 50; contra Propp, "The Rod of Aaron and the Sin of Moses," *JBL* 107 [1988]: 21), at least not at its inception. Both Num 20:24 and 27:14 cast this failure as direct rebellion (√מרה) against Yahweh, and Deut 32:51 understands it as act of treachery (√מעל). Yet to be fair to Propp, the redactors responsible for this sin may well have considered exclusion from the land a "light" punishment (Propp, "Rod of Aaron," 21); after all, Achan acted treacherously (√מעל) when he took some of the חרם from Jericho (Josh 7:1)—an act for which his whole family was executed (Josh 7:25). Here, Frankel's reconstruction of the composite nature of the sin itself is instructive: that the sin now appears minor is a product of the traditioning process, in which an original sin (Frankel argues for a lack of trust [לא האמנתם in v. 12aβ] in Yahweh's "promise of aid") was later augmented by glosses regarding the failure to sanctify Yahweh in v. 12aγ, Num 27:14, and Deut 32:51 (*Murmuring Stories*, 271–284). For further discussion of the composite nature of Num 20:12, 24; 27:14; and Deut 32:51, see p. 212 n. 22 above and p. 215 n. 32 below.

Regarding Num 20:12, Olivier Artus aptly describes its relationship to v. 11 as without transition, brutal, and unexpected[26]; only vv. 8ay and 10b in any way prepare the reader for the sanction in v. 12,[27] and v. 10b only does so on account of Yahweh's instruction in v. 8ay. In other words, by simply altering v. 8ay (cf. p. 212 n. 21 above) an editor could pave the way for inserting v. 12, which would otherwise stand in complete discontinuity with the rest of the narrative.

As for Num 20:24 and 27:14, the tensions these verses introduce into their immediate literary contexts are subtle, but nevertheless present. Scholars as early as Noth have argued that vv. 23aβb-24 are secondary to Num 20:22–29,* though Noth's specific arguments have not found a wide following.[28] This dismissal, however, may stem from how Noth framed his argument. [29] Rather than focusing

---

[26] "Il n'existe aucune transition entre les versets 11 et 12: le changement de thématique est brutal et l'annonce de la sanction qui frappe Moïse et Aaron est, dans l'état actuel du texte, inattendue" (Artus, Etudes sur le livre des Nombres, 237).

[27] Artus' notations are slightly different than the current study's: in Artus' study, v. 8aβ.ay is ודברתם אל־הסלע לעיניהם ונתן מימיו (Etudes sur le livre des Nombres, 283), which this study would denote as v. 8ay-δ. The redundancy that v. 8aδ (= Artus' v. 8ay) forms with v. 8bα (cf. p. 212 n. 21 above) does not contribute to the creation of Moses and Aaron's sin. Likewise, Artus includes the whole of v. 10, but v. 10a shows Moses and Aaron's compliance to Yahweh's instructions to "gather" the congregation / assembly (cf. v. 8aβ and v. 10a); thus, v. 10a contributes nothing to the sin of Moses and Aaron.

[28] E.g., Budd sees no "serious difficulty" in vv. 23–24 (Numbers [WBC 5; Waco: Word Books, 1984], 227); E. W. Davies follows Budd at this point (Numbers [NCB; Grand Rapids: Eerdmans, 1995], 211); Frankel agrees with Noth regarding v. 24b, but sees no problem with v. 24a (Murmuring Stories, 280–281); Knierim and Coats accept Noth's argument that v. 23 is secondary, but reject his reasons for seeing v. 24 as such (Numbers [FOTL 4; Grand Rapids: Eerdmans, 2005], 233–234).

The source critical work of Ludwig Schmidt largely agrees with Noth's findings, but on slightly different grounds. Schmidt sees Num 20:23b as dependent on Num 20:16, which he deems JE; he therefore sees v. 23b as stemming from PentRed who merged JE and P. Schmidt then assigns Num 20:24 to PentRed because it *tones down considerably* ("mildertе [...] erheblich ab") P's rationale in Num 20:12: whereas in v. 12 P accuses Moses and Aaron of disbelief, v. 24 states that Moses and Aaron merely disobeyed Yahweh's command (*Das vierte Buch Mose: Numeri 10,11–36,13* [ATD 7,2; Göttingen: Vandenhoeck & Ruprecht, 2004], 99). While Schmidt's argument is forced—how can rebellion (√מרה) tone down disbelief (√אמן)?—it is significant that he understands v. 24 as secondary to Num 20:22–29*.

[29] Noth founded his argument on four grounds. First, Yahweh addresses both Moses and Aaron in vv. 23aβb-24, instead of just Moses; one would not expect an address to both Moses and Aaron until after v. 25. Second, the geographical annotation in v. 23b appears out of place, as v. 22 is the more logical location; instead, v. 23b depends on the later insertion of vv. 14–21. Third, v. 24 depends on the "waters of Meribah" in Num 20:13, which he asserts is even later than v. 12. Finally, v. 24aα is redundant with v. 26b (Martin Noth, *Das vierte Buch Mose: Numeri* [ATD 7; Göttingen: Vandenhoeck & Ruprecht, 1966], 134).

on narrative logic—specifically, to whom Yahweh speaks and when it would be logical for him to do so—one may simply recognize that v. 24 stands as entirely unnecessary to the text. The first portion of the verse creates redundancy with v. 26b, which is more intrinsic to the narrative than v. 24a. The second half of v. 24b only provides the rationale for Aaron's death outside the land. Since this tradition stands out as secondary in Num 20:12 and Deut 32:51, one rightly suspects it to be secondary in v. 24. This suspicion finds confirmation in that the narrative reads fluidly without v. 24 altogether: in the style of HexRed (cf. Num 33:38a), Num 20:22–23, 25–29 portrays Moses' (and implicitly Aaron's) absolute obedience to the command of Yahweh (ויעש משה כאשר צוה יהוה in Num 20:27a [cf. Num 20:9]),[30] even to the point of Aaron dying outside the land. A similar portrait of Moses' obedient death in fact appears in Deut 34:5b (HexRed).

Finally, Num 27:14 also introduces tensions into Num 27:12–23. Yet unlike Num 20:24 in relation to Num 20:22–29*, the tensions reside within v. 14 itself. Verse 14 twice identifies מדבר צן as the regional setting for Moses and Aaron's sin,[31] and the syntax of v. 14a is awkward at best.[32] Once one recognizes, howev-

---

30 Given the distribution of על־פי יהוה (cf. p. 115 n. 94 above), it may be significant that the phrase כאשר צוא יהוה occurs almost exclusively within the Hexateuch: Exod 7:6, 10, 20; 12:28, 50; 16:34; 34:4; 39:1, 5, 7, 21, 26, 29, 31, 43; 40:19, 21, 23, 25, 27, 29, 32; Lev 8:4, 9, 13, 17, 21, 29; 9:7, 10; 10:15; 16:34; 24:23; Num 1:19; 2:33; 3:42, 51; 8:3, 22; 15:36; 17:26; 20:27; 26:4; 27:11, 22; 31:7, 31, 41, 47; 36:10; Deut 1:19; 5:32; 34:9; Josh 10:40; 11:15, 20; 14:2, 5; 21:8. Of its sixty-one occurrences, only twice is this phrase extant outside the Hexateuch: 2 Sam 24:19 and Jer 13:5.
31 The first instance is in v. 14a, within Yahweh's speech to Moses (כאשר מריתם פי במדבר־צן), while the second appears outside of Yahweh's speech in v. 14b (הם מי־מריבה קדש מדבר־צן). The parenthetical nature of v. 14b occasionally prompts scholar to suggest it as glossic (e.g., Bruno Baentsch, *Exodus – Leviticus – Numeri: übersetzt und erklärt* [HKAT I/2; Göttingen: Vandenhoeck & Ruprecht, 1903], 639; more recently by Timothy R. Ashley, *The Book of Numbers* [NICOT; Grand Rapids: Eerdmans, 1993], 550). Others still see all or part of v. 14 as later than vv. 12–13, but describe that relative diachronic relationship differently; e.g., Noth says v. 14b was added later (*Numeri*, 186); Kratz sees vv. 13b-14 as later than vv. 12–13a (*Komposition der erzählenden Bücher des Alten Testaments: Grundwissen der Bibelkritik* [UTb 2157; Göttingen: Vandenhoeck & Ruprecht, 2000], 111); Schmidt asserts that "V. 14 ist freilich ein Zusatz" (Schmidt, *Numeri*, 167); and finally see for Frankel's view, see p. 215 n. 32 below.
32 The infinitive clause להקדישני במים does not compliment well the verb and direct object מריתם פי. Frankel goes so far as to state "the phrase מריתם פי ... להקדישני can only be: 'You rebelled against my word *by* sanctifying me'" (*Murmuring Stories*, 271), which of course would make no sense. Frankel, however, overstates his case here, as his translation is not the only viable rendering. One can read the infinitive as referencing a command to sanctify him before the congregation ("you rebelled against my command ... to sanctify me"), but as Frankel correctly notes Num 20:1–13 iterates no such command from Yahweh to Moses and Aaron (*Murmuring Stories*, 272).

er, that all other iterations of Moses and Aaron's sin (i.e., Num 20:12, 24; Deut 32:51) are later additions to their immediate literary contexts, there is little reason to suspect otherwise with Num 27:14 as a whole. Moreover, as noted earlier regarding Num 20:24, one can readily excise v. 14 without detriment to the fluid reading of pericope as a whole: Yahweh gives instructions regarding Moses'

It is easier, as Frankel has convincingly shown, to argue that the accusation that Moses and Aaron had failed to sanctify Yahweh before the people (להקדישני לעיני בני ישראל) is glossic in all its occurrences (i.e., Num 20:12; 27:14 and Deut 32:51). In Num 27:14, the phrase "מריתם פי להקדישני ..." is syntactically awkward, regardless how one reads it, and nowhere in Num 20:1–13 does Yahweh give such a command. In Deut 32:51, the failure to sanctify Yahweh (לא קדשתם אותי) reduces the initial accusation that Moses and Aaron had broken faith with him (מעלתם בי); the duplicate phrases על אשר and בתוך בני ישראל, which occur in both halves of v. 51 further supports the glossic nature of v. 51b. Finally, this motif is noticeably absent in the death notice of Aaron (Num 20:24), which may preserve a more original portrayal of the sin. Since this motif is secondary in Num 27:14 and Deut 32:51, Frankel rightly suspects that the failure to sanctify Yahweh in Num 20:12 is secondary as well. Frankel cites additional support for this reconstruction—including the redundant mention of the Israelites and two distinctive sins (i.e., the lack of trust in v. 12aβ versus the failure to sanctify in v. 12aγ)—but the most convincing evidence is the assertion in v. 13b that Yahweh was sanctified. In the end, Frankel suggests that the glossator responsible for these additions may also have found the portrayal of Moses' sin as too egregious to believe, and as a result sought to reduce it (cf. Frankel, *Murmuring Stories*, 271–274). Admittedly, this reconstruction cannot explain why such a glossator did not emend Num 20:24, which also implicates Moses in the 2mp verb מריתם.

Once the failure to sanctify Yahweh is excised, the remaining verbal depictions of Moses and Aaron's sin are variable and therefore require attending. Numbers 20:12 portrays the sin as a lack of faith (לא־האמנתם); Num 20:24 and 27:14 says the sin was rebellion (מריתם); and Deut 32:51 says they broke faith (מעלתם). Here, Thomas Mann's discussion of the verb √מרה is most insightful. Mann observes the verb מרה is typical of Deuteronomy, especially in the wilderness reminiscences in Deut 9:7, 23–24, but P only uses it in reference to the sin of Moses and Aaron. "The priestly explanation would in effect be saying that Moses' denial was not on account of the people's unfaithfulness and rebellion, but due to his own" (Thomas W. Mann, "Theological Reflections on the Denial of Moses," *JBL* 98 [1979]: 485; cf. Frankel, *Murmuring Stories*, 273 n. 33). This confluence of √מרה and √אמן in Deut 9:23 for the spy story—which culminates in the first wilderness generation being denied entry into the Promised Land (cf. Num 14:22–23)—and the portrayal of Moses and Aaron's sin (to the same effect) as √אמן in Num 20:12 and √מרה in Num 20:24 and 27:14 permits speculation. The whole phrase להקדישני לעיני בני ישראל in Num 20:12 may not be a tertiary gloss: instead, a glossator could have altered the verb in v. 12aγ in the same way that post-PentRed altered the verb in v. 8aγ (cf. p. 212 n. 21 above). Such an alteration is less invasive, requiring only the rewriting a form of √מרה with the 1cs pronominal suffix (למרותי or perhaps ומריתם פי; cf. Num 27:14) into the current verb להקדישני.

death; Moses offers no resistance, and his only concern is that Yahweh appoints a successor as he had done with Aaron (Num 27:12–13, 15–23).³³

In short, the sin of Moses and Aaron within the Pentateuch stands out as a literary creation by the hands of post-Pentateuchal redactors, and tradition-historically this assignment is precisely what one would expect given the final stage of M-Mt's tradition-historical development reflected in Deut 32:51 (post-PentRed). Yet this alteration of the P* M-Mt is no artless expansion. With but the alteration of two words in v. 8aγ (from והכית את to ודברתם אל) and the insertion of v. 12, the scribes involved not only provided a final authoritative theological explanation for Moses and Aaron's exclusion from the land, but they also did so via situational irony. Prior to the augmenting of v. 8aγ and the insertion of v. 12, the narrative stood as yet another example of Israelite rebellion in the wilderness (cf. §7.3.2); Moses' censuring the Israelites as *rebels* (המרים) in v. 10b is expected; and the provision of water demonstrates Yahweh is holy among them. After the changes

---

33 Earlier this study concluded that Deut 32:48–50, 52 (*HexRed*) expands upon some form of Num 27:12–14 (see pp. 112–113 above). Here, it becomes clear that the earlier form upon which Deut 32:48–52* depends is Num 27:12–13, not 27:12–14. Yet how can HexRed appropriate Num 27:12–13 for Deut 32:48–50, 52 but not evince awareness of Num 27:12–13 in the priestly itinerary in Numbers 33? After all, Num 33:38–39 (*HexRed* and *PentRed*) is aware of Aaron's death at Mt. Hor? One possible solution that presents itself is that Num 27:12–13—and most likely some form of Num 27:15–23—belonged to P^G; since HexRed appropriated Num 27:12–13 for Deut 32:48–52*, it is unlikely that he would have included in the Hexateuch any portion of Num 27:12–23 relative to its current position. Instead, PentRed appears to have inserted the P^G version into its current location in order to install Joshua with some of Moses' power (מהודך; cf. Num 27:20) before the report of Joshua's commission in Deut 31:14 f. (why HexRed only appropriated Num 27:12–13 rather than 27:12–23*).

The rationale behind commissioning Joshua earlier in the Pentateuch, yet letting Moses continue to live from Numbers 28–Deuteronomy 34, is elusive. Here, Rainer Albertz' recent observations regarding the Pentateuchal redaction in Numbers is particularly helpful. Although Num 27:12–23 "seems somewhat isolated," Albertz argues the insertion in this position was necessary for three reasons: 1) it facilitates Joshua's leadership role in Num 32:28–32 and 34:16–29, and yet 2) permits Moses to live long enough to exact revenge on the Midianites (Num 31:2); and finally 3) it subordinates Joshua to Eleazar the high priest (Num 27:21), which Achenbach demonstrates is the focus of the report because "in all places within Num 26–36, where Joshua is mentioned after his installment, he is preceded by Eleazar (32:12, 28; 34:17)" ("A Pentateuchal Redaction in the Book of Numbers? The Late Priestly Layers of Num 25–36," *ZAW* 125 [2013]: 224–225; cf. Reinhard Achenbach, *Die Vollendung der Tora: Studien zur Redaktionsgeschichte des Numeribuches im Kontext von Hexateuch und Pentateuch* [BZAR 3; Wiesbaden: Harrassowitz Verlag, 2003], 559–560). In short, it appears that PentRed inserted what is now Num 27:12–23* (originally P^G) in order to incorporate further P^G materials into Numbers. This reconstruction provides a configuration which explains why Deut 32:48–52* expands on Num 27:12–14*, and yet Num 27:12–23 appears to have entered the Pentateuch after Deut 32:48–52.

wrought by post-PentRed, however, it is Moses and Aaron who emerge as unbelieving *rebels*—rebels meriting the same fate as those Moses had just condemned.³⁴

7.3.2 The Assemblies against Moses and Aaron in Num 20:2–3 and Numbers 16–17

Once one reconstructs the P* M-Mt narrative without Moses and Aaron's failure—that is, by restoring v. 8aγ and excising v. 12 (cf. §7.3.1 above)—the remaining textual material relays a narrative in which the Israelites assemble against Moses and Aaron (cf. Appendix E). This narrative, as scholars widely recognize, has strong literary connections to the rebellion(s) led by Korah, Dathan, and Abiram and its aftermath in Numbers 16–17³⁵; and together these texts (i.e. Numbers 16–17 and 20:1–13) create themes that frame and anchor the intervening legal material in Numbers 18–19.³⁶ Unique connections³⁷ between Numbers 16–17

---

34 Similarly Blum, who exclaims "Gerade in seinem Eifer, in dem Mose das Volk al 'Widerspenstige' zurechtweisen will und das Zeichen der בני מרי [i.e., Aaron's staff; cf. Num 17:25] in seiner Hand schwingt, ist er selbst 'widerspenstig' gegenüber Jhwh!" (*Studien zur Komposition des Pentateuch* [BZAW 189; Berlin: de Gruyter, 1990], 275). See also p. 215 n. 32 above.
35 For example, see Noth, *Numeri*, 128–129; Budd, *Numbers*, 18; Davies, *Numbers*, 203; Artus, *Etudes sur le livre des Nombres*, 228–229; Horst Seebass, *Numeri 10,11–22,1* (vol. 2. Teilband of *Numeri*; BKAT IV/2; Neukirchen-Vluyn: Neukirchener Verlag, 2003), 281.
  Knierim and Coats, however, see stronger connections to Numbers 13–14, wherein Yahweh passes judgment on the first wilderness generation, with the exception of Caleb and Joshua. From their perspective, Num 20:1–13 now extends this judgment to Moses and Aaron (*Numbers*, 226). While this connection is valid (§7.3.3 below), it ignores the clear literary connections between Num 20:1–13 and the rebellions in Numbers 16–17. For example, they read the staff vv. 8–11 as consistently Moses'—to be fair, so does Levine, who sees connections to Numbers 16–17, but insists the staff is Moses (*Numbers 1–20: A New Translation with Introduction and Commentary* [AB 4; New York: Doubleday, 1993], 489)—but this reading completely overlooks the description of the staff in v. 9 which indicates that it was Aaron's staff, not Moses' (cf. Num 17:22–26 and 20:9). In short, although Knierim and Coats rightly read Num 20:1–13 in light of Numbers 13–14 (cf. §7.3.3 below), the formation of "all the tradition from Num 13:1 through Num 20:22" is more complex than they represent (cf. Knierim and Coats, *Numbers*, 226).
36 See the arguments in Thomas W. Mann, "Holiness and Death in the Redaction of Numbers 16:1–20:13," in *Love and Death in the Ancient Near East* (ed. John Marks and Robert Good; Guilford: Four Quarters Publishing, 1987), 181–190; and more recently in Adriane Leveen, "'Lo we Perish': A Reading of Numbers 17:27–20:29," in *Torah and the Book of Numbers* (ed. Christian Frevel, Thomas Pola, and Aaron Schart; FAT2 62; Tübingen: Mohr Siebeck, 2013), 248–272.

7.3 Literary Analysis of Numbers 20:1–13 — 219

and 20:1–13 include the phrase ויקהלו על־משה ועל־אהרן, which in the Hebrew Bible only occurs in Num 16:3 and 20:2b[38]; the verbs in the people's wish for death in Num 20:3bβ (גוענו בגוע) also occur in their complaint that everyone is dying in Num 17:27–28 (גוענו ... לגוע)[39]; the staff Moses took in v. 9 had been set before Yahweh (ויקח משה את־המטה מלפני יהוה כאשר צוהו), which can only refer to Aaron's staff which Moses had obediently set before Yahweh in Num 17:22–26; Moses' invective in v. 10b begins with שמעו־נא, an imperative Moses also uses in his address to Korah and his supporters in Num 16:8[40]; and finally, Moses calls the assembly "המרים," the participial form of √מרה, from which also derives the nominative מרי, which Yahweh uses to describe the Israelites in Num 17:25 (בני־מרי).[41] Together these literary connections strongly suggest that the hand responsible for inserting Numbers 16–17 (i.e. PentRed) edited Num 20:1–11* + 13 so as to cast

---

37 The appearance of the כבוד־יהוה in Num 20:6 is a motif of P* materials across the Pentateuch —cf. Exod 16:7, 10; 24:16–17; Lev 9:6, 23; Num 14:21; 16:19; and 17:7—so while it affords a connection between Numbers 16–17 and Num 20:1–13, it does not uniquely bind the two texts. The same is applicable to קהל יהוה in Num 20:4; although this phrase elsewhere only occurs in Deut 23:2–4, 9, the Israelites are called the קהל in context of יהוה within P* materials (e.g., Exod 16:3; Lev 4:13; Num 15:15; 19:20).

38 This observation is not contingent on the length of the phrase, as though including Aaron is what limits the intertextual possibilities. Very rarely did the wilderness generation "assemble against" (על + קהל√) anyone; see Exod 32:1; Num 16:3, 19; 17:7; 20:2.

39 Two differences are immediately apparent, but trivial: in Num 20:3b, the infinitive בגוע is temporal (via the ב preposition) and directly follows the finite verb גוענו; in Num 17:27–28, the two instances of the √גוע frame the complaint, with the finite גוענו opening the complaint in v. 27 and the infinitive לגוע closing it in v. 28 by complimenting the finite verb תמנו. The significance lies in frequency of גוע√ in the Wilderness Narrative: aside from Num 17:27–28 and 20:3b, this root elsewhere appears only in Num 20:29, the death report of Aaron.

Frankel's attempt to read v. 3b as a reference to "the scouts who died in a plague 'before the Lord' (Num. 14:37)" is not convincing (*Murmuring Stories*, 292). As Nihan correctly notes, Num 14:37 does not use the verb √גוע (Nihan, *Priestly Torah to Pentateuch*, 28 n. 42). Moreover, the phrase לפני יהוה—which Frankel cites to link Num 20:3b back lexically to 14:37 (*Murmuring Stories*, 292)—is too formulaic to serve as an intertextual indicator. Instead, the *majora consensus*, against which Frankel briefly argues, is preferable: i.e., that Num 20:3b makes reference to the aftermath of the rebellions in Numbers 16–17.

40 Numbers 16:8 and 20:10b are the only times that Moses says שמעו־נא; the only other instance of שמעו־נא in the Wilderness Narrative occurs in Num 12:6, in Yahweh's rebuke to Aaron and Miriam. Frankel also notes this literary connection between Num 16:8 and 20:10b (*Murmuring Stories*, 277 n. 41).

41 In Numbers, the verb √מרה only occurs in texts associated with the P* M-Mt: Num 20:10, 24; and 27:14. It is more typical, however, of Dt/Dtr materials: Deut 1:26, 43; 9:7, 23–24; 21:18, 20; 31:27; Josh 1:18. The nominative מרי only occurs in the Pentateuch in Num 17:25 and Deut 31:27.

the P* M-Mt narrative as a continuation of the rebellion(s) against Moses and Aaron.

Although Numbers 16–17 is composite,[42] its insertion into Numbers—along with the legal material in chs. 18–19, which Numbers 16–17 and 20 frame[43]—is attributable to PentRed on two grounds: namely, 1) its proximate correspondence to PentRed's insertion into the itinerary in Numbers 33, and 2) its motif of aggrandizing Moses and Aaron. First, although the itinerary in Numbers 33 displays no awareness of these specific rebellions, PentRed's addition of eighteen stations in Num 33:18–36 (from רתמה to גבר עציון) corresponds to the material location of Numbers 16–19.[44] The Wilderness Narrative and the itinerary are largely in agreement up through station thirteen—that is, at חצר(ו)ת (cf. Num 12:16; 33:17b-18a)—but the two radically diverge at this point. The next juncture where Wilderness Narrative and the itinerary start agreeing with one another is station thirty-two—that is, at קדש in מדבר־צן (cf. Num 20:1; 33:36b-37a). In other words, the textual material in the Wilderness Narrative which the itinerary is unaware (i.e., Numbers 13–19) corresponds proximately with the stations inserted by PentRed into the itinerary (i.e., stations 14–37). Granted, the toponyms PentRed added to itinerary do not appear in Numbers 16–19 (or chs. 13–15 for that matter),[45] but in no way are the narratives and legal material in chs. 16–19

---

42 Although this study does not support Joel S. Baden's conclusion that a single compiler merged four documents to form the Pentateuch, his analysis of the strata in, and survey of recent scholarship on, Numbers 16–17 is quite helpful (*The Composition of the Pentateuch: Renewing the Documentary Hypothesis* [AYBRL; New Haven: Yale University Press, 2012], 149–168, 221).

43 For a literary reading of Num 17:27–20:29, see Leveen, "'Lo we Perish'," in Frevel, Pola, and Schart, *Torah and Numbers*, 248–272. Leveen observes that while the materials in these chapters are in possession of their "unique language, genre, and concerns," they nevertheless "poignantly come together as a whole" to "produce a richly layered reflection on the reality of death [in the wilderness], the impossibilities of keeping it at bay, and the sobering attempts of an entire people to resign themselves to that fact" ("'Lo we Perish'," in Frevel, Pola, and Schart, *Torah and Numbers*, 271). Leveen's reading is insightful from a synchronic standpoint; diachronically, however, it is significant that Num 17:27–29 not only connects Num 16:1–17:26 to the laws in Numbers 18–19, but it also helps connect Num 20:1–11* + 13 (via v. 3b; cf. p. 219 n. 39 above) to the rebellions in Numbers 16–17. Thus, Num 17:27–29 and Num 20:3b are redactional, binding Numbers 16–20, and most likely stem from the same hand, which this study identifies as PentRed (cf. pp. 219 above – 223 below).

44 See fractures 4a-c in Appendix C.

45 Recall that most of these eighteen toponyms do no occur anywhere within the Wilderness Narrative proper. The only exceptions are stations 26–29 (from מדרות to יטבתה) in Num 33:30b-34a which appear in a different order in Deut 10:6–7 (again, see fractures 4a-c in in Appendix C).

tied to any geographical location. Thus, PentRed's adding eighteen stations in Num 33:18–36 not only elevated the place where Moses died (הרי יעברים) to the fortieth station (cf. pp. 168–170, 183 above), but they also created the narrative space for inserting the Korah, Dathan, and Abiram traditions.⁴⁶

A second rationale for attributing Numbers 16–17 to PentRed is the motif of aggrandizing Moses and Aaron. Already this study has shown that Deut 33:8–10 and 34:7b, 10–12 stem from PentRed—with Deut 33:8–10 advocating Aaronide ascendancy over the Levites (cf. pp. 130–134), and Deut 34:7b, 10–12 canonizing Moses as Israel's greatest prophet (cf. pp. 116–117). Certainly the story of the rebellion(s) of Korah, Dathan, and Abiram rhetorically serve these same purposes: the ground swallows those that directly challenged Moses' leadership, and fire consumed their supporters (Num 16:28–35); a plague then afflicts the entire congregation (Num 17:1–15); and finally the budding of Aaron's staff reconfirms his selection to the priesthood (Num 17:16–27).⁴⁷ In the end, Numbers 16–17 portrays the deaths of more than 264,000 Israelites for challenging Moses and Aaron's leadership (cf. Num 16:31–35; 17:14)! No wonder the Israelites thought they were all perishing (√גוע) in Num 17:28, and no wonder Moses called them "rebels" (המרים) in Num 20:10b for wishing that they had (cf. Num 20:3bβ).

Since PentRed appears to have compiled and inserted Numbers 16–17 into the emerging Pentateuch, it stands to reason that the literary connections that anchor Num 20:1–13* back to Numbers 16–17 also stem from PentRed. This reconstruction explains why each of the unique connections that bind Num 20:1–11*+13 back to Numbers 16–17 (i.e., Num 20:2b, 3bβ, 9, 10b and פעמים in v.11a [?]⁴⁸) creates literary tension within Num 20:1–11, 13. Verse 2b is functionally re-

---

46 This observation is not to suggest that all the material in Numbers 13–19 stem from PentRed. In fact, there is evidence that suggests a Hexateuchal redactor is responsible for compiling and inserting the scouts story and its aftermath in Numbers 13–14 (cf. §7.3.3 below).
47 The interpretation of the Blessing of Levi (Deut 33:8–11) as a programmatic Aaronide text—one that seeks to absorb the Levites *in the creation of a reconciled priesthood, while at the same time maintaining Aaronide ascendancy* (cf. p. 133 above)—finds corroboration within this composite text. On the one hand, Moses decries the Levites' attempt to usurp Aaron and to claim the priesthood for themselves (Num 16:8–11); yet on the other hand, that Aaron's staff buds לבית לוי (Num 17:23) clearly indicates that Aaron himself is representative of the Levites.
48 The reason why Moses strikes the rock "twice" (פעמים) in Num 20:11a invites speculation at this juncture. W. H. Propp notes several possibilities, including that it was a gesture of futility (cf. M. Margaliot, "The Transgression of Moses and Aaron – Num. 20:1–13," *JQR* 74 [1983]: 214); that two strokes may have been necessary to "implicate" both Moses and Aaron in the sin; that there may have been two springs; or even that it may be "a glossator's note that Moses twice performs such an act in the Pentateuch" ("Rod of Aaron," 23 n. 23). To this list I would add that the two strikes may mirror that Moses and Aaron were the target of these rebellions (i.e., Num 16–17 and 20) and perhaps that even both staffs were involved in the miracle (cf.

dundant with v. 3a,[49] which it may be recalled is the only portion of Num 20:1–13 that exhibits extended verbatim correspondence with Exod 17:1–7 and is part of the מריבה coordination (*pre-Hex Supp*) (cf. pp. 185–186, 198–199 above). Verse 3bβ is not a complaint, so it does not follow well upon v. 3a; instead, vv. 4–5 relay the complaint which v. 3a says the people brought to Moses.[50] Verse 9 clarifies the staff Moses used in the miracle was the one set לפמי יהוה, which can only refer to Aaron's staff which Moses set before Yahweh in Num 17:22–26; yet Num 20:11a states that Moses struck the rock with his staff (במטהו).[51] Finally, Moses' speech to the people in v. 10b is unexpected for three reasons: first, Yahweh did not instruct Moses to speak to the people (although neither did he clearly forbid it); secondly, contrary to Moses' rhetoric, Yahweh did instruct him to bring out water from the rock (cf. v. 8b and 10b)[52]; and finally, Moses had brought forth water from a rock earlier in Exod 17:1–7.

---

p. 222 n. 51 below). The nuance of פעמים is subtle, as the two strikes are neither necessary for Aaron's involvement (it is after all Aaron's staff that the Moses is using [v. 9]), nor intrinsic to the sin of Moses and Aaron (cf. §7.3.1 above). Regardless, in the end, there is no denying Propp's initial assessment: "The reason for the 'double stroke' (*paʿāmayim*, literally) is wholly obscure" ("Rod of Aaron," 23 n. 23).

[49] The only conceptual difference between v. 2b (ויקהלו על־משה ועל־אהרן) and v. 3a (וירב העם עם־משה) is the inclusion of Aaron in v. 2b.

[50] Admittedly, v. 3a (וירב העם עם־משה) is singular and focuses on Moses alone, while vv. 4–5 shift to the plural and address both Moses and Aaron. Such a shift, however, is not unprecedented: one need only to look Exod 17:2 for a similar shift in person number.

[51] The deity does not specify which staff to take in v. 8, but v. 9 states that Moses took it מלפני יהוה just as Yahweh commanded him (כאשר צוהו). Thus, v. 8 could prepare the reader for either v. 9 or v. 11a. What makes v. 9 stand out as secondary compared to v. 11a is that there is no mechanism to explain how Aaron's staff could be reinterpreted (purposefully or accidentally) as Moses' staff. It is more difficult to posit במטהו ("with his staff," referring to Moses in v. 11a) is the product of altering some expression connoting Aaron's staff than it is to posit that v. 9 purposely reorients the narrative so that Aaron's staff becomes the primary instrument of the miracle. After all, Aaron's staff is to serve as a sign against the rebels (לאות לבני־מרי; cf. Num 17:25). From the perspective of the final text, it is difficult not to read both staffs involved in the miracle, which could possibly explain פעמים in v. 11a (cf. p. 221 n. 48 above).

[52] The fact that Moses' rhetorical question appears to contradict Yahweh's instructions at this point is difficult to resolve. A helpful comparison is Moses' rhetorical question in Num 16:11b. Moses asks the rebels, "What is he [i.e., Aaron] that you assemble against him?" Grammatically the answer one is to presume is "nothing," but that conclusion would be erroneous. The whole pericope serves to indicate Moses and Aaron's unique status among the Israelites. Rather, Moses' rhetoric reveals Yahweh to be the one against whom the assembly has gathered: to reject Moses and Aaron is to reject Yahweh's appointment of Moses and Aaron, and therefore to reject Yahweh himself (cf. Num 16:11a). It is possible to read Moses' question in Num 20:10b in a similar way.

In summary, PentRed appears to have shaped Num 20:1–11*+13, adding vv. 20:2b, 3bβ, 9, 10b (and perhaps פעמים in v.11a) in order to recast the P* M-Mt tradition so that it reads as a continuation of Numbers 16–17. Corroboration for this reading emerges on two fronts: first, when one excises these accretions from the P* M-Mt narrative, the remaining material (Num 20:1–2a, 3abα, 4–8, 10a, 11*, 13) still reads fluidly; and secondly, the narrative that remains then closely resembles the narrative in Exod 17:1bβ-7.[53] The only residual materials that do not align in any way with Exod 17:1bβ-7 are the following: the travel notice and its corresponding etiological component (Num 20:1a, 13b); Miriam's death notice (v. 1b); and the list of produce in v. 5bα (cf. §5.2.1 and Fig. 5.1 above).[54] Significantly, these remaining non-aligned portions all represent literary connections to the narrative episodes in Numbers 12–14 (cf. §7.3.3).

---

[53] For a discussion on Exod 17:1bβ-7 after the מריבה coordination (*pre-Hex Supp*), see §6.3.2 above; cf. the Meribah Coordination for Exod 17:1–7 in Appendix D with its correlative for Num 20:1–13 in Appendix E. For the effects this coordination had on the P^G M-Mt narrative, see §7.3.4 below.

[54] This observation is not asserting that all non-aligned materials (cf. §5.2.1 above) are attributable to PentRed and post-PentRed. Rather, it merely notes those components that evince no correspondence to *any* section of the Exod 17:1–7. For the sake of computation, the verbatim, approximate, and conceptual correspondences noted in Appendix B are conditioned by proximity, but there are further instances of possible approximate and conceptual correspondences that do not occur in the same proximity within their respective narratives. The clearest example is ואין מים לשתת העם in Exod 17:1bβ and ומים אין לשתות in Num 20:5bβ (cf. §3 and §6 in Appendix B). In order to substantiate this observation here, a fuller treatment of the non-aligned portions of Num 20:1–13 is therefore in order.

The non-aligned portions attributable to post-PentRed are the recasting of v. 8ay and the insertion of v. 12; the non-aligned portions attributable to PentRed are vv. 20:2b, 3bβ, 9, 10b (and perhaps פעמים in v.11a). This leaves non-aligned portions in vv. 1, 4a, 5aβ-5bα, 6ay-b; לעיניהם, להם, and ואת בעירם in 8ay-b; v. 11 (aside from פעמים); and ויקדש בם in v. 13b. The non-aligned portions that possibly evince conceptual correspondence, but do not correspond to proximity include the following: 1) vv. 4a and 5aβ are rhetorically redundant with Num 20:5aα and 4b respectively, which in turn correspond to the people's complaint in Exod 17:3b; 2) the prostration of Moses and Aaron and the כבוד־יהוה in v. 6ay-b is conceptually related to Moses crying out to Yahweh in Exod 17:4a, even though Exod 17:4a corresponds more closely with Num 20:6aαβ; 3) the words לעיניהם and להם in v. 8ay-bα have in view an audience as does Yahweh's instructions to Moses in Exod 17:5; 4) בעירם in v. 8bβ is clearly parallel to מקני in Exod 17:3; and the actions of Moses in v. 11 (aside from פעמים) correspond to the summary statement that Moses ויעש כן in Exod 17:6. In other words, the only non-aligned portions that 1) post-PentRed or PentRed did not provide, and that 2) do not show any correspondence to the Non-P narrative regardless of the proximity, are as follows: the travel notice in Num 20:1a and its corresponding etiological component in v. 13b; Miriam's death notice in v. 1b; and the list of produce in v. 5bα.

7.3.3 The Travel Notice of Num 20:1, the Scouts Story of Numbers 13–14, and the Wilderness Itinerary of Numbers 33

In chapter six, this study concluded that HexRed used an early form of the priestly itinerary in Numbers 33 as a guide to arrange and thereby merge the non-P and P wilderness materials. This merger was a dynamic process, one in which HexRed not only arranged and combined inherited wilderness materials according to the priestly *Ur*-itinerary, but one which also affected the *Ur*-itinerary itself via HexRed's annotations. It was HexRed who relocated what is now Exod 17:1bβ-7 to its current pre-Sinai location, prepending the narrative with the travel notice in 17:1abα and then leaving a corresponding annotation in Num 33:14. It is from this same hand that the travel notice in Num 20:1 stems—the same hand that likewise noted his work in Num 33:36 (cf. §6.3).

Yet Num 20:1, as it now stands, is not without its own tensions. The foremost of these tensions is the date formula, which *appears* to have suffered damage. Although it indicates what month the Israelites entered מדבר־צן—i.e., the first month (בחדש הראשון)—unlike other dates formulas within the Wilderness Narrative, Num 20:1 gives no indication of the year of the sojourn wherein this particular month took place (c.f., Exod 40:17; Num 1:1; 9:1; 10:11; 33:38; Deut 1:3). This apparent omission in the date formula of Num 20:1 has prompted many scholars to suggest, based on the date of Aaron's death (Num 33:38–39), that originally Num 20:1 may have specified the year as the fortieth year of the sojourn.[55]

This reconstruction, however, is not necessary. To begin, Num 20:1 is not the only date formula in wilderness sojourn to mention no year at all: both Exod 16:1 and 19:1 (both HexRed[56]) specify the month, but relatively date it after an event—

---

[55] Scholars have expressed this idea variously. Noth merely acknowledges this speculation (*Numeri*, 127), while both Budd and Levine simply assert that from P's perspective it must have been the fortieth year (Budd, *Numbers*, 217; Levine, *Numbers 1–20*, 488). Like Gray before them, however, E. W. Davies, Schart, and Seebass all suggest the fortieth year was deliberately omitted (George B. Gray, *A Critical and Exegetical Commentary on Numbers* [ICC; New York: Scribner's, 1903], 257–260; E. W. Davies, *Numbers*, 202–203; Aaron Schart, *Mose und Israel im Konflikt: Eine Redaktionsgeschichtliche Studie zu den Wüstenerzählungen* [OBO 98; Göttingen: Vandenhoeck & Ruprecht, 1990], 99 n. 6; Seebass, *Numeri 10,11–22,1*, 280). Frankel, however, correctly dismisses the idea that Num 20:1 once in any way indicated the fortieth year because this idea is wholly predicated on the assumption that the date formula for Aaron's death in Num 33:38–39 was original to the itinerary, which it is not (Frankel, *Murmuring Stories*, 290; cf. G. I. Davies, "The Wilderness Itineraries and the Composition of the Pentateuch," *VT* 33 [198]): 6).

[56] See stations 7 and 11 in Appendix C; cf. Exod 16:1; 19:2; Num 33:11, 15.

namely, after departure from Egypt.⁵⁷ Granted, one could argue that HexRed did not need to specify the year in these instances, since the mention of the departure from Egypt logically implies it was the first year. Nevertheless, a similar convention—i.e., noting the month relative to an event in context, rather than by a specific year—also occurs in date formulas in Joshua (cf. Josh 3:1; 4:19; 5:10).⁵⁸ Consequently, the convention HexRed employed to indicate chronology may not have included the citation of years, but instead noted the month (and perhaps day) subsequent to a major event, such as the departure from Egypt (the beginning of the sojourn), or the departure from Shittim (the end of the sojourn). Further, since in HexRed the events at Sinai represent the mid-point of the Israelite's sojourn (cf. p. 180 n. 55 above), it may not be too much to suggest that the event which antecedes בחדש הראשון in Num 20:1 is in fact the departure from Sinai (cf. Num 10:12–13* [HexRed]⁵⁹).

Two obstacles to this reading require brief attention: namely, conflicts with the calendar of the sojourn, and the material distance of Num 20:1–13 from the departure from Sinai. First, clearly Num 20:1 cannot now function according to this timeline, since it dates the episode at Kadesh to the first month, yet Num 10:11–12 records the Israelites moved on from Sinai, following the cloud of Yahweh, on the twentieth day of the second month of the second year. Yet the date formula and the cloud motif in Num 10:11–12 stands out as a secondary addition to Num 10:12a +13,⁶⁰ prior to which the date formula in what is now Num 20:1 could readily function.

The second obstacle is the material distance between Num 20:1–13* and the departure from Sinai in Num 10:12–13. Yet this study has shown that the material

---

57 The event component in the date formulas of Exod 16:1 and 19:2 are similar: after specifying the month, that month is followed by a form of the infinitive phrase מארץ מצרים + לצאת.
58 The date formulas in Josh 4:19 and 5:10 indicate the crossing of the Jordan and the first Passover observed in the Promised Land occurred during the first month on the tenth and fourteens days of that month respectively. The year relative to the exodus from Egypt or the wilderness sojourn, however, is nowhere indicated. Instead, the calendar of events appears to begin with the departure from Shittim in Josh 3:1 (מהשטים); cf. Num 33:49 (*HexSupp*); for the assignment of Num 33:49 to a Hexateuchal Supplementer, see p. 177 n. 50 above.
59 For the assignment of Num 10:12a+13 to HexRed, see p. 180 n. 54 above.
60 Both the date formula and the cloud motif in vv. 11+12b* appear to be secondary to Num 10:12a + 13. First, the date formula follows the convention of PentRed in Num 33:3aβ-4, 38b-39, while the departure notice in v. 12a has the same formula (ויסעו בני־ישראל למסעיהם) as Exod 17:1 (HexRed), and the keyword למסעיהם in Num 33:2 (HexRed) (cf. p. 180 n. 54). The travelling cloud motif is introduced into Numbers in Num 9:15–22, which along with Numbers 7, is set one month *prior* to the consensus taken in Numbers 1 (cf. Exod 40:17, 35–38; Num 1:1; 7:1; 9:1, 15–22). Thus, this motif is particularly late (provisionally post-PentRed), as its inclusion in Numbers 9 disrupts the more detailed date formulas that PentRed provides.

in Numbers 16–19 is a later insertion by PentRed—an insertion facilitated by accretions to the P* M-Mt narrative in Num 20:2b, 3bβ, 9, 10b (and possibly פעמים in v.11a). Moreover, once one removes the miscellaneous law code in Numbers 15 (which has little anchoring it to its current position in Numbers[61]), then much of the material distance between the initial departure from Sinai and the arrival at Kadesh is eliminated. The resulting narrative would largely conform to HexRed's itinerary for this passage (cf. Num 33:16–18a + 36b), prior to the insertion of PentRed's stations (Num 33:18b-36a): from מדבר סיני (10:12 ‖ 33:16a) to קברת התאוה (11:4–34 ‖ 33:16b), then to חצר(ו)ת (11:35–12:16 ‖ 33:17b), and then to מדבר־צן at קדש (20:1 ‖ 33:36b). The only narratives not accounted for are 1) the failure at תבערה (Num 11:1–3), which has no travel notice, and 2) the scouts narrative and its aftermath in מדבר־פארן (Numbers 13–14), which is qualified as being on route to Kadesh (מדבר־פארן קדשה) in Num 13:26; cf. Num 12:16b; 13:3, 21)—toponyms notably absent from itinerary in Numbers 33. Moreover, since HexRed's annotation equates מדבר־צן with קדש (Num 33:36b-37a; cf. p. 173 n. 42 above), the tension that the episode at מדבר־צן creates compared to the itinerary HexRed had inherited is not unexpected at this point. In other words, before PentRed inserted Numbers 16–19 (and edited Num 20:1–11*+13 to accommodate this insertion), the material of Num 20:1, 2a, 3abα, 4–8, 10a, 11*, 13 mostly likely followed immediately upon the scouts narrative in Numbers 13–14, and Numbers 13–14 in turn appears largely to have been compiled and inserted by HexRed.[62]

Given the possibility that HexRed had compiled and inserted chs. 13–14, and in so doing the likelihood that an early form of the P* M-Mt narrative once immediately followed upon these chapters, it should come as no surprise that

---

61 Budd observes that this legal code reasserts that Israel will indeed inherit the land (cf. Num 15:2). This theological reassurance is especially poignant given the failure of the first wilderness generation and Yahweh's judgment against them in Numbers 13–14 (Budd, *Numbers*, 167; see also, E. W. Davies, *Numbers*, 149). For a recent discussion of the lateness of the legal materials into Numbers—especially Numbers 18 but also Numbers 15—see Christophe Nihan, "The Priestly Laws of Numbers, the Holiness Legislation, and the Pentateuch," in *Torah and the Book of Numbers* (ed. Christian Frevel, Thomas Pola, and Aaron Schart; FAT2 62; Tübingen: Mohr Siebeck, 2013) 109–137.
62 That a similar arrangement of events appears in Deut 1:19–46 corroborates this reconstruction, which admittedly warrants fuller study than can be attempted here. Rudolph and McEvenue arrive at similar conclusions as this study, though by different means, conclusions which Artus finds plausible (cf. Wilhelm Rudolph, *Der 'Elohist' von Exodus bis Joshua* [BZAW 68; Berlin: Töpelmann, 1938], 84; Sean E. McEvenue, *The Narrative Style of the Priestly Author* [AnBib 50; Rome: Biblical Institute Press, 1971], 93; Artus, *Etudes sur le livre des Nombres*, 220). For detailed treatments of the composite nature of Numbers 13–14, see E. W. Davies, *Numbers*, 127–149 and Frankel, *Murmuring Stories*, 119–201.

HexRed would provide accretions within Num 20:1–2a, 3abα, 4–8, 10a, 11*, 13 in order to bind these narratives together. Three such accretions are demonstrable. First, HexRed's supplement to the narrative's travel notice in v. 1aαβ (ויבאו בני־ישראל כל־העדה מדבר־צן בחדש הראשון) contains the station HexRed had inherited in the itinerary (i.e., מדבר־צן in Num 33:36bα) and a date formula similar in form to those HexRed has used elsewhere.[63] The fact that only קדש plays an etiological role in the narrative (cf. v. 13), not מדבר־צן, further suggests v. 1aαβ to be secondary. The second accretion, however, is most likely v. 1b: the death notice of Miriam. This notice in 20:1b and the death of Aaron in 20:22–29* not only frame the events at קדש (cf. 20:1b, 16, 22), but they also close a frame around the scouts story and its aftermath (Numbers 13–14), a frame opened by Miriam and Aaron's rebellion against Moses in Numbers 12.[64] In other words, Num 20:1b may not be as extrinsic as many scholars presume.[65] The third and final accretion is the list of produce in v. 5bα, which exhibits clear connections with Num 13:23. Granted, the individual words grain (זרע), figs (תאנה), vines (גפן), and pomegranates (רמון) occur elsewhere in the Hexateuch, and as a precise constellation they only appear together in Num 20:5bα. Nevertheless, aside from Num 20:5bα, the only texts which evince a significant overlap of these items of produce are Num 13:23 and Deut 8:8—texts pertaining the fertility of the Promised Land.[66] Thus,

---

[63] See p. 173 n. 42. Also, since the region which the scouts explored was from ממדבר־צן עד־רחב לבא חמת (Num 13:21b), and they returned to the main camp at מדבר־פארן "toward" or "near" קדש (literally, וילכו ויבאו ... אל־מדבר פארן קדשה) in Num 13:26, it is logical that the next station where HexRed would have Israel bivouac is "מדבר־צן ... בקדש" in Num 20:1 (cf. Num 33:36b).
[64] Artus also sees a connection between Numbers 12 and the death reports of Miriam and Aaron in Numbers 20, but he argues that Num 20:1αβ-b (וישב העם בקדש ותמת שם מרים ויקבר שם) is a "fragment de texte ancient intégré par un auteur sacerdotal dans l'introduction de son récit" (Artus, *Etudes sur le livre des Nombres*, 221). The reason Artus provides for reading v. 1αβ-b as a single fragment—the succession of three *wayyiqol* verbs—is not convincing. Verse 1αβ (וישב העם בקדש), as Artus also notes, facilitates in pun-like fashion the closure of the narrative, but in this way it also serves a etiological function for the narrative, explaining the toponym via the story of how Yahweh was sanctified at that location. In short, v. 1αβ is intrinsic to the episode.
[65] For a succinct survey, see Artus, *Etudes sur le livre des Nombres*, 221 n. 68.
[66] Deuteronomy 8:8 (*Dt*; cf. Table 3.3 on p. 78 above) preserves the Deuteronomic ideal portrait of the fertility of the promised land, which no doubt would have conditioned the expectations of later tradents regarding the resources one would find in the land. Here in Deut 8:8, among other resources that include water (cf. Deut 8:7–9; cf. Num 20:5bβ), one finds listed תאנה, רמון, and גפן, but not specifically זרע; though one may read "wheat and barley" (חמה ושערה) as conceptually related. In Num 13:23, the scouts return from spying out the land, bearing evidence of the land's fertility. Here in Num 13:23 is the only other place in the Hexateuch—aside from Num 20:5 and Deut 8:8—where one finds תאנה and רמון listed together. Admittedly missing from

the only text which could serve as the narrative antecedent of the Israelite's expectation in Num 20:5bα is Num 13:23.

None of these accretions (i.e., vv. 1aαβ, 1b, 5bα) relate intrinsically to the foundational narrative of Num 20:1–13, which like its Non-P correlative in Exod 17:1–7 concerns water deprivation in the wilderness (see Appendix E). Instead, vv. 1aαβ, 1b, and 5bα only serve to anchor the P* M-Mt narrative back to episodes located in Numbers 12–14. It is, therefore, understandable when scholars like Frankel, Knierim, and Coats particularly read Num 20:1–13 as building primarily upon these episodes,[67] for at one time it most likely did. Thus, in compiling the Non-P and P wilderness traditions, HexRed framed the stay at Sinai-Horeb with episodes of wilderness deprivation, challenges of leadership, and conflict with the Amalekites (cf. Exod 15:22–18:26; Numbers 11–14 + 20:1–13*).[68]

In the end, HexRed's work results in a fluid series of narratives. With but a few innocuous accretions, he brilliantly transformed the P* M-Mt narrative from a complaint over water deprivation into the first expression of the community coping with the loss of their dream. They had seen the bounty of the idyllic Promised Land, but by their own obstinacy they and their leaders would not inherit it; for all but Caleb, Joshua, and their children, the journey was for naught. Yahweh had forgiven them (cf. Num 14:20), so he graciously provides water for them and their cattle, but their fate is sealed. All that remains for them is to live and die in the wilderness (cf. Num 14:20–45*; 20:1b, 22–29; 33:38; Deut 32:48–52*; 34:5).

Num 13:23 is any produce to correspond with זרע, but גפן conceptually relates to the "cluster of grape" (אשכול ענבים) with which the scouts also returned, and which serves as the prompt for the etiological toponym Wadi Eschol (נחל אשכול) in Num 13:24.

[67] See Frankel's argument that Num 20:3b (ולו גוענו בגוע אחינו לפני יהוה) refers to the plague that struck the scouts in Num 14:37 as opposed to the people's outcry in Num 17:27–28 (*Murmuring Stories*, 292; cf. p. 219 n. 39 above for a critique of this position). Likewise, Knierim and Coats argue that "the context for this text [i.e., Num 20:1–13] lies not so much in the legal material in Numbers 17–19, not even in the literary sources in Numbers 16 (J/P) which are harmonious with this story, but rather in Numbers 13–14" (*Numbers*, 226; cf. p. 218 n. 35 for a critique of this position).

[68] Although this study is certainly not derivative of Schart's, see Schart's similar conclusions regarding the concentric arrangement of this material around Sinai (*Mose und Israel*, 49–57).

7.3.4 The מריבה Coordination of Num 20:3–5*+13a and Exod 17:2–7*

This study argues in chapter six that prior to HexRed merging the non-P and P wilderness traditions, the two M-Mt narrative traditions had undergone coordination within their separate literary corpora (cf. §6.3.2 and §6.4). While this editorial process remains to be seen for other wilderness traditions, corroboration of this hypothesis emerges on two fronts. First, all the components of this coordination remain extant at a pre-Hexateuch stage of the P* M-Mt narrative. After removing the alterations / accretions from Num 20:1–13 provided by post-PentRed (vv. 8aγ, 12), PentRed (vv. 2b, 3bβ, 9, 10b), and HexRed (vv. 1aαβ, 1b, 5bα), the remaining textual material is Num 20:1aγ, 2a, 3abα, 4–5a, 5bβ-8*, 10a, 11*, 13. This material reads fairly fluidly as a "preofficial complaint"—in which one party persuades another of the validity of its complaint without arbitration[69]— lodged against Moses and Aaron regarding the lack of water (cf. *The Meribah Coordination* in Appendix E). Yet within this residual complaint narrative lie all the components involved in coordinating the two M-Mt narratives (i.e. vv. 3aα, 4b-5aα, 5bβ, 13a)—components that all bear striking verbal correspondence to the Meribah accretions in Exod 17:1bβ-7 (cf. Fig. 7.1 The מריבה Coordination below). As already noted, the phrase וירב העם עם־משה is the only extended verbatim correspondence between these narratives (17:2aα ‖ 20:3aα; see letter A in Fig. 7.1 below). The infinitive clauses (17:3bβ ‖ 20:4b) display approximate verbal and conceptual correspondences and occur in transposed order with the questions למה העליתנו ממצרים (17:3bα ‖ 20:5aα), which aside from an opening *waw*-conjunction in v. 5aα are consonantly identical (see letter B). The central crisis that opens the non-P M-Mt narrative closes the series of coordinating components in Num 20:2–3 (17:1bβ ‖ 20:5bβ), and these clauses display approximate verbal correspondence (see letter C). Finally, the Meribah supplements to both etiologies (17:7aʸ-bα ‖ 20:13a) also display approximate verbal correspondence (see letter D). In short, these coordinating components account for the highest degrees of verbal correspondence between the two M-Mt narratives, and they were all extant in their respective narratives prior to HexRed.

A second front further corroborates this reconstruction: namely, that the coordinating components in Num 20:3–5, 13 all appear secondary to the residual material. The infinitive clause in v. 4b and the question in v. 5aα are the clearest

---

[69] In which case, Moses and Aaron agree that the people's complaint is legitimate. Moses and Aaron therefore approach the deity for provision, not for arbitration. For a discussion of this form, see pp. 192–195 above, especially nn. 94 and 103. Admittedly, this reconstruction requires a relative particle (באשר [?]) in order to join the infinitive clause in Num 20:5aβ to the coordinating component in v. 5bβ.

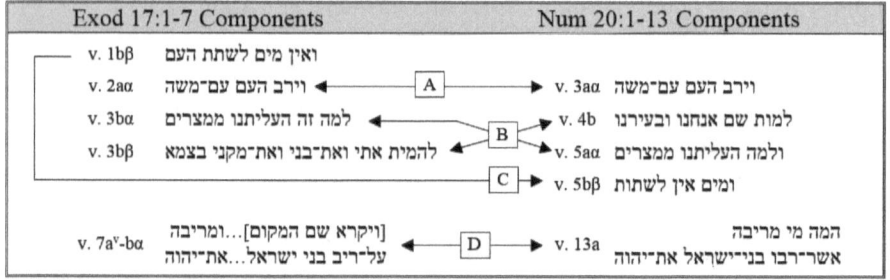

Fig. 7.1: The מריבה Coordination

examples, as both components have functional duplicates within the residual narrative: v. 5aα (ולמה העליתנו ממצרים) rhetorically asks the same question as v. 4a (ולמה הבאתם את־קהל יהוה אל־המדבר הזה); likewise, the infinitive in v. 4b (למות שם אנחנו ובעירנו), which concludes the question of v. 4a, has a grammatical duplicate in v. 5aβ (להביא אתנו אל־המקום הרע הזה). Removing both coordinating components (which are contiguous, so vv. 4b-5aα) therefore results in a single residual question that is both quite intelligible and exhibits its own parallelism: להביא אתנו אל־המקום הרע הזה ‖ למה הבאתם את־קהל יהוה אל־המדבר הזה (vv. 4a + 5aβ).

Granted, the coordinating components in vv. 3aα and 13a do not create such overt redundancies; nevertheless, they do not stand as intrinsic to the residual narrative. Verse 3aα only qualifies the residual question above (vv. 4a + 5aβ) as the initiation of a preofficial complaint; it does not create the primary crisis, which is solely the issue of water deprivation. Instead, the residual v. 2a (ולא־היה מים לעדה)—which in turn renders the coordinating v. 5bβ redundant—iterates this crisis. In other words, one could excise v. 3aα, and the crisis v. 2a introduces would readily lead into the speech formula (ויאמרו לאמר; cf. v. 3aβ) and then into the congregation's residual question (v. 4a + 5aβ). Finally, while v. 13a does not create an overt redundancy, it is to an extent functionally redundant with v. 13b (ויקדש בם), which already provides a nascent etiological explanation for the toponym קדש in the residual v. 1ay (וישב העם בקדש).

In summary, just as the Meribah components in the non-P M-Mt narrative are secondary and build on the preexisting, yet still developing etiology of מסה, so also the Meribah components in P* M-Mt (i.e., vv. 3aα, 4b, 5aα, 5bβ, 13a) build upon a preexisting, yet still developing etiology of קדש.[70] Thus, in the end, the

---

[70] Admittedly, many scholars assign v. 1ay as non-P material, based on the designation העם for the Israelites; e.g. Noth, *Numeri*, 127–128; George W. Coats, *Rebellion in the Wilderness: The Murmuring Motif in the Wilderness Traditions of the Old Testament* (Nashville: Abingdon, 1968), 72–73; Levine, *Numbers 1–20*, 487; Artus, *Etudes sur le livre des Nombres*, 219;

residual narrative lying in the background of this *pre-Hexateuchal Supplemental* coordination is Num 20:1aγ, 2a, 3aβ, 4a, 5aβ, 6–8*, 10a, 11*, 13b—the P^G episode of קדש (cf. Appendix E).

7.3.5 The Formation of the קדש Episode of Num 20:1–11*+13b in Light of Exod 17:2–7's Formative Stages

So far, like its non-P counterpart, the literary development of the P* M-Mt narrative has unfolded through a process of *Fortschreibung*. Yet the history of Num 20:1–13's development has proven to be more dynamic, as well as more protracted. Each stage of literary growth transpired incrementally as its literary horizons increased through time—from an awareness of a separate, yet genetically related non-P tradition, through the many stages that culminated in the Pentateuch's final form.

The question that emerges now is "Did the P^G קדש episode have an even earlier literary history, or was it written whole-cloth as Num 20:1aγ, 2a, 3aβ, 4a, 5aβ, 6–8*, 10a, 11*, 13b?" If Deuteronomy and the literary history of Exod 17:1–7 is any indicator, then the likelihood of the P^G קדש episode having an earlier literary history must be entertained. The first written stage of M-Mt, as preserved in Deut 8:15 and evidenced by the foundational stratum of Exod 17:1–7, was a positive tradition in which the people thirst for water in the wilderness, Moses intercedes, and Yahweh provides. Yet the P^G קדש episode, like the non-P מסה episode, is not necessarily a positive tradition. In the מסה episode, the people make demands that Moses in turn interprets as testing Yahweh; in the same vein, the people in the P^G קדש episode demand to know why Moses and Aaron brought them into the wilderness where there is no water, and only after Moses intercedes does Yahweh provide and is proved holy among them.[71] In the end, these corre-

---

Schmidt, *Numeri*, 88, 91. Nevertheless, in the wake of revisionist studies (cf. §1.3.2), the profiling of such a non-technical term can carry little weight in diachronic analysis. After all, there is nothing to preclude a priestly tradent from occasionally employing this ubiquitous word. Specht agrees, and although I cannot agree with Specht's conclusion that "Num 20,1–13 hat sich als eine in sich kohärente Erzählung erweisen," his critique against assuming that P did not use עם is worth noting: "'Volk' עם ist trotz einiger Infragestellungen bei P durchaus zu finden, und zwar an prägnante Stellen wie in 'Ex 6,7 und Lev 9,22–27', so Schart, *Mose und Israel*, 112 [...] man kann den Stil nicht mögen, sprachstatistich kann mann 'Volk' P nicht absprechen" (Herbert Specht, "Die Verfehlung Moses und Aaron in Num 20,1–13* P," in *Torah and the Book of Numbers* [ed. Christian Frevel, Thomas Pola, and Aaron Schart; FAT2 62; Tübingen: Mohr Siebeck, 2013], 284 n. 29, 311).

71 Cf. *The Massah Episode* in Appendix D with *The Kadesh Episode* in Appendix E.

lations permit speculation as to whether behind the P^G קדש episode may also lie a positive foundational narrative.

Such an inquiry produces yet another correlation between these narratives: the negative components in both stories are at the periphery of the textual material. In the non-P / Dtr–Dtr Supp narrative, the extraction of Exod 17:1bβ and the מסה etiological components in vv. 2 and 7 produced a positive foundational narrative resembling the tradition in Deut 8:15–16 (*Dt*). Likewise, excising the etiological components (i.e. Num 20:1aγ, 13b) and the people's caustic question (vv. 3aβ +4a +5aβ)—components all located at the periphery of the P^G material—produces a foundational narrative core that corresponds with the expected positive tradition (cf. Appendix E). Thus, while less demonstrable than its later developments, a positive foundation narrative (vv. 2a, 6–8*, 10a, 11* [*early-P*]) likely lies behind P^G's קדש episode.

7.4 Toward a Synthesis: The Literary History of Numbers 20:1–13 and its Relationship to Exodus 17:1–7 and Deuteronomy's M-Mt Tradition-historical Framework

The above literary analyses (§7.3) suggest that the P* M-Mt narrative in Num 20:1–13 developed over the course of at least six stages of literary growth (cf. Appendix E: The P* M-Mt Narrative by Stages of Literary Development). Similar to the literary history of the non-P M-Mt narrative in Exod 17:1–7, the formation of the P* M-Mt narrative transpired through a process of *Fortschreibung*, in which Num 20:1–13 grew via incremental accretions as additional texts entered its broader literary context. Unlike its non-P correlative, these accretions occasioned in places a more thorough rewriting of the literary tradition; e.g., revising והכית את to ודברתם אל in v. 8aγ (*Stage 6*). The exact extent and textual parameters of each stage of development must therefore remain malleable. Nevertheless, at the risk of appearing overly precise, the following stages not only limn the development the P* M-Mt, they also explain the internal tensions within Num 20:1–13 and account for the four dynamics which characterize the relationship of the two M-Mt narratives: i.e. *congruity, incongruity, shared literary tension,* and *connectivity*.

Stage 1: The earliest detectable written stage of the P* M-Mt narrative no doubt emerged from the same oral tradition as did the non-P M-Mt narrative, and much like its Deuteronomic counterpart, the priestly foundational narrative was most likely a positive tradition (vv. 2a + 6–8* + 10a + 11* [*early P*]) in which the people thirst for water, Moses (and Aaron) intercedes for them, and then Yahweh provides water from a rock by having Moses strike it with his staff. The Israelites are not culpable of any cultic failure in this primitive episode (cf. Deut 8:15–16); instead, the focus is on the crisis and its miraculous resolution. Although derivative of the same oral tradition, this narrative is not materially related to the non-P narrative or within the purview of the Deuteronomic tradents. This shared oral origin, yet independent transcription, accounts for the M-Mt narratives' *congruity* at the approximate verbal and conceptual levels, as the framework of the tradition found expression via certain common (e. g., מים, מטה, יד, √לקח, √נכה, √יצא, √שתה) and distinct, yet synonymous terms (e. g., סלע for צור).

Stage 2: The formation of an early קדש etiology and the congregation's question (vv. 1aγ + 4a* + 5aβ + 13b [P^G]) reoriented the positive tradition into a negative episode in which the congregation in effect murmurs[72] against its leaders and, by implication of the etiology (ויקדש [יהוה] בם), against Yahweh. This development occurred independently of, yet parallel to, a similar development within the non-P M-Mt narrative, which likewise saw the emergence of the early etiology (i. e., מסה) and the reorientation toward a negative tradition (Exod 17:2, 7; cf. Deut 6:16; 9:22). This similarity becomes more pronounced when one considers that the people's demand in Exod 17:2 is directed toward Moses and a second party (presumably Yahweh), yet Moses' retort and the etiology underscore Yahweh as the true target of the people's aggression (cf. Exod 17:2, 7). A final similarity is that these developments represent peripheral expansions to their respective narrative cores—in other words, at this stage the literary growth of both texts was centrifugal in nature. In the end, despite the *incongruity* of the distinctive etiologies, the M-Mt narratives were still sufficiently recognizable as variants of the same tradition.

Stage 3: This stage of Num 20:1–13's literary growth represents the first of its four *post-P* developments. With the addition of the מריבה etiology and duplicate murmuring components (vv. 3a + 4b + 5bβ* + 13a [*pre-Hex Supp*]), this stage transformed the P^G קדש episode into a story that later texts would variously refer to as the מי מריבה (cf. Deut 33:8; Ps 81:8; 106:32), the מי מריבת קדש (cf. Num 27:14; Deut 32:51; Ezek 48:28), or in one instance מי מריבות קדש (Ezek 47:19). These insertions mirror those that entered Exod 17:1–7 at the same time and represent an attempt to coordinate the two literary versions of the M-Mt. This coordination—which occurred after the development of each text's primary etiology, but prior to the merger of the non-P and P corpora—effectively recast the M-Mt narratives as literary versions of the same successfully levied preofficial, informal ריב. In the end, this stage not only accounts for the strong verbal

---

[72] That Num 20:1–13, even in its final form, does not have the verb √לון, yet has multiple murmuring questions (cf. vv. 4–5a) is striking. Provisionally, it suggests this component of the murmuring motif entered the P* M-Mt at an early stage of this motif's development.

contiguity between the M-Mt narratives, but since the same hand (*pre-Hex Supp*) was responsible for both, it also explains their *shared internal tensions*.

Stage 4: In chapter six, this study argues that HexRed 1) transposed the מסה-מריבה episode (Exod 17:1bβ-7*) into its current pre-Sinai position at רפידים, 2) joined it thematically and lexically to other deprivation stories (Exod 15:22–16:36), and then 3) documented this work in the priestly itinerary (cf. Num 33:14bβ). This chapter has shown HexRed to be responsible for similar redactional procedures in the P* M-Mt narrative. In merging the non-P and P wilderness corpora, HexRed 1) situated the קדש episode (Num 20:1–11* + 13) in a post-Sinai position in מדבר-צן; 2) joined it thematically and lexically to the block of episodes in Numbers 12–14, thereby framing this block with the deprivation episodes in Num 11:4–35 and Num 20:1–11* + 13; and then 3) recorded this editorial activity in the priestly itinerary (Num 33:36bβ). Thus, with the emergence of the Hexateuch, the P* M-Mt narrative acquired vv. 1aαβ + 1b + 5bα (*HexRed*) and by these accretions achieved *connectivity* with Numbers 12–14.

In the end, this arrangement artistically elevated the scouts story and its aftermath (Numbers 13–14) as the devastating anti-climax of the first wilderness generation's sojourn. Aside from Joshua and Caleb, the whole first generation would die in the wilderness—even Moses, with whom Yahweh was angry on the people's account (cf. Deut 1:19–3:29), would die in the wilderness—and it is here in Num 20:1–11* + 13 that the people struggle to come to terms with this fate. Though Yahweh provides water for the congregation, this act of provision testifies to his forgiveness and faithfulness; the divine punishment would irrevocably stand (cf. Num 14:20).

Stage 5: The penultimate stage of the P* M-Mt's literary development took place at the hands of PentRed, who inserted vv. 2b, 3bβ, 9 and 10b (and possibly פעמים in v. 11aβ). These accretions recast Num 20:1–11* + 13 as a story of rebellion against Moses and Aaron, affording the *connectivity* with (and continuation of) the rebellion(s) in Numbers 16–17, which also were compiled and inserted by PentRed. In this *independent development*, the role of Aaron's staff becomes seminal, and the insertion of v. 9—which clarifies the staff Moses used for the miracle was Aaron's (if not also his own)—may well have prompted the gloss-like relative clause in Exod 17:5bα[li-vi], which in turn disambiguates the staff used in Exod 17:1bβ-7 as Moses'.

Rhetorically, the force of these accretions in light of Numbers 16–17 aggrandizes Moses and Aaron, and it is at this stage for the first time that Deuteronomy reflects concrete awareness of the P* M-Mt in Deut 33:8 (PentRed). Since this stage is prior to the innovation of Moses and Aaron's sin (Stage 6), PentRed can cite both M-Mt narratives as examples of Aaron's devout service despite challenges to his divine appointment to the priesthood. Likewise, Moses' rhetorical question in v. 10b not only reveals Yahweh as the one against whom the people are truly rebelling, it also tacitly reaffirms Moses and Aaron as the people's divinely appointed leaders. At this stage, the question expresses no lack of faith on the part of Moses and Aaron.

Stage 6: The final stage of Num 20:1–13's literary development is the innovative creation of Moses and Aaron's sin by modifying v. 8aγ + adding v. 12 (*post-PentRed*). For the first time this accretion connects the deaths of Aaron and Moses to the M-Mt. Prior to this independent development, their deaths outside the land were predicated on the first wilderness generation's refusal to take the land and Yahweh's subsequent, if not misdirected anger. Now Moses and Aaron's punishment mirrors the people's, because in a moment of situational irony, they too have acted faithlessly toward and rebelled against Yahweh (cf. Num 20:24; 27:14; Deut 9:23). In the end, this final stage in the literary history of Num 20:1–13 corresponds to the final stage of the framework of the M-Mt's tradition-historical development preserved in Deuteronomy (cf. Deut 32:51 [*post-PentRed*]).

Again, this reconstruction is quite ambitious; yet the fact that the first five stages of Num 20:1–13's literary development corresponds to the five stages of Exod 17:1–7's literary development corroborates this reconstruction of Num 20:1–13' literary development. From the start, Num 20:1–13 emerged as a distinct literary transcription of the same positive oral tradition upon which Exod 17:1–7 was founded (Stage 1 [*Dt* ∥ *early P*]). The two M-Mt narratives underwent simultaneous independent development, by which they not only acquired their distinctive foundational etiologies, but also took on components which cast Israel in a negative light (Stage 2 [*Dtr–Dtr Supp* ∥ P^G]). Despite their distinct etiologies, scribes understood the two M-Mt narratives as slightly different versions of the same story, so the two versions then underwent coordination within their respective corpora (Stage 3 [*pre-Hex Supp*]). When these corpora were merged in the formation of the Hexateuch, both versions were edited and arranged in relation to materials that are now within their respective broader literary contexts: Exod 15:22–16:36 for Exod 17:1–7 and Numbers 12–14 for Num 20:1–13 (Stage 4 [*HexRed*]). This process continued when Numbers 16–17 entered the literary horizon of Num 20:1–13, resulting in the disambiguation of the staffs used within each text (Stage 5 [*PentRed*]). Only the final stage of Num 20:1–13's literary development is completely non-aligned—i.e, the failure of Moses and Aaron (Stage 6 [*post-PentRed*]—as the P* M-Mt continued to develop even after the non-P M-Mt had stabilized. Yet even this late stage of the M-Mt's tradition-historical development is reflected in the framework of the M-Mt's development detected in Deuteronomy (cf. Deut 32:51). It is to this framework and its implications for future studies that this study now turns.

Chapter Eight: Conclusion

8.1 Summary and Implications of the Current Study

In his 1974 commentary, *The Book of Exodus*, Brevard S. Childs avers that the "variety in the Old Testament's use of the Meribah tradition" is such "that one can suspect a complex history of tradition," but "the evidence for tracing this development is no longer available."[1] Childs is correct as it pertains to the diversity of the M-Mt within the Hebrew Bible and its rich, complex history of development. His assertion that no evidence remains whereby to reconstruct the M-Mt's *Traditionsgeschichte*, however, must be reconsidered. The distribution of the Deuteronomy's six M-Mt reminiscences (i.e., Deut 6:16; 8:15; 9:22; 32:13, 51; and 33:8) across its macro- and micro-redactional strata affords a diachronic framework whereby to reconstruct the major stages of the M-Mt tradition-historical development; that is, at least from the perspective of Deuteronomy's tradents.

At its earliest stage, the M-Mt began as a positive tradition about Yahweh's faithfulness in the wilderness: the experience of deprivation in the wilderness was a divine test, one which the wilderness generation passed, and Yahweh in turn miraculously provided water from a rock (Deut 8:15; 32:13 [Dt]). The second and third stages of the M-Mt's tradition-historical development witnessed radical changes: not only did the M-Mt acquire a primitive toponymic etiology, but it also acquired components which recast the Israelites' role in the tradition negatively (Deut 6:16 [Dtr]; 9:22 [Dtr Supp]). Thus, at this point in M-Mt's development, Yahweh provides water despite the Israelites' faithlessness in the wilderness. The idyllic "honeymoon" period in the wilderness was over (cf. Hos 9:10; Jer 2:5–6, 21a); in fact, it never happened at all (Deut 9:7, 22–24).

Throughout these first three stages, the proprietors of Deuteronomy show no awareness of the P* M-Mt. Instead, they are only aware of the non-P M-Mt as reflected in the early stages of Exod 17:1bβ-7's literary development, when it was joined with the post-Horeb non-P traditions in what is now Numbers 11 (cf. Deut 9:22). Only at the fourth stage in Deut 33:8 (PentRed) does Deuteronomy evince awareness of both the non-P and P* M-Mt narratives. Yet the reminiscence in Deut 33:8 suggests that the non-P M-Mt (and most likely the P* M-Mt) had undergone intermediate stages of development—that is, between the third and

---

[1] Brevard S. Childs, *The Book of Exodus: A Critical, Theological Commentary* (OTL; Louisville: Westminster, 1974), 306.

fourth stages—that are not directly represented in Deuteronomy. Specifically, Deut 33:8 cites the M-Mt narratives as parallel, yet distinct texts that approximate the span of Aaron's faithful service in the wilderness. This perspective could only result from the two M-Mt narratives having been compared and harmonized, and then subsequently anchored into their respective positions within the emerging Pentateuch. In other words, Deut 33:8 presumes both the coordination of the non-P and P* M-Mt (*pre-Hex Supp*) and the merger of the corpora in which they once had independent existence (*HexRed*).

Similar to Deut 33:8, the reminiscence in Deut 32:51 also demonstrates awareness of the P* M-Mt narrative, but this reminiscence stands out as even later than Deut 33:8. Deuteronomy 33:8 aggrandizes Aaron and the Aaronide priesthood; it therefore demonstrates no awareness of Moses and Aaron's sin in the final form of the P* M-Mt narrative. Only Deut 32:51 (*post-PentRed*) demonstrates awareness of this late development of the P* M-Mt, and by so doing constitutes the fifth and final stage of the M-Mt's tradition history to which Deuteronomy bears witness.

In short, Deuteronomy preserves five stages of the M-Mt tradition-historical development, as illustrated in Fig. 8.1 below:

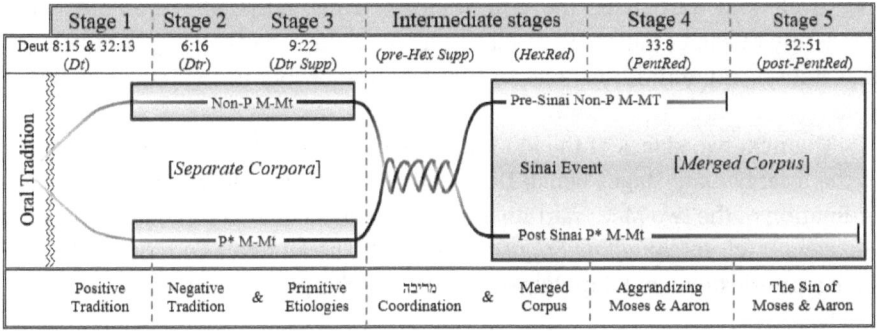

Fig. 8.1: The Framework of the M-Mt's Tradition-historical Development

The *first stage* is the positive non-P tradition (*Dt*); the *second* and *third stages* recast that tradition as an episode of national failure and concretize the מסה etiology (*Dtr–Dtr Supp*); the *fourth stage* occurs much later and is aware of both the non-P and P* M-Mt narratives in their respective places in the Pentateuch (*PentRed*), but the fourth stage is not yet aware of Moses and Aaron's sin; the *fifth stage* witnesses the addition of Moses and Aaron's sin to the P* M-Mt narrative. In the end, these stages represent the witness of Deuteronomy's textual proprietors to the M-Mt's tradition-historical development through time—the progression of which can also be detected in the literary history of the two M-Mt narratives in Exod 17:1–7 and Num 20:1–13.

To begin, the foundational narratives detectable in both M-Mt narratives resemble the positive tradition preserved in the reminiscence of Deut 8:15 and 32:13 (cf. *Stage 1* in Fig. 8.1 above). In the foundational narrative of Exod 17:1–7, the people thirst for water, Moses intercedes, and Yahweh provides.[2] The same crisis and resolution is also in the foundational narrative of Num 20:1–13.[3] These foundational narratives derive from the same oral tradition, as the parallel tradition components relayed with distinctive language indicate. Yet they also emerged independently of each other in the context of separate non-P and P corpora, as the limited purview of Deuteronomy's early textual tradents—signified by their awareness of the non-P corpus alone—would also indicate.

The second stages of Exod 17:1–7's and Num 20:1–13's literary development also transpired independently of each other, yet they correspond lexically and/or functionally to the developments of M-Mt preserved in Deut 6:16 and 9:22 (cf. *Stages 2–3* in Fig. 8.1. above). The accretions that entered Exod 17:1–7 during its second stage of literary growth recast the Israelites' role in the M-Mt negatively and provided the non-P narrative with its מסה etiological components.[4] Similarly, the second stage of Num 20:1–13's literary growth portrayed the people negatively and introduced the קדש etiology.[5] Thus, although developing independently of each other, both M-Mt narratives reflect the same types of changes that the second and third stages of the M-Mt framework in Deuteronomy anticipate.

The next two stages of the M-Mt narratives' literary development correspond to the intermediate stages which Deut 33:8 (*PentRed*) logically presumes: i.e. coordination of the two M-Mt narratives and their subsequent entry into a compiled Hexateuch (cf. *Intermediate Stages* in Fig. 8.1). The Meribah Coordination stems from a pre-Hexateuchal Supplementer (pre-Hex Supp), who compared the two M-

---

[2] The foundational narrative in Exod 17:1–7 is preserved in vv. 3aα + 4aα + 5a-5bα^i + 5bα^{vii}-6 (*Dt*). See Appendix D for a representation of each of Exod 17:1–7's literary stages.
[3] The foundational narrative in Num 20:1–13 is preserved in vv. 20:2a + 6–8* (with והכית את in v. 8 instead of ודברתם אל) + 10a + 11* (minus פעמים in v. 11) (*early-P*). See Appendix E for a representation of each of Num 20:1–13's literary stages.
[4] These accretions are vv. 1bβ + 2aβ-bα + 2bγ + 7a^{i-iv} + 7bβ-γ (*Dtr–Dtr Supp*). When added to the foundational narrative (cf. p. 238 n. 2 above), the resulting textual material approximating this Massah Episode is Exod 17:1bβ + 2aβ-bα + 2bγ + 3aα + 4aα + 5a-5bα^i + 5bα^{vii}-6 + 7a^{i-iv} + 7bβ-γ (cf. Appendix D).
[5] These accretions are vv. 1aγ + 4a* + 5aβ + 13b (P^G). When added to the foundation narrative (cf. p. 238 n. 3 above), the resulting textual material approximating the P^G Kadesh Episode subsequent is Num 20:1aγ + 2a + 4a* + 5aβ + 6–8* + 10a + 11* + 13b (cf. Appendix E).

Mt narratives within their respective non-P and P collections, recognized them as variant expressions of the same tradition, and then coordinated them as successfully levied preofficial complaints.[6] Without this coordination, the M-Mt narratives would have been the מסה and קדש narratives, with little verbal correspondence, and so Deut 33:8 would most likely not have recalled the M-Mt narratives as parallels within a merged corpus.

The merger of the non-P and P corpora into the Hexateuch occasioned changes to both M-Mt narratives, especially to their travel notices, but it also prompted changes in relation to their newly acquired broader literary contexts. The Hexateuchal Redactor (HexRed) transposed Exod 17:1bβ-7* to a pre-Sinai / Horeb location, and in so doing anchored it in the Wilderness Narrative with the travel notice.[7] This transposition transformed the non-P M-Mt into the climax of a series of pre-Sinai deprivation episodes (Exod 15:22–16:36)—episodes compiled on account of their similar motifs and the catchwords √נסע and √לון. Likewise, HexRed anchored Num 20:1ay-11*+13 with accretions that clarify the pre-existing travel notice and that connect the narrative to the scouts story, which at this time immediately preceded it in Numbers 13–14.[8]

The fifth stage of the M-Mt narratives' literary growth aligns with the penultimate stage of the M-Mt tradition-historical framework detected in Deut 33:8 (cf. *Stage 4* in Fig. 8.1 above). As part of the Blessing of Levi, Deut 33:8 not only demonstrates awareness of traditions across the Pentateuch, it also aggrandizes Aaron in the same way that Deut 34:7, 10–12 does Moses. This agenda to aggrandize Moses and Aaron is detectable in the rebellions of Korah, Dathan, and Abiram and its aftermath, which the Pentateuchal Redactor (PentRed) compiled and inserted. At the same time, PentRed also supplemented Num 20:1–11* + 13 with

---

6 In Exod 17:1–7, this coordination resulted in the accretions of vv. 2aα + 2bβ + 3aβ-b + 4aβ-b + 7a^v-bα (*pre-Hex Supp*). When added to the Massah Episode (cf. p. 238 n. 4 above), the resulting textual material approximating the non-P M-Mt after the Meribah Coordination is Exod 17:1bβ-5bα^i + 5bα^{vii}-7 (cf. Appendix D).

In Num 20:1–13, this coordination resulted in the accretions of vv. 3a + 4b + 5bβ* + 13a (*pre-Hex Supp*). When added to the P^G Kadesh Episode (cf. p. 238 n. 5 above), the resulting textual material approximating the P* M-Mt narrative after the Meribah Coordination is Num 20:1ay + 2a + 3a + 4–5aβ + 5bβ* + 6–8* + 10a + 11* + 13.

7 With the addition of the travel notice in v. 1abα, the resulting textual material at this penultimate stage of Exod 17:1–7's literary development is vv. 1–5bα^i + 5bα^{vii}-7 (*HexRed*). The only remaining material development is the relative clause in v. 5bα^{ii-vi} (*PentRed*).

8 The accretions that stem from HexRed are vv. 1aαβ + 1b + 5bα. When added to the P* M-Mt narrative after the Meribah Coordination (cf. p. 239 n. 6), the resulting textual material after HexRed's accretions is Num 20:1–2a + 3a + 4–8* + 10a + 11* + 13.

accretions that anchor it back to these rebellions,⁹ thereby recasting the P* M-Mt narrative as the continuation of these rebellions in which Moses and Aaron's divine appointment as Israel's leaders is challenged and miraculously reconfirmed. Further, since PentRed disambiguates the staff used in the P* M-Mt as Aaron's, the gloss disambiguating the staff in Exod 17:5bα$^{ii\text{-}vi}$ likely stems from the same hand. This glossic addition brings Exod 17:1–7's formative literary history to a close.

Unlike Exod 17:1–7, the literary history of Num 20:1–13 continues to a sixth and final stage—i.e., the failure of Moses and Aaron, the P* M-Mt's most distinctive tradition component—a stage which aligns with Deut 32:51 (cf. *Stage 5* in Fig. 8.1 above). Prior to this development, however, Moses and Aaron's standing before Yahweh had never been called into question via the M-Mt.¹⁰ As radical as this reorientation was for the P* M-Mt tradition, its creation by a post-Pentateuchal Redactor (post-PentRed) required only the editing of v. 8aγ (i.e., rewriting והכית את as ודברתם אל) and the insertion of v. 12. Moreover, since the sin of Moses and Aaron is demonstrably later in all its occurrences (cf. Num 20:24; 27:14; Deut 32:51) than the surrounding texts into which it has been inserted, this tradition stands as particularly late in the Pentateuch. Thus, with this editing, Num 20:1–13's formative literary history not only comes to a close, but so also does the reflections of the M-Mt's development within Deuteronomy.

In summary, the framework of the M-Mt's tradition-historical development preserved in Deuteronomy aligns diachronically with the stages of the M-Mt narratives' literary growth. This confluence not only corroborates the M-Mt framework detected in Deuteronomy, but it also provides a key to understanding the formation of what is arguably one of the Pentateuch's most debated blocks of material: the Wilderness Narrative. From common oral traditions emerged two independent literary corpora (non-P and P*), which underwent successive post-priestly editings that involved coordination, compilation, and expansion—a dynamic process of *Fortschreibung*. Thus, the role that the M-Mt played in the formation of the Pentateuch is therefore paramount and warrants continued consideration.

---

9 The accretions that stem from PentRed are vv. 20:2b, 3bβ, 9 and 10b (and possibly פעמים in v. 11aβ). When added to HexRed's P* M-Mt narrative (cf. p. 239 n. 8 above), the resulting textual material after PentRed's accretions is Num 20:1–11* + 13. The only remaining material development for the P* M-Mt narrative is the creation of Moses and Aaron's sin in vv. 8aγ + 12 (*post-PentRed*).

10 That this development took place after PentRed is the only reason why Deut 33:8 can recall Aaron as Israel's devout one, whom Israel had tested at Massah and contended at the waters of Meribah.

8.2 Trajectories for Further Study

As this study draws to a close, much work still remains before the task of tracing of tradition history of the M-Mt is complete. As the first chapter of this study indicates, the M-Mt is extant throughout the Hebrew Bible, and appears in the Apocrypha, New Testament, Pseudepigrapha, and in the writings of Josephus and Philo. Of course, the remaining explicit and allusive references within the Hebrew Bible—that is, those beyond the Pentateuch—especially merit study in light of this study's diachronic findings.[11] Citations in the Apocrypha, New Testament, and Pseudepigrapha merit treatment as well, along with the citations by Josephus and Philo, but not necessarily within the diachronic confines of the M-Mt's formative stages.[12] Finally, there is a need to develop criteria for confirming and assessing the possible intertextual echoes of this tradition, as texts with constellations of M-Mt components appear in the Hebrew Bible, Apocrypha, and the New Testament.[13]

---

11 The *explicit evocations* of the M-Mt beyond the Pentateuch but within the Hebrew Bible are Ezek 47:19; 48:28; Ps 81:8, 17; 95:8–11; and 106:32. Provisionally, these texts evince components that align with the M-Mt tradition-historical development as follows: Ezek 47:19 and 48:28 reflect the P* M-Mt at a stage after the Meribah coordination; both Ps 81:8, 17 and Ps 95:8–11 also reflect the Meribah coordination, but Ps 81:8, 17 preserves echoes of the earliest forms both the non-P and P* M-Mt, while Ps 95:8–11 reflects the non-P formula in Exod 17:7; and Ps 106:32 demonstrates awareness of Moses and Aaron's sin, so it appears especially late.

The *allusions* to the M-Mt beyond the Pentateuch but within the Hebrew Bible are Isa 48:21; Ps 78:15–16, 20, 35; 105:41; 114:8 and Neh 9:15, 20. Provisionally, Isa 48:21 uses non-P terminology, but its plural בחרבות (*in the wastelands*) and parallel statements regarding the issuance of water may indicate awareness of both non-P and P* traditions (HexRed?); the allusions within Ps 78 (cf. vv. 15–16, 20, 35) display awareness of both M-Mt narratives and focus on the Israelite's rebellion (מרה/ו; cf. vv. 8, 17, 40, 56), and so mirrors PentRed's insertion of Numbers 16–17 and the corresponding accretions to Num 20:1–13; Ps 105:41 reflects the non-P M-Mt but after HexRed's transposition; Ps 114:8 evinces early non-P/Dt language; and Neh 9:15, 20 demonstrates awareness of the entire Hexateuch and the Deuteronomistic History with a preference for P* M-Mt (HexRed).

12 As noted earlier (cf. p. 2 n. 5 above), allusions to the M-Mt are extant in Wis 11:4–10; 2 Esd 1:17–20; 1 Cor 10:4; Heb. 3:7–11 (cf. Ps 95:8–11); *4 Ezra* 1:20; *L.A.B.* 10:7; *Hel. Syn. Pr.* 12:74; *Ant.* 20.8.10 (cf. Ps 95:8–11); *Det.* 115–118.

13 In the Hebrew Bible, possible intertextuality with the M-Mt is discernible in Isa 7:10–14; 43:20; Jer 14:1–12 + 19–22; and Ezek 16:13, 19. In Isa 7:10–14, Ahaz's rejection of the offer for a prophetic sign in Isa 7:12—לא־אנסה את־יהוה—can be read as a first person appropriation of Deut 6:16's לא תנסו את־יהוה. Yet Ahaz's appropriation stops short in that he does not call Yahweh "my God" (אלהי), nor does he cite the precedent of Massah (cf. Deut 6:16's לא תנסו את־יהוה אלהיכם כאשר נסיתם במסה), in which the Israelites had inappropriately tested Yahweh by asking היש יהוה בקרבנו אם־אין (Exod 17:7). The prophet's enraged response carries forward

On one final note, the M-Mt continued to capture the Jewish imagination well after its formative stages had reached completion. Yet it is the dynamic history of the M-Mt's development, as preserved in the Pentateuch itself, which no doubt paved the way for the variety of M-Mt's later appropriations and interpretations.[14] Like the tantalizing glisten of desert mirages, the formative stages of the M-Mt shift on the axis of the human-divine relationship: from moments of divine testing and miraculous provision to those moments of intense human failure, the Massah-Meribah tradition is a mirror in which each generation can gaze and assess whether it is in right relationship with God.

Ahaz's intertext, completing the appropriation of Deut 6:16 and alluding to Exod 17:7. First he evokes אלהי (not יהוה אלהי!) in his rebuke, and then he proceeds to give a sign in the naming of a forthcoming child עמנו אל, which conceptually relates to the question the people ask in Exod 17:7. In short, if viable, this intertext would explain the prophet's otherwise irascible response to Ahaz' refusal, unmasking it as an expression of false piety, and it may reveal why Isaiah chose the symbolic name עמנו אל in the first place, since the oracular context in no way resonates with the symbolic name (cf. Isa 8:1–4; Hos 1:4–2:3, 24–25).

The other possible intertexts within the Hebrew Bible merit briefer attention. In Isa 43:20, the tradition of Yahweh providing נהרות (*rivers*) in the wilderness most likely alludes to the M-Mt tradition, especially in light of the theme of a new exodus from Babylon in Isa 42:14–21. Nevertheless, the connection is conceptual (i.e. running water) as opposed to lexical. In Jer 14:1–12, 19–22, Judah calls on Yahweh—whom she likens to a desert nomad (Jer 14:8)—during a severe drought. Suffering from water deprivation like her ancestors during the wilderness sojourn, Judah appeals to Yahweh, declaring ואתה בקרבנו יהוה (Jer 14:9; cf. Exod 17:7)! Ezekiel 16:13, 19 uses the same mythic language of Yahweh providing honey and oil as does the M-Mt reminiscence preserved in Deut 32:13 (cf. Jason Gile, "Ezekiel 16 and the Song of Moses: A Prophetic Transformation," *JBL* 130 [2011]: 96).

In the Apocrypha, Judith 8–11 appears intertextually related to the M-Mt. David DeSilva notes that this story "provides an important and meaningful layer of intertexture for reading Judith" (*Introducing the Apocrypha: Message, Context, and Significance* [Grand Rapids, MI: Baker Academic, 2002], 97). Judith rebukes the rulers of Bethulia for testing God by promising to surrender in five days to the Assyrians—who had cut off the town's water supply—if God had not delivered them by that time (Jdt 7:17–8:27).

Finally, in the New Testament, the temptation narratives in Matt 4:1–11 and Luke 4:1–13 are intertextually related to the M-Mt. First, Jesus is led up into the desert to be tested (νπειράζω) by the devil, during which time he did not eat, and some minor manuscripts add that he did not drink (ουδε επιεν; cf. f^{13} and a few other texts). In his rebuttal, two of Jesus' quotes are from Deut 8:13 and 6:16—texts closely associated with the story of Massah and the wilderness testing.

14 Here, one only need to look to Paul for an example. In 1 Cor 10:1–5, he allegorically appropriates the wilderness traditions in 1 Cor 10:1–5; nevertheless, he appears to have understood the rock in Exod 17:1–7 and the rock in Num 20:1–13 to be one and the same spiritual source of nutriment. In this regard, his reading is very much akin to Philo's (*Det.* 115–118).

Appendices

Appendix A

Rhythm and Translation of the Ur-ריב of Deuteronomy 32

האזינו השמים ואדברה	1	[3//3]	Give ear, O heavens, and let me speak!
ותשמע הארץ אמרי־פי			Let the earth hear the words of my mouth.
כי שם יהוה אקרא	3	[4//3]	For I will declare the name of Yahweh;
הבו גדל לאלהינו			Ascribe greatness to our God!
הצור תמים פעלו	4	[3//3]	The Rock, his deed is blameless;
כי כל־דרכיו משפט			Indeed, all his ways are just.
אל אמונה ואין עול		[4//3]	A God of faithfulness, without iniquity;
צדיק וישר הוא			righteous and upright is he.
שחת לו לא בניו מומם	5	[5//3]	To him, *they are* ruined, his "no-sons" for their blemish
דור עקש ופתלתל			– a perverse and crooked generation.
הלוא־הוא אביך קנך	6b	[3//3]	Did not he, your father, acquire you?
הוא עשך ויכננך			Did he not make you and establish you?
שאל אביך ויגדך	7b	[3//3]	Ask your father, and he will tell you;
זקניך ויאמרו לך			your elders, and they will speak to you.
בהנחל עליון גוים	8	[3//3]	When Elyon allotted the nations,
בהפרידו בני אדם			when he apportioned the sons of man,
יצב גבלת עמים		[3//3]	He set up the territories of the peoples
למספר בני אלוהים			according to the number of the Sons of God.
כי חלק יהוה עמו	9	[4//3]	Indeed, Yahweh's portion *was* his people,
יעקב חבל נחלתו			Jacob, the lot of his inheritance.
ימצאהו בארץ מדבר	10	[3//3]	He found him in a land of desert,
ובתהו ילל ישמן			in an empty, howling wasteland.
יסבבנהו יבוננהו		[2//3]	He surrounded him, cared for him,
יצרנהו כאישון עינו			guarded him as the pupil of his eye.
כנשר יעיר קנו	11	[3//2]	As an eagle stirs up its nest,
על־גוזליו ירחף			hovering over its young,
יפרש כנפיו יקחהו		[3//2]	He spread out his wings, caught him,
ישאהו על־אברתו			lifting him up on his pinions.
יהוה בדד ינחנו	12	[3//4]	Yahweh alone guided him,
ואין עמו אל נכר			and there was no foreign god with him.
ירכבהו על־במותי ארץ	13	[3//3]	He rode him upon the heights of the earth,
ויאכלהו תנובת שדי			and fed him the produce of the field;
וינקהו דבש מסלע		[3//3]	He suckled him *with* honey from a rock,
ושמן מחלמיש צור			*with* oil from a flinty rock
חמאת בקר וחלב צאן	14	[4//3]	– Curd of cattle, milk of the flock,
עם־חלב כרים ואילים			with fat of lambs and rams,
בני־בשן ועתודים		[2//3]	Sons of Bashan and he-goats
עם־חלב כליות חטה			with fat of choice wheat –
יאכל יעקב וישבע	15	[3//3]	Jacob ate and was satiated;
וישמן ישרון ויבעט			and Jeshurun grew fat and kicked.
ויטש אלוה עשהו		[3//3]	He forsook Eloah *who* made him;
ונבל צור ישעתו			he disregarded the Rock of his salvation.

¹⁶ יקנאהו בזרים בתועבת יכעיסהו	[2//2]	He made him jealous with foreign *gods*; with abominations he provoked him.
¹⁷ יזבחו לשדים לא אלה אלהים לא ידעום	[4//3]	They sacrificed to the *šedim*, a "no-god," gods they had not known,
חדשים מקרב באו לא שערום אבתיך	[3//3]	New ones, *which* had recently come, *whom* your fathers did not dread.
¹⁸ צור ילדך תשי ותשכח אל מחללך	[3//3]	You forgot the Rock *who* bore you; forgot El who birthed you.
¹⁹ וירא יהוה וינאץ מכעס בניו ובנתיו	[3//3]	So Yahweh saw *it* and he spurned *them*, because of the provocation of his sons and daughters.
²⁰ ויאמר אסתיר פני מהם אראה מה אחריתם	[4//3]	And he said, "I will hide my face from them; I will see what their end *will be!*
כי דור תהפכת המה בנים לא־אמן בם	[4//3]	For a generation of perversity are they, sons *with* no faithfulness in them.

Appendix B

Quantitative Analysis of the Verbal and Conceptual Correspondences of Exod 17:1–7 and Num 20:1–13

The following summarizes the per section analysis of the M-Mt narratives' verbal and conceptual correspondence, as illustrated in Fig. 5.1 (for convenience, see Fig. B.1 below). Each section summary below concludes with a synoptic annotation, which uses two parentheses to record the types of correspondence within its respective section of Exodus 17 "in parallel relationship to" (indicated by the symbol ‖) its correlative in Numbers 20. Within each parenthesis is four numbers, which in turn signifies the number of words within the section of Hebrew text that evinces each type of correspondence, with the place values representing first verbatim, then approximate verbal, and then conceptual correspondence, and then finally non-aligned material in a (v/a/c/n) pattern.[1] These values facilitate the quantitative analysis that then follows. (Note for the sake of accuracy the following word counts are not reduced by maqqefs.)

§ 1. *Travel Notice.* Only בני ישראל is verbatim, but the two-word phrase is also clearly formulaic. The *nomen regens* כל עדת approximates the appositive כל העדה, as does ממדבר with מדבר. The verb √חנה is conceptually parallel to √ישב. The remainder is non-aligned. Synopsis: (2/3/1/7) ‖ (2/3/2/5).

§ 2. *Miriam's Death Notice.* Numbers 20:1b is fully non-aligned. Synopsis: (0/0/0/0) ‖ (0/0/0/5).

§ 3. *Crisis Statement.* For consistency and on account of parallel location, מים is noted as verbatim, but it is difficult to imagine another lexeme in this position (e.g. Exod 15:22; Num 21:5; 33:14; Deut 8:15). The correspondence most likely stems from water being a foundational tradition component. The phrase ואין מים לשתת (17:1bβ) receives a double notation: within §3, it bears conceptual correspondence to ולא היה מים, but it also approximately corresponds with ומים אין

---

[1] To illustrate how to read these annotations, consider the annotation for §1, which reads "Synopsis: (2/3/1/7) ‖ (2/3/2/5)." This annotation indicates that two words within §1—that is, Exod 17:1abα ‖ Num 20:1a—correspond at the verbatim level (<u>2</u>/3/1/7) ‖ (<u>2</u>/3/2/5); that three words correspond verbally, but only approximately (2/<u>3</u>/1/7) ‖ (2/<u>3</u>/2/5); that one word in Exod 17:1abα corresponds conceptually to two words in Num 20:1a (2/3/<u>1</u>/7) ‖ (2/3/<u>2</u>/5); and finally that seven words in Exod 17:1abα and five words in Num 20:1a show no correspondence whatsoever and are therefore non-aligned (2/3/1/<u>7</u>) ‖ (2/3/2/<u>5</u>).

DOI 10.1515/9783110463354-010

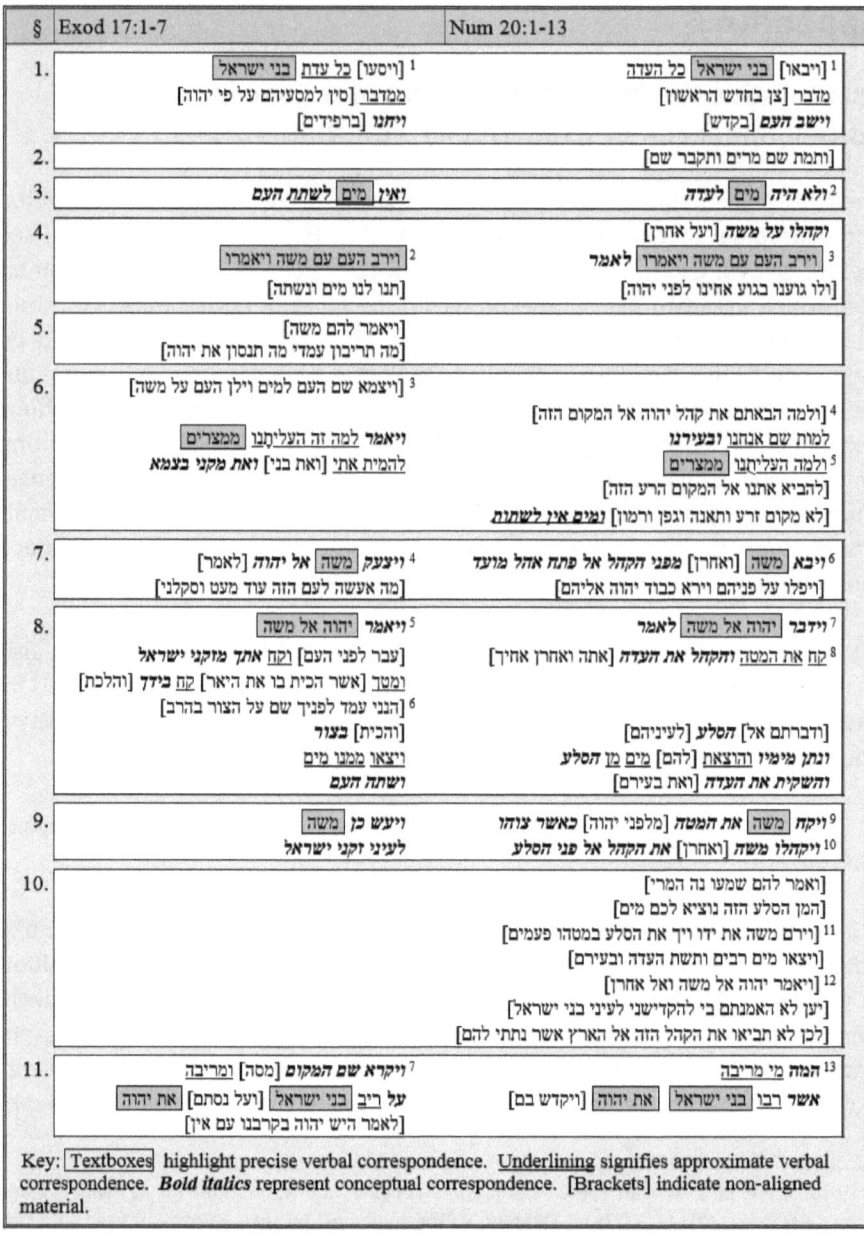

Figure. B.1: The Verbal and Conceptual Correspondences of Exod 17:1–7 and Num 20:1–13

לשתות (20:5bδ) in §6, the main differences being location and the infinitive is *plene*. (The notation only records 17:1bβ's conceptual correspondence within §3, not its approximate correspondence with 20:5bδ in §6.) Finally, העם corresponds conceptually with לעדה. Synopsis: (1/0/3/0) ‖ (1/0/3/0).

§ 4. *Initiation of Complaint*. The largest verbatim correspondence is וירב העם עם משה ויאמרו. Since ויאמרו is formulaic and introduces the non-aligned dialogue, one cannot assume it is part of a quotation. At best, וירב העם עם משה may indicate quotation (although see §6.3.2 above). The act of assembling against Moses (ויקהלו על משה) is conceptually implicit in 17:2, as well as is לאמר which introduces the congregation's complaint. The mention of Aaron (20:2b) and the people's first words to Moses (17:2aβγ; 20:3b) are non-aligned. Synopsis of (5/0/0/4) ‖ (5/0/4/8).

§ 5. *Moses' Response*. Exodus 17:2b is fully non-aligned. Synopsis: (0/0/0/10) ‖ (0/0/0/0).

§ 6. *Formal Complaint*. ממצרים is verbatim, but it is part of the people's formulaic complaint about being brought out from Egypt (cf. Exod 14:11; Num 11:20; 21:5). The rest of the formulary (העליתנו [זה] [למה]) shows approximate correspondence, with the hiphil infinitive differing only vocalically in order to direct the complaint against Aaron as well in 20:5. The speech formula ויאמר in 17:3 is approximately related to ויאמרו לאמר in 20:3 (cf. §4), but since the dialogue in 20:3–5 is uninterrupted, there is no repetition; ויאמר in 17:3b is therefore recorded as conceptual. The people's accusation of Moses attempting to kill them (infinitive √מות) is also approximate, both lexically and locally; this accusation follows the formula in 17:5, but immediately precedes it in 20:4b. The suffixed nominatives מקני and בעירנו are conceptually synonymous. Like its correlative in 17:1bβ (cf. §3 above), ומים אין לשתות in 20:5bδ receives a double notation: it is strikingly approximate to ואין מים לשתת in 17:1bβ, but it also conceptually corresponds to בצמא in the accusation of 17:3. (Only the conceptual correspondence is recorded.) The remainder (17:3a; 20:4a, 5bβ-γ) is non-aligned. Synopsis: (1/5/4/10) ‖ (1/5/4/20).

§ 7. *Moses (and Aaron) before Yahweh*. On account of its parallel location, משה is recorded as verbatim; since Moses is syntactically expected as the subject, it cannot serve as an indicator for dependency. Moses' crying out (√צעק) to Yahweh requires spatial transition, even if in Exodus 17 the אהל מועד has yet to be constructed; 17:4aα and 20:6a are therefore conceptually parallel. The mention of Aaron—as it is in 20:2, 6, 8, 10, 12—is non-aligned, as well as is Moses' appeal to Yahweh (17:4aβ-b) and the appearance of divine כבוד (20:6b). Synopsis: (1/0/3/8) ‖ (1/0/7/8).

§ 8. *Instructions for Redress.* יהוה אל משה is verbatim, but the phrase is part of the speech formula so one cannot assume it to be the product of quotation. The remaining speech formula (ויאמר and לאמר ... וידבר) corresponds conceptually. The commands to take (√לקח) witnesses and the staff also correspond: to take only מזקני ישראל (17:5aγ) as opposed to הקהל את העדה (20:8aα) corresponds conceptually, but to take the מטה—whether Moses' or Aaron's—corresponds approximately. Taking the staff in the hand is implicit in 20:8, so בידך corresponds conceptually, but the reminiscence of the staff having been used to strike the river (17:5bα) is non-aligned. צור and סלע are conceptually parallel, but the description of the issuance in 17:6aδ and 20:8bα is approximate, using the lexemes √יצא, מים, and מן. Num 20:8bα is apposite to מימיו ונתן in 20:8aδ, making 20:8aδ conceptual. That the people will drink (√שתה) in 17:6aε is conceptually parallel to the command for Moses to give the congregation a drink (√שקה) in 20:8bβ; the mention of בעיר in this regard is non-aligned. The remaining material is non-aligned: the mention of Aaron (20:8aβ), the instruction to pass before the people (17:5aβ), the command to go (17:5bγ), Yahweh's promise to stand atop the rock at Horeb (17:6aαβ), and the instructions regarding whether to strike the rock (17:6aγ) or to speak to it (20:8aγ). Synopsis: (3/6/14/17) ‖ (3/6/12/9).

§ 9. *Moses' (and Aaron's) Obedience.* Again, משה is recorded as verbatim, but see the comments in §7 above. The remaining correspondences in this section are conceptual: while 17:6b summarizes Moses' obedience with ויעש כן, 20:9–10a depicts Moses obeying Yahweh's first two commands in v. 8a (קח את המטה והקהל את העדה); and while Moses' obedience unfolds before the זקני ישראל in 17:6b, Moses' and Aaron's obedience unfolds before the קהל in 20:10a. The clarification that the staff was מלפני יהוה (v. 9a) and the mention of Aaron (v. 10a) are non-aligned. Synopsis: (1/0/5/0) ‖ (1/0/12/3).

§ 10. *Failure and Punishment.* Numbers 20:10b-12 is fully non-aligned. Synopsis: (0/0/0/0) ‖ (0/0/0/51).

§ 11. *Etiology.* בני ישראל and את יהוה are verbatim, but as instigator and direct object their correspondence more likely stems from form and syntax than from literary dependency. Technically, מריבה is only approximate: in 17:7a it has the conjunction, but in 20:13 it is *nomen rectum* of the construct מי, for "מי מריבה" not just מריבה. The nominative ריב approximately corresponds to the verb רבו (√ריב). The use of the relative אשר parallels conceptually the preposition על in that both introduce the operative etiological logic. The act of Moses naming the location in 17:7a is conceptually parallel to the etiological declaration of the toponym in 20:13aα. Non-aligned materials include the Massah elements (17:7a, 7bβ), the question regarding the divine presence (17:7by), and the antithetical statement that Yahweh was indeed treated as holy (20:13b; cf. 20:12). Synopsis: (4/2/4/9) ‖ (4/3/2/2).

Together, the above synopses facilitate the following quantitative analysis (cf. Table B.1 below). In their MT forms, Exod 17:1–7 has 133 words, while Num 20:1–13 has 192 words. When comparing the two texts, only 18 words exhibit verbatim correspondence and shared structural proximity: בני־ישראל (17:1a ‖ 20:1a; 17:7bα ‖ 20:13aβ); מים (17:1bβ ‖ 20:2a); וירב העם עם־משה ויאמרו (17:2aα ‖ 20:3a); ממצרים (17:3bα ‖ 20:5aα); משה (17:4aα ‖ 20:6aα; 17:6bα ‖ 20:9a); יהוה אל־משה (17:5aα ‖ 20:7a); and את־יהוה (17:7bβ ‖ 20:13aβ). Approximate verbal correspondence is also fairly limited: only 16 words in Exod 17:1–7 are lexically, yet imprecisely related to 17 words in Num 20:1–13. Loose conceptual overlap is more prevalent in Numbers 20 (by nearly 9%) than Exodus 17, with 46 words in Num 20:1–13 overlapping conceptually (but not lexically) with 21 words in Exod 17:1–7. The verbal and conceptual correspondence can therefore be represented as a ratio of aligned versus non-aligned textual material within each text: in Exod 17:1–7, this ratio is 18 + 16 + 34 to 133 (i.e., verbatim + approximate + conceptual to the total words within the textual unit), which is 68/133 (51.1%); in Numbers 20, this ratio is 18 + 17 + 46 to 192, with is 81/192 (42.2%). Given the subjective nature inherent to assigning conceptual overlaps within the material, a general figure of *50% or less* (50% for Exod 17:1–7; 40% for Num 20:1–13) for material exhibiting any form of correspondence is a fair approximation. By contrast, approximately 50% of Exod 17:1–7 represents distinct, non-aligned material, while the percentage of distinctive, non-aligned within Num 20:1–13 is slightly higher (approximately 60%).[2]

---

[2] These statistics hold even if one eliminates the travel notices and Miriam's death notice (17:1a-bα; 20:1) as secondary to the narratives, as scholars still widely agree. Following the same procedure as above (cf. p. 247 n. 1), without these sections (§1 & 2; cf. Fig. B.1 and Table B.1 above), Exod 17:1bβ-7 has 120 words, while Num 20:1b-13 has 175 words. The subtotals for the varying types of correspondences in 17:1bβ-7 and 20:1b-13 is (16/13/33/58 ‖ 16/14/44/101). Using the above formula for the percentage of corresponding material in each text, 51.7% (16 + 13 + 33 / 120) of Exod 17:1bβ-7 corresponds to 42.2% (16 + 14 + 44 /175) of Num 20:1b-13.

Table B.1: Quantitative Analysis of the Correspondence between Exod 17:1–7 and Num 20:1–13

Sections:	Exodus 17:1-7					Numbers 20:1-13				
	V	A	C	N	§Sub	V	A	C	N	§Sub
§1	2	3	1	7	13	2	3	2	5	12
§2	0	0	0	0	0	0	0	0	5	5
§3	1	0	3	0	4	1	0	3	0	4
§4	5	0	0	4	9	5	0	4	8	17
§5	0	0	0	10	10	0	0	0	0	0
§6	1	5	4	10	20	1	5	4	20	30
§7	1	0	3	8	12	1	0	7	8	16
§8	3	6	14	17	40	3	6	12	9	30
§9	1	0	5	0	6	1	0	12	3	16
§10	0	0	0	0	0	0	0	0	51	51
§11	4	2	4	9	19	4	3	2	2	11
Subtotals:	18	16	34	65	133	18	17	46	111	192
Percentages:	13.5%	12.0%	25.6%	48.9%	100%	9.4%	8.8%	24.0%	57.8%	100%

Key: V = Verbatim; A = Approximate; C = Conceptual; N = non-aligned; and §Sub = section subtotal

Appendix C

Fig. C.1: Fractures and Overlaps in the Wilderness Travel Notices and the Itinerary of Num 33:1–49

Fractures**	Formula*	Travel Notice (TN) Station	TN References	#	Num 33	Itinerary Stations	Itinerary Annotations
	P*	רעמסס (Ramses)	Exod 12:37 (cf. Gen 47:11)	0	v. 5a	רעמסס (Ramses)	Vv. 3-4: PentRed's introduction (cf. p. 180 n. 55).
	P	סכת (Succoth)	Exod 13:20	1	v. 5b	סכת (Succoth)	
1a.	P	אתם (Etham)	Exod 13:20	2	v 6b	אתם (Etham)	Vv. 6bβ, 7aγ-b, 8aβ-bβ, 9bα-β: Clarifies אתם, החירה (פי), the crossing of the ים, the מרה entered afterward, and אלם (cf. fractures 1a-c; pp. 171-172 above).
1b.	P*	פי החירה (Pi-hahiroth)	Exod 14:2	3	v. 7b	פי החירת (Pi-hahiroth)	
	non-P	מרה (Marah)	Exod 15:22	4	v. 8bβ	מרה (Marah)	
1c.	P*	מדבר שור (Wild. of Shur)	Exod 15:23				
	P*	אילם (Elim)	Exod 15:27	5	v. 9b	אילם (Elim)	
				6	v. 10b	ים-סוף (Reed Sea)	
2a.	P*	מדבר סין (Wild. of Sin)	Exod 16:1	7	v. 11b	מדבר-סין (Wild. of Sin)	
				8	v. 12b	דפקה (Dophkah)	
				9	v. 13b	אלוש (Alush)	
2b.	P	רפידים (Rephidim)	Exod 17:1	10	v.14b	רפידם (Rephidim)	V. 14bβ: Clarifies רפידים as a place of water deprivation (cf. 2a-b; pp. 172-173 above).
	P*	מדבר סיני (Wild. of Sinai)	Exod 19:1-2	11	v.15b	מדבר סיני (Wild. of Sinai)	
3a.	P*	מדבר פארן (Wild. of Paran) (תבערה etiology in Num 11:3; no TN)	Num 10:12-13				
3b.		(קברות התאוה etiology in Num 11:34; no TN)		12	v. 16b	קברת התאוה (Kibroth-hattaavah)	
	P	חצרות (Hazeroth)	Num 11:35	13	v. 17b	חצרת (Hazeroth)	
4a-c.	P	מדבר פארן (Wild. Of Paran)	Num 12:16				
				14	v. 18b	רתמה (Rithmah)	4a.
				15	v. 19b	רמן פרץ (Rimmon-perez)	

* TN compared to the priestly itinerary formula: P = uses both √נסע and √חנה; P* = uses either √נסע or √חנה, but not both; non-P = uses neither √נסע nor √חנה.
** For fracture key, see Table C.2 below.

Appendix C

Fractures**	Formula*	Travel Notice (TN) Stations	TN References	#	Num 33	Itinerary Stations	Itinerary Annotations
				16	v. 20b	לִבְנָה (Libnah)	
				17	v. 21b	רִסָּה (Rissah)	
				18	v. 22b	קְהֵלָתָה (Kehelathah)	
				19	v. 23b	הַר־שָׁפֶר (Mt. Shepher)	(4a.)
				20	v. 24b	חֲרָדָה (Haradah)	
				21	v. 25b	מַקְהֵלֹת (Makheloth)	
				22	v. 26b	תָּחַת (Tahath)	
				23	v. 27b	תָּרַח (Terah)	
				24	v. 28b	מִתְקָה (Mithkah)	
				25	v. 29b	חַשְׁמֹנָה (Hashmonah)	(4b.)
				26	v. 30b	מֹסֵרוֹת (Moseroth)	
				27	v. 31b	בְּנֵי יַעֲקָן (Bene-jaakan)	
				28	v. 32b	חֹר הַגִּדְגָּד (Hor-haggidgad)	
				29	v. 33b	יָטְבָתָה (Jotbathah)	
				30	v. 34b	עַבְרֹנָה (Abronah)	(4c.)
				31	v. 35b	עֶצְיֹן גָּבֶר (Ezion-geber)	
(5a.)	non-P (!)	מִדְבַּר־צִן (Wild. of Zin)	Num 20:1	32	v. 36bα	מִדְבַּר־צִן (Wild. of Zin)	V. 36bβ: Equates מִדְבַּר־צִן with קָדֵשׁ (cf. fracture 5a-b; pp. 172-173 above).
(5b.)		(אֶת narrative in Num 20:14-21; no TN)					
(6a.)	P*	הֹר הָהָר (Mt. Hor)	Num 20:22	33	v. 37bα	הֹר הָהָר (Mt. Hor)	Vv. 37bβ, 38-39, 40: Clarifies הֹר הָהָר as bordering אֶרֶץ אֱדוֹם; relays details about Aaron's death; recalls conflict at מְרִיבָה (cf. fractures 6a-b; pp. 173-174 above).
(6b.)	P*	(וַיִּסְעוּ narrative in Num 21:1-3; no TN)					
	P*	הֹר הָהָר (departure only)	Num 21:4				
		(וַיַּחֲנוּ narrative in Num 21:4-9; no station)					
(7a.)	P	אֹבֹת (Oboth)	Num 21:10	34	v. 41b	צַלְמֹנָה (Zalmonah)	
(7b.)	P	עִיֵּי הָעֲבָרִים (Iye-abarim)	Num 21:11	35	v. 42b	פּוּנֹן (Punon)	
(7c.)	P*	נַחַל זֶרֶד (Wadi Zered)	Num 21:12	36	v. 43b	אֹבֹת (Oboth)	
				37	v. 44b	עִיִּים " (Iye-abarim)	

* TN compared to the priestly itinerary formula: P = uses both √נסע and √חנה; P* = uses either √נסע or √חנה, but not both; non-P = uses neither √נסע nor √חנה.
** For fracture key, see Table C.2 below.

Fractures**	Formula*	Travel Notice (TN) Stations	TN References	#	Num 33 Itinerary Stations	Itinerary Annotations
	P*	אַרְנוֹן (the Arnon)	Num 21:13			
7c.	non-P	בְּאֵר (Beer)	Num 21:16			V. 44bβ: Clarifies עִיֵּי הָעֲבָרִים as the entry point into the territory of מוֹאָב (cf. fractures 7b-c; pp. 174-176 above).
	non-P	מַתָּנָה (Mattanah)	Num 21:18			
	non-P	נַחֲלִיאֵל (Nahaliel)	Num 21:19			
	non-P	בָּמוֹת (Bamoth)	Num 21:19			
	non-P	הַגַּיְא אֲשֶׁר בִּשְׂדֵה מוֹאָב (The valley in the region of Moab)	Num 21:20			
8a.		(סיחון & עוג narratives in Num 21:21-35; no TN)				
8b.	P	עַרְבֹת מוֹאָב עַל יַרְדֵּן יְרֵחוֹ (Plains of Moab beyond the Jordan opposite Jericho)	Num 22:1			
		(מדבר & מסע בני ישראל in Numbers 22-25; no TN)				
		(ויחנו על ירדן ערבות מואב in Num 26:3, 63; no TN)				
8c.		(הר העברים in Num 27:12; no TN)				
		(ויחנו בערבות מואב in Num 31:12; no TN)				
		[Transjordanian allotment to Reuben & Gad in Numbers 32 [cf. vv. 34, 38]; no TN]				
				38	v. 45b	דִּיבֹן גָּד (Dibon-gad)
				39	v. 46b	עַלְמֹן דִּבְלָתָיְמָה (Almon-diblathaim)
				40	v. 47b	הָרֵי הָעֲבָרִים (The Mts. of the Abarim)
				41	v. 48b	עַרְבֹת מוֹאָב (Plains of Moab)

Vv. 47bβ, 48bβ, 49: Clarifies the הָרֵי הָעֲבָרִים range as לִפְנֵי נְבוֹ (cf. Deut 32:49; 34:1); the מוֹאָב as עַרְבֹת יְרֵחוֹ יַרְדֵּן; and the bivouacs within עַרְבֹת מוֹאָב as ranging from בֵּית הַיְשִׁמֹת to אָבֵל הַשִּׁטִּים (cf. fractures 8a-c; pp. 176-179).

* TN compared to the priestly itinerary formula: P = uses both √נסע and √חנה; P* = uses either √נסע or √חנה, but not both; non-P = uses neither √נסע nor √חנה.

** For fracture key, see Table C:2 below.

Table C.1: Key to the Fractures and Overlaps in the Wilderness Travel Notices And Itinerary of Num 33:1–49 in Fig. C.1

Fracture #	Description
1a	Departure point from Egypt reoriented from אתם (cf. Exod 13:20–22) to פי החירת (cf. Exod 14:1–2).
1b	After crossing the ים / ים־סוף, the entry point into the wilderness is the מדבר שור in Exod 15:22, but in Num 33:8 the entry point is מדבר אתם.
1c	The Wilderness Narrative has no bivouac between אילם (Exod 15:27) and the מדבר־סין (Exod 16:1), while the itinerary has Station 6 beside the ים סוף (Num 33:10b).
2a	The Wilderness Narrative has no record of Stations 8–9 at דפקה and אלוש (cf. Num 33:12b-13b).
2b	The travel notice in Exod 17:1abα indicates additional stages not represented in the Wilderness Narrative via the phrase למסעיהם על־פי יהוה (cf. fracture 2a). Additionally, Exod 17:6 intrinsically locates the narrative at חרב, but the Israelites have yet to arrive at חרב / סיני (cf. Exod 19:2).
3a	The first departure from מדבר סין in Num 10:12–13 abridges subsequent stages via על־פי יהוה ... למסעיהם (cf. fracture 2b), with the cloud settling in מדבר פארן. Numbers 10:33–34, however, repeats this departure, but the cloud stays over them during the day between campsites; Israel does not enter מדבר פארן until after Miriam's (and Aaron's) failure at הצרות (Num 12:16). The itinerary in Numbers 33 exhibits no awareness or מדבר פארן or the cloud of the Lord.
3b	While Num 33:16b treats קברת התאוה as a station (although not תעברה), the Wilderness narrative provides no travel notice for the *arrival* at either complaint narrative (cf. Num 11:35, which treats קברת התאוה as a station of departure).
4a-c	Stations 14–31 in the itinerary, from רתמה to עציון גבר, do not appear in the Wilderness Narrative. Conversely, the itinerary has no awareness of the narrative materials between Station 13 (חצרת) and station 32 (קדש) (cf. Num 33:17–36), a span which corresponds to the textual material in Numbers 13–19.
4a	Stations 14–25 in the itinerary, from רתמה to חשמנה (cf. Num 33:18–29), are not attested elsewhere in the Hebrew Bible.
4b	Stations 26–29 in the itinerary – i.e., (1) מסרות (2) בני יעקן (3) הר הגדגד, and (4) יטבתה (cf. Num 33:30–33) – elsewhere only appear in Deut 10:6–7, but in a slightly different order and with some variant spellings: (2) בארת בני־יעקן (1) מוסרה (3) הגדגד, and (4) יטבתה.
4c	Station 30, עברנה (Num 33:34–35), does not occur in the Hebrew Bible outside of Num 33:34–35. Station 31, עציון גבר (Num 33:35–36), occurs in Deut 2:8; 1Kgs 9:26 (= 2 Chr 8:17); and 1 Kgs 22:49 (= 2 Chr 20:36); it does not, however, occur again in the Wilderness Narrative.

Table C.1: Key to the Fractures and Overlaps in the Wilderness Travel Notices And Itinerary of Num 33:1–49 in Fig. C.1 *(Continued)*

Fracture #	Description
5a	The travel notice in Num 20:1 locates קדש in מדבר־צן, but Num 13:26 locates קדש in proximity to מדבר פארן. Numbers 33:36b, however, equates מדבר־צן with קדש.
5b	Numbers 20:16, 22 identifies קדש as a city (עיר) on the border of אדום (cf. v. 16) and the location from which Israel departed on its way to הר ההר (cf. v. 22), where Aaron dies (Num 20:22–29; cf Deut 10:6, where Aaron dies at מוסרה [cf. fracture 4b]). Conversely, Num 33:37 locates הר ההר (not קדש) as on the border of אדום (cf. fracture 6a).
6a	Numbers 20:22 sets הר ההר on the border of אדום. Numbers 21:4 reflects this outlying proximity in its travel notice, which records a second *departure* from הר ההר (see fracture 6b) via דרך ים־סוף in order to circumnavigate אדום, but then provides no *arrival* station in which to set the ensuing bronze serpent narrative (cf. Num 21:4–9). The itinerary records Stations 34 and 35 – i.e., צלמנה and פונם (Num 33:36–37) – which is not extant in the Wilderness Narrative, but may have been instrumental in situating the bronze serpent narrative (cf. p. 167 n. 27 above). Immediately after the bronze serpent narrative, the travel notice in Num 21:10 records a departure (נסע√), but no station of departure (originally הר ההר?) from which Israel sets out on their trek to אבת (cf. fracture 7a).
6b	Numbers 21:1 indicates a departure from an unstated location (in context הר ההר in Num 20:22–29) via דרך האתרים, which incites the battle with the King of Arad at חרמה (Num 21:1–3). This initial departure emerges as secondary in context of Num 21:4's departure, which is bound to the previous narrative (cf. Num 20:22 and 21:4). The itinerary does not consider חרמה a station, but demonstrates awareness of this conflict in the annotation in Num 33:40.
7a	While Num 21:10 uses the verbs נסע√ and חמה√ in its travel notice, the station of departure is omitted, or perhaps presumed (cf. fracture 6a).
7b	Numbers 21:11 locates עיי העברים outside the territory of מואב, in the wilderness which is על־פני מואב ממזרח השמש. The itinerary sees עיי העברים as located inside the territory of Moab (בגבול מואב).
7c	The bivouacs in Num 21:12–20, from נחל זרד to הגיא אשר בשדה מואב, are not extant in the itinerary, and the form of the travel notices becomes increasingly terse to the extent of becoming verbless.
8a	There is no awareness of the conflicts with סיהן and עוג in the itinerary between Station 37 (עיי העברים) and Station 38 (דיבן גד). Only the range provided in the annotation of Num 33:49 (*HexSupp*) – namely, בית הישמת (cf. Jos 12:3) and אבל השטים (Num 25:1) – evinces awareness of the conflicts with Sihon and Og, the Balaam cycle, and the Baal-Peor narrative.
8b	Variations of Station 41 and its annotation (בערבת מואב על ירדן ירחו; Num 33:48) become a refrain framing materials of which the itinerary (aside from v. 49; cf.

Table C.1: Key to the Fractures and Overlaps in the Wilderness Travel Notices And Itinerary of Num 33:1–49 in Fig. C.1 *(Continued)*

Fracture #	Description
	fracture 8a) largely shows no awareness: Num 22:1; 26:3, 63; 31:12; 33:50; 35:1; 36:13. The only exception is Num 33:50, which echoes Num 33:48 and introduces a section designed to transition to Deuteronomy. This transition is interrupted by the annotation in Num 33:49 (*HexSupp*) (cf. p. 177 n. 50 above).
8c	In the Wilderness Narrative, Yahweh commands Moses to ascend הר העברים הזה (which is not a wilderness station) in Num 27:12, which in turn occurs *after* the Israelites had arrive at the ערבות מואב לירדן ירחו (Num 22:1; cf. Num 26:3, 63). In the itinerary, הרי העברים is Station 40, at which the Israelites arrive *before* they bivouac at Station 41, the ערבת מואב על ירדן ירחו (cf. Num 33:47–48).

Appendix D

Exodus 17:1-7 by Stages of Literary Development[1]

Foundational Narrative (Dt)

ויצמא שם העם למים ויצעק משה אל־יהוה	And the people thirsted there for water, so Moses
ויאמר יהוה אל־משה עבר לפני העם	cried out to Yahweh. And Yahweh said to Moses,
וקח אתך מזקני ישראל ומטך קח בידך והלכת	"Pass before the people, and take with you some of
הנני עמד לפניך שם על־הצור בחרב	Israel's elders, and take your staff in your hand, and
והכית בצור ויצאו ממנו מים ושתה העם	go. Behold, I will be standing there upon the rock at
ויעש כן משה לעיני זקני ישראל	Horeb, and you will strike the rock, and water will
	go out from it, and the people will drink." Then
	Moses did so before the eyes of Israel's elders.

The Massah Episode (Dtr–Dtr Supp)

<u>ואין מים לשתת העם ויאמרו תנו־לנו מים ונשתה</u>	<u>Now there was no water for the people to drink,</u>
<u>ויאמר להם משה מה־תנסון את־יהוה</u>	<u>so they said 'Give us water, so we may drink!" Then</u>
ויצמא שם העם למים ויצעק משה אל־יהוה	<u>Moses said to them, "Why do you test Yahweh?"</u>
ויאמר יהוה אל־משה עבר לפני העם	But the people thirsted there for water, so Moses
וקח אתך מזקני ישראל ומטך קח בידך והלכת	cried out to Yahweh. And Yahweh said to Moses,
הנני עמד לפניך שם על־הצור בחרב	"Pass before the people, and take with you some of
והכית בצור ויצאו ממנו מים ושתה העם	Israel's elders, and take your staff in your hand, and
ויעש כן משה לעיני זקני ישראל	go. Behold, I will be standing there upon the rock at
<u>ויקרא שם המקום מסה על נסתם את־יהוה</u>	Horeb, and you will strike the rock, and water will
<u>לאמר היש יהוה בקרבנו אם־אין</u>	go out from it, and the people will drink." Then
	Moses did so before the eyes of Israel's elders. <u>And</u>
	<u>Moses called the name of the place "Massah"</u>
	<u>because they had tested Yahweh, saying, "Is Yahweh</u>
	<u>among us for not?"</u>

---

[1] The new materials added at each stage are indicated by underlining.

The Meribah Coordination (pre-Hex Supp)

ואין מים לשתת העם <u>וירב העם עם־משה</u>	Now there was no water for the people to drink, *so the people lodged a complaint with Moses*, and said 'Give us water, so we may drink!" Then Moses said to them, *"Why are you lodging a complaint with me? Why do you test Yahweh?"* But the people thirsted there for water, *and the people murmured against Moses, and they said* "Why then did you bring us up from Egypt? To kill us, our sons, and our cattle with thirst?" Then Moses cried out to Yahweh, *saying, "What am I to do for this people? A little more, and they will stone me!"* And Yahweh said to Moses, "Pass before the people, and take with you some of Israel's elders, and take your staff in your hand, and go. Behold, I will be standing there upon the rock at Horeb, and you will strike the rock, and water will go out from it, and the people will drink." Then Moses did so before the eyes of Israel's elders. And Moses called the name of the place "Massah" *and "Meribah" because of the complaint of the children of Israel*, and because they had tested Yahweh, saying, "Is Yahweh among us for not?"
ויאמרו תנו־לנו מים ונשתה ויאמר להם משה	
<u>מה־תריבון עמדי</u> מה־תנסון את־יהוה	
ויצמא שם העם למים <u>וילן העם על־משה</u>	
<u>ויאמר למה זה העליתנו ממצרים</u>	
<u>להמית אתי ואת־בני ואת־מקני בצמא</u>	
ויצעק משה אל־יהוה <u>לאמר</u>	
<u>מה אעשה לעם הזה עוד מעט וסקלני</u>	
ויאמר יהוה אל־משה עבר לפני העם	
וקח אתך מזקני ישראל ומטך קח בידך והלכת	
הנני עמד לפניך שם על־הצור בחרב	
והכית בצור ויצא ממנו מים ושתה העם	
ויעש כן משה לעיני זקני ישראל	
ויקרא שם המקום מסה <u>ומריבה</u>	
<u>על־ריב בני ישראל</u> ועל נסתם את־יהוה	
לאמר היש יהוה בקרבנו אם־אין	

Transposition of the non-P M-Mt Narrative (HexRed)

<u>ויסעו כל־עדה בני־ישראל ממדבר־סין למעיהם על־פי יהוה
ויחנו ברפידים</u>
ואין מים לשתת העם וירב העם עם־משה
ויאמרו תנו־לנו מים ונשתה ויאמר להם משה מה־תריבון
עמדי מה־תנסון את־יהוה
ויצמא שם העם למים וילן העם על־משה
ויאמר למה זה העליתנו ממצרים
להמית אתי ואת־בני ואת־מקני בצמא
ויצעק משה אל־יהוה לאמר
מה אעשה לעם הזה עוד מעט וסקלני
ויאמר יהוה אל־משה עבר לפני העם
וקח אתך מזקני ישראל ומטך קח בידך והלכת
הנני עמד לפניך שם על־הצור בחרב
והכית בצור ויצאו ממנו מים ושתה העם
ויעש כן משה לעיני זקני ישראל
ויקרא שם המקום מסה ומריבה
על־ריב בני ישראל ועל נסתם את־יהוה
לאמר היש יהוה בקרבנו אם־אין

<u>And all the congregation of the children of Israel journeyed from the Wilderness of Sin, according to their stages at the command of Yahweh, and they camped at Rephidim.</u> And there was no water for the people to drink, so the people lodged a complaint with Moses, and said 'Give us water, so we may drink!" Then Moses said to them, "Why are you lodging a complaint with me? Why do you test Yahweh?" But the people thirsted there for water, and the people murmured against Moses, and they said "Why then did you bring us up from Egypt? To kill us, our sons, and our cattle with thirst?" Then Moses cried out to Yahweh, saying, "What am I to do for this people? A little more, and they will stone me!" And Yahweh said to Moses, "Pass before the people, and take with you some of Israel's elders, and take your staff in your hand, and go. Behold, I will be standing there upon the rock at Horeb, and you will strike the rock, and water will go out from it, and the people will drink." Then Moses did so before the eyes of Israel's elders. And Moses called the name of the place "Massah" and "Meribah" because of the complaint of the children of Israel, and because they had tested Yahweh, saying, "Is Yahweh among us for not?"

The Disambiguation of the Staff (PentRed)

ויסעו כל־עדה בני־ישראל ממדבר־סין למעיהם על־פי יהוה	And all the congregation of the children of Israel journeyed from the Wilderness of Sin, according to their stages at the command of Yahweh,
ויחנו ברפידים	
ואין מים לשתת העם וירב העם עם־משה	and they camped at Rephidim. And there was no water for the people to drink, so the people lodged a complaint with Moses, and said 'Give us water, so we may drink!"
ויאמרו תנו־לנו מים ונשתה	
ויאמר להם משה מה־תריבון עמדי מה־תנסון את־יהוה	
ויצמא שם העם למים וילן העם על־משה	Then Moses said to them, "Why are you lodging a complaint with me? Why do you test Yahweh?"But the people thirsted there for water, and the people murmured against Moses, and they said "Why then did you bring us up from Egypt? To kill us, our sons, and our cattle with thirst?"
ויאמר למה זה העליתנו ממצרים להמית אתי ואת־בני ואת־מקני בצמא	
ויצעק משה אל־יהוה לאמר	
מה אעשה לעם הזה עוד מעט וסקלני	
ויאמר יהוה אל־משה עבר לפני העם וקח אתך מזקני ישראל	Then Moses cried out to Yahweh, saying, "What am I to do for this people? A little more, and they will stone me!" And Yahweh said to Moses, "Pass before the people, and take with you some of Israel's elders, and take your staff <u>(with which you struck the Nile)</u> in your hand, and go. Behold, I will be standing there upon the rock at Horeb, and you will strike the rock, and water will go out from it, and the people will drink." Then Moses did so before the eyes of Israel's elders. And Moses called the name of the place "Massah" and "Meribah" because of the complaint of the children of Israel, and because they had tested Yahweh, saying, "Is Yahweh among us for not?"
ומטך <u>אשר הכית בו־היאר</u> קח בידך והלכת	
הנני עמד לפניך שם על־הצור בחרב	
והכית בצור ויצאו ממנו מים ושתה העם	
ויעש כן משה לעיני זקני ישראל	
ויקרא שם המקום מסה ומריבה	
על־ריב בני ישראל ועל נסתם את־יהוה	
לאמר היש יהוה בקרבנו אם־אין	

Appendix E

Numbers 20:1–13 by Stages of Literary Development[1]

The Foundational Narrative (early-P)

ולא־היה מים לעדה	Now there was no water for the congregation, so
ויבא משה ואהרן מפני הקהל אל־פתח אהל מועד	Moses and Aaron went from the congregation to the
ויפלו על־פניהם וירא כבוד־יהוה אליהם	entrance of tent of meeting, and they fell on their faces.
וידבר יהוה אל־משה לאמר	Then the glory of Yahweh appeared to them, and
קח את־המטה והקהל את־העדה אתה ואהרן אחיך	Yahweh spoke to Moses, saying "Take the staff and
[והכית את]־הסלע לעיניהם ונתן מימיו	assemble the congregation, you and Aaron your
והוצאת להם מים מן־הסלע	brother; then [strike] the rock before their eyes, and it
והשקית את־העדה ואת־בעירם	will yield its water. You will bring out for them water
ויקהלו משה ואהרן את־הקהל אל־פני הסלע	from the rock, and you will provide the congregation
וירם משה את־ידו ויך את־הסלע במטהו	and their livestock a drink."
ויצאו מים רבים ותשת העדה ובעירם	So Moses and Aaron gathered the assembly before
	the rock. Then Moses raised his hand, and he struck the
	rock with his staff, and much water went out, so the
	congregation and their livestock drank.

The Kadesh Episode (P)

וישב העם בקדש ולא־היה מים לעדה	Now the people stayed at Kadesh, and there was no
ויאמרו לאמר למה הבאתם את־קהל יהוה	water for the congregation. And they said, saying "Why
אל־המדבר הזה	did you bring the assembly of Yahweh to this
להביא אתנו אל־המקום הרע הזה	wilderness, to bring us to this wretched place?!"
ויבא משה ואהרן מפני הקהל אל־פתח אהל מועד	So Moses and Aaron went from the congregation to
ויפלו על־פניהם וירא כבוד־יהוה אליהם	the entrance of tent of meeting, and they fell on their
וידבר יהוה אל־משה לאמר	faces. Then the glory of Yahweh appeared to them, and
קח את־המטה והקהל את־העדה אתה ואהרן אחיך	Yahweh spoke to Moses, saying "Take the staff and
[והכית את]־הסלע לעיניהם ונתן מימיו	assemble the congregation, you and Aaron your
והוצאת להם מים מן־הסלע	brother; then [strike] the rock before their eyes, and it
והשקית את־העדה ואת־בעירם	will yield its water. You will bring out for them water
ויקהלו משה ואהרן את־הקהל אל־פני הסלע	from the rock, and you will provide the congregation
וירם משה את־ידו ויך את־הסלע במטהו	and their livestock a drink."
ויצאו מים רבים ותשת העדה ובעירם	So Moses and Aaron gathered the assembly before
[...] <u>ויקדש [יהוה] בם</u>	the rock. Then Moses raised his hand, and he struck the
	rock with his staff, and much water went out, so the
	congregation and their livestock drank. [...] <u>and</u>
	<u>[Yahweh] was proved holy among them.</u>

---

[1] The new materials added or changed at each stage are indicated by underlining. Reconstruction forms are indicated by brackets.

The Meribah Coordination (pre-Hex Supp)

וישב העם בקדש ולא־היה מים לעדה	Now the people stayed at Kadesh, and there
<u>וירב העם עם־משה</u> ויאמרו לאמר	was no water for the congregation, <u>so the people</u>
למה הבאתם את־קהל יהוה אל־המדבר הזה	<u>lodged a complaint with Moses</u> and said, saying
<u>למות שם אנחנו ובעירנו</u>	"Why did you bring the assembly of Yahweh to this
<u>ולמה העליתנו ממצרים</u>	wilderness?! <u>For us and our livestock to die here?!</u>
להביא אתנו אל־המקום הרע הזה	<u>Why did you bring us up from Egypt?!</u> To bring us
[באשר] <u>מים אין לשתות</u>	to this wretched place <u>[where] there is no water to</u>
ויבא משה ואהרן מפני הקהל אל־פתח אהל מועד	<u>drink!"</u>
ויפלו על־פניהם וירא כבוד־יהוה אליהם	So Moses and Aaron went from the
וידבר יהוה אל־משה לאמר	congregation to the entrance of tent of meeting, and
קח את־המטה והקהל את־העדה אתה ואהרן אחיך	they fell on their faces. Then the glory of Yahweh
[והכית את]־הסלע לעיניהם ונתן מימיו	appeared to them, and Yahweh spoke to Moses,
והוצאת להם מים מן־הסלע	saying "Take the staff and assemble the
והשקית את־העדה ואת־בעירם	congregation, you and Aaron your brother; then
ויקהלו משה ואהרן את־הקהל אל־פני הסלע	[strike] the rock before their eyes, and it will yield
וירם משה את־ידו ויך את־הסלע במטהו	its water. You will bring out for them water from
ויצאו מים רבים ותשת העדה ובעירם	the rock, and you will provide the congregation and
<u>המה מי מריבה אשר־רבו בני־ישראל את־יהוה</u>	their livestock a drink."
ויקדש בם	So Moses and Aaron gathered the assembly
	before the rock. Then Moses raised his hand, and
	he struck the rock with his staff, and much water
	went out, so the congregation and their livestock
	drank.
	<u>These are the waters of Meribah, where the</u>
	<u>children of Israel lodged a complaint with Yahweh,</u>
	but he was proved holy among them.

The Wilderness of Zin (HexRed)

ויבאו בני־ישראל כל־העדה מדבר־צן בחדש הראשון	<u>Now the children of Israel, all the congregation,</u>
וישב העם בקדש <u>ותמת שם מרים ותקבר שם</u>	<u>came to the Wilderness of Zin in the first month</u>, and
ולא־היה מים לעדה וירב העם עם־משה	the people stayed at Kadesh. <u>And Miriam died there,</u>
ויאמרו לאמר למה הבאתם את־קהל יהוה	<u>and there she was buried.</u>
אל־המדבר הזה למות שם אנחנו ובעירנו	And there was no water for the congregation, so
ולמה העליתנו ממצרים	the people lodged a complaint with Moses and said,
להביא אתנו אל־המקום הרע הזה	saying "Why did you bring the assembly of Yahweh to
<u>לא מקום זרע ותאנה וגפן ורמן</u> ומים אין לשתות	this wilderness?! For us and our livestock to die here?!
ויבא משה ואהרן מפני הקהל אל־פתח אהל מועד	Why did you bring us up from Egypt?! To bring us to
ויפלו על־פניהם וירא כבוד־יהוה אליהם	this wretched place?! <u>It is not a place of grain, figs,</u>
וידבר יהוה אל־משה לאמר	<u>vines, or pomegranates;</u> and there is no water to
קח את־המטה והקהל את־העדה אתה ואהרן אחיך	drink!"
[והכית את]־הסלע לעיניהם ונתן מימיו	So Moses and Aaron went from the congregation
והוצאת להם מים מן־הסלע	to the entrance of tent of meeting, and they fell on their
והשקית את־העדה ואת־בעירם	faces. Then the glory of Yahweh appeared to them,
ויקהלו משה ואהרן את־הקהל אל־פני הסלע	and Yahweh spoke to Moses, saying "Take the staff
וירם משה את־ידו ויך את־הסלע במטהו	and assemble the congregation, you and Aaron your
ויצאו מים רבים ותשת העדה ובעירם	brother; then [strike] the rock before their eyes, and it
המה מי מריבה אשר־רבו בני־ישראל את־יהוה	will yield its water. You will bring out for them water
ויקדש בם	from the rock, and you will provide the congregation
	and their livestock a drink."
	So Moses and Aaron gathered the assembly
	before the rock. Then Moses raised his hand, and he
	struck the rock with his staff, and much water went
	out, so the congregation and their livestock drank.
	These are the waters of Meribah, where the
	children of Israel lodged a complaint with Yahweh,
	but he was proved as holy among them.

The Assembly against Moses & Aaron (PentRed)

ויבאו בני־ישראל כל־העדה מדבר־צן בחדש הראשון	Now the children of Israel, all the congregation,
וישב העם בקדש ותמת שם מרים ותקבר שם	came to the Wilderness of Zin in the first month, and the people stayed at Kadesh. And Miriam died there,
ולא־היה מים לעדה <u>ויקהלו על־משה ועל־אהרן</u>	and there she was buried.
וירב העם עם־משה ויאמרו לאמר	And there was no water for the congregation, <u>so</u>
<u>ולו גוענו בגוע אחינו לפני יהוה</u>	<u>they gathered against Moses and Aaron.</u> Then the
ולמה הבאתם את־קהל יהוה אל־המדבר הזה	people lodged a complaint with Moses and said,
למות שם אנחנו ובעירנו	saying <u>"If only we had died when our brothers died</u>
ולמה העליתנו ממצרים	<u>before Yahweh!</u> And why did you bring the assembly
להביא אתנו אל־המקום הרע הזה	of Yahweh to this wilderness?! For us and our
לא מקום זרע ותאנה וגפן ורמון ומים אין לשתות	livestock to die here?! Why did you bring us up from
ויבא משה ואהרן מפני הקהל אל־פתח אהל מועד	Egypt?! To bring us to this wretched place?!
ויפלו על־פניהם וירא כבוד־יהוה אליהם	It is not a place of grain, figs, vines, or pomegranates;
וידבר יהוה אל־משה לאמר	and there is no water to drink!"
קח את־המטה והקהל את־העדה אתה ואהרן אחיך	So Moses and Aaron went from the congregation
[והכית את]־הסלע לעיניהם ונתן מימיו	to the entrance of tent of meeting, and they fell on
והוצאת להם מים מן־הסלע	their faces. Then the glory of Yahweh appeared to
והשקית את־העדה ואת־בעירם	them, and Yahweh spoke to Moses, saying "Take the
<u>ויקח משה את־המטה מלפני יהוה כאשר צוהו</u>	staff and assemble the congregation, you and Aaron
ויקהלו משה ואהרן את־הקהל אל־פני הסלע	your brother; then [strike] the rock before their eyes,
<u>ויאמר להם שמעו־נא המרים</u>	and it will yield its water. You will bring out for them
<u>המן־הסלע הזה נוציא לכם מים</u>	water from the rock, and you will provide the
וירם משה את־ידו ויך את־הסלע במטהו <u>פעמים</u>	congregation and their livestock a drink."
ויצאו מים רבים ותשת העדה ובעירם	<u>So Moses took the staff from before Yahweh, just</u>
המה מי מריבה אשר־רבו בני־ישראל את־יהוה	<u>as he had commanded him.</u> Then Moses and Aaron
ויקדש בם	gathered the assembly before the rock, <u>and Moses</u>
	<u>said to them, "Listen now, you rebels! Are we to</u>
	<u>provide you water from this rock?!"</u> Then Moses
	raised his hand, and he struck the rock with his staff
	<u>twice</u>, and much water went out, so the congregation
	and their livestock drank.
	These are the waters of Meribah, where the
	children of Israel lodged a complaint with Yahweh,
	but he was proved holy among them.

The Failure of Moses and Aaron (post-PentRed)

ויבאו בני־ישראל כל־העדה מדבר־צן בחדש הראשון	Now the children of Israel, all the congregation, came to the Wilderness of Zin in the first month, and
וישב העם בקדש ותמת שם מרים ותקבר שם	the people stayed at Kadesh. And Miriam died there,
ולא־היה מים לעדה ויקהלו על־משה ועל־אהרן	and there she was buried.
וירב העם עם־משה ויאמרו לאמר	And there was no water for the congregation, so
ולו גוענו בגוע אחינו לפני יהוה	they gathered against Moses and Aaron. Then the
ולמה הבאתם את־קהל יהוה אל־המדבר הזה	people lodged a complaint with Moses and said,
למות שם אנחנו ובעירנו	saying
ולמה העליתנו ממצרים	"If only we had died when our brothers died before
להביא אתנו אל־המקום הרע הזה	Yahweh! Why did you bring the assembly of Yahweh
לא מקום זרע ותאנה וגפן ורמון	to this wilderness?! For us and our livestock to die
ומים אין לשתות	here?! Why did you bring us up from Egypt?! To
ויבא משה ואהרן מפני הקהל אל־פתח אהל מועד	bring us to this wretched place?! It is not a place of
ויפלו על־פניהם וירא כבוד־יהוה אליהם	grain, figs, vines, or pomegranates; and there is no
וידבר יהוה אל־משה לאמר	water to drink!"
קח את־המטה והקהל את־העדה אתה ואהרן אחיך	So Moses and Aaron went from the
ודברתם אל־הסלע לעיניהם ונתן מימיו	congregation to the entrance of tent of meeting, and
והוצאת להם מים מן־הסלע	they fell on their faces. Then the glory of Yahweh
והשקית את־העדה ואת־בעירם	appeared to them, and Yahweh spoke to Moses,
ויקח משה את־המטה מלפני יהוה כאשר צוהו	saying "Take the staff and assemble the
ויקהלו משה ואהרן את־הקהל אל־פני הסלע	congregation, you and Aaron your brother; then
ויאמר להם שמעו־נא המרים	<u>speak to</u> the rock before their eyes, and it will yield
המן־הסלע הזה נוציא לכם מים	its water. You will bring out for them water from the
וירם משה את־ידו ויך את־הסלע במטהו פעמים	rock, and you will provide the congregation and
ויצאו מים רבים ותשת העדה ובעירם	their livestock a drink."
<u>ויאמר יהוה אל־משה ואל־אהרן</u>	So Moses took the staff from before Yahweh, just
<u>יען לא־האמנתם בי להקדישני לעיני בני־ישראל</u>	as he had commanded him. Then Moses and Aaron
<u>לכן לא תביא את־הקהל הזה</u>	gathered the assembly before the rock, and Moses
<u>אל־הארץ אשר־נתתי להם</u>.	said to them, "Listen now, you rebels! Are we to
המה מי מריבה אשר־רבו בני־ישראל את־יהוה	provide you water from this rock?!" Then Moses
ויקדש בם	raised his hand, and he struck the rock with his staff
	twice, and much water went out, so the congregation
	and their livestock drank.
	<u>Then Yahweh said to Moses and to Aaron,</u>
	<u>"Because you did not believe me enough to prove me</u>
	<u>holy before the children of Israel, you will therefore</u>
	<u>not bring this assembly to the land which I have</u>
	<u>given them."</u>
	These are the waters of Meribah, where the
	children of Israel lodged a complaint with Yahweh,
	but he was proved holy among them.

Bibliography

Aberbach, M., and L. Smolar. "Aaron, Jeroboam, and the Golden Calves." *Journal of Biblical Literature* 86 (1967): 129–140.
Achenbach, Reinhard. *Die Vollendung der Tora: Studien zur Redaktionsgeschichte des Numeribuches im Kontext von Hexateuch und Pentateuch.* Beihefte zur Zeitschrift für Altorientalische und biblische Rechtgeschichte 3. Wiesbaden: Harrassowitz Verlag, 2003.
—, *Israel zwischen Verheißun und Gebot: Literarkritische Untersuchungen zu Deuteronomium 5–11.* Europäische Hochschulschriften: Reihe 23, Theologie 422. Frankfurt am Main: Peter Lang, 1991.
Ahlström, Gösta W. *The History of Ancient Palestine.* Edited by Diana Edelman. Minneapolis: Fortress Press, 1993.
Albertz, Rainer. "A Pentateuchal Redaction in the Book of Numbers? The Late Priestly Layers of Num 25–36." *Zeitschrift für die alttestamentliche Wissenschaft* 125 (2013): 220–233.
—, "Das Buch Numeri jenseits der Quellentheorie Eine Redaktionsgeschichte von Num 20–24 (Teil 1)." *Zeitschrift für die alttestamentliche Wissenschaft* 123 (2011): 171–183.
—, "Das Buch Numeri jenseits der Quellentheorie Eine Redaktionsgeschichte von Num 20–24 (Teil II)." *Zeitschrift für die alttestamentliche Wissenschaft* 123 (2011): 336–347.
Albertz, Rainer, James D. Nogalski, and Jakob Wöhrle, eds. *Perspectives on the Formation of the Book of the Twelve.* Beihefte zur Zeitschrift für die alttestamentliche Wissenschaft 433. Berlin–New York: de Gruyter, 2012.
Albright, W. F. "Some Remarks on the Song of Moses in Deuteronomy." *Vetus Testamentum* 9 (1959): 339–346.
Allen, David M. *Deuteronomy and Exhortation in Hebrews: A Study of Narrative Re-presentation.* Wissenschaftliche Untersuchungen zum Neuen Testament 2. Reihe 238. Tübingen: Mohr Siebeck, 2008.
Allen, Leslie C. *Psalms 101–150.* Word Biblical Commentary 21. Waco: Word Books, 1983.
Alt, Albrecht. "Josua." Pages 13–29 in *Werden und Wesen Des Alten Testaments.* Edited by Paul Volz, Friedrich Stummer, and Johannes Hempel. Beihefte zur Zeitschrift für die alttestamentliche Wissenschaft 66. Berlin: Alfred Töpelmann, 1936.
—, *Kleine Scriften zur Geschichte des Volkes Israels.* 2 vols. Münich: C. H. Beck, 1953.
Altmann, Alexander, ed. *Biblical Motifs: Origins and Transformations.* Studies and Texts 3. Cambridge: Harvard University Press, 1966.
Altmann, Peter. "What do the 'Levites in your Gates' Have to do with the 'Levitical Priests'? An Attempt at European-North American Dialogue on the Levites in the Deuteronomic Law Corpus." Pages 135–154 in *Levites and Priests in Biblical History and Tradition.* Edited by Mark A. Leuchter and Jeremy M. Hutton. Society of Biblical Literature Ancient Israel and its Literature 9. Leiden–Boston: Brill, 2012.
Anderson, A. A. *The Book of Psalms: Volume 2.* New Century Bible. London: Oliphant, 1972.
Anderson, Bernard W. "Introduction: Martin Noth's Traditio-Historical Approach in the Context of Twentieth-Century Biblical Research," pages xiii-xxxii in *A History of Pentateuchal Traditions,* by Martin Noth. Translated by Bernard W. Anderson. Stuttgart: Verlag, 1948. Repr., Englewood Cliffs: Prentice-Hall, 1972.
Anderson, Bernhard W. and Walter Harrelson, eds. *Israel's Prophetic Heritage: Essays in Honor of James Muilenburg.* London: SCM Press, 1962.

Artus, Olivier. *Etudes sur le livre des Nombres: Récit, Histoire et Loi en Nb 13,1–20,13.* Orbis biblicus et orientalis 157. Göttingen: Vandenhoeck & Ruprecht, 1997.
Ashley, Timothy R. *The Book of Numbers.* New International Commentary on the Old Testament. Grand Rapids: Eerdmans, 1993.
Astruc, Jean. *Conjectures sur les mémoires originaux dont il paroit que Moyse s'est servi pour composer le livre de la Genèse.* Brussels, 1753.
Aurelius, Erik. *Der Fürbitter Israels: Eine Studie zum Mosebild im Alten Testament.* Coniectanea biblica: Old Testament Series 27. Stockholm: Almqvist & Wiksell, 1988.
Bacon, Benjamin W. "JE in the Middle of the Pentateuch. III. From Egpyt to Sinai: Analysis of Exodus XII.37–XVII.16." *Journal of Biblical Literature* 11 (1892): 177–200.
Baden, Joel S. *J, E, and the Redaction of the Pentateuch.* Forschungen zum Alten Testament 68. Tübingen: Mohr Siebeck, 2009.
—, *The Composition of the Pentateuch: Renewing the Documentary Hypothesis.* Anchor Yale Bible Reference Library. New Haven–London: Yale University Press, 2012.
—, "The Violent Origins of the Levites: Text and Tradition." Pages 103–116 in *Levites and Priests in Biblical History and Tradition.* Edited by Mark A. Leuchter and Jeremy M. Hutton. Society of Biblical Literature Ancient Israel and its Literature 9. Leiden–Boston: Brill, 2012.
Baentsch, Bruno. *Exodus – Leviticus – Numeri: übersetzt und erklärt.* Handkommentar zum Alten Testament I/2. Göttingen: Vandenhoeck & Ruprecht, 1903.
Baltzer, Klaus. *The Covenant Formulary in Old Testament, Jewish and Early Christian Writings.* Philadelphia: Fortress, 1971.
Barr, James, ed. *Language and Meaning: Studies in Hebrew Language and Biblical Exegesis: Papers Read at the Joint British-Dutch Old Testament Conference at London, 1973.* Oudtestamentische Studiën 19. Leiden: Brill, 1974.
Barrick, W. Boyd. *BMH as Body Language: A Lexical and Iconographic Study of the Word BMH When Not a Reference to Cultic Phenomena in Biblical and Post-biblical Hebrew.* Library of Hebrew Bible / Old Testament Studies 477. London–New York: T & T Clark, 2008.
Bartelmus, Rüdiger, Thomas Krüger, and Helmut Utzschneider, eds. *Konsequente Traditionsgeschichte: Festschrift für Klaus Baltzer zum 65. Geburtstag.* Orbis biblicus et orientalis 126. Göttingen: Vandenhoeck & Ruprecht, 1993.
Bartlett, J. R. "The Wadi Arabah in the Hebrew Scriptures." Pages 151–156 in *Crossing the Rift: Resources, Routes, Settlement Patterns and Interaction in the Wadi Arabah.* Edited by Piotr Bienkowski and Katharina Galor. Levant Supplementary Series 3. Oxford: Oxbow, 2006.
Baumgarten, Joseph M. *Qumran Cave 4, XIII, The Damascus Document (4Q266–273).* Discoveries in the Judaean Desert XVIII. Oxford: Clarendon Press, 1996.
Beaucamp, E. *Le Psautier: Ps 73–150.* Sources bibliques. Paris: Gabalda, 1976.
Begg, Christopher T. "Contributions to the Elucidation of the Composition of Deuteronomy with special attention to the significance of the Numeruswechsel." Ph.D. diss., Katholieke Universiteit te Leuven, 1978.
—, "The Significance of the Numeruswechsel in Deuteronomy: The "Pre-History" of the Question." *Ephemerides theologicae lovanienses* 55 (1979): 116–124.
Begrich, Joachim. *Studien zu Deuterojesaja.* Beiträge zur Wissenschaft vom Alten (und Neuen) Testament 4 Folge, Heft 25 [77]. Stuttgart: W. Kohlhammer, 1938.
Bellinger, W. H. Jr. *Psalms: Reading and Studying the Book of Psalms.* Peabody: Hendrickson, 1990.

Beuken, W. A. M. "Exodus 16:5, 23: A Rule Regarding the Sabbath." *Journal for the Study of the Old Testament* 32 (1985): 3–14.
Beuken, W. A., and H. W. van Grol. "Jeremiah 14,1–15,9: A Situation of Distress and its Hermeneutics; Unity and Diversity of Form: Dramatic Development." Pages 297–342 in *Le Livre de Jeremie: le prophete et son milieu, les oracles et leur transmission*. Edited by Pierre Maurice Bogaert. Louvain: Leuven University Press, 1981.
Beyerle, Stefan. *Der Mosesegen im Deuteronomium: Eine text-, kompositions- und formkritische Studie zu Deuteronomium 33*. Beihefte zur Zeitschrift für die alttestamentliche Wissenschaft 250. Berlin–New York: DeGruyter, 1997.
—, "Evidence of a Polymorphic Text: Towards the Text-History of Deuteronomy 33." *Dead Sea Discoveries* 5 (1998): 215–232.
Biddle, Mark E. *Deuteronomy*. Smyth & Helwys Bible Commentary. Macon: Smyth & Helwys, 2003.
—, *Polyphony and Symphony in Prophetic Literature: Rereading Jeremiah 7–20*. Studies in Old Testament Interpretation 2. Macon: Mercer University Press, 1996.
Bienkowski, Piotr and Katharina Galor, eds. *Crossing the Rift: Resources, Routes, Settlement Patterns and Interaction in the Wadi Arabah*. Levant Supplementary Series 3. Oxford: Oxbow, 2006.
Blenkinsopp, Joseph. "An Assessment of the Alleged Pre-Exilic Date of the Priestly Material in the Pentateuch." *Zeitschrift für die alttestamentliche Wissenschaft* 108 (1996): 495–518.
—, *Ezra – Nehemiah*. Old Testament Library. Louisville: Westminster Press, 1988.
—, *Isaiah 1–39: A New Translation with Introduction and Commentary*. Anchor Bible 19. New York: Doubleday, 2000.
—, *Isaiah 40–55: A New Translation with Introduction and Commentary*. Anchor Bible 19 A. New York: Doubleday, 2002.
—, *Isaiah 56–66: A New Translation with Introduction and Commentary*. Anchor Bible 19B. New York: Doubleday, 2003.
—, *The Pentateuch: An Introduction to the First Five Books of the Bible*. Anchor Bible Reference Library. New York: Doubleday, 1992.
Block, Daniel I. *The Book of Ezekiel: Chapters 25–48*. New International Commentary on the Old Testament. Grand Rapids: Eerdmans, 1998.
Blum, Erhard. *Die Komposition der Vätergeschichte*. Wissenschaftliche Monographien zum Alten und Neuen Testament 57. Neukirchen-Vluyn: Neukirchener, 1984.
—, "Pentateuch – Hexateuch – Enneateuch? Oder: Woran erkennt man ein literarisches Werk in der hebräischen Bibel." Pages 67–97 in *Les dernièrs rédactions du Pentateuque, de L'Hexateuque et de L'Ennéateuque*. Edited by Thomas Römer and Konrad Schmid. Bibliotheca ephemeridum theologicarum lovaniensium 203. Paris: Leuven University, 2007.
—, "Pentateuch – Hexateuch – Enneateuch? Or: How Can One Recognize a Literary Work in the Hebrew Bible." Pages 43–71 in *Pentateuch, Hexateuch, or Enneateuch? Identifying Literary Works in Genesis through Kings*. Edited by Thomas B. Dozeman, Thomas Römer, and Konrad Schmid. Society of Biblical Literature 8. Atlanta: Society of Biblical Literature, 2011.
—, *Studien zur Komposition des Pentateuch*. Beihefte zur Zeitschrift für die alttestamentliche Wissenschaft 189. Berlin: de Gruyter, 1990.
Bogaert, Pierre Maurice, ed. *Le Livre de Jeremie: le prophete et son milieu, les oracles et leur transmission*. Louvain: Leuven University Press, 1981.

Boorer, Suzanne. "The Place of Numbers 13–14* and Numbers 20:2–13* in the Priestly Narrative (Pg)." *Journal of Biblical Literature* 131 (2012): 45–63.

—, *The Promise of the Land as Oath: A Key to the Formation of the Pentateuch*. Beihefte zur Zeitschrift für die alttestamentliche Wissenschaft 205. Berlin–New York: de Gruyter, 1992.

Boston, James R. "The Wisdom Influence upon the Song of Moses." *Journal of Biblical Literature* 87 (1968): 198–202.

Botterweck, G. Johannes and Helmer Ringgren, eds. *Theological Dictionary of the Old Testament*. Translated by John T. Willis. 15 vols. rev. ed. Stuttgart: Verlag W. Kohlhammer, 1970. Repr., Grand Rapids: Eerdmans, 1977.

Boyarin, Daniel. "The Gospel of the Memra: Jewish Binitarianism and the Prologue of John." *Harvard Theological Review* 94 (2001): 243–284.

Braulik, Georg, ed. *Bundesdokument und Gesetz: Studien zum Deuteronomium*. Herders biblische Studien 4. Freiburg–New York: Herder, 1995.

Britt, Brian. *Rewriting Moses: The Narrative Eclipse of the Text*. Journal for the Study of the Old Testament: Supplement Series 402. London–New York: T & T Clark, 2004.

Brown, Francis, S. R. Driver, and Charles A. Briggs, eds. *A Hebrew and English Lexicon of the Old Testament*. 1968. London: Oxford University Press, 1907.

Brown, Raymond E. *An Introduction to the Gospel of John; Edited, Updated, Introduced, and Concluded by Francis J. Maloney*. Anchor Bible Reference Library. New York: Doubleday, 2003.

Brown, Raymond E. *The Gospel According to John (i-xii): Introduction, Translation, and Notes*. Anchor Bible 29. New York: Doubleday, 1966.

Brueggemann, Walter. *A Commentary on Jeremiah: Exile and Homecoming*. Grand Rapids: Eerdmans, 1998.

—, *Deuteronomy*. Abingdon Old Testament Commentaries. Nashville: Abingdon Press, 2001.

Budd, Philip J. *Numbers*. Word Biblical Commentary 5. Waco: Word Books, 1984.

Buis, P. "Les conflits entre Moïse et Israël dans Exode et Nombres." *Vetus Testamentum* 28 (1978): 257–270.

Burden, Terry L. *The Kerygma of the Wildernss Traditions in the Hebrew Bible*. American University Studies, Series VII, Theology and Religion 163. New York: Peter Lang, 1994.

Burnett, Joel S., W. H. Bellinger Jr., and Dennis Tucker Jr., eds. *Diachronic and Synchronic: Reading the Psalms in Real Time: Proceedings of the Baylor Symposium on the Book of Psalms*. New York–London: T & T Clark, 2007.

Butler, James T., Edgar W. Conrad, and Ben C. Ollenburger, eds. *Understanding the Word: Essays in Honour of Bernhard W. Andersen*. Journal for the Study of the Old Testament: Supplement Series 37. Sheffield: JSOT Press, 1985.

Campbell, Antony F., and Mark A. O'Brien. *Unfolding the Deuteronomistic History: Origins, Upgrades, Present Text*. Minneapolis: Fortress, 2000.

Caquot, André. "Les bénédictions de Moïse (Deutéronome 33, 6–25). I – Ruben, Juda, Lévi, Benjamin." *Semitica* 32 (1982): 67–81.

Carr, David M. "Controversy and Convergence in Recent Studies of the Formation of the Pentateuch." *Religious Studies Review* 23 (1997): 22–31.

—, *Reading the Fractures of Genesis: Historical and Literary Approaches*. Louisville: Westminster John Knox, 1996.

—, *The Erotic Word: Sexuality, Spirituality, and the Bible*. New York: Oxford University, 2003.

—, *The Formation of the Hebrew Bible: A New Reconstruction.* New York: Oxford University Press, 2011.
—, "The Moses Story: Literary Historical Reflections." *Hebrew Bible and Ancient Israel* 1 (2012): 7–36.
—, *Writing on the Tablet of the Heart: Origins of Scripture and Literature.* New York: Oxford University, 2005.
Carroll, Robert P. *Jeremiah: A Commentary.* Old Testament Library. London: SCM Press Ltd, 1986.
Cassuto, Umberto. "Il capitolo 33 del Deuteronomio e la festa del Capo d'anno nell'antico Israele." *Revista degli studi orientali* 11 (1926–1928): 233–253.
Chapman, Stephen B. *The Law and the Prophets: A Study in Old Testament Canon Formation.* Forschungen zum Alten Testament 27. Tübingen: Mohr Siebeck, 2000.
Charlesworth, James H., ed. *The Old Testament Pseudepigrapha.* 2 vols. Anchor Bible Reference Library. New York: Doubleday, 1983.
Childs, Brevard S. *Introduction to the Old Testament as Scripture.* Philadelphia: Fortress, 1979.
—, *Isaiah.* Old Testament Library. Louisville: Westminster, 2001.
—, *The Book of Exodus: A Critical, Theological Commentary.* Old Testament Library. Louisville: Westminster, 1974.
Christensen, Duane L. "Two Stanzas of a Hymn in Deuteronomy 33." *Biblica* 65 (1984): 382–389.
—, *Deuteronomy 1–11.* Word Biblical Commentary 6a. Dallas: Word Books, 1991.
—, *Deuteronomy 1:1–21:9.* 2nd ed. Word Biblical Commentary 6a. Nashville: Thomas Nelson, 2001.
—, *Deuteronomy 21:10–34:12.* Word Biblical Commentary 6b. Nashville: Thomas Nelson, 2002.
—, "Deuteronomy in Modern Research: Approaches and Issues." Pages 3–17 in *A Song of Power and the Power of Song: Essays on the Book of Deuteronomy.* Edited by Duane L. Christensen. Sources for Biblical and Theological Study 3. Winona Lake: Eisenbrauns, 1993.
Christensen, Duane L., ed. *A Song of Power and the Power of Song: Essays on the Book of Deuteronomy.* Sources for Biblical and Theological Study 3. Winona Lake: Eisenbrauns, 1993.
Clements, R. E. *Deuteronomy.* Old Testament Guides. Sheffield: JSOT, 1989.
—, *Isaiah 1–39.* New Century Bible. Grand Rapids: Eerdmans, 1980.
Coats, George W. "An Exposition for the Wilderness Traditions." *Vetus Testamentum* 22 (1972): 288–295.
—, *Exodus 1–18.* Forms of the Old Testament Literature IIA. Grand Rapids: Eerdmans, 1999.
—, *Rebellion in the Wilderness: The Murmuring Motif in the Wilderness Traditions of the Old Testament.* Nashville: Abingdon, 1968.
—, "The Wilderness Itinerary." *Catholic Biblical Quarterly* 34 (1972): 135–152.
Cornill, C. H. "Beiträge zur Pentateuchkritik." *Zeitschrift für die alttestamentliche Wissenschaft* 11 (1891): 1–34.
Craigie, Peter C., Page H. Kelly, and Joel F. Drinkard. *Jeremiah 1–25.* Word Biblical Commentary 26. Nashville: Thomas Nelson, 1991.
Cross, Frank M. Jr. *Canaanite Myth and Hebrew Epic: Essays in the History of the Religion of Israel.* Cambridge: Harvard University Press, 1973.

Cross, Frank M. Jr., and David Noel Freedman. "The Blessing of Moses." *Journal of Biblical Literature* 67 (1948): 191–210.
Dahood, Mitchell. *Psalms II: 51–100*. Anchor Bible 17. Garden City: Doubleday, 1968.
Davies, Eryl W. *Numbers*. New Century Bible. Grand Rapids: Eerdmans, 1995.
Davies, G. I. "The Wilderness Itineraries and Recent Archaeological Research." Pages 161–176 in *Studies in the Pentateuch*. Edited by J. A. Emerton. Supplements to Vetus Testamentum 41. Leiden: Brill, 1990.
—, "The Wilderness Itineraries and the Composition of the Pentateuch." *Vetus Testamentum* 33 (1983): 1–13.
—, *The Way of the Wilderness: A Geographical Study of the Wilderness Itineraries in the Old Testament*. Society for Old Testament Studies Monograph Series 5. New York: Cambridge University Press, 1979.
—, "The Wilderness Itineraries: A Comparative Study." *Tyndale Bulletin* 25 (1974): 46–81.
DeClaissé-Walford, Nancy L. *Introduction to the Psalms*. St. Louis: Chalic Press, 2004.
DeSilva, David A. *Introducing the Aprocrypha: Message, Context, and Significance*. Grand Rapids: Baker Academic, 2002.
DeVries, S. J. "The Origin of the Murmuring Tradition." *Journal of Biblical Literature* 87 (1968): 51–58.
Diamond, A. R. Pete, Kathleen M. O'Connor, and Louis Stulman, eds. *Troubling Jeremiah*. Journal for the Study of the Old Testament: Supplement Series 260. Sheffield: Sheffield Academic Press, 1999.
Dijkstra, Meindert. "The Geography of the Story of Balaam: Synchronic Reading as a Help to Date a Biblical Text." Pages 72–97 in *Synchronic or Diachronic? A Debate on Method in Old Testament Stuides*. Edited by Johannes C. De Moor. Oudtestamentische Studiën 34. Leiden: Brill, 1995.
Dotan, Aron. "Reflections Towards a Critical Edition of Pentateuch Codex Or. 4445." Pages 39–51 in *Estudios masoréticos (X Congreso de la IOMS): En memoria de Harry M. Orlinsky*. Edited by E. F. Tejero and M. T. O. Monasterio. Textos y Estudios "Cardenal Cisneros" 55. Madrid: Instituto de Filogía del CSIC, 1993.
Dozeman, Thomas B. *Exodus*. Eerdmans Critical Commentary. Grand Rapids: Eerdmans, 2009.
—, "Geography and Ideology in the Wilderness Journey from Kadesh through the Transjordan." Pages 173–190 in *Abschied vom Jahwisten: Dis Komposition des Hexateuch in der jüngsten Diskussion*. Edited by Jan Christian Gertz, Konrad Schmid, and Markus Witte. Beihefte zur Zeitschrift für die alttestamentliche Wissenschaft 315. Berlin–New York: de Gruyter, 2002.
—, "Hosea and the Wilderness Wandering Tradition." Pages 55–70 in *Rethinking the Foundations: Historiography in the Ancient World and in the Bible*. Edited by Steven L. McKenzie and Thomas Römer. Beihefte zur Zeitschrift für die alttestamentliche Wissenschaft 294. Berlin–New York: de Gruyter, 2000.
—, "The Priestly Wilderness Itineraries and the Composition of the Pentateuch." Pages 257–288 in *The Pentateuch: International Perspectives on Current Research*. Edited by Thomas B. Dozeman, Konrad Schmid, and Baruch J. Schwartz. Forschungen zum Alten Testament 78. Tübingen: Mohr Siebeck, 2011.
Dozeman, Thomas B. and Konrad Schmid, eds. *A Farewell to the Yahwist? The Composition of the Pentateuch in Recent European Interpretation*. Society of Biblical Literature Symposium Series 34. Atlanta: Society of Biblical Literature, 2006.

Dozeman, Thomas B., Konrad Schmid, and Baruch J. Schwartz, eds. *The Pentateuch: International Perspectives on Current Research*. Forschungen zum Alten Testament 78. Tübingen: Mohr Siebeck, 2011.

Dozeman, Thomas B., Thomas Römer, and Konrad Schmid, eds. *Pentateuch, Hexateuch, or Enneateuch? Identifying Literary Works in Genesis through Kings*. Society of Biblical Literature 8. Atlanta: Society of Biblical Literature, 2011.

Drazin, Israel. *Targum Onkelos to Deuteronomy: An English Translation of the Text with Analysis and Commentary*. New York: Ktav Publishing House, 1982.

Duncan, Julie A. "New Readings for the "Blessing of Moses" from Qumran." *Journal of Biblical Literature* 114 (1995): 273–290.

Durham, John I. *Exodus*. Word Biblical Commentary 3. Waco: Word Books, 1987.

Ederer, Matthias. *Aufbrüche zur Exodustheologie: Das Itinerar Num 33.1–49 als theologische Deutung der Wüstenzeit Israels*. Stuttgarter Bibelstudien 231. Stuttgart: Katholisches Bibelwerk, 2014.

Eichhorn, J. Gottfried. *Einleitung ins Alte Testament*. 3 vols. Leipzig: Bey Weidmanns erben und Reich, 1780–1783.

Eissfeldt, Otto. *Einleitung in das Alte Testament, unter Einschluß der Apokryphen und Pseudepigraphen sowie der apokryphen- und pseudepigraphenartigen Qumrān-Schriften*. Edited by Rudolf Bultmann. 3rd ed. Neue theologische Grundrisse. Tübingen: J. C. B. Mohr, 1964.

—, *The Old Testament: An Introduction including the Apocrypha and Pseudepigrapha, and also the works of similar type from Qumran*. Translated by P. R. Ackroyd. 3rd ed. Tübingen: Mohr, 1934. Repr., New York: Harper & Row, 1965.

Emanuel, David. "An Unrecognized Voice: Intra-textual and Intertextual Perspectives on Psalm 81." *Hebrew Studies* 50 (2009): 85–120.

Emerton, J. A., ed. *Studies in the Pentateuch*. Supplements to Vetus Testamentum 41. Leiden: Brill, 1990.

Emmrich, Martin. "The Case against Moses Reopened." *Journal of the Evangelical Theological Society* 46 (2003): 53–62.

Fishbane, Michael. *Biblical Interpretation in Ancient Israel*. Oxford: Clarendon Press, 1985.

—, "The Well of Living Water: A Biblical Motif and Its Ancient Transformations." Pages 3–16 in *"Sha'arei Talmon": Studies in the Bible, Qumran, and the Ancient Near East Presented to Shemaryahu Talmon*. Edited by Michael A. Fishbane, Emanuel Tov, and Weston Fields. Winona Lake: Eisenbrauns, 1992.

Fishbane, Michael A., Emanuel Tov, and Weston Fields, eds. *"Sha'arei Talmon": Studies in the Bible, Qumran, and the Ancient Near East Presented to Shemaryahu Talmon*. Winona Lake: Eisenbrauns, 1992.

Fistill, Ulrich. *Israel und das Ostjordanland: Untersuchungen zur Komposition von Num 21,21–36,13 im Hinblick auf die Entstehung des Buches Numeri*. Österreichische biblische Studien 30. Frankfurt: Peter Lang, 2007.

Flint, Peter W. and Patrick D. Miller, eds. *The Book of Psalms: Composition and Reception*. Leiden–Boston: Brill, 2005.

Fohrer, George. *Einleitung in das Alte Testament: begründet von Ernst Sellin; neubearbeitung von Georg Fohrer*. 11th ed. Heidelberg: Quelle & Meyer, 1969.

Fokkelman, J. P. *Major Poems of the Hebrew Bible: At the Interface of Hermeneutics and Structural Analysis: Volume 1: Ex. 15, Deut. 32, and Job 3*. Studia semitica neerlandica 37. Assen: Van Gorcum, 1998.

Frankel, David. "The Destruction of the Golden Calf – A New Solution." *Vetus Testamentum* 44 (1994): 330–339.
—, *The Murmuring Stories of the Priestly School: A Retrieval of Ancient Sacerdotal Lore.* Supplements to Vetus Testamentum 89. Leiden–Boston–Köln: Brill, 2002.
Freedman, David Noel. "The Poetic Structure of the Framework of Deuteronomy 33." Pages 85–107 in *Divine Commitment and Human Obligation, vol. 2: Poetry and Orthagraphy.* Edited by J. Huddlestun. Grand Rapids: Eerdmans, 1997.
—, "Archaic Forms in Early Hebrew Poetry." *Zeitschrift für die alttestamentliche Wissenschaft* 72 (1960): 101–107.
Freedman, David Noel, ed. *Anchor Bible Dictionary.* 6 vols. New York: Doubleday, 1992.
Fretheim, Terence E. *Jeremiah.* Smyth & Helwys Bible Commentary. Macon: Smyth & Helwys, 2002.
Frevel, Christian. *Mit Blick auf das Land die Schöpfung erinnern: Zum Ende der Priestergrundschrift.* Herders biblishce Studien 23. Freiburg: Herder, 2000.
Frevel, Christian, Thomas Pola, and Aaron Schart, eds. *Torah and the Book of Numbers.* Forschungen zum Alten Testament 2. Reihe 62. Tübingen: Mohr Siebeck, 2013.
Fritz, Volkmar. *Israel in der Wüste: Traditiongeschichtliche Untersuchung der Wüstenüberlieferungen des Jahwisten.* Marburger theologische Studien 7. Marburg: N. G. Elwert, 1970.
Fuhs, H. F. "Qadesh – Materialen zu den Wüstentradition Israels." *Biblische Notizen* 9 (1979): 54–70.
Fuller, Russell. "The Blessing of Levi in Dtn 33, Mal 2, and Qumran." Pages 31–44 in *Konsequente Traditionsgeschichte: Festschrift für Klaus Baltzer zum 65. Geburtstag.* Edited by Rüdiger Bartelmus, Thomas Krüger, and Helmut Utzschneider. Orbis biblicus et orientalis 126. Göttingen: Vandenhoeck & Ruprecht, 1993.
Fuss, Werner. *Die deuteronomistische Pentateuchsredaktion in Exodus 3–17.* Beihefte zur Zeitschrift für die alttestamentliche Wissenschaft 126. Berlin: de Gruyter, 1972.
Gall, August Freiherrn von hrsg. *Der Hebräische Pentateuch der Samaritaner.* Giessen: Alfred Töpelmann, 1918.
Galling, Kurt. *Die Erwählungstraditionen Israels.* Beihefte zur Zeitschrift für die alttestamentliche Wissenschaft 48. Giessen: A. Töpelmann, 1928.
García López, Félix. "Analyse littéraire de Deutéronome, V-XI." *Revue biblique* 84 (1977): 481–522.
—, "Analyse littéraire de Deutéronome, V-XI." *Revue biblique* 85 (1978): 5–49.
—, "Deut., VI et la tradition-rédaction du Deutéronome." *Revue biblique* 85 (1978): 161–200.
—, "La Place du Lévitique et des Nombres dans la Formation du Pentateuque." Pages 75–98 in *The Books of Leviticus and Numbers.* Edited by Thomas Römer. Bibliotheca ephemeridum theologicarum lovaniensium 215. Leuven: Peeters, 2008.
—, "Yahvé, fuente última de vida análisis de Dt 8." *Biblica* 62 (1981): 21–54.
Garton, Roy E. "Rattling the Bones of the Twelve: Wilderness Reflections in the Formation of the Book of the Twelve." Pages 237–251 in *Perspectives on the Formation of the Book of the Twelve.* Edited by Rainer Albertz, James D. Nogalski, and Jakob Wöhrle. Beihefte zur Zeitschrift für die alttestamentliche Wissenschaft 433. Berlin–New York: de Gruyter, 2012.

Gerstenberger, Erhard. *Psalms: Part 1: With and Introduction to Cultic Poetry*. Forms of the Old Testament Literature 14. Grand Rapids: Eerdmans, 1988.
—, *Psalms: Part 2: and Lamentations*. Forms of the Old Testament Literature 15. Grand Rapids: Eerdmans, 2001.
Gertz, Jan Christian. *Tradition und Redaktion in der Exoduserzählung: Untersuchungen zur Endredaktion des Pentateuch*. Forschungen zur Religion und Literatur des Alten und Neuen Testaments 186. Göttingen: Vandenhoeck & Ruprecht, 2000.
Gertz, Jan Christian, Konrad Schmid, and Markus Witte, eds. *Abschied vom Jahwisten: Dis Komposition des Hexateuch in der jüngsten Diskussion*. Beihefte zur Zeitschrift für die alttestamentliche Wissenschaft 315. Berlin–New York: de Gruyter, 2002.
Gese, H. and H. R. Rüger, ed. *Wort und Geschichte: Festschrift für Karl Elliger zum 70. Geburtstag*. Alter Orient und Altes Testament 18. Neukirchen-Vluyn: Neukirchener Verlag, 1973.
Gile, Jason. "Ezekiel 16 and the Song of Moses: A Prophetic Transformation." *Journal of Biblical Literature* 130 (2011): 87–108.
Ginzberg, Louis. *The Legends of the Jews*. 7 vols. Philadelphia: Jewish Publication Society, 1909-1938. Repr., Baltimore: Johns Hopkins University Press, 1998.
Golka, Friedemann W. "The Aetiologies in the Old Testament: Part 1." *Vetus Testamentum* 26 (1973): 410–428.
—, "The Aetiologies in the Old Testament: Part 2." *Vetus Testamentum* 27 (1977): 36–47.
Gordley, Matthew E. *Teaching through Song in Antiquity*. Wissenschaftliche Untersuchungen zum Neuen Testament 2. Reihe 302. Tübingen: Mohr-Siebeck, 2011.
Graf, Karl H. *Die geschichtlichen Bücher des Alten Testaments. Zwei historisch-kritische Untersuchungen*. Leipzig: T. O. Weigel, 1866.
Gray, George Buchanan. *A Critical and Exegetical Commentary on Numbers*. International Critical Commentary. New York: Charles Scribner's Sons, 1903.
Gressmann, Hugo. *Mose und seine Zeit: Ein Kommentar zu den Mose-Sagen*. Forschungen zur Religion und Literatur des Alten und Neuen Testaments 18. Göttingen: Vandenhoeck & Ruprecht, 1913.
Gunkel, Hermann. *Genesis: Übersetzt und Erklärt*. 3rd ed. Göttingen: Vandenhoeck & Ruprecht, 1910.
—, *Schöpfung und Chaos in Urzeit und Endzeit: Eine religionsgeschichtliche Untersuchung über Gen 1 und Ap Joh 12*. Göttingen: Vandenhoeck & Ruprecht, 1895.
Gunkel, Hermann, and Joachim Begrich. *Einlietung in die Psalmen: Die Gattungen der religösen Lyrik Israels*. Göttingen: Vandenhoeck & Rurprecht, 1933.
Hals, Ronald. *Ezekiel*. Forms of the Old Testament Literature 19. Grand Rapids: Eerdmans, 1988.
Haran, Menahem. "Ezekiel, P, and the Priestly School." *Vetus Testamentum* 58 (2008): 211–218.
Harvey, John E. *Retelling the Torah: The Deuteronomistic Historian's Use of Tetrateuchal Narratives*. Journal for the Study of the Old Testament: Supplement Series 403. London–New York: T & T Clark, 2004.
Haudebert, Pierre, ed. *Le Pentateuque: débats et recherches: XIVe Congrìs de l'ACFEB, Angers (1991)*. Lectio divina 151. Paris: Cerf, 1992.
Hausmann, Jutta and Hans-Jürgen Zobel, eds. *Alttestamentlicher Glaube und biblische Theologie: Festschrift für Horst Dietrich Pruess zum 65. Geburtstag*. Stuttgart: Kohlhammer, 1992.

Helfgot, Nathaniel. "'And Moses Struck the Rock': Numbers 20 and the Leadership of Moses." *Tradition* 27 (1993): 51–58.
Herrmann, Siegfried. "Die konstruktive Restauration: Das Deuteronomium als Mitte biblischer Theologie." Pages 155–170 in *Probleme biblischer Theologie. Gerhard von Rad zum 70. Geburtstag*. Edited by Hans Walter Wolff. Munich: Kaiser Verlag, 1971.
Herrmann, Wolfram. "Ex 17,7bβ und die Frage nach der Gegenwart Jahwes in Israel." Pages 46–55 in *Alttestamentlicher Glaube und biblische Theologie: Festschrift für Horst Dietrich Pruess zum 65. Geburtstag*. Edited by Jutta Hausmann and Hans-Jürgen Zobel. Stuttgart: Kohlhammer, 1992.
Hoffmeier, James K. *Ancient Israel in Sinai: The Evidence for the Authenticity of the Wilderness Tradition*. Oxford: Oxford University Press, 2005.
Holladay, William L. *Jeremiah 1: A Commentary on the Book of the Prophet Jeremiah Chapters 1–25*. Hermanthena. Philadelphia: Fortress Press, 1986.
—, *Jeremiah 2: A Commentary on the Book of the Prophet Jeremiah: Chapters 26–52*. Edited by Paul D. Hanson. Hermeneia. Minneapolis: Fortress, 1989.
Hossfeld, Frank L., and Eric Zenger. *Psalms 2: A Commentary on Psalms 51–100*. Translated by Linda M. Maloney. Hermeneia. Minneapolis: Fortress, 2005.
Houtman, Cornelius. *Exodus – Vol. 2: Chapters 7:14–19:25*. Translated by Sierd Woudstra. Historical Commentary of the Old Testament. Kampen: KOK Kampen, 1996.
—, *Exodus*. Translated by Sierd Woudstra. 4 vols. Historical Commentary on the Old Testament. Kampen: KOK Publishing, 1996.
Huddlestun, J., ed. *Divine Commitment and Human Obligation, vol. 2: Poetry and Orthagraphy*. Grand Rapids: Eerdmans, 1997.
Huffmon, H. B., F. A. Spina, and A. R. W. Green, eds. *The Quest for the Kingdom of God: Studies in Honor of G. E. Mendenhall*. Indiana: Eisenbrauns, 1983.
Hummel, Horace D. *Ezekiel 21–48*. Concordia Commentary. St. Louis: Concordia Publishing House, 2007.
Hupfeld, Hermann. *Die Quellen der Genesis und die Art ihrer Zusammensetzung*. Berlin: Wiegandt und Grieben, 1853.
Hyatt, J. Philip. *A Commentary on Exodus*. New Century Bible. London: Oliphants, 1971.
Ilgen, Carl David. *Die Urkunden des jerusalemischen Templearchivs in ihrer Urgestalt. 1, Die Urkunden des ersten Buchs von Moses in ihrer Urgestalt*. Halle: Hemmerde & Schwetschke, 1798.
Johnstone, William. *1 and 2 Chronicles: Volume 2: 2 Chronicles 10–36: Guilt and Atonement*. Journal for the Study of the Old Testament: Supplement Series 254. Sheffield: Sheffield Academic Press, 1997.
—, *Chronicles and Exodus: An Analogy and its Application*. Journal for the Study of the Old Testament: Supplement Series 275. Sheffield: Sheffield Academic, 1998.
—, "From the Sea to the Mountain: Exodus 15,22–19,2: A Case-Study in Editorial Techniques." Pages 245–264 in *Studies in the Book of Exodus: Redaction – Reception – Interpretation*. Edited by Marc Vervenne. Bibliotheca ephemeridum theologicarum lovaniensium 126. Leuven: Leuven University, 1996.
—, "Reactivating the Chronicles Analogy in Pentateuchal Studies, with Special Reference to the Sinai Pericope in Exodus." *Zeitschrift für die alttestamentliche Wissenschaft* 99 (1987): 16–37.
—, "The Use of the Reminiscences in Deuteronomy in Recovering the Two Main Literary Phases in the Production of the Pentateuch." Pages 247–273 in *Abschied vom*

Jahwisten: Dis Komposition des Hexateuch in der jüngsten Diskussion. Edited by Jan Christian Gertz, Konrad Schmid, and Markus Witte. Beihefte zur Zeitschrift für die alttestamentliche Wissenschaft 315. Berlin-New York: de Gruyter, 2002.

Jones, Douglas R. *Jeremiah.* New Century Bible. Grand Rapids: Eerdmans, 1992.

Joüon, Paul, and Tamitsu Muraoka. *A Grammar of Biblical Hebrew.* 3rd repr. of 2nd ed. with corrections. Subsidia biblica 27. Rome: Gregorian & Biblical Press, 2011.

Judaeus, Philo. *The Works of Philo: Complete and Unabridged.* Translated by C. D. Yonge. New upd. ed. Peabody: Hendrickson, 1993.

Kessler, Martin. "From Drought to Exile: A Morphological Study of Jer 14:1–15:4." Pages 501–526 in *Book of Seminar Papers.* Edited by Lane C. McGaughy. Los Angeles: Society of Biblical Literature, 1972.

Keßler, M. and M. Wallraff, eds. *Biblische Theologie und historisches Denken: Wissenschaftsgeschichtliche Studien aus Anlass der 50. Wiederkehr der Basler Promotion von Rudolf Smend.* Studien zur Geschichte der Wissenschaften in Basel. Neue Folge 5. Basel: Schwabe Verlag, 2008.

Khan, Geoffrey and Diana Lipton, eds. *Studies on the Text and Versions of the Hebrew Bible in Honour of Robert Gordon.* Supplements to Vetus Testamentum 149. Leiden–Boston: Brill, 2012.

Kiesow, Klaus. *Exodustexte im Jesajabuch: Literarkritische und motivgeschichtliche Analysen.* Orbis biblicus et orientalis 24. Göttingen: Vandenhoeck & Ruprecht, 1979.

Klein, Michael L. *The Fragment-Targums of the Pentateuch according to their Exant Sources.* 2 vols. Analecta biblica 76. Rome: Biblical Institute Press, 1980.

Knierim, Rolf P., and George W. Coats. *Numbers.* Forms of the Old Testament Literature 4. Grand Rapids: Eerdmans, 2005.

Knight, Douglas A. "Introduction: Tradition and Theology." Pages 1–8 in *Tradition and Theology in the Old Testament.* Edited by Douglas Knight. Philadelphia: Fortress, 1977.

—, *Rediscovering the Traditions of Israel.* 3rd ed. Society of Biblical Literature Studies in Biblical Literature 16. Atlanta: Society of Biblical Literature, 2006.

—, "The Pentateuch." Pages 261–296 in *The Hebrew Bible and its Modern Interpreters.* Edited by Douglas A. Knight and Gene M. Tucker. Philadelphia: Fortress, 1985.

—, "Tradition History." Pages 633–638 in vol. 6 of *Anchor Bible Dictionary.* Edited by David Noel Freedman. 6 vols. New York: Doubleday, 1992.

Knight, Douglas A. and Gene M. Tucker, eds. *The Hebrew Bible and its Modern Interpreters.* Philadelphia: Fortress, 1985.

Knight, Douglas, ed. *Tradition and Theology in the Old Testament.* Philadelphia: Fortress, 1977.

Koch, Christoph. *Treueid und Bund: Studien zur Rezeption des altorientalischen Vertragsrechts im Deuteronomium und zur Ausbildung der Bundestheologie im Alten Testament.* Beihefte zur Zeitschrift für die alttestamentliche Wissenschaft 383. Berlin–New York: de Gruyter, 2008.

Kohata, F. "Die priesterschriftliche Uberlieferungsgeschichte von Numeri XX 1–13." Pages 3–34 in *Annual of Japanese Biblical Institute: Vol. III.* Edited by M. Sekine and A. Satake. Tokyo: Yamamoto Shoten, 1977.

Kratz, Reinhard G. *Komposition der erzählenden Bücher des Alten Testaments: Grundwissen der Bibelkritik.* Uni-Taschenbücher 2157. Göttingen: Vandenhoeck & Ruprecht, 2000.

—, *The Composition of the Narrative Books of the Old Testament.* Translated by John Bowden. Göttingen: Vandenhoeck & Ruprecht, 2000. Repr., New York: T & T Clark, 2005.

—, "The Pentateuch in Current Research: Consensus and Debate." Pages 31–61 in *The Pentateuch: International Perspectives on Current Research*. Edited by Thomas B. Dozeman, Konrad Schmid, and Baruch J. Schwartz. Forschungen zum Alten Testament 78. Tübingen: Mohr Siebeck, 2011.

Kraus, Hans-Joachim. *Psalmen*. 2 vols. 2nd ed. Biblischer Kommentar Altes Testament XV. Neukirchen: Neukirchener Verlag, 1961.

Kupfer, Christian. *Mit Israel auf dem Weg durch die Wüste: Eine leserorientierte Exegese der Rebellionstexte in Exodus 15:22–17:7 und Numeri 11:1–20:13*. Oudtestamentische Studiën 61. Leiden–Boston: Brill, 2012.

Labuschagne, C. J. "The Tribes in the Blessing of Moses." Pages 97–112 in *Language and Meaning: Studies in Hebrew Language and Biblical Exegesis: Papers Read at the Joint British-Dutch Old Testament Conference at London, 1973*. Edited by James Barr. Oudtestamentische Studiën 19. Leiden: Brill, 1974.

—, "The Tribes in the Blessing of Moses." *Old Testament Studies* 19 (1974): 108–112.

Larbig, Torsten and Siegfried Wiedenhofer, eds. *Tradition and Tradition Theories: An International Discussion*. Studien zur Traditionstheorie 1. Berlin–Münster: Lit Verlag, 2006.

Leal, Robert Barry. *Wilderness in the Bible: Toward a Theology of Wilderness*. Studies in Biblical Literature 72. New York: Peter Lang, 2004.

Leder, Arie. "The Desert Itinerary Notices of Exodus: Their Narrative, Semiotic, and Theological Functions." *Estudios bíblicos* 68 (2010): 291–311.

Lee, Nancy C. "Exposing a Buried Subtext in Jeremiah and Lamentations: Going after Baal and . . . Abel." Pages 87–122 in *Troubling Jeremiah*. Edited by A. R. Pete Diamond, Kathleen M. O'Connor, and Louis Stulman. Journal for the Study of the Old Testament: Supplement Series 260. Sheffield: Sheffield Academic Press, 1999.

Lehming, Sigo. "Massa und Meriba." *Zeitschrift für die alttestamentliche Wissenschaft* 73 (1961): 71–77.

Lenchak, Timothy A. *"Choose Life": A Rhetorical-Critical Investigation of Deuteronomy 28,69–30,20*. Analecta biblica 129. Rome: Pontificio Istituto Biblico, 1993.

Leuchter, Mark A. and Jeremy M. Hutton, eds. *Levites and Priests in Biblical History and Tradition*. Society of Biblical Literature Ancient Israel and its Literature 9. Leiden–Boston: Brill, 2012.

Leveen, Adriane. "'Lo we Perish': A Reading of Numbers 17:27–20:29." Pages 248–272 in *Torah and the Book of Numbers*. Edited by Christian Frevel, Thomas Pola, and Aaron Schart. Forschungen zum Alten Testament 2. Reihe 62. Tübingen: Mohr Siebeck, 2013.

—, *Memory and Tradition in the Book of Numbers*. New York: Cambridge University Press, 2008.

Levenson, Jon D. "Who Inserted the Book of the Torah." *Harvard Theological Review* 68 (1975): 203–233.

Levine, Baruch A. *Numbers 1–20: A New Translation with Introduction and Commentary*. Anchor Bible 4. New York: Doubleday, 1993.

—, *Numbers 21–36: A New Translation with Introduction and Commentary*. Anchor Bible 4 A. New York: Doubleday, 2000.

Lim, Timothy H. "Deuteronomy in the Judaism of the Second Temple Period." Pages 6–26 in *Deuteronomy in the New Testament: The New Testament and Scriptures of Israel*. Edited by Maarten J. J. Menken and Steve Moyise. Library of New Testament Studies 358. London–New York: T & T Clark, 2007.

Lipschits, Oded., Gary Knoppers, and Rainer Albertz, eds. *Judah and the Judeans in the Fourth Century B.C.E.* Winona Lake: Eisenbrauns, 2007.
Loersch, Sigrid. *Das Deuteronomium und seine Deutungen. Ein forschungs-geschichtlicher Überblick.* Stuttgarter Bibelstudien 22. Stuttgart: Katholisches Bibelwerk, 1967.
Lohfink, Norbert. "'Ich bin Jahwe, dein Artzt': Gott, Gesellschaft und menschliche Gesundheit in nachexilischen Pentateuchbearbeitung." Pages 11–73 in *Ich will euer Gott werden: Beispiele biblischen Redens von Gott.* Edited by Norbert Lohfink et al. Stuttgart Bibelstudien 100. Stuttgart: Verlag Katholisches Bibelwerk, 1981.
—, *Das Hauptgebot: Eine Untersuchung literarischer Einleitungsfragen zu Dtn 5–11.* Analecta biblica 20. Rome: Pontifical Biblical Institute, 1963.
—, "Der Bundesschluß im Land Moab: Redaktionsgeschictliches zu Dt 28,69–32, 47." *Biblische Zeitschrift* 6 (1962): 32–56.
Lohfink, Norbert and et al, eds. *Ich will euer Gott werden: Beispiele biblischen Redens von Gott.* Stuttgart Bibelstudien 100. Stuttgart: Verlag Katholisches Bibelwerk, 1981.
Lohfink, Norbert, ed. *Das Deuteronomium: Entstehung, Gestalt, und Botschaft.* Bibliotheca ephemeridum theologicarum lovaniensium 68. Leuven: Leuven University Press, 1985.
Long, Burke O. *The Problem of Etiological Narrative in the Old Testament.* Beihefte zur Zeitschrift für die alttestamentliche Wissenschaft 108. Berlin: Töpelmann, 1968.
Lull, David J., ed. *Society of Biblical Literature: 1990 Seminar Papers.* Atlanta: Scholars Press, 1990.
Lundbom, Jack R. *Deuteronomy: A Commentary.* Grand Rapids: Eerdmans, 2013.
—, *Jeremiah 1–20: A New Translation with Introduction and Commentary.* Anchor Bible 21a. New York: Doubleday, 1999.
Luyten, Jos. "Primeval and Eschatological Overtones in the Song of Moses (DT 32,1–43)." Pages 341–347 in *Das Deuteronomium: Entstehung, Gestalt, und Botschaft.* Edited by Norbert Lohfink. Bibliotheca ephemeridum theologicarum lovaniensium 68. Leuven: Leuven University Press, 1985.
MacDonald, Burton. *"East of the Jordan": Territories and Sites of the Hebrew Scriptures.* ASOR Books 6. Boston: American Schools of Oriental Research, 2000.
MacDonald, Nathan. "Anticipations of Horeb: Exodus 17 as Inner-Biblical Commentary." Pages 7–19 in *Studies on the Text and Versions of the Hebrew Bible in Honour of Robert Gordon.* Edited by Geoffrey Khan and Diana Lipton. Supplements to Vetus Testamentum 149. Leiden–Boston: Brill, 2012.
Maillot, Alphonse, and André Lelièvre. *Les Psaumes.* 3 vols. 2nd ed. Genève: Labor et Fides, 1972.
Mann, Thomas W. "Holiness and Death in the Redaction of Numbers 16:1–20:13." Pages 181–190 in *Love & Death in the Ancient Near East: Essays in Honor of Marvin H. Pope.* Edited by John H. Marks and Robert M. Good. Guilford: Four Quarters, 1987.
—, "Theological Reflections on the Denial of Moses." *Journal of Biblical Literature* 98 (1979): 481–494.
Margaliot, M. "The Transgression of Moses and Aaron – Num. 20:1–13." *Jewish Quarterly Review* 74 (1983): 196–228.
Margalit, Baruch. "Ugaritic Contributions to Hebrew Lexicography (with special reference to the poem of Aqht)." *Zeitschrift für die alttestamentliche Wissenschaft* 99 (1987): 391–404.
Marks, John and Robert M. Good, eds. *Love and Death in the Ancient Near East.* Guilford: Four Quarters Publishing, 1987.

Mayes, A. D. H. *Deuteronomy.* New Century Bible. Grand Rapids: Eerdmans, 1979.
—, "Deuteronomy 4 and the Literary Criticism of the Deuteronomy." *Journal of Biblical Literature* 100 (1981): 23–51.
McCann, Clinton J., ed. *The Shape and Shaping of the Psalter.* Journal for the Study of the Old Testament: Supplement Series 159. Sheffield: JSOT Press, 1993.
McCarthy, Carmel. *Biblia Hebraica Quinta, Fascicle 5: Deuteronomy.* Stuttgart: Deutsche Bibelgesellschaft, 2007.
McConville, J. G. *Law and Theology in Deuteronomy.* Journal for the Study of the Old Testament: Supplement Series 33. Sheffield: JSOT, 1984.
McEvenue, Sean E. *The Narrative Style of the Priestly Author.* Analecta biblica 50. Rome: Biblical Institute Press, 1971.
McGaughy, Lane C., ed. *Book of Seminar Papers.* Los Angeles: Society of Biblical Literature, 1972.
McKenzie, Steven and M. Patrick Graham, eds. *The History of Israel's Traditions: The Heritage of Martin Noth.* Journal for the Study of the Old Testament: Supplement Series 182. Sheffield: Sheffield Academic, 1994.
McKenzie, Steven L. and Thomas Römer, eds. *Rethinking the Foundations: Historiography in the Ancient World and in the Bible.* Beihefte zur Zeitschrift für die alttestamentliche Wissenschaft 294. Berlin–New York: de Gruyter, 2000.
McNamara, Martin. *Targum and Testament Revisited: Aramaic Paraphrases of the Hebrew Bible.* Grand Rapids: Eerdmans, 2010.
Menken, Maarten J. J. and Steve Moyise, eds. *Deuteronomy in the New Testament: The New Testament and Scriptures of Israel.* Library of New Testament Studies 358. London–New York: T & T Clark, 2007.
Milgrom, Jacob. "Magic, Monotheism, and the Sin of Moses." Pages 251–265 in *The Quest for the Kingdom of God: Studies in Honor of G. E. Mendenhall.* Edited by H. B. Huffmon, F. A. Spina, and A. R. W. Green. Indiana: Eisenbrauns, 1983.
—, *Numbers: The Traditional Hebrew Text with the New JPS Translation.* JPS Torah Commentary. Philadelphia: Jewish Publication Society, 1990.
Miller, J. Maxwell. "The Israelite Journey through (around) Moab and Moabite Toponymy." *Journal of Biblical Literature* 108 (1989): 577–595.
Mitchell, H. G. "The Use of the Second Person in Deuteronomy." *Journal of Biblical Literature* 18 (1899): 61–109.
Mittmann, Siegfried. "Num 21,14–21 – eine redaktionelle Kompilation." Pages 143–149 in *Wort und Geschichte: Festschrift für Karl Elliger zum 70. Geburtstag.* Edited by H. and H. R. Rüger Gese. Alter Orient und Altes Testament 18. Neukirchen-Vluyn: Neukirchener Verlag, 1973.
Moenikes, Ansgar. "Das Tora-Buch aus dem Temple. Zu Inhalt, geschichtlichen Hintergrund und Theologie des sogenannte Ur-Deuteronomium." *Theologie und Glaube* 96 (2006): 40–55.
—, *Tora ohne Mose: Zur Vorgeschichte der Mose-Tora.* Bonner biblische Beiträge 149. Berlin: Philo, 2004.
Moor, Johannes C. De, ed. *Synchronic or Diachronic? A Debate on Method in Old Testament Stuides.* Oudtestamentische Studiën 34. Leiden: Brill, 1995.
Mynatt, Daniel S. *The Sub Loco Notes in the Torah of Biblia Hebraica Stuttgartensia.* Bibal Dissertation Series 2. Louisville: Bibal Press, 1994.

Müller, Reinhard, Juha Pakkala, and Bas ter Haar Romeny. *Evidence of Editing: Growth and Change of Texts in the Hebrew Bible*. Society of Biblical Literature Resources for Biblical Study 75. Atlanta: Society of Biblical Literature, 2014.
Najjar, Mohammad, and Thomas E. Levy. "Condemned to the Mines: Copper Production and Christian Persecution." *Biblical Archaeology Review* 37 (Nov / Dec 2011): 30–39.
Nelson, Richard D. *Deuteronomy*. Old Testament Library. Louisville: Westminster John Knox, 2002.
Nicholson, Ernest. W. *Deuteronomy and Tradition*. Philadelphia: Fortress, 1967.
—, *The Pentateuch in the Twentieth Century: The Legacy of Julius Wellhausen*. New York: Clarendon-Oxford, 1998.
Nielsen, Eduard. *Deuteronomium*. Handbuch zum Alten Testament I/6. Tübingen: Mohr-Siebeck, 1995.
Nigosian, S. A. "The Song of Moses (Dt 32): A Structural Analysis." *Ephemerides theologicae lovanienses* 72 (1996): 5–22.
Nihan, Christophe. *From Priestly Torah to Pentateuch: A Study in the Composition of the Book of Leviticus*. Forschungen zum Alten Testament 2. Reihe 25. Tübingen: Mohr Siebeck, 2007.
—, "The Priestly Laws of Numbers, the Holiness Legislation, and the Pentateuch." Pages 109–137 in *Torah and the Book of Numbers*. Edited by Christian Frevel, Thomas Pola, and Aaron Schart. Forschungen zum Alten Testament 2. Reihe 62. Tübingen: Mohr Siebeck, 2013.
Nodet, Etienne. "Israelites, Samaritans, Temples, Jews." Pages 121–171 in *Samaria, Samarians, Samaritans: Studies on Bible, History and Linguistics*. Edited by Jósef Zsengellér. Studia Judaica 66. Berlin–Boston: De Gruyter, 2011.
Noth, Martin. *A History of Pentateuchal Traditions*. Translated by Bernard W. Anderson. Stuttgart: Verlag, 1948. Repr., Englewood Cliffs: Prentice-Hall, 1972.
—, *Das vierte Buch Mose: Numeri*. Das Alte Testament Deutsch 7. Göttingen: Vandenhoeck & Ruprecht, 1966.
—, *Das zweite Buch Mose: Exodus*. Das Alte Testament Deutsch 5. Göttingen: Vandenhoeck & Ruprecht, 1958.
—, "Der Wallfahrtsweg zum Sinai." *Palästina-Jahrbuch* 36 (1940): 5–28.
—, *Überlieferungsgeschichte des Pentateuch*. Stuttgart: W. Kohlhammer, 1948.
—, *Überlieferungsgeschichtliche Studien. I. Die sammelnden und bearbeitenden Geschichtswerke im Alten Testament*. Schriften der Königsberger Gelehrten Gesellschaft: Geisteswissenschaftliche Klasse 18. Halle: M. Niemeyer, 1943.
O'Brien, Mark. *The Deuteronomistic History Hypothesis: A Reassessment*. Orbis biblicus et orientalis 92. Göttingen: Vandenhoeck & Ruprecht, 1989.
O'Connell, Robert H. "Deuteronomy IX 7–X 7, 10–11: Panelled Structure, Double Rehearsal and the Rhetoric of Covenant Rebuke." *Vetus Testamentum* 42 (1992): 492–509.
—, "Deuteronomy VIII 1–20: Assymmetrical Concentricity and the Rhetoric of Providence." *Vetus Testamentum* 40 (1990): 437–452.
Oblath, Michael D. *The Exodus Itinerary Sites: Their Locations from the Perspective of the Biblical Sources*. Studies in Biblical Literature 55. New York: Peter Lang, 2004.
Olmo Lete, Gregorio del. "La unidad literaria de Jer 14–17." *Estudios bíblicos* 30 (1971): 3–46.
Oswalt, John N. *The Book of Isaiah: Chapters 1–39*. New International Commentary on the Old Testament. Grand Rapids: Eerdmans, 1986.

Otto, Eckart. *Das Deuteronomium im Pentateuch und Hexateuch: Studien zur Literargeschichte von Pentateuch und Hexateauch im Lichte des Deuteronomiumrahmens*. Forschungen zum Alten Testament 30. Tübingen: Mohr Siebeck, 2000.

—, *Das Deuteronomium: Politische Theologie und Rechtsreform in Juda und Assyrien*. Beihefte zur Zeitschrift für die alttestamentliche Wissenschaft 284. Berlin–New York: de Gruyter, 1999.

—, *Deuteronomium 1–11: Erster Teilband: 1,1–4,43*. Herders theologischer Kommentar zum Alten Testament. Freiburg–Basel–Wien: Herder, 2012.

Pakkala, Juha. "The Date of the Oldest Edition of Deuteronomy." *Zeitschrift für die alttestamentliche Wissenschaft* 121 (2009): 388–401.

Pakkala, Juha and Martti Nissinen, eds. *Houses Full of All Good Things: Essays in Memory of Timo Veijola*. Publications of the Finnish Exegetical Society 95. Göttingen: Vandenhoeck & Ruprecht, 2008.

Parke-Taylor, Geoffrey H. *The Formation of the Book of Jeremiah: Doublets and Recurring Phrases*. Edited by Terence Fretheim. Society of Biblical Literature Monograph Series 51. Atlanta: Society of Biblical Literature, 2000.

Perlitt, Lothar. *Bundestheologie im Alten Testament*. Wissenschaftliche Monographien zum Alten und Neuen Testament 36. Neukirchen-Vluyn: Neukirchener, 1969.

—, "Priesterschrift im Deuteronomium." *Zeitschrift für die alttestamentliche Wissenschaft* 100 (1988): 65–88.

Person, Raymond F. Jr. *The Deuteronomic School: History, Social Setting, and Literature*. Studies in Biblical Literature 2. Atlanta: Society of Biblical Literature, 2002.

Pola, Thomas. *Die ursprüngliche Priesterschrift: Beobachtungen zur Literarkritik und Traditionsgeschichte von P^g*. Wissenschaftliche Monographien zum Alten und Neuen Testament 70. Neukirchen-Vluyen: Neukirchener Verlag, 1995.

Preuss, Horst D. *Deuteronomium*. Erträge der Forschung 164. Darmstadt: Wissenschaftliche Buchgesellschaft, 1982.

Propp, William H. C. *Exodus 1–18: A New Translation with Introduction and Commentary*. Anchor Bible 2. New York: Doubleday, 1999.

—, *Exodus 19–40: A New Translation with Introduction and Commentary*. Anchor Bible 2a. New York: Doubleday, 2006.

—, "The Priestly Source Recovered Intact." *Vetus Testamentum* 46 (1996): 458–478.

—, "The Rod of Aaron and the Sin of Moses." *Journal of Biblical Literature* 107 (1988): 19–26.

—, *Water in the Wilderness: A Biblical Motif and its Mythological Background*. Harvard Semitic Monographs 40. Atlanta: Scholars Press, 1987.

Pury, Albert de. "PG as the Absolute Beginning." Pages 99–128 in *Les dernièrs rédactions du Pentateuque, de L'Hexateuque et de L'Ennéateuque*. Edited by Thomas Römer and Konrad Schmid. Bibliotheca ephemeridum theologicarum lovaniensium 203. Paris: Leuven University, 2007.

Pury, Albert de, ed. *Le Pentateuque en question: Les origines et la composition des cinq premiers livres de la Bible à la lumière des recherches récentes*. Le Monde de la Bible 19. Geneva: Labor et Fides, 2002.

Pury, Albert de, Thomas Römer, and Jean-Daniel Macchi, eds. *Israël construit son histoire: L'historiographie deûteronomiste à la lumière des recherches récentes*. Le Monde de la Bible 34. Geneva: Labor et Fides, 1996.

Qimron, Elisha, and John Strugnell. *Qumran Cave 4.V: Miqṣat Ma'aśe ha-Torah*. Discoveries in the Judaean Desert X. Oxford: Clarendon, 1994.
Rad, Gerhard von. *Das formgeschichtliche Problem des Hexateuchs*. Beiträge zur Wissenschaft vom Alten (und Neuen) Testament 4.26. Stuttgart: W. Kohlhammer, 1938.
—, *Das fünfte Buch Mose: Deuteronomium*. Das Alte Testament Deutsch 8. Göttingen: Vandenhoeck & Ruprecht, 1964.
—, *Deuteronomy: A Commentary*. Translated by Dorothea Barton. Old Testament Library. Göttingen: Vandenhoeck & Ruprecht, 1964. Repr., Philadelphia: Westminster Press, 1966.
—, *Die Priesterschrift im Hexateuch: Literarisch untersucht und theologisch gewertet*. Beiträge zur Wissenschaft vom Alten (und Neuen) Testament 4.13. Stuttgart–Berlin: W. Kohlhammer, 1934.
—, *Old Testament Theology: Volume 1: The Theology of Israel's Historical Traditions*. Translated by D. M. G. Stalker. Munich: Chr. Kaiser Verlag, 1957. Repr., New York: Harper & Row, 1962.
—, "The Beginnings of Historical Writing in Ancient Israel." Pages 166–204 in *The Problem of the Hexateuch and Other Essays*. Edited by Gerhard von Rad. Translated by E. W. Trueman Dicken. Munich: Kaiser Verlag, 1958. Repr., New York: McGraw-Hill, 1966.
—, "The Form-Critical Problem of the Hexateuch." Pages 1–74 in *The Problem of the Hexateuch and Other Essays*. Edited by Gerhard von Rad. Translated by E. W. Trueman Dicken. Munich: Kaiser Verlag, 1958. Repr., New York: McGraw-Hill, 1966.
—, *Theologie des alten Testaments*. 2 vols. München: Chr. Kaiser, 1957.
Rad, Gerhard von, ed. *The Problem of the Hexateuch and Other Essays*. Translated by E. W. Trueman Dicken. Munich: Kaiser Verlag, 1958. Repr., New York: McGraw-Hill, 1966.
Rendtorff, Rolf. *Das überlieferungsgeschichtliche Problem des Pentateuch*. Beihefte zur Zeitschrift für die alttestamentliche Wissenschaft 147. Berlin–New York: de Gruyter, 1976.
—, *The Problem of the Process of Transmission in the Pentateuch*. Translated by John L. Scullion. Journal for the Study of the Old Testament: Supplement Series 89. Berlin: de Gruyter, 1977. Repr., Sheffield: Sheffield Academic, 1990.
Robertson, David A. *Linguistic Evidence in Dating Early Hebrew Poetry*. Society of Biblical Literature Dissertation Series 3. Missoula: Society of Biblical Literature, 1972.
Robker, Jonathan M. "The Balaam Narrative in the Pentateuch / Hexateuch / Enneateuch." Pages 335–366 in *Torah and the Book of Numbers*. Edited by Christian Frevel, Thomas Pola, and Aaron Schart. Forschungen zum Alten Testament 2. Reihe 62. Tübingen: Mohr Siebeck, 2013.
Rofé, Alexander. *Deuteronomy: Issues and Interpretation*. Old Testament Studies. London–New York: T & T Clark, 2002.
—, *Introduction to the Composition of the Pentateuch*. Translated by H. N. Bock. Sheffield: Sheffield Academic, 1999.
Rollston, Christopher A. *Writing and Literacy in the World of Ancient Israel: Epigraphic Evidence from the Iron Age*. Society of Biblical Literature Archaeology and Biblical Studies 11. Atlanta: Society of Biblical Literature, 2010.
Rose, Martin. *Deuteronomist und Jahwist:Untersuchungen zu den Berührungspunkten beider Literaturwerke*. Abhandlungen zur Theologie des Alten und Neuen Testaments 67. Zürich: Theologischer Verlag, 1981.

Roskop, Angela R. *The Wilderness Itineraries: Genre, Geography and the Growth of Torah*. History, Archaeology, and Culture of the Levant 3. Winona Lake: Eisenbrauns, 2011.

Rudolph, Wilhelm. *Der 'Elohist' von Exodus bis Joshua*. Beihefte zur Zeitschrift für die alttestamentliche Wissenschaft 68. Berlin: Töpelmann, 1938.

Römer, Thomas. "Le Deutéronome à la quête des origines." Pages 65–98 in *Le Pentateuque: débats et recherches: XIVe Congrìs de l'ACFEB, Angers (1991)*. Edited by Pierre Haudebert. Lectio divina 151. Paris: Cerf, 1992.

—, "The Book of Deuteronomy." Pages 178–212 in *The History of Israel's Traditions: The Heritage of Martin Noth*. Edited by Steven McKenzie and M. Patrick Graham. Journal for the Study of the Old Testament: Supplement Series 182. Sheffield: Sheffield Academic, 1994.

—, "The Elusive Yahwist: A Short History of Research." Pages 9–27 in *A Farewell to the Yahwist? The Composition of the Pentateuch in Recent European Interpretation*. Edited by Thomas B. Dozeman and Konrad Schmid. Society of Biblical Literature Symposium Series 34. Atlanta: Society of Biblical Literature, 2006.

—, *The so-called Deuteronomistic History: A Sociological, Historical and Literary Introduction*. London–New York: T & T Clark, 2005.

—, "La construction du Pentateuque, de l'Hexateuque et de l'Ennéateuque: Investigations préliminaires sur la formation des grands ensembles littéraires de la Bible hébraïque." Pages 9–34 in *Les derniers rédactions du Pentateuque, de L'Hexateuque et de L'Ennéateuque*. Edited by Thomas Römer and Konrad Schmid. Bibliotheca ephemeridum theologicarum lovaniensium 203. Paris: Leuven University, 2007.

Römer, Thomas, ed. *The Books of Leviticus and Numbers*. Bibliotheca ephemeridum theologicarum lovaniensium 215. Leuven: Peeters, 2008.

—, *The Future of the Deuteronomistic History*. Bibliotheca ephemeridum theologicarum lovaniensium 147. Leuven-Louvain: Leuven University Press, 2000.

Römer, Thomas and Albert de Pury. "L'Historiographie deutéronomist (HD): Historie de la recherche et enjeux de débat." Pages 9–122 in *Israël construit son histoire: L'historiographie deûteronomiste à la lumière des recherches récentes*. Edited by Albert de Pury, Thomas Römer, and Jean-Daniel Macchi. Le Monde de la Bible 34. Geneva: Labor et Fides, 1996.

Römer, Thomas and Konrad Schmid, eds. *Les derniers rédactions du Pentateuque, de L'Hexateuque et de L'Ennéateuque*. Bibliotheca ephemeridum theologicarum lovaniensium 203. Paris: Leuven University, 2007.

Römer, Thomas and Marc Z. Brettler. "Deuteronomy 34 and the Case for a Persian Hexateuch." *Journal of Biblical Literature* 119 (2000): 401–419.

Rose, Martin. *Deuteronomist und Jahwist: Untersuchungen zu den Berührungspunkten beider Literaturwerke*. Abhandlungen zur Theologie des Alten und Neuen Testaments 67. Zürich: Theologischer Verlag, 1981.

Sakenfeld, Katharine D. "Theological and Redactional Problems in Numbers 20:2–13." Pages 133–154 in *Understanding the Word: Essays in Honour of Bernhard W. Andersen*. Edited by James T. Butler, Edgar W. Conrad, and Ben C. Ollenburger. Journal for the Study of the Old Testament: Supplement Series 37. Sheffield: JSOT Press, 1985.

Samuel, Harald. *Von Priestern zum Patriarchen: Levi und die Leviten im alten Testament*. Beihefte zur Zeitschrift für die alttestamentliche Wissenschaft 448. Berlin–Boston: de Gruyter, 2014.

Sanders, Paul. *The Provenance of Deuteronomy 32*. Oudtestamentische Studiën 37. Leiden: Brill, 1996.
Schart, Aaron. *Mose und Israel im Konflict: Eine Redaktionsgeschichtliche Studie zu den Wüstenerzählungen*. Orbis biblicus et orientalis 98. Göttingen: Vandenhoeck & Ruprecht, 1990.
Schmid, Hans Heinrich. *Der sogenante Jahwist: Beobachtungen und Fragen zur Pentateuchforschung*. Zürich: Theologischer Verlag, 1976.
Schmid, Konrad. *Literaturgeschichte des Alten Testaments: Eine Einführung*. Darmstadt: Wissenschaftliche Buchgesellschaft, 2008.
—, "The Emergence and Disappearance of the Separation between the Pentateuch and the Deuteronomistic History in Biblical Studies." Pages 11–24 in *Pentateuch, Hexateuch, or Enneateuch? Identifying Literary Works in Genesis through Kings*. Edited by Thomas B. Dozeman, Thomas Römer, and Konrad Schmid. Society of Biblical Literature 8. Atlanta: Society of Biblical Literature, 2011.
—, "The Late Persian Formation off the Torah: Observations on Deuteronomy 34." Pages 237–251 in *Judah and the Judeans in the Fourth Century B.C.E.* Edited by Oded Lipschits, Gary Knoppers, and Rainer Albertz. Winona Lake: Eisenbrauns, 2007.
Schmidt, Ludwig. "Die Priesterschrift – kein Ende am Sinai." *Zeitschrift für die alttestamentliche Wissenschaft* 120 (2008): 481–500.
—, *Das vierte Buch Mose: Numeri 10,11–36,13*. Das Alte Testament Deutsch 7,2. Göttingen: Vandenhoeck & Ruprecht, 2004.
—, *Studien zur Priesterschrift*. Beihefte zur Zeitschrift für die alttestamentliche Wissenschaft 214. Berlin–New York: de Gruyter, 1993.
Schuller, Eileen M., and Carol A. Newsom. *The Hodayot (Thanksgiving Psalms): A Study Edition of 1QH^a*. Society of Biblical Literature Early Judaism and its Literature 36. Atlanta: Society of Biblical Literature, 2012.
Seebass, Horst. *Numeri 10,11–22,1*. Vol 2. Teilband of *Numeri*. Biblischer Kommentar, Altes Testament IV/2. Neukirchen-Vluyn: Neukirchener Verlag, 2003.
Seeligmann, I. L. "A Psalm from Pre-Regal Times." *Vetus Testamentum* 14 (1964): 75–92.
Seitz, Gottfried. *Redaktionsgeschichtliche Stüdien zum Deuteronomium*. Beiträge zur Wissenschaft vom Alten (und Neuen) Testament 5. Heft 13. Stuttgart: W. Kohlhammer, 1971.
Sekine, M. and A. Satake, eds. *Annual of Japanese Biblical Institute: Vol. III*. Tokyo: Yamamoto Shoten, 1977.
Sellin, Ernst, and Georg Fohrer. *Einleitung in das Alte Testament: begründet von Ernst Sellin; neubearbeitung von Georg Fohrer*. 11th ed. Heidelberg: Quelle & Meyer, 1969.
Ska, Jean-Louis. *Introduction to Reading the Pentateuch*. Translated by Pascale Dominque. Winona Lake: Eisenbrauns, 2006.
—, "Un nouveau Wellhausen." *Biblica* 72 (1991): 253–263.
Skehan, Patrick W. "A Fragment of the "Song of Moses" (Deut. 32) from Qumran." *Bulletin of the American Schools of Oriental Research* 136 (1954): 12–15.
Skehan, Patrick W., Eugene Ulrich, and Judith E. Sanderson. *Qumran Cave 4, IV: Palaeo-Hebrew and Greek Biblical Manuscripts*. Discoveries in the Judaean Desert IX. Oxford: Clarendon Press, 1992.
Smith, Mark S. *The Ugaritic Baal Cycle: Volume 1: Introduction with Text, Translation and Commentary of KTU 1.1–1.2*. Supplements to Vetus Testamentum LV. Leiden–New York–Köln: Brill, 1994.

Smith, Mark S. with contributions by Elizabeth M. Block Smith. *The Pilgrimage Pattern in Exodus*. Journal for the Study of the Old Testament: Supplement Series 239. Sheffield: Sheffield Academic, 1997.

Smith, Mark S. and Wayne T. Pitard. *The Ugaritic Baal Cycle: Volume II: Introduction with Text, Translation and Commentary of KTU/CAT 1.3–1.4*. Supplements to Vetus Testamentum 114. Leiden: Brill, 2009.

Soggin, J. Alberto. "Kultätiologische Sage und Katechese im Hexateuch." *Vetus Testamentum* 10 (1960): 341–347.

Sparks, Kent. "Genesis 49 and the Tribal List Tradition in Ancient Israel." *Zeitschrift für die alttestamentliche Wissenschaft* 115 (2003): 327–347.

Specht, Herbert. "Die Verfehlung Moses und Aaron in Num 20,1–13* P." Pages 273–313 in *Torah and the Book of Numbers*. Edited by Christian Frevel, Thomas Pola, and Aaron Schart. Forschungen zum Alten Testament 2. Reihe 62. Tübingen: Mohr Siebeck, 2013.

Sperber, Alexander. *The Bible in Aramaic: The Pentateuch according to the Targum Onqelos, vol. 1*. Leiden: Brill, 1992.

Stackert, Jeffrey. *Rewriting the Torah: Literary Revision in Deuteronomy and the Holiness Legislation*. Forschungen zum Alten Testament 52. Tübingen: Mohr Siebeck, 2007.

Staerk, W. *Das Deuteronomium – Sein Inhalt und seine literarische Form: Eine kritische Studie*. Leipzig: Hinrichs, 1894.

Stahl, Rainer. "Aspekte der Geschichte deuteronomistischer Theologies: Zur Traditionsgeschichte der Terminologie und zur Redaktionsgeschichte der Redekompositionen." Ph.D. diss., Jena, 1982.

Steck, Odil Hannes. *Exegeses des Alten Testaments: Leitfaden der Methodik: Ein Arbeitbuch für Proseminare, Seminare, und Vorlesungen*. 12., überarbeitete und erweiterte Auflage 1989. Neukirchen-Vluyn: Neukirchener Verlag, 1971.

—, *Exegeses des Alten Testaments: Leitfaden der Methodik: Ein Arbeitbuch für Proseminare, Seminare, und Vorlesungen*. 13., überarbeitete und erweiterte Auflage 1993. Neukirchen-Vluyn: Neukirchener Verlag, 1971.

—, *Old Testament Exegesis: A Guide to Methodology*. Translated by James D. Nogalski. 2nd ed. Society of Biblical Literature Resources for Biblical Study 39. Atlanta: Scholars Press, 1998.

Steuernagel, C. *Der Rahmen des Deuteronomiums: Literarcritische Untersuchungen über seine Zusammensetzung und Entstehung*. Halle: J. Krause, 1894.

—, *Übersetzung und Erklärung der Bücher Deuteronomium und Josua und Allgemeine Einteilung in den Hexateuch*. Handkommentar zum Alten Testament I.3. Göttingen: Vandenhoeck & Ruprecht, 1900.

Stoellger, Philipp. "Deuteronomium 34 ohne Priesterschrift." *Zeitschrift für die alttestamentliche Wissenschaft* 105 (1993): 26–51.

Struppe, Ursula. *Die Herrlichkeit Jahwes in der Priesterschrift. Eine semantische Studie zu kebôd YHWH*. Österreichische biblische Studien 9. Klosternneuberg: Österreichisches Katholisches Bibelwerk, 1988.

Stulman, Louis. *Jeremiah*. Abingdon Old Testament Commentaries. Nashville: Abingdon Press, 2005.

Suzuki, Yoshihide. "The 'Numeruswechsel' in Deuteronomy." Ph.D. diss., Claremont Graduate School, 1982.

Sweeney, Marvin A. *Isaiah 1–39: With an Introduction to Prophetic Literature*. Forms of the Old Testament Literature 16. Grand Rapids: Eerdmans, 1996.

—, *The Twelve Prophets*. Edited by David W. Cotter. 2 vols. Berit Olam. Collegeville: Liturgical Press, 2000.
—, "The Wilderness Traditions of the Pentateuch: A Reassessment of their Function and Intent in Relation to Exodus 32–34." *Society of Biblical Literature Seminar Papers* 28 (1989): 291–299.
Talmon, Shemaryahu. "The Desert Motif in the Bible and in Qumran Literature." Pages 31–63 in *Biblical Motifs: Origins and Transformations*. Edited by Alexander Altmann. Studies and Texts 3. Cambridge: Harvard University Press, 1966.
Tejero, E. F. and M. T. O. Monasterio, eds. *Estudios masoréticos (X Congreso de la IOMS): En memoria de Harry M. Orlinsky*. Textos y Estudios "Cardenal Cisneros" 55. Madrid: Instituto de Filogía del CSIC, 1993.
Thiessen, Matthew. "The Form and Function of the Song of Moses (Deuteronomy 32:1–43)." *Journal of Biblical Literature* 123 (2004): 401–424.
Thompson, J. A. *The Book of Jeremiah*. New International Commentary on the Old Testament. Grand Rapids: Eerdmans, 1980.
Tigay, J. H. *Deuteronomy* דברים. JPS Torah Commentary. Philadelphia: Jewish Publication Society, 1996.
Tillesse, G. Minette de. "Sections 'tu' et sections 'vous' dans le Deutéronome." *Vetus Testamentum* 12 (1962): 29–87.
Toorn, Karel van der. *Scribal Culture and the Making of the Hebrew Bible*. Massachusetts: Harvard University, 2007.
Tov, Emanuel. *Textual Criticism of the Hebrew Bible*. 3rd, rev. and exp. Minneapolis: Fortress, 2012.
Tov, Emanuel, Martin G. Jr. Abegg, Armin Lange et al. *The Texts from the Judaean Desert: Indices and an Introduction to the Discoveries in the Judaean Desert Series*. Discoveries in the Judaean Desert 39. Oxford – New York: Oxford University Press, 2002.
Uhlig, Torsten. *The Theme of Hardening in the Book of Isaiah*. Forschungen zum Alten Testament 2. Reihe 39. Tübingen: Mohr Siebeck, 2009.
Ulrich, Eugene, and Frank Moore Cross et al. *Qumran Cave 4, IX: Deuteronomy, Joshua, Judges, Kings*. Discoveries in the Judaean Desert XIV. Oxford: Clarendon Press, 1995.
Ulrich, Eugene, F. M. Cross, et al. *Qumran Cave 4, VII: Genesis to Numbers*. Discoveries in the Judaean Desert XII. Oxford: Clarendon Press, 1994.
Van Seters, John. "The Conquest of Sihon's Kingdom: A Literary Examination." *Journal of Biblical Literature* 91 (1972): 182–197.
—, *Abraham in History and Tradition*. New Haven-London: Yale University, 1975.
—, "Once again – the Conquest of Sihon's Kingdom." *Journal of Biblical Literature* 99 (1980): 117–119.
—, "Law and the Wilderness Rebellion Tradition: Exodus 32." Pages 583–591 in *Society of Biblical Literature: 1990 Seminar Papers*. Edited by David J. Lull. Atlanta: Scholars Press, 1990.
—, *Prologue to History: The Yahwist as Historian in Genesis*. Louisville: Westminster John Knox, 1992.
—, "Studien zur Komposition des Pentateuch" (review of Erhard Blum, *Studien zur Komposition des Pentateuch*). *Journal of Biblical Literature* 111 (1992): 122–124.
—, *The Life of Moses: The Yahwist as Historian in Exodus – Numbers*. Louisville: Westminster John Knox, 1994.

—, *The Pentateuch: A Social-Science Commentary.* Trajectories 1. Sheffield: Sheffield Academic, 1999.
—, "The Redactor in Biblical Studies: A Nineteenth Century Anachronism." *Journal of Northwest Semitic Languages* 29 (2003): 1–19.
—, "The Report of the Yahwist's Demise has been Greatly Exaggerated." Pages 143–157 in *A Farewell to the Yahwist? The Composition of the Pentateuch in Recent European Interpretation.* Edited by Thomas B. Dozeman and Konrad Schmid. Society of Biblical Literature Symposium Series 34. Atlanta: Society of Biblical Literature, 2006.
Vang, Carsten. "The So-called 'Ur-Deuteronomy' – Some Reflections on its Content, Size, and Age." *Hiphil* 6 (2009): 1–22.
Vaulx, J. de. *Les Nombres.* Sources bibliques. Paris: J. Gabalda, 1972.
Veijola, Timo. "'Der Mensch lebt nicht von Brot allein': Zur literarischen Schichtung und theologischen Aussage von Deuteronomium 8." Pages 143–158 in *Bundesdokument und Gesetz: Studien zum Deuteronomium.* Edited by Georg Braulik. Herders biblische Studien 4. Freiburg – New York: Herder, 1995.
—, *Das fünfte Buch Mose: Deuteronomium / Übersetzt und erklärt von Timo Veijola.* Das Alte Testament Deutsch 8/1. Göttingen: Vandenhoeck & Ruprecht, 2004.
Vervenne, Marc, ed. *Studies in the Book of Exodus: Redaction – Reception – Interpretation.* Bibliotheca ephemeridum theologicarum lovaniensium 126. Leuven: Leuven University, 1996.
Vogt, Peter T. *Deuteronomic Theology and the Significance of Torah: A Reprisal.* Winona Lake: Eisenbrauns, 2006.
Volz, Paul, Friedrich Stummer, and Johannes Hempel, eds. *Werden und Wesen Des Alten Testaments.* Beihefte zur Zeitschrift für die alttestamentliche Wissenschaft 66. Berlin: Alfred Töpelmann, 1936.
Von Gall, August Freiherrn. *Der Hebräische Pentateuch der Samaritaner.* Giessen: Alfred Töpelman, 1918.
Walsh, J. T. "From Egypt to Moab: A Source Critical Analysis of the Wilderness Itinerary." *Catholic Biblical Quarterly* 39 (1977): 20–33.
Waltke, Bruce K., and M. O'Connor. *An Introduction to Biblical Hebrew Syntax.* Winona Lake: Eisenbrauns, 1990.
Washburn, David L. *A Catalog of Biblical Passages in the Dead Sea Scrolls.* Society of Biblical Literature Text-Critical Studies 2. Atlanta: Society of Biblical Literature, 2002.
Watts, James W. "Scripturalization and the Aaronide Dynasties." *Journal of Hebrew Scriptures* 13.6 (2013): 1–16.
Watts, John D. W. *Isaiah 34–66.* Word Biblical Commentary 25. Waco: Word Books, 1987.
Weber, Beat. "Psalm 78 als 'Mitte' des Psalters? – ein Versuch." *Biblica* 88 (2007): 305–325.
Weimar, Peter. *Studien zur Priesterschrift.* Forschungen zum Alten Testament 56. Tübingen: Mohr Siebeck, 2008.
Weinfeld, Moshe. *Deuteronomy 1–11: A New Translation with Introduction and Commentary.* Anchor Bible 5. New York: Doubleday, 1991.
—, *Deuteronomy and the Deuteronomic School.* Clarendon Press: Oxford, 1972.
—, "Deuteronomy, Book Of." Pages 168–183 in vol. 2 of *Anchor Bible Dictionary.* Edited by David Noel Freedman. 6 vols. New York: Doubleday, 1992.
Weiser, Artur. *The Psalms: A Commentary.* Translated by Herbert Hartwell. Old Testament Library. Göttingen: Vandenhoek & Ruprecht, 1959. Repr., Philadelphia: Westminster, 1962.

Weisman, Z. "A Connecting Link in an Old Hymn: Deuteronomy XXXIII 19a, 21b." *Vetus Testamentum* 28 (1978): 365–368.
Weissenberg, Hanne von. "Deuteronomy at Qumran and in MMT." Pages 520–537 in *Houses Full of All Good Things: Essays in Memory of Timo Veijola*. Edited by Juha Pakkala and Martti Nissinen. Publications of the Finnish Exegetical Society 95. Göttingen: Vandenhoeck & Ruprecht, 2008.
Weitzman, Michael P. *The Syriac Version of the Old Testament: An Introduction*. University of Cambridge Oriental Publications 56. Cambridge: Cambridge University Press, 1999.
Wellhausen, Julius. "Die Composition des Hexateuchs." *Jahrbuch für deutsche Theologie* 21 (1876): 392–450, 531–602.
—, "Die Composition des Hexateuchs." *Jahrbuch für deutsche Theologie* 22 (1877): 407–479.
—, *Die Composition des Hexateuchs und der historischen Bücher des Alten Testaments*. 3rd ed. Berlin: Georg Reimer, 1899.
—, *Geschichte Israels: in zwei Bänden*. Berlin: Druck und Verlag von G. Reimer, 1878.
—, *Skizzen und Vorarbeiten. Zweites Heft. Die Compositions des Hexateuchs*. Berlin: G. Reimer, 1885.
Wenham, Gordon J. *Genesis 16–50*. Word Biblical Commentary 2. Dallas: Word Books, 1994.
Westermann, Claus. *Forschung am Alten Testament: gesammelte Studien*. Theologische Bücherei: Alten Testament 24. München: Kaiser, 1964.
Wette, W. M. L. de. *Dissertatio critico-exegetica qua Deuteronomium a prioribus pentateuchi libris diversum, alius cuiusdam recentioris auctoris opusesse monstratur*. Ph.D. diss., Jena, 1805.
Wevers, John W. *Notes on the Greek Text of Deuteronomy*. Society of Biblical Literature Septuagint and Cognate Studies 39. Atlanta: Scholars Press, 1995.
Wevers, John W., ed. *Numeri*. Septuaginta III, 1. Göttingen: Vandenhoeck & Ruprecht, 1982.
Wevers, John W., ed. *Deuteronomium*. Vol. III, 2 of *Septuaginta: Vetus Testamentum Graecum*. Auctoritate Academiae Scientiarum Gottingensis editum. Göttingen: Vandenhoeck & Ruprecht, 1977.
—, *Exodus*. Septuaginta: Vetus Testamentum Graecum Auctoritate Academiae Scientiarum Gottingensis editum II, 1. Göttingen: Vandenhoeck & Ruprecht, 1991.
Whybray, Roger N. *The Making of the Pentateuch: A Methodological Study*. Journal for the Study of the Old Testament: Supplement Series 53. Sheffield: Sheffield Academic, 1987.
Wiedenhofer, Siegfried. "Tradition – History – Memory: Why do we need a Complex Theory of Tradition." Pages 375–398 in *Tradition and Tradition Theories: An International Discussion*. Edited by Torsten Larbig and Siegfried Wiedenhofer. Studien zur Traditionstheorie 1. Berlin – Münster: Lit Verlag, 2006.
Wijngaards, John. "הוציא and העלה: A Twofold Approach to the Exodus." *Vetus Testamentum* 15 (1965): 91–102.
Williamson, H. G. M. *Ezra-Nehemiah*. Word Biblical Commentary 16. Nashville: Thomas Nelson, 1985.
—, *The Book Called Isaiah: Deutero-Isaiah's Role in Composition and Redaction*. New York: Oxford University Press, 2005.
Wilson, Gerald H. *The Editing of the Hebrew Psalter*. Society of Biblical Literature Dissertation Series 76. Chico: Scholars Press, 1985.
Wolff, Hans Walter, ed. *Probleme biblischer Theologie. Gerhard von Rad zum 70. Geburtstag*. Munich: Kaiser Verlag, 1971.

Wright, David P. *Inventing God's Law: How the Covenant Code of the Bible Use and Revised the Laws of Hammurabi*. Oxford-New York: Oxford University, 2009.
Wright, G. E. "The Lawsuit of God: A Form-Critical Study of Deuteronomy 32." Pages 26–67 in *Israel's Prophetic Heritage: Essays in Honor of James Muilenburg*. Edited by Bernhard W. Anderson and Walter Harrelson. London: SCM Press, 1962.
Wynn-Williams, Damian J. *The State of the Pentateuch*. Beihefte zur Zeitschrift für die alttestamentliche Wissenschaft 249. Berlin – New York: de Gruyter, 1997.
Yadin, Yigael. "The Expedition to the Judaean Desert, 1961. 'Expedition D – The Cave of the Letters.'" *Israel Exploration Journal* 12 (1962): 227–257.
Yoo, Philip Y. "The Four Moses Death Accounts." *Journal of Biblical Literature* 131 (2012): 423–441.
Young, Edward J. *The Book of Isaiah*. 2 vols. New International Commentary on the Old Testament. Grand Rapids: Eerdmans, 1969.
Zenger, Erich. *Israel am Sinai. Analysen und Interpretationen zu Exodus 17–34*. Altenberge: CIS-Verlag, 1982.
Ziegler, Joseph, ed. *Ezechiel*. Septuaginta XVI, 1. Göttingen: Vandenhoeck & Ruprecht, 1952.
Zimmerli, Walter. *Ezekiel 2: A Commentary on the Book of the Prophet Ezekiel, Chapters 25–48*. Translated by Walter Zimmerli. Hermeneia. Neukirchener-Vluyn: Neukirchener, 1969. Repr., Philadelphia: Fortress Press, 1983.
Zsengellér, Jósef, ed. *Samaria, Samarians, Samaritans: Studies on Bible, History and Linguistics*. Studia Judaica 66. Berlin–Boston: De Gruyter, 2011.

Index of names

Achenbach, Reinhard   69, 74, 106 f., 111 f., 138, 152, 162 f., 217
Albertz, Rainer   168, 178 f., 217
Allen, David M.   97
Altmann, Peter   127
Artus, Olivier   148, 150 f., 195, 206, 212, 214, 218, 226 f., 230
Ashley, Timothy R.   32, 169, 215
Astruc, Jean   47 f.
Aurelius, Erik   64, 67, 69, 71, 73 f., 151

Bacon, Benjamin W.   150, 210
Baden, Joel S.   11, 33, 127 f., 219
Baentsch, Bruno   215
Baltzer, Klaus   45
Bartlett, J. R.   167
Begg, Christopher T.   44
Begrich, Joachim   192 f.
Beyerle, Stefan   47, 120 f., 123
Biddle, Mark E.   95
Blenkinsopp, Joseph   29
Block-Smith, Elizabeth M.   16
Blum, Erhard   16–19, 22, 30, 35, 37, 151, 153, 155, 210, 218
Boorer, Suzanne   73–75, 150, 210 f.
Boston, James R.   86, 95, 97
Boyarin, Daniel   105
Britt, Brian   86, 95
Brown, Raymond E.   105
Budd, Philip J.   162–164, 214, 218, 224, 226

Campbell, Antony F.   38, 56
Caquot, André   123
Carr, David M.   2, 4, 42, 67, 79, 106–108, 153 f.
Cassuto, Umberto   125
Chapman, Stephen B.   46
Childs, Brevard S.   9 f., 14 f., 21 f., 147, 183, 194, 236
Christensen, Duane L.   40, 45 f., 57, 64, 96, 124

Coats, George W.   10, 13–15, 22, 64, 142 f., 161, 183, 191–196, 198, 208, 214, 218, 228, 230
Cornill, C. H.   150, 210
Craigie, Peter C.   86
Cross, Frank M. Jr.   122–125, 128, 161, 163 f., 167, 169, 203, 210

Dahmen, Ulrich   126, 132 f.
Davies, Eryl W.   109, 148, 152, 162 f., 170, 214, 218, 224, 226
Davies, G. I.   147, 161–165, 167, 169 f., 175, 224
DeSilva, David A.   242
DeVries, S. J.   13
Dijkstra, Meindert   177 f.
Dotan, Aron   158
Dozeman, Thomas B.   16, 21, 127 f., 147, 151, 161 f., 164 f., 169, 172, 174, 182
Drazin, Israel   90, 92, 122, 135
Duncan, Julie A.   120 f.
Durham, John I.   9

Ederer, Matthias   163, 170
Eichhorn, J. Gottfried   47 f.
Eissfeldt, Otto   29, 44, 106, 147
Emanuel, David   86
Emmrich, Martin   32

Fistill, Ulrich   166, 168, 177 f.
Fohrer, George   3 f.
Fokkelman, J. P.   96
Frankel, David   21 f., 48, 127 f., 151–153, 206 f., 209–216, 219, 224, 226, 228
Freedman, David Noel   122–125, 128
Frevel, Christian   106 f., 110, 113, 148, 151, 195, 206
Fritz, Volkmar   13, 150 f., 183
Fuhs, H. F.   150
Fuller, Russell   121, 125, 127

Galling, Kurt   12
García López, Félix   41 f., 53 f., 56 f., 59, 67, 69, 73 f., 76 f., 113

Garton, Roy E. 2f., 59
Gertz, Jan Christian 107, 148, 195f.
Gile, Jason 242
Golka, Friedemann W. 182
Gordley, Matthew E. 96
Graf, Karl H. 10, 15, 47f., 84
Gray, George Buchanan 150, 210, 224
Gressmann, Hugo 10f., 22, 33, 183
Gunkel, Hermann 10–12, 14, 33

Haar Romeny, Bas ter 155
Haran, Menahem 109
Harvey, John E. 95, 106, 113, 115
Helfgot, Nathaniel 32
Herrmann, Wolfram 59, 193
Houtman, Cornelius 150
Hupfeld, Hermann 48

Ilgen, Carl David 47f.

Johnstone, William 20–22, 33, 73, 80f., 127f., 147, 163f., 182, 188–191

Klein, Michael L. 90, 122, 131, 135
Knierim, Rolf P. 196, 198, 214, 218, 228
Knight, Douglas A. 3, 32–34
Kratz, Reinhard G. 30f., 33–37, 41f., 45–47, 110, 151f., 215
Kupfer, Christian 22, 182

Labuschagne, C. J. 1, 95, 121, 123–126
Leder, Arie 17
Lehming, Sigo 10, 12f., 20, 134, 183
Lenchak, Timothy A. 44f.
Leveen, Adriane 115, 133, 218, 220
Levenson, Jon D. 100
Levine, Baruch A. 218, 224, 230
Levy, Thomas E. 167
Lim, Timothy H. 91
Lohfink, Norbert 41f., 44, 53–55, 65–67, 69, 73–77, 96, 100, 210
Lundbom, Jack R. 178

MacDonald, Burton 174f., 178
MacDonald, Nathan 130, 183
Mann, Thomas W. 216, 218
Margaliot, M. 32, 210, 221

Margalit, Baruch 86f.
Mayes, A. D. H. 38, 41f., 44–47, 56f., 60–62, 66, 68f., 74, 76f., 86, 95–97, 109, 121, 123, 125f., 132
McCarthy, Carmel 1, 53, 65, 89f., 93, 96–99, 104, 121f., 125
McEvenue, Sean E. 226
McNamara, Martin 178
Milgrom, Jacob 210
Miller, J. Maxwell 174f., 178
Mitchell, H. G. 44f.
Mittmann, Siegfried 152, 175
Moenikes, Ansgar 41–44
Müller, Reinhard 155

Najjar, Mohammad 167
Nelson, Richard D. 38, 41f., 45–47, 56, 66–69, 73f., 86, 95, 97, 100, 114, 121, 123, 125–127, 129, 132
Newsom, Carol A. 89
Nicholson, Ernest. W. 16, 18, 29, 54
Nielsen, Eduard 38, 43, 47, 56, 59, 68, 73f., 77, 96, 116, 121, 123, 132
Nigosian, S. A. 95, 97
Nihan, Christophe 106–108, 110f., 116f., 148, 152, 194–196, 206–208, 211, 213, 219, 226
Nodet, Etienne 126
Noth, Martin 10, 12–14, 22, 31, 33, 36f., 44, 47, 64, 84, 106, 109, 111f., 142, 147f., 150f., 161–163, 167, 170, 173, 180, 182f., 192, 195, 214f., 218, 224, 230

O'Brien, Mark 38, 45, 56
O'Connell, Robert H. 67, 74f.
Otto, Eckart 41–43, 85, 110f., 116

Pakkala, Juha 36, 155
Perlitt, Lothar 16, 106, 109, 112, 116
Person, Raymond F. Jr. 31, 43, 62
Pitard, Wayne T. 93
Pola, Thomas 110, 152
Preuss, Horst D. 38, 41f., 47, 56, 74, 76f., 106, 123

Index of names

Propp, William H. C.   10, 15, 22, 79, 109, 116, 127, 186, 210, 213, 221, 222
Pury, Albert de   16, 36 f., 44, 54

Rad, Gerhard von   10 – 12, 14, 19, 33, 84, 103, 106
Rendtorff, Rolf   14, 16, 33
Robertson, David A.   47
Robker, Jonathan M.   177
Rofé, Alexander   29, 43, 57, 210
Rollston, Christopher A.   123
Römer, Thomas   16, 31, 36 – 46, 49, 54, 107, 114 – 117, 152
Rose, Martin   16
Roskop, Angela R.   147, 161 – 168, 174 – 176
Rudolph, Wilhelm   148, 150, 195, 226

Sakenfeld, Katharine D.   151
Samuel, Harald   5, 127, 130, 132 f.
Sanders, Paul   47, 86 – 90, 93, 95 – 97, 100
Schart, Aaron   16 f., 20, 22, 151, 224, 226, 228, 231
Schmid, Hans Heinrich   16
Schmid, Konrad   19, 84 f., 106 f., 116
Schmidt, Ludwig   109 f., 112, 148, 150, 195, 214 f., 231
Schuller, Eileen M.   89
Seebass, Horst   150, 218, 224
Seeligmann, I. L.   124
Seitz, Gottfried   42, 54 – 58, 61, 67 f., 74, 76 f.
Sellin, Ernst   3
Ska, Jean-Louis   18 f.
Skehan, Patrick W.   91, 93
Smith, Mark S.   16, 93 f.
Soggin, J. Alberto   55
Sparks, Kent   123, 126
Specht, Herbert   231
Sperber, Alexander   90
Stackert, Jeffrey   44 f.
Staerk, W.   44

Steck, Odil Hannes   3 f., 33
Steuernagel, C.   44, 124
Stoellger, Philipp   112, 114, 116
Suzuki, Yoshihide   54

Thiessen, Matthew   95
Tigay, J. H.   98
Tillesse, G. Minette de   44, 53 f., 59, 73
Toorn, Karel van der   40, 42
Tov, Emanuel   52 f., 89

Van Seters, John   13, 16, 18 – 20, 22, 29, 33, 39 f., 45 f., 127 f., 147, 151, 161 f., 175
Vang, Carsten   57, 69
Vaulx, J. de   177
Veijola, Timo   42, 56, 59, 67 – 69, 73 f., 76 f.
Vogt, Peter T.   45

Walsh, J. T.   161
Watts, James W.   132
Weber, Beat   6
Weimar, Peter   109
Weinfeld, Moshe   38 f., 47, 69
Weisman, Z.   124
Weissenberg, Hanne von   52
Wellhausen, Julius   10 – 12, 15, 18, 47 f., 84, 150
Wenham, Gordon J.   186
Westermann, Claus   33, 182
Wette, W. M. L. de   36, 48
Wevers, John W.   90, 92, 104
Whybray, Roger N.   29
Wiedenhofer, Siegfried   32
Wijngaards, John   2, 68
Wright, David P.   44
Wright, G. E.   95, 97

Yadin, Yigael   203
Yoo, Philip Y.   116

Zenger, Erich   110, 148, 195

Index of ancient sources

Hebrew Bible

Genesis
4:14   99
6:3   106, 117
7:13   109
12:7   114f.
13:7–10   186
13:7   186
13:10   186
17:23   109
17:26   109
19:37–38   182
26:20–22   182, 184, 186
26:20–21   186
26:22   186
28:19   190
29:31–30:24   182
32:3   190
34:2   131
34:25–31   129
36:43   109
38   131
47:11   109, 253
49:5–7   125
49:26   125
50:13   109

Exodus
1–24   30
2:1   130
3:1   161
4   107
4:1–9   107
4:2–4   196
4:2–3   211
4:14   130, 132
4:17   196
4:27–31   107
6:7   231
7:1   138
7:6   215
7:7   106
7:8–13   196
7:9   196
7:10   215
7:14–18   196, 201
7:15   196
7:19   196, 211
7:20   196, 201, 215
8:5–6   196
8:5   211
8:12–13   211
8:16–17   196
8:16   196
9:23   196, 211
10:13   196, 211
12:17   109
12:41   109
12:51   109
12:26   55
12:28   215
12:37   253
12:50   215
13:14   55
13:17   172
13:20–22   256
13:20   165, 172, 253
14:1–2   165, 172, 256
14:1   172
14:2   165, 253
14:6–7   147
14:11–12   80
14:11   144, 165, 249
14:16   196, 211
15:1   208
15:4–5   11
15:8–10   11
15:12–16   11
15:18   155
15:22–19:2   21, 81, 189
15:22–18:26   228
15:22–17:7   24, 148, 181, 188, 199, 200
15:22–16:36   234f., 239

15:22–26   80 f., 181
15:22–25   17, 19
15:22   80, 165, 172 f., 247, 253, 256
15:23–26   15
15:23–25   182
15:23   253
15:24–25   181
15:24   148, 159, 189
15:25–26   17
15:25   148
15:27   147, 167, 169, 253, 256
16   21, 187, 211
16:1–36   71
16:1–15   17
16:1   144, 147, 172, 224 f., 253, 256
16:2–17:13   134
16:2–36   181, 187
16:2   130, 144, 148, 181, 184
16:3   80, 187, 207 f., 219
16:4   148, 181
16:6   187
16:7   148, 181, 219
16:8   148, 181, 187
16:9   144
16:10   144, 219
16:12–13   187
16:16–31   17
16:20   187
16:23–24   187
16:34   215
17–19   162
17   4, 14, 87, 128, 146 f., 150, 153, 194, 196, 247, 249, 251
17:1–7   1, 4, 9, 12 f., 15, 17–21, 24, 31 f., 35, 51, 56, 59, 64, 72, 79–82, 99, 128–131, 134, 136, 138, 141–144, 146–160, 162, 181–183, 186, 188–191, 193 f., 197–203, 205, 207 f., 222–224, 228 f., 231–236, 238–240, 242, 251
17:1–5   239
17:1–3   186, 194
17:1–2   147, 150, 160, 186 f., 192, 194, 195
17:1   5, 17, 72, 115, 143 f., 146–151, 160–163, 165, 167, 172 f., 180, 182, 185–188, 194, 197, 199, 205, 213, 223–225, 229, 232, 238 f., 247, 249, 251, 253, 256
17:2–7   15, 84, 143, 150, 188, 190 f.

17:2–6   17
17:2–3   130, 147, 158, 181, 183, 208
17:2   13, 17, 130, 134, 142–144, 146–148, 151, 158–160, 182–189, 191– 195, 197 f., 207 f., 222, 229, 232 f., 238 f., 249, 251
17:3–6   17, 150, 160, 182
17:3–4   192, 195
17:3   6, 80, 130, 143 f., 147 f., 150 f., 159 f., 189, 192–195, 197 f., 204, 207, 223, 229, 238 f., 249, 251
17:4–7   150 f., 188
17:4   144, 160, 188 f., 193, 195, 197 f., 223, 238 f., 249, 250 f.
17:5–7   239
17:5–6   160, 191–193, 196 f., 238
17:5   130, 143 f., 148, 150, 160, 182, 189, 192, 195–197, 199–201, 223, 234, 238–240, 249–251
17:6   5 f., 17, 72, 130, 144, 147, 161 f., 173, 189, 191, 193, 211, 223, 250 f., 256
17:7   6, 13, 15, 20, 59, 80, 82, 116, 130 f., 134, 141–144, 147 f., 150, 160, 181–194, 197 f., 208, 229, 232 f., 238 f., 241 f., 250 f.
17:8–16   17
17:8   148, 205
17:9–12   196
17:9–11   211
17:10–12   130
17:14–24   148
18   17
18:5   161
18:27   17
19:1–2   17, 147, 161, 173, 253
19:1   172, 181, 224
19:2   80, 205, 224 f., 256
19:8   159
19:19   159
20–23   30
20:3   58
20:4   58
20:5   58
20:20   148
20:23–23:19   45
22:20–33   45
23:9–31   45

24:7   159
24:9–11   130
24:16–17   219
28:3   132
28:30   131f.
29–30   133
29   110
32–34   79
32   14f.
32:1   80, 130, 159, 219
32:7   130
32:20   130
32:22   159
32:23   80, 130
32:25–29   80f., 128f., 190f., 195
32:26–29   8, 128f., 131
32:26–28   80
32:27–29   129
32:27   129
32:29   129
32:35   80
33:1   130
33:3   130
33:5   130
33:19   130
33:21   130
33:22   130
34:2   130
34:4   215
34:9   130
34:14   48
39:1   215
39:5   215
39:7   215
39:21   215
39:26   215
39:29   215
39:31   215
39:43   215
40   110
40:17   147, 224
40:19   215
40:21   215
40:23   215
40:25   215
40:27   215

40:29   215
40:32   215

Leviticus
1–9   133
2:5–9   45
2:13–16   45
4:13   219
8:4   215
8:8   131
8:9   215
8:13   215
8:17   215
8:21   215
8:29   215
9   110
9:6   219
9:7   215
9:10   215
9:22–27   231
9:23   219
10:10–11   133
10:15   215
16   110
16:34   215
18:7–23   45
21:1–12   134
21:1–4   132
21:2–3   132
21:10–12   132
21:11   132
22:32   107
23:14   109
23:21   109
23:28   109
23:29   109
23:30   109
24:12   115
24:23   215

Numbers
1–10   111, 203
1   225
1:1   147, 224f.
1:19   215
2:33   215
3:16   115

3:39   115
3:42   215
3:51   115, 215
4:37   115
4:41   115
4:45   115
4:49   115
7   225
7:1   225
8:3   215
8:6–26   133
8:22   215
9   225
9:1   147, 224 f.
9:15–22   225
9:18   115
9:20   115
9:23   115
10:11–23   17
10:11–12   172, 223
10:11   147, 180, 224 f.
10:12–13   180, 225, 253, 256
10:12   147, 165, 180, 225 f.
10:13   115, 213, 225
10:29–32   17
10:33–11:35   24
10:33–11:3   162
10:33–34   256
10:33   165
11–36   203
11–25   7, 111
11–14   228
11   17, 19, 21, 80, 128, 181, 189 f., 197, 200 f., 236
11:1–35   83
11:1–34   79, 190 f.
11:1–3   21, 79, 128, 188 f., 191, 226
11:1   80, 198
11:3–4   20
11:3   20, 73, 80, 189–191, 198, 253
11:4–35   21, 187 f., 234
11:4–34   79, 128, 189, 191, 226
11:4–10   188
11:4–6   80
11:4   20, 73, 80, 189–191, 198
11:7–9   187
11:7–8   71

11:10   198
11:11–12   188
11:13   188, 191
11:14–17   188
11:16   191
11:18–23   188
11:18   80
11:20   80, 144, 191, 198, 249
11:21–22   198
11:21   191
11:24–30   188
11:24–25   191
11:24   198
11:30–31   198
11:30   191
11:31–35   188
11:32   198
11:33–34   80
11:33   191, 198
11:34   190, 198, 253
11:35–12:16   226, 256
11:35   253
12–14   24, 149, 223, 228, 234 f.
12   138, 227
12:1–15   149
12:6–8   138
12:6   219
12:16   147, 165, 172, 220, 226, 253, 256
13–19   220 f., 256
13–15   220
13–14   21, 79, 161, 218, 221, 226–228, 234, 239
13   205
13:1   218
13:3   115, 226
13:21   226 f.
13:23   149, 173, 205, 227 f.
13:24   228
13:26   144, 147, 149, 161, 173, 206, 226 f., 257
14:2–4   80
14:2   184, 189
14:7   144
14:20–45   228
14:20–36   71
14:20–35   80
14:20   228, 234

14:21   219
14:22 – 23   216
14:22   7, 148
14:25   165
14:26 – 35   7
14:27   189
14:29   189
14:36   189
14:37   219, 228
14:39 – 45   17
14:41   115
15   226
15:2   226
15:15   219
15:25   144
15:32 – 36   17
15:36   215
16 – 20   220
16 – 19   220, 226
16 – 17   21, 24, 149, 196 f., 199, 201, 205, 208, 218 – 221, 223 – 235, 241
16   228
16:1 – 17:26   220
16:1   199
16:3   149, 184, 208, 219
16:7   199
16:8 – 11   221
16:8   199, 217, 219
16:10   199
16:11   189, 222
16:19   219
16:22   107
16:28 – 35   221
16:31 – 35   221
17 – 19   228
17:1 – 15   221
17:1 – 10   149
17:2 – 10   196 f.
17:6 – 7   184
17:6   144, 189
17:7   219
17:10 – 11   197
17:14   221
17:16 – 27   221
17:16 – 26   208
17:20   189
17:22 – 26   206, 218 f., 222

17:22 – 24   206
17:23 – 24   206
17:23   221
17:25 – 26   206, 210
17:25   206, 208, 218 f., 222
17:26   206, 215
17:27 – 20:9   220
17:27 – 29   220
17:27 – 28   208, 219, 228
17:27   219
17:28   219, 221
18 – 19   218, 220
18   226
19:20   219
20   4 f., 21, 87, 108, 110, 135, 146 f., 150, 206, 220 f., 227, 247, 251
20:1 – 13   1, 4, 8, 13, 15, 17 f., 20 – 22, 24, 31 f., 35, 46, 51, 64, 72, 80, 105, 107 f., 111 f., 119, 128, 134, 136, 138, 141 – 144, 146, 148 – 157, 171, 173, 185 – 187, 194, 196 – 203, 205 – 211, 215 f., 218 f., 221 – 223, 225, 228 f., 231 – 233, 235, 238 – 242, 251
20:1 – 11   80 f., 212, 219 – 221, 223, 226, 234, 239, 240
20:1 – 2   223, 226 f., 239
20:1   5, 72, 111, 144, 146 – 151, 161, 171 – 173, 206, 209, 220, 223 – 234, 238 f., 247, 251, 254, 257
20:2 – 13   12, 149, 151, 211
20:2 – 5   147, 184 – 187, 194, 198, 207 – 209
20:2 – 3   229
20:2   6, 144, 147, 149 – 151, 184, 205 – 208, 219, 221 – 223, 226, 229 – 232, 234, 238 – 240, 249, 251
20:3 – 5   159, 229, 249
20:3 – 4   207 f.
20:3   134, 143 f., 146 f., 150 f., 154, 185 f., 194, 206 – 209, 219 – 223, 226 – 234, 239 f., 249, 251
20:4 – 8   223, 226 f., 239
20:4 – 7   151
20:4 – 5   80, 194 f., 207 f., 222, 229 f., 233, 239
20:4   147, 150 f., 194, 204, 206 – 209, 219, 223, 229 – 233, 238 f., 249
20:5 – 8   229

20:5   6, 143f., 147, 149–151, 173, 186, 194, 205–209, 223, 227–234, 238f., 249, 251
20:6–8   209, 231f., 238f.
20:6   144, 150f., 219, 223, 249–251.
20:7–8   203
20:7   143f., 150f., 251
20:8–13   210
20:8–11   6, 72, 195f., 200, 207, 218
20:8–9   150, 212
20:8   142, 148–151, 195, 204, 206f., 209–211, 214, 216–218, 222f., 229, 235, 238, 240, 249, 250
20:9–10   250
20:9   144, 148–151, 195–197, 199, 201, 205f., 208f., 215, 218f., 221–223, 226, 229, 234, 240, 250f.
20:10–12   250
20:10   150f., 153f., 204, 206–210, 214, 217, 219, 221–223, 226f., 229, 231f., 234f., 238–240, 249f.
20:11   148, 150f., 195, 197, 204–207, 209, 212, 214, 221–223, 226f., 229, 231f., 234, 238–240
20:12–13   208
20:12   107f., 111, 119, 137f., 147–152, 172f., 205–207, 209–218, 223, 229, 235, 240, 249, 251
20:13   1, 7, 107, 111, 131, 134, 143f., 147f., 150f., 171, 173, 182–184, 203, 206–209, 211f., 214, 216, 219–221, 223, 226f., 229–234, 238–240, 250f.
20:14–21   214, 254
20:16   173, 214, 227, 257
20:22–29   24, 105–108, 111f., 119, 135, 148, 171, 214f., 227f., 257
20:22–23   215
20:22   109, 144, 214, 218, 227, 254, 257
20:23–24   214
20:23   109, 214
20:24   1, 4, 20, 31f., 136f., 141, 143, 149, 171, 183, 205, 208f., 211, 213–216, 219, 235
20:25–29   215
20:25   109, 214
20:26   214f.
20:27   109, 215
20:29   117, 119, 219
21–25   178
21   176
21:1–3   174, 254, 257
21:1   174, 257
21:2   159
21:3   190
21:4–9   167, 174, 191, 254, 257
21:4   109, 165, 174, 254, 257
21:5   80, 130, 144, 159, 173, 184, 204, 247, 249
21:7   159
21:9   167
21:10–20   161
21:10–13   175
21:10   254, 257
21:11–20   175
21:11–13   174
21:11   174–176, 254, 257
21:12–20   175, 257
21:12–13   164, 175f.
21:12   254
21:13–15   176
21:13   175f., 255
21:14–15   175
21:16–20   176
21:16–18   17, 175f.
21:16   173, 255
21:18–20   164, 175f., 178
21:18   255
21:19   255
21:20   165, 175–178, 255
21:21–36:13   166
21:21–35   175f., 255
21:21–34   169f.
21:21–24   176
21:24   176
21:25–32   176
21:27–30   167
21:30   167
21:32   176
21:33–35   176
22–36   178
22–25   177, 179, 255
22–24   175, 177
22:1–3   176
22:1   110, 114, 165, 172, 178f., 255, 258

22:3–20   177
22:4   178
22:7   178
22:18   115
22:22–35   177
22:35–24:25   177
22:41   175, 178
23:10   99
23:14   175, 178
23:28   175, 178
24:13   115
25–36   168, 178
25   178
25:1–18   170, 178
25:1–5   168
25:1   177 f., 257
25:6   144
25:7–15   131
25:16–18   178
26–36   111, 168, 178 f., 217
26:2   144
26:3   110, 114, 178 f., 255, 258
26:4   215
26:9   184
26:63   110, 114, 178 f., 255, 258
27   108, 110, 112
27:11   215
27:12–23   105, 177, 215, 217
27:12–14   1, 4, 18, 20, 23 f., 31 f., 47, 50, 84, 104–106, 108–113, 118 f., 136, 141, 148, 168, 177, 179, 217
27:12–13   177, 212, 215, 217
27:12   112, 118, 168, 174, 176, 179, 255, 258
27:13–14   171, 183, 215
27:13   109
27:14   6, 104, 109, 111, 118 f., 134, 137, 143, 149, 205, 208 f., 211–216, 219, 233, 235
27:15–23   106–108, 119, 177, 217
27:17   107
27:18   117
27:20   144, 217
27:21   131, 217
27:22   215
31:1   177
31:2   217
31:7   215
31:8   177

31:12   110, 114, 178 f., 255, 258
31:16   107, 177 f.
31:31   215
31:41   215
31:47   215
32:1–38   168
32:2   116
32:3   168
32:7–15   79
32:12   217
32:28–32   217
32:28–30   177
32:28   217
32:33   170
32:34–38   168
32:34–36   168
32:34   168, 170, 255
32:37–38   168
32:38   116, 168, 255
33   18, 109, 146–149, 162–165, 179, 181, 201, 212, 217, 220, 224, 226, 256
33:1–49   161–166, 168, 179, 181
33:1–18   171
33:1–4   166, 171, 180
33:1   180 f.
33:2   115, 180 f., 213, 225
33:3–49   162
33:3–5   180 f.
33:3–4   170 f., 180, 225, 253
33:3   170, 180 f.
33:4   170
33:5–49   161, 168, 171, 175, 179 f., 199
33:5–18   171, 180 f.
33:5   169, 170, 180, 253
33:6–9   171, 172
33:6   165, 170–172, 181, 199, 253
33:7   164, 170–172, 181, 199, 253
33:8   165, 170–172, 181, 199, 253, 256
33:9   164, 167, 169–172, 181, 199, 253
33:10–11   165
33:10   167, 172, 253, 256
33:11–13   169
33:11   224, 253
33:12–13   163, 167, 256
33:12   253
33:13   253
33:14–15   1, 162

33:14   5, 24, 136, 141, 148, 170–173, 180 f., 199, 224, 234, 247, 253
33:15   173, 224, 253
33:16–18   226
33:16   226, 253, 256
33:17–36   256
33:17–18   147, 220
33:17   226, 253
33:18–36   166, 168, 170 f., 180 f., 220 f., 226
33:18–35   171
33:18–30   163
33:18–29   256
33:18   253
33:19   253
33:20   254
33:21   254
33:22   254
33:23   254
33:24   254
33:25   254
33:26   254
33:27   254
33:28   254
33:29   254
33:30–34   166, 220
33:30–33   256
33:30   171, 254
33:31   109, 254
33:32   254
33:33   254
33:34–35   256
33:34   254
33:35–36   256
33:35   254
33:36–49   24, 149, 171 f.
33:36–48   180 f.
33:36–40   171
33:36–37   171, 220, 226
33:36   5, 136, 141, 170–173, 181, 199, 224, 226 f., 234, 254, 257
33:37   109, 170–174, 181, 199, 254, 257
33:38–40   166
33:38–39   136, 169–174, 180 f., 199, 212, 217, 224 f., 254
33:38   109, 115, 147, 171, 180 f., 212 f., 215, 224, 228

33:39   109
33:40   170–174, 181, 199, 254, 257
33:41–48   171
33:41–47   163
33:41–43   174
33:41–42   167
33:41   109, 254
33:42   254
33:43   254
33:44   170–172, 174 f., 181, 199, 254 f.
33:45–46   167, 168
33:45   170, 255
33:46   136, 168, 255
33:47–48   258
33:47   116 f., 168–172, 174, 176 f., 179, 181, 199, 255
33:48–49   166, 177
33:48   110, 114, 169–172, 174, 177–179, 181, 199, 255, 257 f.
33:49   110, 169–172, 174, 177 f., 180 f., 199, 225, 255, 257 f.
33:50–56   170
33:50   110, 114, 169, 177–179, 258
34:7   109
34:8   109
34:15   178
34:16–29   217
34:16   177
34:17   217
35:1   110, 114, 178 f., 258
36:5   115
36:6–13   179
36:10   215
36:13   110, 114, 178 f., 258

Deuteronomy
1–28   57
1–11   85
1–4   39, 46, 113 f.
1–3   39, 41, 105, 113 f.
1:1–5   43
1:3   147, 170, 224
1:4   170
1:5   109
1:6–4:40   38 f.
1:6–3:29   43
1:8   62, 115

1:19 – 3:29   234
1:19 – 46   226
1:19 – 40   46
1:19   215
1:26   115, 219
1:34 – 37   5, 114, 116, 137
1:35   62
1:43   115, 219
2 – 3   175
2   175
2:2 – 6   204
2:8 – 9   176
2:8   166, 256
2:13 – 18   176
2:13 – 14   175
2:24 – 3:10   170
2:24   175 f.
2:35   175
3:8   175
3:12   175
3:14   182
3:16   175
3:20   114
3:21 – 22   5
3:23 – 29   46, 114
3:23 – 28   112
3:24 – 28   203
3:25   114
3:26 – 29   116, 137
3:26   5
3:27 – 19   119
3:27 – 28   114
3:27   114 f., 118, 174, 204
3:28   204
3:29   115, 178
4   23, 39, 41, 62
4:1 – 40   44, 56, 60 – 62, 69
4:3 – 4   78
4:3   178
4:9   55, 61
4:10   61
4:19   61
4:21 – 22   5, 46, 128
4:21   114, 116, 137
4:22   61 f.
4:23   58, 62
4:24   58, 61

4:25 – 26   67
4:25   61
4:26   61 f.
4:31   61
4:38   61
4:40   61
4:44 – 30:20   53
4:44 – 28:68   38 f.
4:44   40
4:45   40, 42
4:46 – 49   170
4:46   178
4:48   175
5 – 28   38
5 – 26   38
5 – 11   23, 29, 39 – 41, 49, 51 f., 75, 84
5   40, 43, 56
5:1 – 11:25   75
5:1 – 6:9   43
5:1 – 5   41
5:1   41 f.
5:6 – 21   41, 84
5:7   58, 62
5:8   58
5:9   58
5:32   215
6 – 11   42 f.
6 – 7   53
6   55 f., 69 f.
6:1 – 25   75
6:1 – 4   76
6:1 – 3   41, 76
6:1   41 f., 76
6:2   59
6:3   92
6:4 – 7:26   41
6:4 – 25   53 f., 61, 63, 71, 84
6:4 – 13   56
6:4 – 11   52
6:4 – 9   40, 42, 52, 54 – 56, 63, 70, 76, 78
6:4 – 5   41 – 43, 63, 70 f., 75 – 78, 82
6:4   43, 53
6:5 – 6   70
6:5   42, 76
6:6 – 25   76
6:6 – 9   63, 70 f.
6:6 – 7   70

6:7–9   52, 63, 70
6:7   55
6:10–11:32   40
6:10–25   54f.
6:10–19   55–57, 60–63, 65, 69, 71, 76
6:10–18   54–57, 60f., 69, 76
6:10–16   54
6:10–15   69
6:10–13   56, 63, 65, 69, 71, 76, 78
6:10–12   61f.
6:10–11   54, 56f., 63, 69
6:10   55–57, 61, 69, 71, 92, 115
6:11   60, 69, 71
6:12–16   54
6:12–15   78
6:12–13   56f.
6:12   55, 60–63, 65, 68, 69
6:13   54, 58, 61, 63
6:14–19   56f., 76
6:14–16   128
6:14–15   67, 69
6:14   53–61, 63, 71, 76, 78
6:15   54–59, 61–65, 71, 76, 78, 82, 184f., 198
6:16–17   53–57, 59, 61
6:16   1, 5, 18, 20, 23, 31f., 40, 49–53, 55–60, 62–65, 71–73, 76–83, 119f., 135–138, 141, 183–185, 192, 198, 200, 208, 233, 236, 238, 241f.
6:17–19   55, 63, 65, 71, 78
6:17–18   56f., 76
6:17   43, 53–61, 63, 65, 76, 78
6:18–19   42, 57
6:18   54–57, 60f., 63, 76
6:19   55, 60f.
6:20–25   54f., 63, 70f., 76, 78
6:20–24   11, 42, 76
6:20–22   43
6:20–21   70
6:20   53–55, 59, 70, 76
6:21–25   54, 76
6:21–24   63
6:21–23   63
6:23–24   67, 70
6:23   70
6:24–25   43, 70
6:24   63, 67, 70

6:25   76
7   63, 67
7:1–11   43
7:1–6   56
7:1–3   42
7:1–2   67
7:1   56, 170
7:3   56
7:4–5   56, 61
7:6   42, 56
7:7–15   61
7:7–8   56
7:11–13   41
7:11   44
7:12   56
7:16–24   67
7:17–24   42
7:17–19   69
7:25–26   56, 61, 67
8   60, 65–69
8:1–20   65–67, 69, 71, 76f., 84, 191
8:1–6   61, 76
8:1–4   116
8:1   41–44, 56, 66–68, 70f., 76, 78
8:2–20   41
8:2–18   63, 65, 67–72, 78, 136
8:2–6   66, 68, 70, 76
8:2–5   68
8:2–4   66f., 70
8:2   63, 66f., 70, 72
8:3–4   72, 82
8:3   66, 82, 115
8:4–6   66
8:4   66
8:5–7
8:5   67, 70
8:6–7   70
8:6   66–68, 70
8:7–18   65, 69, 71, 76
8:7–13   56
8:7–11   42, 56, 67–69, 76
8:7–10   66, 68, 70
8:7–9   66–69, 76, 92, 227
8:7–8   76
8:7   68f., 76
8:8–9   66
8:8   149, 227

8:9–10   76
8:9   66
8:10   65f., 68f., 76
8:11–18   70
8:11–16   76
8:11–14   60f,, 65
8:11   41, 56, 59–61, 65f., 68f., 76
8:12–18   67f., 76
8:12–16   68
8:12–14   42, 60, 68f., 76
8:12–13   67–69
8:12   56, 60, 65f., 69, 71
8:13–14   60
8:13   56, 66, 242
8:14–17   67
8:14–16   61, 66, 68, 76
8:14   60, 67–70, 76
8:15–16   5, 65, 68, 70, 72, 76f., 82, 129, 191, 193, 197, 232
8:15   1, 18, 20, 23, 31f., 40, 49–52, 62, 65f., 71f., 77, 81–83, 85, 87, 103f., 119, 135f., 138, 141, 191f., 231, 236, 238, 247
8:16   63, 66, 68, 70, 72, 82
8:17–18   42, 56, 66, 68f., 76
8:17   67f., 70
8:18–20   61, 67, 76
8:18   66, 68, 70, 76
8:19–20   41, 56, 66–69, 71, 76, 78
8:19   66, 69
9–10   39
9:1–10:11   73, 75, 77, 84
9:1–8   76f.
9:1–7   42, 74, 76
9:1–6   74, 76. 78
9:1–3   76
9:1   76
9:2   76
9:3–6   76
9:4–7   76
9:4–6   76
9:4   76
9:5   62, 115
9:7–10:11   41, 73f., 79f.
9:7–29   76
9:7–24   79f.
9:7–23   5
9:7–21   162

9:7–8   56, 75f.
9:7   74–76, 78–80, 216, 219, 236
9:8–10:11   42, 78
9:8–21   75
9:8–19   78
9:8–9   162
9:8   74, 76, 79, 181
9:9–21   75
9:9–19   75f.
9:9–18   75f.
9:9–12   76
9:9   74–76
9:10   76
9:11   74–76
9:12   74, 76
9:13–14   42, 74, 76
9:15–19   76
9:15–17   74, 76
9:15   76
9:16–17   76
9:16   76
9:17   76
9:18–19   74, 76
9:18   74
9:20–28   73
9:20   56, 74–76, 78
9:21   20f., 75f.
9:22–24   20, 56, 74–79, 236
9:22–23   8
9:22   1, 5, 18, 20, 23f., 31f., 40, 49–52, 64, 72–75, 77–81, 83, 119f., 135–138, 141, 162, 171, 181, 183–185, 187f., 191f., 198, 200, 208, 233, 236, 238
9:23–24   216, 219
9:23   79, 115, 216, 235
9:24   14, 74, 75
9:25–10:7   75
9:25–10:5   75
9:25–29   75f., 78
9:25   75f.
9:26–29   42, 74, 76
9:27   115
10:1–5   74–76, 78
10:5   76
10:6–9   74–76, 133
10:6–7   74, 76, 78, 166, 220, 256
10:6   46, 76, 109, 166, 171, 174, 257

Index of ancient sources

10:7   76, 166
10:8–11   76
10:8–9   74, 76, 78
10:8   133
10:10–11   42, 75f., 78
10:10   74–76
10:11   62, 74, 76
10:12–11:32   61
10:12–21   56
10:12–13   74
10:12   56, 78
10:13–19   56
10:19   61
10:20   56
10:21–22   56
10:21   56
11:1–28   56
11:2–7   41
11:8–9   41
11:8   42
11:9–12   92
11:16–17   41
11:19   55
11:22–25   41, 43
11:29–30   61
11:31–32   56
11:32–12:1   43
12–28   75
12–26   38–42, 126, 153
12:1–19:13   43
12:1   40
12:2   170
12:8–12   43
12:12–19   126
12:29   170
13:2–10   43
13:2   62
13:6   62
14:22–23   43
14:27–29   126
14:28–29   43
15:19–23   43
16:1–17   43
16:11   126
16:14   126
17:3   62
17:9   126

17:18   133
18:1–2   126
18:6–7   126
18:11   115
18:15   111, 116
18:18   213
18:20   62
19:14–25:19   43
21:5   126
21:18   219
21:20   219
23:2–4   219
23:2   208
23:3   208
23:4   208
23:4–5   177
23:9   208, 219
24:8   126
24:14   133
26   39
26:1–11   43
26:3–4   126
26:3   62
26:5–9   11
26:9   92
26:11–13   126
26:14   115
26:15   92
26:16–19   61
27   39
27–30   39, 41
27–28   39
27:3   92
27:9–10   61
28   38–40, 43, 153
28:1–6   61
28:3–6   43
28:11   62
28:14   62
28:15–19   61
28:15   43
28:16–19   43
28:20–44   43
28:36   62
28:69–30:20   43
28:69   109
29–31   39

29–30   38 f.
29   46
29:1–30:20   61
29:7–8   170
29:12   115
29:28   40
30–34   39
30   40
30:20   115
31–34   29, 38–41, 46, 49, 84 f., 112
31   46, 100
31:1–34:12   46
31:1–30   46
31:1–22   46
31:1–13   38
31:1–8   43, 46
31:1   213
31:2   46, 116, 119, 137
31:4   170
31:7–8   177
31:9–13   43
31:9   133
31:14–23   38, 177
31:14–16   46
31:14–15   43
31:14   46, 217
31:15–23   177
31:16–22   99 f.
31:16   46, 99 f.
31:17–18   97, 99
31:17   99 f.
31:18   62, 100
31:20–23   62
31:20   62, 100
31:21   99 f.
31:22   46
31:23–30   46
31:23   43
31:24–29   38
31:24–26   133
31:27–29   99 f.
31:27   219
31:28   100
31:29   100
32–33   39, 46
32   43, 46
32:1–44   23

32:1–43   5, 38, 46, 49, 84 f.
32:1–26   96 f.
32:1–20   136
32:1–3   91, 95
32:1   46, 98–101
32:2   97, 99 f.
32:3–26   99
32:3–20   99 f.
32:3   91, 98, 101
32:4–18   88
32:4–6   95
32:4   5, 94, 101
32:5   100
32:6–18   100 f., 103
32:6–8   91
32:6–7   98, 100
32:6   98 f.
32:7–14   95
32:7–8   91
32:7   98 f.
32:8–9   101
32:8   88, 94, 99
32:9–10   91
32:10–25   100
32:10–18   86
32:10–14   6
32:10–11   91, 101, 103
32:10   86, 89
32:11   89, 101
32:12   86, 100 f.
32:13–18   101
32:13–15   101
32:13–14   88, 91 f., 101, 103
32:13   1, 5–7, 23, 31 f., 40, 47, 49 f., 72, 84–95, 101, 103 f., 119, 135, 138, 141, 236, 238, 242
32:14–20   91
32:14   88, 90, 98–100
32:15–18   95
32:15–17   101
32:15   5 f., 94, 98–101
32:16–18   99
32:17–29   91
32:17–18   91, 98, 100 f.
32:17   98 f.
32:18   5 f., 94, 98 f.
32:19–25   95

32:19–20   101
32:19   100 f.
32:20–26   97
32:20   97–101
32:21–26   97–100
32:21–25   96
32:21   99
32:22–23   91
32:22   91
32:24   99
32:25–43   97
32:25–27   91
32:25   95 f.
32:26–43   100
32:26–27   97
32:26   96 f.
32:27–43   97, 99 f.
32:27   96 f.
32:28–29   99
32:29   95
32:30–31   6
32:30   5, 94
32:31   5, 94
32:32–33   91, 99
32:33–35   91
32:37–43   91
32:38–39   98 f.
32:38   98
32:39   98
32:43   88 f., 94, 98
32:44–33:1   46
32:44–47   104
32:44   177
32:45–47   38, 61
32:47–49   179
32:47   114
32:48–52   18, 31 f., 38, 40, 47, 50, 84 f., 104–106, 108–113, 117–119, 122, 170, 176 f., 212, 217, 228
32:48–51   109, 111
32:48–50   85, 105, 113, 119, 135, 137, 199, 213, 217
32:48   109, 112, 117
32:49–50   117, 174
32:49   109 f. 112, 114, 116 f., 169, 171, 174, 176, 255
32:50   109, 112, 118, 171

32:51   1, 4, 6, 20, 23, 46–50, 84 f., 104 f., 109, 111, 118–120, 135, 137 f., 141, 143, 171, 183, 201, 205, 209 f., 212 f., 215–217, 233, 235–237
32:52   85, 105, 112 f., 115, 117–119, 135, 137, 199, 213, 217
33   5, 23, 43, 46, 49, 125 f., 128
33:1–29   38, 113
33:2–29   46, 84 f.
33:2–5   124
33:2   1
33:6–25   124
33:7   121, 125 f.
33:8–11   5, 8, 11, 85, 122–124, 127, 129 f., 133, 199
33:8–10   122–126, 129 f., 133 f., 221
33:8–9   12, 128, 132–134, 190
33:8   1, 7, 13, 15, 18, 20 f., 23, 31 f., 40, 47, 49 f., 80 f., 84 f., 119–122, 124–138, 141, 143, 183 f., 190 f., 199–201, 213, 233 f., 236–240
33:9–10   132–134
33:9   122, 129, 131 f.
33:10   124, 127, 132 f.
33:11   123–127, 129, 132
33:12   121
33:13   121
33:15–16   94
33:16   125
33:17   125
33:18   121
33:22   121
33:23   121
33:24   121
33:26–29   124
33:28   92
34   38 f., 46 f., 105, 110, 112–114, 116, 119
34:1–12   43, 46, 169, 212
34:1–9   106, 108, 112 f., 116 f., 119, 122
34:1–6   46, 113 f., 119, 174
34:1–5   117
34:1–3   114, 116, 118, 155
34:1   106 f., 110, 112–114, 116 f., 171, 176, 179, 255
34:2   114
34:3   114
34:4   62, 109, 113–116, 118

34:5–6   113, 115, 174
34:5   109, 115, 118, 213, 215, 228
34:6   109, 117, 178
34:7–9   106f., 110, 113
34:7   46, 106, 113, 116, 119f., 134, 137, 170, 213, 221, 239
34:8–9   113, 116f.
34:8   110, 117, 119
34:9   106f., 117, 119, 215
34:10–12   113, 116, 120, 134, 137, 170, 213, 221, 239
34:10   116, 138
34:11–12   116

Joshua
1:1   115
1:13   115
1:15   115
1:18   219
2:10   170
3:1   225
4:6   55
4:19   225
4:21   55
5:6   92
5:9   190
5:10   225
5:11   109
7:1   213
7:25   213
7:26   182
8:31   115
8:33   115
9:10   170
9:14   115
10:27   109
10:40   215
11:12   115
11:15   215
11:20   215
12:1–6   170
12:3   169, 178, 257
12:6   115
13–22   178
13:8–12   170
13:8   115
13:20   178
13:22   177
13:24–28   170
13:32   110, 178, 179
14:2   215
14:5   215
14:7   115
15:13   115
16:1   178
17:4   115
17:14   159
18:7   115
19:50   115
20:8   178
21:3   115
21:8   215
22:2   115
22:4   115
22:5   115
22:7   178
22:9   115
22:16–17   107
22:24   55
24:2–13   11
24:9–10   177
24:13   92
24:16   159
24:19–20   58
24:19   58
24:21–22   159
24:24   159
24:29   115

Judges
1:26   182
2:5   182
2:8   115
2:16–16:31   8
9:18   189
10:3–5   182
11   175
11:15–18   174
11:18–19   176
11:18   176
11:19–23   170
15:19   182
18:12   182
20:8–10   159

1 Samuel
2:9 131
8:19–20 159
11:12 159
12:8 11
12:19 159
13:1 116

2 Samuel
3:10 92
3:12 92
6:8 182
18:3 159
19:9–10 159
22:26 131
24:19 215

1 Kings
4:19 170
9:26 166, 256
11:18 121
12:4 159
12:16 159
22:27 107
22:49 166, 256

2 Kings
18:12 115
18:32 92
24:3 213

Isaiah
1:2–20 95
1:2 98
7:10–14 1f., 6, 241
7:12 241
7:14 6
8:1–4 241
8:17–22 99
42:14–21 242
43:20 1, 7, 20, 241f.
48:21 1, 5, 141, 241
54:8 99
58:14 92f.

Jeremiah
2:2–8 59

2:4–13 95
2:5–6 236
2:21 236
3:12 131
5:31 99
13:5 215
14:1–12 1, 6, 241f.
14:1–9 2
14:8 242
14:9 6, 242
14:19–22 1f., 6, 241f.
16:10 159
22:21 59
33:18 133
48:45 170

Ezekiel
16 6, 59
16:4–8 59
16:13 1, 5f., 241f.
16:19 1, 5f., 241f.
16:43 59
23:8 59
24:2 109
24:19 159
39:23–24 99
39:25 58
39:29 99
40:1 109
42:2 109
47:19 1, 6, 134, 141, 143, 183, 233, 241
48:28 1, 6, 134, 141, 143, 183, 233, 241

Hosea
1:4–2:3 242
2:16–17 59
2:24–25 241
9:10 59, 236
10:11 101
11:1–5 59
13:4–6 59

Amos
4:13 91, 93f.

Micah
1:3 91, 93f.

6:1–8 95
7:2 131

Nahum
1:2 58

Habakkuk
3:9 212

Malachi
2 133

Psalms
4:4 131
12:2 131
13:2–3 99
16:10 131
18:26 131
27:9 99
30:5 131
30:8–10 99
31:24 131
32:6 131
37:28 131
43:1 131
44:25–26 99
50 6, 95
50:5 131
52:11 131
73–89 6
73–83 6
78 6, 11, 241
78:8 241
78:13–31 72
78:15–16 1, 141, 241
78:15 6
78:16 20
78:17 241
78:19–20 6
78:20 1, 20, 141, 241
78:35 6, 141, 241
78:36 6
78:40 241
78:56 241
79:2 131
81 6f., 87
81:8 1, 7, 87, 134, 141, 143, 183, 233, 241

81:17 1, 7, 87, 141, 241
85:9 131
86:2 131
88:15–19 99
89:20 131
89:47 99
90–106 7
95 7
95:8–11 1f., 83, 141, 241
95:8–9 7
95:8 143, 183
95:10–11 7
97:10 131
104:29 99
105 7, 11
105:1 7
105:2 7
105:5 7
105:37–42 7
105:41 1, 7, 141, 241
105:42 7
106 7, 11, 134
106:7–12 7
106:7 7
106:13–33 7
106:13 7
106:14 7
106:19–20 7
106:21 7
106:31–32 128
106:32–33 7f.
106:32 1, 7, 141, 143, 183, 233, 241
106:34–46 7
106:45 7
107–150 8
114:1 8
114:3 8
114:4 8
114:5 8
114:6 8
114:8 1, 8, 72, 103, 141, 241
116:15 131
132:9 131
132:16 131
135:11–12 170
136 11
136:17–22 170

145:10   131
145:17   131
148:14   131
149:1   131
149:5   131
149:9   131

Job
26:9   87

Proverbs
17:14   187

Canticles
1:7   42
3:1–4   42

Ezra
2:63   131

Nehemiah
7:65   131
8:7–9   133
9   8
9:6   8

9:13–14   11
9:14–15   8
9:15–17   8
9:15   1, 8, 141, 241
9:18–20   8
9:18   8
9:20   1, 8, 141, 241
9:22   170
9:26–31   8

1 Chronicles
6:78   178

2 Chronicles
1:3   115
6:4   131
8:17   166, 256
10:10   159
10:16   159
20:36   166, 256
24:6   115
29:24   121
31:2   133
31:4   133

Texts from the Judean Desert

By Numbering
1Q5 (1QDeut^b)   91, 96 f.
4Q11 (4QpaleoGen – Exod^l)   159
4Q14 (4QExod^c)   159
4Q22 (4QpaleoExod^m)   130, 158 f., 184
4Q27 (4QNum^b)   203 f.
4Q29 (4QDeut^b)   91
4Q30 (4QDeut^c)   73, 91
4Q32 (4QDeut^e)   65
4Q35 (4QDeut^h)   120 f., 131
4Q37 (4QDeut^j)   88, 91
4Q38 (4QDeut^{k1})   91
4Q43 (4QDeut^p)   52
4Q44 (4QDeut^q)   88 f., 91
4Q45 (4QpaleoDeut^r)   91, 93
4Q130 (4Qphyl^c)   52
4Q141 (4Qphyl^n)   91, 99

4Q142 (4Qphyl^o)   52
4Q175 (4QTest)   120 f., 130
4Q364 (4QRP^b)   73
4Q365 (4QRP^c)   159
4Q428 (1QH^a XXIV)   89
5Q1 (5QDeut)   65
5/6ḤevNum^a (5/6Ḥev1^a)   203
Mur4 (Murphyl)   52
Naḥal Ḥever   73

By Sigla
1QDeut^b (1Q5)   91, 96 f.
1QH^a XXIV (4Q428)   89
4QDeut^b (4Q29)   91
4QDeut^c (4Q30)   73, 91
4QDeut^e (4Q32)   65
4QDeut^h (4Q35)   120 f., 131

4QDeutʲ (4Q37)   88, 91
4QDeutᵏ¹ (4Q38)   91
4QDeutᵖ (4Q43)   52
4QDeutᑫ (4Q44)   88f., 91
4QExodᶜ (4Q14)   159
4QNumᵇ (4Q27)   203f.
4QpaleoDeutʳ (4Q45)   91, 93
4QpaleoExodᵐ (4Q22)   130, 158f., 184
4QpaleoGen – Exodˡ (4Q11)   159
4Qphylᶜ (4Q130)   52
4Qphylⁿ (4Q141)   91, 99
4Qphylᵒ (4Q142)   52
4QRPᵇ (4Q364)   73
4QRPᶜ (4Q365)   159
4QTest (4Q175)   120f., 130
5QDeut (5Q1)   65
5/6Ḥev1ᵃ (5/6ḤevNumᵃ)   203
Mur4 (Murphyl)   52
Naḥal Ḥever   73

Ancient Versions

Samaritan Pentateuch
Exod 17:2   130, 158f., 184
Exod 20   158
Exod 20:17   158
Num 20:13ᵇ   203f.
Num 33:41–42   167
Deuteronomy 2–3   204
Deut 2:2–6   204
Deut 3:24–28   203f.
Deut 8:15   65
Deut 9:22   73
Deut 11   158
Deut 27   158
Deut 32:7   98
Deut 32:8   88
Deut 32:38   168
Deut 32:13   91, 93
Deut 32:15   99
Deut 32:20   97
Deut 32:51   104
Deut 33:8   121

Septuagint
Gen 4:23   204
Gen 23:8   204
Exod 17:2   130, 158f., 184
Exod 17:3   159
Num 20:4   204
Num 20:8   204
Num 20:10   204
Num 20:11   204f.
Num 27:14   104
Num 33:41–42   167
Deut 8:15   65
Deut 9:22   73
Deut 12–26 (A)   91
Deut 27–34 (A)   91
Deut 32:7   98
Deut 32:8   88, 99
Deut 32:13–14   92
Deut 32:13   89–93
Deut 32:13 (α')   92f.
Deut 32:13 (B)   93
Deut 32:14   90
Deut 32:15   99
Deut 32:43   89
Deut 32:51   104
Deut 32:51 (α')   104
Deut 33:3   1
Deut 33:8   120–122, 130
Deut 33:8 (σ')   122
Judg 9:7   204
1 Chr 28:2   204
2 Chr 15:2   204
2 Chr 20:20   204
2 Chr 28:11   204
Jdt 7:17–8:27   242
Jdt 8–11   2, 242
Ps 33:12   204
Ps 34:10   204
Ps 94   7
Odes 2:13   92
Job 21:2   204
Job 32:10   204

Job 34:2   204
Wis 11:4–10   2, 241
Amos 4:13   91
Mic 1:3   91
Isa 46:3   204
Isa 46:12   204
Isa 49:1   204
Isa 51:1   204
Isa 51:4   204
Isa 55:2   204
Isa 58:14   92
Dan 11:19 (θ')   92

Syriac
Exod 17:2   130, 158 f., 184
Exod 17:3   159
Num 20:2   204
Num 20:3   204
Num 33:41–42   167
Deut 9:22   73
Deut 32:51   104

Deut 32:38   168
Deut 33:8   122

Targumim
Exod 17:2   130, 158 f., 184
Exod 17:3   159
Deut 9:22   73
Deut 32:13–14   92
Deut 32:13   90, 92 f.
Deut 32:15   99
Deut 32:51   104 f.
Deut 33:8–9   128
Deut 33:8   122, 135
Deut 33:9   131

Vulgate
Exod 17:2   130, 158 f., 184
Exod 17:3   159
Deut 9:22   73
Deut 32:51   104

New Testament

Matthew
4:1–11   2, 242

Mark
1:1   154

Luke
4:1–13   2, 242

1 Corinthians
10:1–5   242
10:4   2, 241

Hebrews
3:7–4:15   7
3:7–11   2, 241

Various

Ancient Near Eastern
Baal Cycles 1.1–1.6   94
Baal Cycle 1.4:VII.33–34   93
Baal Cycle 1.4:VII.34   93
Baal Cycle 1.6:III:6–7   87 f.
Baal Cyle 1.6:III:12–13   87 f.
Sefîre 1B.21–45   45

Classical Greek
Homer, *Illiad* 27.1–2   45
Sophocles, *Oedipus* 23.2–3   45
Xenophon, *Xenophon* 25.1   45

Old Testament Pseudepigrapha
2 Esdras 1:17–20   2, 241
4 Ezra 1:20   2, 241
Hellenistic Synagogal Prayers 12:74   2, 241

Liber antiquitatum biblicarum (Pseudo – Philo)
    10:7   2, 241
Testament of Levi   133

Philo
Quod deterius potiori insidari soleat (Det.)
    115 – 118   2, 241f.

Josephus
Jewish Antiquities (Ant.) 20.8.10   2, 241

British Museum Codex (Or. 4445)
Gen 39:20 – Deut 1:33   158
Exod 17:2   158
Exod 17:3   159
Num 7:46 – 73   158
Num 9:12 – 10:18   158

1599 Geneva
2 Kgs 11:6   1

1899 Douay – Rheims American Edition
Deut 6:16   64

www.ingramcontent.com/pod-product-compliance
Lightning Source LLC
Chambersburg PA
CBHW031722230426
43669CB00007B/213